MICROCOMPUTERS AND LIBRARIES:
A Bibliographic Sourcebook

by
Thomas L. Kilpatrick

The Scarecrow Press, Inc.
Metuchen, N.J., & London
1987

Library of Congress Cataloging-in-Publication Data

Kilpatrick, Thomas L., 1937–
    Microcomputers and libraries.

    Includes index.
    1. Microcomputers--Library applications--
Bibliography. 2. Libraries--Automation--
Bibliography. 3. Library science--Data processing--
Bibliography. I. Title.
Z678.93.M53K54 1987   016.025'02'0285416   86-31341
ISBN 0-8108-1977-5

To

Michael E. Bullard

who was inadvertently omitted

in 1979

CONTENTS

INTRODUCTION

The microcomputer is a phenomenon of the 1970s and 1980s which holds far more potential than has yet been realized. In fewer than fifteen years after it came onto the market, it has revolutionized the information industry and has had major impact on office management, industrial design and technology, entertainment, and dozens of other industries and services, including libraries.

Microcomputers have been readily accepted in the library workplace, where they have been adapted for use in all phases of library work from office word processing, fund accounting, and projecting of trends for the future to cataloging, circulation, reference, online searching, and bibliographic instruction. The options seem endless. This becomes obvious when one reviews the literature and sees the variety of subjects treated and the volume of writing concerning microcomputers in libraries. In 1983 a comprehensive bibliography concerning libraries and microcomputers was published in ACCESS: Microcomputers in Libraries. That bibliography contained 312 entries, many of them announcements of equipment purchases by individual libraries and the applications which were made of the new acquisitions. Since that time, library journals have begun publishing microcomputer articles on a regular basis; several journals devoted exclusively to library applications of microcomputers have begun publication; and monographs, proceedings of conferences, and other types of information sources are appearing regularly. In three short years the volume of publication has increased to the point that one person can no longer keep up with the literature; and the type of material being written has changed so drastically that it hardly seems related to that which was being published just three to five years earlier.

This publication represents an attempt at covering the literature of microcomputer technology as it

is related to, and as it has influenced libraries,
library services, and library personnel since the late
1970s. No claim at comprehensiveness is made, for
there are several items which are known to be missing;
and there must be others lurking in obscurity, still
unknown to the compiler of this bibliography.

A word concerning methodology may give the reader
some indication of what has been included here.
Sixty-one journals were scanned regularly since 1980
for items related to microcomputers and libraries.
These were English language publications of national
scope, concerning libraries or libraries and microcomputers. Manual searches were performed periodically
on such standard library science/information science
indexes as Library Literature, and Library and Information Science Abstracts. Annual online searches
were done in the ERIC, Dissertation Abstracts, and
Microcomputer Index databases. Finally, bibliographies, footnotes, and other references from the literature in hand were routinely checked for previously
undiscovered items. Known omissions fall into three
categories: (1) items which could not be verified
through standard bibliographic tools or obtained
through library acquisitions or interlibrary loan
sources, (2) items where were unobtainable because of
copyright/photocopy restrictions, (3) and a few late
1985 publications which arrived too late to meet the
February, 1986, cut-off date for inclusion.

A project of this nature could never be completed
without the cooperation of a variety of people. Among
those who must be acknowledged are Kenneth G. Peterson, Dean of Library Affairs at Southern Illinois University at Carbondale, and Darrell Jenkins, Director
of Library Services, who offered continuing support
for this project through their offices; and the faculty and staffs of every department and division of
Library Services, who contributed help and support
through the purchase of materials, the placement of
subscriptions, the routing of journals, the rush
cataloging of books, and dozens of other services
which made necessary materials readily accessible.

A superior secretarial staff in Library Affairs/
Library Services contributed to the ease with which

the project was completed. Thanks to Camille Hedden, Mary Clancy, and Henrietta Miller for use of their office word processors, and for taking time to deal with many of the frustrations of last-minute manuscript preparation in their usual efficient, professional ways.

My staff, the Research and Reference/Interlibrary Loan Department, deserve special recognition for processing the hoards of interlibrary loan requests that I submitted, and for supporting and encouraging me, even when they weren't certain what I was doing. Special thanks to Robert L. Keel, Jane Reed, Tammy Young, Diane Mansfield, David Brossart, Joyce Thiems, Joy Oetelaar, Betsy Hutton, and the part-time student staff who has each contributed to this effort.

Finally, a special word of appreciation to Diane Voth, for her consistently high quality research assistance, and for a beautiful job of word processing on the final manuscript.

OVERVIEWS AND GENERAL

1   "AT/L Subscriber Survey: Public Libraries Lead
     Microcomputer Boom; Academics, Specials Lag
     Behind." Advanced Technology/Libraries 12
     (March 1983): 1-3.
        The results of a questionnaire concerning
     microcomputers, distributed by the editors of
     Advanced Technology/Libraries in December 1982,
     reveals early data on microcomputer ownership,
     library applications, and reasons for slow growth
     in micro use.

2   ANDERSON, ERIC S. "Eric (Not ERIC): You Can't
     Go Home Again (With Apologies to Thomas
     Wolfe)." OCLC Micro 1 (May 1985): 5-6.
        Anderson examines progress and obsoles-
     cence in the microcomputer industry, using as
     examples his preference for the Macintosh over
     the Apple IIc and the Apple II+, and Apples'
     experimental copyright statement accompanying
     APPLEWORKS software.

3   ANDREW, GEOFF, and ATTENBOROUGH, COLIN. "Wide-
     spread and Varied Initiatives--But There
     Should Have Been More Involvement." Library
     Association Record 85 (June 1983): 221-24.
        1982 was Information Technology Year in
     Great Britain, and the authors review activities
     and progress made in information technology
     during the year, including ComputerTown instal-
     lations and developments in microcomputing and
     word processing.

4   AVALLONE, SUSAN. "The Trial 'by' Error Phase."
     Library Journal 110 (May 1, 1985): 96-97; and
     School Library Journal 31 (May 1985): 126-27.
        A recent survey concerning microcomput-
     ers in public and academic libraries is reported
     by an editorial coordinator for Library Journal.
     Based on responses from 46 academic and 42 public
     libraries, the report addresses numbers and
     brands, applications, software, and problems.

1

5   BEAUMONT, JANE, and KRUEGER, DONALD R. <u>Microcom-</u>
    <u>puters for Libraries: How Useful are They?</u>
    Ottawa: Canadian Library Association, 1983.
    124p.
        Ten articles concerning the use of micro-
    computers in libraries deal specifically with
    such areas as research, library management, pro-
    fessional development, communications, bulletin
    board systems, library applications, and soft-
    ware. Bibliographies.
        CONTENTS: Introduction, by Donald R.
    Krueger.--Microcomputers in Libraries: How Useful
    are They? by Howard Fosdick.--Communications
    Software for Microcomputers in Libraries, by Roy
    E. Metcalfe.--Microcomputers and Professional
    Development, by Gene Wilburn and Marion Wilburn.
    --The Microcomputer as a Management Tool, by Ken
    Frost.--Application Software for Microcomputers
    in Libraries, by Jane Beaumont.--Data Base Man-
    agement Systems, by Jane Beaumont.--Microcomput-
    ers in Library Research, by Timothy C. Craven.--
    Microcomputer-Based Bulletin Board Systems, by
    Gene Wilburn and Marion Wilburn.--Microcomputers
    in Libraries: A Showcase, by John Black.

6   BERGLUND, PATRICIA. "Special Report: An Expert
    Talks About Micros: Interview with Allan
    Pratt." <u>Wilson Library Bulletin</u> 58 (January
    1984): 345-47.
        In the interview format Allan Pratt
    identifies his personal hardware and software
    choices, discusses circulation of software, makes
    recommendations on catalog conversion, and deals
    with numerous other microcomputer topics.

7   BERRY, JOHN. "Library Use of Microcomputers:
    Massive and Growing." <u>Library Journal</u> 110
    (February 1, 1985): 48-49.
        A 1984 survey concerning microcomputer
    use in libraries, sponsored by the R. R. Bowker
    Company and conducted by McGraw-Hill, reports the
    number of micros in service in libraries in 1984,
    and identifies the most popular brands, most
    popular software, popular public access programs,
    and other statistics.

8   BLACK, JOHN B. "New Information Technologies:
     Some Observations on What is in Store for
     Libraries." INSPEL 15, no. 3 (1981): 145-53.
     A survey of past developments and future
     trends in library automation touches on equip-
     ment (including minicomputers, microcomputers,
     and word processing systems), the development of
     networks, the changing shape of information, and
     libraries of the future.

9   BLAIR, JOHN C., Jr. "Micro Magic (Sometimes
     Also Known as 'Micro Misery')." Online 5
     (October 1981): 90-94.
     This general overview of microcomputers
     in libraries addresses justification, purchase,
     staffing needs, hardware components, software
     operation, and remote access to stored data.

10   BLAIR, JOHN C., Jr. "Micros, Minis, and Main-
     frames. . .A Newcomers Guide to the World of
     Computers--Especially Micros." Online 6
     (January 1982): 14-26.
     This overview puts the microcomputer into
     perspective, touching on differences in micros,
     minis, and mainframes; suggesting selection pro-
     cedures for microcomputer equipment and software;
     discussing languages, networking, hard disks, and
     other technological topics; and describing a va-
     riety of library applications, from text editing
     and accounting to data storage and retrieval.
     A glossary of terms is appended. Bibliography.

11   BOSS, RICHARD W. "Microcomputers in Libraries:
     The Quiet Revolution." Wilson Library
     Bulletin 59 (June 1985): 653-60.
     Boss provides a broad overview of micro-
     computer technology for libraries, considering
     single board, desktop, and multi-user systems,
     memory expansion, limitations, standards,
     applications, downloading, and other topics of
     interest to librarians.

12   "British Library News (from BLR and D Newsletter,
     No. 25, December 1982)." Electronic Library
     1 (April 1983): 100-01.

Two microcomputer related grants are announced by the British Library. The first, an award to the Polytechnic of Central London, is for the development of a microcomputer-based online catalog; the second, an award to Paul F. Burton, is for a survey of microcomputer use in British school and academic libraries.

13   "British Library Support for Micro Projects." Electronic Library 3 (January 1985): 24. Three microcomputer projects sponsored by the British Library Research and Development Department are briefly described. The projects concern the development of a microcomputer facility for small libraries, an examination of the usefulness of program generators, and a study of the feasibility of local area networks.

14   BURTON, PAUL F., and PETRIE, J. HOWARD. Introducing Microcomputers: A Guide for Librarians. Wokingham: Van Nostrand Reinhold, 1984. 243p. A thorough introduction to microcomputers in libraries from the British perspective, this volume treats development and technology, operating systems, data management and information retrieval, library applications, software and hardware selection, and management techniques. Bibliography.

15   CELLENTANI, DIANE. "Survey Results: Over Half of OCLC Members Own Micros." OCLC Newsletter no. 156 (February 1985): 14. A random sampling of 365 OCLC member and 148 nonmember libraries was surveyed in 1984 concerning microcomputer ownership (including number and brands), usage, and future plans. The results are summarized.

16   CELLENTANI, DIANE. "Survey Results: Two-Thirds of OCLC Members Own Micros. . ." OCLC Newsletter no. 159 (October 1985): 12. A 1985 survey of OCLC member libraries to determine microcomputer ownership and use is reported, and results are compared to results of similar surveys conducted in 1983 and 1984.

17 CHEN, CHING-CHIH. "Editorial." Microcomputers
    for Information Management 1 (March 1984):
    iii-iv.
        This editorial deals briefly with the
    burgeoning microcomputer marketplace, the adapta-
    tion of the technology to library and information
    management functions, and the need for a journal
    devoted exclusively to a library and information
    management audience.

18 CHEN, CHING-CHIH. "Microcomputer Use in Librar-
    ies in the US: Current and Future Trends."
    Program 19 (January 1985): 29-38.
        Chen surveys microcomputer development
    and implementation in American libraries, and
    speculates on the future. Both hardware and
    software are considered, as are various library
    applications. Bibliography.

19 CHEN, CHING-CHIH, and BRESSLER, STACEY E.
    Microcomputers in Libraries. New York: Neal-
    Schuman Publishers, 1982. 259p.
        Thirteen articles by authorities in
    library and information science provide current
    information on microcomputer hardware and soft-
    ware, applications of microcomputers in librar-
    ies, influences of technology on staff and
    staffing, and planning for automation. Appendi-
    ces include comparison charts, illustrations of
    microcomputer hardware, and a bibliography.
        CONTENTS: An Introduction to Microcomput-
    ers, by Leonard J. Soltzberg.--Microcomputers--
    Their Selection and Evaluation, by Barbara
    DeYoung.--Library Administrative Concerns on
    Hardware Acquisition, by James R. Kennedy.--Soft-
    ware--What's Available, by David Kelley.--Looking
    Ahead With Microcomputers, by Donald W. Kaiser.--
    Microcomputers in Academic Libraries, by Barbara
    Stecconi Koven.--The Impact of Microcomputers on
    Public Libraries, by Barbara DeYoung.--Microcom-
    puter Applications in School Library Media
    Centers, by Martha Stanton.--Applications of
    Microcomputers in Special Libraries, by J. H.
    Katayama.--Technology: Staff Issues, by Inabeth
    Miller.--Staff Training and Automation: Issues

and Concerns for Library Managers, by Val Urbanek
.--Strategic Planning: A Key to Successful Auto-
mation, by Ann Wolpert.--Conclusion, by Stacey E.
Bressler.--Introduction to Hardware Comparison,
by Stacey E. Bressler and Ching-chih Chen.--
Questionnaire Survey of Participants in the
Institute on Microcomputers in Libraries Held at
Simmons College, Boston, November 6-7, 1981, by
Candy Schwartz and Susanna Schweizer.--Quick
Survey on the Potential Use of Microcomputers in
Libraries, by Ching-chih Chen.

20   COSTA, BETTY, and COSTA, MARIE. A Micro Handbook
     for Small Libraries and Media Centers. Little-
     ton, CO: Libraries Unlimited, 1983. 216p.
     The Costas present a concise handbook
concerning microcomputer use in small libraries,
addressing the development of microcomputer technology, software, hardware, library applications,
choosing and implementing systems, and a case
study of Betty Costa's experiences with COMPUTER
CAT at Mountain View Elementary School, in Broomfield, Colorado. Approximately 1/3 of the volume
is appendices, which include a glossary, bibliography, sample software evaluation charts, and information on the care of the microcomputer.
Bibliography.

21   CYSNEIROS, LUIZ FERNANDO. "Mini- and Micro-
     Computers in Information, Documentation and
     Libraries in Brazil--An Overview." The
     Application of Mini- and Micro-Computers in
     Information, Documentation and Libraries.
     Proceedings of the International Conference on
     the Application of Mini- and Micro-Computers
     in Information, Documentation and Libraries,
     Tel-Aviv, Israel, 13-18 March 1983. New York:
     North Holland, 1983. Pp. 373-75.
     The state of automation in Brazil is
analyzed, considering the application of mini-
and microcomputers in libraries and information
centers, and addressing the creation of databases
and the dissemination of database services via
automated methods.

22 DOOLEY, ANN. "Mitre Report Indicates: Number of
    Micros Growing in Libraries." Computerworld
    13 (April 23, 1979): 81-82.
          George A. Simpson's Microcomputers in
    Library Automation is summarized. The advantages
    of using microcomputers in library automation are
    presented, along with requirements for micro-
    based circulation, cataloging, acquisitions, and
    serials control systems.

23 EYRE, JOHN J. "The Impact of Automation on
    Libraries--A Review." Journal of Library and
    Information Science 5 (April 1979): 1-15.
          The growth of automation in libraries is
    reviewed from the introduction of the early main-
    frame to the present microcomputer revolution,
    along with an analysis of the impact of computers
    on library staff. Bibliography.

24 FOSDICK, HOWARD. "Library Microcomputers: Some
    Notes Gained from Experience." Wilson Library
    Bulletin 58 (April 1984): 558-61.
          Nine questions, from "How could our
    library totally mess up with micros?" to "How
    will micros be used in libraries in the future?"
    are addressed in this practical, advice-filled
    article for the layman. Obsolescence, security,
    selection, and copyright are some of the topics
    included.

25 FOSDICK, HOWARD. "The Microcomputer Catalyst."
    New Information Technologies--New Opportuni-
    ties. Clinic on Library Applications of Data
    Processing, 1981. Urbana, IL: University of
    Illinois Graduate School of Library and Infor-
    mation Science, 1981, v. 18. Pp. 13-27.
          Progress in microcomputer technology is
    occurring so rapidly that no one can be certain
    of the course for change or the implications for
    the future. Fosdick attempts to analyze trends
    and predict developments--some ordinary; others
    imaginative.

26 FOSDICK, HOWARD. "The Microcomputer Revolution."
    Library Journal 105 (July 1980): 1467-72.

The author explains the differences
between mini- and microcomputers, describes the
applications of minicomputers to libraries, then
predicts the future of the microcomputer, for
which the technology is only now being developed
and new library applications being made. Bibliography.

27 GORDON, HELEN A. "Microcomputer Survey Results."
    Online 7 (May 1983): 8-11.
        The results of a microcomputer survey
    distributed to attendees of ONLINE '82 in Atlanta
    are reported. Although the 75 valid returns rep-
    resent less than 10% of the surveys distributed
    the results provide information on levels of
    expertise and trends in microcomputing.

28 GRANT, CARL, and KLEVORN, THOMAS. "Library
    Automation in Missouri: A Survey." Show-Me
    Libraries 35 (October/November 1983): 7-14.
        A survey to determine the extent of
    automation in Missouri libraries is summarized in
    tables, with a brief introduction and concluding
    statement.

29 GRANT, CARL, and KLEVORN, THOMAS. "Microcomput-
    ers and Library Automation." Show-Me Librar-
    ies 31 (August 1980): 10-14.
        This general introduction to the concept
    of library microcomputing stresses necessary
    system components and suggests applications for
    the technology.

30 GRIFFITHS, JOSE-MARIE. "Applications of Mini and
    Micro Computers to Information Handling."
    Communicating Information. Proceedings of the
    43rd ASIS Annual Meeting. White Plains, NY:
    Knowledge Industry Publications, 1980, v. 17.
    Pp. 306-09.
        Historic development of computer hardware
    and software, applications of mini- and microcom-
    puter technology to various library processes,
    and the future of small computer systems in
    libraries are considered briefly. Bibliography.

31 HERTHER, NANCY K. "New Technology for Library
    Microcomputers: Artificial Intelligence."
    Small Computers in Libraries 5 (June 1985):
    12-15.
        Artificial intelligence is explained in
    layman's terms, with definitions, applications,
    background, languages, and the future of the
    technology addressed. Its potential for librar-
    ies is considered briefly, but its practical
    application to library functions is predicted to
    be far in the future. Bibliography.

32 HORSNELL, VERINA. "New Technology: A Personal
    View." Library Association Record 82 (August
    1980): 359.
        Developments and improvements in computer
    technology since the 1950s have vastly increased
    the usefulness of computers in libraries; how-
    ever, lack of adequate programming, shortage of
    skilled operators, rising software costs, and
    noncompatibility of commercially prepared pro-
    grams are slowing progress in adapting automated
    procedures.

33 HUDSON, RICHARD. "Micro Computer Systems."
    Vine no. 37 (February 1981): 37-38.
        This early article concerning the micro-
    computer characterizes it as a simple version of
    the mini and mainframe; suggests criteria for
    determining uses and need; recommends it to li-
    brary schools for computer education; and defines
    it in terms of cost and storage media.

34 HUME, STEPHEN. "Microcomputers." State Librar-
    ian 27 (November 1979): 30-32; and Serials
    Review 6 (October/December 1980): 45-47.
        A general introduction to microcomputer
    technology is followed by suggested applications
    in library cataloging, circulation, administra-
    tive, and serials areas. Bibliography.

35 INTNER, SHEILA S. "Microcomputers in the Li-
    brary." RTSD Newsletter 10, no. 5 (1985): 56-
    58.
        Intner surveys developments and trends in

this literature review concerning microcomputers
in the library. The issues which she emphasizes
are cataloging and circulation of microcomputer
software and continuing education for librarians.
Bibliography.

36   LaRUE, JAMES. "Words in Process: The Science of
      Serendipity." Library Software Review 3
      (September 1984): 385-89.
      Imagination provides the key to the
      library of the future, and LaRue imagines a sys-
      tem in which a home computer can provide patron
      access to the local library's mainframe, search
      remote online databases, download to a note file
      provide word processing, spreadsheet, graphics,
      and printing options, and answer the telephone.

37   LEGGATE, PETER, and DYER, HILARY. "The Microcom-
      puter in the Library." Electronic Library 3
      (July 1985): 200-09.
      The first in a series of six articles in-
      tended to provide an appreciation of microcomput-
      ers in libraries, this overview of microcomputer
      development considers components, operating
      systems, hardware, history, applications, per-
      formance, and integrated systems. Bibliography.

38   LEGGATE, PETER, and DYER, HILARY. "The Micro-
      computer in the Library: II, Hardware and
      Operating Systems." Electronic Library 3
      (October 1985): 260-74.
      The second in a series of articles con-
      cerning microcomputers in the library considers
      the major components of a microcomputer system,
      emphasizes ergonomic factors in keyboard and
      visual display unit design, and stresses the
      importance of the operating system in microcom-
      puter operation. Bibliography.

39   LUNDEEN, GERALD. "The Role of Microcomputers in
      Libraries." Wilson Library Bulletin 55
      (November 1980): 178-85.
      A brief but informative introduction to
      microcomputers provides basic history and termi-
      nology; describes current library uses in cata-

loging, circulation, acquisitions, serials, and reference functions; and predicts trends, including the development of the microcomputer as another media device with on-site and remote hookups. Bibliography.

40   MAGGIO, TERI. "Microcomputers and Other Automated Computer Systems in Louisiana Libraries." Louisiana Library Association Bulletin 46 (Summer 1983): 5-10.
The results of a survey concerning computer ownership and applications in Louisiana libraries are reported. 226 libraries were surveyed, with major emphasis on microcomputer usage, although mini- and mainframe data were gathered and reported.

41   MARTIN, SUSAN K. "Convergence/Divergence: The Adolescence of Library Automation." Information Technology and Libraries 2 (December 1983): 347-48.
In a guest editorial Martin points up the 1970s trend toward library cooperation and shared systems, which seems to be reversing in the 1980s because of the development of the inexpensive microcomputer. She draws parallels between automation and the adolescent, and speculates on the future of automation in libraries.

42   MASON, ROBERT M. "Prospects for 1985." Library Journal 110 (January 1985): 60-61.
Mason predicts what 1985 holds for library microcomputer users. He notes emphasis on developing library-specific software, increased knowledge on the part of the user, and a stepped up pace of technological development. He specifically emphasizes local area networks (LANs), improved operating systems, and optical disc storage.

43   MASON, ROBERT M. "What Good are Microcomputers, Anyway?" Library Journal 108 (January 15, 1983): 108-10.
A new column called "Mason on Micros" is introduced, with a general discussion of the

impact of microcomputer technology on libraries
and a rationale for the column. Distinctions are
drawn between personal computers, desktop computers, and home computers.

44 MATHEWS, WILLIAM D. "Advances in Electronic
    Technologies." Journal of Library Automation
    11 (December 1978): 299-307.
        Mathews examines the use of microproces-
    sors, new storage techniques, and digital trans-
    mission of data, then predicts their combined
    impact on the future of library information
    processing.

45 MATHEWS, WILLIAM D. "Information Technologies
    for the 1980s: Lasers and Microprocessors."
    Arlington, VA: ERIC Document Reproduction
    Service, ED 187 320, 1979.
        The development of laser and micro-
    processor technologies and the impact of these
    developments on libraries and library services
    are discussed in this early, intuitive paper.

46 MATTHEWS, JOSEPH R. "You're in the Chips; or,
    The Computer: What It Is and What It Can Do."
    Drexel Library Quarterly 17 (Fall 1981): 5-
    17.
        A basic introduction to computers, this
    article defines terms, distinguishes types of
    computers from micros to mainframes, describes
    basics of operation, identifies uses, provides
    hints on purchase, and projects the future of
    the technology. Bibliography.

47 McCRACKIN, MARK. "Just Imagine. . .The Implica-
    tions of Technological Changes in Computing
    and Telecommunications." Top of the News 39
    (Summer 1983): 347-51.
        McCrackin predicts only innovations which
    are already in prototype, still the list is im-
    pressive. Predictions include smaller, cheaper,
    more powerful, and more numerous computers, vast
    changes in input modes, optical disc technology
    for library storage, the expansion of networks,
    and the development of the information utility.

48 MESSERSMITH, PAUL. "Microcomputers: Make Sure
    You Understand the Answers!" ACCESS: Micro-
    computers in Libraries 1 (July 1981): 16, 18.
        Messersmith poses several microcomputer
    problems that he would like to see considered in
    the literature.

49 "Microcomputer Evolution and Libraries; or, Can
    You Spare 16-Bits?" Small Computers in
    Libraries 2 (July 1982): 4-5.
        A brief history of the microcomputer
    traces its development from the early 1970s, when
    it was basically a hobbyist's toy, to the pres-
    ent, in which it is making a real impact on
    business, education, and libraries. The emerging
    total-system concept is explored as a trend for
    the future.

50 "Micros in Libraries: British Library Support."
    Electronic Library 3 (July 1985): 165.
        Six microcomputer related research and
    development projects sponsored by the British
    Library are reviewed briefly.

51 MILLER, EDWARD P. "A Computer Caveat and a Call
    to Action." Show-Me Libraries 33 (September
    1982): 14-16.
        The impact of the microcomputer on
    American life is the topic of this article which
    considers the possibilities of computer assisted
    instruction, electronic mail, dial-up informa-
    tion, and other innovations. A major concern is
    the negative impact of such a change on the poor,
    who cannot afford the equipment or the access
    fees for electronic education, mail delivery, or
    library services.

52 MILLIOT, JIM. Micros at Work; Case Studies of
    Microcomputers in Libraries. Introduction by
    Allan D. Pratt. White Plains, NY: Knowledge
    Industry Publications, 1985. 148p.
        In 1984 questionnaires concerning micro-
    computer ownership and use were sent to 220
    libraries in the United States and Canada. 64
    usable responses were received and tabulated for

statistical purposes. Respondents contributed
brief descriptions of their library's microcomputer programs. Bibliography.

53 NEIHENGEN, TOM. "We Must be Micro-Computerized."
      Catholic Library World 55 (October 1983):
      134-36.
         The value of the microcomputer as a labor
saving device for librarians is stressed, and a
variety of problems involving software adaptability and hardware and software purchases are
addressed. Critical comments by six other
practicing librarians are appended.

54 NEUSTADT, RICHARD M. "The Third Revolution in
      Information: A Challenge to Libraries."
      Library Journal 106 (July 1981): 1375-76.
         The third revolution in information
technology began with the invention of the
telegraph about 100 years ago, but has escalated
dramatically in recent years because of developments in information storage and retrieval. The
revolution's challenge to libraries is to supply
the needs of clientele, whether those needs are
for retrieval of bibliographic data, full text
retrieval, or the provision of microcomputers for
patron use.

55 "1985: New Technology for Libraries." Library
      Journal 105 (July 1980): 1473-78.
         Five information company executives
predict how libraries will look in the future,
and which technologies will have the greatest
impact on library development. Two of the
five envision microcomputers having a major
influence.

56 OPPENHEIM, CHARLES. "New Technology: Trends,
      Limits, and Social Effects." International
      Forum on Information and Documentation 7
      (October 1982): 20-25.
         Recent developments in microcomputing,
telecommunications, and graphics storage have
made the paperless society technically feasible.
The possibility of a paperless society is discus-

sed, its probable impact on librarianship and
information science is noted, and reasons for its
slow development are detailed. Bibliography.

57 PEMBROKE, JILL. "Public Databases: Your Elec-
      tronic Library." Small Systems World 11
      (September 1983): 30-34.
        The hard copy library is compared to the
electronic library, factors are discussed which
are making the electronic library a reality, and
access to electronic data is described.

58 PRATT, ALLAN D. "Microcomputers in Libraries."
      Annual Review of Information Science and Tech-
      nology. White Plains, NY: Knowledge Industry
      Publications, 1984, v. 19. Pp. 247-69.
        A recognized authority reviews the liter-
ature of microcomputers in libraries, considering
the development of the technology and its integration into library operations. Software and
applications are reviewed, information sources
are considered, and the future of the micro is
predicted. Bibliography.

59 PRATT, ALLAN D. "The Use of Microcomputers in
      Libraries." Journal of Library Automation 13
      (March 1980): 7-17.
        Pratt considers advantages of microcom-
puters and potential for improvement of library
service through their use, along with suggested
applications, including text editing, biblio-
grapic compilation, and on-line database searching. Bibliography.

60 RABIG, ANTHONY. "The Printed Word on the Infer-
      nal Machine." Show-Me Libraries 34 (August
      1983): 31-34.
        Rabig considers the impact of microcom-
puter technology, particularly communications and
database availability, on society and libraries.

61 RAITHEL, FREDERICK J. "Personal Microcomputers
      in the Library Environment." Journal of
      Library Automation 13 (September 1980): 196-
      97.

As early as 1977 cooperative microcomputer projects made news in mid-Missouri. The first was a software sharing project; the second was a microcomputer-based professional development network for librarians. Both are evaluated in this short article.

62   "Research in the UK." Small Computers in Libraries 1 (October 1981): 3.
      Library microcomputer research projects funded by the British Government are listed and briefly described.

63   RICHMOND, PHYLLIS A. "Library Automation in the United States of America." Program 15 (January 1981): 24-37.
      A review of library automation, past and future, begins with networking, touches on the development of database services and document delivery. The impact of mini- and microcomputer technology is considered, but the major theme of the article is the development of user-friendly software and interfaces which will permit easy access to any information from any terminal. Bibliography.

64   SATYANARAYANA, R. "Microprocessors and Word Processors--Their Use in Information Retrieval Systems." Annals of Library Science and Documentation 27 (March/December 1980): 118-23.
      This article written for the purpose of raising awareness of word processors and microprocessors in India, identifies components, defines terms, and describes applications. Bibliography.

65   SCHOENLY, STEVEN B. "Automation on a Small Scale." Mississippi Libraries 43 (Autumn 1979): 163-66.
      An early advocate of microcomputer utilization in libraries draws attention to advantages of the technology, suggesting time savings, low cost, ease of programming, and local autonomy as positive arguments for automation via microcomputer. Bibliography.

66 SCHOENLY, STEVEN B. "Toward an Appreciation of
    Microcomputers." Arkansas Libraries 38
    (September 1981): 12, 14, 16.
        Schoenly speculates on the future of
    libraries and the role of the microcomputer in
    library development. Bibliography.

67 SHEROUSE, VICKI M. "Deja Vu." Ohio Media Spec-
    trum 33 (July 1981): 22-23.
        The microcomputer revolution of the 1980s
    is compared to the audiovisual explosion of the
    1960s, and a strong justification is made for
    accepting the technology as yet another medium
    for learning.

68 SIMPSON, GEORGE A. "Microcomputers in Library
    Automation." Arlington, VA: ERIC Document
    Reproduction Service, ED 174 217, 1978.
        A short, informative introduction written
    in nontechnical terms, this report deals with a
    multitude of microcomputer topics including types
    of hardware, common hardware configurations,
    principles of storage, input/output equipment,
    and software. Current and future uses for micro-
    computers are suggested and described for every
    library area, and the future of the microcomputer
    in libraries is discussed briefly. The glossary
    of terms, list of acronyms, and list of vendors
    are useful. Changes have occurred in the field
    since this was published in 1978, but the report
    is still useful for basic principles of microcom-
    puter application to libraries. Bibliography.

69 SPELLER, BENJAMIN F., Jr. "Microcomputing in
    North Carolina Libraries." North Carolina
    Libraries 40 (Fall/Winter 1982): 189-90.
        This lead article for an issue of North
    Carolina Libraries devoted entirely to the topic
    of microcomputers in libraries introduces the
    authors and themes of the six other articles
    which constitute the issue. Bibliography.

70 STANDING, ROY A. "Briefing: Microprocessors."
    American Society for Information Science
    Bulletin 8 (April 1982): 19-24.

In a briefing session for a 1981 American
Society for Information Science meeting, Standing
predicts the inevitable growth of microcomputer
use in business offices and educational settings,
describes the workings of a micro, notes improvements in the technology, and stresses the importance of sound software selection. A hardware
comparison chart is appended.

71 STOKES, ADRIAN V. "Characteristics of Micros and
    Their Applications." Minis, Micros and Termi-
    nals for Libraries and Information Services.
    Proceedings of the Conference Organized Joint-
    ly by the Institute of Information Scientists
    and the Information Retrieval Specialist Group
    of the British Computer Society, Held at the
    National Computing Centre, Manchester, 6-7
    November 1980. Chichester: Heyden, 1981. Pp.
    47-54.
       A brief history of the microcomputer,
    physical limitations which restrict its useful-
    ness, developments which are expanding its
    application, and standards for production and
    manufacture are considered. Bibliography.

72 SWEENEY, RICHARD T. "The Electronic Library."
    Online '81 Conference Proceedings, Dallas,
    2-4 November 1981. Weston, CT: Online, Inc.,
    1981. Pp. 214-25.
       The impact of videotex on the role of
    traditional libraries is the theme of this
    article which describes what the library of the
    future will become, and discusses ways in which
    libraries should be changing to meet the chal-
    lenge of the new technology. Although micro-
    computers are referred to only briefly, they will
    play a major role in videotex access, according
    to the author.

73 TAITT, HENRY A. "Children--Libraries--Comput-
    ers." Illinois Libraries 62 (December 1980):
    901-03.
       The evolution of the library from print
    to computer orientation will be dramatic, and
    Taitt projects how the library of the future will

operate, accessed from home via micro interface
with the library's super computer.

74 TURNER, JUDITH AXLER. "Electronic Library Plan-
     ned for Researchers." The Chronicle of Higher
     Education 29 (November 14, 1984): 16.
     Frederick G. Kilgore, former president
of OCLC, describes an electronic library which
permits researchers to access journals and monographs in their homes, offices, laboratories, or
dormitory rooms using personal computers. Development of the library, called the Electronic Information Delivery Online System (EIDOS) is being
funded through OCLC, and may eventually lead to
the disappearance of printed books as we now know
them.

75 "Urban Libraries Survey Reports Heavy Computer
     Use." Library Journal 110 (February 15,
     1985): 100.
     A survey sponsored by the Urban Libraries
Council provides information on the prevalence of
micro-, mini-, and mainframe computers in libraries, and the uses that are being made of them.

76 VICKERY, A., and BROOKS, H. "Microcomputer,
     Liberator or Enslaver." Proceedings of the
     4th International Online Information Meeting,
     London, 9-11 December 1980. Medford, NJ:
     Learned Information, 1980. Pp. 387-96.
     The role of the microcomputer in library
information centers is assessed, and advantages
and disadvantages are weighed. Bibliography.

77 WHITLOCK, JOHN A. "Micros in Libraries?"
     Proceedings of the National Conference on
     Library and Bibliographic Applications of
     Minicomputers, Sydney, 22-24 August 1979.
     Sydney, Australia: University of New South
     Wales School of Librarianship, 1979. Pp.
     175-89.
     Definitions, applications, evaluations,
and the future of microcomputer technology in
libraries are considered from an Australian
perspective.

78 WINFIELD, R. P. "An Informal Survey of Opera-
    tional Microprocessor-Based Systems, Autumn
    1979." Program 14 (July 1980): 121-29.
        A 1979 survey of microprocessor-based
    systems in British Libraries indicates the volume
    of use and various applications of microcomputers
    and word processors in libraries at that time.

79 WOODS, LAWRENCE A., and POPE, NOLAN F. The Li-
    brarian's Guide to Microcomputer Technology
    and Applications. White Plains, NY: Published
    for American Society for Information Science
    by Knowledge Industry Publications, 1983.
    209p.
        Microcomputer technology is addressed in
    basic terms, including chapters on hardware,
    software, and the impact on libraries. Applica-
    tions for public services, technical services,
    and management are discussed, as are trends for
    the future. Appendices include a directory of
    libraries with major microcomputer installations,
    lists of vendors, a glossary, and a bibliography.

80 "Your Rapidly Appreciating Micro Investment."
    Technicalities 4 (September 1984): 1-2.
        The usefulness of the microcomputer as a
    library tool is noted, and the trend among li-
    brary book and serial vendors to replace turnkey
    systems with micros is a strong indication that
    the micro is the computer of the future.

81 ZURKOWSKI, PAUL G. "The Library Context & the
    Information Context: Bridging the Theoretical
    Gap." Library Journal 106 (July 1981): 1381-
    84.
        The author outlines a brief history of
    information storage from pre-Gutenberg days to
    the present, and beyond. In considering the
    future of the library in a technological age, he
    suggests enhancing information literacy through
    use of microcomputers and the creation and
    manipulation of local databases. In this new
    age the librarian becomes teacher/facilitator
    for those clients with information needs.

PLANNING, IMPLEMENTATION, AND MANAGEMENT

82 ANDERSON, ERIC S. "Eric (Not ERIC): The Woebe-
    gone Librarian." OCLC Micro 1 (December 1985):
    4-5.
        Anderson discusses the advantages and
    limitations of hard disk drives, and provides
    practical advice on determining the need for one.

83 ANGLIN, RICHARD V. "Cooperate and Plan Before
    You Buy Anything: Computer Commandments."
    Library Journal 109 (October 1, 1984): 1821-
    22.
        Anglin provides a basic planning guide
    for purchase and introduction of microcomputers
    into library management and service, along with
    nine commandments for accomplishing the task with
    ease. Common themes which run throughout are the
    sharing of information with neighboring libraries
    and the utilization of local services.

84 ANSFIELD, PAUL J. "Humanizing the Installation
    of Microcomputers." Catholic Library World 54
    (November 1982): 151-54.
        The psychology of change as it affects
    the employee confronted with microcomputer auto-
    mation is the topic of this article. The frus-
    tration, stress, and loss of self-esteem which
    accompany change are acknowledged, and methods of
    reducing anxiety are explored. Bibliography.

85 ARMSTRONG, C. J. "Micro-Automation--The Problems
    of Selection." Electronic Library 2 (July
    1984): 165-74.
        The microcomputer has made automation
    possible for libraries which could never consider
    it before. Armstrong reviews the decision making
    process, then presents and discusses five options
    for automating the small library. Bibliography.

86 BEISER, KARL. "Choosing a Computer System."
    Library Software Review 3 (September 1984):
    332-38.

21

Beiser discusses the process he followed in choosing a microcomputer for the Maine Regional Library System. The steps include a needs analysis and the selection of appropriate software to perform each necessary function—database management, word processing, and accounting—before the selection of the hardware and peripherals. He also considers system installation and the purchase of additional software after the system is in place.

87 BERRY, JOHN. "The Local Option." Library Journal 106 (September 1, 1981): 1583.

This editorial explores the possibilities and advantages of employing microcomputers at the local level to accomplish library processes which are currently being brokered nationwide by large networks.

88 BILLS, LINDA G. "Making Decisions About Automation for Small Libraries." Library Resources and Technical Services 29 (April/June 1985): 161-71.

As computers have decreased in price and commercial programs have become more adaptable, automation has come within the realm of an increasing number of libraries. This article suggests some practical considerations for determining need, becoming acquainted with the world of automation, and selecting the system which best fits your library environment. Bibliography.

89 BLAIR, JOHN C., Jr. "Selection of Microcomputer Software and Hardware." Online '81 Conference Proceedings, Dallas, 2-4 November 1981. Weston, CT: Online, Inc., 1981. Pp. 298-99.

Sound advice for the novice hardware and software shopper includes such basic tips as: call the producer of the product to see if it is available locally; check to see how warranty repair work is handled; shop for off-the-shelf software; purchase hardware on which you have seen the software demonstrated; and always maintain service contracts.

90   BOCHER, ROBERT F. "Microcomputers: Guidelines
        for the Planning Process and Software Selec-
        tion." Wisconsin Library Bulletin 78 (Summer
        1983): 59-61.
            Guidelines for planning the purchase and
    installation of a microcomputer and for selecting
    quality software to meet the needs of the library
    are outlined and discussed.

91   BREAM, ELIZABETH. "Microcomputers in Libraries."
        Emergency Librarian 10 (January/February
        1983): 30-33.
            In the first of what is to be a feature
    column in Emergency Librarian, Elizabeth Bream
    deals with the problems inherent in the decision
    to get involved in microcomputing. Especially
    useful are suggestions for learning microcomputer
    usage locally.

92   BUNSON, STANLEY N. "Put a Micro Lab in the Media
        Center." Instructional Innovator 29 (January
        1984): 29-30.
            Finding space and determining physical
    design and layout for a microcomputer lab in a
    community college media center are the topics of
    this article which considers present and future
    usage and needs.

93   BYERS, EDWARD W. "Our Microcomputer." Wyoming
        Library Roundup 37 (Spring 1982): 40-42.
            The introduction of microcomputer appli-
    cations to a library operation with increasing
    needs and a set financial base is described, and
    the positive impact that an Altos micro with a
    database management system, word processing
    package, and bookkeeping features has had on the
    work flow and morale of a busy staff is told.

94   CHENEY, HAL. "User-Friendly? Designer-Friendly!"
        Library Software Review 3 (September 1984):
        339-45.
            The concept of user-friendliness is
    relative to the user and the computer system, and
    must be judged in terms of the users' needs and
    expectations, and the machine's capabilities.

Cheney provides a casual but workable model for analyzing the friendliness of hardware, operating systems, and applications software.

95 "Choosing the Most 'Useful' Micro." Library Systems Newsletter 3 (May 1983): 38.
A survey conducted by the Washington Post in 1983 identifies the most useful microcomputer hardware based on the number of compatible software programs.

96 CLARK, PHILIP M. "Training Library Staff to Use a Microcomputer." Top of the News 39 (Summer 1983): 329-31.
Games, finger exercises, small and large group sessions, individual practice, and other techniques for teaching microcomputer use are recommended and described, with helpful suggestions for making the training effective.

97 CLINE, SHARON D. "What to do Before the Micro Comes." Online '84 Conference Proceedings, San Francisco, 29-31 October, 1984. Weston, CT: Online, Inc., 1984. Pp. 54-59.
Planning for library automation is essential, no matter what size system is considered. Among considerations which are identified and discussed are space and environment, applications, software selection, staff training, and planning for future needs and expansion.

98 CONGER, LUCINDA D. "The Micro Choice." Database 8 (August 1985): 73-74.
Choosing a microcomputer system is not as difficult as it was before IBM entered the marketplace. The decision is now largely a choice of an appropriate operating system and compatible software. Conger points out the differences in the four most popular operating systems, discusses software and reviewing tools, and considers advantages and disadvantages of microcomputing.

99 COSTA, BETTY. "Open Letter to the Library Community." OCLC Micro 1 (September 1985): 2.
Library functions are frequently auto-

mated with little or no planning for those times when the system goes down. Costa addresses this problem, suggesting the development of alternative systems, manual contingency systems, and planning for down time, repairs, and system replacement.

100 CRAWFORD, WALT. "Common Sense Planning for a Computer; or, What's it Worth to You?" Library Hi Tech 2, no. 3, issue 7 (1984): 79-86.

Crawford outlines a practical, dollars-and-cents method for determining the value of a microcomputer to an individual or organization in this article concerning planning for automation.

101 CRAWFORD, WALT. "Commonsense System Pricing; or, How Much Will That $1,200 Computer Really Cost?" Library Hi Tech 2, no. 2, issue 6 (1984): 27-32.

Microcomputer shoppers may encounter drastic differences in stated price because of variations in pricing practices. Three pricing methods are identified; shopping for a complete microcomputer system is recommended over shopping for individual components; and examples of systems are provided, with estimated costs.

102 CULLEN, PATSY. "Are We Ready for the Micro?" Audiovisual Librarian 10 (Winter 1984): 30-33.

Just another piece of office equipment; or, a major influence on the nature of learning—two opposing viewpoints of the microcomputer are presented. Innovative uses are suggested, and questions are asked which should help the librarian in an educational institution determine the role of the microcomputer in the library. Bibliography.

103 DOUGLAS, SHIRLEY, and NEIGHTS, GARY. "Microcomputer Reference: A Guide to Microcomputers." Arlington, VA: ERIC Document Reproduction Service, ED 205 203, 1980.

A guide for educational practitioners, including librarians, this publication provides general information about microcomputers, help in conducting a needs assessment, and criteria for microcomputer selection. Bibliography.

104 EDMONDS, LESLIE. "Taming Technology: Planning for Patron Use of Microcomputers in the Public Library." Top of the News 39 (Spring 1983): 247-51.
In the 1970s the Rolling Meadows (IL) Public Library added a dial-up terminal in order to access the local high school's computer. Although it was not a successful experiment, it paved the way for the introduction of microcomputer technology in the 1980s. The selection of hardware, the building of a software collection, regulations for the use of equipment, and training information are presented.

105 ENG, SIDNEY. "Micro-Hysteria in Libraries." Catholic Library World 55 (December 1983): 224-25, 229.
The author points up the work which goes into creating microcomputer files, the slowness of the equipment, and the expense of a micro beyond the initial cost of the system. Comments of five other librarians are included.

106 ENG, SIDNEY. "Micro-Hysteria, One Year Later." Catholic Library World 56 (February 1985): 294-97.
Eng reiterates his hesitancy to incorporate microcomputer technology into the library, and justifies his stance by noting rapid changes, built-in obsolescence of hardware, and the growing sophistication of software demanding strong operator skills for full utilization. Five other librarians comment on his views.

107 FALK, HOWARD. "Computer Software and Equipment Considerations." School Library Journal 28 (November 1981): 29-32.
Factors in selecting a library computer system, mini or micro, are presented. Software, printing capabilities, storage, and maintenance are considered.

108 FONDIN, HUBERT. "The Impact of New Information
   Systems on the Training of Future Information
   Professionals." Journal of Information Science 8 (March 1984): 49-55.
      The training of information professionals
   in the use of new information systems is examined, with the impact of microcomputers, electronic
   publishing, the end user, the information utility, and new types of data being primary concerns.
   Bibliography.

109 FREEDMAN, MARY, and CARLIN, LARRY. "An Interview
   in Four Voices." Library Journal 110 (May 1,
   1985): 40-41.
      In the interview format the authors pre-
   sent their views on selecting microcomputer hardware and software for a library.

110 FREEDMAN, MARY, and CARLIN, LARRY. "A Micro for
   Warminster." Library Journal 110 (April 1,
   1985): 54-55.
      In two dialogs between a librarian shop-
   ping for a microcomputer and a salesman in a
   computer store, the authors of this article
   contrast ideal customer-salesman interaction
   with the less-than-perfect interaction which is
   often found in reality.

111 GATES, HILARY. "Factors to Consider in Choosing
   a Microcomputer for Library Housekeeping and
   Information Retrieval in a Small Library:
   Experience in the Cairns Library." Program 18
   (April 1984): 111-23.
      In 1982 the Cairns Library, which serves
   the John Radcliffe Hospital, Oxford, England, began a project to develop a microcomputer system
   suitable for use in small libraries. Planning,
   hardware selection, software development and
   selection, and system analysis are considered.
   Bibliography.

112 GIBB, FORBES. "Choosing a Microcomputer for the
   Library." State Librarian 29 (July 1981):
   19-21.
      How to determine the best microcomputer

system for a library is the topic of this article
which touches on hardware, storage media, and
software, and lists sources of additional help
and guidance.

113 GRANT, CARL. "Library Automation: The Definition
of Needs." Show-Me Libraries 34 (June 1983):
15-19.
    A step-by-step plan for defining library
needs and translating those needs into a winning
proposal for an automated system is presented by
a librarian who has been through the process.
Although not micro-specific, the information is
applicable to the writing of a proposal for a
microcomputer system.

114 GRANT, CARL. "Library Automation: The Hardware."
Show-Me Libraries 34 (September 1983): 15-18.
    The second in a series of articles
concerning the selection of library automated
systems, this article deals with hardware.

115 GRANT, CARL. "Library Automation: The Software."
Show-Me Libraries 35 (August 1984): 28-31.
    The third in a series of articles which
also covers the performing of a needs assessment
and the selection of computer hardware, this
article concerns software selection. Topics
considered are the user evaluation, technical
evaluation, training, documentation, costs, and
company support and reputation.

116 GRIFFITHS, JOSE-MARIE, and KING, DONALD W. "New
Technologies and Libraries: A Framework for
Decision Making." Microcomputers for Information Management 1 (June 1984): 95-107.
    Library automation has escalated with the
introduction of the microcomputer into the library environment, and the options for automation
in today's market are overwhelming. Griffiths
and King present a model for decision making
which takes into consideration library functions,
services, products, activities, resource components, costs, performance measures, attributes,
and effectiveness. Applying the model, cost ef-

fectiveness of various automated systems can be
figured. Bibliography.

117 HOLLAND, MAURITA PETERSON, and BEAN, MARGARET
     HELMS. "The IBM Personal Computer in a Large
     Academic Library." Online '83 Conference
     Proceedings, Chicago, 10-12 October, 1983.
     Weston, CT: Online, Inc., 1983. Pp. 118-23.
     When the University of Michigan's Engi-
     neering Libraries received two IBM PCs in 1982,
     staff faced the task of integrating them into
     library routines. Holland and Bean discuss
     their experiences with VISICALC, WORDSTAR, dBASE
     II, and other commercial software, and address
     training of personnel, software development,
     computer-to-computer communications, professional
     literature, and the future of microcomputing in
     the Engineering Libraries. Bibliography.

118 ISSHIKI, KOICHIRO. "Justifying the Purchase of a
     Micro, Part I." ACCESS: Microcomputers in
     Libraries 2 (January 1982): 7, 23-24.
     A feasibility study to determine need and
     possible applications is the first step in pre-
     paring for the purchase of a microcomputer. Is-
     shiki outlines the procedure step by step.

119 ISSHIKI, KOICHIRO. "Justifying the Purchase of a
     Micro, Part II: Selling the Idea." ACCESS:
     Microcomputers in Libraries 2 (April 1982):
     8-9, 17.
     A problem-solution approach to justifying
     the purchase of a microcomputer is presented,
     with valuable supporting information and hints
     for strengthening the justification and improving
     the presentation of the information.

120 KESNER, RICHARD M. "The Computer and the Library
     Environment: The Case for Microcomputers."
     Journal of Library Administration 3 (Summer
     1982): 33-50.
     Library administrators' perceptions of
     automation are surveyed, and the place of the
     microcomputer in library automation is consid-
     ered. Bibliography.

121 KESNER, RICHARD M., and JONES, CLIFTON H. <u>Micro-</u>
<u>computer Applications in Libraries: A Manage-</u>
<u>ment Tool for the 1980s and Beyond</u>. New Direc-
tions in Librarianship, no. 5. Westport, CT:
Greenwood Press, 1984. 250p.
Microcomputer applications in libraries
are justified, planning and implementation strategies are discussed, a variety of applications
are suggested, and computer assisted instruction
is considered. Bibliography.

122 KRUEGER, DONALD R. "Issues and Applications of
Microcomputers for Libraries." <u>Canadian</u>
<u>Library Journal</u> 38 (October 1981): 281-85.
Applications of microcomputer technology
to library functions and the impact they will
have on library services, personnel, and budgets
are the issues called to the attention of library
administrators in this early article.

123 MARCUM, DEANNA H., and BOSS, RICHARD W. "Information Technology." <u>Wilson Library Bulletin</u>
56 (January 1982): 364-65.
Marcum and Boss address the six major
elements--1) hardware, 2) software, 3) performance, 4) convenience, 5) reliability, and 6) cost
--to be considered in purchasing a microcomputer
for library use.

124 MARCUM, DEANNA H., and BOSS, RICHARD W. "Information Technology." <u>Wilson Library Bulletin</u>
57 (January 1983): 414-15, 447.
Problems of library management are addressed, and the emerging role of the microcomputer in easing the burden of those problems
through word processing, accounting, statistical
analysis, information storage, and electronic
mail is presented.

125 MASON, ROBERT M. "The Challenge of the Micro
Revolution." <u>Library Journal</u> 109 (June 15,
1984): 1219-20.
Microtechnology has brought the library
world to a time of crisis. New hardware, software, systems, and services are revolutionizing

the information industry, and library administrators must decide whether their libraries will become a part of the revolution or remain simply repositories for books.

126 MASON, ROBERT M. "Choosing a Microcomputer: A Success Story." Library Journal 108 (February 15, 1983): 356-58.
Mason narrates briefly the frustrations and satisfaction accompanying his first microcomputer purchase, and shares practical advice on choosing a microcomputer system based on a needs assessment.

127 MASON, ROBERT M. "Choosing a Vendor: Where to Buy a Micro." Library Journal 108 (March 15, 1983): 560-62.
Mason discusses the advantages and disadvantages of purchasing microcomputer equipment from manufacturers' representatives, computer stores, general retail stores, and mail order vendors. Criteria for choosing a vendor are provided. Second-hand purchases are considered.

128 MASON, ROBERT M. "Dear Colleague." American Society for Information Science Bulletin 8 (April 1982): 10-13.
Mason discusses considerations in choosing microcomputer hardware, describes his own personal system, and makes general recommendations for others who might be in the market for a microcomputer.

129 MASON, ROBERT M. "Human Resources and the Micro System." Library Journal 110 (March 15, 1985): 44-45.
Mason recommends a job study and redesign of work flow when automation is introduced into the workplace. To that end, he discusses techniques of job design and the use of the microcomputer as a motivator.

130 MASON, ROBERT M. "The Micro Manager." Library Journal 109 (April 15, 1984): 794-95.
Librarians often acquire microcomputer

hardware with little lead time for planning. This article deals with the details of formulating a policy and procedures for effective use of micro equipment.

131 MATHESON, NINA W. "Midwinter Musing on Microcomputers and Memex." Medical Library Association Bulletin 72 (April 1984): 214-16.
    A realistic approach to microcomputer use is presented in this brief article which compares expectations and realities, and suggests possible applications for home and office applications for the technology.

132 "Michigan Library Consortium Lends Funds for Automation." Library Journal 109 (May 1, 1984): 840.
    The Michigan Library Consortium has announced a financial loan program for its members to aid in the purchase of OCLC terminals and microcomputer equipment for online reference services.

133 "Micro Training Project Receives $38,000 Grant." School Library Journal 29 (May 1983): 17-18.
    The awarding of a $38,000 grant to the Innovative Technology Project for Western Pennsylvania Schools is announced. For the purpose of training media specialists and teachers in the use of microcomputers, the grant will help support the purchase of equipment and software, curriculum and program development, and a software previewing center.

134 Microcomputers for Libraries; Product Review and Procurement Guide. Powell, OH: James E. Rush Associates, 1984. Loose leaf.
    This valuable guide to microcomputers, written for the librarian, combines basic information with product reviews of software, hardware, systems, and peripherals. Addresses of hardware manufacturers, software vendors, and sources of supplies are included, along with substantial sections on telecommunications, hardware and software selection, and other topics. Pub-

lished in loose-leaf, the volume can be easily updated as new and revised sections are produced. Bibliography.

135   "N. Y. Challenge: LSCA for Micros." Library Journal 107 (October 1, 1982): 1804.
      $100,000 in LSCA grants have been made available to New York libraries with innovative microcomputer projects, according to this news release from the New York State Library.

136   NASH, JOHN C., and NASH, MARY M. "Libraries and Small Computers--A Perspective for Decision-Making." Canadian Library Journal 38 (August 1981): 207-11.
      In applying computer technologies to library processes, it is better to adapt the computer to the library than to adapt the library to the computer. In order to aid librarians in deciding what functions to convert, the authors have described microcomputer capabilities and costs and included a case study as a practical guide. Bibliography.

137   "NETWORds: When One PC Is Not Enough." OCLC Micro 1 (November 1985): 6-7.
      When an operation outgrows its microcomputer, there are several options which may be considered. Among the options are adding a hard disk drive for more storage space, buying a second micro, or converting to a local area network. The advantages of each are considered, with suggestions for appropriate equipment and software.

138   PALMOUR, VERNON E. "Planning Automated Information Systems." The Application of Mini- and Micro-Computers in Information, Documentation and Libraries. Proceedings of the International Conference on the Application of Mini- and Micro-Computers in Information, Documentation and Libraries, Tel-Aviv, Israel, 13-18 March 1983. New York: North-Holland, 1983. Pp. 495-501.
      A process for planning and implementing

small automated systems in libraries and information centers is outlined. Based on participative management techniques, the process involves pre-planning, setting goals, determining needs, developing and evaluating alternatives, and implementing the plan. Bibliography.

139 PALO, ERIC E. "Hidden Computer Costs." Small Computers in Libraries 4 (November 1984): 8-9.
Palo reviews the hidden costs in implementing a library microcomputer project. Costs for service, training, security, peripherals, and software are discussed. A listing of possible expenses, with estimated costs, is appended.

140 PAUSTIAN, P. ROBERT, and HILBURN, PATRICK M. "Computer Literacy at the UMKC Library: An Administrative Approach." Show-Me Libraries 35 (October/November 1983): 36-39.
Interest in word and data processing was generated among the staff of the University of Missouri at Kansas City Library when an IBM Displaywriter was purchased for office use. To capitalize on that interest, a computer literacy program was launched to familiarize personnel with capabilities of microprocessor equipment. A committee was chosen to study and recommend the purchase of the first micro, with the possibility of additional equipment purchases as needs arose. The shared equipment program and on-going computer literacy program for staff are described.

141 PEMBERTON, JEFFERY K. "Spread of Microcomputers . . .Fast and Wide." Database 5 (August 1982): 6-7.
A fact-filled article gives practical advice on getting into microcomputing, useful hardware features, and outstanding software packages.

142 POPE, NOLAN F. "Selecting a Microcomputer System." Special Libraries Association Florida Chapter Bulletin 14 (April 1982): 80-86.
Pope considers issues to be resolved before choosing a library microcomputer system. He recommends a needs assessment based on staff ex-

pectations, projected life span of the system,
expansion options, and database design. Vendor
reliability is considered, and an evaluation of
the stability of possible vendors is recommended.

143 PRITCHER, PAMELA N. "Integrating Microcomputers
     and the Information Professional: Strategies
     for Training Information Managers to Use the
     PC." Online 9 (March 1985): 15-22.
          In 1983 an Information Research Center
     was established by Bell Communications Research
     Inc., with each information management profes-
     sional on the staff supplied with an IBM PC.
     This article deals with the integration of the
     micro into the IRC, and the training program
     established by the company to help researchers
     adapt to the new technology.

144 RAPPAPORT, SUSAN. "Getting Librarians Involved
     With Computers." Library Journal 110 (June
     15, 1985): 44-45.
          Staff acceptance of computers is often
     the major hurdle in automating a library. Rap-
     paport discusses a microcomputer training project
     for staff of the New York Public Library which
     consists of hands-on workshops, video games, and
     other techniques designed to break down fears and
     prejudices.

145 RORVIG, MARK E. Microcomputers and Libraries: A
     Guide to Technology, Products and Applica-
     tions. White Plains, NY: Knowledge Industry
     Publications, 1981. 134p.
          A thorough but somewhat dated reference
     concerning microcomputer applications to library
     functions, this work provides a basic guide for
     librarians considering the purchase of microcom-
     puter equipment. An introduction to the technol-
     ogy is followed by reviews of specific library
     software, case studies of libraries that are cur-
     rently using micros, and reviews of hardware sys-
     tems. Appendices include charts which provide
     quick comparisons of systems, sources of software
     and hardware, a list of microcomputer journals
     and a glossary. Bibliography.

146 ROSASCHI, JIM. "Avoid Worthless Micro-Related
     Purchases." ACCESS: Microcomputers in Librar-
     ies 2 (January 1982): 6, 26-27.
     Considerations which will help the micro-
computer novice avoid unwise purchases are followed by a recommended list of sources for equipment and software reviews, evaluations, and comparisons. Bibliography.

147 RUSH, JAMES E. "Evaluation of Integrated Online
     Library Systems: Minis and Micros, Part 1."
     Second National Conference on Integrated On-
     line Library Systems Proceedings, Atlanta,
     Georgia, 13-14 September 1984. Canfield, OH:
     Genaway & Associates, 1984. Pp. 306-11.
     In the first of two presentations, Rush
defines integration, distinguishes among various
types or levels of integration--hardware, software, data, functional, operational, managerial--
and recommends an analysis to determine needs.

148 RUSH, JAMES E. "Evaluation of Integrated Online
     Library Systems: Minis and Micros, Part 2."
     Second National Conference on Integrated On-
     line Library Systems Proceedings, Atlanta,
     Georgia, 13-14 September 1984. Canfield, OH:
     Genaway & Associates, 1984. Pp. 312-23.
     In the second of two presentations, Rush
provides a model with which to analyze the functions and needs of a library in preparation for
implementing an integrated online system.

149 SCHUYLER, MICHAEL. "Workshop Reports: Microcom-
     puters." PNLA Quarterly 47 (Winter/Spring
     1983): 33-34.
     Schuyler summarizes considerations for
evaluation and purchase of functional library
microcomputer hardware--quality and availability
of support services, versatility and compatibility, and software availability--and suggests
basic types of software for first purchase.

150 "Selecting a Micro for Office and Management
     Applications." Library Systems Newsletter 3
     (October 1983): 73-75.

Six criteria for selecting a library microcomputer are enumerated and discussed, and several specific brands of hardware are recommended for library management applications.

151 SHARPE, DAVID M., and SMITH, SHIRLEE. "Technical Spotlight: Microcomputers? Test Drive Before You Buy." CMLEA Journal 3 (Spring 1980): 20-21.
Shopping for a microcomputer is compared to buying a new car. The components necessary for a workable system are discussed, and the selection process is outlined, with practical advice for decision making.

152 SHREEVE, ROBIN. "Advent of Micros Offers Many Possibilities." Educational Computing 2 (June 1981): 37-38.
The library of the West Suffolk College of Further Education was one of the early users of microcomputer technology in the United Kingdom. The librarian discusses the decision to automate using a microcomputer, and relates the library's experiences in programming and implementing applications such as the serial control file.

153 SLOAN, BERNARD G. "Micromania: A Manager's Perspective." Library Journal 110 (July 1985): 30-32.
Microcomputer selection, hardware compatibility, security, and training are among the potential problem areas for the library manager considering automation via microcomputer. Sloan suggests administrative support for microcomputer education, promotion, consulting, development, and information distribution as the major coping strategy for dealing with these areas.

154 SMARDO, FRANCES A. "Children and Computers: Competencies, Perceptions, and Attitudes." Public Libraries 23 (Spring 1984): 23-25.
Library administrators faced with implementing microcomputer use must become familiar with research on the topic. The author points up

the lack of substantial research on library automation and reviews the literature on microcomputers and childhood education. Bibliography.

155 SPELLER, BENJAMIN F., Jr. "Planning for Technology: Manager's Resources Review." Public Libraries 22 (Summer 1983): 59-60.
    This survey of literature concerning library automation is intended for directors and personnel of small to medium-sized public libraries, and concentrates on microcomputer technology and automated circulation systems. Bibliography.

156 SULLIVAN, ROLL A. Microcomputer Applications in Library Administration. A. M. A. Research Report, no. 34. Washington, DC: American Microcomputer Association, 1981. 76p.
    This consideration of automation of library administrative processes via microcomputer provides information on functions which should and those which should not be automated. Standalone installations, systems, and networks are considered. Software, implementation, training, maintenance, and other concerns are addressed.

157 SUTTON, ROGER. "Beyond the Hype of Microwares." School Library Journal 31 (September 1984): 54.
    Sutton encourages librarians to avoid purchasing microcomputer equipment and software simply because everyone else is doing it, and to analyze the current and future potential of the micro before making a purchase.

158 TEBBETTS, DIANE R., and CHEN, CHING-CHIH. "Microcomputers and Integrated Library Systems in New England ARL Libraries: Current Status and Management Consideration." Microcomputers for Information Management 2 (September 1985): 137-51.
    A research project investigating the plans of nine New England ARL libraries to integrate microcomputers into automated library systems reveals that microcomputer technology is generally being used in stand-alone situations,

with no plan for integration. Case studies are
included. Bibliography.

159 Turnkey Trends." Small Computers in Libraries 2
(February 1982): 5.
The trend toward total systems packages
is discussed, and purchasers of library automation systems are advised to rely on vendor supplies and services rather than attempt do-it-
yourself projects.

160 "Two Year Colleges and Libraries in California
May Get Free Micros." Library Journal 109
(June 1, 1984): 1070.
A bill in the California legislature to
extend legislation offering tax credits for gifts
of microcomputers to schools, may also include
gifts to junior colleges and libraries, according
to this news note.

161 VAVREK, BERNARD. "Microcomputer for Sale." Library Journal 108 (November 1, 1983): 2025-26.
Vavrek enumerates many of the problems
and pitfalls of microcomputer utilization in libraries, and recommends caution, particularly in
public service areas.

162 VAVREK, BERNARD. "Microcomputers and Rural Libraries." Technicalities 2 (July 1982): 5-6,
16.
The coordinator of the Center for the
Study of Rural Libraries reveals his personal
conversion to microcomputer use, discusses some
of the problems of small rural libraries, suggests programs which might be useful in small
libraries, recommends study before purchase, and
cautions against bandwagon purchasing.

163 VEANER, ALLEN B. "Management and Technology."
IFLA Journal 7, no. 1 (1981): 32-37.
In libraries, the management of technology, from micro to mainframe, ultimately becomes
the responsibility of the library director or
department administrator, who must approve system selection, provide funding for one-time and

on-going expenses, educate staff, and integrate programs. Veaner provides sound advice on how to accomplish these tasks effectively.

164 WALTON, ROBERT A. "Integrating the Micro into the Existing Workforce." Online '82 Conference Proceedings, Atlanta, 1-3 November 1982. Weston, CT: Online, Inc., 1982. Pp. 209-14.
        Walton identifies two employee groups who are potential problems when planning the integration of microcomputers into the workplace. He discusses the bases of their attitudes, then outlines a workable plan for introduction and integration of the new technology. Bibliography.

165 WALTON, ROBERT A. "Keeping Costs Down by Keeping Track of Supplies." Technicalities 3 (November 1984): 9, 13.
        Costs of microcomputing run far in excess of the price of hardware. Supplies (ribbons, paper, diskettes, etc.) represent on-going costs which must be worked into the budget. Walton lists three categories of supplies (mandatory, suggested, and extravagant) and offers some practical suggestions for the first-time purchaser.

166 WALTON, ROBERT A. Microcomputers: A Planning and Implementation Guide for Librarians and Information Professionals. Phoenix, AZ: Oryx Press, 1983. 96p.
        In a style which the novice can understand Walton explains the basics of microcomputer technology for the librarian or information specialist. He considers hardware, software, and implementation of a computer system in three sections, with chapters devoted to such topics as keyboards and displays, printers, library applications software, purchasing a system, and integrating micros into the workplace. Bibliography.

167 WALTON, ROBERT A. Microcomputers and the Library: A Planning Guide for Managers. Austin, TX: Texas State Library, Library Development Division, 1982. 96p.; and Arlington, VA: ERIC Document Reproduction Service, ED 225 539, 1982.

A brief introduction to the theory of microcomputer technology precedes general discussions of hardware and software usage and sections on library software development, equipment and software selection, and program implementation and management. This document provided the basis for Walton's later book, Microcomputers: A Planning and Implementation Guide for Librarians and Information Professionals. Bibliography.

168 WALTON, ROBERT A. "A Simple (But Complete) Guide to Acquiring and Running a Micro System." Online '83 Conference Proceedings, Chicago, 10-12 October 1983. Weston, CT: Online, Inc., 1983. Pp. 302-04.
Walton outlines the right way and the wrong way to select and implement a library microcomputer system.

169 WARDEN, WILLIAM H. III, and WARDEN, BETTE M. "Selecting the Right Microcomputer." Georgia Libraries 21 (February 1984): 10-14.
Selection criteria and sound advice for purchasing a microcomputer system to meet present and future library needs are the emphases of this article which outlines the selection process for clarity and ease of use. Bibliography.

170 "Wayne State Invests Heavily in Staff Computer Literacy." Library Journal 108 (February 15, 1983): 336.
A computer literacy project for the Wayne State University Library staff is described, and the anticipated benefits to the library are reviewed.

171 "What Now? vs. Which One? (Part I)." Small Computers in Libraries 1 (July 1981): 1-2.
For the librarian who has fallen heir to microcomputer facilities without knowledge of the uses they may serve, this article advises the exercise of caution when choosing functions to automate, and encourages the use of commercially produced rather than homemade programs to achieve desired results.

172 "What Now? vs. Which One? (Part II)." Small Com-
       puters in Libraries 1 (August 1981): 1-2.
            Specifications for an office or library
     microcomputer system, along with practical advice
     on shopping for and purchasing microcomputer
     equipment make this a valuable article for the
     inexperienced librarian about to enter the micro-
     computer age.

173 "What Seems to Work." Small Computers in Librar-
       ies 3 (February 1983): 7.
            Practical advice on getting the greatest
     return from a microcomputer includes giving in-
     terested staff members time to experiment, adapt-
     ing commercial software to local needs, and
     learning BASIC programming in order to create
     software when the need arises.

174 WILLIAMS, PHILIP W. "The Effect of Micro-Tech-
       nology on Information Handling." Microproces-
       sors and Intelligence. Proceedings of an
     AsLib Seminar, Slough, 14-15 May 1979.
     London: AsLib, 1980. Pp. 22-29.
            In general terms Williams describes the
     impact of the microprocessor on information hand-
     ling, problems of implementing a micro-based sys-
     tem, and the role of the manager in planning and
     coordinating for maximum utilization and benefit.

175 WILLIAMS, PHILIP W. "Information Technology--
       Problems and Opportunities." Minis, Micros
       and Terminals for Libraries and Information
       Services. Proceedings of the Conference
     Organized Jointly by the Institute of Infor-
     mation Scientists and the Information Re-
     trieval Specialist Group of the British Com-
     puter Society, Manchester, England, 6-7 Novem-
     ber 1980. London: Hayden, 1980. Pp. 1-11.
            Costs of computer equipment have dropped
     steadily during recent years, making automation
     a reality for large numbers of offices and li-
     braries. Williams discusses new possibilities
     for automation, identifies problems that may be
     encountered, and makes suggestions for trouble-
     free implementation. Bibliography.

176 WISMER, DONALD. "Microcomputers With a Bald
     Face; or, You've Got to Begin Somewhere." On-
     line 7 (September 1983): 52-59.
          Justification for implementing a micro-
     computer project, practical uses for the tech-
     nology, and a case study of the Maine State Li-
     brary's experience make up this down-to-earth
     introduction to low cost computing.

ACADEMIC LIBRARIES

177 "Academic Libraries in the Computer Age." College and Research Libraries News 42 (February
1981): 29-31.
The impact of the computer on academic
libraries is predicted, with views ten and fifty
years into the future.

178 ALEXANDER, WILLIAM, and ROSE, GREG. "Micros in
the Media Center." Small Computers in Libraries 3 (January 1983): 2-3.
The authors consider standard and innovative uses of the microcomputer in a community
college media center. Emphasis is placed on
graphics and other microcomputer aids to media
production.

179 ALLEN, KIMBERLY G. "Micros at Michigan: Developing Computer Literacy in the Library Staff."
Technicalities 3 (March 1983): 14-15.
In an attempt to respond to the needs of
staff members at the University of Michigan Graduate Library, administrators purchased two Osborne microcomputers and a printer to circulate
among the staff as needed. This article describes
the staff orientation offered, some uses made of
the equipment, and plans for expansion of the
program.

180 ASSOCIATION OF RESEARCH LIBRARIES. OFFICE OF
MANAGEMENT STUDIES. SYSTEMS AND PROCEDURES
EXCHANGE CENTER. Microcomputers in ARL Li-
braries. SPEC Kit, no. 104. Washington, DC:
Association of Research Libraries, Office of
Management Studies, 1984.
The results of a survey concerning micro-
computer use in academic libraries is reported.
Policy statements, planning specifications, and
staff training programs from leading ARL member
libraries provide guidance for others. Bibliog-
raphy.

181 ASSOCIATION OF RESEARCH LIBRARIES. OFFICE OF
MANAGEMENT STUDIES. SYSTEMS AND PROCEDURES
EXCHANGE CENTER. The Use of Small Computers
in ARL Libraries. SPEC Kit, no. 77. Washington, DC: Association of Research Libraries,
Office of Management Studies, 1981.
A general introduction to the use of
small computers in libraries, this publication
emphasizes microcomputers. Included are advantages and limitations of the technology, needs
and trends for the future, and thirteen articles
describing local applications of mini and micro
systems. Bibliography.

182 BURTON, PAUL F. Microcomputer Applications in
Academic Libraries. Library and Information
Research Report, no. 16. London: British Library, 1983. 125p.
A survey of 742 academic libraries in the
United Kingdom indicates current and planned applications of microcomputers, types of hardware,
system benefits, and other data. Also included
are a list of microcomputer organizations and the
names and addresses of librarians who are available for advice and consulting. Bibliography.

183 GUSKIN, ALAN E., STOFFLE, CARLA J., and BARUTH,
BARBARA E. "Library Future Shock: The Microcomputer Revolution and the New Role of the
Library." College and Research Libraries 45
(May 1984): 177-83.
Information technology and the development of the microcomputer will have dramatic impact on the academic library of the future. The
authors call upon librarians to recognize the potential of the library and make it the central
campus resource for the new technology. Bibliography.

184 MARCOTTE, FREDERICK A. "A Microcomputer in a
Micro-Sized Library." Small Computers in Li-
braries 5 (February 1985): 6-8.
In the first segment of a three-part
article concerning automation in the library of
Clermont College, the author describes how the

hardware was selected, the kind of hardware chosen, software purchases, and serials check-in and communication applications.

185 MARCOTTE, FREDERICK A. "A Microcomputer in a Micro-Sized Library, Part II." Small Computers in Libraries 5 (March 1985): 5-8.
The second installment of a three-part series on automation in the library at Clermont College considers government document control using DATATREK serials software.

186 MARCOTTE, FREDERICK A. "A Microcomputer in a Micro-Sized Library, Part III." Small Computers in Libraries 5 (April 1985): 4-6.
The third installment of a three-part series concerning automation in the Clermont College Library describes an unsuccessful cooperative project between the library and a computer science class.

187 "Michigan Acquires Zenith Microcomputers." Wilson Library Bulletin 59 (April 1985): 520.
The University of Michigan Library's purchase of 70 Zenith-150 microcomputers for staff use, and a gift from the manufacturer of 50 more for the Undergraduate Library's microcomputer center, are reported by Richard Dougherty, the library's director.

188 "Micros in Academic Libraries." Small Computers in Libraries 1 (August 1981): 4-5.
Preliminary results of an Association of Research Libraries, Office of Management Studies survey of microcomputer uses in ARL member libraries are summarized.

189 PATRICK, RUTH J., and BOOTH, ROBERT E. "The Impact of Microcomputers in Academic Libraries. Final Report." Arlington, VA: ERIC Document Reproduction Service, ED 247 932, 1984.
A research project conducted at Wayne State University to determine the potential of microcomputer technology in academic libraries is reported. The report addresses user motiva-

tion, training, guidelines for library use, implementation, and problems.

190　"U. of M. Library Acquires 70 Z-150's." Small
　　　Computers in Libraries 5 (May 1985): 3.
　　　　　The University of Michigan Library has
purchased 70 Zenith-150 microcomputers for staff
use; the Library School purchased similar Zenith
equipment for its faculty; and Zenith has given
the Undergraduate Library 50 micros for its computer center, according to this brief note.

191　"U. of Michigan Acquires 150 Zenith Micros." Li-
　　　brary Journal 110 (May 1, 1985): 22.
　　　　　Michigan-made Zenith microcomputers have
been purchased for staff use in the University of
Michigan's Library, and 50 additional machines
have been donated by the company for use in a
Library Microcomputer Center, according to this
brief article.

192 ANDERSON, ERIC S. "The Amazing Library Computer: Part 2 of a Two Part Series." Electronic Learning 2 (March 1983): 68-71.

School library management tasks suitable for a microcomputer are examined in terms of the availability of off-the-shelf hardware, size of the task to be performed, and the amount of storage space required. Popular library application programs are listed in chart form for easy comparison.

193 ANDERSON, ERIC S. "The Microcomputer: One More Piece of AV Equipment." Book Report 1 (September/October 1982): 28-31.

Anderson makes a strong case for integrating the microcomputer with other equipment in the media center, and offers guidelines for following through with the plan.

194 ANDERSON, ERIC S. "Putting Micros to Work in the Media Center." Computing Teacher 9 (May 1982): 13-14.

Apple II Plus micros purchased for the Dakota (IL) Community Unit School District are being used primarily for instruction, although administrative and library functions are being phased into the program. Anderson describes the school's microcomputer program, including processing of overdue notices, word processing, and production of bibliographies for the library.

195 ANDERSON, ERIC S. "Sharing the Future." Book Report 4 (May/June 1985): 28.

Anderson predicts the impact of microcomputer technology on the school library of the future, and encourages librarians to begin now to learn how to use a word processor, a spreadsheet, a database manager, and to share worthwhile projects with other librarians with similar needs and interests.

196 ANDERSON, ERIC S. "Wonderful Welling." Computing Teacher 10 (January 1983): 32-33.
          A high school librarian reports positive-
ly on the accomplishments of one student with a
knack for microcomputing, and the challenge and
assistance he presents to the school, to other
students, and to the librarian.

197 BARRETTE, PIERRE P. "Microcomputers in the
School Media Program." Catholic Library World
53 (October 1981): 125-32.
          Barrette addresses microcomputer technol-
ogy in education and school media centers, point-
ing out the need for greater utilization of the
technology, calling attention to major problems,
and discussing the professional development needs
of educators confronted with rapidly changing
equipment and procedures. Bibliography.

198 BAUCKHAM, MARY. "The Changing Role of the Computing Librarian." Computing Teacher 13
(December 1985/January 1986): 39-40.
Bauckham tells of the development of a computing center in her middle school, and describes
the evolution of the library staff to accommodate
the needs of the new center and its patrons.

199 BENSON, LAURA M. "Erwin Open School Computer
Program." Educational Computer Magazine 2
(May/June 1982): 22-23.
          A practical discussion concerning intro-
duction and maintenance of microcomputers in an
elementary school media center is provided by a
center coordinator, who describes her plans to
use public service, computer literacy equipment
for library management tasks.

200 BERGLUND, PATRICIA. "School Library Technology."
Wilson Library Bulletin 58 (February 1984):
427-29.
          Three school librarians discuss experi-
ences in integrating microcomputers into their
libraries. Each has taken a different approach,
and each has been successful because of personal
innovativeness and system versatility.

201 BERGLUND, PATRICIA. "School Library Technology."
     Wilson Library Bulletin 58 (April 1984): 571-
     73.
          The introduction of microcomputers into
     elementary school libraries has sometimes drawn
     negative reactions from teachers, parents, and
     librarians themselves. Three elementary librar-
     ians tell how they planned programs to introduce
     microcomputer learning into their schools, and
     note the positive responses that their programs
     elicited.

202 BERGLUND, PATRICIA. "School Library Technology."
     Wilson Library Bulletin 59 (November 1984):
     202-03.
          Berglund deals with many of the fears and
     hesitancies of people encountering the microcom-
     puter for the first time.

203 BEST, TIM. "Computers, Libraries, and You."
     Book Report 1 (September/October 1982): 22-23.
          Best encourages school librarians to take
     the initiative in introducing computer management
     techniques into their libraries, and provides
     sound advice on implementing the plan.

204 BOEHMER, M. CLARE. "Computerizing the Small-
     School Library; Computerizing on a Shoe-
     string." Catholic Library World 54 (November
     1982): 162-65.
          The economics of automating a small
     school library via microcomputers is addressed,
     and advice on planning and developing a workable
     public access program for students is provided.

205 BOEHMER, M. CLARE. The Micro in Your Library.
     Pocatello, ID: Contemporary Issues Clearing-
     house, 1983. 38p.
          A general introduction to the concept of
     the microcomputer in the school library, this
     publication considers personnel for microcomputer
     supervision, criteria for hardware and software
     selection, development of in-house software,
     funding for the program, implementation, expan-
     sion, and maintenance.

206 BRICKLEY, RICHARD R. "Schools, Computers, and
Libraries: Selected Resources from Course Projects Developed by Students in L. S. 8064-90,
Villanova University, Fall Term, 1980." Arlington, VA: ERIC Document Reproduction Service, ED 200 194, 1981.
Nine class projects concerning the use of
computers in educational or library settings cover a variety of subjects and applications. Two
projects concerning micros are especially applicable: "Design of Microcomputer Inventory of
Media/AV Equipment in a Junior High School," and
"Teachers Resource List of Supplementary Materials for Courses Using Microcomputer." Bibliography.

207 BRODIE, LINDA. "High Tech and Hair Dryers."
Voice of Youth Advocates 7 (June 1984): 78-79.
Most school media personnel have to be
innovative in ways other than teaching, and Linda
Brodie is no exception. In this entertaining
article she describes a very active microcomputer
program that she has developed for the Roosevelt
Junior High School in Eugene, Oregon, despite
less than perfect physical facilities.

208 CLYDE, LAUREL A., and JOYCE, D. JOAN. "Computers
and School Libraries." COMLA Newsletter 45
(September 1984): 2, 14.
Microcomputer use in Australian public
schools is increasing rapidly, making dissemination of microcomputer information essential.
The authors summarize developments and applications, discuss the growing number of workshops
and conferences, and address the need for better
indexing and bibliographic control of the literature. Bibliography.

209 COHEN, FRANCES LIEBERMAN. "Bank Street Writer:
An Elementary School Program." School Li-
brary Media Quarterly 13 (Spring 1985):
99-101.
Library staff at Shady Grove Elementary
School in Wissahickon School District, near
Philadelphia, plan to teach word processing to

the entire student enrollment of fifth and sixth
graders, using two Franklin Ace 100's and one
Commodore Pet, with BANK STREET WRITER software.
The project is outlined, and advantages and disadvantages are presented. Bibliography.

210 "Computer Placement Focus of '82-'83 Study."
    School Library Journal 31 (December 1984): 15.
        A research survey concerning placement of
microcomputers in schools indicates greatest use
of the equipment when located in a laboratory or
library setting. Results of the survey are summarized briefly.

211 "Computers and Library Management." Book Report
    4 (November/December 1985): 22-29.
        In symposium format five practicing
librarians address the use of microcomputers in
school library management. Database management,
circulation, ergonomics, and cataloging and circulation of software are some of the topics considered.
        CONTENTS: Becoming Literate in Data Man-
agement Programs, by Deborah M. Cooke.--Practical
Applications of a Database, by John A. Nied.--
One Library's Experiences With CIRCULATION PLUS,
by Martha H. Bailey.--Ergonomics and Computers,
by Eugene LaFaille.--Setting Up a Software Lending Library, by Marilyn Nicholson.

212 COOK, BETH, and TRUETT, CAROL. "Media Special-
    ists and Microcomputers: 13 Aspects of a
    Changing Role." Media and Methods 21 (Decem-
    ber 1984): 26, 31-33.
        School librarians and media specialists
must determine their roles in providing microcomputer services based on personal, departmental,
and school needs and expectations. Thirteen
alternatives are discussed; two programs are analyzed. Bibliography.

213 CRAWFORD, RON. "Microcomputers in the School
    Library." The Revolting Librarian 7 (Summer
    1980): 8-9.
        A school librarian provides his rationale

for purchasing a microcomputer for the library, describes how the funds were raised, and illustrates a variety of applications.

214 DEACON, JAMES. "Coping With the Computer in the School Media Center." Book Report 1 (September/October 1982): 17-38.
    Five of seven articles in this symposium on computers in the school library concern some aspect of microcomputer utilization.
    CONTENTS: Wake Up Educators: The Microcomputer Is Here, by Paula Galland.--Computers, Libraries and You, by Tim Best.--Introducing the Media Specialist to the Microcomputer, by Paula R. Grookett.--One More Piece of AV Equipment, by Eric S. Anderson.--How to Fund Those Microcomputer Projects, by James Deacon.--Going On-Line With a Computerized Library Network, by Hugh Durbin.--The View From the OCLC Terminal, by Kimberly Greene.

215 DEACON, JAMES. "How to Fund Those Microcomputer Projects." Book Report 1 (September/October 1982): 32-33.
    Outside sources of funding for school library microcomputer projects are suggested. Local and community support groups, block grants, foundations, and industry are discussed.

216 DEACON, JAMES. "If I Had an Apple, What Would I Do With It?" Educational Computer Magazine 1 (September/October 1981): 15, 23.
    A media coordinator considers practical uses for a micro in his media center and decides on library orientation and circulation projects as first priorities. The founding of "The Computers and the Media Center Task Group" is identified as an outgrowth of this project.

217 DIXON, SCOTT. "How to Organize an Efficient, Smooth-Running Computer Room." Electronic Learning 2 (October 1982): 64-65, 84.
    The computer room in the Media Center of Boulder, Colorado's Centennial Junior High School logs an average of 350 hours per month of patron

use on the Center's three microcomputers. Organization makes the project run smoothly, and the priorities of the organization are explained by math teacher, Scott Dixon.

218   DOYEN, SALLY, and ROUSE, JOYCE. "Microcomputers in Libraries and Media Centers." Miami University School of Education and Allied Professions Review 19 (Spring 1983): 19-23.
      The introduction of the microcomputer into the school library environment has altered the operation of the library, the expectations of the students, and the skills needed by librarians to be fully effective. Doyen and Rouse look at the changes and consider the impact of microcomputers on school libraries of the future.

219   FUCHS, CURTIS RAY. "Microcomputer Futures: Predictions of Selected Faculty Members in Missouri Secondary Schools." Ph. D. dissertation, University of Missouri, 1982.
      The purpose of this study was to predict the future of microcomputers in the business and mathematics curricula and the school libraries of Missouri. A Delphi method was used. It was found that each department predicted growing dependency on micros, with business teachers expressing the greatest need and predicting the earliest integration of the equipment into their curriculum. Librarians associated micros with increased efficiency and better service, and predicted that they would be indispensable by 1987. Bibliography.

220   FUCHS, CURTIS RAY. "School Libraries and Microcomputers." Show-Me Libraries 35 (October/ November 1983): 58-60.
      The reluctance of some school librarians to accept microcomputers is noted, and curricular implications and library uses are discussed. Bibliography.

221   GERHARDT, LILLIAN N. "Dreaming Professionally." School Library Journal 31 (November 1984): 2.
      The editor of School Library Journal

presents findings from a survey conducted by
R. R. Bowker Co. The survey indicates that elementary and college libraries are far ahead of
high school libraries in microcomputer use. This
calls for immediate attention to planning for
automation on the part of high schools in order
to meet the needs of computer proficient students
who will soon be enrolling.

222 GERHARDT, LILLIAN N. "On Form, Size, and Propor-
tion." School Library Journal 30 (December
1983): 2.
In a brief editorial school librarians
are encouraged to incorporate microcomputer technology into their libraries, but to do it in such
a way that the technology is kept in perspective.

223 GILMAN, JAMES A. Information Technology and the
School Library Resource Centre: The Microcomputer as Resourcerer's Apprentice. CET
Occasional Paper, no. 11. London: Council for
Educational Technology, 1983. 289p.
Uses and treatment of microcomputer resources in schools is addressed, with emphasis on
the role of the school library resource center.
The author considers computer literacy and computer aided instruction, hardware, software, online services, administration and management, and
implications of microcomputers in the school li-
brary/media center, all from the British perspective. Bibliography.

224 GILMAN, JAMES A. "The Resourcerer's Apprentice."
Education Libraries Bulletin 25, no. 3 (1982):
1-11.
Gilman predicts that microcomputer technology will relieve the school librarian from
clerical duties and allow for greater attention
to professional activities. He analyzes these
activities and the impact they may have on school
librarianship and the educational profession.

225 GRAHAM, JUDY. "My Micro Chased the Blues Away!"
School Library Journal 29 (February 1983):
23-26.

The Point Pleasant (WV) High School librarian writes of her experiences in planning,
seeking funding, and setting up a microcomputer-
based system to perform circulation, reporting,
and other functions. Equipment needs, problems,
future applications, and funding are treated.

226 GRAY, ROBERT A. "Microcomputers: A Primer for
     Instructional Media Specialists." Interna-
     tional Journal of Instructional Media 8, no.
     3 (1980-81): 207-12.
        The concept of the microcomputer system
     is explored, with information on selection and
     utilization, and sources for additional reading.
     Bibliography.

227 GROOKETT, PAULA R. "Introducing the Media Spe-
     cialist to the Microcomputer." Book Report 1
     (September/October 1982): 25-27.
        Grookett describes the integration of
     micros into 41 South Carolina media centers.

228 HANSON, MARY. "Impact of Computers on Media
     Skills." Media Spectrum 11 (Fourth Quarter
     1984): 9.
        The impact of microcomputer technology on
     education is far reaching. Hanson discusses
     change in the elementary curriculum as typing and
     computing skills are added, change in teaching
     methods as teachers adopt micros as teaching de-
     vices, and change in media center operation as
     media specialists adapt micros to media produc-
     tion, recordkeeping, and management functions.

229 HARRIS, MARY CLAIRE. "An Apple for the Librar-
     ian." Sourdough 18 (October 1981): 10, 16.
        An elementary school librarian briefly
     describes her first year using an Apple II micro-
     computer. Various library uses for a file man-
     agement program are listed, and her first pro-
     gramming experiences are told.

230 HAYCOCK, KENNETH R. "Micros: The New Status Sym-
     bol." Emergency Librarian 10 (January/Febru-
     ary 1983): 5.

In editorial style Haycock addresses
questions which may aid librarians and media specialists in determining the value of the micro in
the school library.

231 HELLER, NORMA. "Computers in an Urban Library
     Media Center." Computing Teacher 10 (February
     1983): 51-55.
     The media specialist in an inner city
school, in which a major portion of the students
have learning or emotional difficulties, provides
an impression of the impact of the media center's
microcomputer project on children with special
needs. Useful software is reviewed. Original
contributions by students are included.

232 HINO, JEFF, and BOSS, JACQUELINE A. "Summer Fun
     on Micros for Kids and Parents." Computing
     Teacher 9 (May 1982): 26-30.
     Two school media specialists describe
their microcomputer summer school program conducted for children in grades 2 through 8.

233 HOPKINS, DEE. "Micros in the Elementary Media
     Center? Somebody Pop the Bubble. . .Problems
     Do Exist." Indiana Media Journal 7 (Winter
     1984): 3-6.
     The microcomputer has created problems in
many school libraries and media centers. Hopkins
cites noise, poor utilization of equipment by
students and teachers, demands on the time of the
librarian/media specialist, and drain on other
programs when the microcomputer program must be
funded and maintained with existing resources.
Bibliography.

234 HORNER, G., and TESKEY, F. J. "Micro-Computers
     and the School Library." School Librarian 27
     (December 1979): 339-40.
     Horner and Teskey consider microcomputer
software another form of educational media, and
the microcomputer another type of teaching machine. They make a strong case for the housing,
cataloging, and circulation of these items in the
school media center.

235 HUG, WILLIAM E. "Videodiscs, Microcomputers, and
     Media Program: District and School." Indiana
     Media Journal 3 (Fall 1980): 3-5.
          Hug takes the stance that videodisc and
     microcomputer technologies can provide the qual-
     ity school media program outlined in the AASL/
     AECT publication, Media Programs: District and
     School (1975). Bibliography.

236 JOHNS HOPKINS UNIVERSITY. CENTER FOR SOCIAL
     ORGANIZATION OF SCHOOLS. "School Uses of
     Microcomputers: Reports from a National
     Survey. Issue No. 5." Alexandria, VA: ERIC
     Document Reproduction Service, ED 246 886,
     1984.
          Location of microcomputer equipment in a
     school has an impact on its effectiveness and
     use. This study compares microcomputer usage
     when equipment is located in classrooms, the
     library/media center, in micro labs, rotated from
     room to room, and dispersed throughout the build-
     ing in areas where needs have been identified.

237 JONES, MILBREY L. "The Non-Debate About Place-
     ment of Microcomputers in Libraries and
     Schools." Catholic Library World 54 (November
     1982): 145-46.
          Jones assumes a middle-of-the-road stance
     on the debate concerning placement of and respon-
     sibility for microcomputer equipment in a school,
     saying that micros should be in all locations
     where they are needed, whether it be classroom,
     media center, or both.

238 JONES, MILBREY L., and SIMMONS, BEATRICE. "Uti-
     lizing the New Technologies in School Library
     Media Centers: A Report to the Association."
     School Media Quarterly 9 (Summer 1981): 331-
     34.
          The impact of microcomputers and other
     recent technological developments on the school
     library is the concern of this report on a
     special meeting of the American Association of
     School Librarians held at ALA Midwinter, 1981.
     Bibliography.

239 KARAS, FRANK. "Microcomputers and the Teacher-
Librarian: Panacea or Pandora's Box." School
Libraries in Canada 3 (Autumn 1982): 20-23;
and MSLAVA Journal 10 (June 1983): 12-19.
Karas places the responsibility for computer education with the teacher, although he
states that the school librarian will be expected
to assume responsibility for the resource services aspects of a microcomputer program. The
responsibilities of the school librarian are presented here, and librarians are encouraged to
become resource persons, with emphasis on consulting and management. Bibliography.

240 KINZLER, MILT. "The Microcomputer and the Building Media Specialist." School Learning Resources 1 (Spring 1982): 24.
Kinzler addresses basic philosophical issues concerning the responsibility for a computer
literacy program in a school, and the roles of
the media center and the building media specialist in the program.

241 KONOPATZKE, PAT. "Elmira High School Media Center
Computer Program." Educational Computer Magazine 1 (July/August 1981): 8-9.
A justification for locating public-use
microcomputers in the media center, a discussion
of the media specialist's role in administering
the program, and a description of a workable computer literacy program constitute this article.

242 LEHMANN, RICHARD. "What I've Learned After Nine
Months With an Apple." Ohio Media Spectrum 34
(Spring 1982): 30-31.
In 1981 the library in Westerville,
Ohio's South High School acquired an Apple II
microcomputer. After one school year of use, the
media specialist offers practical suggestions on
a variety of microcomputer topics, including purchase, scheduling, control, and security.

243 LOPEZ, ANTONIO M., Jr. "Microcomputers: Tools of
the Present and Future." School Media Quarterly 9 (Spring 1981): 164-67.

Lopez describes changes that microcomputers are bringing to education and predicts additional developments, including the evolution of the library as we presently know it into the computerized information center of the future. Bibliography.

244 MACON, MYRA, and LESTER, GLENDA. "The Microcomputer: Its Role in Education and the School Media Center." Arkansas Libraries 39 (September 1982): 22-24.
The growing importance of the microcomputer in education is discussed, and applications of the technology to school library/media center programs are explored. Bibliography.

245 MACON, MYRA, and LESTER, GLENDA. "The Role of the Microcomputer in School Library Media Centers." Technicalities 3 (August 1983): 11-13.
The integration of the microcomputer into the school library media center is essential to the development of quality library media programs, and the librarian is the catalyst which determines the degree of success and acceptance of the technology. This article addresses the total integration of the micro, including training of library media center staff, development of computer literacy through library instruction programs, integration of various management applications into library routines, and offering micro services such as networking. Bibliography.

246 McCULLOCH, ARETA, and GRIEVE, ANN. "Getting Ready: Computers and the School Library." School Library Bulletin 13 (September 1981): 1-7.
The authors analyze school library functions to determine which are adaptable to computerization, and outline a computer preparedness program to pave the way for automation.

247 "Micro Use Is Up 75% School Survey Shows." School Library Journal 32 (December 1985): 12.
A survey of 15,275 school districts con-

cerning the use of microcomputers indicates major increases in microcomputer utilization. This article briefly summarizes the findings of the survey, and provides purchase information for the complete survey report.

248 The Microelectronics Revolution and Its Implications for the School Library. London: Library Association, School Libraries Group, 1982. 11p.
   The role of the microcomputer in British education is reviewed, and implications for teaching and administrative use in the school library are explored. Bibliography.

249 MILLER, GLORIA. "No One Said It Was Easy." School Library Journal 31 (November 1984): 62-64, 66.
   Planning, implementing, and coordinating a microcomputer program for students and personnel of the Charlotte-Mecklenburg (NC) School System was begun in 1982, after several microcomputer systems had already been purchased. Miller describes a faculty/staff training program which was instrumental in getting the microcomputer project started. She writes candidly of problems, and projects what the future may hold for the school system.

250 MILLER, INABETH. "An Examination of Microcomputers in Educational Settings with Particular Focus Upon Library/Media Operations: Realities and Possibilities--State of the Art." Ed. D. dissertation, Boston University, 1982.
   Data from two national surveys, site visits to major microcomputer centers, and other methods of data collection are the bases for this model for decision making for microcomputer utilization in educational institutions, with emphasis on the library/media center. Bibliography.

251 MILLER, INABETH. Microcomputers in School Library Media Centers. New York: Neal-Schuman, 1984. 165p.
   Based on the author's doctoral disserta-

tion, but written in a popular rather than a research study format, this book contains a wealth
of information on microcomputers in education.
The author deals with the problems of selection
and preparation, including such matters as selection committees and teacher and staff training.
Chapters on computer assisted instruction, microcomputers in the school library, and micros in
alternative settings provide information on state
of the art educational applications. Chapters on
software include information on reviewing tools,
previewing, choosing a vendor, and copyright.
Bibliography.

252 MILLER, MARILYN L., and MORAN, BARBARA B. "Expenditures for Resources in School Library
Media Centers FY '82-83." School Library
Journal 30 (October 1983): 105-14.
A national survey of general expenditures
in school library media centers provides text and
several charts concerning location, management,
and application of microcomputers in media centers in the United States. Bibliography.

253 MILLER, MARILYN L., and MORAN, BARBARA B. "Expenditures for Resources in School Library
Media Centers FY '83-84." School Library
Journal 31 (May 1985): 19-31.
The second of School Library Journal's
surveys of expenditures for school libraries in
the United States is reported here. The report
covers various resources, including books, periodicals, audiovisual equipment and materials,
services, and staff, with a substantial section
devoted to microcomputers and software.

254 NAUMER, JANET NOLL. Media Center Management With
an Apple II. Littleton, CO: Libraries Unlimited, 1984. 236p.
This practical handbook on the use of the
Apple II microcomputer as a management tool in a
school media center provides basic information on
the development of a system, and care and maintenance of equipment and software, but the major
portion of the book is devoted to database management, spreadsheet, and word processing pack-

ages and their applications to media center functions. Bibliography.

255 NICHOLSON, MARILYN. "The Librarian and Special
Education--Computers Bring Us Together." Computing Teacher 10 (May 1983): 47-48.
Microcomputer technology has provided one
school librarian with the means to improve library services to special education teachers and
students, according to this article which summarizes software selection activities, data gathering and recordkeeping opportunities, and other
services.

256 NICHOLSON, MARILYN. "Library Word Processing
Center Enriches Publications Class." Computing Teacher 10 (May 1983): 46-47.
A microcomputer center in the library/
media center at Danville, California's Los Cerros
Intermediate School, has heightened junior high
school students' interests in both microcomputing
and writing. The school librarian describes how
word processing skills are taught to students in
a Yearbook/Publications class, which can be
utilized in general classwork.

257 NICKLIN, R. C., and TASHNER, JOHN H. "Micros in
the Library Media Center?" School Media
Quarterly 9 (Spring 1981): 168-72, 177-81.
Nicklin and Tashner consider factors to
be examined when proposing the purchase of microcomputers for instructional purposes in a school
media center. Bibliography.

258 NIERENGARTEN, JOHN A. "Micro Computers in School
Media Centers." Wisconsin Library Bulletin 76
(November/December 1980): 273-74.
A basic introduction to microcomputer use
in school libraries and media centers, this article defines and describes hardware, identifies
what microcomputers can do, and provides tips for
first time purchasers.

259 OLDS, MICHAEL. "Microcomputers Enhance Learning,
Administration in School Media Centers and

Classrooms." <u>American Libraries</u> 11 (November 1980): 634-35.
The microcomputer is extolled as a major labor saving device for school administrators, media specialists, and librarians, and a popular teaching tool for classrooms and media centers.

260 ORWIG, GARY. "The Microcomputer and the Media Center." <u>Florida Media Quarterly</u> 6 (Spring 1981): 7-9.
The integration of the microcomputer into the school media center is described, along with methods of utilization including an online catalog, shelf lists, production of bibliographies, word processing, circulation, and instruction. Bibliography.

261 PATTIE, KENTON, and ERNST, MARY. "Chapter II Grants: Libraries Gain." <u>School Library Journal</u> 29 (January 1983): 17-20.
Chapter II, a federal aid to education program created in 1981 by the consolidation of twenty-eight small aid programs into one large Block Grant, is a program through which school libraries may obtain funds for materials and equipment. The authors explain the program, tell how libraries may benefit from it, and explain how funding for microcomputer equipment might be obtained through Chapter II.

262 PILKINGTON, MARGARET. "Using a Micro-Computer in a School Resource Centre." <u>Society for Mass Media and Resource Technology Journal</u> 11, no. 4 (1981): 23-26.
A basic evaluation of early microcomputer effectiveness in a school media center is presented in this article which addresses uses, advantages, limitations, and practical difficulties, but concludes with a positive recommendation. Bibliography.

263 SAUNDERS, JEREMY. "Information and the Librarian." <u>Educational Computing</u> 3 (July/August 1982): 22-23.
Saunders summarizes the proceedings of a

weekend microcomputer seminar for school librarians at Nottingham University in April, 1982. The eighty librarians in attendance considered the role of the librarian in microcomputer usage, and identified four essential activities: consulting, reference, in-house database management, and software control.

264 SCHLESSINGER, JUNE H., and SCHLESSINGER, BERNARD S. "Use of Microcomputers in Schools--Library Interaction with Subject Areas." The Application of Mini- and Micro-Computers in Information, Documentation and Libraries. Proceedings of the International Conference on the Application of Mini- and Micro-Computers in Information, Documentation and Libraries, Tel-Aviv, Israel, 13-18 March 1983. New York: North-Holland, 1983. Pp. 447-54.

The perception that the microcomputer is a tool of the science and business curricula in the public schools is tested by means of a survey of randomly selected secondary schools in Texas. Library involvement in microcomputer use is also surveyed, and found to be infrequent and unimaginative. Innovative uses of micros in libraries and departments of English are recommended, and cooperative projects between libraries and humanities teaching areas are suggested.

265 SHEROUSE, VICKI M. "Purchasing a Microcomputer for the School Media Center." Ohio Media Spectrum 34 (Spring 1982): 7-9.

Computer literacy, programming, computer-assisted instruction, and administrative support are identified as the four major applications for microcomputers in school media centers. Hardware is considered for each application, and selection of hardware components is addressed.

266 SHEROUSE, VICKI M. "Support for Your Local Computer Revolution." Book Report 1 (September/October 1982): 40-42.

Sherouse suggests software, books, periodicals and other media to support microcomputer programs in school libraries.

267 SHEROUSE, VICKI M., and POST, RICHARD. Micro-
     computers in the Media Center. Columbus, OH:
     Ohio Educational Library Media Association,
     1983. 60p.
         Eleven short articles by authorities in
     the field of microcomputers provide an overview
     of microcomputer applications in schools and
     media centers. Bibliography.
         CONTENTS: The Microcomputer and the
     School Media Center, by Vicki Sherouse.--Select-
     ing a Microcomputer for the Media Center, by
     Vicki Sherouse.--Computer Software Selection, by
     Richard Post.--Cataloging and Storing Microcom-
     puter Materials, by Kathy Kneil.--Microcomputer
     Management, by Roger Burgess.--Using a Microcom-
     puter for Media Center Administration, by Vicki
     Sherouse.--Setting Up In-Service Programs About
     Computers, by Steven Hawley.--Microcomputer Lan-
     guages, by Fred Williams.--Troubleshooting Micro-
     computers, by Weston Orloff.--Networking: Vital
     Links to a Total Information System, by Keith
     Bernhard.--Interactive Video, by Richard Post.

268 SIMMONS, DEBRA. "The Library, the Computer, and
     Utopia." Emergency Librarian 10 (January/
     February 1983): 11-12.
         The author questions the practice of add-
     ing the microcomputer to traditional educational
     settings and the decision to place responsibility
     for the computer program with the school librar-
     ian. She recommends an evaluation of a school's
     needs and a revision of its philosophy to accom-
     modate the new technology. Bibliography.

269 SKAPURA, ROBERT. "Somewhere Between Doonesbury
     and Time Magazine." Computing Teacher 10
     (March 1983): 49-51.
         Skapura supports the placement of a
     school's first micro in the media center, pre-
     sents an example of shared usage, and estimates
     present and future impact of the technology.

270 SKAPURA, ROBERT. "Start Small and Be Very, Very
     Good." Computing Teacher 10 (April 1983):
     57-58.

Skapura provides practical advice on
getting started in microcomputing, along with
several suggested media center functions which
lend themselves to automation.

271 SMITH, LOTSEE, and SWIGGER, KEITH. "Microcomputers in School Library Media Centers." Drexel
Library Quarterly 20 (Winter 1984): 7-15.
Microcomputer applications in school library media centers are surveyed in this literature review, which attempts to identify the extent of micro use in American school libraries,
and examines the instructional and managerial
functions served. Bibliography.

272 STARKEY, FLO. "Microcomputers in School Library
Long Overdue." New Mexico Library Association
Newsletter 10 (December 1982): 1.
In 1982 microcomputers were purchased for
the secondary school libraries of the Roswell
(NM) Independent School District, where they are
used for processing overdues, maintaining circulation statistics, and performing other clerical
tasks. The impact of the micro on student morale
is mentioned, and popularity of an extracurric-
ular computer literacy program is told.

273 SUGRANES, MARIA R. "Microcomputer Applications
at Ocean View High School Media Center."
CMLEA Journal 3 (Spring 1980): 9-11.
An Apple II (48K) microcomputer with disk
drive, printer, and micromodem, provides Ocean
View High School students with access to instructional programs in the school district's IBM 370
computer, as well as access to commercially produced programs on floppy disks, and the opportunity to practice programming individually. Librarians are using the system for searching databases and creating bibliographies. Other uses
are envisioned. Bibliography.

274 "TRS-80 at NYC School." Small Computers in Li-
braries 2 (January 1982): 7.
The Dalton School Library is using Radio
Shack TRS-80 equipment for such activities as

library competency testing, maintaining a calen-
dar of events, periodical listing, and information retrieval, in addition to providing online
access to a variety of databases.

275 THOMASON, NEVADA WALLIS. <u>Microcomputer Information for School Media Centers</u>. Metuchen,
NJ: Scarecrow, 1985. 316p.
     Twenty-five articles reprinted from a
variety of library and educational journals provide an overview of microcomputer technology and
applications in the school library media center.
     CONTENTS: Child's Play, by Harry C.
Broussard.--Debunking Some Common Computer Myths,
by M. Clare Boehmer.--Microcomputers and Automation in the School Library Media Center, by Nevada Thomason.--From the Beginning, by Bill Burns
and Mike Sharp.--The Use of Microcomputers in Libraries, by Allan D. Pratt.--Microcomputers in
Libraries and Media Centers, by Sally Doyen and
Joyce Rouse.--Computerizing on a Shoestring, by
M. Clare Boehmer.--Administering the Microcomputer Program--Assessing for Direction and Policy: A
Checklist, by Hilda L. Jay and Judith M. Bury.--
Information Technology, by Deanna Marcum and
Richard Boss.--The Microcomputer: One More Piece
of AV Equipment, by Eric S. Anderson.--Microcom-
puters for Media Centers, by William T. Cound.--
The Terrible Ten in Educational Programming, by
Ann Lathrop.--Library Applications of Microcom-
puters, by Theodore C. Hines, Lois Winkel, Rosann
W. Collins, and Francis A. Harvey.--Microcomput-
ers: Library Management Tools of the Future, by
Jewel H. Harris.--Tending Apples in the Library,
by William M. Fabian.--TRS-80 at the Maine State
Library, by Donald Wismer.--Computers and the
Media Center: A Principal's Perception, by Gary
Zosel.--If I Had an Apple, What Would I Do With
It? by Jim Deacon.--"Card" Catalog on a Micro-
computer--So Easy a Child Can Use It, by Betty
Costa and Marie Costa.--A Complete Guide to the
Disk, by Carlene Char.--Monitors: The Better to
See Your Data With, by David Gabel.--The CP/M
Operating System, by Mark Dahmke and Ed Jones.--
If It's Worth Its Weight in Paper..., by David

Gabel.--System Software for Local Educational
Microcomputer Networks: What It Is, What We Have,
What We Need, by Hugh Garraway.--Maintenance
Alternatives for Personal Computers, by Lewis A.
Whitaker.

276   THOMASON, NEVADA WALLIS.   "Microcomputers and
      Automation in the School Library Media
      Center." School Library Media Quarterly 10
      (Summer 1982): 312-19.
         An historic overview of library automa-
      tion introduces a detailed discussion of library
      uses of the microcomputer, particularly in school
      media centers and libraries. The author discus-
      ses technology, hardware, journals, and includes
      a glossary. Bibliography.

277   TOLER, DONNA J.   "So You Want to Buy a Microcom-
      puter!" Florida Media Quarterly 6 (Spring
      1981): 11-12.
         The media specialist in a school is the
      logical person to supervise the purchase of
      microcomputer equipment. Toler reviews basics of
      materials selection and the elements of a micro-
      computer which a media specialist should know.

278   TROUTNER, JOANNE JOHNSON.   The Media Specialist,
      the Microcomputer, and the Curriculum.   Edited
      by Shirley L. Aaron. Littleton, CO: Libraries
      Unlimited, 1983. 181p.
         The introduction of microcomputers into
      the school curriculum via the school media center
      is the theme of this volume, which deals with the
      media specialist's role in implementing a micro-
      computer program, selection of hardware and soft-
      ware, computer literacy, and curricular and ad-
      ministrative applications. Bibliography.

279   TRUETT, CAROL.   "The Computer as Library Aide."
      Classroom Computer News 3 (March 1983): 73-74.
         The microcomputer is recommended to
      school librarians for assistance in such routine
      functions as cataloging, circulation, and inven-
      tory control. Several suitable programs are rec-
      ommended.

280 TRUETT, CAROL. "Computer Games in the Learning
Resources Center? You Bet!" ACCESS: Microcomputers in Libraries 2 (October 1982): 9-10,
17-19.
A short history of games, a justification
for including microcomputer games and simulations
in the school resource center, and suggested curriculum oriented games appropriate for libraries
and media centers make up this article. Bibliography.

281 TRUETT, CAROL. "How Well Do Media Specialists
Meet the Challenge of the Computer?" Instructional Innovator 28 (February 1983): 14-16.
A study of 144 media specialists in Nebraska examines the accessibility, utilization,
personnel needs, and future of the microcomputer
in public school media centers.

282 TRUETT, CAROL. "Managing the Media Center: New
Software for School Librarians." ACCESS:
Microcomputers in Libraries 3 (Spring 1983):
7-11.
Based on a survey of Nebraska school
librarians and media specialists, this article
evaluates present microcomputer use and predicts
future developments. Especially useful is a
bibliography of database management software arranged by function to which it is applicable.

283 TWADDLE, DAN R. "School Media Services and Automation." School Media Quarterly 7 (Summer
1979): 257-68, 273-76.
The development of automation in school
libraries and media centers is analyzed, and a
lengthy annotated bibliography of pertinent literature is provided. The microcomputer, although
mentioned, is generally neglected. Bibliography.

284 WALL, ELIZABETH. "When the Micro Comes, Where
Will it Go?" Educational Computer Magazine 1
(November/December 1981): 47-48.
Schools in which a limited number of
microcomputers are expected to serve the entire
faculty and student body are encouraged to place

the equipment in the media center. The decision is justified by the author.

285 WOOLLS, BLANCHE E. "The Use of Microcomputers in Elementary and Secondary School Libraries." The Bowker Annual of Library and Book Trade Information. 28th edition. New York: R. R. Bowker, 1983. Pp. 26-80.

The growing prevalence of microcomputer technology in schools is discussed, and leading curriculum projects are noted. In addition to instructional uses, administrative and housekeeping applications in school libraries and media centers are discussed, with specific examples.

286 ZOSEL, GARY. "Computers and the Media Center: A Principal's Perception." Computing Teacher 9 (March 1982): 34-37.

A high school principal justifies the location of the microcomputer lab in the school's media center, suggests possible computer-aided instruction applications in several subjects, and makes recommendations for media specialists wanting to establish micro labs in their own schools.

287 "Another Administrative Apple." <u>Small Computers in Libraries</u> 1 (December 1981): 3.
  The Willard Public Library of Battle Creek, Michigan, announces the purchase of an Apple II microcomputer for producing periodical holdings lists, book lists, and mailing lists.

288 BALL, ALAN J. S. "Automation of Small Public Libraries in Canada." <u>Canadian Journal of Information Science</u> 5 (May 1980): 145-58.
  An overview of automation in small public libraries in Canada considers funding, problems, and the future of library automation, putting the microcomputer into perspective with minis, mainframes, and library networks. Bibliography.

289 BORGMAN, CHRISTINE L., and KORFHAGE, ROBERT R. "The Public Library Interface to Personal Computer Systems." <u>The Information Age in Perspective</u>. Proceedings of the 41st ASIS Annual Meeting. White Plains, NY: Knowledge Industry Publications, 1978, v. 15. Pp. 41-43.
  The proliferation of home computer systems will lead to greatly expanded retrieval and analysis of information--information which the public library should take an active role in supplying. As technological changes are implemented, they will impact upon and in turn be influenced by culture, technology, economics, law, and politics. These influences are the topic of this paper.

290 CHRISTIAN, DEBORAH. "The Microcomputer at Oakridge, Oregon." <u>Library Journal</u> 105 (July 1980): 1470-71.
  An Ohio Scientific C2-8PDF microcomputer has solved many of the circulation, accounting, recordkeeping, and acquisitions problems of this small public library serving a population of 4,000. It has the potential for still greater

use with the addition of new hardware and software.

291 CURRY, BETSY; MOELLER, EDWARD R.; and WILLIAMS,
    VICKI L. "Microcomputers in Public Libraries
    in Georgia--Survey, 1983--Summary." Georgia
    Librarian 21 (May 1984): 36-37.
        The results of a microcomputer survey
    sent to fifty county and regional library direc-
    tors in Georgia are reported. The survey con-
    cerned ownership, applications, training, public
    use equipment, hardware, software circulation
    policies, and other topics.

292 GODWIN, MARY JO. "Microcomputers Go Public."
    North Carolina Libraries 40 (Fall/Winter
    1982): 198-202.
        The microcomputer has revolutionized the
    small library just as the mainframe and national
    networks have revolutionized major research
    facilities. Godwin describes microcomputer ap-
    plications at four small North Carolina public
    libraries. These applications range from mailing
    lists to bookkeeping to card catalog production
    to computer literacy programs. A section on
    access to databases is included. Bibliography.

293 HOLLIS, TRICIA. "Greenwood-Leflore Computerizes
    on a Budget." Mississippi Libraries 44 (Sum-
    mer 1980): 66-67.
        Wayne Skelton, Director of the Greenwood-
    Leflore (MS) Public Library, illustrates how a
    small library can automate on a budget by instal-
    ling a microcomputer for book ordering, online
    searching, statistical recordkeeping, and book-
    keeping.

294 "Iowa Apple-Cable System." Small Computers in
    Libraries 2 (December 1982): 2.
        The author describes some creative tele-
    vision publicity and programming for the Iowa
    City (IA) Public Library, made possible through
    microcomputer technology, the interest of volun-
    teer microcomputer enthusiasts, and library-cable
    tv system cooperation.

295 KOENIG, JUDITH. "Microcomputers Have a Place in
the Small Public Library." Canadian Library
Journal 40 (June 1983): 169-71.
Microcomputer technology has made automation possible for the small public library. The
basics for setting up a microcomputer system are
reviewed, and benefits of database management are
told. Bibliography.

296 "Micros in Libraries." Online Review 7 (April
1983): 78.
The Bedfordshire County (UK) Library
Service was the recipient of a $140,000 grant for
the purchase of microcomputer hardware, software
for development of in-house databases, and for
public access programs. Basic project guidelines
are included.

297 "Prince George's County Library Gets $25,000 for
Branch Micros." Library Journal 109 (July
1984): 1280.
The Prince George's County (MD) Memorial
Library reports receiving a $25,000 grant from
the Washington Post newspaper to purchase software and hardware for two branch libraries.

298 RAYMOND, CHADWICK T. "Automation at Addison."
Library Journal 108 (June 15, 1983): 1220.
Addison (IL) Public Library's automation
program is outlined, including a CLSI system for
circulation control and an Alpha Micro Operating
System (AMOS) for business applications, library
functions, and a computer literacy program for
youth.

299 ROWBOTTOM, MARY. "Use of Microcomputers in Public Libraries." Vine no. 55 (October 1984):
30-35.
In 1984 the Library Association sponsored
a survey of public libraries in Great Britain to
determine the prevalence and use of microcomputers. This report summarizes the data, including
information on numbers and brands of hardware,
peripherals, software, and applications to library functions.

300 SAGER, DONALD J. "Public Library Service to the
Microchip Generation." <u>Top of the News</u> 39
(Summer 1983): 307-14.

     The automation of functions in the public
library may have a negative impact on the services available to children and young people unless the library staff has a strong commitment to
making systems accessible to all. Sager discusses the possible negative impact of automation,
along with the dichotomy of the large automated
resource sharing networks and the stand-alone
systems which are proliferating libraries today.
Bibliography.

301 COLE, DAVID H. "IBM PC in St. Cloud, MN." Small
Computers in Libraries 3 (July 1983): 1.
Cole describes Great River Regional Library's use of the IBM Personal Computer for
indexing new books prior to their addition to the
library's COM Catalog, and indexing of the St.
Cloud Daily Times, as well as plans for expansion
into word processing, statistics maintenance, and
budgeting.

302 "Coop Project in Rochester, N. Y." Small Computers in Libraries 2 (January 1982): 2-3.
The Rochester Area Resource Exchange, a
four-year pilot project to encourage multi-type
library cooperation, is using Apple II Plus hardware for word processing, directory maintenance
and compilation of a union list of serials. Plans
call for a union list of non-print media, a film
booking program, and an accounting system.

303 "IBM PC in Canada." Small Computers in Libraries
2 (June 1982): 5-6.
The purchase of an IBM Personal Computer
by the Georgian Bay Regional Library System provides word and statistical processing necessary
for the system, and holds the potential for interlibrary communication, a cooperative collection development program, and access to a mini-
computer-based acquisitions system.

304 "Mid-Mississippi Aims for Low Cost Micro-Based
Automation." Library Journal 108 (December 1,
1983): 2202.
Plans for automating the Mid-Mississippi
Regional Library System are announced. The pro-
ject, which will cost some $20,000, will use IBM
micros and Peachtree, Information Unlimited,
WORDSTAR, and INFOSTAR software.

305 MINGES, JAMES. "Microcomputers for Regional
      Service." Technicalities 4 (September 1984):
      10-11, 15.
         In 1981 the Northwest Missouri Library
   Network purchased an Apple II microcomputer for
   telecommunications purposes. Within a year and a
   half it had paid for itself in telecommunications
   savings, and its use had been expanded to include
   word processing, file management, accounting, and
   other functions.

306 MINGES, JAMES. "Microcomputers for Regional
      Service: Northwest Missouri." Show-Me Librar-
      ies 34 (January 1983): 7-9.
         The use of an Apple II Plus microcomputer
   by the Northwest Missouri Regional Library Network has proven both economical and efficient.
   The library coordinator outlines applications for
   word processing, PFS, and VISICALC software, and
   presents some guidelines for decision making.

307 NICKEL, EDGAR. "Apples for Librarians Too!"
      Technicalities 2 (August 1982): 4, 9.
         In 1980 the Northwest Kansas Library Sys-
   tem purchased an Apple II microcomputer to access
   the Kansas Informational Circuit for interlibrary
   loan purposes. Since purchase of the micro, the
   library staff has automated talking book circulation records and completed a union list of serials for the twenty-six system members using the
   equipment.

308 CLEMENTS, DAVID W. G. "Automation in the Reference Division British Library." The Application of Mini- and Micro-Computers in Information, Documentation and Libraries. Proceedings of the International Conference on the Application of Mini- and Micro-Computers in Information, Documentation and Libraries, Tel-Aviv, Israel, 13-18 March 1983. New York: North-Holland, 1983. Pp. 437-42.

Clements reviews the application of computers in the Reference Division of the British Library, touching briefly on mainframe operations with microcomputer interfaces, discussing retrospective conversion with minicomputers, and addressing the various housekeeping, management, and information retrieval activities performed with microcomputers.

309 TURNER, PHILIP A. "The Use of Mini and Microcomputers at the USDA National Agricultural Library." The Application of Mini- and Micro-Computers in Information, Documentation and Libraries. Proceedings of the International Conference on the Application of Mini- and Micro-Computers in Information, Documentation, and Libraries, Tel-Aviv, Israel, 13-18 March 1983. New York: North-Holland, 1983. Pp. 257-65.

The National Agricultural Library has used minicomputers since the early 1970s to create records for the AGRICOLA database. This program is described, as is the use of microcomputers for word processing, financial analysis, and software development. Expansion of programs is also considered. Bibliography.

310 WISMER, DONALD. "TRS-80 at the Maine State Library." Small Computers in Libraries 2 (November 1982): 2-5.

The Maine State Library's Coordinator of

Automated Data Services justifies the library's choice of microcomputer hardware, discusses current uses, describes software problems and local programming changes, and evaluates the library's program.

311 BICKERSTAFF, MOLLIE. "Setting Up and Running an
    Information Centre in a Large UK Chartered
    Accountancy Practice." Aslib Proceedings 37
    (March 1985): 147-55.
        Experiences in establishing and operating
    an information center for a British accounting
    firm are related by one of the firm's partners.
    Microcomputer services, programming, and use are
    stressed.

312 BOYNE, WALTER J., and OTANO, HERNAN. "Direct
    Document Capture and Full Text Indexing: An
    Introduction to the National Air and Space
    Museum System." Library Hi Tech 2, no. 4,
    issue 8 (1984): 7-14.
        The National Air and Space Museum has
    established as its goal the development of the
    world's leading respository for materials con-
    cerning the history of air and space technology.
    To that end, the museum established a videodisc
    project for preserving and distributing materi-
    als. The choice of playback and indexing equip-
    ment for this project fits into the scope of this
    bibliography since it involves surveying and
    selecting microcomputer equipment.

313 CHAN, ANNA. "dBASE II in a Small Library."
    Small Computers in Libraries 3 (August 1983):
    4-5.
        The automation of cataloging and acquisi-
    tions functions of the Transportation Safety Col-
    lection in the Department of Civil Engineering at
    the University of Toronto was accomplished using
    IBM PC hardware and dBASE II software. The pro-
    ject is described and evaluated. Bibliography.

314 DAEHN, RALPH M. "Technology and Microcomputers
    for an Information Centre/Special Library."
    Canadian Library Journal 41 (February 1984):
    39-43.

The library of the Ontario Centre for
Farm Machinery and Food Processing Technology, is
effectively using microcomputers to compensate
for limited storage space. With a SUPERBRAIN QD
II micro and appropriate software, the library is
providing online search services, interlibrary
loan through electronic mail, an in-house database of peripheral literature concerning farm
machinery and food technology, and VIDEOTEX. The
library's operation is described. Bibliography.

315 DOUGLASS, REBECCA S., and FAY, JIM. "A Curriculum Center Emerges into the Microcomputer
Age." Technicalities 3 (June 1983): 13-14.
The experiences of the Illinois Vocation-
al Curriculum Center in expanding to meet the demands for microcomputer information are told by
the Center's director and microcomputer specialist. The goals are discussed; the beginnings of
the program, including a cooperative arrangement
with the Central Illinois Computer Consortium,
are told; equipment and peripherals are described; and recommendations are made for others
who may be considering similar projects.

316 ELAZAR, DAVID H. "Downloading and Uploading:
Experience of the Technical Information Center
of Israel Aircraft Industries (Abstract)."
Downloading/Uploading Online Databases and
Catalogs. Proceedings of the Congress for
Librarians, St. John's University, Jamaica,
New York, 18 February 1985. Library Hi Tech
Special Studies Series, no. 1. Ann Arbor, MI:
Pierian Press, 1985. Pp. 58-59.
The Technical Information Center of
Israel Aircraft Industries has automated library
services with a CDC CYBER mainframe, but acqui-
sitions, cataloging, and circulation functions
are performed on a multi-terminal microcomputer
with uploading and downloading capabilities. The
system is described.

317 ERTEL, MONICA M. "Apples in the Apple Library--
How One Library Took a Byte." Online 7 (March
1983): 20-29.

Apple Computer's corporate librarian relates some of the problems and pleasures involved
in establishing a library for one of the world's
major microcomputer manufacturers. Automation of
circulation, cataloging, reference, and other
functions are detailed and illustrated through
charts and figures.

318 GILLMAN, PETER L. "Microcomputers in Special Li-
        braries: A Means to an End?" Electronic Li-
        brary 2 (July 1984): 197-203.
            Library microcomputers are often pur-
chased with great expectations but little knowledge of their capabilities, their limitations, or
their compatibility with other equipment. Gillman examines current microcomputer applications
and makes some practical suggestions for evaluation prior to purchase. Bibliography.

319 GREEN, KEVIN E., and WHITING, JOYCE. "Combined
        Production of a Current Awareness Bulletin and
        Database on a Microcomputer." Program 18 (Oc-
        tober 1984): 298-307.
            A microcomputer is employed by the GEC
Engineering Research Centre Library to maintain
an in-house bibliographic database of pertinent
journal articles and create a weekly bulletin.
Choice of the Torch C-68000 microcomputer and
WORDSTAR and SUPERFILE software is related, creation of the database and bulletins is described,
and other applications are projected. Bibliography.

320 KAUFFMAN, S. BLAIR. "Planning for Automation:
        Microcomputers in the Law Library." Law Li-
        brary Journal 77, no. 1 (1985): 6-25.
            Kauffman outlines procedures for planning
microcomputer purchase and integration into a law
library. He considers what functions to automate,
system availability and costs, financing, system
and vendor selection, and implementation of the
system.

321 "Medical Library Apples." Small Computers in
        Libraries 1 (November 1981): 1.

This short article describes innovative uses of microcomputers in two Wisconsin hospital libraries.

322 ROGERS, CARL D., Jr. "Microcomputers in Special Libraries: A Survey." North Carolina Libraries 40 (Fall/Winter 1982): 203-09.
This research article reports the results of a survey of 121 special libraries in North Carolina concerning the prevalence of microcomputer use, types of hardware, applications, library demographics, and user satisfaction. Bibliography.

323 ROYLE, MARY ANNE. "Speak Memory: Microcomputers in Law Library Automation." Law Library Journal 74 (Winter 1981): 101-20.
An overview of developments in computer technology and the adaptation of computers to library procedures leads into a review of the major microcomputer systems currently available, with brief comparative information in chart form. Bibliography.

324 SMITH, LIBBY. "Microcomputer Applications in Special Libraries." North Carolina Libraries 40 (Fall/Winter 1982): 210-13.
A survey of special libraries in North Carolina indicates that the most common uses of the microcomputer are word processing, data transmission and receiving, automation of routing functions, and office management and bookkeeping. Several special libraries are cited as examples.

325 STEWART, ALAN K., and STRYCK, B. CAMILLE. "Micro- and Minicomputers for Online Information Center Operations." Library Management Bulletin 6 (Fall 1982): 4-5.
The Amoco Research Center's Information Center used the company's mainframe for word processing and other library functions, but found the system troublesome to use. The Center's conversion to a Digital Equipment Corporation WS-200 mini and DECMATE micros is related, with information on planned and unplanned uses.

326 TAWYEA, EDWARD W. "Public Service Applications
of a Microcomputer in a Medical Library."
Medical Library Association Bulletin 70 (July
1982): 321-22.
The process of implementing and integrating microcomputer capabilities into the North-
western University Medical Library's public service program is described, including information
on hardware selection, automation of specific
functions, future applications, and the impact of
the commitment to automation via microcomputer on
the total library program. Bibliography.

327 WALLACE, DANNY P. "Small Computers in Illinois
Special Libraries; The Results of a 1984
Survey." Illinois Library Statistical Report,
no. 18. Springfield, IL: Illinois State Library, 1985. Pp. 111-50.
This survey concerns automation of special libraries in Illinois, but concentrates on
micro- and minicomputers. Sponsored by the Special Libraries Association, Illinois Chapter, the
survey includes responses from 555 libraries, and
analyzes geographical distribution, library size,
access to micro- and minicomputers, uses, brands
of computers, software, and other data.

328 WILLIAMS, THOMAS. "Microcomputer Applications in
a Hospital Library." Medical Library Association Bulletin 73 (April 1985): 207-10.
The planning and implementation of a
microcomputer system in the library of the Veterans Administration Medical Center in New York
City is related by the hospital librarian, who
made the selection, wrote the proposal, and su-
pervised the integration of the system into the
library. Several suggestions for selection and
implementation are provided.

APPLICATIONS

329 ADAMS, R. "Leicester Polytechnic Library's Pet
     Solutions." Vine no. 44 (August 1982): 41-45.
          In 1982 the Leicester Polytechnic Insti-
     tute Library purchased a Commodore Pet microcom-
     puter for interlibrary loan transmission, word
     processing, input to PRESTEL, and budget applica-
     tions. Applications are described and evaluated,
     and plans for future developments are outlined.

330 "Aloha dBASE II." Small Computers in Libraries
     3 (May 1983): 5.
          Programs developed by staff of the Hawaii
     Medical Library to perform indexing, catalog card
     maintenance, and borrower list maintenance are
     described. Programs are written for Kaypro II
     hardware.

331 "Apple DBMS Use in Ontario." Small Computers in
     Libraries 2 (May 1982): 6.
          Librarians at L'amoreaux Collegiate In-
     stitute, Agincourt, Ontario, report using THE
     DATA REPORTER and MODIFIABLE DATABASE for book
     orders, circulation statistics, and overdues.

332 ASHBY, JOHN M. "Micros Are Not Just for Teach-
     ing." Instructional Innovator 28 (February
     1983): 23-24.
          An educational media specialist considers
     imaginative uses for the microcomputer in a media
     production center. Applications range from in-
     dexing photographs to lighting control.

333 BARNARD, ROY S. "The Apple at Calvin T." Ne-
     braska Library Association Quarterly 13 (Win-
     ter 1982): 10-11, 24.
          An Apple II Plus microcomputer, purchased
     by Kearney State College Library in 1982 to fa-
     cilitate online searching, interlibrary lending,
     and serial ordering, has been called into service
     for maintaining bindery records, storage lists,

duplicate exchange lists, and student hours.
Other uses are planned for the future.

334   BEISER, KARL.   "256 Kilobytes and a MULE."
      Library Journal 110 (May 1, 1985): 117; and
      School Library Journal 31 (May 1985): 147.
            The microcomputer is recommended as a
      time saver for the small library, and twenty-nine
      suggested applications are listed to illustrate
      its value and versatility. Also included are
      tips to help the novice have a successful and
      satisfying initial experience.

335   BLAIR, JOHN C., Jr.   "MOMS--Multifunction Office
      Management System: Software and Hardware Inte-
      gration for Database Management." Online '82
      Conference Proceedings, Atlanta, 1-3 November
      1982. Weston, CT: Online, Inc., 1982. Pp.
      244-50.
            MOMS, a microcomputer-based system devel-
      oped for the Texas A & M University Medical Sci-
      ences Library, combines the database management
      capabilities of CONDOR and dBASE II software with
      other single-function commercial programs to
      achieve a total office management system.

336   BREAM, ELIZABETH.   "The Marvelous Micro (And Why
      You Should Buy One Now!)" Emergency Librarian
      10 (January/February 1983): 6-8.
            A positive argument in favor of microcom-
      puter use in libraries addresses advantages of
      applying the technology to word processing, data
      management, communications, and bulletin board
      activities. Bibliography.

337   BURNETT, STEPHEN L., and PETIT, MICHAEL J.   "The
      Use of Microcomputers at George Mason Univer-
      sity Law Library." Law Library Journal 77,
      no. 1 (1985): 132-45.
            In 1983 the staff of the George Mason
      University Law Library launched automated serials
      control and acquisitions projects using micro-
      computer technology. Implementation of the in-
      house system is described, including staff
      training, software adaptation, record inputting

and maintenance, and report generation. Also
included are sections concerning claims reports,
payment records, bindery records, and other related topics.

338 BURTON, PAUL F. "Information Retrieval Using
       Petaid." Educational Computing 3 (May 1982):
       34-35.
       Burton demonstrates the versatility of
the microcomputer and PETAID database management
software by describing library applications for
the program, including a journal index, acquisitions system, and serials control file. Problems
encountered with PETAID are also recounted.

339 BURTON, PAUL F. "The Microcomputer in the
       Smaller Library." Scottish Library Associa-
       tion News no. 160 (November/December 1980):
       175-78.
       The Senior Librarian at Leith Nautical
College describes his library's use of the microcomputer for periodical indexing and acqisitions
control.

340 BURTON, PAUL F. "Using the PET at Leith Nautical
       College." Small Computers in Libraries 2
       (January 1982): 4.
       The Senior Librarian at Leith Nautical
College describes use of a Commodore PET 3032
system for indexing journals and maintaining book
order files. Bibliography.

341 BURTON, PAUL F. "A Versatile Pet." Vine no. 40
       (October 1981): 26-29.
       Leith Nautical College Library has been a
leader in microcomputer use in the British Isles.
In this article the librarian explains how he
automated acquisitions and serials control and
created a periodicals index and union catalog
with a Commodore Pet micro and PETAID software.

342 CARTER, ELEANOR M. "Application of Micros in
       Libraries and Learning Resource Centers."
       Microcomputer Applications in Administration
       and Instruction. New Directions for Community

Colleges, no. 47. San Francisco: Jossey-Bass, 1984. Pp. 71-80.

Possible microcomputer applications in a community college library and resource center include direct patron use, administrative applications and support services. Carter discusses these applications and specific functions as they have been implemented in the Learning Resource Center at the State University of New York's Cobleskill campus. Bibliography.

343 CHEN, CHING-CHIH. "Microcomputer Library Systems and Subsystems: Trends and Developments." Second National Conference on Integrated On-line Library Systems Proceedings, Atlanta, Georgia, 13-14 September 1984. Canfield, OH: Genaway & Associates, 1984. Pp. 39-52.

Microcomputers are viable machines which have a place in integrated library systems according to this author, who points out their advantages and limitations, suggests applications, and points out trends for greater development in integrated, in-house, and modular type systems, along with micro-based subsystems. Bibliography.

344 CIPOLLA, KATHARINE G. "Our Readers Report." Classroom Computer News 1 (March/April 1981): 19.

Several readers have written to Classroom Computer News to report microcomputer projects in their libraries. Among them are a report of a survey of equipment and software usage, a program that generates overdues, and a computer-based personnel development program. Some of the items are reported in greater detail elsewhere.

345 COOPERATIVE LIBRARY AGENCY FOR SYSTEMS AND SERVICES (CLASS). Directory of Microcomputer Applications in Libraries. San Jose, CA: CLASS, 1984. 128p.

Attendees at a 1982 microcomputer seminar and all CLASSONLINE subscribers were surveyed concerning microcomputer applications in their libraries. This publication provides a compilation of that data. Four sections provide com-

plete entries for responding libraries, with
entries indexed by hardware, software, and application.

346 CORBIN, BILL J. "Microcomputers: Non-Traditional
       Applications for Libraries." Arkansas Librar-
       ies 38 (September 1981): 18-21.
            Several microcomputer applications to
       library functions are discussed, including word
       processing, statistical analysis, report genera-
       tion, file management, instruction, scheduling,
       database searching, and mailing list maintenance.
       The future of micros in libraries and the lack of
       library oriented software are touched on briefly.
       Bibliography.

347 "County Library Uses Microcomputer." Information
       Retrieval and Library Automation 16 (October
       1980): 4.
            In this brief news note various microcom-
       puter applications at the St. Louis County (MO)
       Public Library are described.

348 CRAIG, KENT. "TRS-80 II in Tennessee." Small
       Computers in Libraries 3 (October 1983): 5-7.
            The Williamson County (TN) Public Library
       reports automation of a variety of functions with
       TRS-80 hardware and PROFILE PLUS, SCRIPSIT, and
       several locally produced software programs.
       Functions include maintenance of genealogy lists,
       serials lists, and borrower files, data manipula-
       tion for reports, cataloging functions, indexing,
       and processing of overdues.

349 "Creative Librarians and the Micro." Technicali-
       ties 4 (July 1984): 1.
            In this editorial the editors present the
       microcomputer as a tool with vast potential for
       librarians, and challenge the profession to think
       creatively in developing new and innovative ap-
       plications.

350 DAMIANS, GUY F. J. "T.A.M.I.L.: A Tiny Automatic
       System on Micro-Computer for Information
       Processing in Libraries." The Application of

Mini- and Micro-Computers in Information,
Documentation and Libraries. Proceedings of
the International Conference on the Applica-
tion of Mini- and Micro-Computers in Informa-
tion, Documentation and Libraries, Tel-Aviv,
Israel, 13-18 March 1983. New York: North-
Holland, 1983. Pp. 103-08.
T.A.M.I.L., a microcomputer-based online
catalog and circulation system developed in
France, is described in detail.

351 DWYER, JAMES R. "Micros: Applications Tomorrow."
ACCESS: Microcomputers in Libraries 1 (October
1981): 3, 26-27.
Current use and future potential of the
micro is considered in circulation, acquisitions,
cataloging, networking, and document delivery.

352 EDGERTON, MARY. "Adventures with the M300 Workstation." OCLC Micro 1 (May 1985): 9-11, 23.
Edgerton, an avowed computer novice, describes her experiences integrating the M300
Workstation into the cataloging department of the
SUNY College at Purchase Library, and adapting to
its versatility. Word processing with WORDSTAR
software is considered, with printer compatibility problems noted.

353 ERTEL, MONICA M. "A Small Revolution: Microcomputers in Libraries." Special Libraries 75
(April 1984): 95-101.
The impact of microcomputer technology on
libraries is considered, particularly in the
areas of communication, word processing, administration, and data management. Bibliography.

354 "Florida Art School Automates with CASTLE System." Library Journal 109 (February 1, 1984):
134.
The library of the Ringling School of Art
and Design, Sarasota, Florida, has installed a
micro-based integrated computer system which provides online catalog and circulation capabilities
with inventory and management control, according
to this brief article.

355 HANIFAN, THOMAS. "Apple System in Iowa." Small
Computers in Libraries 3 (March 1983): 3-4.
Muscatine Community College Library's
microcomputer system is described, and word processing, online searching, and data management
applications are discussed.

356 HARVIE, BARBARA. "Library Applications of Microcomputers." Collegiate Microcomputer 1 (Aug-
gust 1983): 235-37.
A survey of school and public libraries
by People's Computer Company revealed many innovative applications of microcomputers to library
functions. Twenty-five of these are listed; the
reminder to choose software before choosing hardware is repeated; and addresses of two dozen
software sources are provided.

357 HINES, THEODORE C.; WINKEL, LOIS; COLLINS, ROSANN
W.; and HARVEY, FRANCIS A. "Library Applications of Microcomputers." Wyoming Library
Roundup 37 (Spring/Summer 1982): 33-40.
A similar article to ones which appeared
in ACCESS: Microcomputers in Libraries and Classroom Computer News, this one provides 33 ideas
for using a microcomputer in a library setting.
Advice on getting started, an equipment list, and
several general suggestions are included.

358 HINES, THEODORE C.; WINKEL, LOIS; COLLINS, ROSANN
W.; and HARVEY, FRANCIS A. "Micros: Applications Today." ACCESS: Microcomputers in Libraries 1 (October 1981): 2, 21-22.
Thirty-one library applications for the
microcomputer are suggested and described, ranging from catalog card production to interlibrary
loan borrowing to patron lists to inventories.
Practical discussions of equipment needs, recommended brands, and cost estimates are included.

359 HINES, THEODORE C.; WINKEL, LOIS; COLLINS, ROSANN
W.; and HARVEY, FRANCIS A. "Putting Microcom-
puters to Work in the Library--31 Ideas for a
Start." Classroom Computer News 2 (January/
February 1982): 44-46.

The authors list and briefly describe applications of microcomputers to various library functions. This is a revision of an article which appeared earlier in ACCESS.

360 HYMAN, MIKE A. "A Computer for Every Library--A Practical Reality at Last?" Proceedings of the 4th International Online Information Meeting, London, 9-11 December 1980. Medford, NJ: Learned Information, 1980. Pp. 235-43.
    Microcomputer technology has made automation a realistic objective for even the smallest library. The author considers equipment and costs, but concentrates on applications, particularly bibliographic access. Bibliography.

361 INCE, DAVID. "Library Applications for Microcomputers." Georgia Libraries 21 (February 1984): 6-8.
    Applications of microcomputer technology to library administration, public services, computer assisted instruction, circulation, and acquisitions functions, are suggested. An integrated system for a small library is proposed.

362 JUDY, DICK. "Conceptual Invention: A Change in Computing Concepts." ACCESS: Microcomputers in Libraries 2 (July 1982): 4, 16.
    The introduction of the intelligent terminal into a computer system alters the concept of concentrated intelligence in the central host computer, decentralizing intelligence and sharing it with the local terminal at the bottom of the system architecture. This requires a drastic readjustment of user concepts, but makes the computer more adaptable to user needs, provided the user will employ both perceptual and conceptual processes in developing and adapting computer applications.

363 "Kansas Apples." Small Computers in Libraries 1 (November 1981): 1.
    This brief note describes how the Apple II Plus is being used for circulation of talking book materials, automatic telephone answering,

interlibrary loans, compiling union lists, order
control, and communication with TI Silent 700
terminals in the Northwest Kansas Library System.

364 KAYSER, JOHN. "Fund Accounting Program." Small
     Computers in Libraries 3 (May 1983): 1.
        A search for a microcomputer-based fund
     accounting system for the Plainview-Old Bethpage
     (NY) Public Library lead ultimately to the pur-
     chase of an integrated system from IMS Interna-
     tional Microsystems which offers the required
     fund accounting, with word processing, database
     management, and other office functions offered as
     a bonus. The system configuration, functions,
     and cost are discussed.

365 KENT, ANTHONY K. "Strategies for the Development
     of Micro-Computer Systems for Use in Infor-
     mation Processing." The Application of Mini-
     and Micro-Computers in Information, Documenta-
     tion and Libraries. Proceedings of the Inter-
     national Conference on the Application of
     Mini- and Micro-Computers in Information,
     Documentation and Libraries, Tel-Aviv, Israel,
     13-18 March 1983. New York: North-Holland,
     1983. Pp. 481-87.
        The author encourages librarians and
     information and documentation specialists to
     address the small problems in their fields of
     expertise using microcomputers. For maximum ef-
     fectiveness, he recommends in-house programming
     or program development, with the user employing
     versatile commercial programs, since no one
     understands the problems and needs of a user
     better than the user himself.

366 LANGDON, LINDA. "Commodore Micros in North Bay,
     Ontario." Small Computers in Libraries 3
     (April 1983): 6-7.
        Fourteen microcomputer programs developed
     for the West Ferris Secondary School Library, of
     North Bay, Ontario, are described. Written for
     Commodore hardware, the software provides circu-
     lation, cataloging, ordering, processing, and
     other functions.

367 LANGDON, LINDA. "Library Programs from Canadian School." ACCESS: Microcomputers in Libraries 3 (Spring 1983): 3, 30.
      This is a slightly edited version of an article which also appeared in the April, 1983 issue of Small Computers in Libraries.

368 LATHROP, ANN, and F. MAY, CURTIS. "The Amazing Library Computer; 1st of a 2-Part Series." Electronic Learning 2 (February 1983): 68-71.
      The microcomputer is considered as a teaching device and as a library management tool with four short case studies illustrating the versatility of the technology.

369 LAYTHE, ROSAMOND. "Heavy Apple Use at SUI." Small Computers in Libraries 1 (April 1981): 4-5.
      The Assistant Director for Public Services at Southern Illinois University at Edwardsville enumerates and briefly describes ten current and six proposed applications of Apple II microcomputer equipment to functions in the SIUE library.

370 "Library Microcomputer Applications Using DEC Rainbow 100's." Small Computers in Libraries 4 (June 1984): 5.
      Applications for Rainbow 100 and Rainbow 100+ microcomputer equipment in administration and public services at the University of Winnipeg Library are described. SELECT, dBASE, and LOTUS 1-2-3 software provide word processing, financial, and recordkeeping capabilities; POLYXFER CP/M COMM provides online searching, downloading, printing and electronic mail.

371 LODDER, N. M. "Microcomputers: Their Application in Libraries." South African Journal for Librarianship and Information Science 50 (April 1983): 171-75.
      General microcomputer applications to library management are considered, and specific applications to libraries in South Africa are reviewed. Bibliography.

372 LUNDEEN, GERALD. "Microcomputers in Personal
     Information Systems." Special Libraries 72
     (April 1981): 127-37.
          Lundeen examines the personal information
     and indexing needs of the researcher and discus-
     ses the adaptability of microcomputer hardware
     and software to those needs. Bibliography.

373 MAXEY, VIVIAN. "Winn With a Micro." Louisiana
     Library Association Bulletin 46 (Summer 1983):
     11-12.
          In the spring of 1982 the Winn Parish
     (LA) Library purchased a TRS-80 microcomputer,
     which is used for maintaining patron files, the
     annual budget, an equipment inventory, and a sup-
     plies inventory. Presented is a profile of the
     library, which helped justify the purchase of the
     micro, and a brief description of each applica-
     tion.

374 MICHELS, FREDRICK. "Developing Inhouse Systems
     Using Micros." Library Hi Tech 3, no. 1,
     issue 9 (1985): 83-91.
          Possibilities for library automation have
     expanded enormously, and librarians are encour-
     aged in this article to develop the microcomputer
     to its full potential through in-house program-
     ming and utilization of inexpensive single ap-
     plication programs and versatile commercial soft-
     ware such as dBASE II. Two serials programs are
     included to illustrate the ease of programming.

375 "Microcomputers for Small Libraries." New York
     Library Association Bulletin 30 (June 1982):
     1, 6-7.
          Database management, word processing, and
     accounting are identified as the three most
     important library functions for microcomputers.
     Various applications of these are discussed.

376 "Micros at Scott Community College." Small Com-
     puters in Libraries 3 (January 1983): 1.
          At Scott Community College, Bettendorf,
     Iowa, Apple and Atari microcomputers are being
     used for control of overdues, film rental, verti-

cal file processing, periodical holdings lists,
acquisitions, bibliographies, and word processing, according to Scott's librarian.

377 "Micros in South Carolina Libraries." Small Com-
      puters in Libraries 2 (August 1982): 2.
         Microcomputer applications are reported
by the University of South Carolina College of
Librarianship, Newberry College's Wessels Library, the Cherokee County Public Library, and
Richland County Public Library.

378 NEVINS, KATE. "Microcomputers in the Mainframe
      Environment." Proceedings of the 8th Inter-
      national Online Information Meeting, London,
      4-6 December 1984. Medford, NJ: Learned
      Information, 1984. Pp. 321-30.
         The impact of the OCLC M300 Workstation
on terminal usage, staff needs, costs, and
efficiency are considered for both interlibrary
loan and cataloging operations using MICRO EN-
HANCER software.

379 PANCHAPAKESAN, S.; RAO, N. V. SRINIVASA; SRINI-
      VASAN, R.; BAPAT, GOPAL; and SOMASEKAR, S.
      "Micro-Processor Based Information Handling
      System." Library Science With a Slant to
      Documentation 17 (December 1980): 97-101.
         A micro-processor based information sys-
tem is described, which was designed for the Information Centre for Aeronautics at the National
Aeronautics Laboratory, Bangalore, and is capable
of handling the Centre's circulation, acquisitions, and information searching.

380 PENNIMAN, W. DAVID. "Microcomputers in Librar-
      ies: If They Are the Answer, What Is the
      Question?" Microcomputers for Information
      Management 1 (March 1984): 31-38.
         The microcomputer is a diverse tool which
has been adapted to both traditional and non-traditional uses in libraries. Several OCLC applications are described, and sources for information about additional applications are suggested.
Innovation is encouraged. Bibliography.

381 POST, RICHARD. "Microcomputer Uses." Ohio Media
Spectrum 34 (Spring 1982): 10-12.
Microcomputer applications can be grouped
into four functional categories. Repetitive processes, control tasks, sequential problems, and
storage retrieval are addressed. Applications
are discussed which fall into each category.

382 PRATT, ALLAN D. "Microcomputers as Information
Dissemination Tools." Communicating Information. Proceedings of the 43rd ASIS Annual
Meeting. White Plains, NY: Knowledge Industry
Publications, 1980, v. 17. Pp. 314-16.
Microcomputers are demonstrated to be
adaptable in local and network information handling, particularly in the areas of word processing, indexing of local materials, and online
searching of brokered databases. Bibliography.

383 "Program Alert: PNBC Computer Survey Finds Widespread, Varied Use." Library Journal 107
(March 15, 1982): 590.
A survey concerning the use of microcomputers in libraries of the Pacific Northwest
indicates that Apple micros are being used for a
variety of applications including interlibrary
loan, circulation backup, cataloging, maintenance
of public service files, statistics, accounting,
budgeting, word processing, data management, and
online searching. Eight libraries are mentioned
for their innovative uses of the technology.

384 RAITHEL, FREDERICK J. "The Implications of
Microcomputers for Libraries." Show-Me Libraries 29 (March 1978): 3-4.
In this early article one of the pioneers
of microcomputing in libraries addresses possible
uses of the technology, including computer-
assisted instruction, graphics, and a project of
his own involving development of an automated library acquisitions system.

385 ROWAT, MARTIN J. "Microcomputers in Libraries and
Information Departments." Aslib Proceedings
34 (January 1982): 26-37.

The potential of the microcomputer in libraries and information centers is the theme of this paper, which concentrates on library processes and implementation of appropriate programs to meet defined needs. Bibliography.

386 ROWBOTTOM, MARY. "Microcomputers in British Libraries." Small Computers in Libraries 1 (September 1981): 6.
Information retrieval is the major use made of microcomputers in Great Britain, although other uses are becoming prevalent. Although potential is great, development has been delayed by the lack of quality software.

387 ROYLE, MARY ANNE. "Microcomputers and Law Library Automation: New Directions." Law Library Journal 77, no. 1 (1985): 104-31.
Law libraries have been slow to automate because of the costs of mini and mainframe systems and the relatively small size of most law collections. Microcomputers offers new options to law libraries. Royle considers microcomputer alternatives and library functions which lend themselves to automation via microcomputer.

388 SARGEANT, ARTHUR. "Advice from a Trying Librarian." Educational Computing 3 (May 1982): 35.
Never at a loss for ideas to utilize a library microcomputer, the author explains how he and other members of the Ilkley College Library staff adapted to automation, and describes applications implemented by them, including an automated serials control system, a list of missing books, an index to microcomputer articles, and an index of career materials held by the library.

389 SCACCIA, JOSEPH F. "The Uses and Limitations of Microcomputers in Libraries." Road Runner 26 (April 1981): 24-34.
The components and operation of a microcomputer system are briefly described, hardware and software limitations are considered, and actual and potential microcomputer applications are discussed. Bibliography.

390 SCHUYLER, MICHAEL. "An Apple for the Public
   Library." Educational Computer Magazine 2
   (July/August 1982): 16.
      When the Kitsap (WA) Regional Library's
Board of Trustees voted to purchase a microcom-
puter in 1981, an Apple II was chosen, along with
VISICALC, DATA FACTORY, ZARDAX, VISITREND/VISI-
PLOT, and READABILITY software programs. Schuy-
ler discusses the uses made of each software
package and estimates its value to the total
library program.

391 SPENCER, WILLIAM A. "Library Applications for
   Communicating Micros." American Society for
   Information Science Bulletin 9 (December
   1982): 48.
      Spencer elaborates on his thesis that the
microcomputer is the key to providing information
quickly, easily, and inexpensively, even in the
smallest library. Several applications are
suggested.

392 STEUDEL, CONNIE. "Apple Automation on a Limited
   Budget." Technicalities 4 (May 1984): 13-14.
      An opportunity to purchase Apple II hard-
ware at a reduced price encouraged librarians at
Springfield College in Illinois to automate, despite budgeting problems and little opportunity
for prior planning. The author describes automation of circulation and serials control, and
touches briefly on audiovisual inventory and bibliographic instruction applications.

393 "TRS-80 in Use at Glendora (CA) PL." Small Computers in Libraries 1 (April 1981): 7.
      A news brief announces and describes the
use of a TRS-80 microcomputer for order control,
catalog card production, online searching, and
electronic mail at the Glendora (CA) Public
Library.

394 "Tacoma PL Ties WLN to DataPhase Circ System."
   Small Computers in Libraries 1 (October 1981):
   2.
      A microcomputer-based interface between

the WLN cataloging network and the Tacoma (WA) Public Library's DataPhase circulation system provides automated transfer of data to the circulation files, as well as information for order forms, accounting, and catalog cards.

395 TAYYEB, RASHID. "Microcomputers: Implications for Technical Services." Canadian Library Journal 40 (April 1983): 64.
   The growing familiarity of the general public with the operation and versatility of the microcomputer is creating increasing pressures in libraries to computerize operations for faster and easier access. Tayyeb discusses these pressures and how they impact on the library, particularly technical services.

396 THOMPSON, JAMES. "Microcomputer Use at Rice University." Vine no. 47 (March 1983): 30-31.
   The Rice University Library is using a Philips MICOM 2002 word processor for a variety of office automation functions in addition to word processing. The author reviews serials, personnel, and acquisitions functions which are performed with the MICOM 2002, and considers future potential for the hardware.

397 WEISSMAN, AARON. "TALK is Cheap." OCLC Micro 1 (May 1985): 21.
   Weissman documents the M300's versatility, describing experiences in online searching, file creation, and word processing using PC-TALK, PC-FILE III, and PC-WRITE software.

398 "What Not to Computerize." Small Computers in Libraries 5 (March 1985): 8-9.
   Seven types of library tasks are identified and discussed which are best left as manual operations.

399 WILLIAMS, PHILIP W. "The Potential of the Microprocessor in Library and Information Work." Aslib Proceedings 31 (April 1979): 202-09.
   The development of the integrated circuit has drastically reduced the costs of automating

library processes. Williams suggests some library functions which lend themselves to microcomputer aided storage and retrieval, including
patron files, circulation, cataloging, mailing
lists, and acquisitions.

400 WISMER, DONALD. "The TRS-80 and State Library
       Applications." Online '83 Conference Pro-
       ceedings, Chicago, 10-12 October 1983. Wes-
       ton, CT: Online, Inc., 1983. Pp. 314-17.
            In 1981 the Maine State Library purchased
       a Radio Shack TRS-80 microcomputer for general
       use. Applications are described, including mail-
       ing lists, serials control, printed catalog pro-
       duction, union listings, statistics, and invoice
       production. Plans for the future are discussed.

401 WOODROW, MARTIN. "Application of the Apple."
       Library Association Record 84 (January 1982):
       21-22.
            The Hertfordshire County (UK) Information
       Librarian describes his experiences in choosing
       and installing a microcomputer for online search-
       ing, then expanding its use as other applications
       were realized.

402 WOODS, LAWRENCE A. "Applications of Microcomput-
       ers in Libraries." New Information Technolo-
       gies--New Opportunities. Clinic on Library
       Applications of Data Processing: 1981. Urbana,
       IL: University of Illinois Graduate School of
       Library and Information Science, 1981, v. 18.
       Pp. 28-42; and Special Libraries Association
       Florida Chapter Bulletin 14 (April 1982):
       64-79.
            Woods discusses the problems inherent in
       using microcomputers in libraries, then summa-
       rizes progress made in developing microcomputer
       applications for each function of the library,
       considering technical and public services, man-
       agement, and peripheral areas.

403 WRIGHT, JAN C. "Rainbows in the Mountains."
       Small Computers in Libraries 4 (September
       1984): 10-11.

The Learning Resources Center of Colorado Mountain College's Alpine Campus is making use of microcomputer technology, both in teaching and managerial functions. Such library applications as acquisitions, word processing, overdues, and reserve lists are handled via microcomputer, while students and faculty are provided access to software and hardware in a computer lab situation. Use policies, maintenance statistics, and other apsects of public use micros are addressed.

404 YARBOROUGH, CYNTHIA COX. "Library Automation at Presbyterian College." Small Computers in Libraries 3 (September 1983): 6-7.

Yarborough describes Presbyterian College's use of Apple II Plus hardware and a combination of commercial and locally produced software to accomplish automated catalog card production, book label printing, book list production, periodical listings, word processing, and other functions.

405 YOTHER, LARRY W. "Systems Development at the Grom Hayes Library: A Mini System Adaptable to Micros." ACCESS: Microcomputers in Libraries 2 (January 1982): 5, 20-23.

Programs developed for the Grom Hayes Library of Hartford State Technical College provide automated circulation, cataloging and processing, acquisitions, serials control, word processing, and other functions. Although designed for the Digital PDP-11/70 minicomputer, the programs are adaptable to micro systems.

406 "Acquisitions on an Apple." Library Journal 109
      (February 15, 1984): 314.
           The Bel Air Branch of the Harford County
      (MD) Library has instituted an in-house acquisi-
      tions system which runs on an Apple II microcom-
      puter. The program is used to maintain order in-
      formation, produce cards, record books received
      and produce acquisitions lists.

407 ALLMAN, LINDA K., and FREEMAN, GRETCHEN L.
      "Standing Orders With 'ListHandler'." Small
      Computers in Libraries 4 (October 1984): 8-10.
           The Richland County (SC) Public Library
      uses an online automated acquisitions system for
      book acquisitions, but needed additional internal
      records for standing order information. Allman
      and Freeman tell how their needs have been met
      through the use of an Apple II Plus microcomputer
      with LIST HANDLER software.

408 BEDNAR, COLLEEN F. "Acquisition Lists Produced
      on Apple." RTSD Newsletter 9, no. 8 (1984):
      93.
           The Howe Library of the Shenandoah Col-
      lege and Conservatory of Music is using an Apple
      IIe microcomputer, with QUICK FILE II and APPLE
      WRITER II software, to produce acquisitions lists
      for distribution to faculty. Hardware require-
      ments and software capabilities are told.

409 BIELENBERG, W. LARRY. "BISAC Transmission at
      Concordia Seminary." Information Technology
      and Libraries 2 (June 1983): 173-76.
           In 1980 the Concordia Seminary Library
      implemented a microcomputer-based acquisitions
      system which now operates on a Helix micro. In
      1982 the acquisitions staff began transmitting
      order records to Midwest Library Service in BISAC
      format using a Bell 212A dialup connection. The
      system is described and evaluated, with both
      advantages and shortcomings presented.

410 BURTON, PAUL F. "Commodore Pet + Petaid = Automated Acquisitions File." Technicalities 2
(September 1982): 10-11.
Automation of the acquisitions function
at the Leith Nautical College Library, Edinburgh,
Scotland, is described by the librarian. Reasons
for choosing PETAID software are told, basics of
the conversion process and advantages of the new
procedure are discussed.

411 CAMPBELL, MARY E., and DOLL, L. F. "Rewards and
Pitfalls of Turning Toward a Micro (and Away
from Integrated Systems) for Acquisitions: The
Ideal vs. the Affordable." (Networking +
Integrating) * (Systems + Society). Proceed-
ings of the 12th Annual Canadian Conference of
Information Science, Toronto, 14-16 May 1984.
Alexandria, VA: ERIC Document Reproduction
Service, ED 244 636, 1984. Pp. 121-40.
The decision-making process is explored
which led to the choice of a stand-alone, micro-
computer-based acquisitions system over an inte-
grated system in the Library of the Ontario
Institute for Studies in Education. The micro-
based system is evaluated; advantages and disadvantages are examined. Bibliography.

412 D'ANCI, MARJORIE. "Acquisitions With an Apple."
Technicalities 4 (August 1984): 9, 11.
The Harford County (MD) Library System
has revolutionized its acquisition functions
through the application of an Apple IIe microcomputer and PERSONAL FILE SYSTEM software to
the operation. THe library system's centralized
acquisition system is described, and a mock-up
of the revised order form is included.

413 FRECHETTE, JAMES. "Library Acquisitions on a
Micro Scale." Library Journal 110 (November
1, 1985): 154-55; and School Library Journal
32 (November 1985): 142-43.
The Community College of Rhode Island's
Learning Resources Center launched its initial
microcomputer automation program with an acquisitions project. The Apple II Plus micro

and IFO file management system proved unsuccessful, but were upgraded with a hard disk and dBASE
II software to make the project workable. Frechette reviews ordering and receiving procedures,
and discusses advantages of the automated file
system for acquisitions.

414 FREUND, ALFRED L. "Ramapo Catskill Library Sys-
        tem--OZZ Book Order System." Small Computers
        in Libraries 2 (July 1982): 6.
            The Director of the Ramapo Catskill Li-
    brary System outlines the move from a manual book
    ordering procedure to a jobber supplied online
    system to an in-house microcomputer-based program
    using Commodore CBM 8032 hardware and OZZ data
    management software.

415 GILLESPIE, JIM. "Fine Tuning the Book Budget
        with dBASE and Supercalc." Small Computers in
        Libraries 5 (May 1985): 6-7.
            Gillespie demonstrates the use of the
    dBASE file manager and the SUPERCALC spreadsheet
    in keeping track of book orders, encumbrances,
    and payments in a library acquisitions depart-
    ment.

416 "Interview: Jenko Lukac." ACCESS: Microcomputers
        in Libraries 1 (July 1981): 8-9.
            Jenko Lukac, author of the Computerized
    Library Acquisitions System (CLAS) program,
    answers questions about himself, the CLAS soft-
    ware, and the potential of the microcomputer in
    library management.

417 JACOBS, NAOMI. "Developing a Customized Mono-
        graphic Acquisitions System Using dBASE II and
        the IBM PC XT Microcomputer." Proceedings of
        the 6th National Online Meeting, New York,
        30 April-2 May 1985. Medford, NJ: Learned
        Information, 1985. Pp. 241-49.
            An in-house acquisitions system, devel-
    oped for the Research Library at the National
    Center for Research in Vocational Education on
    the Ohio State University campus, is described.
    Using an IBM XT microcomputer and dBASE II soft-

ware, a menu driven program was developed to automate acquisitions procedures which were previously done manually. Planning and design of the database is discussed, sample menus and reports are provided, and pilot testing of the program is described.

418 MASON, THOMAS R., and NEWTON, EVAN. "Forecasting Library Futures: Participative Decisionmaking With a Microcomputer Model. Background Paper. Workshop 3." Arlington, VA: ERIC Document Reproduction Service, ED 238 444, 1983.

A paper presented at the 11th Conference of the Association for Institutional Research in the Upper Midwest, this document describes a microcomputer program used to project library collection growth at Cornell University through the year 2002.

419 MILLER, BRUCE CUMMINGS. "Book Order Distribution --Frequency Curves: A BASIC Program." Library Software Review 3 (September 1984): 379-84.

Miller describes an in-house microcomputer program for analyzing performance of book and materials suppliers through the analysis of library acquisitions data. A printed copy of the program written to run on a Timex/Sinclair micro accompanies the text.

420 MILLER, BRUCE CUMMINGS. "Key Variable Changes in a Spreadsheet Model of Library Acquisitions." Library Software Review 3 (December 1984): 527-31.

Using a microcomputer and spreadsheet software, Miller has devised a model for comparing the cost of library acquisitions performed manually and acquisitions performed via OCLC. The model is adaptable to any library acquisitions department.

421 MOSKOWITZ, MICKEY, and ALCORN, CYNTHIA. "The Collection Manager's Micro." Technicalities 5 (March 1985): 11-13.

VISICALC, PFS: FILE, and PFS: REPORT have proven useful to the Emerson College Library's

collection development librarian for maintaining
acquisitions records and statistics, inventory
records, a weeding file, and an out-of-print
needs list.

422 NEILL, CHARLOTTE; CALLAWAY, ANN; and ALGERMISSEN,
VIRGINIA. "Creation of a Book Order Management System Using a Microcomputer and a DBMS."
Library Software Review 4 (March/April 1985):
71-78.
    In 1982 the Medical Sciences Library of
Texas A & M University automated book ordering
with a microcomputer and database management
system. The acquisitions system, called BOOK-
DIRT, is described and illustrated, and its
benefits are pointed out. Bibliography.

423 NILES, JUDITH. "Acquisitions Fund Accounting on
a Word Processor." Library Hi Tech 1 (Fall
1983): 10-13.
    Rice University's Fondren Library employs
a Philips 2002 word processor for fund accounting
in its acquisitions department. Encumbrances,
accounting, reports, and other functions are described, and the system's versatility is applaud-
ed. Bibliography.

424 PERRY-HOLMES, CLAUDIA. "LOTUS 1-2-3 and Decision
Support: Allocating the Monograph Budget."
Library Software Review 4 (July/August 1985):
205-13.
    Spreadsheets can provide the library ad-
ministrator with valuable information for planning because of the ease with which statistical
and numerical projections can be figured. The
author demonstrates how LOTUS 1-2-3 can be applied to the process to determine a library's
budget for monographic purchases. Bibliography.

425 St. CLAIR, GLORIANA, and BOLLAND, NANCY. "A 3-
Step Process for Fund Reporting." OCLC Micro
1 (May 1985): 12-15.
    St. Clair and Bolland describe a process
for downloading financial information and statistical data from the OCLC Acquisition Subsystem

using the M300 Workstation, then manipulating the data using LOTUS 1-2-3 to produce financial reports.

426 SCHUYLER, MICHAEL. "Purchase Order Numbers Program." ACCESS: Microcomputers in Libraries 2 (April 1982): 14.
     A simple program written in APPLESOFT BASIC provides unique purchase order numbers for libraries using the WLN acquisitions system.

427 SHAW, DEBRA S. "Visicalc and the Library Acquisitions Budget." Online '83 Conference Proceedings, Chicago, 10-12 October 1983. Weston, CT: Online, Inc., 1983. Pp. 266-70.
     Use of the VISICALC spreadsheet in allocating library book funds to academic departments is described by a university librarian who explains the technique and the advantages of the program.

428 SUKOVICH, JOHN E. "Acquisitions With dBASE II." Small Computers in Libraries 3 (August 1983): 7.
     Newberry College's automated acquisitions system is described. The system, which employs an Apple II Plus micro with a Corvus 20 megabyte hard disk is evaluated positively, although limitations are noted.

429 "TRS-80 Microcomputer at Lorain Keeps Track of Standing Orders." Library Journal 108 (December 15, 1983): 2292.
     The Lorain (OH) Public Library reports successful use of a Radio Shack TRS-80 to consolidate standing orders in the main library and five branches.

430 WALKER, STEPHEN. "A Microcomputer Based Library Acquisition System." Vine 34 (May 1982): 39-41; and Small Computers in Libraries 2 (August 1982): 6.
     A microcomputer-based acquisition system designed by the Central Information Services of the University of London for the University's

Institute of Advanced Legal Studies is described.
The possibility of marketing the system is suggested.

431 WELSCH, ERWIN K.; CROSSFIELD, NANCY L.; and FRA-
ZIER, KENNETH L. "Microcomputer Use in Collection Development." Library Resources and
Technical Services 29 (January/March 1985):
73-79.
Microcomputers are used in three of the
libraries at the University of Wisconsin-Madison
to perform collection development and acquisitions. The authors describe these uses and
stress the variety in hardware, software, and
techniques used to perform similar functions.
Bibliography.

432 "Western Maryland College Puts Microcomputer to
Work." Library Journal 107 (December 1,
1982): 2216.
Western Maryland College's Hoover Library
is using a TRS-80 Model II microcomputer for
accounting and acquisitions, according to this
brief news item.

433 KESNER, RICHARD M. "Microcomputer Applications
in Archives: Towards an International Information Retrieval Network." The Application of
Mini- and Micro-Computers in Information,
Documentation and Libraries. Proceedings of
the International Conference on the Application of Mini- and Micro-Computers in Information, Documentation and Libraries, Tel-Aviv,
Israel, 13-18 March 1983. New York: North-
Holland, 1983. Pp. 707-16.
    Automation is a recent phenomenon in
archives, and most archivists are facing the task
of integrating microcomputers into the workplace
with no former experience on which to rely.
Kesner considers the problems of internal integration and the greater problems posed by networking of archival data, supporting his thesis
with research when possible. Bibliography.

434 KESNER, RICHARD M. "Microcomputer Archives and
Records Management Systems: Guidelines for
Future Development." American Archivist 45
(Summer 1982): 299-311.
    The development of the Microcomputer
Archives Records Management Systems (MARS) is
outlined, its value as a tool for archivists is
explored, and its future is suggested.

435 KESNER, RICHARD M., and HURST, DON. "Microcomputer Applications in Archives: A Study in
Progress." Archivaria 12 (Summer 1981): 3-19.
    The value of the microcomputer is recog-
nized in archival work, and its application as an
archival tool is demonstrated through a detailed
description of the Microcomputer Archives and
Records Management Systems (MARS) at the Archives
of Appalachia. Bibliographic notes.

436 WILSON, ARNOTT T.; HEJAZIAN, KHOSROW; and FIND-
LAY, CLAIRE E. "PARCH--A Package for Archi-

vists, Researchers, Companies, and Historians." <u>The Application of Mini- and Micro-Computers in Information, Documentation and Libraries</u>. Proceedings of the International Conference on the Application of Mini- and Micro-Computers in Information, Documentation and Libraries, Tel-Aviv, Israel, 13-18 March 1983. New York: North-Holland, 1983. Pp. 129-39.

A general evaluation of the microcomputer in archival work, including both advantages and limitations, is followed by a description of the microcomputer-based system, called PARCH, in use in the Glasgow University Archives, Glasgow, Scotland. Bibliography.

437 "AV Control System on an Apple." Small Computers
in Libraries 1 (October 1981): 4.
The Central Iowa Regional Library in Des
Moines announces the use of a microcomputer for
circulation control of its audiovisual media and
equipment. The program is briefly described.

438 BUNTING, LARRY. "How to Computerize Media Management." Instructional Innovator 29 (May
1984): 39-40.
A microcomputer-based scheduling system
for media equipment and materials in the Scottsdale (AZ) Community College media center is
described and evaluated, and plans for further
development are told.

439 DEWEY, PATRICK R., and GARBER, MARVIN. "Easy to
Use Microcomputer Generated 'Subject Guide'
Wall Chart." Online 7 (March 1983): 32-43.
A micro-based subject guide, developed
with an Apple II and DATA FACTORY software, is
used to produce quick reference wall charts listing call numbers for frequently requested subjects. A copy of the chart from the Chicago Public Library's North-Pulaski Branch is included.

440 EMMENS, CAROL A. "Microcomputer Can Sub for
Character Generators." School Library Journal
30 (May 1984): 47.
A microcomputer can be used to do titles,
credits, and graphics for locally produced video
and other media productions, if a school or media
center does not have access to a character generator. Method is discussed, along with advantages and disadvantages.

441 "Film Booking on an Apple." Library Journal 109
(April 15, 1984): 761.
The State Library of Ohio reports doing
film booking on an Apple IIe microcomputer using

Software Publishing Corp.'s File, Report, and
Graph software.

442   FISHER, MARJORIE. "The Computer and the 16mm
        Film." Small Computers in Libraries 2 (June
        1982): 4.
              An Indiana film cooperative reports a 40%
      increase in use following automation of their
      film catalog and distribution to member teachers
      of printouts listing films appropriate to their
      subjects and grade levels.

443   HINES, THEODORE C.; WINKEL, LOIS; and COLLINS,
        ROSANN W. "The Children's Media Data Bank."
        Top of the News 36 (Winter 1980): 176-80.
              The Children's Media Data Bank, a comput-
      er-based bibliographic control system for pre-
      school and elementary level media, is described.
      Although originally set up on an IBM 370/165
      computer, it has been adapted to microcomputer.

444   HUNTZINGER, RALPH. "KCLS' Film Reservation Sys-
        tem." ACCESS: Microcomputers in Libraries 2
        (April 1982): 6-7, 20-24.
              Coordinator of Non-Book Media Services
      for the King County (WA) Library System provides
      a detailed description of KCLS, King County's
      microcomputer-based booking system for media.

445   "Kansas Uses Apple Computer for Talking Books
        Circulation." Library Journal 107 (January
        15, 1982): 134.
              An Apple II 48K microcomputer is being
      utilized successfully in the circulation control
      of the talking books program at the Northwest
      Kansas Library System in Norton, according to
      this news brief.

446   LANGDON, LINDA. "Audio Visual Union List--Micro
        to Mini Communication." Electronic Library 2
        (October 1984): 255-56.
              The creation of a union catalog of audio-
      visual materials for the Nipissing County (Ontar-
      io) School District and its automation using the
      District's VAX 11/780 minicomputer, are described

by the librarian who conceived and executed the
idea. The catalog is accessed via microcomputer.

447 SCHUYLER, MICHAEL. "Slides from the Screen."
     Small Computers in Libraries 2 (June 1982):
     3-4.
          Schuyler describes an easy technique for
     producing black-and-white or color slides from a
     microcomputer screen.

CATALOGING AND PROCESSING

448 ANDERSON, ERIC S. "Catalog Cards by Computer: A Look at the Offerings." Book Report 3 (January/February 1985): 63-64.

Cataloging standards and selection criteria for cataloging software are considered, nine cataloging software programs are reviewed, and the best of the group are chosen.

449 AVENEY, BRIAN, and DREW, SALLY. "Automated Resource Sharing: Wisconsin Spreads its Nets." Wilson Library Bulletin 57 (May 1983): 742-43.

The authors describe the creation of WISCAT, a computer output microform union catalog for 137 libraries in Wisconsin, and WISCAT maintenance using Apple microcomputers and a software system called MITINET/retro. Plans for a related interlibrary loan network are also disclosed.

450 BAZILLION, RICHARD J. "Microcomputer-Based Recon With Ocelot: A Case Study." Library Software Review 4 (May/June 1985): 125-27.

In 1984 Algoma University College Library began a retrospective conversion project using an Ocelot Library System. The project is described, and time and cost for completing the project are estimated. Besides the cataloging module, Ocelot's circulation and acquisitions modules are considered, and price comparisons with other systems are provided.

451 BAZILLION, RICHARD J., and SCOTT, SUSAN. "Ocelot Unleashed." Canadian Library Journal 42 (June 1985): 155-58.

The Algoma University College Library, Sault Ste. Marie, Ontario, has undertaken a retrospective conversion project using IBM PC XT hardware and OCELOT software. Equipment specifications, cost estimates, staffing, record format, and problems are addressed, and the future with OCELOT is predicted.

452 BJORNER, SUSAN N. "DB-Master Database for Library Cataloging." Small Computers in Libraries 1 (December 1981): 1.
    The librarian at the Massachusetts Vocational Curriculum Resource Center describes how DB MASTER software is used for cataloging and production of a printed catalog. Advantages and disadvantages of the program are discussed.

453 "Cataloguing System." InCite 3 (August 6, 1982): 2.
    MICROMARC, a microcomputer-based cataloging system designed and installed at the Colac Technical School, Colac, Victoria, Australia, is described briefly. The system can handle about 30,000 items, and can be expanded to accommodate circulation and accounting functions.

454 DESMARAIS, NORMAN. "BiblioFile for Retrospective Conversion." Small Computers in Libraries 5 (December 1985): 24-28.
    In 1985 the Providence College Library acquired and implemented BIBLIOFILE, a compact disc read-only-memory system for retrospective conversion of cataloging records to machine-readable form. The system and its use are described in detail.

455 DUKE, JOHN K. "NAF Card: A Microcomputer-Based Reference Card Generator." Technical Services Quarterly 1 (Summer 1984): 73-82.
    NAF CARD, a microcomputer program developed at Iowa State University, is described and evaluated. Designed to print authority control and cross reference cards for the card catalog, the program is written in Microsoft BASIC and runs on an IBM PC.

456 ENDELMAN, JUDITH E., and BAUERLE, DIANE K. "Computerized Access to a Chapbook Collection." College and Research Libraries News 46 (July/August 1985): 340-42.
    In 1983 Indiana University's Lilly Library acquired the Elizabeth Ball collection of children's literature, which included 2000 chap-

books. Because of the special nature of the collection, AACR2 cataloging with input into OCLC
did not seem feasible. The staff chose instead
to create a microcomputer-based catalog using an
IBM XT and dBASE software. The catalog is described and its use explained.

457 FINN, MAUREEN. "21 Institutions to Convert 2.1
    Million Titles Via MICROCON." OCLC Newsletter
    no. 158 (July 1985): 9.
        OCLC's MICROCON Service, a microcomputer-
    based retrospective conversion method offered by
    OCLC, is described, and 21 libraries using the
    service are listed.

458 GILNER, DAVID J.; KOVACIC, ELLEN S.; and ZAFREN,
    HERBERT C. "Hebrew Cataloging via Microcom-
    puter." Small Computers in Libraries 3 (Sep-
    tember 1983): 3-5.
        Utilization of online cataloging facili-
    ties for processing non-Roman alphabet materials
    has long been a problem for libraries. The Hebrew
    Union College Library has addressed and found a
    solution to the problem of cataloging books in
    Hebrew using standard Apple II Plus hardware, in-
    novative programming, and specially designed
    character sets for monitor and printer. The sys-
    tem is described and evaluated.

459 HACKLEMAN, DEBBIE. "Staff Help Develop Catalog-
    ing Procedures: Using the Cataloging Micro
    Enhancer Software." OCLC Micro 1 (November
    1985): 18-19, 30.
        When the Oregon State University Li-
    brary's Cataloging Department purchased an M300
    Workstation and cataloging MICRO ENHANCER, full-
    time staff and student workers were asked to
    participate in planning for its implementation.
    The procedure is described, and problems are
    analyzed.

460 HELLMAN, JEREMY M. "Library Catalog: A Program
    for Creating a Personal Computer-Based Library
    Catalog." Creative Computing 9 (March 1983):
    216, 218, 220, 222, 225-26, 228-30, 232, 234,

236, 238, 240, 242, 244, 246, 248, 250, 252, 254-55.
A microcomputer program for cataloging and organizing a home library using Apple II Plus hardware is described, and the program is reproduced in full.

461 "IBM PC Duplicates Catalog Cards at Massillon, Ohio Library." Library Journal 109 (July 1984): 1280.
The director of the Massillon (OH) Public Library reports the development of a program which duplicates catalog card sets using an IBM PC, and NEC 7730 printer designed to accommodate card stock.

462 "Johns Hopkins Goes With REMARC and Gets Free Apples." Library Journal 107 (October 1, 1982): 1804.
Library Director Susan Martin announces Johns Hopkins' decision to do retrospective conversion of catalog records through the REMARC database using Apple micros for entering search keys.

463 LAI, SHEILA. "MICROCON Project Under Way in California." OCLC Newsletter no. 158 (July 1985): 9.
The Library at California State University, Sacramento, began a retrospective conversion project in 1985 using OCLC's MICROCON Service. The project is described briefly, with notes on planning, hit rate, and progress.

464 LIM, SUE. "Control Cataloging Backlogs With ME." OCLC Micro 1 (November 1985): 15.
Cataloging librarians at California State Polytechnic University have devised a method of controling cataloging backlog and re-searching OCLC non-hits using MICRO ENHANCER software. The method is shared.

465 LIM, SUE. "The OCLC M300 Cataloging Microenhancer." M300 and PC Report 2 (June 1985): 6-8.
The California State Polytechnic Univer-

sity Library was one of the first to install an
M300 Workstation, and served as one of twelve
nationwide test sites for OCLC cataloging using
the new equipment. This, part one of a two-part
article, describes the impact of the M300 and
cataloging MICRO ENHANCER software on the morale
of the cataloging staff and the workflow within
the department.

466 LIM, SUE. "The OCLC M300 Cataloging Microenhanc-
       er, Part II." M300 and PC Report 2 (July/
       August 1985): 6-7.
            Part two of a two-part article, this sec-
     tion addresses the impact of the cataloging MICRO
     ENHANCER on workflow. Special functions and
     problems are also considered.

467 LUTHIN, PATRICIA. "Students Say 'Let ME Do It!'"
       OCLC Micro 1 (May 1985): 19-20.
            Georgetown University Library was a test
     site for the cataloging MICRO ENHANCER software.
     The head of cataloging at Georgetown describes
     routines for checking Library of Congress copy,
     revising, editing, and producing records using
     the MICRO ENHANCER. Procedures for conducting
     additional searches are also detailed.

468 "Maxwell Software Makes TRS-80 into an OCLC
       Terminal." Library Journal 107 (September 1,
       1982): 1589-90.
            Maxwell Library Systems of Cambridge,
     Massachusetts announces the development of new
     software that allows the TRS-80 microcomputer to
     serve as an OCLC Terminal. The major advantage
     is the ability to download information from the
     OCLC database to a floppy disk, which can serve
     in lieu of an archive tape for recently added
     records.

469 McTIGUE, ELIZABETH; ROBINSON, MARY ELIZABETH;
       SAVER, BARRY; and SCHULTZ, CLAIRE K. "Catalog
       Card Production with a Programmable Terminal."
       Medical Library Association Bulletin 65 (Janu-
       ary 1977): 13-16.
            Cataloging library materials using a Com-

putek 200 programmable terminal and a program
written by a computer science student is described in this article concerning early use of
small computers for library functions. Bibliography.

470 "New MICRO-MARC Service Announced." Small Computers in Libraries 4 (May 1984): 5.
MicroMARC, a new cataloging service with
microcomputer access, is announced by Library
Systems and Services, Inc.

471 NEWBY, JILL. "O[u]R Procedure for Cataloging
Analytics." OCLC Micro 1 (May 1985): 8.
Newby outlines a procedure developed at
Oregon State University for producing catalog
analytics using the OCLC MICRO ENHANCER.

472 NEWTON, GEORGE. "Using TRS-80 Scripsit for Book
Labels." Small Computers in Libraries 3
(November 1983): 2.
Newton describes the use of a TRS-80
microcomputer with SCRIPSIT word processing soft-
ware to produce book labels for the Sacramento
(CA) Public Library. Other functions are also
mentioned briefly.

473 "Printing Catalog Cards." Small Computers in
Libraries 4 (May 1984): 2.
Printers suitable for catalog card production are discussed, along with features to
look for in printer selection. A word about
printer tables is also included.

474 "RLG Announces IBM PC Version of RLIN Terminal."
Electronic Library 3 (July 1985): 156.
The Research Libraries Group (RLG) announces the availability of software that will
allow the IBM PC to function as a terminal to
access RLIN. The necessary hardware configuration is outlined. Plans for future enhancements
are revealed.

475 "RLG Announces IBM PC Version of RLIN Terminal."
Wilson Library Bulletin 59 (April 1985): 522.

The Research Libraries Group (RLG) announces plans to distribute software which will
enable an IBM PC to function as a terminal for
access to the RLIN database. Plans for later
development call for support of Cyrillic and
Asian alphabet input and searching via IBM PC.

476 "RLG Terminal Emulation Software for IBM." Small
      Computers in Libraries 5 (May 1985): 3-4.
      The Research Libraries Group (RLG) an-
nounces a new software package for the IBM PC
which will permit RLIN libraries to do cataloging
off-line, then upload into the RLIN database.
Hardware specifications are listed.

477 ROGERS, BARRY. "Morwell High School Computer
      Cataloguing Program." School Library Bulletin
      13 (September 1981): 41-43.
      An Australian school librarian describes
the use of TRS-80 hardware and LIBDATA software
for cataloging and LIBPRINT for catalog card production. The program and the process is evaluated, and expanded use of the micro is predicted
for the future.

478 SALAS, RICARDO. "A Library Cataloging System
      Using Microcomputers. Analysis of an Experi-
      ence." The Application of Mini- and Micro-
      Computers in Information, Documentation and
      Libraries. Proceedings of the International
      Conference on the Application of Mini- and
      Micro-Computers in Information, Documentation
      and Libraries, Tel-Aviv, Israel, 13-18 March
      1983. New York: North-Holland, 1983. Pp.
      351-57.
      The library of the Pontificia Universidad
Catolica de Chile has launched a project to automate cataloging functions using microcomputers,
with the goal of ultimately developing an integrated microcomputer-based system merging cataloging, acquisitions, circulation, and information retrieval. Planning and implementing the
first phase of the project is described, and
progress toward future developments is discussed.
Bibliography.

479 SILVERMAN, KAREN SANDLIN. "A Photographic Ar-
     chives Goes Online." Library Software Review
     4 (September/October 1985): 274-79.
          In 1984 the Academy of Natural Sciences
     of Philadelphia Library was awarded a government
     grant to organize its photograph collection. The
     choice and implementation of a microcomputer-
     based system for cataloging and control of the
     collection was a high priority of the project.
     The process is described, along with descriptions
     of the data entry processes and an evaluation of
     SIRE, the data management program which became
     the basis for the project. Bibliography.

480 SKOPP, SAM. "Play It Again. . ." OCLC Micro 1
     (July 1985): 9.
          MICRO ENHANCER software permits a central
     processing center to catalog multiple copies of a
     title at different times without re-editing data.
     The procedure is explained.

481 SUTTON, COLIN. "Computer in the Library."
     Australian School Librarian 17 (Spring 1980):
     97-98.
          A TRS-80 microcomputer, purchased for
     word processing in a school administrative of-
     fice, is being utilized for the production of
     catalog cards for the school's library. Three
     programs: LIBDATA, LIBPRINT, AND LIBACC process
     the data, produce catalog cards, and print
     accession lists.

482 THOMAS, JOSEPH W. "Mixing It Up--Retrospective
     Conversion and Current Cataloging." OCLC
     Micro 1 (May 1985): 15.
          The OCLC MICRO ENHANCER enables catalog-
     ers to record retrospective conversion records
     and current cataloging production onto a single
     disk and upload both at once. Automated proce-
     dures sort and record appropriate charges, but
     OCLC generated statistics will be misleading.

483 VAN ARSDALE, DENNIS. "A Convenient Method for
     Inputting Search Keys." OCLC Micro 1 (July
     1985): 10.

A list of ISBNs or OCLC numbers entered onto a MICRO ENHANCER data disk at the time a book is ordered provides quick and easy access to OCLC catalog copy at processing time, according to this brief article.

484 WANG, ANDREW. "New Microcomputer-Based Retrospective Conversion Service to Be Offered This Fall." OCLC Newsletter no. 154 (September 1984): 9.

OCLC's microcomputer-based retrospective conversion program, begun in 1984, is announced. Advantages of the program are listed, terms of the contract are summarized, and operation of the microcomputer program is described.

485 WATKINS, DEANE. "Let ME Do It." OCLC Micro 1 (July 1985): 14-15.

The assimilation of the M300 Workstation and MICRO ENHANCER software into a cataloging department may require study and reorganization of the workflow to make the best use of the new equipment. Watkins tells how this was accomplished at Oregon State University. A flowchart is included.

486 "Word Processing Eases Librarians' Catalogue Problem." Business Equipment Digest 19 (April 1979): 56.

The Southeast Thames Regional Library and Information Service provides various services to its fifty member libraries, including centralized cataloging and processing of materials for fourteen of its medical library members. A new BDP 90-02 word processing system has streamlined the procedure, and is being considered for other functions as well.

487 ALABI, G. A. "Design of a Microcomputer-Based
Circulation System for Nigerian Academic
Libraries." Microcomputers for Information
Management 2 (March 1985): 43-52.
The design of an experimental microcomputer-based circulation system for use in the
academic libraries of Nigeria is outlined, with
information on the program structure, file structure and organization, and system functions. A
brief evaluation of the pilot installations at
the Ibadan University Library and other sites is
provided in the conclusion. Bibliography.

488 "Apples Back Up CLSI Circ System." Small Computers in Libraries 1 (April 1981): 5.
A brief news note announces the purchase
of two Apple microcomputers with Computer Trans-
lations, Inc. software to back up the Tucson (AZ)
Public Library's CLSI circulation system.

489 BAGNALL, J., and SPRING, M. "New Circulation
System at Newcastle University." Vine no. 37
(February 1981): 12-18.
The authors describe the automated circu-
lation system at England's Newcastle University
Library. Based on a DEC PDP 11/03 minicomputer,
the system employs microcomputers equipped with
OCR scanners and keypads for data entry and short
term storage.

490 BARGHOORN, TERESA; HOKE, KATHY; JOHNSON, CHERYL;
and HEARON, MARY ANN. "Converting to Computer
Circulation." Book Report 3 (March/April
1985): 23-25, 27.
To aid in the selection of computer-based
circulation management systems for their school
district, two Texas school librarians conducted
pilot programs using different circulation systems. The systems tested were Follett Book Company's BOOK TRAK and Winnebago Software Company's

LIBRARY CIRCULATION SYSTEM. Evaluation criteria are outlined. Conclusions and recommendations are summarized.

491 BASHIA, BEVERLY. "Using a Microcomputer to Handle Overdues: The Pierce Junior High School Experience." Indiana Media Journal 5 (Fall 1982): 20-25.
   A software program written by a math teacher solved the problem of producing overdue notices for one junior high school. The program is illustrated and evaluated.

492 "CLSI Demonstrates New Products at ALA Midwinter Meeting." Information Technology and Libraries 2 (June 1983): 219-20.
   New CLSI products introduced at ALA Midwinter, 1983, include an Apple II-based circulation backup, which is described here.

493 CARLSON, GARY. "Circulation Systems on Microcomputers." Drexel Library Quarterly 20 (Fall 1984): 34-47.
   Microcomputer-based circulation systems are increasing in popularity as greater power and storage capacity make them practical for small and medium-sized libraries. This article considers system requirements, advantages, limitations, and selection criteria for automation of circulation functions with microcomputer equipment. Bibliography.

494 CHENG, CHIN-CHUAN, and MURPHY, KURT R. "The IBM PC as a Public Terminal on LCS." Information Technology and Libraries 3 (March 1984): 62-68.
   The interfacing of the IBM PC with the University of Illinois' Library Computer System (LCS) to provide microcomputer capabilities for public access to data is described, along with a description of the programming and an introduction to the LCS system.

495 COVINO, JOSEPH, and INTNER, SHEILA S. "An Informal Survey of the CTI Computer Backup System."

Journal of Library Automation 14 (June 1981):
108-10.

Before investing in a Computer Translation, Inc. microcomputer-based backup for its
CLSI LIBS 100 circulation system, the Great Neck
(NY) Public Library surveyed eleven other libraries that owned CTI systems, asking about applications and satisfaction. Results of the survey
are reported here, with Great Neck's decision.

496 EARNEST, PATRICIA H. "Use of the Microcomputer
for Bibliographic Data Input." Information
Choices and Policies. Proceedings of the 42nd
ASIS Annual Meeting. White Plains, NY: Knowledge Industry Publications, 1979, v. 16. P.
289.

A project to create a shared circulation
database for five California State University
campuses using microcomputers for input and editing is abstracted.

497 HOLMEN, DON. "Circulation Management System at
Waunakee High School." Small Computers in
Libraries 2 (December 1982): 6.

The Waunakee (WI) High School's Materials
Center Director describes the center's new circu-
lation system which uses CIRCULATION MANAGEMENT
SYSTEM software with Apple II Plus equipment.

498 INTNER, SHEILA S. "Microcomputer Backup to Online
Circulation." Journal of Library Automation
14 (December 1981): 297-99.

Because of excessive downtime on the CLSI
LIBS 100 circulation system, the Great Neck (NY)
Public Library installed a backup system based on
Apple II Plus hardware, with mini-disk drives, a
monitor, and a switching system. This has solved
many of the library's circulation problems, and
the hardware can be used in other ways when the
CLSI system is functioning. Bibliography.

499 KLASING, JANE P., and SCHWARTZ, JOE. "Control
Overdues with a Microcomputer." Florida Media
Quarterly 6 (Spring 1981): 19-21.

A microcomputer program written by a

student at Cooper City (FL) High School manages overdues for the high school library. Operation of the program is described, and the program is reproduced in full.

500 LEE, LEONA. "A Microcomputer Handles Overdues." School Library Journal 27 (April 1981): 42.
At Monroe Township High School, Jamesburg, New Jersey, a micro is used in the school media center for circulation control and overdues by entering bibliographic data under student name in the patron file when materials are taken out, and printing overdues from the file when materials are not returned on time.

501 LINKLATER, WILLIAM. "An Australian Online Circulation System Using OCR-A." Vine no. 27 (March 1979): 36-40.
The Swinburne College of Technology Library's microprocessor-based circulation system is described in considerable detail. Based on NCR 2151 hardware with Intel 8080A microprocessors, the system recognizes information input via OCR wand or keyboard. The system also includes a set of software packages for housekeeping tasks.

502 LINKLATER, WILLIAM. "Microprocessor-Based Library Circulation System." LASIE 9 (November/ December 1978): 36-41.
A microprocessor-based circulation system developed and installed in the Library of Swinburne College of Technology, Hawthorn, Victoria, Australia, is justified in comparison to other possible choices, and is described in detail.

503 "Low-Cost Microcomputer System Automates Library Services." Design News (May 8, 1978): 54-55.
A microcomputer-based circulation system, built by Decicom Systems, has been installed at the East Meadow, Long Island (NY) Public Library. Functions of the system are described and a system profile is provided.

504 LUNDEEN, GERALD, and TENOPIR, CAROL. "Microcomputer-Based Library Catalog Software." Micro-

computers for Information Management 1 (September 1984): 215-28.

The authors consider factors in selecting software for circulation systems, and evaluate and compare eight microcomputer-based circulation programs.

505 "Microcomputers May be Better for Circ than Minis." Library Journal 103 (October 15, 1978): 2030-31.

This article summarizes a research report entitled Automated Circulation Systems in Public Libraries, by the MITRE Corp., points out the problems with turnkey systems, and describes the potential of the microcomputer for circulation control.

506 NELMS, WILLIE. "Overdues Procedures Using a Microcomputer." Library and Archival Security 6 (Summer/Fall 1984): 91-95.

Librarians at the Sheppard Memorial Library, Greenville, North Carolina, have applied microcomputer technology and the CONDOR database management program to the problem of overdues, and are saving about $1200 annually. Step-by-step procedures are outlined.

507 "On-line OCLC-CLSI Interface." Small Computers in Libraries 1 (August 1981): 3-4.

An Apple-based microcomputer interface between OCLC cataloging terminals and a CLSI LIBS-100 circulation system provides transfer of information from OCLC to the circulation computer at the William F. Maag Library, Youngstown State University.

508 PIEMONTE, KAY. "Our Experiences With Book Trak." Book Report 3 (March/April 1985): 26-27.

In 1984 the Salem (MA) High School's Instructional Media Center implemented a BOOK TRAK circulation system. This article describes the system as it operates in the Center, discusses changes in the Center's operation that were made to accommodate the system, and evaluates the system from the perspective of the librarian.

509 "Portable Terminals Cut Downtime for Tempe, Arizona Library." Library Journal 107 (November 1, 1982): 2036.
    The Tempe (AZ) Public Library reports the use of MSI Corporation portable terminals with 68K of memory for circulation backup and bookmobile circulation.

510 "RLIN-CLSI Interface at San Francisco PL." Small Computers in Libraries 2 (January 1982): 7.
    A TPS-400 microcomputer interface developed by TPS Electronics is being used to transfer cataloging records from the RLIN database to a CLSI circulation system at the San Francisco Public Library.

511 ROURKE, HELEN. "Micros on the Way in at Ku-Ring-Gai Municipal Library." LASIE 11 (May/June 1981): 18-20.
    Rourke describes the Ku-Ring-Gai (New South Wales) Municipal Library's transition from an outdated Regiscope circulation system to a new automated system employing microcomputers for charging and discharging, with data storage in a UNIVAC 90/30 mainframe.

512 SEALS, J. H., and WOOD, L. R. "A Micro-Based Online Circulation System at Aston." Vine no. 41 (December 1981): 9-13.
    A locally developed, microcomputer-based circulation system for the University of Aston (UK) Library is described and discussed. Hardware, files, operation, and costs are reviewed. Disadvantages are considered.

513 SKAPURA, ROBERT. "The Overdue Writer: A Program Long Overdue." School Library Media Quarterly 10 (Summer 1982): 347-50.
    The development of software to monitor circulation and produce overdue notices using Apple or TRS-80 hardware is described by the librarian who wrote the program.

514 STEVENS, MARY. "University Welcomes Downloaders." American Libraries 15 (November 1984): 702.

Ontario's York University has made provision for anyone having a microcomputer or terminal with communication capabilities to access the library's circulation system, YORKLINE. Access, innovative uses, and future plans are addressed.

515 THOMASON, NEVADA WALLIS. Circulation Systems for School Library Media Centers; Manual to Microcomputers. Littleton, CO: Libraries Unlimited, 1985. 169p.

This thorough consideration of small circulation systems particularly suited to school libraries traces the development of library circulation from the manual system to the microcomputer. Circulation policies, statistics, audiovisual systems, and special circulation problems are considered. Semi-automatic systems are discussed. Microcomputer systems are introduced and illustrated, with notes on hardware, software, types of systems, and system selection. Bibliography.

516 "UNIFACE: A Circulation System/WLN Interface." ACCESS: Microcomputers in Libraries 1 (October 1981): 5.

The Tacoma (WA) Public Library and Boeing Computer Services have developed an interface between the Washington Library Network's computer and the library's DataPhase system. Called UNIFACE, it employs a Terak 8510a microcomputer to transfer WLN data into the library's database. This article briefly describes how the interface is used in the library's circulation and acquisition operations, specifies hardware necessary for the interface, and provides purchase information for the software.

517 WALTON, ROBERT A. "Circulation and Overdue Materials Software for Microcomputers." Technicalities 5 (January 1985): 12.

Twenty-one microcomputer-based circulation and overdue programs are listed, with producer addresses, hardware requirements, and prices.

518 WARD, JOSEPH H., Jr. "Microcomputer Use at
     Wilcox High School." CMLEA Journal 3 (Spring
     1980): 12-14.
          The tediousness of preparing overdue no-
     tices has been greatly reduced in one California
     high school by use of a microcomputer to perform
     the task; and some valuable circulation statis-
     tics can be captured in the bargain, according to
     the school librarian.

519 WILSON, CHRIS W. J. "Developments at Harwell."
     Vine no. 36 (December 1980): 11-12.
          The upgrading of an outmoded circulation
     system at the Harwell (UK) Public Library is
     outlined, and the features of the new system, a
     Digital PDP/03 microcomputer with two floppy
     disks, printer, and two VDUs are described.

520 WILSON, CHRIS W. J.; HAYNES, E. M.; and TESKEY F.
     N. "Harwell Automated Loans System--HAL,
     Using STATUS." Program 15 (April 1981):
     43-65.
          The Harwell (UK) Public Library's transi-
     tion from batch-processed teletype circulation to
     a microcomputer-based system using STATUS soft-
     ware is told in detail. Hardware and software
     are described; reasons for the change, system
     design, implementation, problems, and costs are
     discussed.

521 WOOD, LAWRENCE. "A Circulation Control System
     on an ACT Apricot." Vine no. 57 (December
     1984): 4-12.
          A microcomputer-based circulation system
     installed in the Stockport College of Technology
     Library in 1984 is described and evaluated. The
     program, which runs on an ACT-Apricot micro, with
     hard disk and Epson HX-20 peripherals, provides
     capacity for 60,000 circulation records and
     10,000 borrowers in a menu driven system.

GRAPHICS

522 DISKIN, JILL A., and FITZGERALD, PATRICIA. "Library Signage: Applications for the Apple Macintosh and MacPaint." Library Hi Tech 2, no. 4, issue 8 (1984): 71-77.

       Carnegie-Mellon University Libraries is using Apple Macintosh microcomputers with MACWRITE word processing and MACPAINT graphics software to produce signs, posters, letterhead stationery, office memos, and other instructional, informational, and promotional printing. Various applications are described and illustrated.

523 EMMENS, CAROL A. "Computer Graphics Jazz Up Video Productions." School Library Journal 31 (April 1985): 50.

       The versatility and usefulness of computer generated graphics is demonstrated, several microcomputer graphics programs are mentioned, and a method of providing videotapes using a computer graphics program is described.

524 JOHNSON, HARRIET, and JOHNSON, RICHARD D. "Mac Graphics in the Library." Small Computers in Libraries 5 (October 1985): 14-16.

       Using MACPAINT graphics and MACWRITE word processing programs with an Apple Macintosh microcomputer, an innovative librarian can create professional looking signs, charts, stationery, and other printed forms. The authors provide suggestions and illustrations, with brief instructions concerning some forms. Bibliography.

525 RAPPAPORT, SUSAN. "Computer Graphics for the Novice." Library Journal 110 (September 1, 1985): 146-47.

       Computer graphics have been possible for years with mini and mainframe computers, but have only become practical with the development of the micro. Rappaport discusses several graphics programs and peripherals, including KOALAPAD, ZOOM GRAFIX, MACPAINT, PRINT SHOP, and PFS: GRAPH.

526 AMYX, RICHARD. "Indexing Information With a
     TRS-80." Personal Computing 5 (May 1981):
     57, 60.
          In order to make a software manual more
     useful, the author wrote a program for the TRS-80
     which enabled him to create an index for the man-
     ual where none had been provided. He describes
     the program, then shares it with readers who
     may need it for indexing books, papers, recipes,
     journal articles, or other collections.

527 ARMSTRONG, C. J. and KEEN, E. M. Workbook for
     NEPHIS and KWAC: Microcomputer Printed Subject
     Indexes Teaching Package, Part 1. British Li-
     brary Research & Development Report, no. 5710.
     London: British Library, 1982. 57p.
          Intended for use in teaching indexing by
     microcomputer, this workbook provides instruc-
     tion, examples, and exercises for developing
     skills in Nested Phrase Indexing System (NEPHIS)
     and Keyword and Context (KWAC).

528 ARMSTRONG, C. J. and KEEN, E. M. Manual for
     Teaching NEPHIS and KWAC: Microcomputer Print-
     ed Subject Indexes Teaching Package, Part 2.
     British Library Research & Development Report,
     no. 5711. London: British Library, 1982. 59p.
          A teacher's guide for teaching NEPHIS and
     KWAC indexing, this publication is intended to
     accompany the Workbook for NEPHIS and KWAC listed
     above.

529 BATTY, DAVID. "Microcomputers in Index Language
     Design and Development." Microcomputers for
     Information Management 1 (December 1984):
     303-12.
          Arguments and a case study are presented
     in support of microcomputer use in the production
     of indexes, the development of controlled vocabu-
     laries, and the generation of references.

530 BEVERSDORF, ANNE. "Index or VISIDEX: Gaining Access to Periodical Records." <u>ACCESS: Microcomputers in Libraries</u> 2 (April 1982): 10-11, 25.
     A peripheral use of a microcomputer purchased for the Research Department of the Agency for Instructional Television in Bloomington, Indiana, has been the indexing of a periodical collection in the agency's library, using the VISIDEX program available from Personal Software.

531 CARTER, NANCY F. "Sheet Music Index on a Microcomputer." <u>Information Technology and Libraries</u> 2 (March 1983): 52-55.
     The planning and implementation of an automated index for the University of Colorado Library's sheet music collection is described. A TRS-80 Model II micro and PROFILE software were used for the project. Advantages and disadvantages of the micro are discussed, and examples of a printout and an input worksheet are provided.

532 CRAVEN, TIMOTHY C. "Automatic NEPHIS Coding of Descriptive Titles for Permuted Index Generation." <u>American Society for Information Science Journal</u> 33 (March 1982): 97-101.
     Craven discusses his work in a project to automate the title coding function for NEPHIS, an index generation program developed at the University of Western Ontario. Bibliography.

533 CRAVEN, TIMOTHY C. "Microcomputer Customizing of Permuted Index Displays." <u>Information Interaction</u>. Proceedings of the 45th ASIS Annual Meeting. White Plains, NY: Knowledge Industry Publications, 1982, v. 19. Pp. 63-65.
     Customizing online network index displays using a microcomputer is described, with various options and illustrations. Bibliography.

534 CRAVEN, TIMOTHY C. "Microcomputer-Generated Graphic Displays as an Aid in String Indexing." <u>American Society for Information Science Journal</u> 31 (March 1980): 123-24.
     Human error is often difficult to detect in index construction, but can be reduced by

using a microcomputer and a string index language. The author demonstrates index validation
through the creation of graphic displays of concept links using the NEPHIS string index language
and a Pet 2001-8 microcomputer. Bibliography.

535 CRAVEN, TIMOTHY C. "Microcomputer Simulation of
Large Permuted Indexes." Information Choices
and Policies. Proceedings of the 42nd ASIS
Annual Meeting. White Plains, NY: Knowledge
Industry Publications, 1979, v. 16. Pp.
168-73.
Simulations of large indexes and index
evaluation are demonstrated through the NEPHIS
index simulator program, which was developed at
the University of Western Ontario for a PET
2001-8 microcomputer using Commodore BASIC
language. Bibliography.

536 FAULKNER, RONNIE W. "dBASE III and Newspaper
Indexing." Library Software Review 4 (Septem-
ber/October 1985): 280-84.
The Library Director at Glenville (VA)
State College tells of the decision to automate
certain library processes and the selection of
IBM hardware for the purpose, along with dBASE
III data management software for indexing and
listing functions. The automation of a local
newspaper index using the system forms the major
portion of the article, which describes the project in detail. Bibliography.

537 FETTERS, LINDA K. "A Guide to Seven Indexing
Programs. . .Plus a Review of the 'Professional Bibliographic System'." Database 8 (December 1985): 31-38.
The development of microcomputer programs
for book and journal indexing is discussed, and
three types of software are identified. Guidelines for selection of indexing software are outlined, and several appropriate programs are reviewed. Programs included are: BOOKDEX, NEWSDEX,
THE INDEX EDITOR, INDEX PREPARATION SYSTEM, MICRO
INDEXING SYSTEM, MICREX, MACREX, BNS COMPUTER-
ASSISTED INDEXING PROGRAM, FOXON-MADDOCKS INDEX

PREPARATION SYSTEM, ININDEX, and PROFESSIONAL
BIBLIOGRAPHIC SYSTEM.

538 FLOWER, ERIC, and MENCHEN, GARY. "A Simple Newspaper Index Using dBASE II." Small Computers
in Libraries 4 (December 1984): 6-8.
Flower and Menchen provide a detailed
account of the creation and operation of an
indexing project at the University of Maine at
Orono for the Maine Times. File creation, data
entry, and printing are addressed.

539 "Grant for Micro Study." Library Association
Record 86 (February 1984): 53.
R. F. Guy and the College of Librarianship Wales have been awarded a grant to develop
microcomputer software for production of printed
subject indexes, according to this news item.

540 HALES, DAVID, and ARTMAN, BRENDA. "Alaska Newspaper Index: Microcomputers and Information
Access Company." RSR: Reference Services
Review 11 (Fall 1983): 48-52.
The need for indexing of Alaskan newspapers is expressed, and several early individual
and group indexing projects are described. The
current Alaska Newspaper Indexing Project, a
microcomputer-based system, which provides data
to the Information Access Company for inclusion
in DIALOG's "Local News Index File," is described.

541 HINES, THEODORE C., and WINKEL, LOIS. "Micro-
computer-Aided Production of Indexes." Indexer 11 (October 1979): 198-201.
An inexpensive hardware configuration and
software program for compiling book indexes is
described by two experienced indexers and microcomputer programmers. Bibliography.

542 HINES, THEODORE C.; WINKEL, LOIS; and COLLINS,
ROSANN W. "Microcomputers and the Serials Librarian." Serials Librarian 4 (Spring 1980):
275-79.
The use of microcomputers in indexing

periodicals is described, and the ease with which
camera-ready copy can be produced for publication
purposes is lauded.

543 "Newspaper Indexing With dBASE II." Small Com-
puters in Libraries 2 (May 1982): 1.
Employing a CompuStar microcomputer sys-
tem with dBASE II software, the University of
Arizona Library is indexing the local newspaper.
Details of the project are provided.

544 POWELL, ANTOINETTE. "The KAES Indexing Project."
M300 and PC Report 2 (May 1985): 3-4.
An indexing project using an M300 Workstation with a hard disk drive for index construction is described by the University of
Kentucky's Agriculture Librarian. Still in the
planning stage when the article was written,
plans are to follow AGRICOLA format and make the
information available through AGRICOLA when the
project is completed.

545 PURTON, A. CAMPBELL. "Microcomputers for Home
Indexing: A Report and Guide." Indexer 13
(April 1982): 27-31.
Portions of the task of compiling a book
index are mechanical. Purton describes how these
mechanical operations can be expedited by using
a microcomputer, and considers hardware and software suitable for the task.

546 SAUVE, DEBORAH. "Private Files in Bilingual Education." Special Libraries Association Florida Chapter Bulletin 15 (January 1983): 24-29.
When the National Clearinghouse for Bilingual Education began its machine-readable
database in 1977-78, the Clearinghouse contracted
with Bibliographic Retrieval Service (BRS) for
data storage, but decided to create the files in-
house using an Alpha-Micro System AM-100 microcomputer. The process is described and evaluated.

547 THOMPSON, JUDITH. "Index Creation on the Wang
OIS 130." Electronic Library 1 (July 1983):
181-86.

Guidelines are provided for the use of the index generator option on the Wang OIS 130 word processor for production of book indexes.

548 TOMASELLI, MARY F. "Microcomputer-Based Indexing and Abstracting." Indexer 14 (April 1984): 30-34.

In 1983 a project to index the masters theses and masters papers submitted to the Queens College Graduate School of Library and Information Studies was begun by a faculty member, with the assistance of two graduate students. This project, which was carried out on an Apple II microcomputer with LIBRARY MATE software, is described, with examples of the final document.

549 "Univ. of Arizona Installs CompuStar for Indexing." Small Computers in Libraries 2 (March 1982): 6.

An Intertec CompuStar system has been purchased by the University of Arizona Library for use in an Arizona newspaper indexing project and word processing functions.

550 WOODROW, MARTIN. "Stansted Inquiry: Indexing Documents Using a Microcomputer." Indexer 13 (October 1982): 104-06.

Details are provided concerning an indexing project of some 1800 documents for the Hertfordshire (UK) Library Service. An Apple micro and DB MASTER software were used. Routines and and problems are described.

551 YERKEY, A. NEIL. "A Preserved Context Indexing System for Microcomputers: PERMDEX." Information Processing and Management 19, no. 3 (1983): 165-71.

PERMDEX, a non-commercial microcomputer program for creating permuted indexes, is described in considerable detail by its author, who says that it assists the indexer in the indexing process, then handles the tasks of creating, sorting, storing, and arranging data, and printing the finished copy.

552 EVANS, ELIZABETH A. "Microcomputers: An Interlibrary Loan Application." Special Libraries
75 (January 1984): 17-27.
Processing interlibrary loan requests on
ALA forms has been automated and streamlined
through the application of dBASE II to the function. The author describes her program, reviews
changes made when it was adopted by two North
Carolina libraries, and includes mockups of forms
generated by the system. Bibliography.

553 GADSDEN, S. R., and ADAMS, ROY J. The Administration of Interlending by Microcomputer.
Library and Information Research Report, no.
30. Boston Spa: British Library, 1984. 58p.
Gadsden and Adams describe the design and
development of a microcomputer system to adminis-
ter interlibrary borrowing and lending in Great
Britain. A needs survey, software choice, and
system operation are considered. Bibliography.

554 GIVENS, BETH. "Micros and Interlibrary Loan in
Montana." ACCESS: Microcomputers in Libraries
2 (July 1982): 5-7, 24.
The interlibrary loan network in Montana
converted from TWX to Apple microcomputers to ex-
pediate communications and save money. Givens
describes the conversion process and the network
structure, then evaluates the system.

555 GIVENS, BETH. "Montana's Use of Microcomputers
for Interlibrary Loan Communications." Information Technology and Libraries 1 (September
1982): 260-64.
Montana's new resource sharing network
based on microcomputer technology and electronic
mail is outlined, and the network configuration
is described. Advantages of the new Apple-based
system over TWX communication are presented, and
further advancements are foreseen. Bibliography.

556 GOSZ, KATHLEEN M. "Apple ILL Net in Wisconsin."
Small Computers in Libraries 2 (December
1982): 1-2.
The establishment of the Waukesha County
(WI) Library System and the system's installation
of a microcomputer-based interlibrary loan network are related by the system's director.

557 GOSZ, KATHLEEN M. "Microcomputer Network Supports ILL for Waukesha County Library System."
Wisconsin Library Bulletin 78 (Summer 1983):
65-67.
The Waukesha County (WI) Library System's
conversion from telefacsimile to microcomputers
for transmission of interlibrary loan requests is
outlined, and the new system is evaluated.

558 HUND, FLOWER. "Apple ILLNET in Missouri." Small
Computers in Libraries 2 (November 1982): 1.
A Missouri interlibrary loan network
based on an electronic mail system utilizing Apple II Plus microcomputers is described and evaluated by one of the participants.

559 "IBM PCs and Apples in ILL Net." Small Computers
in Libraries 4 (March 1984): 3.
Two microcomputer-based resource sharing
projects by Colorado library systems are described. One is a cooperative local area network
linking libraries in two library systems to expedite interlibrary loan; the second is a joint online catalog linking two other systems.

560 KANE, MATTHEW J. "Database Management for Interlibrary Loan." Information Technology and
Libraries 3 (September 1984): 297-99.
The Altoona Area (PA) Public Library's
experience in automating its interlibrary loan
records using an Apple III microcomputer and PFS:
FILE software is shared, and its positive impact
is told.

561 MARNEY, DEAN. "DB MASTER for Mail Order Library."
Small Computers in Libraries 2 (December
1982): 3-4.

Details are provided concerning the automation of the Mail Order Library's inventory file at the North Central (WA) Regional Library, using DB MASTER software with an Apple II Plus micro and a Corvus Mass Storage Disk System/20MB.

562 MATTHEWS, JOSEPH R. "Resource Sharing in Montana: A Study of Interlibrary Loan and Alternatives for a Montana Union Catalog." Arlington, VA: ERIC Document Reproduction Service, ED 198 821, 1980.

The Montana plan for sharing of library resources within the state is outlined in detail. Of particular interest is the interlibrary loan network utilizing microcomputers as the major mode of communication. Bibliography.

563 METRICS RESEARCH CORP. "Study of the Communications Needs of the Fox Valley Interlibrary Loan Network." Arlington, VA: ERIC Document Reproduction Service, ED 233 718, 1982.

A survey of the libraries in the Fox Valley Interlibrary Loan Network reveals that communication technology is seen as the network's greatest need. Four types of communication configurations are described and compared. Results indicate that microcomputer nodes with communications software could fill the communications needs, with other online and offline functions provided as a bonus.

564 "Micros are Telecommunications Link for NYSILL and RML Networks in NY." Library Journal 108 (May 15, 1983): 940.

A microcomputer-based telecommunication link for the New York Interlibrary Loan System and the Regional Medical Network is announced in this brief news item.

565 MINNERATH, JANET, and PARKER, PHILLIP. "What Smartcom Never Showed Us." OCLC Micro 1 (September 1985): 18-20.

Staff of the University of Oklahoma Health Sciences Library are using an M300 Workstation with WORDSTAR and SMARTCOM II to create and transmit interlibrary loan requests. The authors provide step-by-step instructions for the procedure and an example to illustrate the form as transmitted.

566 "New Technology: Montana Uses Micros for Interlibrary Loan." Library Journal 108 (January 15, 1983): 88.
   The conversion of the Montana Resource Sharing Network from teletype to microcomputer is told, and the program is evaluated briefly.

567 PISTORIUS, J. M., and SMITH, J. W. "Microcomputer Application in a Library for Document Ordering and Delivery." Electronic Library 3 (October 1985): 290-95.
   The Document Delivery Service of South Africa's Centre for Scientific and Technical Information installed a microcomputer in 1984 when its manual system for handling requests became ineffective because of increasing volume. A program developed locally has solved the problem, providing for automated request handling, recordkeeping, invoicing, and referral. Automatic transmission of requests is considered, as are peripheral, in-house uses of the system.

568 RICE-LIVELY, MARY LYNN. "Dallas Public Library's Chapter in the History of the MicroEnhancer." Texas Libraries 45 (Fall 1984): 83-85.
   In 1983 the Dallas (TX) Public Library agreed to be a test site for OCLC's interlibrary loan MICRO ENHANCER software. Dallas Public's interlibrary loan service is described before and after the implementation of the program. Preparation, costs, and evaluation are addressed.

569 "State Supplied Micros to Speed Kansas Interloan." Library Journal 109 (February 1, 1984): 135.
   The Kansas State Library has purchased Zenith Z-100 microcomputers for the seventeen libraries on the Kansas Information circuit to enhance interlibrary loan communication, according to this brief note.

570 ANDERSON, ERIC S. "What a Spreadsheet Is and Why
You Might Care." OCLC Micro 1 (November
1985): 24-25.
In this brief article Anderson defines
spreadsheets and illustrates how one may be used
to maintain circulation statistics.

571 BERNHARD, KEITH E. "Computer Applications in the
Library Media Center: An Introduction to Electronic Spreadsheets." School Library Media
Quarterly 12 (Spring 1984): 222-26.
This article analyzes what a spreadsheet
does, how it works, how it can be applied to
school library/media situations, and how to determine its value to your operation. Examples
and illustrations are included. Bibliography.

572 CASTLE, WALLACE I.; CASTLE, MARY K.; and PAYNE,
LEILA M. "The Use of Simulation as a Decision
Support Aid." Technicalities 1 (June 1981):
12-14.
The use of microcomputer simulation for
administrative problem solving and decision
making is explained and demonstrated by posing a
hypothetical staffing problem in a cataloging department, setting up a model, and working through
the simulation to its logical conclusion, which
provides information to support and guide the
decision maker in exercising personal judgment.

573 CLARK, PHILIP M. Microcomputer Spreadsheet
Models for Libraries: Preparing Documents,
Budgets, and Statistical Reports. Chicago:
American Library Association, 1985. 118p.
Beginning with a basic introduction to
spreadsheets and their use in library management,
this book presents thirty detailed models for
budgeting, statistical analysis, projections, and
other functions, all of which are easily adaptable to VISICALC, SUPERCALC, MULTIPLAN, PERFECT
CALC, OR LOTUS 1-2-3.

574 FREUND, ALFRED L. "Microcomputers: A New Era at
     Ramapo Catskill." Library Journal 108 (June
     15, 1983): 1217-19.
          The Ramapo Catskill (NY) Library System's
     office automation project is described, including
     the rationale for the project and various appli-
     cations for which micros have been adapted.

575 GIBSON, LARRY M. "Electronic Spreadsheet Pack-
     ages for Microcomputers." Drexel Library
     Quarterly 20 (Fall 1984): 64-73.
          The concept of the spreadsheet is analy-
     zed, its development is traced, library applica-
     tions are suggested, and its future is predicted.
     A substantial spreadsheet glossary is appended.

576 LAW, D. "A Library Accounts Package for Micros."
     Vine no. 45 (October 1982): 49-50.
          A microcomputer-based accounting package
     developed for the Edinburgh University Library is
     described. The program, which has subsets for
     commitments, expenditures, sales, and serials,
     and can accommodate 900 different funds, will run
     on Apple II or Sirius hardware.

577 MALINCONICO, S. MICHAEL. "Decisions Under Un-
     certainty." Library Journal 109 (November
     15, 1984): 2129-31.
          The value of a microcomputer in adminis-
     trative decision-making is discussed and demon-
     strated through the application of micro-based
     projection techniques using a spreadsheet to
     solve two hypothetical library problems.

578 "Microcomputer Timetabling." CABLIS 72 (April
     1982): 12.
          A microcomputer is being used at the
     Fairport (NY) Public Library to schedule library
     assistants for work hours. A task which once
     took five hours now consumes twenty minutes,
     according to this news item.

579 MILLER, BRUCE CUMMINGS. "Spreadsheet Models of
     Library Activities." Library Hi Tech 1
     (Spring 1984): 19-25.

Spreadsheet capabilities and their uses in library management and planning are presented, with models for five functions which can easily be adapted to an individual library's needs.

580 MILLS, CLAUDIA. "Brave New Office." Show-Me Libraries 35 (October/November 1983): 61-64.
The automated office of the future is predicted and described, with health concerns, adaptation to automation, and the psychological impact of the computer considered.

581 RAYMOND, CHADWICK T. "Automated Business Functions with Alpha Micro." Small Computers in Libraries 3 (August 1983): 6-7.
Raymond describes the automation of payroll, general accounting, inventory, and personnel functions for the Addison (IL) Public Library, using an Alpha Micro 100T and AMOS (Alpha Micro Operating System).

582 RICHMOND, RICK. "Office Automation Software for Public Libraries." Wyoming Library Roundup 39 (Spring/Summer 1984): 42-45.
This article reviews the most common library office activities and suggests computer applications to reduce the workload. Word processing, calculating and forecasting, data management, and communications are considered.

583 "Roanoke Apple IIe and Visicalc Aid Output Measures Control." Library Journal 109 (July 1984): 1280.
The Roanoke County (VA) Public Library reports that use of an Apple IIe micro and VISICALC software enables them to keep and analyze circulation and reference statistics and provide monthly reports to aid in implementing quality control measures.

584 SCHUYLER, MICHAEL. "Apple Experiences at Kitsap." Small Computers in Libraries 2 (January 1982): 1.
The purchase of an Apple microcomputer, with VISICALC and DATA FACTORY software, allowed

the Kitsap Regional Library in Bremerton, Washington, to automate budget, circulation statistics, vacation records, mailing lists, accounts payable, and payroll.

585 SCHUYLER, MICHAEL. "The Evolution of Spreadsheets." Microcomputers for Information Management 2 (March 1985): 11-23.
        The spreadsheet has contributed substantially to the acceptance of microcomputer technology and its integration into the office. The evolution of the spreadsheet is traced from the earliest VISICALC edition, emphasizing the impact of VISICALC, LOTUS 1-2-3, and SYMPHONY on the development of microcomputing in general.

586 SCHUYLER, MICHAEL. "Visicalc: Uses for an Electronic Spreadsheet in the Library." Technicalities 2 (November 1982): 6-8.
        Schuyler demonstrates spreadsheet applications to cataloging and circulation statistics, discusses spreadsheet construction, memory requirements, and compatibility with other programs such as WORDSTAR and DATASTAR.

587 STRAZDON, MAUREEN E. " A Library Application of the Apple VisiCalc Program." Drexel Library Quarterly 17 (Winter 1981): 75-86.
        The VISICALC program, written expressly for mathematical calculation and manipulation with Apple hardware, is described, and its applications to statistical recordkeeping and the library budget at the Vane B. Lucas Memorial Library of the American College is evaluated.

588 SWERSEY, PATRICIA JOHNSON. "Learning to Use Your Spreadsheet." Library Software Review 4 (September/October 1985): 291-93.
        Swersey considers a variety of methods of learning spreadsheet operation. These include studying the manual, using software tutorials, taking classes, and relying on newsletters, books, and other materials for help.

ONLINE CATALOGS

589 "Apple Replaces Library Card Catalog." Apple
Education News 3 (January 1982): 8.
This article discusses the computeriza-
tion of the card catalog at the Mountain View
Elementary School in Broomfield, Colorado. Jus-
tification is provided, and advantages are told.

590 ARMSTRONG, MARGARET, and COSTA, BETTY. "Computer
Cat at Mountain View Elementary School." Library Hi Tech 1 (Winter 1983): 47-52.
The automated catalog at Broomfield, Colorado's Mountain View Elementary School is described. Advantages over the traditional card
catalog are noted, as are positive user reac-
tions. Bibliography.

591 BAKER, PATTI R. "A Software Filing System for
Elementary Schools." Educational Computer
Magazine 3 (September 1983): 46-47, 50, 91.
A fourth grade teacher at Centerburg (OH)
Elementary School describes an automated catalog
she developed for her school's growing software
collection using a microcomputer with PFS: FILE
and PFS: REPORT software.

592 ". . .But Try Them Instead of Dewey Decimals."
Education USA 24 (October 12, 1981): 52.
The Mountain View Elementary School's
online library catalog is briefly described, and
advantages over the traditional card catalog are
discussed.

593 "A Computerized Card Catalog." Personal Computing 5 (December 1981): 99-100.
The computerized catalog at Broomfield,
Colorado's Mountain View Elementary School Library is described briefly.

594 COSTA, BETTY. "Catalogs via Microcomputers."
School Library Journal 27 (March 1981): 71.
In a letter to the editor, Betty Costa

reviews the microcomputer-based catalog at the
Mountain View Elementary School, Broomfield,
Colorado.

595 COSTA, BETTY. "Microcomputer in Colorado--It's
       Elementary!" Wilson Library Bulletin 55 (May
       1981): 676-78, 717.
            The Mountain View Elementary School
     microcomputer project is described in detail,
     including the development of specifications for
     the system, its operation, and plans for future
     expansion.

596 COSTA, BETTY. "An Online Catalog for an Elemen-
       tary School Library Media Center." School Li-
       brary Media Quarterly 10 (Summer 1982): 337-
       40, 345-46.
            Betty Costa answers frequently asked
     questions about COMPUTER CAT, the microcomputer-
     based online catalog at the Mountain View Elemen-
     tary School, Broomfield, Colorado. Bibliography.

597 COSTA, BETTY, and COSTA, MARIE. "'Card' Catalog
       on a Microcomputer--So Easy a Child Can Use
       It!" Catholic Library World 54 (November
       1982): 166-69.
            COMPUTER CAT, the online catalog at
     Mountain View Elementary School, in Broomfield,
     Colorado, is described, and its advantages for
     the librarian are outlined. Bibliography.

598 COSTA, BETTY, and COSTA, MARIE. "Computer Cat in
       Colorado; An Online Catalog for Students."
       ACCESS: Microcomputers in Libraries 1 (July
       1981): 4-6.
            Basically a reprint of an article which
     appeared earlier in Wilson Library Bulletin, this
     contains an evaluative section which did not ap-
     pear in the earlier version.

599 COSTA, BETTY, and COSTA, MARIE. "Microcomputers
       in Libraries." Technicalities 1 (October
       1981): 16.
            The Costas consider problems of auto-
     mating a small library, discuss advantages of

automation, and offer COMPUTER CAT as a viable system for libraries which cannot justify a mini or mainframe computer.

600   COSTA, MARIE, and COSTA, BETTY. "The Microcomputer in the School Media Centre." Review 10 (June 1982): 23-24.
　　　　In this journal published by the Library Services Division of the South Australian Department of Education, Costa and Costa provide an overview of COMPUTER CAT, the microcomputer-based library catalog at Broomfield, Colorado's Mountain View Elementary School. The various program components are defined, user orientation is described, technical problems and acceptance of the program are reviewed. Bibliography.

601   "Developing Micro-Based On-Line Catalogs." Small Computers in Libraries 4 (January 1984): 4-5.
　　　　While little or no software exists for creating and maintaining small online catalogs for libraries, interest and demand are increasing and will eventually lead to the production of such programs. The editors of Small Computers in Libraries have considered the development of online catalog software and written some basic specifications for it.

602   DURBIN, HUGH. "There's a Computer in Your Future." Ohio Media Spectrum 34 (Spring 1982): 24-25.
　　　　Durbin shares his impressions of the microcomputer-based online catalog at Broomfield, Colorado's Mountain View Elementary School.

603   EDMONTON (ALBERTA) PUBLIC SCHOOLS. "Utilization of a Microcomputer in an Elementary School Learning Resource Centre." Arlington, VA: ERIC Document Reproduction Service, ED 239 601, 1983.
　　　　A study to determine the educational value of a microcomputer-based library catalog over a traditional card catalog is reported. Increased interest, ease of use, and greater use of nonfiction materials are noted.

604 EMBAR, INDRANI. "Online Catalog Using dBASE II."
    Small Computers in Libraries 3 (May 1983): 6.
          The use of dBASE II database management
    system to create an online catalog for the Re-
    search Library of Chicago's Boston Consulting
    Group is told by the library's technical librar-
    ian. Pros and cons are considered.

605 ENGLE, MARY. "Microcomputers and MELVYL." DLA
    Bulletin 3 (October 1983): 6, 13.
          The use of microcomputers as terminals to
    access MELVYL, the University of California's on-
    line catalog, is described. Necessary hardware
    and software are discussed, and the advantages of
    a micro over a terminal are told.

606 FREUND, ALFRED L. "A Regional Bibliographic
    Database on Videodisc." Library Hi Tech 3,
    no. 2, issue 10 (1985): 7-9.
          The creation of an automated union cata-
    log for a three system, eight county area of
    southeastern New York state is reviewed by the
    director of the Ramapo Catskill Library System.
    The catalog is produced in COM and videodisc
    formats. The videodisc version will operate on
    an industrial quality videodisc player with an
    IBM PC interface for searching.

607 GARTEN, EDWARD D. "Using a Microcomputer and In-
    telligent Terminals to Enhance Public Catalog
    and Reference Support Within the LAMBDA Online
    Catalog System." Proceedings of the Confer-
    ence on Integrated Online Library Systems,
    Columbus, Ohio, 26-27 September 1983. Can-
    field, OH: Genaway & Associates, 1983. Pp.
    121-29.
          The Local Access to and Management of
    Bibliographic Data and Authorities (LAMBDA) Pro-
    ject, SOLINET's pilot project to establish re-
    gional catalog databases, is described by the
    director of Tennessee Tech University Library, a
    LAMBDA participant. Although LAMBDA is resident
    on a mainframe conputer, a microcomputer inter-
    face at Tennessee Tech provides public access
    and special features for patrons and reference

librarians. The interface and features are described and briefly evaluated. Bibliography.

608 GONDER, PEGGY ODELL. "Library Computer Saves Time, Prevents Frustration." Rocky Mountain News (Denver) 28 September 1981, pp. 48-49.
Operation of the online catalog at Broomfield Colorado's Mountain View Elementary School is explained, and its advantages over the traditional card catalog are told.

609 GORMAN, MICHAEL. "Microcomputers and Online Catalogs." Drexel Library Quarterly 20 (Fall 1984): 25-33.
The advantages of an online library catalog are acknowledged, but unfamiliar functions and commands are recognized as discouraging factors for many library users. Using the University of Illinois' LCS online catalog and circulation system as a point of reference, Gorman proposes a hypothetical microcomputer interface which would reduce computer commands to standard English and take much of the frustration out of online catalog searching.

610 "Interview: Betty Costa." ACCESS: Microcomputers in Libraries 1 (July 1981): 7, 20.
Betty Costa answers questions about the Mountain View Elementary School's microcomputer-based online catalog, including plans for adding circulation and acquisitions capabilities to the present system.

611 LaRUE, JAMES. "Dialing for Data." Library Software Review 4 (January/February 1985): 14-17.
In 1978 the Lincoln Library, Springfield, Illinois, automated circulation with a CLSI system. Since that time, they have upgraded to provide a public online catalog, and are now providing dialup access from personal computer. Background of the project is reviewed, and the dialup program is evaluated.

612 LAUGHLIN, PATRICIA. "Design and Implementation of the Milwaukee Public Museum's Automated Map

Catalog." SLA Geography and Map Division
Bulletin 130 (December 1982): 20-30.
The Milwaukee (WI) Public Museum's automated map catalog is the result of a gift of a
used Commodore Pet 32K microcomputer. The design
and implementation of the catalog project are
reviewed, and guidelines for accepting gifts of
microcomputer equipment are presented.

613 MALSAM, MARGARET. "A Computer First for an Ele-
mentary School: Microcomputer Replaces Card
Catalog." Educational Computer Magazine 1
(September/October 1981): 40-41, 53.
The Mountain View Elementary School's
Apple-based online catalog is publicized. Dia-
grams provide information on searching the data-
base and creating records.

614 MALSAM, MARGARET. "The Computer Replaces the Card
Catalog in One Colorado Elementary School."
Phi Delta Kappan 63 (January 1982): 321; and
Ohio Media Spectrum 34 (Spring 1982): 22-23.
The public relations specialist of School
District 12, Northglenn, Colorado, describes and
evaluates COMPUTER CAT, the Mountain View Elemen-
tary School's microcomputer-based online library
catalog.

615 MASON, ROBERT M. "Laser Disks for Micros." Library Journal 110 (February 15, 1985): 124-25.
Laser disc technology is addressed, and
its advantages and disadvantages for data storage are considered. New developments and applications are described, including the Library
Corporation's BIBLIOFILE microcomputer software,
which provides for the creation of an online
catalog using combined microcomputer/laser technology.

616 "Microcomputer Replaces Card Catalog." Media and
Methods 18 (September 1981): 2.
This news brief announces the microcom-
puter-based online catalog installed at Broom-
field, Colorado's Mountain View Elementary
School, and briefly describes its opertation.

617 MILLER, LESLIE, and KUN-WOO PARK CHOI. "A Microcomputer Based Reserve System for University
Branch Libraries." Information Interaction.
Proceedings of the 45th ASIS Annual Meeting.
White Plains, NY: Knowledge Industry Publications, 1982, v. 19. Pp. 195-96.
        The authors describe a microcomputer-
based bibliographic control system for a reserve
book room, which provides multiple access points
including author, title, key-word, course, and
teacher. Advantages and restrictions of the system are noted. Bibliography.

618 MURPHY, BROWER. "CD-ROM and Libraries." Library
Hi Tech 3, no. 2, issue 10 (1985): 21-26.
        The compact laserdisc is described, and
its potential for large volume data storage in
libraries is discussed. BIBLIOFILE, a compact
disc-read only memory system for storing and accessing MARC data, is also described. BIBLIOFILE
combines Hitachi and IBM PC hardware.

619 PEMBERTON, JOHN E. "Selecting Software for a
Micro-Based Library Catalogue." Law Librarian
14 (December 1983): 34-38.
        The experiences of the staff of the
University of Buckingham's Denning Law Library in
choosing software and implementing a micro-based
library catalog are shared by the librarian. The
software, a Eurotec Consultants program called
LIBRARIAN is described, record conversion is
illustrated, and searching is briefly discussed.
Bibliography.

620 PENNOCK, ANNE, and McKINNIE, WILLIAM G. "Automating Access to a Small Church Library."
Small Computers in Libraries 5 (May 1985): 8.
        Creating an online catalog for a church
library using dBASE II and an IBM PC is described
by the librarians who performed the task.

621 PIPER, ANTHONY. "An Idea for a Library Package
Based on the 380-Z." Educational Computing 3
(May 1982): 34-35.
        Piper outlines the functioning of a

microcomputer-based online catalog which permits
a patron to place data into a request file for
materials not owned by the library.

622 RAITHEL, FREDERICK J. "Integrated Information
       Retrieval Networks: An Experiment in the
       Decentralized Library." Show-Me Libraries 35
       (May/June 1984): 12-14.
         The Small Farms Studies Library at the
University of Missouri Columbia has automated its
catalog through the university's mainframe computer, then downloaded the data onto IBM PCs and
stored it on diskettes. Copies are available to
faculty and students who want them for office or
research use, along with a public domain searching program which is distributed free of charge
with each catalog copy.

623 "School Uses Microcomputer to Replace Card Cata-
       log." American Libraries 12 (May 1981): 293-
       94.
         The computerized catalog developed for
Broomfield, Colorado's Mountain View Elementary
School is described, including public utiliza-
tion, data input, costs, and other factors.

624 "School Uses Microcomputer to Replace Card Cata-
       log in Library." Small Computers in Libraries
       1 (May 1981): 1.
         Betty Costa provides a description of the
microcomputer-based online catalog at Mountain
View Elementary School, Broomfield, Colorado.

625 "School Uses Microcomputer to Replace Card Cata-
       log in the Library Media Center." School
       Media Quarterly 9 (Summer 1981): 219-20.
         The relief of catalog frustration for
both patron and library staff is one of the major
benefits of automation, according to Betty
Costa, who describes the online catalog project
at Mountain View Elementary School near Denver.

626 SMITH, EILEEN. "Career Key: A Career Library
       Management System." Vocational Guidance
       Quarterly 32 (September 1983): 52-56.

Career Key, a microcomputer cataloging
system used at the Career Development Library of
Florida State University, is described by the
Career Development Librarian. The program, de-
signed specifically for cataloging, storing, and
retrieving career materials, runs on an Apple II
Plus microcomputer with a Corvus hard disk drive.
Bibliography.

627 "Springfield, Ill. Micro Users Can Tap Library
        CLSI Database." Library Journal 109 (Septem-
        ber 1, 1984): 1590.
            Springfield, Illinois' Lincoln Library
offers dial-up access to its CLSI circulation
database and an online index to local newspapers,
according to this news brief which describes the
services and tells how to get more information.

628 STEVENS, BOB. "Microcomputers for Alternatives
        to the Card Catalogue." School Libraries in
        Canada 3 (Winter 1983): 9-10.
            A microcomputer-based online catalog
program for small libraries, under development
when the article was written, is described by its
developer. Obvious problems--length of MARC
records, limited storage on floppy disks, and in-
ability to produce subject lists--are discussed.
Developments leading up to the online catalog are
mentioned.

629 SWORTS, NANCY. "School Children Handling Computer
        Technology." Denver Post. Neighbors--Boulder
        Valley Section, 11 March 1981, p. 9.
            The online catalog at Broomfield, Colo-
rado's Mountain View Elementary School is reviewed for the general public in this newspaper
article. The problem of obtaining school board
approval for the system is dealt with briefly.

630 "Test Project Thrives in Denver Elementary School
        Library." Electronic Learning 1 (March/April
        1982): 12, 14.
            The microcomputer-based online catalog at
Broomfield, Colorado's Mountain View Elementary
School is described in this news item.

631 TUROCK, BETTY J., and SHELTON, HILDRED. "Online
     Catalog in the Small Public Library: Enhanced
     Subject Access Via Microcomputer." Proceed-
     ings of the 5th National Online Meeting, New
     York, 10-12 April 1984. Medford, NJ: Learned
     Information, 1984. Pp. 405-11.
          The Pittsylvania County (VA) Library has
     developed an online catalog with enhanced subject
     access, using an Apple II microcomputer and PFS:
     FILE software. The catalog is described, with
     emphasis on subject searching. Bibliography.

632 VENNER, GILLIAN, and WALKER, STEPHEN. "Microcom-
     puter Networking in Libraries II: A Public
     Access Catalogue System." Vine no. 48 (May
     1983): 22-26.
          The authors describe the development of
     an online public access library catalog using
     microcomputers in a local area network configura-
     tion. Hardware, software, file construction,
     file searching, and maintenance are addressed.

633 BAGGARLEY, RICHARD, and McKINNEY, JOANNE. "Micro-
computerized Periodical Management." The
Information Community: An Alliance for Progress. Proceedings of the 44th ASIS Annual
Meeting. White Plains, NY: Knowledge Industry
Publications, 1981, v. 18. Pp. 248-49.
The authors describe Avery International
Research Center's serials control project, an
Apple II-based system which permits serial check-
in and cataloging; routinely generates routing
slips, claim letters, and subscription expiration
warnings; and is capable of producing printed
holdings lists, statistics, budget information,
and other data on demand.

634 CIMPL, KAY. "The GENERAL MANAGER and an Apple
II+ = Library Organization." Small Computers
in Libraries 5 (October 1985): 17-21.
Staff of the Clinical Sciences Center Library of the University of Wisconsin/Madison used
GENERAL MANAGER software with an Apple microcomputer to create a local holdings file for health
related serials in seventeen branch libraries on
the University of Wisconsin campus. The author
considers software selection and describes database design and operation. Bibliography.

635 COLE, SUSIE, and HILL, CINDY. "Automating Library Systems with PFS." ACCESS: Microcomputers in Libraries 2 (October 1982): 11-14.
The authors describe how they solved many
of the problems of serial acquisitions, control,
routing, and recordkeeping for the Acurex Corporation Library through use of the PFS database
management system and an Apple II Plus micro.

636 GADIKIAN, RANDY. "Development of a Periodicals
List in dBASE II." Library Software Review 4
(May/June 1985): 139-42.
Gadikian reviews the decision to convert

the State University of New York College at Buffalo periodical list from mainframe to micro, describes the procedure, and evaluates the results.

637 HOLMQUIST, LENNART JOHAN. "Periodical Management at the Apple Computer Library." Database 7 (December 1984): 31-36.
An Apple III microcomputer and PFS: FILE are used in Apple Computer's Corporate Library for periodical management. This article reviews PFS: FILE briefly and illustrates its application to the problem of serials control in a special library setting.

638 KELLEY, GLORIA A. "Serials Management: A Microcomputer Application." South Carolina Librarian 28 (Fall 1984): 6-9.
Winthrop College, in Rock Hill, South Carolina, uses the OCLC Serials Control System for serials check-in, but the program provides no financial or statistical data. In order to gain this information for budgeting and acquisitions purposes, files were created using MULTIPLAN and DB MASTER software. The project is described and results are evaluated.

639 LEATHERBURY, MAURICE C. "Serials Control Systems on Microcomputers." Drexel Library Quarterly 20 (Fall 1984): 4-24.
Eight microcomputer-based serials control systems are compared in text and chart format, using cataloging, check-in, searching, claims, routing, bindery control, duplicates control, financial control, ordering, subscription payment, vendor records, and reports as the bases for comparison. Systems considered are CLASS's CHECKMATE, DataTrek's SERIAL MODULE--CARD CATALOG, Follett's MAGAZINE CONTROL, Gaylord's GS-600 SERIALS CONTROL SYSTEM, Innovative Interface's INNOVACQ, Maxwell Library Systems' PERIODICALS CONTROL, Meta Micro's SERIALS CONTROL SYSTEM, and Richmond's MAGAZINE CONTROL SYSTEM. Bibliography.

640 LENZINI, REBECCA, and RAKAUSKAS, GEORGE. "Personal Computers and Faxon's LINX Network." In-

formation Technology and Libraries 3 (March 1984): 58-62.

The Faxon Company's work in integrating the IBM PC into their LINX network as an interactive terminal offering features unique to the system is described.

641 McQUEEN, JUDY, and BOSS, RICHARD W. "Serials Control in Libraries: Automated Options." Library Technology Reports 20 (March/April 1984): 89-282.

The problems of serials control are addressed, with emphases on bibliographic control and automation of serials records. Forty-eight serials control systems, representing the 1984 state-of-the-art and including both microcomputer-based and turnkey systems, are evaluated.

642 MOORE, BRIAN P. "Microcomputer Database Management for Union Listing." Technicalities 2 (September 1982): 8-9, 11.

In 1981 the Rochester (NY) Regional Research Library Council purchased an Apple II Plus, with DB MASTER software, to facilitate the creation of an automated union list of serials for high school and public libraries in the region. The article details problems inherent in using a commercial software package, describes how the format for the union list was developed, and evaluates the finished product.

643 MOULES, MARY L. "Producing a Local Union List of Serials with Word Processing Equipment." Serials Librarian 7 (Winter 1982): 27-34.

The planning and implementation of a union list of serials for the 72-member Illinois Valley Library System is the subject of this article. Produced on an IBM Office System 6 word processor, the project was designed to accommodate parameters of the existing software and the variety of serials records kept by the system's member libraries.

644 "Projects at Univ. of Minn-Duluth." Small Computers in Libraries 2 (April 1982): 7.

Information stored in the University of Minnesota at Duluth's mainframe computer is being updated and made accessible through two microcomputer projects. One project supplies subject indexing for the library's periodical indexes; the other updates periodical subscription information.

645 SCHRIEFER, KENT. "INNOVACQ: Serials Control at Boalt Hall." Serials Review 10 (Winter 1984): 51-68.

In 1983/84 the University of California, Berkeley Law Library installed a microcomputer-based INNOVACQ serials control system. This article justifies the purchase, reviews each of its functions, describes search procedures, and provides examples to illustrate output and forms.

646 STEPHENSON, MARY SUE, and PURCELL, GARY R. "The Automation of Government Publications: Functional Requirements and Selected Software Systems for Serial Controls." Government Information Quarterly 2, no. 1 (1985): 57-76.

A void exists in the development of microcomputer-based control systems for government documents, although serials control systems are generally adaptable. The authors consider turnkey and mini or microcomputer network options, problems associated with automating documents, and functional requirements for a document system. Abstracts of fourteen serials systems are presented, with hardware requirements ranging from micro to mainframe. Bibliography.

647 VOGEL, J. THOMAS, and BURNS, LYNN W. "Serials Management by Microcomputer: The Potential of DBMS." Online 8 (May 1984): 68-71.

Librarians at the Philadelphia College of Textiles and Science relate how they automated serials holdings lists with an Apple II Plus microcomputer and PFS software, added check-in and claiming functions, then expanded their operation with dBASE II, adding subscription information and lending files. Examples of forms are provided.

648 BRANDEHOFF, SUSAN E. "'Rehabilitation Community'
      Focus of Computer Literacy Project." American
      Libraries 13 (December 1982): 711.
          Rockville (MD) Regional Library's "Com-
puter Literacy for the Rehabilitation Community,"
a program designed to address the needs of disabled library patrons, is described. The project
currently runs on two TRS-80 microcomputers, with
a modem, an appropriate software collection, volunteer help, and lots of enthusiasm; however,
many innovations such as a type-and-talk box for
non-verbal people are planned.

649 BREWER, JAMES. "Printed Bibliographies: Produc-
      tion from an Online Data Base Using Techniques
      of Uploading/Downloading." Downloading/Upload-
      ing Online Databases and Catalogs. Proceedings
      of the Congress for Librarians, St. John's
      University, Jamaica, New York, 18 February
      1985. Library Hi Tech Special Studies Series,
      no. 1. Ann Arbor, MI: Pierian Press, 1985.
      Pp. 30-39.
          Procedures for processing entries for the
Festschrift Project at the University of Wiscon-
sin/Madison Memorial Library illustrate downloading, data manipulation, and uploading procedures
for creating a printed bibliography. Records are
downloaded from OCLC, altered to include contents
notes and subject information using a microcomputer, then stored on the University's mainframe,
where the sorting and production of the final
bibliography is accomplished.

650 CHAN, JULIE M. T. "The Promise of Computers for
      Reluctant Readers." Library Journal 110
      (November 1, 1985): 132, 134-35, 137-38, 140,
      142-43; and School Library Journal 32 (Novem-
      ber 1985): 120, 122-23, 125-26, 128, 130-31.
          The use of microcomputers with reluctant
readers is considered, summarizing the value and

applications of the technology, suggesting criteria for software selection, and discussing the development of a software collection suitable for use with reluctant readers. Specific titles are discussed; review sources are listed; a directory of publishers is provided.

651 DOWLIN, KENNETH E., and HAWLEY, BRENDA G. "The Use of Portable Microcomputers for Library Inventory." Microcomputers for Information Management 1 (March 1984): 67-73.
    Application of a TRS-80 Model 100 portable microcomputer to the inventory function at Pikes Peak Library District, Colorado Springs, is described and evaluated. Bibliography.

652 EMMENS, CAROL A. "Computer Programs for Video Production." School Library Journal 32 (November 1985): 46.
    Microcomputers have found a place in video production which may be included among the activities of a media center. Applications include scriptwriting, budgeting/scheduling, teleprompting, filing, and cataloging. Appropriate software is recommended for each activity.

653 FREEMAN, STEVE. "The 'Apple Corps' at St. Louis." Library Journal 110 (May 1, 1985): 110-12; and School Library Journal 31 (May 1985): 140-42.
    A remedial teaching program, which has long been a service of the St. Louis (MO) Public Library, has been automated through the addition of microcomputers for patron use. The remedial program is described, the introduction of micros is discussed, and the change is evaluated.

654 GOLDHOR, HERBERT. "Patrons Use Micros to Answer Library Survey." American Libraries 16 (October 1985): 668.
    2,500 library patrons of 62 Illinois public libraries were surveyed in March 1985 about their use of books and libraries. The survey was conducted using microcomputer diskettes rather than printed questionnaires, and the process is reported here rather than the results.

655 GOLDSTEIN, CHARLES M., and PRETTYMAN, MAUREEN. "Processing Downloaded Citations." Download-ing/Uploading Online Databases and Catalogs. Proceedings of the Congress for Librarians, St. John's University, Jamaica, New York, 18 February 1985. Library Hi Tech Special Studies Series, no. 1. Ann Arbor, MI: Pierian Press, 1985. Pp. 40-49.

Downloading of bibliographic data may be a time and cost saver to the researcher, but the citations seldom print out in standard biblio-graphic form. However, through the use of word processing or bibliographic formatting software, citations can easily be reformatted. The authors discuss the process, which consists of parsing the citations and formatting the references. Three methods are presented. Bibliography.

656 HIGGINS, BARBARA J. "'Pick Quick': A User Guid-ance Program." School Library Journal 29 (April 1983): 35.

A computerized bibliography dealing with the problems of young people is described and illustrated. The program is written for the Apple II, but is adaptable.

657 HOOKER, FRAN. "Computerized Braille: The Boulder Story." Wilson Library Bulletin 59 (April 1985): 527-30.

The Boulder (CO) Public Library's Braille Computer Center is described. One of the first of its kind in the United States, the Center uses an Apple IIe microcomputer with an Echo II voice synthesizer, an IBM PC with Braille software, and a Thiel Braille Embosser to enable visually hand-icapped patrons to achieve a degree of independ-ence in reading and writing.

658 KURKUL, DONNA LEE. "The Development of a Comput-er-Based Library System: LCDF--Library Collec-tion Distribution Formulas." MLS thesis, State University of New York at Albany, 1982.

Library Collection Distribution Formulas (LCDF), a software package designed to calculate and aid in the planning of book distribution prior to shifting a collection, is described in detail by its creator. Written in Standard Pascal, the program will run on either a mainframe or a microcomputer with a Pascal compiler. Bibliography.

659 MARKLUND, KARI. "Dimensional Flowcharting to Improve Library Performance." Microcomputers for Information Management 2 (June 1985): 113-28.
Flowcharts may be used to describe graphically a series of routines in a work situation, culminating in an end product. A microcomputer-based flowchart program is introduced and applied to an interlibrary loan situation to demonstrate its applicability to libraries. Bibliography.

660 MARX, PATRICIA C., and MARX, JOHN N. "Automating the Production of Bindery Slips." Technicalities 5 (March 1985): 15-16.
A program developed at Texas Tech University for automating bindery control and producing bindery slips is described by its creators. The program, an adaptation of a data management program written by a Texas Tech chemistry professor, runs on a TI 99/4A microcomputer.

661 "Micros and the Learning Disabled." Small Computers in Libraries 2 (July 1982): 3.
A short article on the use of microcomputers with autistic children calls attention to applications which librarians and teachers may wish to explore further.

662 MILLER, BRUCE CUMMINGS. "Disk Capacity in File Design: A Spreadsheet Model." Library Software Review 4 (July/August 1985): 202-04.
Miller presents a spreadsheet model which may help the librarian designing a data file define field lengths for maximum flexibility and space utilization.

663 "NYDISK Project to Automate N. Y. Library Data Collection." Library Journal 109 (December 1984): 2204.

A project to develop standardized procedures for gathering and reporting library statistics via microcomputer is announced by New York's
Southern Tier Library System.

664　POTTER, WILLIAM GRAY. "Modeling Collection Over-
lap on a Microcomputer." Information Technology and Libraries 2 (December 1983): 400-07.
　　　A study of title duplication in 23 academic library collections in Illinois was performed using an IBM Personal Computer interfaced
with Illinois' statewide Library Computer System
(LCS). Some of the findings are revealed, but
the major purpose of this article is to demonstrate the microcomputer's versatility in analyzing a large database. Bibliography.

665　REGEN, SHARI S., and CHEN, CHING-CHIH. "Microcomputers: Independence and Information Access
for the Physically Handicapped." Microcomputers for Information Management 1 (December
1984): 285-301.
　　　The development of technology for the
physically handicapped is reviewed, with emphasis
on microprocessor-based products. The potential
for the technology is discussed, and implications
for libraries are considered. Bibliography.

666　ROMANIUK, ELENA. "Analysis of Survey Results
Using a Microcomputer." Information Technol-
ogy and Libraries 4 (September 1985): 233-36.
　　　In 1983 the Newspapers Committee of the
British Columbia Library Association sent out a
survey to libraries in the province prior to
launching a preservation and access project.
This article concerns the analysis of the survey,
using an Apple microcomputer with PFS: FILE and
PFS: REPORT software. Bibliography.

667　ROSENBERG, VICTOR. "The Scholar's Workstation."
College and Research Libraries News 46 (November 1985): 546-59.
　　　There are many similarities in research
methods, whether in the sciences or the humanities, and the microcomputer as a tool of scholar-

ship is cutting across disciplinary lines to aid researchers in all areas. Rosenberg considers a scholar's workstation, with a microcomputer as the focal point, identifying and discussing the common tasks of all researchers, and explaining how the microcomputer can ease the workload and speed the task of research production.

668 SCHUYLER, MICHAEL. "Computer Applications of Readability." ACCESS: Microcomputers in Libraries 2 (April 1982): 12-13, 18-19.
An Apple II microcomputer program employing nine different readability formulas evaluates the reading level of written materials. Bibliography.

669 "TRS-80 Light Switch Monitor Saves Library $90,600/Year." Library Journal 109 (April 1, 1984): 619.
Use of a TRS-80 Model II microcomputer to activate the lighting in the University of South Carolina's central library is the topic of this news note.

670 TASHNER, JOHN H. "Using Computers with Gifted Students." Top of the News 38 (Summer 1982): 318-24.
Tashner outlines three major microcomputer applications to a program for the gifted, and identifies the librarian's roles in those programs. Bibliography.

671 TOBIN, CAROL; TIPPET, HARRIET; CULKIN, PATRICIA; and WALKER, ELIZABETH. "The Computer and Library Instruction." RSR: Reference Services Review 12 (Winter 1984): 71-78.
Four reference librarians write on three different aspects of computer use in library patron education. Tobin considers education of the end user in online bibliographic searching; Tippet considers word processing and records management applications for preparing instructional aids; Culkin and Walker consider computer assisted instruction. Only Tippet deals directly with micros. Bibliography.

672 WILLIAMS, STEVE. "Computer Determination of
Reading Levels." Media Spectrum 9 (First
Quarter 1982): 13, 16.
A microcomputer program for determining
the reading level of printed material using the
Bormuth, Fry, Flesch, and Fogg readability for-
mulas has been developed and implemented in the
media center of the Plymouth Salem High School,
Canton, MI. The program is described and evalua-
ted, and further information is offered.

673 WISMER, DONALD. "Labels from the Electronic Yellow Pages: A BASIC Routine." Online 8 (July
1984): 36-40.
Two versions of a program for the TRS-80
III microcomputer to download data and print
address labels from the Electronic Yellow Pages
are included and discussed, along with examples
of the end product.

674 YARNALL, GAIL. "Kurzweil Computer Products."
Library Hi Tech News no. 11/12 (December 1984/
January 1985): 1, 12.
The Kurzweil Reading Machine has become
standard equipment in libraries with a high number of visually impaired patrons, but the value
of the machine can be extended dramatically
with a little ingenuity. Yarnall describes how
the Kurzweil Reading Machine can be interfaced
with a microcomputer to do online searching for
blind patrons and produce Braille text when a
Braille printer is available.

WORD PROCESSING

675 ANDERSON, DAVID, and LANDIS, KAY. "The Use of
    the IBM Displaywriter in a Special Library."
    Productivity in the Information Age. Proceed-
    ings of the 46th ASIS Annual Meeting. White
    Plains, NY: Knowledge Industry Publications,
    1983, v. 20. Pp. 48-50.
        Staff of the Ashland Chemical Company's
    Technical Information Center use an IBM Display-
    writer for a variety of functions, including
    memo/report writing, creating bibliographies,
    journal control, and communications. TEXTPACK,
    ASYNCHRONOUS COMMUNICATIONS PROGRAM, and REPORT
    PACK software are described and evaluated in
    light of the needs of a special library.

676 BECKER, JOSEPH, and KATZENSTEIN, GARY. "Word
    Processors for Libraries." Library Technology
    Reports 19 (March/April 1983): 121-88.
        This article on word processor use in li-
    braries provides background information on the
    technology, discusses selection criteria, reviews
    six word processor systems, and includes a bibli-
    ography for further reference.

677 BLAIR, JOHN C., Jr. "Text Processing & Format-
    ting: Composure, Composition & Eros." Online
    8 (September 1984): 19-26.
        In a seemingly frivolous manner Blair
    presents sound advice on learning and adapting to
    a word processing system, then turns to word pro-
    cessing software, matching functions and features
    with off-the-shelf word processing packages.

678 BLOCK, DAVID, and KALYONCU, AYDAN. "Selection of
    Word Processing Software for Library Use."
    Information Technology and Libraries 2 (Sep-
    tember 1983): 252-60.
        Library applications are considered for
    word processing software, and factors which in-
    fluence software selection are discussed. APPLE

WRITER II, WORDSTAR, MAGIC WAND, and SCREEN WRIT-
ER II are reviewed. Bibliography.

679 BOSS, RICHARD W. "Selecting Word Processing Software." Software Review 2 (March 1983): 4-9.
The process of evaluating and selecting a
word processing software package is reviewed,
from the initial needs assessment through the examination and comparison of programs. A dozen
popular packages are listed at the end of the
article.

680 "EE Word Processing Guide." Electronic Education
4 (September 1984): 36-37.
Twenty word processing programs are compared in easy to interpret chart format.

681 GALLOWAY, SARAH BETH. "Using a Word Processor in
Library Management." Library Journal 108
(November 1, 1983): 2028-30.
The director of the Roswell (NM) Public
Library describes the selection procedure which
led to the purchase of an IBM Displaywriter word
processing system. Implementation, evaluation,
and future potential are addressed.

682 GORDON, HELEN A. "Improving Searcher's Productivity Using Microcomputer Word Processing
Systems." Online '82 Conference Proceedings,
Atlanta, 1-3 November 1982. Weston, CT: Online, Inc., 1982. Pp. 64-68.
Applications of word processing systems
to an online searching operation are discussed,
including use for data capture and editing, letter writing, and document production, formatting,
and editing. Selection criteria for word processing software are considered.

683 GREEN, LISA ANN. "Computer Meets Book: Some Implications for Publishing in the Electronic
Age." Top of the News 39 (Summer 1983): 333-
36.
The impact of microcomputers and word
processors on the publishing industry is discussed, and the implications for libraries,

particularly in speed of production, costs, and types of publishing are told.

684 HINES, THEODORE C.; WINKEL, LOIS; and COLLINS, ROSANN W. "Word Processing Roles in Information Management." ACCESS: Microcomputers in Libraries 2 (July 1982): 8-9, 20-22.

Word processing capabilities are a necessity for libraries, although stand-alone word processing equipment may not be the most economical and functional purchase for a library. The authors discuss word processing functions most often required in libraries and microcomputer software packages which are adaptable to those applications.

685 HINES, THEODORE C.; WINKEL, LOIS; COLLINS, ROSANN W.; and HARVEY, FRANCIS A. "Quiet Please: Computer at Work." Desktop Computing 1 (October 1981): 46-47.

The advantages of using word processing software with a microcomputer are presented, with labor saving tips and library uses for which word processing is ideal.

686 JEWELL, JOHN. "Automating I & R Files: Word Processing, a First Step (Fresno County Information & Referral Network)." RQ 21 (Winter 1981): 135-40.

Word processing equipment provides the means for producing a semiannual 900 page community resources directory for the Fresno County (CA) Free Library, according to this paper presented at the 1981 ALA Conference as part of a symposium on automation of information and referral files.

687 KIDDER, AUDREY J. "Using Word Processors in Libraries." Illinois Libraries 65 (April 1983): 248-51.

An overview of word processing in libraries is provided in this article which describes the hardware and its development. Uses are suggested, including letter and report writing, mailing list maintenance, production of overdue notices, recordkeeping, and storage of ledgers. Hints are given on selection of word processing equipment. Bibliography.

688 MARCUM, DEANNA B. "Word Processing in Libraries." Library Technology Reports 16 (July/August 1980): 299-301.
The advantages of word processing over straight copy typing are explained, and uses of word processing equipment in the libraries at Emory and Johns Hopkins Universities, and pro-proposed uses at New York and Detroit public libraries are enumerated.

689 MASON, ROBERT M. "Choosing Software for Text Processing." Library Journal 108 (September 1, 1983): 1665-66.
A general discussion of data entry, text editing, and document formatting leads into comparisons of WORDSTAR, PEACHTEXT, PERFECTWRITER, and SELECT word processing software and PERFECT-SPELLER, PEACHTEXT 5000, and WORD PLUS spelling programs.

690 McCUNN, DONALD H. "Evaluating Equipment: Criteria for Word Processing Hardware." ACCESS: Microcomputers in Libraries 2 (July 1982): 14-16.
A trend in library computing has been the adaptation of microcomputers to word processing functions by use of word processing software. This article provides practical information on evaluating the adaptability of microcomputer hardware to text manipulation.

691 MOSKOWITZ, MICKEY. "Use an Apple to Save a Tree: Word Processing With the Microcomputer." Technicalities 3 (January 1983): 11-12.
The addition of word processing capability to an existing microcomputer system is simple, inexpensive, and cost effective. The author discusses word processing applications in libraries, necessary hardware and software, and staff adjustment to the new procedures and equipment. Bibliography.

692 MOULTON, LYNDA W. "Word Processing Equipment for
   Information Centers." Special Libraries 71
   (November 1980): 492-96.
        Word processing equipment in a small
   special library can be adapted to the production
   of catalog cards, newsletters, memos, technical
   data, bibliographic data printouts, and indexes,
   and provide the capability to create and search
   local databases, according to Moulton.

693 NASH, SARAH HENDRICKSON. "Selecting and Implementing a Word Processor in the Library."
   Electronic Library 1 (October 1983): 265-73.
        The word processor is an ideal tool for
   small libraries without access to automated library systems, according to this writer who uses
   hers for producing catalog cards, accession
   lists, mailing labels, subscription lists, re-
   ceipts, and other functions. The selection process including needs analysis, equipment comparisons, and justifications is discussed.

694 POLLARD, RICHARD. "Word Processing for Microcomputers: An Assessment of Current Trends and
   Future Potential." Microcomputers for Information Management 2 (September 1985): 189-200.
        Second generation software has vastly im-
   proved the quality of word processing by microcomputer. Pollard compares seven word processing
   programs against a dedicated word processor, considering features, ease of use, training, and
   technical support. Compared are WORDSTAR 3.3,
   DISPLAYWRITER 2, MICROSOFT WORD 1.0, MULTIMATE
   3.3, SAMNA WORD III, WORD PERFECT 4.0, and WORD-
   STAR 2000. Bibliography.

695 "SCIL's Microcomputer." Small Computers in Libraries 2 (June 1982): 5.
        The editor of Small Computers in Librar-
   ies describes methods employed in producing the
   newsletter, and the micro's role in the process.

696 SCHUYLER, MICHAEL. "Evaluating Word Processors."
   ACCESS: Microcomputers in Libraries 2 (July
   1982): 12-13, 18-20.

The basic components of word processing software are detailed, and the ZARDAX and SUPER TEXT word processing programs, designed for use with Apple hardware, are evaluated and compared.

697 STEENSLAND, M. C., and SPAITH, T. G. "Application of a Personal/Business Computer in Library Automation. Updating a Mainframe Resident Authority File." Electronic Library 2 (October 1984): 279-84.
In 1982 Chemical Abstracts Service made editorial and procedural changes which made it necessary to edit the authority file resident on their mainframe computer. This was accomplished using word processing equipment. The decision to use word processors is discussed, and implementation is briefly outlined. Bibliography.

698 "Survey of Word Processing Equipment." Library Technology Reports 16 (July/August 1980): 303-435.
A thorough treatment of state-of-the-art word processing in 1980, this lengthy article contains a good introduction to the development of the word processor, a handy glossary of terms, a survey of 100 different models of word processors produced by 27 different companies, and a comparison of those models. Although some of the material is dated, the introductory matter, glossary, and manufacturers list are still current.

699 THOMPSON, RICHARD E. "Word Processors in the Public Library." Technicalities 3 (March 1983): 3-4, 10.
In 1981 the Wilmette (IL) Public Library purchased a CPT 8100 word processor for its administrative office. An evaluation one year later relates incentives for the purchase; describes the selection process, the equipment, and its capabilities; and suggests applications and capabilities in addition to text processing.

700 WHITEHEAD, JOHN B. "Developments in Word Processing Systems." Program 17 (July 1983): 130-53.
Whitehead considers word processor usage

in libraries and information centers in 1983.
Available systems and applications are described;
rapid technological development and system selection are discussed; the choice between word
processing equipment and microcomputer hardware
with word processing capabilities is weighed.

701   WHITEHEAD, JOHN B. "Developments in Word Processing Systems and Their Application to Information Needs." Aslib Proceedings 32 (March
1980): 118-33.
        Development of the word processor and its
versatility as a library tool are described. Its
use as a small stand-alone computer is discussed,
along with several library applications, including order processing, online searching, serials
control, and book catalog production. Bibliog-
graphy.

702   WHITEHEAD, JOHN B. "Progress in Documentation--
Word Processing: An Introduction and Apprais-
al." Journal of Documentation 36 (December
1980): 313-41.
        The advantages of the word processor over
the typewriter in the business office is discussed, along with suggested library uses including
acquisitions, budget control, producing catalogs,
auditing and stock control, serials control,
circulation, information storage and retrieval,
and online database searching. Bibliography.

703   WHITEHEAD, JOHN B. "Word Processing and Information Management." Aslib Proceedings 33 (September 1981): 325-42.
        The word processor is often viewed as
little more than an upgraded typewriter; however,
that view is dispelled as the components of a
word processing system are described, potential
library applications are told, and examples of
prototype library systems are reviewed. Bibliography.

704   WHITSED, N. "Reflections on Word Processing: The
Experience of a Small Medical Library." Aslib
Proceedings 34 (September 1982): 415-19.

Characteristics of the Philips word processor are discussed, and reasons for its being chosen by the Charing Cross (UK) Hospital Medical School Library are provided. Applications described, in addition to traditional word processing, include catalog card production and statistical report generation. Bibliography.

705 WILLIAMS, E. M. "The Application of Word Processors in Library and Information Work." South African Journal of Librarianship and Information Science 50 (April 1983): 176-78.
    The worth of word processing equipment in a library is expressed in the variety of tasks to which it may be applied. Besides general office typing, the author suggests book catalog production and maintenance, indexing, list production, form letters, circulation, and serial management. Bibliography.

706 "Word Processing for the Apple II." Small Computers in Libraries 1 (May 1981): 7.
    This brief article explains the difficulties and limitations of using the Apple II as a word processor, suggests extra hardware which makes it more adaptable to the function, and recommends two suitable software programs.

REFERENCE AND PUBLIC SERVICES

707   ANDREWS, KAREN L.; ARMSTRONG, JUNE; and BENEN-
FELD, ALAN R. "Microcomputers, Minicomputers,
or Private Database Services in Reference
Work: Some Decision Factors." Communicating
Information. Proceedings of the 43rd ASIS
Annual Meeting. White Plains, NY: Knowledge
Industry Publications, 1980, v. 17. Pp. 310-
13.
      The development of a rationale for the
use of small computer systems in library reference work is combined with information and a comparative summary of mini and microcomputer use
with in-house files and online database services
purchased from a vendor. Bibliography.

708   "Apple Bulletin Board System at Chicago PL."
Small Computers in Libraries 1 (December
1981): 3.
      The North-Pulaski Branch of the Chicago
Public Library announces the installation of a
dialup APPLE BULLETIN BOARD SYSTEM for distributing public service messages.

709   BIVINS, KATHLEEN T., and ERIKSSON, LENNART. "REF-
LINK: A Microcomputer Information Retrieval
and Evaluation System." Information Processing
and Management 18, no. 3 (1982): 111-16.
      REFLINK, an expanded and enhanced version
of the REFLES system developed at UCLA, is described in detail. Bibliography.

710   BIVINS, KATHLEEN T., and ERIKSSON, LENNART. "REF-
LINK: A Microcomputer Information Retrieval
System." Proceedings of the 2nd National Online Meeting, New York, 24-26 March 1981.
Medford, NJ: Learned Information, 1981. Pp.
73-80.
      The authors explain REFLINK, a sophisti-
cated information retrieval system utilizing
inexpensive microcomputer hardware, along with
REFLES, the system on which REFLINK is based.

711 BIVINS, KATHLEEN T., and ERIKSSON, LENNART. "REF-
LINK: Small-Scale Computing in Information
Environments Provides the 'Missing Link'." The
Information Community: An Alliance for Pro-
gress. Proceedings of the 44th ASIS Annual
Meeting. White Plains, NY: Knowledge Industry
Publications, 1981, v. 18. Pp. 245-47.
REFLINK, a microcomputer system designed
to interface with a variety of on- and off-line
databases, is analyzed, and its use in the infor-
mation and library reference context is illustra-
ted with examples. Bibliography.

712 BIVINS, KATHLEEN T., and PALMER, ROGER C. "A
Microcomputer Alternative for Information
Handling: REFLES." Information Processing
and Management 17, no. 2 (1981): 93-101.
The prototype REFLES system, a microcomputer-based program designed at the UCLA Graduate
School of Library and Information Science for enhancement of reference services, is described in
detail. Bibliography.

713 BIVINS, KATHLEEN T., and PALMER, ROGER C.
"REFLES: An Individualized Microcomputer Sys-
tem for Fact Retrieval." Proceedings of the
3rd International Online Information Meeting,
London, 4-6 December 1979. Medford, NJ:
Learned Information, 1979. Pp. 231-38; and
Online Review 4 (December 1980): 357-65.
The Reference Librarian Enhancement System (REFLES) is an in-house system for hard-to-
find, ephemeral, and rapidly changing reference
information which employs Radio Shack TRS-80
hardware and a software package developed by the
UCLA Graduate School of Library and Information
Science. Details of the file structure and program functions are presented, as are examples of
data entry and data manipulation. REFLES' future
is predicted. Bibliography.

714 BIVINS, KATHLEEN T., and PALMER, ROGER C.
"REFLES (Reference Librarian Enhancement
System)." Information Choices and Policies.
Proceedings of the 42nd ASIS Annual Meeting.

White Plains, NY: Knowledge Industry Publications, 1979, v. 16. Pp. 58-65.

The major portion of this article consists of a proposal for the development, demonstration, and evaluation of REFLES, a prototype microcomputer-based online reference database at UCLA.

715 "Booklist On-Line in Chicago." Small Computers in Libraries 4 (November 1984): 5-6.

The North-Pulaski Branch of the Chicago Public Library is now offering microcomputer book reviews from Booklist via their electronic bulletin board. This and other services are discussed. Access is described.

716 CONVEY, JOHN. "Microcomputer and Community Information in the Public Library." Proceedings of the 6th International Online Information Meeting, London, 7-9 December 1982. Medford, NJ: Learned Information, 1982. Pp. 365-71.

The use of a microcomputer to maintain community information files and local directories is considered, and a working project at the Lancashire (UK) Library is described. Bibliography.

717 DEWEY, PATRICK R. "Dear ABBS: Marketing, Maintenance, and Suggestions." Small Computers in Libraries 2 (September 1982): 1-3.

Branch Librarian for Chicago Public's North-Pulaski Neighborhood Library describes the APPLE BULLETIN BOARD SYSTEM in operation in his library, evaluates the service and the system, and makes recommendations to others considering similar projects.

718 DEWEY, PATRICK R. "The Electronic Bulletin Board Arrives at the Public Library: The North-Pulaski Library Prototype." Library Hi Tech 1 (Spring 1984): 13-17.

The electronic bulletin board at Chicago Public Library's North-Pulaski Branch is described, with access routines, menu displays, commands, security, and censorship statements discussed and illustrated. Bibliography.

719 D'URSO, LAWRENCE A. "The Application of Micro-
        computers to New I & R Files: A Beginner's
        Experience." RQ 21 (Winter 1981): 143-46.
        The Chicago Public Library's establish-
     ment of a reference file concerning American
     Indian groups and the automation of the file
     using an Apple II microcomputer are described.
     The author relates the difficulties encountered
     when attempting to use a locally produced pro-
     gram, and the staffs' relief when adaptable, com-
     mercially produced software was substituted.
     Bibliography.

720 "Electronic Bulletin Board Accessed by Home
        Micros." Library Journal 109 (May 15, 1984):
        938.
        An electronic bulletin board program at
     the Spokane (WA) Public Library is described, and
     the software on which it operates is reviewed.

721 "Electronic Bulletin Board in Liverpool, New
        York." Library Journal 110 (May 1, 1985): 21.
        The Liverpool (NY) Public Library's elec-
     tronic bulletin board is described. The first
     such facility to be installed in a library east
     of Chicago, the bulletin board has been well re-
     ceived in the area.

722 ENSOR, PAT. "The Expanding Use of Computers in
        Reference Service." RQ 21 (Summer 1982):
        365-72.
        The importance of computers in library
     reference service is stressed in this article
     which addresses online database searching, devel-
     opment of local databases, and cooperative online
     reference. The microcomputer is put into per-
     spective, and its importance for the future of
     library reference is noted.

723 "Free Apple Software Offered Via Phone Call at
        Chicago Branch." Library Journal 109 (March
        1, 1984): 422.
        A new service offered through the elec-
     tronic bulletin board of Chicago Public Library's
     North-Pulaski Branch is the downloading of free

programs from the library's Apple microcomputer. A contact person is named should more information be wanted.

724 HINES, THEODORE C.; WINKEL, LOIS; and COLLINS, ROSANN W. "Microcomputers for Reference and Adult Services." RQ 22 (Summer 1983): 360-63.
With the exception of online searching, microcomputers have had little impact on library public services. The authors attempt to dispel some misconceptions about microcomputers, and suggest indexing, computer aided instruction, bulletin board services, and bibliography projects which could easily be done on a public service micro.

725 KITTLE, PAUL W. "Putting the Medical Library Online: Electronic Bulletin Boards. . .and Beyond." Online 9 (May 1985): 25-30.
The Loma Linda University Medical Center Library has established a bulletin board service using THE BREAD BOARD SYSTEM (TBBS) communications software. Included in the service are a general file containing public information and hospital news, a private message file for physicians only, and a staff news bulletin.

726 KRIZ, HARRY M., and KOK, VICTORIA T. "The Computerized Reference Department: Buying the Future." RQ 25 (Winter 1985): 198-203.
The Science and Technology Library of the Virginia Polytechnic Institute and State University is using microcomputers and the university's mainframe to automate reference, collection development, and management functions. The project is described, and available functions are outlined. Bibliography.

727 "Librarians' Bulletin-Board System." Small Computers in Libraries 2 (October 1982): 5.
INFOPORT, a computerized bulletin board system at the Royal Ontario Museum Library, is designed to supply information concerning events in the Toronto area. Dial access is free except for line charges.

728 "Libraries Extend Their Reach With Bulletin Board
     Systems." Bulletin Board Systems 3 (June
     1985): 1-2.
         A microcomputer-based bulletin board sys-
     tem is an excellent method of expanding a library
     outreach program. Two successful bulletin board
     systems, located at the North-Pulaski Branch of
     the Chicago Public Library and at the Liverpool
     (NY) Public Library, are described, with details
     of online items and sources of more information.

729 LIGHT, JANE IRBY. "Online: Creating Community
     Information Databases." Online '81 Conference
     Proceedings, Dallas, 2-4 November 1981. Wes-
     ton, CT: Online, Inc., 1981. Pp. 211-13.
         The author presents a wealth of informa-
     tion concerning local information and referral
     files. Included are such topics as types of
     local databases, designing an automated file,
     collecting and updating information, and a ra-
     tionale for the development of an I & R file in a
     library.

730 MAGRATH, LYNN L. "A Public Library in Your Home?"
     Media Spectrum 9 (Fourth Quarter 1982): 15,
     24.
         A pilot project to permit microcomputer
     dial-up access to the mainframe of the Pikes Peak
     Library District, in Colorado Springs, Colorado,
     is described and evaluated. Six files are acces-
     sible, including holding and circulation records,
     a calendar, and course lists at local colleges.

731 MERSHON, LORETTA K. "A Model Automated Resource
     File for an Information and Referral Center."
     Special Libraries 71 (August 1980): 335-44.
         Automation of the data file for an infor-
     mation and referral center is discussed, includ-
     ing advantages, standards, file content, and con-
     struction. Bibliography.

732 MOORE, CATHY. "Get Good Programs for the Price
     of a Phone Call." OCLC Micro 1 (September
     1985): 14-17, 25.
         Electronic bulletin boards are often good

sources of free public domain software and other valuable information and services which may be obtained by dialing the bulletin board number and downloading onto your own disk. Moore describes and provides access information for two bulletin boards located in Wisconsin, plus the OCLC Bulletin Board, and the FEDLINK Bulletin Board.

733 PRATT, ALLAN D. "Community Service and Small Computer Systems." Journal of Library and Information Science 6 (October 1980): 154-62.

The establishment of local information and referral files in libraries is justified, and the microcomputer is presented as an easy and efficient tool for providing I & R services. Bibliography.

734 RIECHEL, ROSEMARIE. "Online in the Public Library: Automating the General Reference Desk." Proceedings of the 4th National Online Meeting, New York, 12-14 March 1983. Medford, NJ: Learned Information, 1983. Pp. 445-55.

An Apple II Plus microcomputer, printer, modem, and selected software were purchased for reference services of the Queens Borough (NY) Public Library in 1982. This article describes integration of the hardware into the reference operation, implementation of a computer literacy program for reference personnel, and the development of a community information file project.

735 "San Bernardino Home Micros Swamp Library MICRO-LINK." Library Journal 110 (July 1985): 19.

In its first year and a half, the San Bernardino (CA) Public Library's Microcomputer Information Center (MICROLINK) has handled some 9,000 requests. The service provides a bulletin board with listings of community events, book reviews, and microcomputer programs. In addition, reference questions can be left for librarians, who respond through the system's Message Base.

736 SHIRINIAN, GEORGE N. "Toronto CBBS for Librarians --A User View." Small Computers in Libraries 2 (December 1982): 6-7.

INFOPORT, a microcomputer-based bulletin board service offered by the Toronto Public Library, is evaluated by a user from a neighboring community.

737 SHRODER, EMELIE J. "Community Information in the '80s: Towards Automation of Information and Referral Files." RQ 21 (Winter 1981): 135-55.
Papers by John Jewell, Cynthia Slater, Lawrence A. D'Urso, and Jane Irby Light and Carol Yamamoto, presented at the 1981 ALA Conference in San Francisco, represent four methods of automating in-house information and referral files.

738 SHRODER, EMELIE J. "Online I & R in Your Library: The State of the Art." RQ 21 (Winter 1981): 128-33.
Prototype mini and microcomputer-based information and referral systems are described. Charts of costs, capacities, advantages, and disadvantages provide information concerning hardware and software for both types of systems. Bibliography.

739 SMITH, DANA E., and HUTTON, STEVE M. "Back at 8:00 AM: Microcomputer Library Reference Support Programs." Collegiate Microcomputer 2 (November 1984): 289-94.
A microcomputer project at Purdue University Libraries to support reference service at various points throughout the library, particularly during periods when reference service is not normally available, is described and evaluated by its developers.

740 TRAUTMAN, RODES. "A How-To on Using the Micro in Creating a Reference Tools Database." Online '84 Conference Proceedings, San Francisco, 29-31 October 1984. Weston, CT: Online, Inc., 1984. Pp. 247-51.
Reference librarians can develop a database of reference sources using a microcomputer and programmable word processing software such as PMATE. Trautman describes the procedure and reviews advantages of maintaining such a database.

741 TRAUTMAN, RODES, and GOTHBERG, HELEN M. "A Reference Tools Database: A Proposed Application for a Microcomputer at the Reference Desk." Reference Librarian 5/6 (Fall/Winter 1982): 195-98.

A library reference database tailored to an individual library's reference collection and accessible via microcomputer is proposed. Structure and use are described. Bibliography.

742 WALTER, VIRGINIA. "From Ghostbusters to BUSTER: A Micro Connection." OCLC Micro 1 (November 1985): 16-17.

The Los Angeles Public Library's Central Branch is a major resource library serving the city and much of southern California. However, its location makes access extremely difficult. BUSTER (Business/Science and Technology Electronic Reference) a microcomputer-based reference service for the Business and Science Branches of the Library has eased the patron pressure drastically. The service is described and evaluated by the manager of the Business and Economics Department.

COMPUTER LITERACY AND PUBLIC ACCESS MICROS

743 ABERNETHY, JANET. "Computer Literacy and Chil-
      dren." Canadian Library Journal 41 (February
      1984): 26-29.
            As a cultural and educational resource,
      the public library has the responsibility for
      providing computer literacy opportunities for all
      ages. The library's role in providing computer
      literacy programs is discussed, and some success-
      ful projects are reviewed. Bibliography.

744 "Apple to Donate Micros to 9000 California
      Schools." School Library Journal 30 (October
      1983): 73.
            The Apple Computer Company's "Kids Can't
      Wait" program, which offers free microcomputers
      to qualifying California schools, is described.

745 "Apples in Baltimore County: Coin-Operated Serv-
      ice." Library Journal 107 (June 15, 1982):
      1174.
            Coin-operated microcomputer equipment in-
      stalled at public libraries in Catonsville, North
      Point, and Cockeysville, Maryland represent the
      first such installations in the state, according
      to this news note.

746 AVALLONE, SUSAN. "Public Access to Microcomput-
      ers." Library Journal 110 (May 1, 1985): 105-
      06; and School Library Journal 31 (May 1985):
      135-36.
            A survey of academic and public libraries
      concerning public use of microcomputers provides
      data on philosophies, practices, popular brands
      of equipment, circulation/use policies, popular
      programs, and problems.

747 BAKER, ELAINE. "From Victrola to Microcomputer:
      Rural Libraries & New Technology." Library
      Journal 109 (July 1984): 1288-93.
            In 1982 the Southern Adirondack Library

System received a $41,000 LSCA Title I grant from the State of New York to promote computer literacy. Design of the project, use of the funds, and benefits derived by the participating libraries are all told in this report on the project.

748 BARNES, MARTHA. "Computer Literacy: An Introduction." Top of the News 39 (Spring 1983): 237-40.
The basic terminology of microcomputers is addressed in this article which briefly explains memory, languages, programming, hardware, and time sharing. A glossary of fifty additional terms round out the presentation.

749 BENNETT, CHARLES. "A Bite Off the Apple." Scottish Library Association News 180 (March/April 1984): 7-8.
In December 1982 the Motherwell (Scotland) District Library received an Apple II microcomputer system on loan for a six-month period. The public use program, which was developed as a result, is described and evaluated, and plans for the future are told.

750 BLAIR, MARJORIE. "ComputerTown Puts Fun Back Into Learning." Electronic Education 2 (March/April 1983): 69, 92-94.
The philosophy of ComputerTown, its beginnings, and its development from 1979 to 1983 are summarized, with a value statement and positive expression of hope for continued growth.

751 BOSS, JACQUELINE A. "Order of the Apple." Computing Teacher 11 (October 1983): 41-43.
Jacqueline Boss outlines the computer literacy program she developed for her middle school media center, and relates its success despite a shortage of equipment and the absence of a place for computer learning in the curriculum.

752 BOSS, JACQUELINE A. "Sexism Among the Micros." Computing Teacher 9 (January 1982): 55-57.
A school media specialist acknowledges male domination of microcomputer equipment in her

media center, and addresses the problem with an analysis of the reason. A weekly programming contest for her students bears out her observation of sexism, but has encouraged some girls to participate.

753 "Broadneck, Md. New Library to be First with Computers & CATV." Library Journal 107 (December 1, 1982): 2215.
    The Broadneck Branch of the Annapolis/Anne Arundel County (MD) Public Library announces plans for public access to microcomputers and CATV in its new facility.

754 BURGMAN, CAROLYNE C. "Humble Beginnings: Lessons in Computer Utilization." North Carolina Libraries 42 (Fall 1984): 118-20.
    Dealing with adult negative attitudes may be the most difficult task in implementing a computer literacy program in a school. Carolyne Burgman, media specialist at the F. D. Bluford School in Greensboro, North Carolina, describes how the task was accomplished in her school, through trial and error, with lots of enthusiasm and public support. Lessons learned along the way are printed in bold type.

755 BURTON, LOUISE. "Computertown, U.S.A.!" Recreational Computing 8 (July/August 1979): 10-11; and Computing Teacher 7 (September 1979): 32.
    The value, appeal, and versatility of the microcomputer for educational and recreational purposes is amply demonstrated in this illustrated article concerning ComputerTown installations and activities in Menlo Park, California.

756 "CAI at Texas A & M." Small Computers in Libraries 3 (April 1983): 4-5.
    Following one semester's use, the staff of Texas A & M University Library's Learning Resources Department have evaluated their new public-access microcomputer center. Facilities are described briefly; volume of use is reported; types of use and users are analyzed; and scheduling is addressed.

757 CARPENTER, JENNIFER K. "Microcomputers in Public
      Libraries for Public Access: A Survey." North
      Carolina Libraries 42 (Winter 1984): 185-90.
            A nationwide survey of libraries with
      public access microcomputer programs yielded 36
      responses, which are analyzed in this research
      report. The survey considers project goals,
      software, hardware selection, user fees, circula-
      tion policies, staffing, and other topics. Bib-
      liography.

758 "Chicago Computer Center." ACCESS: Microcomput-
      ers in Libraries 2 (April 1982): 3.
            The establishment of the Personal Comput-
      er Center at Chicago Public Library's North-
      Pulaski Branch is announced, equipment and serv-
      ices are described, and the Library's online bul-
      letin board is discussed.

759 "Chicago, Illinois Has Thriving Computer Center."
      Library Journal 107 (April 1, 1982): 674.
            Statistics are provided to support a
      positive evaluation of the public access micro-
      computer project at Chicago Public Library's
      North-Pulaski Branch.

760 "Children Computer Volunteers Help Janesville,
      Wisc. Program." Library Journal 108 (October
      1, 1983): 1832.
            A Janesville (WI) Public Library summer
      volunteer program for children and young people
      interested in microcomputers provided computer
      literacy instruction for students and valuable
      assistance for library staff, according to this
      brief news item.

761 CIMBALA, DIANE J. "There Goes the Neighborhood!"
      Technicalities 5 (June 1985): 9-10, 12, 16.
            The microcomputerization of Augusta Col-
      lege is related, from the initial decision to
      house the microcomputer lab in the library, to
      the implementation of the project, to the making
      of policy decisions concerning cataloging and
      circulation of software. Problems of the project
      and unforeseen benefits are identified.

762 CLEAVER, BETTY. "Microcomputers and Teacher Preparation." Ohio Media Spectrum 34 (Spring 1982): 16-18.

The microcomputer instructional laboratory, established at Ohio State University as part of the Edgar Dale Media Center, is the topic of this short article. Equipment selection, facilities planning, and access procedures are addressed.

763 COHEN, DOREEN. "ComputerTown USA! Menlo Park Revisited." ACCESS: Microcomputers in Libraries 2 (October 1982): 5-6, 19.

The ComputerTown USA! microcomputer demonstration project at Menlo Park (CA) Public Library has evolved from a video game center to an integral part of the library's services. The author describes the changes and current services offered. Bibliography.

764 "Coin Devices for Micros." Library Systems Newsletter 2 (August 1982): 58-59.

For libraries wishing to provide coin-operated microcomputer services, three coin devices--Mark Time, CompuVend, and XCP--are evaluated.

765 "Coin/Mac." Small Computers in Libraries 5 (September 1985): 21.

COIN/MAC, of Chicago, announces the development of a coin-operated Macintosh micro. Special features, programs, and options are noted.

766 "Coin-Op Apples for Libraries." Small Computers in Libraries 2 (February 1982): 3.

Micro Timesharing Company announces the development of coin-operated Apple microcomputers available for installation in libraries.

767 "Coin-Op Computer Desk." Small Computers in Libraries 1 (October 1981): 1.

A coin-operated microcomputer available through CompuVend Computer Systems is announced and described.

768 "Coin-Op Computer in Public Library." Small Computers in Libraries 1 (May 1981): 5.
What is believed to be the first coin-operated microcomputer installed in a public library is announced by the Tredyffrin Public Library of Strafford, Pennsylvania.

769 "Coin-Op Word Processing." Library Journal 110 (February 15, 1985): 100.
Coin-operated word processors available in the University of Connecticut Library are discussed briefly.

770 "Coin-Operated Micros." ACCESS: Microcomputers in Libraries 2 (April 1982): 3.
Micro Timesharing Company announces a coin-operated Apple II Plus micro, and provides information on its anticipated market, lease arrangements, and a contact for more information.

771 "Community Development $$ Buys Computers for Lorain, Ohio." Library Journal 107 (October 1, 1982): 1804.
Lorain (OH) Public Library's first venture in providing microcomputing equipment for public use has been successful in attracting Community Development Department funding for expansion of the service, according to this news note.

772 "Compumat Coin-Op Apples Picked by San Diego County." Library Journal 109 (June 1, 1984): 1070.
The San Diego County (CA) Public Library system has contracted with the Compumat Company to install coin-operated microcomputers in five branch libraries, according to this news brief.

773 "Computer Assisted Instruction at the Texas A & M University Library." Electronic Library 1 (July 1983): 169-70.
The public access microcomputer project at Texas A & M University's Sterling C. Evans Library is described and evaluated following one semester of operation. Hardware, software, and patron use are considered.

774 "Computer Lit for Handicapped Offered by Buffalo
      & Erie Co." Library Journal 108 (October 15,
      1983): 1911.
         A new Apple II-based microcomputer liter-
      acy program for handicapped patrons is reported
      by the Buffalo and Erie County (NY) Public Li-
      brary.

775 "Computer Literacy Focus of Scottsdale PL."
      School Library Journal 29 (April 1983): 11.
         The Scottsdale (AZ) Public Library's com-
      puter literacy program is described. Intended
      for educational purposes, the program focuses on
      children, but the future includes plans for ex-
      tending the program to adults.

776 "Computer Literacy Serves Literacy at Scottsdale,
      Ariz. Public Library." Library Journal 108
      (March 15, 1983): 536.
         The Scottsdale (AZ) Public Library has
      instituted a microcomputer program to improve
      language skills for children and adults, accord-
      ing to this brief news note.

777 "Computer Tie-In Makes Program in Lincoln City,
      Nebraska a Success." Library Journal 108
      (January 1, 1983): 12.
         The Lincoln (NE) City Libraries report a
      positive response to a youth program called "Byte
      into Reading," which awards computer time for
      books read.

778 "Computers for Kids at Adrian (MI) PL." Small
      Computers in Libraries 1 (December 1981): 7.
         A two-week course, "Computers for Kids,"
      proved so successful at the Adrian (MI) Public
      Library that the local school district loaned the
      library four microcomputers for an indefinite
      period to allow them to continue the program.

779 "ComputerTown International to Offer New Serv-
      ices." Small Computers in Libraries 2 (April
      1982): 2-3.
         ComputerTown, USA! has been so successful
      that ComputerTown International has been founded

in the hope of continuing the program after National Science Foundation funding ends in 1983. The major services of ComputerTown International are described here.

780 "ComputerTown, OK!" Oklahoma Librarian 32 (May/ June 1982): 1.
A ComputerTown microcomputer project at the Norman (OK) Public Library is described.

781 "ComputerTown USA!" Small Computers in Libraries 1 (October 1981): 1.
The purpose for the development of ComputerTown, USA! is discussed, and the success of several installations is considered.

782 "Corpus Christi: Computer Literacy." Library Journal 109 (September 15, 1984): 1716.
The Corpus Christi (TX) Public Library will launch a five-year computer literacy program, made possible through the Junior League, whose members will provide training sessions and patron assistance in the use of microcomputers.

783 CURTIS, HOWARD. "The Mann Library Microcomputer Center." Small Computers in Libraries 4 (December 1984): 8-9.
A recently opened microcomputer center in Cornell University's Mann Library is described. Facilities, services, instructional programs and the software collection are discussed.

784 DERTIEN, JIM. "Microcomputer at the Bellevue Public Library." Nebraska Library Association Quarterly 12 (Summer 1981): 28-29.
The Bellevue (NE) Public Library's computer literacy program, based on a TI/4 microcomputer, is described, with additional information on finance of the program and peripheral services.

785 DEWEY, PATRICK R. "Computers, Fun, & Literacy." School Library Journal 29 (October 1982): 118.
Chicago Public Library's North-Pulaski Neighborhood Branch combined computer instruction

and game time with books and reading for a very
successful summer reading program. The program,
"Computers are Fun!" is described here.

786 DEWEY, PATRICK R. "How to Install a Microcomputer for Public Use and Survive!" Online '83
Conference Proceedings, Chicago, 10-12 October
1983. Weston, CT: Online, Inc., 1983. Pp.
43-46.
         Dewey considers several examples of pub-
lic use microcomputer facilities in libraries and
provides guidelines for establishing similar facilities in libraries where none now exist.

787 DEWEY, PATRICK R. Kids, Libraries, & Microcomputers: A Formula for Success. Pocatello, ID:
Contemporary Issues Clearinghouse, 1983. 7p.
         A plan for a children's computer literacy
program in a public library is presented by a librarian who has proven the value of such a project. Intended to cover a six-week period, activities are outlined for each meeting. Suggestions for puzzles and games are also included, as
are a list of resources.

788 DEWEY, PATRICK R. "A Microcomputer in the
Chicago Public Library for Staff and Public
Use." Illinois Libraries 64 (September 1982):
880-83.
         The public access microcomputer project
at the North-Pulaski Branch of the Chicago Public
Library is described in detail. Bibliography.

789 DEWEY, PATRICK R. "The Personal Computer Center
at the North-Pulaski Library." Educational
Computer Magazine 3 (March/April 1983): 28-29.
         Dewey provides details of the microcom-
puter pilot project at Chicago's North-Pulaski
Branch Library, including hardware and software
selection, location, staffing, publicity, public
use, and staff projects.

790 DEWEY, PATRICK R. "Problems in the Personal Computer Center." Small Computers in Libraries 2
(April 1982): 1-2.

After six month's experience with micros
in a public access setting, the staff of the
Chicago Public Library's North-Pulaski Neighborhood Library have identified the major problems
with such a project. These problems are shared,
along with methods of solving or avoiding them.

791 DEWEY, PATRICK R. Public Access Microcomputers:
A Handbook for Librarians. White Plains, NY:
Knowledge Industry Publications, 1984. 151p.
A practical treatment of public access
microcomputer programs in public libraries,
Dewey's book addresses the basics of establishing
a microcomputer center, software and hardware
selection, and project management. Descriptions
of several established public access projects are
included, as are suggestions for creating and
maintaining interest, and possible additional
services such as electronic bulletin boards and
database searching. Valuable appendices include
a model grant proposal, hardware and software
sources, a glossary, and a selected bibliography.

792 DEWEY, PATRICK R. "Public Access Microcomputers:
The Mouse That Roared." Public Libraries 24
(Fall 1985): 118-21.
Dewey notes the impact that public use
microcomputers have had on the public library,
and considers planning processes to meet current and future needs.

793 DEWEY, PATRICK R. "Public-Access Micros." American Libraries 15 (November 1984): 704.
The public-access microcomputer project
at Chicago Public Library's North-Pulaski Branch
is described, including the electronic bulletin
board, a public domain software copy center, word
processing seminars, game days, programming clas-
ses, computer clubs, and demonstrations. Equipment and programs are evaluated.

794 DEWEY, PATRICK R. "Public Access to Microcomputers: Thoughts from the North-Pulaski
Experience." RSR: Reference Services Review
11 (Fall 1983): 21-24.

Dewey discusses various aspects of public access microcomputer service in public libraries, including tutoring, reference, troubleshooting, and guidance in software selection. Purchasing equipment, supervision, coin-op vs. free use, and other topics are addressed. Bibliography.

795 DIMICK, BARBARA. "The Microcomputer in the Public Library: A Children's Room Experience." Top of the News 39 (Spring 1983): 253-59.
In 1982 the Madison (WI) Public Library acquired an Apple II Plus microcomputer for its Children's Room. This article describes and evaluates the experience, dealing with the initial purchase, software, copyright, scheduling, and user issues. A list of the library's soft-software is included. Bibliography.

796 DOYLE, JANET, and SYMONDS, TERRY. "Summer Student Projects Leading up to 'Read to Lead'." Canadian Library Journal 41 (April 1984): 85-89.
"Read to Lead," an outreach program for inner-city children in the area of Halifax, Nova Scotia's North Branch Library, incorporated a microcomputer component into its programming in 1982. The total program is described, including the microcomputer component, which is evaluated.

797 DUNCAN, CAROL S. "COMPULIT: Computer Literacy for Tacoma." Library Journal 109 (January 1984): 52-54.
The development of COMPULIT, Tacoma (WA) Public Library's micro-based computer literacy pilot project, is described, including various computer courses offered, available hardware and software, long range plans, and a brief evaluation of the project.

798 EBRAHIM, HEIDI. "Bedfordshire County Library Microcomputer Project." Program 19 (April 1985): 150-59.
In the early 1980s the Bedfordshire County (UK) Library System launched a public access microcomputer project intended to provide

microcomputer facilities for patrons of its larger branch libraries. Planning and implementation of the project are treated, with information provided on aims and objectives, hardware, software, staffing, staff training, and public use. Problems are related, and a good overall evaluation is included.

799 EMMENS, CAROL A. "Home Computers Find a New Home--Public Libraries." Collection Building 5 (Summer 1983): 18-23.
Seven case studies of public libraries which offer public access microcomputer facilities are presented. The libraries offer a diversity of services, from coin operated micros to programs offering free use within the library, to a rental program for hardware and software, to online searching performed by library personnel. Despite the diversity, all programs have been judged successful and the services in great demand.

800 ENGLISH, JEANNE. "Reference and Information Services in the Information Society: Possibilities for the School Library Media Center." Bookmark 41 (Winter 1983): 99-105.
Justification for including the school media specialist in planning for computer literacy, and consideration of the media center as the logical site for generation of the literacy program are discussed. Components of a program for training media specialists for their new role in microcomputer literacy are proposed, and some model literacy programs are considered. Bibliography.

801 "First Public Computers Put in Oklahoma Library." Library Journal 107 (March 15, 1982): 591.
This news item gives details concerning Norman (OK) Public Library's purchase of several TRS microcomputers for public use in both the adult and children's sections, and the increase in public interest which came as a result. An increase in tax support for the library is attributed to the program.

802 "Forsyth County, N. C. Installs Public Computers." Library Journal 107 (February 15,
1982): 393-94.
The Forsyth County (NC) Public Library
announces the installation of two microcomputers
for public use. Goals and user policies are
stated, popular programs are identified, and an
in-house micro-related project is discussed.

803 FOWLER, BONNIE S., and SMITH, DUNCAN. "Microcomputers for the Public in the Public Library." Information Technology and Libraries
2 (March 1983): 46-52.
The Forsyth County (NC) Public Library's
public access microcomputer project, offered as a
service of the Adult Continuing Education Department, is described and evaluated by two librarians who work with the project. Background,
goals, and services are described, use and user
data are provided, and a word on software selection is added. Bibliography.

804 GIACOMA, PETE. "Computers, Computer Literacy,
and Access in the Children's Room." Top of
the News 41 (Fall 1984): 53-59.
Microcomputers are being added to children's library facilities at an astounding rate,
often with little or no thought to philosophy,
goals, or impact. Giacoma addresses the problem
of planning for computer literacy and computer
aided instruction programs in libraries, and
presents some thoughtful suggestions for launching a program successfully. Bibliography.

805 GIBBS, SALLY. "Computer in the Library as
Indispensable Hub of the School." Library
Association Record 86 (February 1984): 71-72.
The negative image of the school library
in Great Britain is noted, and the influence of
public access microcomputers on reversing that
image is discussed. Bibliography.

806 GRAF, NANCY. "Computers and Media Centers--A
Winning Combination." Computing Teacher 11
(May 1984): 42-44.

The development and implementation of computer literacy and computer aided instruction programs at the Chief Joseph Junior High School in Richland, Washington is the theme of this article which offers practical suggestions for an effective program.

807   HARVIE, BARBARA. "Out of the Arcades and into the Library." American Libraries 12 (November 1981): 602-05.

In 1979 the Menlo Park (CA) Public Library became permanent host to a ComputerTown model public access computer project through the efforts of two concerned citizens and the generosity of several local vendors. This article describes the project and its impact on the library.

808   HARVIE, BARBARA, and ANTON, JULIE. "Is There a Microcomputer in Your Future? ComputerTown Thinks the Answer is 'Yes'." Top of the News 39 (Spring 1983): 275-81.

The role of the computer in the children's and young people's sections of a public library is briefly stated, advantages of a ComputerTown installation are told, and details of funding, hardware and software selection, administration, and problems are discussed.

809   HEGARTY, KEVIN. "Computer Literacy." Online '83 Conference Proceedings, Chicago, 10-12 October 1983. Weston, CT: Online, Inc., 1983. Pp. 90-112.

In 1982 the Tacoma (WA) Public Library launched a computer literacy program through a Library Services and Construction Act (LSCA) grant. Details of the proposal, justification, and early steps toward implementation are considered, as are guidelines for computer use, equipment lists, and available software.

810   HEINS, ETHEL L. "Bits and Bytes--And Books?" Horn Book 59 (April 1983): 134-35.

Computer literacy has become one more component in a liberal education; however, the

author warns against over reliance on technology
to the detriment of traditional literacy.

811 "Herds of Micros at Texas A & M Supporting Teaching Programs." Library Journal 108 (March 15,
1983): 538.
A public use microcomputer program at the
Texas A & M University Library is described, and
a variety of uses are discussed.

812 "Humanities Faculty Targeted for Computer Literacy at Mason." Library Journal (February 1,
1984): 133.
A computer literacy program for the
humanities faculty of George Mason University is
described. The program is made available through
the University's Fenwick Library.

813 JAROS, JOE. "Surviving Unprecedented Growth at
Texas A & M Library." Wilson Library Bulletin
58 (June 1984): 719-22.
An article which deals with the expansion
of library facilities at Texas A & M University
Library considers collection development, staffing, and automation. Among the automated programs and services considered are the library's
microcomputer center and the end user online
search service.

814 JARTZ-HORVATH, LOUISA. "Live Wires: Children and
Computers in Libraries." Ohio Library Association Bulletin 51 (July 1981): 19-22.
Justification for providing microcomputer
programs and equipment in public libraries is
given by a strong proponent who cites successful
examples and quotes staunch supporters of the
technology.

815 JOHNSON, STEPHEN C. "Computers and the Public."
Sightlines 17 (Spring 1984): 12-14.
Microcomputer programs in Norman, Oklahoma; Caldwell, Idaho; and Lorain, Ohio, are
surveyed, along with the "Public Access Microcomputers" project of Illinois' Lincoln Trails Library System to indicate the proliferation of the

technology. Two problems--financing the programs
and copyright issues--are addressed.

816 JULIEN, DON. "Expanding Service: Public Access
     Microcomputers." Wilson Library Bulletin 59
     (February 1985): 381-85.
         A morphological approach is applied to
     the problem of establishing a public service
     microcomputer program. The elements of the
     project--needs, clientele, skill level, type of
     service, type of equipment, and location--are
     considered individually, and notes on using the
     model are included.

817 JULIEN, DON, and SCHAUER, BRUCE. "Microcomputers
     Come to Kings County." Library Journal 108
     (June 15, 1983): 1214-16.
         An evaluation of King County (WA) Library
     System's public access microcomputer project pro-
     vides a rationale and objectives for the project
     and addresses hardware and software needs, staff
     training, policies, and general operation and
     maintenance. Bibliography.

818 "Kids' Computer Program Opens at Starkville PL."
     School Library Journal 27 (August 1981):
     12-13.
         The success of a recent microcomputer
     literacy project in the children's room of the
     Starkville (MO) Public Library is related, and
     mounting interest among adults is told in this
     brief news story.

819 "King County Goes Online: Reference Services and
     Apple IIs." Library Journal 107 (August
     1982): 1370.
         The King County (WA) Library System re-
     ports the addition of free online searching to
     its information services, and the installation
     of public access Apple II microcomputers in two
     of its branches.

820 KUSACK, JAMES M., and BOWERS, JOHN S. "Public
     Microcomputers in Public Libraries." Library
     Journal 107 (November 15, 1982): 2137-41.

A general overview of public access microcomputers in public libraries reports the results of a survey of some 100 libraries concerning number and type of equipment, usage, problems, benefits, costs, and demand. Bibliography.

821   LaPIER, CYNTHIA. "The Care and Maintenance of an Apple Orchard." Reference Librarian 5/6 (Fall/Winter 1982): 51-56.

Practical suggestions concerning necessary equipment and add-ons are coupled with sound advice on equipment and software maintenance for for Apple microcomputers, particularly those in public use areas of libraries.

822   LAZERICK, BETH. "Facing the Future: One School's Commitment to Computer Education." Top of the News 39 (Spring 1983): 261-63.

The computer literacy program at Shaker Heights, Ohio's Moreland Elementary School is described and evaluated after two years of operation.

823   LINCOLN TRAIL LIBRARIES SYSTEM. Public Access Microcomputers: A Planning Guide. Champaign, Illinois: Lincoln Trail Libraries System, 1983.

This guide to the planning and implementation of public access microcomputer projects in public libraries deals with hardware and software selection, funding, site preparation, publicity, and other topics. Bibliography.

824   LOOP, LIZA. "ComputerTown, USA!" Instructional Innovator 27 (February 1982): 22-23.

The philosophy behind ComputerTown, USA!, a history of its development, and its prospects for the future are summarized.

825   LOOP, LIZA, and ANTON, JULIE. "ComputerTown, USA! Bringing Computers to the People." Classroom Computer News 3 (September/October 1982): 29-30, 86.

The philosophy behind ComputerTown, USA!,

history of its development, and its potential for the future are enthusiastically described by its technical coordinator.

826 LOOP, LIZA; ANTON, JULIE; and ZAMORA, RAMON.
ComputerTown: A Do-It-Yourself Community Computer Project. Menlo Park, CA: People's Computer Co., 1982. 105p.
ComputerTown, a microcomputer-based public access computer literacy project made available to libraries, museums, and other educational organizations by People's Computer Company, is treated in this do-it-yourself handbook which deals with planning, funding, installing, and managing of a ComputerTown installation.

827 LOOP, LIZA; ANTON, JULIE; and ZAMORA, RAMON.
ComputerTown: Bringing Computer Literacy to Your Community. Reston, VA: Reston Publishing Co., 1983. 160p.
The ComputerTown concept is treated thoroughly in this description and analysis, which emphasizes definitions and descriptions of the program, with information on planning, finance, implementation, and maintenance. Bibliography.

828 MacLEOD, MARCIA. "Computer Literacy: Is it Our Duty to Teach Bits and Bytes?" Library Association Record 86 (August 1984): 295-97.
MacLeod does not answer her own question directly, but considers the merits of computer literacy programs in light of existing projects in several British libraries.

829 "Making Kids Computer-Wise: Plattsburgh Buys Apple II." Library Journal 105 (March 15, 1980): 669.
An Apple II microcomputer, purchased for the Clinton-Essex-Franklin Library System of Plattsburgh, New York and placed in the children's room, was so well received by children and adults alike, that a grant was submitted to the Board of Cooperative Educational Services for funding to add computer training programs for all interested patrons.

830 "Mankato State University in Minnesota Has an Active Microcomputer Lab." Library Journal 108 (May 1, 1983): 862, 864.
Mankato State University's microcomputer laboratory is described by the University's Audiovisual Services Coordinator.

831 MARCHBANK, ALAN M. "Libraries and Micros." Scottish Library Association News 181 (May/June 1984): 13-18.
Marchbank addresses the responsibilities of the library and library staff to the personal computer user. Among the questions considered are the library's responsibility for supplying space, power hookups, security, appropriate furniture, compatible equipment, peripherals, and software for those patrons who own and bring their own micro to the library.

832 MASON, ROBERT M. "Traveling Apple's LISA, Public Micros." Library Journal 108 (June 15, 1983): 1235-36.
The "Public Micros" section of this article briefly describes public access microcomputer projects at the Mansfield-Richland County (OH) Public Library and the Baltimore County (MD) Public Library.

833 McCANN, SUE. "Portsmouth (NH) PL Public Access." Small Computers in Libraries 3 (March 1983): 1.
Two Apple II Plus microcomputers and four smaller VIC-20s form the basis for the automation program at the Portsmouth (NH) Public Library. One Apple is reserved for staff use. The other is dedicated to in-house public access, while the VIC-20s circulate to patrons. Workshops and self-help sessions round out the program.

834 "Micro Services at Texas A & M Library." ACCESS: Microcomputers in Libraries 3 (Spring 1983): 30-31.
In 1982 the Sterling C. Evans Library at Texas A & M University completed its first semester of providing microcomputer access to

students and faculty through the library's
Learning Resources Department. The program is
described and evaluated, and greater use and
expansion is projected.

835 "Microcomputers for Rent at San Francisco Public." Library Journal 108 (March 15, 1983):
536, 538.
The coin-op microcomputer program at the
San Francisco (CA) Public Library is announced
and described.

836 "Microcomputers Take Off in Tacoma COMPULIT Program." Library Journal 108 (August 1983):
1414.
The Tacoma (WA) Public Library's eight-
week microcomputer literacy program for adults
is outlined briefly.

837 "Micros Tested for School Library Databases."
Online Review 7 (December 1983): 443-44.
A project of the School of Librarianship
and Information Studies at Robert Gordon's Institute of Technology, Aberdeen, will employ KWIRS
software and Apple II micros to develop small
online databases for use in school libraries to
teach information retrieval skills to school
children.

838 MILLER, JOHN. "Motivating Students to Learn
Proper Computer Operation Skills." School
Library Media Quarterly 12 (Fall 1983): 82-83.
When a variety of microcomputer hardware
was purchased for Deer Park, Ohio's Amity Elementary School Library, librarian and teachers were
concerned about proper care. Introductory lessons and a test of microcomputer skills devised
to teach proper use are described, and their success is told.

839 MILLER, JOHN, and PARK, WILLIAM. "License Your
Computer Students." Ohio Media Spectrum 36
(Spring 1984): 35-36.
When a computer literacy component was
added to the curriculum at Amity Elementary

School in Deer Park, Ohio, a videotape show illustrating the proper use of the equipment, a test on basic use of the equipment, and a computer-user license were produced to aid in teaching and insuring good user techniques. The project is described and the license is reproduced.

840 "Montgomery Co. Brings Computers to the Disabled Population." Library Journal 108 (January 1, 1983): 11-12.
　　　The Rockville (MD) Public Library reports the success of a computer literacy program for the disabled, which was made possible through LSCA funding.

841 MORGENROTH, LYNDA. "Using Computers at the Library: More Than Just Books." New Library Scene 3 (June 1984): 14.
　　　An article reprinted from the Boston Globe describes coin operated microcomputer facilities at the Newton (MA) Free Library, stressing their acceptance by the general public.

842 MOSES, RICHARD. "Steam Engines in the Public Library; or, Computers, Children and Library Services." Emergency Librarian 10 (January/February 1983): 13-16.
　　　The development of a microcomputer program to encompass the needs of a total public library clientele is the vision of the staff of Oakville (Ontario) Public Library. An overview of the program is provided, including descriptions of services for preschool children, the elderly, and the handicapped.

843 "Niles PL Undertakes Computer Literacy Program." Wilson Library Bulletin 58 (February 1984): 395.
　　　The Niles (IL) Public Library announces a computer literacy program implemented in 1983 in its main library and branches. Apple IIe and Texas Instrument micros are provided free of charge to patrons, as are word processing, database management, and educational courseware programs.

844 "Oakville, Ontario Library to Set Up 'Electronic Branch'." Library Journal 108 (May 1, 1983): 860, 862.
A microcomputer center in a local shopping mall provides microcomputer training and access for patrons of all ages, according to an Oakville (Ontario) Public Library spokesperson.

845 "Ohio Puts LSCA Money into Computer Literacy." Library Journal 107 (November 15, 1982): 2133.
Richard Cheski, Ohio State Librarian, announces the awarding of LSCA grants to fifteen Ohio public libraries for the purchase of microcomputer systems. Cheski provides justification for the expenditure.

846 "Ohio's Mansfield-Richland County Meets Need for Computer Training." Library Journal 108 (May 1, 1983): 858, 860.
Mansfield-Richland County (OH) Public Library personnel tell of the positive public response to the library's microcomputer literacy program.

847 OPOCENSKY, VIRGINIA. "Byte Into Reading." School Library Journal 29 (May 1983): 39.
"Byte Into Reading," Lincoln (NE) City Library's microcomputer program for Summer, 1982, is reviewed and evaluated. Advanced planning, publicity, staffing, problems, and rewards are considered.

848 PANTELIDIS, VERONICA SEXAUER. Microcomputer Essentials. 3rd ed. Greenville, NC: East Carolina University, Department of Library and Information Studies, 1985. 98p.
A basic manual for use in teaching/ learning microcomputer operation, this publication addresses Acorn, Apple, Commodore, IBM, and TRS-80 hardware. Although written for college level computer literacy programs, it is easily adaptable to adults and young adults.

849 "Personal Computer in the Children's Room." LJ/ SLJ Hotline 10 (March 2, 1981): 4.

A personal computer donated by the Palo Alto (CA) Public Library's Friends organization has made possible a children's public access microcomputer project, according to this news note.

850 PIELE, LINDA J. "Circulating Microcomputer Software." ACCESS: Microcomputers in Libraries 2 (October 1982): 7-8, 20-23.
The establishment of a microcomputer center in the University of Wisconsin-Parkside Library/Learning Center is described, including decisions on choice of equipment, circulation of software, cataloging of programs, staff training, use policies, user orientation, security, and maintenance. Bibliography.

851 POLLY, JEAN ARMOUR. "Burning-In: Four Years at the Public Library's Microcomputer." Small Computers in Libraries 5 (September 1985): 13-15, 22.
In 1981 the Liverpool (NY) Public Library began a public access microcomputer program that has become a model for others. The library's assistant director shares insights and wisdom concerning planning, equipment, patron needs, budgeting, collection development, and processing of software, gathered from four years of experience.

852 "Public Access Microcomputers." UNABASHED Librarian no. 47 (1983): 15-17.
Dan Zack, of the Burlington (IA) Public Library; Faye Clow, of the Bettendorf (IA) Public Library; and Dennis Davis, of the Ottumwa (IA) Public Library summarize presentations they made at 1983 computer workshops. Their presentations concern selection of microcomputer systems for public access, introductory projects, and regulation of public microcomputer usage.

853 "Public Access Microsystem Offered by Newly Merged Firm." Library Journal 108 (August 1983): 1414.
Maxwell Library Systems and Boston Copyco announce their merger and a new coin-operated

microcomputer service available to libraries
wanting to offer public access hardware.

854 RAMSEY, JERRY D., and DARLING, JOHN R. "Develop-
     ing a Multipurpose Microcomputer Learning
     Laboratory." Collegiate Microcomputer 2
     (November 1984): 295-300.
          The authors describe a microcomputer
     learning laboratory established in the Texas Tech
     University Library. Facility design, rules and
     procedures, and a special faculty training pro-
     gram are considered. Bibliography.

855 RAPPAPORT, SUSAN. "Literacy and Computers."
     Library Journal 110 (October 1, 1985): 74-75.
          Director of the microcomputer project
     at the New York Public Library, describes the
     establishment and growth of the project, and
     illustrates its value through a case study.

856 RAPPAPORT, SUSAN. "Software for the People."
     Library Journal 110 (February 1, 1985): 56-58.
          The New York Public Library's public ac-
     cess microcomputer project is considered, with
     particular attention to the development of soft-
     ware collections.

857 RAPPAPORT, SUSAN. "Software to Teach Problem
     Solving." Library Journal 110 (May 15, 1985):
     44-45.
          Public libraries have a commitment to
     computer literacy programs for adults as well as
     children. This includes not only providing hard-
     ware, but also high quality, appropriate soft-
     ware. Rappaport suggests logic and problem
     solving software which should appeal to adult
     learners.

858 RILEY, JEAN. "Computers in the Library." T.H.E.
     Journal: Technological Horizons in Education
     11 (November 1983): 123-24.
          Cumberland College Library's eleven pub-
     lic service microcomputers have proven sufficient
     for the computing needs of faculty and students
     in this small church college, and low use periods

provide librarians the opportunity for dial-up access to an online catalog system and other library applications.

859 RILEY, JEAN. "Microcomputers in the Cumberland College Library." UNABASHED Librarian no. 47 (1983): 6.
    Riley addresses educational and recreational uses made of eleven public service microcomputers available to students and faculty of Cumberland College. The article is similar to one which appeared in T.H.E. Journal.

860 ROMANS, ANNE F., and RANSOM, STANLEY A. "An Apple a Day: Microcomputers in the Public Library." American Libraries 11 (December 1980): 691-93.
    To accomplish its goal of bringing basic computer literacy to local children, the Plattsburgh (NY) Public Library launched a microcomputer project for its Children's Room in early 1980. The authors describe the hardware and software, discuss problems, and evaluate the overall success of the project.

861 ROMANS, ANNE F., and RANSOM, STANLEY A. "Apple in Plattsburg, (NY) PL." Small Computers in Libraries 1 (April 1981): 5.
    "Apple in Plattsburg" is a synopsis of a longer article by Romans and Ransom which appeared in American Libraries, December 1980.

862 ROSE, PHILLIP E. "Microcomputers--One Library's Approach." Online 8 (January 1984): 30-32.
    The ComputerTown USA concept is explored, its adaptation to local facilities is discussed, and Aurora (CO) Public Library's experience in developing a ComputerTown program is told.

863 ROSENBERG, VICTOR. "Word Processing for Library Patrons." Library Hi Tech 2 no. 2, issue 6 (1984): 25-26.
    Libraries are encouraged to provide public service word processors, bibliographic formatting software, and terminal to terminal

interface capabilities to support scholars and
scholarship.

864 "San Bernardino PL & Schools Cooperate on
      Micros." Small Computers in Libraries 2
      (January 1982): 3.
          Microcomputers installed in branch facil-
      ities of the San Bernardino (CA) Public Library
      provide added opportunity for students to study
      for proficiency exams according to this brief
      news item.

865 SATHER, RUTH. "Microcomputer, Media Center, and
      Kids!" Computing Teacher 9 (December 1981):
      23-26.
          A project to introduce a computer litera-
      cy program into an elementary school is described
      by the school's media specialist. Acquiring
      funding from the PTA, setting up criteria for
      software selection, introducing the microcomputer
      program to students and teachers, and organizing
      the program to accommodate the needs of all users
      are discussed.

866 SATHER, RUTH. "Student Computer User Group."
      Computing Teacher 9 (May 1982): 10-11.
          An elementary school media specialist
      describes a method for heightening microcomputer
      awareness, interest, and use through a Microcom-
      puter Club. Bibliography.

867 SAVAGE, G. SUSAN. "Microcomputers." Public
      Library Quarterly 5 (Summer 1984): 43-45.
          A public access microcomputer program at
      the Dallas (TX) Public Library is described and
      evaluated briefly; the evolution of the micro is
      reviewed from the early 4-bit machines through
      the current supermicro.

868 SCHAEFER, MARY TONNE. "Public-Access Microcom-
      puters in Libraries." Information Retrieval
      and Library Automation 18 (January 1983): 1-2.
          Three public access microcomputer pro-
      jects in Maryland and Pennsylvania libraries are
      described and evaluated.

869 "School-Library Computervan." American Libraries
14 (September 1983): 546.
A van equipped with ten Apple microcomputers is being utilized by libraries in the Mid-
Hudson (NY) Library System to provide computer
instruction and experience to children ages six
through thirteen, according to this brief news
item.

870 SCOTT, MARY-ANNE. "Having a Go: Micros at
Irvine." Scottish Library Association News
171 (September/October 1982): 23-24.
A public access microcomputer project at
the Irving (Scotland) Branch Library is detailed.

871 SHEA, TOM. "Educating a Community." InfoWorld 6
(April 2, 1984): 31-34.
The microcomputer pilot project at Chicago Public Library's North-Pulaski Branch is described. Innovative applications have been
tried, including public access use, an electronic
bulletin board, development of extensive software
collections, and the production of subject and
software wall guides for quick reference.

872 SIEGFRIED, PAT. "Computers and Children: Problems and Possibilities." Top of the News 39
(Spring 1983): 241-46.
A discussion of the pros and cons of
computer literacy in school leads into a presentation concerning current trends and future
possibilities. Bibliography.

873 SIMMONS, ROSETTA. "Community College Library
Initiates Computer Literacy Program." Show-Me
Libraries 35 (September 1984): 33-37.
The need for a computer literacy program
at Flat River, Missouri's Mineral Area College
was obvious from the demand for computer education. It was the librarian who organized a program to fill the need. This article describes
the initial proposal, development of the program,
implementation, advantages and disadvantages, and
the future of the program as an extension of
library services. Bibliography.

874 SKLARZ, DAVID P. "The Apple (Computer) Orchard
    is Bearing Fruit in Our School." Clearing
    House 57 (February 1984): 284-85.
        The microcomputer lab, an extension of
    the library-media center in Connecticut's East
    Ridge Junior High School, is the subject of this
    article which describes efforts at improving com-
    puter literacy among students and teachers.

875 SKLARZ, DAVID P. "This Apple Orchard is Bearing
    Fruit." Instructional Innovator 29 (January
    1984): 33.
        A positive microcomputer-based computer
    literacy program, which is an extension of the
    library/media center in Ridgefield, Connecticut's
    East Ridge Junior High School, is described. The
    major obstacle to initiating the program was the
    teaching faculty, but a training program designed
    to meet their needs provided the expertise to
    integrate computer literacy into the curriculum.

876 SKVARIA, DONNA. "ComputerTown, OK!" Catholic
    Library World 54 (November 1982): 170-74.
        A ComputerTown, USA! installation, initi-
    ated and implemented by the Norman (OK) Public
    Library for both adults and children, is de-
    scribed and evaluated, with successes and prob-
    lems considered. Bibliography.

877 SMITH, LUCIA WALKER. "Microcomputers in the
    Elementary School." CMLEA Journal 3 (Spring
    1980): 7-8.
        A microcomputer awareness program for
    gifted students, created by an enthusiastic
    school principal and coordinated by a progressive
    librarian, combines theory and hands-on experi-
    ence into a six-week course for fourth and fifth
    grade children, which has proven so successful
    that more advanced units are being developed.
    Bibliography.

878 SNELSON, PAMELA. "Microcomputer Centers in Aca-
    demic Libraries, Part I." Small Computers in
    Libraries 5 (June 1985): 6-9.
        Hal Hall, of Texas A & M; Howard Curtis,

of Cornell; and DeeDee Pannell, of Florida Institute of Technology respond to questions concerning their local microcomputer programs and services. Written in a question/answer format, the article is a report of a panel presentation at the Library Software Conference held in Columbus, Ohio, October, 1984, and deals with the location of micros in libraries, the purpose of a microcomputer center, microcomputer instruction, and software sources.

879 SNELSON, PAMELA. "Microcomputer Centers in Academic Libraries, Part II." Small Computers in Libraries 5 (July/August 1985): 7-9.
      Hal Hall, Howard Curtis, and DeeDee Pannell continue their interview concerning microcomputer centers in their libraries, addressing cataloging, circulation, copyright, licensing arrangements, and other issues.

880 "South Adirondack Library System Reports Rural Micro Project." Library Journal 108 (August 1983): 1414.
      "People and Computers," a microcomputer literacy program for adults, sponsored by the Southern Adirondack Library System in Saratoga Springs, New York, is described.

881 STAFFORD, JOHN. "ComputerTown Worcester!" Assistant Librarian 75 (March 1982): 36-37.
      The purpose of ComputerTown, UK!, a spin-off of ComputerTown, USA!, which was developed in Menlo Park, California, is to provide a network of computer literacy centers throughout the United Kingdom. The installation at the Worcester (UK) City Library is described, and future installations are envisioned.

882 STRONG, GARY E., and GIBSON, LIZ. "Adult Computer Literacy: The California State Library Commitment." Microcomputers for Information Management 1 (June 1984): 143-53.
      The California State Librarian has awarded LSCA grants to 85 libraries to support adult microcomputer literacy programs and twelve re-

source centers. The project is described, libraries are identified, and the involvement of People's Computer Company is explained.

883 "Summer Library Program Teaches Computer Basics." School Library Journal 30 (November 1983): 14.
The Prince George's County (MD) Library System's 1983 summer computer program is described, including how it was provided through volunteer staffing. Similar programs are planned for the future.

884 "TRS-80 III at Lorain Public." Small Computers in Libraries 2 (February 1982): 3.
The public access microcomputer program at the Lorain (OH) Public Library is described, including the hardware, the software collection, orientation, and plans for expansion.

885 TANJI, VIRGINIA M. "Independent Microcomputer Use by Library Users." Medical Reference Services Quarterly 3 (Fall 1984): 91-94.
When the Hawaii Medical Library switched from Apple to Kaypro hardware, reference librarians decided to convert the Apple to public use. The author provides background information, a profile of users, a listing of available software, and an evaluation of the impact of the service on the library's image.

886 THOMPSON, RICHARD E. "A Room of Their Own: Optimal Settings for Patrons and Patron Computers." Technical Services Quarterly 2 (Spring/Summer 1985): 73-91.
The Wilmette (IL) Public Library is providing specially designed facilities for its microcomputer users. Designed for minimum confusion and noise and maximum visibility, the room provides library owned equipment or plug-in facilities for microcomputers. Services, policies, and software are described.

887 TILLMAN-WINNINGHAM, LAURA. "Computers & Children: A Compatible Twosome." School Library Journal 30 (March 1984): 123-24.

A public access microcomputer program for children at the Glendora (CA) Public Library and Cultural Center is described, from the filing system for software to the sponsorship of a library computer club for children and young people. Five initial steps to follow in establishing a public access microcomputer program offer practical advice for librarians needing help in planning.

888 TROUTNER, JOANNE JOHNSON. "Helping Teach Computer Literacy, Part I." Educational Computer Magazine 3 (July/August 1983): 33-34.
The author defines computer literacy and identifies the school media specialist's role in developing a computer literacy program. A good selective bibliography of computer materials for middle school grades is included.

889 TROUTNER, JOANNE JOHNSON. "Helping Teach Computer Literacy, Part II." Educational Computer Magazine 3 (September 1983): 30.
The author encourages team teaching efforts, particularly between the classroom teacher and the media specialist. She describes one team-taught computer literacy unit that proved successful; and she suggests other phases of computer education which lend themselves to the team teaching approach. Bibliography.

890 "Two N. Y. Libraries Provide Computer Education." Library Journal 107 (June 1, 1982): 1041.
Microcomputer programs at Penfield and Fairport (NY) public libraries are announced, and positive patron response is described in this news item.

891 "Use of Micros in Rural Libraries Focus of Illinois Pilot Project." Library Journal 108 (February 15, 1983): 338-39.
The Lincoln Trail Library System, Champaign, Illinois, reports the receipt of a $37,782.65 LSCA grant to fund a demonstration project on the use of public access microcomputers in rural libraries.

892 VERBESEY, J. ROBERT. "Public Microcomputers on
      Long Island." Library Journal 108 (June 15,
      1983): 1211-13.
          A public access microcomputer project at
      the Mastics-Moriches-Shirley (NY) Community Li-
      brary is justified and evaluated. Patron accep-
      tance, scheduling, software care and security,
      and male domination of the equipment are a few of
      the topics treated.

893 WHITE, WALLACE. "'What's That Funny Noise?'
      Videogames in the Library." Library Journal
      106 (April 15, 1981): 859-60.
          In 1980 the Piqua (OH) Public Library in-
      stalled microcomputer equipment, and purchased
      entertainment programs and video games for the
      purpose of attracting greater numbers of junior
      high school students. White describes and evalu-
      ates the program after one year of operation.

894 YEOH, JOSEPHINE W. "Microcomputer Applications."
      Medical Library Association Bulletin 71 (April
      1983): 221.
          The development of a computer literacy
      program at Columbus, Ohio's Riverside Methodist
      Hospital is discussed, and the librarian's role
      in the program is outlined.

895 ZABINSKI, TOBY F., and ZABINSKI, MICHAEL P. "A
      Coin Operated Computer in a Public Library."
      Library Journal 104 (October 15, 1979):
      2174-75.
          One of the first coin-operated microcom-
      puter installations in a public library is de-
      scribed and evaluated. A Wang PCS 1 was bought
      for the Milford (CT) Public Library for recrea-
      tional and educational purposes, and could be
      used for programming or running commercial pro-
      grams. The cost was prohibitive for serious use,
      but the original purpose, to provide hands-on ex-
      perience with computers, was achieved.

896 ZAMORA, RAMON. "ComputerTown, USA! Using Person-
      al Computers in the Public Library." School
      Library Journal 27 (April 1981): 28-31.

Ramon Zamora, Project Director for ComputerTown USA, a microcomputer-based computer
literacy project funded by the National Science
Foundation, describes and evaluates the Menlo
Park (CA) Public Library's ComputerTown, USA!
operation.

COMPUTER AIDED INSTRUCTION

897 ARNOTT, PATRICIA D., and RICHARDS, DEBORAH E.
     "Using the IBM Personal Computer for Library
     Instruction." RSR: Reference Services Review
     13 (Spring 1985): 69-72.
         For several years the University of Del-
     aware used library instruction lessons resident
     on PLATO for teaching basic library skills to
     freshman English students. In 1983 librarians
     began a project to convert the programs for use
     on IBM microcomputers. The project is justified,
     the complexities are discussed, and the final
     products are evaluated.

898 "CAI at the Univ of Michigan." Small Computers
     in Libraries 3 (July 1983): 7.
         The computer assisted instruction program
     offered by the University of Michigan's Instruc-
     tional Strategy Services is outlined. Hardware,
     software, orientation programs, and services are
     reviewed.

899 "Columbus Literacy Project to Enlist Computer
     Aid." Library Journal 107 (November 15,
     1982): 2134.
         The Public Library of Columbus and Frank-
     lin County (OH) announces a microcomputer-based
     reading and literacy program for adults with
     reading difficulties.

900 ENG, SIDNEY. "CAI and the Future of Bibliograph-
     ic Instruction." Catholic Library World 55
     (May/June 1984): 441-44.
         Computer assisted instruction (CAI) is
     considered in detail, and its future impact on
     bibliographic instruction and bibliographic in-
     struction librarians is noted. Bibliography.

901 ERSKINE, JOHN. "Learning by Microcomputer: The
     Role of the Library." An Leabharlann 10
     (Autumn 1981): 96, 98-102, 104-06, 108-11.

The purchase and installation of a microcomputer for computer assisted instruction in a library is justified. Hardware, programming, software, applications, and other topics are considered. Bibliography.

902 FABIAN, WILLIAM M. "Tending Apples in the Library." Educational Computer Magazine 2 (September/October 1982): 35-36.

In a case study format the author discusses the development of a high school level computer assisted instruction program for his learning resources center. He relates successes, problems, uses, and plans for the future, and provides practical hints on organizing, maintaining, and making optimum use of the equipment and software.

903 FLATH, PATRICIA C. "Library Orientation to the Technical Literature." Journal of Chemical Education 59 (June 1982): 516-17.

The author describes a library orientation program designed to introduce chemistry students to the literature of the discipline. The program is written for a Radio Shack TRS-80 microcomputer.

904 MACHALOW, ROBERT. "The Library Microcomputer: Bibliographic Instruction." M300 and PC Report 2 (June 1985): 1-2.

The M300 workstation can be used for bibliographic instruction when not in use for technical processing and database searching. This article explains how the new application can be implemented, with word processing software and the M300.

905 MANDER, CHRIS. "An Oakville Enterprise: Computers Teach Pre-Schoolers to Read and Write." Canadian Library Journal 39 (February 1982): 17-18.

A microcomputer-based reading readiness program for 3-5 year olds, which was inaugurated by the Oakville (Ontario) Public Library in 1979, is described and evaluated.

906 MOSKOWITZ, MICKEY. "Library Orientation Program
        Evaluation." ACCESS: Microcomputers in Li-
        braries 1 (October 1981): 10-13, 23-26.
            The author describes a microcomputer
     program used to evaluate the effectiveness of
     library orientation for 10th grade high school
     students in the Bradford Library, Quincy, Massa-
     chusetts. The LIBRARY ORIENTATION EVALUATION
     PROGRAM is reproduced in its entirety, with docu-
     mentation. Bibliography.

907 NELSON, W. DALE. "Sharpening Reading Skills."
        Wilson Library Bulletin 59 (April 1985): 534.
            A microcomputer program developed by the
     U. S. Navy to improve the reading skills of re-
     cruits has been adapted by the Enoch Pratt Free
     Library in Baltimore for an adult literacy pro-
     gram, and is being considered by other libraries
     for the same purpose.

908 "North York Library Uses Apple II to Develop Lit-
        eracy Program." Library Journal 108 (April
        15, 1983): 786.
            The North York (Ontario) Public Library's
     microcomputer-based literacy program is de-
     scribed. The program currently serves about
     sixty people with access to spelling, grammar,
     and other types of educational programs.

909 ROBERTS, KEN. "The Oakville Public Library's
        Computer Program for Young People: A
        Critique." Emergency Librarian 10 (January/
        February 1983): 16-17.
            The Oakville (Ontario) Public Library's
     pre-school microcomputer program is evaluated,
     and its popularity and value is acknowledged, but
     the claim that "When the preschool child has com-
     pleted the program satisfactorily he will have
     the skills necessary to begin to read," is ques-
     tioned.

910 ROSS, JANE E. "Micro Software for Library Skills
        Instruction." School Library Journal 31
        (November 1984): 68-73.
            This annotated bibliography of 34 off-

the-shelf software programs for teaching library
skills should prove valuable to the school librarian responsible for library instruction.

911 SCHOENLY, STEVEN B. "A Library Tour and Orientation Program for Small Computers." Software
Review 1 (February 1982): 44-57.
A microcomputer-based library orientation
program, developed by the University of Mississippi Graduate School of Library and Information
Science and based on commercially available video
game concepts, is described in detail.

912 SINNETT, DENNIS, and EDWARDS, SHEILA. "Authoring
Systems: The Key to Widespread Use of Interactive Videodisc Technology." Library Hi Tech
2, no. 4, issue 8 (1984): 39-50.
Interactive video systems are considered
as a method of communication and teaching. This
article reviews and recommends microcomputers
which are appropriate as control devices, and
discusses authoring systems, which are software
programs written to aid non-programmers in setting up interactive video presentations using
micros.

913 SNELSON, PAMELA. "Microcomputers in an Academic
Setting: The Computer Initiative at Drew University." Library Hi Tech 2 no. 3, issue 7
(1984): 73-77.
Beginning with the fall of 1984, Drew
University has issued each entering freshman an
Epson QX-10 microcomputer to facilitate learning
in Drew's newly initiated computer-integrated
curriculum. Snelson, a librarian at Drew, discusses the decision and implementation of the
curriculum, along with the library's involvement
in the initiative.

914 STAHL, J. NATALIA, and VALENTE, RICHARD D.
"Plug-In Center for Students." American
Libraries 15 (November 1984): 724.
Clarkson University's decision to supply
each incoming student with a microcomputer, the
corresponding establishment of an Educational

Resources Center, and their impact on the library are discussed.

915 THOMPSON, GLENN J. "Bibliographic Instruction: Computer Use in LMED 100, How to Use the Library." College and Research Libraries News 45 (February 1984): 83.

LMED 100, University of Wisconsin at Eau Claire's library orientation course, was computerized in 1983 using the university's mainframe; however, lessons are also made available on disk for use with the IBM PC. An automated program for checking and recording student achievement is in place, and communication is accomplished through an interactive electronic mail system.

916 TROUTNER, JOANNE JOHNSON. "The Issue of Teaching Typing." Educational Computer Magazine 3 (November/December 1983): 14, 48.

As school library media centers automate catalogs and circulation and add public access computer centers for CAI programs, students who do not know the typewriter keyboard are at a disadvantage. Troutner predicts that typing will soon become a part of the elementary curriculum, and suggests aids available to the media specialist to assist in teaching typing skills. Bibliography.

917 TROUTNER, JOANNE JOHNSON. "The Magic of Interactive Video." Top of the News 39 (Summer 1983): 337-40.

A method of developing interactive video lessons is outlined, and the configuration of an interactive video system, employing an Apple II Plus micro with an interface card for videotape or videodisc, a television monitor, and a videotape player, is described.

918 ZSIRAY, STEPHEN W., Jr. "A Comparison of Three Instructional Approaches in Teaching the Use of the Abridged Readers' Guide to Periodical Literature." Journal of Educational Technology Systems 12, no. 3 (1983-84): 241-47.

Three different methods of teaching a

library skill were tested on a random sampling of
eighth grade English students. There was no dif-
ference found in the effectiveness of the lecture
method as compared to a microcomputer tutorial,
but both lecture and micro proved more effective
than independent reading as a method of learning.
Bibliography.

919 ZSIRAY, STEPHEN W., Jr. "Using the Microcomputer
to Develop Library Media/Information Research
Skills." Computing Teacher 9 (May 1982): 15-
19.
        A microcomputer-based library instruction
program for a middle school library/media center
is described, and the program for teaching use of
the Abridged Readers' Guide is included. Bibliography.

COMMUNICATIONS AND ONLINE SEARCHING

920 ATKINSON, STEVEN D., and WATKINS, STEVEN G.
"Managing Database Information: A Microcomputer Application in a Computer Search Service."
Online 9 (January 1985): 52-66.
The authors describe a microcomputer-
based program for maintaining current information
concerning online databases. The program runs on
an Osborne Executive I microcomputer with PERSON-
AL PEARL software. Bibliography.

921 BASCH, REVA. "For Electronic Cottages: Kudos and
Caveats." Technicalities 4 (May 1984): 10-11.
Telecommuting, working at home and communicating via microcomputer with the workplace,
is addressed. Advantages and disadvantages are
explored, and the concept is discussed in reference to librarianship.

922 BEAN, CHRISTOPHER A. "Softerm and Its Use in
Online Searching." Online 8 (September 1984):
52-56.
Sweet Briar College has been using an
Apple IIe microcomputer and SOFTERM communication
software for online database searching since
March, 1983. A step-by-step description of
search techniques is provided, including both
downloading and uploading procedures. A word on
macros is added. Bibliography.

923 BEARD, JOSEPH J. "Copyright Law and Downloading." Downloading/Uploading Online Databases
and Catalogs. Proceedings of the Congress for
Librarians, St. John's University, Jamaica,
New York, 18 February 1985. Library Hi Tech
Special Studies Series, no. 1. Ann Arbor, MI:
Pierian Press, 1985. Pp. 60-67.
The history of the computer data/copy-
right issue is traced from the 1960s, in order to
provide background for the author's discussion of
ownership and copyright protection of databases,

user restrictions, the doctrine of fair use, and
the role of the courts in moderating the controversy. Bibliography.

924 BELL, A. J.; BELL, ANNE; and SMITH, N. R. "Using
a General Purpose Microcomputer to Aid the
Searching of Bibliographic Databases." Program 16 (October 1982): 200-08.
       The use of a micro for online searching
is studied. Log-on commands and search strategies
may be placed on a disk then transmitted to the
host computer utilizing a program called LIB. The
product of the search can then be downloaded onto
a disk and printed out at the searcher's convenience. Details of sending, interrupting, and al-
tering a search are provided, as is an evaluation
of the total search procedure. Bibliography.

925 BENDIG, MARK. "Using Your Personal Computer for
OCLC Dial Access--What Do You Press After You
Press Return?" OCLC Micro 1 (March 1985): 10-
11, 18.
       As OCLC dial-access users consider
switching from dumb terminals to microcomputers,
they want to know what software best suits
their needs, and how the programs operate. In
response, Bendig recommends three communications
packages, then adds a discussion of control keys
and macros.

926 BENSON, JAMES A. "Glossary of Uploading/Down-
loading." Downloading/Uploading Online Databases and Catalogs. Proceedings of the Congress for Librarians, St. John's University,
Jamaica, New York, 18 February 1985. Library
Hi Tech Special Studies Series, no. 1. Ann
Arbor, MI: Pierian Press, 1985. Pp. 96-101.
       Definitions of words commonly encountered
in the literature of online searching, downloading, and uploading are presented in concise terms
easily understood by the layperson.

927 BENSON, JAMES A. "Terminology of Downloading/
Uploading." Downloading/Uploading Online
Databases and Catalogs. Proceedings of the

Congress for Librarians, St. John's University, Jamaica, New York, 18 February 1985. Library Hi Tech Special Studies Series, no. 1. Ann Arbor, MI: Pierian Press, 1985. Pp. 1-6.

The terminology of downloading and uploading of data is presented categorically, addressing the broad areas of telecommunications hardware, telecommunications software, applications software, and specialized library bibliographic software.

928 BENSON, JAMES A., and WEINBERG, BELLA HASS. "Downloading Policies." Downloading/Uploading Online Databases and Catalogs. Proceedings of the Congress for Librarians, St. John's University, Jamaica, New York, 18 February 1985. Library Hi Tech Special Studies Series, no. 1. Ann Arbor, MI: Pierian Press, 1985. Pp. 75-95.

The downloading policies of twenty representative online databases and database vendors are presented. Among those included are Chemical Abstracts Service, Dialog Informations Services, Excerpta Medica, Newsnet, and PsychINFO.

929 BLAIR, JOHN C., Jr. "Interfacing Micros and Mainframes; Downloading and Uploading; New Ways to Distribute Databases via Floppy Disks and Video Disks." Database 5 (December 1982): 76-81.

The use of the microcomputer as an interface to mainframes is considered, with methods of communication, operating software, preprocessing, downloading, and video technology addressed.

930 BROOKS, KRISTINA M. "The Online Transfer of Machine Readable Data: A Pandora's Box." Database 5 (February 1982): 18-21.

The author discusses problems of online transfer of machine-readable data from a vendor file to a local computer for reformatting and local use. A 1975 project conducted by the Oregon State University Library is cited, and recent microcomputer procedures are discussed. Bibliography.

931 BRUMAN, JANET L. "Communications Software for
      Microcomputers." Arlington, VA: ERIC Docu-
      ment Reproduction Service, ED 234 740, 1983.
        Use of the microcomputer as a smart
terminal for online searching in libraries is
analyzed, including the software necessary, its
functions, and its operation. Additional functions such as electronic mail, bulletin boards,
and file transfers are also discussed. Software
evaluation and selection are considered, and purchase information is provided on seventy-five
communications programs.

932 BRUMAN, JANET L. "Communications Software:
      Keeping in Touch with the Outside World."
      Online '82 Conference Proceedings, Atlanta,
      1-3 November 1982. Weston, CT: Online, Inc.,
      1982. Pp. 112-19.
        The functions of a microcomputer communi-
cations package are considered, from such basics
as communications protocols, screen display, uploading, downloading, editing, and printer controls, to enhancements and advanced options.
Bibliography.

933 BRUMAN, JANET L. "Smart Terminal Software Pack-
      ages for Microcomputers." Proceedings of the
      4th National Online Meeting, New York, 12-14
      April 1983. Medford, NJ: Learned Information,
      1983. Pp. 75-81.
        Functions of communications software for
the microcomputer are explained. Discussed are
features and options which enhance operation and
influence selection of communications packages.

934 BUCKINGHAM, SARAH. "Choosing an End-User On Line
      Searching System." Education Libraries 10,
      no. 2/3 (1985): 41-44.
        The number and type of end user oriented
online search services is increasing steadily,
and the librarian wanting to offer end user access is faced with choosing a service or services
which respond to the needs of both the patron and
the library. This article outlines criteria for
evaluating end user services, and provides infor-

mation about the four major categories of end
user systems: software, gateways, user friendly
vendors, and straight vendors. An appendix is
included which lists several search systems, with
addresses for further inquiries.

935 BURNAM, JUDY K.; FARRELL, EILEEN; and LEVINE,
EMIL H. "Enhancing Online Searching and Other
Library Operations Using an Intelligent Floppy
Disk System." Proceedings of the 3rd National
Online Meeting, New York, 30 March-1 April
1982. Medford, NJ: Learned Information, 1982.
Pp. 41-46.
The Trendata Flexible Disk System, an
intelligent unit which can interface with a dumb
terminal to enhance online searching and communications, is described. Applications to online
searching, circulation, interlibrary loan, cataloging, acquisitions, electronic mail, and office
management are suggested. Bibliography.

936 CAPUTO, ANNE S. "Online Goes to School: Instruction and Use of Online Systems in Secondary
and Elementary Education." Proceedings of the
6th National Online Meeting, New York, 30
April-2 May 1985. Medford, NJ: Learned Information, 1985. Pp. 85-90.
Interest in searching online databases is
growing in many secondary schools. Such student
benefits as gaining a better understanding of research methods, greater awareness of information
sources, and enjoyment of research are often bal-
anced by cost barriers, lack of curriculum support, and conflict/competition between teachers
and librarians for computer literacy responsibilities. Caputo discusses benefits, barriers, and
the future of online services in secondary and
elementary schools.

937 CARL, DAVID L. "Library Media Specialists and
Instructional Development: A Probe of the Lit-
erature via Microcomputer." School Library
Media Quarterly 10 (Winter 1982): 158-63.
An example of an interactive microcom-
puter search program is provided for study.

938 CASBON, SUSAN. "Online Searching With a Micro-
computer--Getting Started." Online 7 (November 1983): 42-46.
The basics of online searching by microcomputer are treated. The trend toward microcomputer use is acknowledged, advantages and disadvantages are explored, legal implications are
considered, and selection of equipment and software is discussed. Bibliography.

939 "Center for Rural Librarianship Offers Electronic
Mail Service." Wilson Library Bulletin 59
(December 1984): 250.
Ruraline, an electronic mail service
which employs microcomputer technology for transmission, is announced and described in this news
item. Established by Clarion University's Center
for the Study of Rural Librarianship, the service
is a part of TYMNET's OnTyme-II network.

940 "Challenge of Data Downloading." Electronic
Library 1 (October 1983): 226.
Carlos Cuadra suggests that microcomputer
technology could lead to large-scale piracy of
database information if database vendors don't
make and enforce user policies and guidelines for
downloading.

941 CHRISTIAN, DEBORAH. "Dial-Up Databases: Delving
into the Utility Concept." ACCESS: Microcomputers in Libraries 1 (July 1981): 3, 19.
The three major bibliographic utilities
now offer dial-up access to their databases,
which can be achieved by use of microcomputer
equipment. However, input requirements are re-
strictive, and user charges are prohibitive for
small libraries. An alternative is the establishment of an independent dial-up utility, which
the author proposes and encourages potential
users to promote.

942 CITROEN, CHARLES L. "Multiuser Microcomputer-
Assisted Access to Online Systems." Proceedings of the 7th International Online Information Meeting, London, 6-8 December 1983.

Medford, NJ: Learned Information, 1983. Pp.
37-44.
    A microcomputer-based online search sys-
tem developed for the Centre for Information and
Documentation-The Netherlands Organization (CID-
TNO) is described. The system offers large volume data storage, extensive text editing capabilities, and simultaneous searching by multiple
users. Bibliography.

943 COLLINS, JOHN. "Personal Computers and Remote
     Library Access: What If You Had a Library and
     Nobody Came?" Education Libraries 9 (Spring
     1984): 19-20.
        Technology has made possible remote
access to libraries via telecommunications and
the home microcomputer. This is seen as a trend
for the future. Basics of the technology are explained; library involvement is encouraged. Bibliography.

944 CRAWFORD, WALT. "Common Sense and Telecommunica-
     tions; or, Reach Out, But Watch Your Wallet."
     Library Hi Tech 3, no. 1, issue 9 (1985):
     69-77.
        Crawford does a thorough cost analysis of
online searching with a microcomputer. He considers necessary hardware and software, discussing a range of options based on price, then
identifies standard information services with
access costs. Bibliography.

945 CROOKS, JAMES E. "End User Searching at the
     University of Michigan Library." Proceedings
     of the 6th National Online Meeting, New York,
     30 April-2 May 1985. Medford, NJ: Learned
     Information, 1985. Pp. 99-110.
        During the fall term of 1984 the Univer-
sity of Michigan Library offered free access to
the BRS/AFTER DARK database to faculty, staff,
and students wishing to do independent online
searching. The project is outlined. Data gathering and analysis techniques are described, but
neither results of the data analysis nor conclusions are reported.

946 CUADRA, CARLOS A. "The Microcomputer Link: Online Database Services and Local Electronic
Libraries." National Forum: Phi Kappa Phi
Journal 63 (Summer 1983): 23-24, 32.
The historical development of online
searching and online bibliographic databases
is summarized, specific databases are described
in order to illustrate the variety available,
and the impact of the microcomputer on database
development and online searching is related.

947 CUADRA ASSOCIATES. "Downloading Policy Study."
Library Hi Tech News 1 (May 1984): 1, 10-11.
The issues involved in the downloading of
copyrighted data from online databases are summarized, and several questions pertaining to the
problem are posed. A research study by Cuadra
Associates, which supplies answers to such questions as volume, reasons for downloading, and use
of downloaded data, is described and reviewed.

948 "Cuadra Associates Launches Multiclient Study of
'Downloading'." Online Review 7 (June 1983):
196-97.
The ethics of downloading from online
databases via microcomputer are addressed. A
study of the problem is announced, to be conducted by Cuadra Associates.

949 "Cuadra Calls for Ground-Rules on Downloading."
Electronic Library 1 (April 1983): 90-91.
In a speech given at the Online '82
Conference, Carlos Cuadra encouraged database
publishers to address the problem of downloading,
which has become prevalent with the increased
popularity of microcomputers in libraries. The
speech is summarized.

950 "Cuadra Looks at Database Downloading." Infor-
mation Retrieval and Library Automation 19
(December 1983): 4-5.
At the Information Industry Association
Annual Meeting, held in November, 1983, Judith
Wanger, vice-president of Cuadra Associates, de-
scribed a project concerning downloading of data

from online databases. She defines the problem and states the objectives of the study, but provides little information concerning the findings. The full report is available from Cuadra Associates for $1450.

951 DesCHENE, DORICE. "Online Searching by End Users." RQ 25 (Fall 1985): 89-95.
The trend toward end user online searching is escalating with the proliferation of microcomputers and the increased efforts of vendors to promote their services. DesChene addresses the questions of funding, staffing, staff roles, training, equipment, and space responsibilities that libraries face because of increasing end user expectations. Bibliography.

952 DEWEY, PATRICK R. "A Professional Librarian Looks at the Consumer Online Services. . .The Source, CompuServe, Apple Bulletin Board, et al." Online 7 (September 1983): 36-41.
Differences between online databases and consumer network services are pointed up; THE SOURCE and COMPUSERVE are evaluated in detail; GAMEMASTER is described; and such bulletin board services as APPLE BULLETIN BOARD SYSTEM and PEOPLE'S MESSAGE SYSTEM are compared. Bibliography.

953 DOLAN, DONNA R. "Downloading and Integrated Software." Database 8 (June 1985): 86-89.
Integrated software has enhanced the process of searching and downloading from online databases. Dolan identifies eleven integrated software packages that support downloading, reviews downloading applications, and provides guidelines for selecting integrated software with telecommunications capabilities.

954 "ERIC to SCIL--Without Retyping." Small Computers in Libraries 1 (October 1981): 4-6.
The editor of Small Computers in Libraries describes how he conducted an ERIC search through DIALOG using a microcomputer. Entries were stored on the microcomputer's floppy disk, edited, and a paper copy was printed out for

publication without retyping. The bibliography
is included.

955 EISENBERG, MICHAEL. "The Direct Use of Online
Bibliographic Information Systems by Untrained
End Users." The Application of Mini- and
Micro-Computers in Information, Documentation
and Libraries. Proceedings of the International Conference on the Application of Mini-
and Micro-Computers in Information, Documentation and Libraries, Tel-Aviv, Israel, 13-18
March 1983. New York: North-Holland, 1983.
Pp. 611-17.
        In this review of the literature concern-
ing end user access to online bibliographic utilities, Eisenberg identifies problems and solutions, considers training for users, and suggests
modifications to make systems user friendly. In
the process, he identifies the role of microcomputer technology in developing easily accessible
systems. Bibliography.

956 "Electronic Mail for Libraries in the West."
Small Computers in Libraries 1 (December
1981): 6.
        The electronic mail system, offered by
the California Library Authority for Systems and
Services (CLASS) and used by many libraries
throughout the midwest and west for interlibrary
loan, is described.

957 "Enhancement of On-line Information Retrieval
Using a Microprocessor-Assisted Terminal."
British Library Research and Development
Newsletter 20 (May 1980): 6.
        This brief news note announces a British
Library grant to Dr. P. W. Williams of the University of Manchester to study use of the microcomputer in automatic translation of command
languages and the use of simplified dialogues in
online searching.

958 EVANS, NANCY, and PISCIOTTA, HENRY. "Search
Helper: Testing Acceptance of a Gateway Software System." Proceedings of the 6th National

Online Meeting, New York, 30 April-2 May 1985. Medford, NJ: Learned Information, 1985. Pp. 131-36.

In order to test the acceptance of end user online searching, SEARCH HELPER software was made available to Carnegie-Mellon University Library patrons, for their use, with little or no instruction or assistance. A survey of users was conducted, and the results, indicating a generally high level of satisfaction, are reported here. Bibliography.

959 FEENEY, MARY J., and MILLER, RUTH. "Downloading: Piracy or Panacea?" Journal of Information Science 8 (February 1984): 7-11.

The copying of data from an online source onto private disks for later manipulation and use is examined from both the vendor and the user perspective. Copyright laws are reviewed. User practices and vendor policies are considered. Bibliography.

960 FENICHEL, CAROL HANSEN. "Using a Microcomputer to Communicate: Part I: The Basics." Microcomputers for Information Management 2 (June 1985): 59-76.

The author considers the advantages of using a microcomputer as a terminal for online searching, the peripherals necessary for such a project, and features to look for in choosing communications software. Appendices provide source information for modems and software packages. Bibliography.

961 FENICHEL, CAROL HANSEN, and MURPHY, JOHN J. "Using a Microcomputer to Communicate: Part 2: Specialized Software." Microcomputers for Information Management 2 (September 1985): 155-70.

This second installment of a series on online communication via microcomputer considers front end and gateway software written specifically to expedite online searching of remote databases. Specific functions of these software programs are considered. An appendix provides purchase information for several popular examples. Bibliography.

962 FERGUSON, CHERYL L., and BALLARD, ROBERT M. "Downloading and Copyright: A Selected Survey of Special Librarians and Database Suppliers." Sci-Tech News 39 (January 1985): 17-19.
Database vendors have become concerned with the loss of property rights since microcomputer access to online databases made downloading a reality. A survey of selected special librarians and database vendors examines the extent of downloading and possible violation of rights by librarians and the policies of vendors regarding downloading and possible infringement. Bibliography.

963 FERRANTE, BARBARA K.; CARLE, LEONARD W.; KUBLI, MARY K.; and VECHT, EMMA S. "Hardware for Downloading/Uploading." Downloading/Uploading Online Databases and Catalogs. Proceedings of the Congress for Librarians, St. John's University, Jamaica, New York, 18 February 1985. Library Hi Tech Special Studies Series, no. 1. Ann Arbor, MI: Pierian Press, 1985. Pp. 7-12.
The authors define downloading and uploading, and consider the host processor, the communications link, and the local system (microcomputer or terminal and modem), which are essential to the task. Downloading and uploading procedures are considered step by step. Solutions to some possible problems are suggested.

964 FOSTER, ALLAN. "Extending the Electronic Library by Downloading: Its Advantages and Disadvantages." Library Association Record 86 (September 1984): 358-59.
Foster reviews the literature of downloading via microcomputer, discussing its merits, legal aspects, and economics, with a section about downloading from bibliographic utilities, and another concerning software. Bibliography.

965 FRIEND, LINDA. "Independence at the Terminal: Training Student End Users to Do Online Lit-

erature Searching." Journal of Academic
Librarianship 11 (July 1985): 136-41.
A program instituted at Pennsylvania
State University to teach students the basics of
online searching through microcomputer access to
BRS/AFTER DARK is described and evaluated. Teaching methodology is described, mechanics of data
gathering is explained, and data analysis is presented, with conclusions. Bibliography.

966 GARMAN, NANCY J., and PASK, JUDITH M. "End User
Searching in Business and Management." Proceedings of the 6th National Online Meeting,
New York, 30 April-2 May 1985. Medford, NJ:
Learned Information, 1985. Pp. 161-65.
As a unit in an investment class in
Purdue University's School of Management, librarians taught students how to search the DOW JONES
NEWS/RETRIEVAL SERVICE database using the library's microcomputer and DSNLink software. The
authors describe the project and report the
results of a survey of participants indicating
positive responses to the experience. Bibliography.

967 GENAWAY, DAVID C. "Microcomputers as Interfaces
to Bibliographic Utilities (OCLC, RLN, etc.)."
Online 7 (May 1983): 21-27.
Options for interfacing with bibliographic utilities via microcomputer are increasing.
This article lists several of the interface systems available, describes the TPS system in
detail, suggests criteria for choosing a system,
and discusses advantages and limitations of
interfacing. Bibliography.

968 GILLETTE, MEREDITH. "The Use of Microcomputers
for Online Demonstrations and Instruction."
Online '82 Conference Proceedings, Atlanta,
1-3 November 1982. Weston, CT: Online, Inc.,
1982. Pp. 341-43.
Gillette describes the use of the microcomputer at the University of Wisconsin-Oshkosh
Library to demonstrate searching of both commercial and in-house files. Problems encountered

and obstacles overcome are given equal time.
Bibliography.

969 GLOSSBRENNER, ALFRED. The Complete Handbook of
Personal Computer Communications: Everything
You Need to Go Online With the World. New
York: St. Martin's, 1983. 325p.

An introduction to online communications
via microcomputer provides information on necessary software and peripherals, types of online
information and services available, and how to
access information sources. THE SOURCE, COMPU-
SERVE, THE DOW JONES NEWS/RETRIEVAL SERVICE,
DIALOG, BRS, ORBIT, and other online information
sources are described in individual chapters, and
eight appendices discuss such topics as the ASCII
Code Set, using Telenet and Tymnet, and using the
personal computer as a typesetter.

970 GRIFFITH, JEFFREY C. "The Impact of the Enduser
on the Online Profession." Online '84 Conference Proceedings, San Francisco, 29-31
October 1984. Weston, CT: Online, Inc., 1984.
Pp. 129-33.

Three factors--the increase in the amount
of machine readable data, the development of
online catalogs in libraries, and the proliferation of the microcomputer--are fostering the
growth of end user demand for database access.
These are leading to increased online use by non-
professionals, combined online services, easier
access, simpler pricing, and a need for standards
for both the user and vendor.

971 GRIFFITH, JEFFREY C. "Why Can't I Do It?
Emerging Training Concerns of End Users and
Online Professionals." Online '83 Conference
Proceedings, Chicago, 10-12 October 1983.
Weston, CT: Online, Inc., 1983. Pp. 77-81.

As microcomputers become prevalent in
homes, offices, and libraries, and online vendors
take steps to accommodate the potential end user
market, user demographics will change. Griffith
analyzes these changes, considers the training
necessary to do end user searching, and predicts

the simplification of system mechanics to implement ease of access. Bibliography.

972 GRIFFITHS, JOSE-MARIE. "Microcomputers and Online Activities." American Society for Information Science Bulletin 10 (April 1984): 11-14.
The parallel growth of the online information and microcomputer industries and the impact of one upon the other make an examination of their interrelationships essential to understanding trends in their development. The author considers the relationship from the perspective of the database creator, the service or network operator, the librarian or information broker, and the end user. Bibliography.

973 GROTOPHORST, CLYDE W. "Another Method for Editing Downloaded Files." Online 8 (September 1984): 85-93.
The editing and reformatting of downloaded bibliographic data with word processing software is time consuming and costly. A program written at George Mason University eases the process enabling librarians to download, edit, and produce bibliographies for patron and vertical file use. The program is included.

974 GROTOPHORST, CLYDE W. "Training University Faculty as End-Use Searchers: a CAI Approach." Proceedings of the 5th National Online Meeting, New York, 10-12 April 1984. Medford, NJ: Learned Information, 1984. Pp. 77-82.
Fenwick Library of George Mason University has instituted an end user online search program for its faculty. The program, which includes written instruction, consultation between trainee and an experienced searcher, and access to equipment and passwords, is described and evaluated, and the future of the program is discussed. Bibliography.

975 HALPERIN, MICHAEL, and PAGELL, RUTH A. "Free 'Do-It-Yourself' Online Searching. . .What to Expect." Online 9 (March 1985): 82-84.
The Lippincott Library of the University

of Pennsylvania began offering free end user online searching in April, 1984. In this article
two librarians discuss the databases offered,
consider policies and procedures, and share their
impressions of the benefits, drawbacks, and the
value of the project. Bibliography.

976 HANDZEL, RUTH; ZAKHEM, RINA; and SUPINO, GIULIO.
"Preliminary Report: Microcomputer Software
for Online Information Retrieval." The Application of Mini- and Micro-Computers in Information, Documentation and Libraries. Proceedings of the International Conference on the
Application of Mini- and Micro-Computers in
Information, Documentation and Libraries, Tel-
Aviv, Israel, 13-18 March 1983. New York:
North-Holland, 1983. Pp. 619-24.
     The development of an in-house micro-
computer software package for performing online
database searches is described by librarians of
the Life Sciences Library of Tel-Aviv University.
Bibliography.

977 HAWKINS, DONALD T. "To Download or Not to Download Online Searches." Online '82 Conference
Proceedings, Atlanta, 1-3 November 1982.
Weston, CT: Online, Inc., 1982. Pp. 3-7.
     Advantages and disadvantages of down-
loading search results from online databases are
considered, with disadvantages seemingly out-
weighing advantages. Major advantages are the
ability to reformat and repackage search results
and the ability to transmit the results to the
requestor via micro communications. Disadvantages are the cost of the equipment and software,
time required to manipulate and print data after
downloading, and possible copyright infringement.
Bibliography.

978 HAWKINS, DONALD T., and BLAIR, JOHN C., Jr. "A
Poetic View of Downloading Online Searches."
Online 7 (March 1983): 64.
     Hamlet's Soliloquy provides form, if not
substance, for this poetic justification for the
use of micros in online searching.

979 HAWKINS, DONALD T., and LEVY, LOUISE R. "Front
End Software for Online Database Searching,
Part 1: Definitions, System Features, and
Evaluation." Online 9 (November 1985): 30-37.
The first in a series of three articles
concerning front end and gateway systems for
online searching, this article provides background information including history, definitions, and a description of front end software,
discussing the features which every good front
end program should provide.

980 "Hertfordshire Library Service." Vine no. 42
(March 1982): 41-42.
Hertfordshire (UK) Library Service began
offering online searching in 1981, using an Apple
II microcomputer with OWLTERM and VISITERM software. A special feature of the service is a
chart, prepared on the micro, which provides
staff and patrons with cost approximations prior
to going online.

981 HLAVA, MARJORIE M. K. "State of the Art 1985:
Special Libraries/Online Technologies."
Special Libraries 76 (Spring 1985): 121-25.
Hlava surveys the use of online technology in special libraries, providing historical
background and future projections concerning
online searching, analyzing the changes wrought
by improved telecommunications technology, and
predicting increased productivity as librarians
begin telecommuting via microcomputer.

982 HOLMES, P. L. "The Re-Use of Machine Readable
Data and Copyright—A Pragmatic Approach to
the Problems." Proceedings of the 4th International Online Information Meeting, London,
9-11 December 1980. Medford, NJ: Learned
Information, 1980. Pp. 1-13.
Holmes acknowledges the growing number of
microprocessors used in accessing online databases, and discusses the impact of copyright on
access to and use of the acquired data. He
offers solutions and alternatives to the problems
which confound most users. Bibliography.

983 HULEATT, RICHARD S. "Data Downloading: A Report
on Who Does What. . .To Whom." Online '81
Conference Proceedings, Dallas, 2-4 November
1981. Weston, CT: Online, Inc., 1981. Pp.
173-75.
Downloading of information from online
resources is becoming increasingly popular with
the growing use of microcomputers. Users, particularly librarians, are encouraged to become
aware of any restrictions written into contracts
with online vendors, and to be cautious about
downloading and distributing copyrighted data.

984 HUNTER, JANNE A. "What Did You Say the End-User
Was Going to Do at the Terminal, and How Much
is it Going to Cost?" Proceedings of the 4th
National Online Meeting, New York, 12-14 April
1983. Medford, NJ: Learned Information, 1983.
Pp. 223-29.
The quality of an online search is not
necessarily related to the status of the searcher, although an intermediary is more likely than
a less experienced end user to perform an effective and efficient search. Hunter addresses the
difficulties of searching large databases, and
considers developments which seem necessary
before end user searching becomes widespread.

985 HUNTER, JANNE A. "When Your Patrons Want to
Search--The Library as Advisor to End Users
. . .A Compendium of Advice and Tips." Online
8 (May 1984): 36-41.
End user database searching is growing
popular as microcomputers proliferate, as demands
on intermediaries increase, and as database vendors recognize the potential of the market. Hunter addresses the services libraries should provide the end user, including guidance in file
selection and equipment use, training in online
search strategies, equipment, software, and document delivery. Bibliography.

986 INKELLIS, BARBARA G. "Legal Issues of Downloading Online Search Results." Online '82
Conference Proceedings, Atlanta, 1-3 November

<u>1982</u>. Weston, CT: Online, Inc., 1982. Pp.
91-92.
An analogy is drawn between downloading
data from online databases and the photocopying
of materials which appear in printed form. Sections of the Copyright Revision Act of 1976 concerning photocopy are applied to the copying of
machine-readable data via microcomputer.

987 JAMIESON, STEPHEN H., and ODDY, ROBERT N. "Low-
Cost Implementation of Experimental Retrieval
Techniques for Online Users." <u>Proceedings of
the 4th International Online Information Meeting, London, 9-11 December 1980.</u> Medford, NJ:
Learned Information, 1980. Pp. 201-09.
A research project which employs a micro
to translate non-Boolean search strategies into
a series of Boolean statements for online search
purposes is described. Bibliography.

988 JANKE, RICHARD V. "Just What <u>Is</u> an End User?"
<u>Online '84 Conference Proceedings, San Fran-
cisco, 29-31 October 1984.</u> Weston, CT: Online, Inc., 1984. Pp. 148-54.
Janke traces the do-it-yourself trend
in libraries from the early 1900s, when patrons
wanted and were encouraged to use the card catalog and indexes, to the present, in which libraries are making public use micros available
for do-it-yourself online searching. He then
concludes that the do-it-yourself patron or end
user is a library standard, and is here to stay.
Bibliography.

989 JANKE, RICHARD V. "Online After Six at the University of Ottawa." <u>Online '83 Conference
Proceedings, Chicago, 10-12 October 1983.</u>
Weston, CT: Online, Inc., 1983. Pp. 124-29.
In March 1983 the University of Ottawa
Library launched Online After Six, a pilot project to determine interest in end user online
search services. Janke summarizes the project,
addressing method, publicity, planning, regulations, patron training, and acceptance. Bibliography.

990 JANKE, RICHARD V. "Online After Six: End User
Searching Comes of Age." Online 8 (November
1984): 15-29.
   The University of Ottawa pioneered end
user searching in 1983. After a year, the project was evaluated, and the results reported,
addressing such issues as cost, regulation, staff
training, publicity, and implications for the
library. A feature of the article is a comparison of online searching performed by end users
and by trained intermediaries. Bibliography.

991 JANKE, RICHARD V. "Presearch Counseling for
Client Searchers (End-Users)." Online 9
(September 1985): 13-26.
   The University of Ottawa Libraries, one
of the pioneers in end user searching via microcomputer, has developed a presearch counseling
program to help end users make the best use of
their time. Janke defines presearch counseling,
compares it to the presearch interview performed
by an online intermediary, and outlines a typical
presearch counseling session. Bibliography.

992 JANSEN, ARNOLD A. J. "Problems and Challenges of
Downloading for Database Producers." Electronic Library 2 (January 1984): 41-51.
   Downloading of data from online databases
may constitute a violation of copyright. Since
microcomputers are increasing the instances of
downloading, database producers must consider new
guidelines and price structures for the use of
their services. The problem is discussed and
solutions are proposed. Bibliography.

993 KAPLAN, ROBIN. "Online Searching: Introducing
the Inevitable." Library Journal 110 (May 1,
1985): 122-23; and School Library Journal 31
(May 1985): 152-53.
   This introduction to online searching via
microcomputer deals with equipment, database vendors, the product, and the reference interview.

994 KESSELMAN, MARTIN. "Front-End/Gateway Software:
Availability and Usefulness." Library Soft-

ware Review 4 (March/April 1985): 67-70.
Kesselman differentiates between front-
end and gateway systems for use with microcomputers in online searching, and reviews several
front-ends and gateways, including IN SEARCH, PC
NET/LINK, SEARCH HELPER, SEARCH MASTER, SCI-MATE,
SUPERSCOUT, and EASYNET. Selection criteria are
also considered.

995 KETCHELL, DEBRA S. "Online Searching by Microcomputer." Medical Library Association
Bulletin 72 (October 1984): 370-72.
The Savitt Medical Library of the University of Nevada is using an IBM PC microcomputer
with a Hayes Smartmodem and SMARTCOM II software
for online searching. Advantages, special features, and limitations of the system are considered.

996 KEYHANI, ANDREA. "Dial Access to OCLC With Your
Own Microcomputer or an M300." M300 and PC
Report 2 (June 1985): 3-5.
Dial access to OCLC's database is now
possible, and more than 20% of OCLC's member libraries are taking advantage of the option, using
microcomputers and M300s as terminals. This
article describes the method, lists equipment
requirements, considers benefits, and discusses
the M300 as a dial-up terminal.

997 KILLEN, DIANA. "Copyright and Computers: The Use
of Machine-Readable Databases." Australian
Library Journal 32 (August 1983): 15-22.
The law has failed to keep pace with
technology in the area of copyright, and Killen
discusses the problems from an Australian perspective, with frequent references to American
database services and law. Bibliography.

998 KIRKENDALL, CAROLYN. "Online Reference Services'
Impact on Bibliographic Instruction." Research Strategies 3 (Winter 1985): 40-43.
The increasing availability of online
search services will impact on the demand for
bibliographic instruction, as well as on methods

and content of BI programs in libraries. Five
librarians respond to these and other issues in
symposium style.

999 KLAUSMEIER, JANE A. "ERIC MICROsearch: Searching
ERIC on a Microcomputer." Library Software
Review 4 (March/April 1985): 63-66.
    A thorough explanation of ERIC MICRO-
search is found in this article. Step-by-step
procedures, with prompts and explanatory notes
lead the reader through the program from booting
up to printing data.

1000 KLAUSMEIER, JANE A. "Microcomputer Based System
for End User Training." Proceedings of the
6th National Online Meeting, New York, 30
April-2 May 1985. Medford, NJ: Learned Information, 1985. Pp. 265-71.
    Thirty-five library schools, academic
libraries, and secondary schools known to use the
MICROsearch system for online searching and end
user training were surveyed concerning primary
uses, satisfaction, and shortcomings. Research
concerning simulators for online training is reviewed, and interviews with survey respondents
are summarized. Bibliography.

1001 KLAUSMEIER, JANE A. "MICROsearch: ERIC's Approach
to the Downloading Dilemma." Proceedings of
the 5th National Online Meeting, New York, 10-
12 April 1984. Medford, NY: Learned Information, 1984. Pp. 149-54.
    Downloading concerns of both the online
vendor and the user are expressed, and the MICRO-
search program designed by ERIC to help alleviate
the problem is explained. The philosophy behind
MICROsearch, required hardware, benefits, and
limitations are addressed. Bibliography.

1002 KLAUSMEIER, JANE A. "MICROsearch: The Many Uses
of a Downloaded Database." Microcomputers for
Information Management 2 (March 1985): 25-32.
    MICROsearch, a program developed by the
Educational Resources Information Center (ERIC)
to provide subscribers with ERIC bibliographic

data on floppy disks, is described, and such uses as bibliographic updates, bibliographic searching, and instruction in online search techniques are discussed. Bibliography.

1003 KLEINER, JANE P. "User Searching: A Public Access Approach to Search Helper." RQ 24 (Summer 1985): 442-51.
In 1983 the Troy H. Middleton Library of Louisiana State University instituted end user searching of online databases with SEARCH HELPER software. Kleiner evaluates the project after a year, addressing the library's organizational efforts, publicity, problems, and results. Bibliography.

1004 KOLNER, STUART J. "The IBM PC as an Online Search Machine--Part 1: Anatomy for Searchers." Online 9 (January 1985): 37-42.
The author addresses the question, "Why IBM?" then considers each component--the computer, the keyboard, the monitor, the printer, the modem--essential to an IBM online search system.

1005 KOLNER, STUART J. "The IBM PC as an Online Search Machine--Part 2: Physiology for Searchers." Online 9 (March 1985): 39-46.
A practical guide for the selection and installation of an IBM PC for online searching, this article addresses purchase (including a list of necessary components), unpacking, and assembly of the system.

1006 KOLNER, STUART J. "The IBM PC as an Online Search Machine--Part 3: Introduction to Software." Online 9 (May 1985): 44-50.
The third in a series of articles concerning the IBM PC as an online searching tool addresses general software needs, categories of software, software selection and purchase, copyright, operating systems, disk preparation, and related topics.

1007 KOLNER, STUART J. "The IBM PC as an Online Search Machine--Part 4: Telecommunications

and Crosstalk XVI." Online 9 (July 1985):
27-34.
Telecommunications software is defined,
and the functions it performs are considered.
Several communications software packages are
mentioned, but only CROSSTALK XVI, the best of
the group, is considered in detail.

1008 KOLNER, STUART J. "The IBM PC as an Online
Search Machine--Part 5: Searching Through
CROSSTALK." Online 9 (November 1985): 42-50.
The fifth and last article in a series
concerning the use of the IBM PC in searching
online databases describes the performance of an
online search using CROSSTALK XVI software.
Step-by-step procedures are outlined, options
are defined, function keys are identified, and
problems are discussed.

1009 KRIEGER, TILLIE. "Using Microcomputers With
Online Systems." Louisiana Library Association Bulletin 46 (Summer 1983): 13-15.
This early article concerning online
database searching with a microcomputer describes
in simple terms the equipment necessary for online searching, briefly outlines the procedure,
and recommends some suitable search software.

1010 LANDRUM, HOLLIS. "ISRS: A Review." M300 and PC
Report 2 (November 1985): 5-8.
TGM Communication is producing a new
Interactive Simultaneous Remote Search (ISRS)
device which permits an online search to be
initiated from a remote location and conducted
while the patron remains in contact with the
intermediary. Hardware specifications, telecommunications programs, system operation, and
interactive searching are addressed.

1011 LESSIN, BARTON M., and GORDON, KELLY L. "Three
Micros and a Hard Disk Do Not a System Make."
Proceedings of the Conference on Integrated
Online Library Systems, Columbus, Ohio, 26-27
September 1983. Canfield, OH: Genaway &
Associates, 1983. Pp. 161-87.

Establishing a microcomputer-based remote access system to provide library services to students and faculty in off-campus programs is detailed. Using Radio Shack equipment, the Central Michigan University provides word processing, a selected online database, and spreadsheet capabilities. The system is described in full, with emphasis on remote access to the library's facilities.

1012 LEVY, LOUISE R. "Gateway Software: Is It for You?" Online 8 (November 1984): 67-79.
Gateway software, programs which interface between the user and the online vendor to expedite searching, are becoming increasingly popular. The author addresses features and capabilities of search software, using IN-SEARCH, THE UNIVERSAL ONLINE SEARCHER, SEARCH HELPER, and microDISCLOSURE as examples. Bibliography.

1013 LUCIA, JOSEPH, and ROYSDON, CHRISTINE. "Online Searching as an Educational Technology: Teaching Computer-Wise End Users." Proceedings of the 5th National Online Meeting, New York, 10-12 April 1984. Medford, NJ: Learned Information, 1984. Pp. 187-93.
A project to teach online searching to end users at Lehigh University is described. Taught by librarians using DECwriters, a Televideo 925 CRT, and an Apple II Plus microcomputer, the one credit hour course was taken largely by education graduate students interested in ERIC searching. Course mechanics, student response, and course and student evaluations are addressed.

1014 MACHALOW, ROBERT, and STIEGELBAUER, ALYCE. "Smartcom II for Database Searching: An Introduction." M300 and PC Report 2 (October 1985): 1-3.
Setting up SMARTCOM II software for online searching can be a problem for the novice. To help alleviate the frustration for the user, the authors provide step-by-step instructions for defining communications sets, originating a call, downloading, and printing.

1015 MARX, B; GHIRARDI, L.; and WOLFF-TERROINE, M. "A
    Computer-Aided Instruction Program for Devel-
    oping Use of Databases." Proceedings of the
    6th International Online Information Meeting,
    London, 7-9 December 1982. Medford, NJ:
    Learned Information, 1982. Pp. 135-42.
        A software tutorial written for the nov-
    ice user of online search services is described.
    Written in four modules, only the second, "Initi-
    ating an Online Search," is treated in detail.
    The program is written in BASIC and runs on a
    Fontaine microcomputer. Bibliography.

1016 MASON, ROBERT M. "Communications Software:
    Bringing the Outside World Into Your Micro."
    Online '83 Conference Proceedings, Chicago,
    10-12 October 1983. Weston, CT: Online, Inc.,
    1983. Pp. 193-97.
        The basics of an online communication
    system are explained in simple terms, covering
    definitions, functions, and features. Three
    communications programs--XMODEM, CROSSTALK, and
    MITE--are presented as examples.

1017 MASON, ROBERT M. "Communications Software: Link-
    ing Your Micro to Other Computers." Library
    Journal 108 (October 1, 1983): 1855-56.
        Linkage of an office micro with other
    computers for expanded storage is considered.
    Software is available for the purpose, but should
    be purchased with caution. Such necessary con-
    siderations as baud rate, parity, data bits, and
    stop bits are discussed, along with optional fea-
    tures such as storage of parameters, help files,
    documentation, and buffers.

1018 McKINNIE, WILLIAM G. "Online Bibliographic
    Searching in Secondary School Resource Cen-
    tres." Emergency Librarian 10 (January/
    February 1983): 8-11.
        A review of research on the topic of
    online searching in school libraries synthesizes
    several research articles on the topic. The
    microcomputer is recognized as a major influence
    in making the service possible. Bibliography.

1019 MELIN, NANCY. "Enlarging Micros: The Mainframe
     Connection." Wilson Library Bulletin 59
     (January 1985): 315-18.
     The merits of both the mainframe and the micro-
     computer are recognized, and methods of interfac-
     ing the two to achieve the best of both worlds
     are considered. Technology, software, and appli-
     cations are discussed.

1020 MILLER, RALPH. "Designing Your Own Low Cost
     Front-End Software." Online 9 (March 1985):
     94-98.
     Most commercial front-end software for
     online searching is only adequate, according to
     Ralph Miller. Miller recommends designing an
     in-house system using INSTANTCOM and PC WRITE.
     He justifies the recommendation, describes the
     operation of the in-house system, and compares
     it to commercial packages.

1021 "Modems, Hertz, and Bauds." Small Computers in
     Libraries 2 (April 1982): 4-6.
     The fundamentals of computer-to-computer
     communication are explained, including the devel-
     opment and use of various types of modems and
     acoustic couplers.

1022 MORTENSEN, ERIK. "Downloading in Online Search-
     ing: A Review of the Literature." Proceedings
     of the 8th International Online Information
     Meeting, London, 4-6 December 1984. Medford,
     NJ: Learned Information, 1984. Pp. 331-42.
     Mortensen considers the issues involved
     in downloading from online databases, including
     technical advantages, improved communication
     software, copyright, and the need for pricing
     guidelines. Bibliography.

1023 MURR, KENNETH R. "After Downloading; How to
     Get the Most Out of Your Microcomputer."
     Proceedings of the 5th National Online Meet-
     ing, New York, 10-12 April 1984. Medford, NJ:
     Learned Information, 1984. Pp. 243-46.
     Murr describes a microcomputer-based pro-
     ject underway at Clemson University to manipulate

downloaded data, using word processing software
to produce professional looking bibliographies
for the patron. Current procedures permit elimination of unwanted records, searching of the
library's database for holdings, the addition of
call numbers for hits, and the printing of an
enhanced citation in correct bibliographic form.

1024 "NFAIS' New EasyNet Retrieval Service." Small
Computers in Libraries 5 (January 1985): 7.
The National Federation of Abstracting
and Information Services announces a toll free
number which provides access to major online
vendors such as DIALOG, BRS, and NEWSNET.

1025 NEMZER, DANIEL E. "Accessing CAS ONLINE with an
M300 Workstation." OCLC Micro 1 (March 1985):
14.
The OCLC M300 Workstation can be used as
a terminal to search online databases through
DIALOG, SDC, and other vendors, without purchasing additional hardware. However, access to
graphic displays available on Chemical Abstracts
Service's CAS ONLINE requires special terminals
or add-ons, which are described.

1026 NICHOLSON, D. M., and PETRIE, J. HOWARD. "Using
a General Purpose Microcomputer for Online
Searching." Aslib Proceedings 35 (September
1983): 354-57.
An online search program developed for
the University of Strathclyde is described in
detail. The program, which runs on a Cifer 2684
with a CP/M operating system, features storage of
log-on procedures, offline creation of search
strategies, downloading, data manipulation, and
uploading. The program can also be used for
interlibrary borrowing. Bibliography.

1027 Online Micro-Software Guide & Directory 1983-
84. Weston, CT: Online, Inc., 1982. Annual
Supplements.
Specifications for commercial microcomputer software packages constitute the major portion of this important reference book. Feature

articles cover such topics as purchasing computer
equipment, how to deal with software problems,
and microcomputer applications. Comparison
charts, a bibliography, a glossary, and indexes
of software producers and distributors complement
the text.

1028 OSBORNE, LARRY N. "Downloading Overview."
Journal of Library Administration 6 (Summer
1985): 13-21.
Issues involved in the transfer of
machine-readable data are analyzed in light of
federal copyright laws and guidelines. Differences in file transfer and data capture are explained, legal uses of downloaded data are presented, moral and legal aspects of downloading
data are discussed, and the literature of downloading and copyright is reviewed. Bibliography.

1029 PEMBERTON, JEFFERY K. "Case for the Dumb (But
Not Stupid) Terminal." Online 7 (November
1983): 6-7.
Pemberton identifies circumstances in
which a dumb terminal might be a better purchase
than a microcomputer for online searching, then
recommends the DECwriter Correspondent over
other terminals he has used.

1030 PEMBERTON, JEFFERY K. "Should Your Next Terminal Be a Computer?" Database 4 (September
1981): 4-6.
The author answers his question affirm-
atively, then proceeds to tout the versatility of
the microcomputer over the limited uses of the
dumb terminal or the video terminal and slave
printer. After making his case for the micro, he
provides seven hints on purchasing micro equipment.

1031 PETRIE, J. HOWARD, and COWIE, J. "A Microcomputer
Based Terminal for Assisting Online Informa-
tion Retrieval." Journal of Information
Science 4 (March 1982): 61-64.
A microcomputer software package for the

Cifer 2684 provides economical, efficient online
searching. The program offers storage of user
IDs, passwords, and search strategies, and the
downloading of data. Bibliography.

1032 PISCIOTTA, HENRY; EVANS, NANCY; and ALBRIGHT,
MARILYN. "Search Helper: Sancho Panza or
Mephistopheles?" Library Hi Tech 2, no. 3,
issue 7 (1984): 25-32.
In a test to see how library patrons will
accept end user searching of commercial online
databases, the Carnegie-Mellon University Library
began providing access to hardware and SEARCH
HELPER software for patrons to do their own online searching. This article reports on a survey
of users of the service, along with suggestions
for enhancing the program.

1033 PREECE, SCOTT E., and WILLIAMS, MARTHA E. "Software for the Searcher's Workbench." Communicating Information. Proceedings of the 43rd
ASIS Annual Meeting. White Plains, NY: Knowledge Industry Publications, 1980, v. 17. Pp.
403-05.
THE SEARCHER'S WORKBENCH, a microcomputer-based system for interfacing with multiple
information databases, is described. A system
based on this prototype, which employs an Alpha
Microsystems microcomputer and a specially designed language called CROSSTALK, may be marketed
in the future. Bibliography.

1034 PRUITT, ELLEN C., and DOWLING, KAREN. "Searching
for Current Information Online. . .How High
School Library Media Centers in Montgomery
County, Maryland are Solving an Information
Problem by Using DIALOG." Online 9 (March
1985): 47-60.
In 1982 the senior high schools of Montgomery County, Maryland, began offering online
search services to students. The rationale for
the decision: to introduce online searching and
expand available resources. The decision is
justified; the online solution to the information
problem is discussed; illustrations are included.

1035 "Reformatting Remote Search Results." Library Systems Newsletter 2 (April 1982): 29-30.
   Three hardware options for performing online searches and manipulating the data for greater readability are proposed and evaluated. They are: (1) using a microcomputer as a terminal (2) using a word processing system as a terminal, and (3) upgrading an existing terminal to operate as a microcomputer.

1036 RILEY, CONNIE; BELL, MARGARET; and FINUCANE, TOM. "Elimination of Duplicate Citations from Cross Database Searching Using an 'Intelligent' Terminal to Produce Report Style Searches." Online 5 (October 1981): 36-41.
   Details are given for searching databases using a microcomputer, storing the searches on cassettes or floppy disks, then manipulating the data to eliminate duplicate entries. The program for eliminating duplicates is provided.

1037 ROSENBERG, VICTOR. "A System for Editing Search Results and Compiling Bibliographies." Proceedings of the 2nd National Online Meeting-New York, 24-26 March 1981. Medford, NJ: Learned Information, 1981. Pp. 409-14.
   An early technique is outlined for downloading and editing bibliographic data from a commercial database using a microcomputer, then storing the data in a mainframe computer where it is easily accessible for future use. Rosenberg notes the question of appropriate uses of databases and stresses that this is an experimental project. Bibliography.

1038 ROSENBERG, VICTOR, and BENSON, PEGGY. "The Professional Bibliographic System and Biblio-Link: Information Management for Downloaded Records." Downloading/Uploading Online Databases and Catalogs. Proceedings of the Congress for Librarians, St. John's University, Jamaica, New York, 18 February 1985. Library Hi Tech Special Studies Series, no. 1. Ann Arbor, MI: Pierian Press, 1985. Pp. 50-55.

The development and maintenance of a local catalog or database, using downloading procedures, are illustrated using BIBLIO-LINK and
THE PROFESSIONAL BIBLIOGRAPHIC SYSTEM to capture
data from OCLC, RLIN, and DIALOG databases and
merge them into one file. The potential for uploading is also demonstrated through a project to
upload data to a mainframe for typesetting. Bibliography.

1039 ROWELL, PETER P., and UTTERBACK, NANCY. "Scientific Literature Currency and Organization
Using a Microcomputer." Online 8 (January
1984): 18-21.
A procedure for performing monthly database searches, downloading, formatting, merging
and printing of data using microcomputer technology is outlined in detail.

1040 "Ruraline Now in Operation." Wilson Library
Bulletin 59 (March 1985): 444.
Ruraline, an electronic mail system
established and operated by the Center for the
Study of Rural Librarianship at Clarion Univer-
sity, is announced and described. Part of
TYMNET's OnTyme-II network, Ruraline is accessed
via microcomputer.

1041 SAFFADY, WILLIAM. "Communications Software Packages for the IBM Personal Computer and Compatibles." Library Technology Reports 21 (July/
August 1985): 355-456.
Communications hardware and software are
treated thoroughly in this article concentrating
on IBM and IBM compatible computers. Hardware,
modems, installation, file transfers, printer
controls, documentation, and other technological
concerns are dealt with in the article's introduction, followed by reviews of seventeen communication programs. Programs reviewed are: ASCII
PRO, BIBLIO-LINK, PROFESSIONAL BIBLIOGRAPHIC
SYSTEM, GEORGE, IMPERSONATOR, I/O EXPRESS, MICRO
LINK II, MITE, PC-DIAL, PC-TALK III, PRO SEARCH,
RESPOND/TTY, RESPOND/ASYNC, SMARTCOM II, SMARTERM
100, TELIOS, VTERM II.

1042 SAFFADY, WILLIAM. "Microcomputers as Terminals."
Library Technology Reports 21 (January/Febru-
ary 1985): 42-46.
    A section of a longer article on costs
of online searching, this deals with the use of
the microcomputer as an online search terminal.
The author addresses hardware configuration and
costs, communications packages, gateways, vendor
charges, and the possibility of hardware and
software rental.

1043 SCHARFF, L.; MAHON, B.; and THOMAS, J. R. "The
Use of Microcomputers for Information Retrieval." Electronic Library 1 (April 1983): 109-
15.
    Members of the Euronet-Diane Launch Team
describe the hardware and software chosen to
automate online searching functions of the data
network, and discuss problems encountered in
their efforts to make the network accessible
online.

1044 SHEPHERD, MICHAEL A., and WATTERS, CAROLYN.
"PSI: A Portable Self-Contained Intermediary
for Access to Bibliographic Database Systems."
Online Review 8 (October 1984): 451-63.
    PSI, a portable self-contained intermedi-
ary designed to provide a single command language
for access to a variety of online databases, is
described. The system includes a single board
computer designed specifically for PSI, but the
software will operate on a microcomputer. Bibliography.

1045 SLEETH, JIM, and LaRUE, JAMES. "The ALL-OUT
Library: A Design for Computer-Powered, Multi-
dimensional Services." American Libraries 14
(October 1983): 594-96.
    An electronic library is described which
is capable of providing remote access to library
files via microcomputer or terminal. Among the
services envisioned are electronic bulletin
boards, catalog searching, material location, and
reference. General specifications for the system
are provided.

1046 SLINGLUFF, DEBORAH; LEV, YVONNE; and EISAN,
ANDREW. "An End User Search Service in an
Academic Health Sciences Library." Medical
Reference Services Quarterly 4 (Spring 1985):
11-21.
To supplement the mediated component of
its online service, the University of Maryland at
Baltimore Health Sciences Library implemented
end user searching using BRS/AFTER DARK. This
article describes the program and evaluates it on
the bases of librarians' observations and exit
interviews with patrons, gathered over a three
month period. Bibliography.

1047 SPIGAI, FRANCES G. "Downloading: Tempest in a
Teapot?" Online '83 Conference Proceedings,
Chicago, 10-12 October 1983. Weston, CT:
Online, Inc., 1983. Pp. 278-79.
Downloading and piracy issues are re-
viewed and their impact on the information indus-
try and market are evaluated.

1048 SPIGAI, FRANCES G. "Downloading Revisited, 1984:
Practices and Policies." Online '84 Conference Proceedings, San Francisco, 29-31 October
1984. Weston, CT: Online, Inc., 1984. Pp.
228-31.
The issue of downloading data from online
databases has been debated, studied, and generally resolved, as reuse contracts and policies have
been developed by database vendors. Spigai re-
reviews the issue and suggests further readings.
Bibliography.

1049 STABLER, KAREN CHITTICK. "The Continuation of
Librarians as Intermediaries." Proceedings of
the 5th National Online Meeting, New York, 10-
12 April 1984. Medford, NJ: Learned Information, 1984. Pp. 375-81.
The debate over end user as opposed to
intermediary conducted online searching is far
from being resolved. In this article the arguments for the intermediary are presented, stressing specialized training and background of the
intermediary, quality of the search, and aid in

locating references after the search has been
completed. Bibliography.

1050 SWIGGER, KEITH. "Micros and Information Utilities in the Schools." Educational Computer 3
(October 1983): 12, 14, 68.
The microcomputer as a communication medium in a school library is the topic of this
article which addresses equipment and cost, evaluates such utilities as COMPUSERVE, THE SOURCE,
BRS, DIALOG, and ORBIT from a public school
perspective, considers appropriate communication
software, and details the benefits and liabil-
ities connected with their use.

1051 TALAB, ROSEMARY STURDEVANT. "Copyright and
Database Downloading." Library Journal 110
(November 1, 1985): 144-47; and School Library
Journal 32 (November 1985): 132-35.
Talab highlights the issues of downloading and copyright infringement, touching briefly
on detection methods, status of database copyright, data storage, fair use of material protected under copyright, and implications for the
future. Bibliography.

1052 TEDD, LUCY A. "Online Databases and Library
User Education--An Introduction." User Education in the Online Age II. Proceedings of the
International Association of Technological
University Libraries Seminar, Delft, The
Netherlands, 30 July-2 August 1984. Goteborg,
Sweden: IATUL, 1985, v. 17. Pp. 121-27.
Education for online database searching
with emphasis on the library user is the theme of
this article, which analyzes the topic in general
terms but emphasizes the impact of microcomputer
systems, database creation, and use. Bibliography.

1053 TEDD, LUCY A. "Thinking Big, Micro-Wise."
Library Association Record 84 (January 1982):
18-19.
Tedd considers hardware and software
options for local and online systems, and reviews

British Library Research and Development Department projects concerning online searching and
local database development. Bibliography.

1054 "Telecommunications Basics." Small Computers in
Libraries 3 (December 1983): 5-6.
   Basics of telecommunications are considered, including such topics as terminals, parity,
the echo option, and the break character.

1055 TENOPIR, CAROL. "Online Searching With a Microcomputer." Library Journal 110 (March 15,
1985): 42-43.
   Microcomputers are fast replacing dumb
terminals as the hardware of choice by online
search intermediaries. Tenopir addresses the
benefits of the microcomputer over the dumb terminal, discusses the essential hardware, software, and modem, and estimates the cost of three
popular systems. Bibliography.

1056 TENOPIR, CAROL. "Online Searching With a Microcomputer: Downloading Issues." Microcomputers
for Information Management 2 (June 1985): 77-
89.
   The ability to download information from
an online database is one of the benefits derived
from the use of micros for online searching. However, the implications of downloading are far
reaching, touching on copyright laws, vendor policies, and pricing. This article addresses the
implications of downloading, and its effects on
the information industry. Bibliography.

1057 TENOPIR, CAROL. "Software for Online Searching."
Library Journal 110 (October 15, 1985): 52-53.
   Tenopir stresses the need for online
search intermediaries to become expert in evaluating communications packages usable in their
work. The value of workshops is discussed for
maintaining awareness, but for those librarians
who can't readily attend workshops on communications software, three programs are reviewed.
They are SEARCHWARE, PRO-SEARCH, and BIBLIO-LINK
used with PROFESSIONAL BIBLIOGRAPHIC SOFTWARE.

1058 TENOPIR, CAROL. "Systems for End Users: Are
There End Users for the Systems?" Library
Journal 110 (June 15, 1985): 40-41.
Tenopir explains the differences in
front-end, intermediary, and gateway systems for
online searching, evaluates BRS/BRKTHRU and EASY-
NET, and discusses the potential demand for end
user searching.

1059 "Terminals--Dumb, Smart & Otherwise." Small
Computers in Libraries 3 (January 1983): 3-7.
The development of the computer terminal
and improvements in communication techniques and
equipment provide background for this discussion
of equipment needs for interactive communications
using a microcomputer as a terminal.

1060 TRAUTMAN, RODES; BALDWIN, CHARLENE M.; and JONES,
DOUGLAS E. "Uploading and Downloading for
Computer-Assisted Reference Service." Down-
loading/Uploading Online Databases and Catalogs. Proceedings of the Congress for Librarians, St. John's University, Jamaica, New
York, 18 February 1985. Library Hi Tech Special Studies Series, no. 1. Ann Arbor, MI:
Pierian Press, 1985. Pp. 13-21.
The application of three software packages, 1DIR, CROSSTALK XVI, and PMATE, to an online search service at the University of Arizona
is described by the developers of the program.
Each package is considered briefly and its function defined, but the service capabilities
achieved through their integration constitute the
major emphasis of this article. Bibliography.

1061 "Userkit-A New Device to Make Online Searching
Cheaper and Easier." Online Review 4 (December 1980): 407.
USERKIT, a microcomputer attachment which
plugs into a system between the terminal and the
accoustic coupler to expedite log-on and online
search procedures, is reviewed and recommended.

1062 "'USERKIT' Reduces On-Line Costs." Small Computers in Libraries 2 (May 1982): 6.

USERKIT, a microcomputer attachment which stores log-on commands, standard search strategies, and other message strings and runs them on command, is recommended as an economy measure for libraries using micros for online database searching.

1063 WALES, J. L. "Using a Microcomputer to Access Bibliographic Databases: Experience With Userlink Software in the ICI Organics Division Information and Library Services Unit." Program 18 (July 1984): 247-57.
    The microcomputer is recommended and justified for online searching, the USERLINK interface is suggested as an effective tool for in-house and external communication, and enhancement software which provides downloading and data manipulation is described. Bibliography.

1064 WALTON, ROBERT A. "Electronic Mail: Choosing the System to Meet Your Library's Needs." Technicalities 4 (May 1984): 5-7.
    Electronic mail is defined and described, its impact on the future of libraries is predicted, several negative arguments are mentioned, and three alternative configurations--the local area network, the distributed system, and the central electronic mailbox--are outlined.

1065 WANGER, JUDITH. "Downloading: The Migration Problem of the 1980s?" Proceedings of the 7th International Online Information Meeting, London, 6-8 December 1983. Medford, NJ: Learned Information, 1983. Pp. 45-51.
    A vice-president of Cuadra Associates addresses the problems created by the practice of downloading from online databases, and announces a forthcoming Cuadra-sponsored study on the topic.

1066 WARRICK, THOMAS S. "Large Databases, Small Computers and Fast Modems. . .An Attorney Looks at the Legal Ramifications of Downloading." Online 8 (July 1984): 58-70.
    An attorney deals with legal aspects of

downloading online database information in light
of the current copyright laws. Bibliography.

1067 WILBURN, GENE. "Terminal Emulator Software for
the TRS-80 Model III: A Look at Eight Telecommunication Programs." Software Review 2
(March 1983): 14-23.
Features to look for in communication
software are identified and discussed, and eight
packages compatible with the TRS-80 Model III
microcomputer are evaluated.

1068 WILLIAMS, MARTHA E., and PREECE, SCOTT E. "A
Mini-Transparent System Using an Alpha Microprocessor." Proceedings of the 2nd National
Online Meeting, New York, 24-26 March 1981.
Medford, NJ: Learned Information, 1981. Pp.
499-502.
THE SEARCHER'S WORKBENCH, a mini-transparent system employing a microcomputer to provide access to online systems and databases, is
addressed, with an overview of the development
project and a survey of the system's features.
Bibliography.

1069 WILLIAMS, PHILIP W. "Intelligent Access to Online Systems." Proceedings of the 4th International Online Information Meeting, London,
9-11 December 1980. Medford, NJ: Learned
Information, 1980. Pp. 397-407.
Williams describes the USERKIT, a Z80
microprocessor which plugs into a system between
terminal and modem or acoustic coupler, to provide communication capabilities.

1070 WILLIAMS, PHILIP W. "A Microcomputer System to
Improve the Recall Performance of Skilled
Searchers." Proceedings of the 4th National
Online Meeting, New York, 12-14 April 1983.
Medford, NJ: Learned Information, 1983. Pp.
581-90.
Williams seeks to improve the performance
of skilled online searchers by employing database
feedback to modify search profiles. The success
of the project is reported, strengths and weak-

nesses are reviewed, and future directions are proposed. Bibliography.

1071 WILLIAMS, PHILIP W. "Microprocessor Assisted Terminals for Online Information Systems." Proceedings of the 3rd International Online Information Meeting, London, 4-6 December 1979. Medford, NJ: Learned Information, 1979. Pp. 139-46.

The use of a microcomputer for online database searching provides for automatic log-on, offline search formulation, and greater opportunity for user assistance. The development of online search programs for unskilled users is discussed, as are copyright issues. Bibliography.

1072 WILLIAMS, PHILIP W. "A Model for an Expert System for Automated Information Retrieval." Proceedings of the 8th International Online Information Meeting, London, 4-6 December 1984. Medford, NJ: Learned Information, 1984. Pp. 139-49.

A model microcomputer-based online search program, intended for use by unskilled as well as skilled searchers, is described. Bibliography.

1073 WILLIAMS, PHILIP W. "A New Device to Simplify Online Searching and Reduce Costs." Proceedings of the 2nd National Online Meeting, New York, 24-26 March 1981. Medford, NJ: Learned Information, 1981. Pp. 503-14.

Desirable features of microcomputer software to enhance online database searching are discussed. OL'SAM, THE SEARCHER'S WORKBENCH, and other online search systems are considered briefly. The USERKIT system is described in detail. Bibliography.

1074 WILLIAMS, PHILIP W. "Recent Developments in the Use of Microcomputers to Access Online Systems." The Application of Mini- and Micro-Computers in Information, Documentation and Libraries. Proceedings of the International Conference on the Application of Mini- and Micro-Computers in Information, Documentation and Libraries, Tel-Aviv, Israel, 13-18 March 1983. New York: North-Holland, 1983. Pp. 645-53.

Williams addresses the problems of searching online systems, expresses user expectations of databases and access hardware, and explains how USERLINK effectively interfaces the access terminal with the database. Bibliography.

1075 WILLIAMS, PHILIP W. "The Use of Microcomputers for Online Computer Access." Proceedings of the 3rd National Online Meeting, New York, 30 March-1 April 1982. Medford, NJ: Learned Information, 1982. Pp. 559-68.

This early article concerning the use of microcomputers in online searching and communication with mainframe computers explains advantages of micro use and discusses the USERKIT interface, which facilitates access.

1076 WILLIAMS, PHILIP W. "The Use of Microelectronics to Assist Online Information Retrieval." Online Review 4 (December 1980): 393-99.

In an early article on the use of the microcomputer for online searching, Williams discusses the advantages, which include savings of up to 50% on line charges, coupled with increased convenience, efficiency, and search quality. Bibliography.

1077 WILLIAMS, PHILIP W. "User Trials of the OASIS Search System." Proceedings of the 5th National Online Meeting, New York, 10-12 April 1984. Medford, NJ: Learned Information, 1984. Pp. 437-52.

A prototype online search system designed for the unskilled user is described by one of its developers. Called OASIS, the system performs the search interview, formulates the search strategy, and performs the search automatically, requiring little or no expertise on the part of the user. Bibliography.

1078 WILLIAMS, PHILIP W, and GOLDSMITH, GERRY. "A Completely Automatic Information Retrieval

System for the Unskilled User." Proceedings
of the 6th International Online Information
Meeting, London, 7-9 December 1982. Medford,
NJ: Learned Information, 1982. Pp. 263-72.
    Research concerning online database
searching by unskilled users is summarized, and
a microcomputer program to enable unskilled users
to perform their own searching is described.

1079 WILLIAMS, PHILIP W., and GOLDSMITH, GERRY.
    "Information Retrieval on Mini- and Micro-
    computers." Annual Review of Information
    Science and Technology. White Plains, NY:
    Knowledge Industry Publications, 1981, v. 16.
    Pp. 85-111.
    A survey of small computer technology is
followed by detailed reviews of the minicomputer
and microcomputer literature in information retrieval, including access to both in-house and
dial-up databases. Bibliography.

1080 WISMER, DONALD. "A Basic Program for Invoicing
    Dialog Subscription Accounts." Online 7 (July
    1983): 51-59.
    A program written for the Maine State
Library to figure and prepare online search in-
voices for the fifteen member libraries of the
Maine Online Consortium is described and reproduced in full. Information concerning the consortium and its use of DIALOG search services is
also provided.

1081 WISMER, DONALD. "The In-House Impact of Online
    Searching." Online 9 (May 1985): 38-40.
    Twenty-seven percent of the online
searching done by the Maine State Library staff
is initiated in-house, for purposes of interlibrary loan verification, document delivery, reference, book selection, or other library needs.
These searches are analyzed and justified for
others who might be considering broadening their
library's use of online services.

1082 WOOLPY, SARA, and TAYLOR, NANCY. "Enduser
    Searching: A Study of Manual vs. Online

Searching By Endusers and the Role of the Intermediary." <u>Online '84 Conference Proceedings, San Francisco, 29-31 October 1984.</u> Weston, CT: Online, Inc., 1984. Pp. 243-45.

In order to evaluate the quality of end user searching, a comparative study of manual and online search results was conducted at Earlham College. Techniques and results are summarized. The role of the librarian in the procedure is defined. Methods of improving end user searching are suggested.

DATABASES AND INFORMATION UTILITIES

1083 "Affordable Databases: Information Utilites and
     Bibliographic Retrieval." ACCESS: Microcom-
     puters in Libraries 1 (October 1981): 7-9, 20,
     22, 27-28.
          The addition of a modem to a microcompu-
     ter system provides communication capabilities to
     individuals and libraries. This article de-
     scribes the services available to dial-up users
     from THE SOURCE, COMPUSERVE, DIALOG, SDC, and
     RLIN.

1084 "Affordable Databases: Information Utilities and
     Bibliographic Retrieval, Part II." ACCESS:
     Microcomputers in Libraries 2 (January 1982):
     8.
          BRS access is described, and services are
     reviewed.

1085 ANDERSON, ERIC S. "MICROsearch." Computing
     Teacher 12 (March 1985): 62-63.
          Anderson evaluates MICROsearch in terms
     of ease of use, low cost, adaptability to in-
     struction in online searching, and patron use in
     updating bibliographic data.

1086 "BRS and DIALOG Personal Computer Search Services
     Announced at ONLINE '82." Online 7 (January
     1983): 10.
          BRS/AFTER DARK and DIALOG's KNOWLEDGE
     INDEX, online search services designed for home
     computer users, are announced and described.

1087 "BIOSIS Data on Floppy Disks." Small Computers
     in Libraries 2 (May 1982): 7.
          BioSciences Information Service announces
     a new system of distributing BIOSIS data on flop-
     py disks. The service, called BITS, is based on
     individual interest profiles submitted at the
     time the subscription is placed. Prices and sub-
     scription information are provided.

1088 "BIOSIS Formalises Downloading." Electronic Library 1 (October 1983): 227-28.
    BIOSIS has addressed the problem of downloading from the BIOSIS database, and offers an alternative service, for a fee.

1089 "BIOSIS Studies Downloading Its Data to Micros." Online 6 (September 1982): 12, 67.
    BIOSIS, a major database producer in the life sciences, is studying the feasibility of marketing monthly database searches on floppy disks. The service, called BITS, would be provided by subscription, based on subscriber interest profiles.

1090 "BITS (BIOSIS) CP/M Programs." Small Computers in Libraries 2 (May 1982): 3.
    Kent-Barlow Information Associates announce two new data retrieval and storage programs--one for use with BIOSIS (BITS) files, the other for local files. Hardware specifications are included.

1091 BOAZ, MARTHA. "PRESTEL and the Trend Toward Personal Computers." Special Libraries 71 (July 1980): 310-14.
    PRESTEL, a public data service developed by the British Post Office and accessible via microcomputer, is described. Its potential for libraries is considered, and its use by libraries encouraged. Bibliography.

1092 BONIN, DENISE. "COMPULINE Records Use of Microcomputer Systems in British Columbia Libraries." PNLA Quarterly 49 (Spring 1985): 40.
    COMPULINE, a database concerning microcomputer use in libraries, is briefly described. The article considers the types of library applications included in the database, common types of information requests received by COMPULINE, and a contact address and telephone number.

1093 BURKE, BARBARA. "The Menu: The International Software Database." Library Software Review 3 (September 1984): 362-70.

THE MENU, a database listing more than
50,000 mini and microcomputer software packages,
is reviewed, and its development traced from
1979 to 1984. Now available online through DIA-
LOG, under the name INTERNATIONAL SOFTWARE DATA-
BASE, file 232, it is recommended over other
similar files.

1094 CHEN, CHING-CHIH, and HU, CHENGREN. "A Statistical Profile of Micro-Based Software."
Microcomputers for Information Management 1
(September 1984): 199-214.
A statistical analysis of the 1500 software programs listed in the MICROUSE database
provides information on the types and availability of software, cost analyses, vendor/producer
statistics, and software-hardware relationships.
Trends for the future are also predicted. Bibliography.

1095 CHEN, CHING-CHIH, and WANG, XIAOCHU. "MicroUse:
The Database on Microcomputer Applications in
Libraries and Information Centers." Microcomputers for Information Management 1 (March
1984): 39-56.
MICROUSE, a microcomputer database developed at Simmons College, concerns applications of
microcomputers in libraries. In this article two
of its developers discuss hardware and software
selection for the project, system configuration,
the multi-file structure, records, and search
procedures.

1096 CLARK W. BRUCE. "ERIC for Microcomputer--A
Pilot Project." Online '81 Conference Proceedings, Dallas, 2-4 November 1981. Weston,
CT: Online, Inc., 1981. Pp. 41-47.
A pilot project at the ERIC Clearinghouse
for Information Resources has resulted in the
development of MICROsearch, a menu driven software package to be used with small databases in
high interest subject areas distributed by the
Clearinghouse. The project, which was field
tested in the early 1980s, is described, and its
applicability to research and study evaluated.

1097 CLARK, W. BRUCE. "Exploration of Problems and
Issues Involved in Searching Remote Databases
via Microcomputer." The Application of Mini-
and Micro-Computers in Information, Documentation and Libraries. Proceedings of the International Conference on the Application of
Mini- and Micro-Computers in Information, Documentation and Libraries, Tel-Aviv, Israel,
13-18 March 1983. New York: North-Holland,
1983. Pp. 625-30.
Two pilot projects launched by ERIC
Clearinghouses to make information more accessible are justified and compared, although they are
quite different. The Clearinghouse on Information Resources developed MICROsearch, a plan to
distribute small data files on floppy disks, with
appropriate search software for local use. The
Clearinghouse for Science, Mathematics, and
Environmental Science made their data available
online through COMPUSERVE. Merits of both are
considered, although MICROsearch is treated in
more detail.

1098 CLARK, W. BRUCE. "MICROsearch--A Project to
Extend the ERIC Database to Microcomputers."
Information Interaction. Proceedings of the
45th ASIS Annual Meeting. White Plains, NY:
Knowledge Industry Publications, 1982, v. 19.
Pp. 60-62.
MICROsearch, a programming project spon-
sored by the ERIC Clearinghouse on Information
Resources, makes possible downloading from the
ERIC database to microcomputer diskette for eco-
nomical and simplified ERIC searching. The pro-
ject is described and evaluated. Bibliography.

1099 "The Computer Database." Information Intelligence Online Libraries and Microcomputers 1
(September 1983): 12.
The COMPUTER DATABASE, DIALOG file 275,
is announced and briefly described, with a Fall,
1983 projected date for going online.

1100 "Data Bases for Home Computer Users." Software
Review 2 (June 1983): 92-93.

Profiles of BRS/AFTER DARK and DIALOG's
KNOWLEDGE INDEX are provided in one article, for
easy comparison.

1101 DEWEY, PATRICK R.   "The Source."   RQ 22 (Summer
     1983): 418-19.
          THE SOURCE, a consumer database catering
     to commercial clients during the day and computer
     enthusiasts during the evening, is reviewed by
     a public librarian who describes the service,
     points out several disadvantages, and recommends
     shopping around before making a commitment.

1102 "Directory of Microcomputer Applications in
     Educational Settings."   Library Software
     Review 3 (June 1984): 151.
          The DIRECTORY OF MICROCOMPUTER APPLICA-
     TIONS IN EDUCATIONAL SETTINGS, a database com-
     piled by the Harvard Graduate School of Educa-
     tion, is announced, with a Fall, 1984 date for
     going online.

1103 DOLAN, DONNA R.   "A Guide to Locating Mini/Micro
     Information in Online Databases."   Online 7
     (March 1983): 78-81.
          Strategies are provided for retrieving
     mini and microcomputer literature through BRS.
     A list of BRS databases is included, with hints
     on the types of microcomputer information found
     in each.

1104 "ERIC Files on the Apple."   Small Computers in
     Libraries 2 (November 1982): 6-7.
          MICROsearch, a microcomputer program
     designed to simplify ERIC searching and make data
     available for sale on floppy disks, is described,
     evaluated, and future developments predicted.

1105 "ERIC to Mount Three Databases on CompuServe. . .
     Files May Be Downloaded to Apple Micros."   On-
     line 6 (March 1982): 9-10, 58.
          The ERIC Clearinghouse for Science, Math-
     ematics, and Environmental Education is planning
     to offer three ERIC databases through COMPUSERVE
     to encourage greater access.   The files can then

be downloaded to microcomputer disks to avoid
high connect time and line charges. Pre-packaged
diskettes are also being considered by the clearinghouse.

1106 ELY, DONALD P. "MICROsearch: Extending the ERIC
Database to Microcomputers." Technicalities 4
(February 1984): 11-12.
MICROsearch, a program to market bibliographic data from the ERIC Clearinghouse on
Information Resources on floppy disks for local
searching, is described and evaluated. Background of the project, necessary hardware configuration, and searching strategies are considered.
Merits and limitations of the program are addressed.

1107 FALK, HOWARD. "The Source v. CompuServe." Online Review 8 (June 1984): 214-24.
THE SOURCE and COMPUSERVE, competing online information utilities, are compared on the
bases of services, price, education related
features, computing, personal data storage, and
other factors.

1108 FERRARINI, ELIZABETH. "Doing Research With an
On-Line Library." Business Computer Systems
2 (February 1983): 39-40, 42.
A general introduction to searching
DIALOG, this article examines some of the available databases, touches briefly on microcomputer,
word processor, and terminal hardware configurations, and provides a sample DIALOG search.

1109 FISCHER, RUSSELL G. "The Librarian as Entrepre-
neur: Joe Ward & Microcomputer Index." Library
Journal 110 (September 1985): 47-50.
Joe Ward, the developer of MICROCOMPUTER
INDEX, DIALOG's file 233, is the subject of this
biographical sketch, which relates how he became
interested in microcomputers, how he combined his
interest with his profession as a librarian, and
how this led to the founding of MICROCOMPUTER
INDEX and involvement in related microcomputer
businesses.

1110 FOLKE, CAROLYN WINTERS. "Online Microcomputer
     Information Answers the Call for Help." Wis-
     consin Library Bulletin 78 (Summer 1983): 62-
     64.
          The problem of locating microcomputer
     literature is addressed, and four online data-
     bases are reviewed. Two of the databases, MICRO-
     COMPUTER INDEX and DISC, index journal litera-
     ture; two others, RESOURCES IN COMPUTER EDUCATION
     (RICE) and INTERNATIONAL SOFTWARE DATABASE (ISD),
     index software reviews and information.

1111 "Free-Access Software-Locator Service Goes On-
     line." Library Software Review 3 (December
     1984): 462.
          SOFTWARE LIBRARY, an online database for
     software identification and location, is an-
     nounced and reviewed. Maintained by Searchmart
     Corporation, a marketing firm specializing in
     computer readable-databases, the file contains
     producer supplied information rather than evalua-
     tive data. Access information is provided.

1112 FROST, STANLEY P. "Online Microcomputer Software
     Guide and Directory (SOFT)." RQ 24 (Winter
     1984): 221-22.
          File SOFT, a directory of currently
     available software, which corresponds to the
     printed Online Microcomputer Software Guide and
     Directory, is reviewed. The database, which
     covers from October, 1983 to the present and is
     updated monthly, is available through BRS for
     $40 per connect hour.

1113 GILLETTE, MEREDITH. "Micros On-Line: A Compari-
     son of Available Citations." ACCESS: Micro-
     computers in Libraries 1 (July 1981): 10-12,
     19.
          A DIALOG search on the topic of micro-
     computers in libraries was done in the ERIC,
     NTIS, SOCIALSCISEARCH, CDI, and LISA databases
     then followed up by a manual search on the same
     topic. Combined computer and manual searches
     produced fifty-five bibliographic citations which
     are provided here, along with some interesting

data concerning duplication of entries from database to database and completeness of the various databases. Bibliography.

1114 GORDON, HELEN A. "SOFT: A Microcomputer Software Database Review." Online '83 Conference Proceedings, Chicago, 10-12 October 1983. Weston, CT: Online, Inc., 1983. Pp. 74-75.
File SOFT, an online directory of microcomputer software, is reviewed, and its use is briefly explained. The database, which contained information on approximately 1400 software programs when the review was written, is available through BRS.

1115 GREENGRASS, LINDA. "Creating a Database With Children." Library Journal 110 (May 1, 1985): 113-16; and School Library Journal 31 (May 1985): 143-46.
The librarian at the Bank Street College's laboratory school describes the construction and use of a student-generated database of the students' favorite books.

1116 GRIEVES, ROBERT T. "Short Circuiting Reference Books." Time 121 (June 13, 1983): 76.
The Academic American Encyclopedia, available online through the Dow Jones News/Retrieval Service or BRS and accessible via micro, is reviewed and compared to printed encyclopedias. Its popularity among students is noted, and librarians' impressions are included.

1117 "Index and Directory to List Micro Articles, Programs." Interface Age 8 (July 1982): 22, 26.
MICROCOMPUTER INDEX, file 233, available through DIALOG, is announced and briefly described. A subject and abstract guide to microcomputer magazines, the database covers the years 1980 to the present, with updates made quarterly.

1118 JANKE, RICHARD V. "BRS/After Dark: The Birth of Online Self-Service." Online 7 (September 1983): 12-29.
BRS/AFTER DARK, an online search service

directed at the home computer market and after hours workplace, is described and compared to KNOWLEDGE INDEX, its counterpart available from DIALOG. Appendices include a comparison chart and results of end user and librarian evaluations from a University of Ottawa survey. Bibliography.

1119 KAPLAN, ROBIN. "Knowledge Index: A Review." Database 8 (June 1985): 122-28.
KNOWLEDGE INDEX, a low-cost, after hours information service, is reviewed in detail, considering library uses, available databases, costs, downloading, document delivery, documentation and service, and ease of use.

1120 KESSELMAN, MARTIN. "Online Update." Wilson Library Bulletin 60 (November 1985): 38-39.
WILSONLINE, the H. W. Wilson Company's online search service, is evaluated, with attention to enhancements and special features.

1121 KESSELMAN, MARTIN. "Online Update: BRS/After Dark." Wilson Library Bulletin 58 (May 1984): 652-53, 687.
Kesselman reviews BRS/AFTER DARK, considering databases, ease of use, plans for expansion, and pricing.

1122 "LSCA Funds a Micro." Library Journal 107 (November 15, 1982): 2132.
The Worthington (OH) Public Library has established a microcomputer-based online database concerning local businesses through a $12,897 LSCA grant, according to this news item.

1123 "Libraries and Micros." Electronic Library 3 (January 1985): 25.
The MICROUSE database, developed by the Simmons College Graduate School of Library and Information Science, is announced and described.

1124 "Library Micro Applications Database." American Libraries 15 (March 1984): 185-86.
The MICROUSE database is reviewed.

1125 MADER, SHARON, and PARK, ELIZABETH. "BRS/After
     Dark: A Review." RSR: Reference Services
     Review 13 (Spring 1985): 25-28.
        BRS/AFTER DARK, a bibliographic search
     service intended for end user access, is reviewed
     by librarians who question its effectiveness and
     its possible negative impact on library online
     services. However, contents, ease of use, the
     print option, costs, and user services are re-
     viewed positively. Problems are addressed.

1126 "Micro Program Catalog On-Line." Small Computers
     in Libraries 4 (November 1984): 4.
        DATA COURIER, DIALOG's file 256, is an-
     nounced. Containing descriptions of business
     related software, it is available for $51 per
     connect hour.

1127 "Micro Software Database Online." Small Compu-
     ters in Libraries 3 (December 1983): 1-2.
        File SOFT, BRS' microcomputer software
     database, is reviewed in terms of uses, size, and
     cost.

1128 "Microcomputer Databases." Information Tech-
     nology and Libraries 1 (March 1982): 71.
        The MICROCOMPUTER INDEX, DIALOG file 233,
     and the INTERNATIONAL MICROCOMPUTER SOFTWARE
     DIRECTORY, DIALOG file 232, are announced and
     reviewed.

1129 "Microcomputer Files Up on Dialog." Small Com-
     puters in Libraries 3 (February 1983): 4.
        The INTERNATIONAL SOFTWARE DATABASE, file
     232, and the MICROCOMPUTER INDEX, file 233,
     available through DIALOG, are announced and
     reviewed.

1130 "Microcomputer Information to be Available on
     DIALOG Information Retrieval Service." Infor-
     mation Retrieval and Library Automation 17
     (January 1982): 8.
        MICROCOMPUTER INDEX, file 233, available
     from DIALOG since Spring 1982, is announced and
     reviewed.

1131 "Microcomputer Software Database from Online
     Inc." Library Software Review 3 (March
     1984): 21-22.
          File SOFT, an online database of micro-
computer software information, is announced. A
profile is provided.

1132 "Microcomputer Software Database Goes Online."
     Online Review 8 (February 1984): 25.
          BRS' File SOFT, an online database of
microcomputer software information, is announced
and described. Uses are suggested; access information is provided; it is compared to Online
Micro-Software Guide and Directory, its counterpart in print.

1133 "Micros in Libraries Database." Electronic
     Library 2 (April 1984): 70.
          MICROUSE database is announced, sources
of information and funding are described, and
information on applications of microcomputers
in libraries is requested.

1134 "Micros in Libraries/Infocenters Topic of New
     Database." Information Retrieval and Library
     Automation 19 (March 1984): 4.
          MICROUSE, a microcomputer-based database
designed to provide information on microcomputer
use in libraries and information centers, is described briefly. Funding, staff, purposes, and
instructions for submitting information are
included.

1135 "MicroUse Database on OCLC." Library Software
     Review 3 (March 1984): 5-6.
          OCLC has given the Simmons College Grad-
uate School of Library and Information Science a
$3,300 grant to help support the development of
the MICROUSE database, designed to provide information concerning microcomputer applications in
libraries.

1136 "MicroUse Database to Provide Libraries with Use-
     ful Information on Micro Applications." OCLC
     Newsletter no. 150 (February 1984): 4.

MICROUSE, and online database developed
at Simmons College to provide information on
applications of microcomputers in libraries, is
announced, and its value to OCLC libraries is
estimated.

1137 "Moonlight Searching." Small Computers in
Libraries 2 (November 1982): 5-6.
BRS/AFTER DARK and DIALOG's KNOWLEDGE
INDEX are each announced, and their services are
described briefly. The possible impact of after
hours searching is noted, as is DIALOG's position
on copyright.

1138 "New Micro SDI from BIOSIS: Model for All Disci-
plines?" Library Journal 108 (November 15,
1983): 2124.
BIOSIS database announces a new Selective
Dissemination of Information program that offers
monthly updates on floppy disks to subscribers in
the biological sciences.

1139 NITECKI, DANUTA A. "WILSONLINE." American
Libraries 16 (December 1985): 804-06, 808-09.
A thorough evaluation of the H. W.
Wilson Company's WILSONLINE online search service
is provided, considering the seventeen databases
offered, and addressing quality, thoroughness,
ease of use, marketing, and future developments.
Bibliography.

1140 OJALA, MARYDEE. "Knowledge Index: a Review."
Online 7 (September 1983): 31-34.
DIALOG's KNOWLEDGE INDEX, an after-hours
search service designed for the novice or home
computer user, is reviewed by a reference librarian who points up its uses, the ways in which it
differs from daytime DIALOG searching, and the
databases which are available. A shorter review
of BRS/AFTER DARK is included for comparative
purposes.

1141 O'LEARY, MICK. "CompuServe and The Source: Data-
banks for the End-User." Database 8 (June
1985): 100-06.

COMPUSERVE and THE SOURCE, two vendors competing for the same clientele, are compared in terms of features, information, and services.

1142 "Online Micro-Software Guide and Directory Goes Online With BRS." Online 7 (September 1983): 10.

File SOFT, an online file of software information based on the Online Micro-Software Guide and Directory, is announced for September, 1983. The database is described, and price information is provided.

1143 "Pergamon VIDEO PATSEARCH Converts to IBM Personal Computer." Information Retrieval and Library Automation 19 (November 1983): 2-3.

VIDEO PATSEARCH, an online search service for British patents, is now fully accessible on an ordinary IBM PC according to this news note. Prior to 1983 a specifically designed micro was required.

1144 REGAZZI, JOHN J. "WILSONLINE: A Review of Features." Library Hi Tech 3, no. 1, issue 9 (1985): 101-12.

WILSONLINE, the H. W. Wilson Company's online bibliographic utility, is described, including search procedures, search categories, the online thesaurus, ranging, displaying and printing records, saving searches, and Wilson's support services.

1145 RICKER, ANN. "Microcomputer Index/DISC." RQ 22 (Summer 1983): 415-17.

MICROCOMPUTER INDEX, available through DIALOG, and DISC available through BRS, are reviewed together and compared for size, currency, titles indexed, format, and special features.

1146 ROTHENBERG, DIANNE. "MICROsearch." RQ 22 (Summer 1983): 417-18.

MICROsearch, an ERIC Clearinghouse on Information Resources program to provide ERIC bibliographic data on diskette in lieu of online, is described, with information on necessary hard-

ware, search strategies, fields in each record,
limitations, benefits, and cost.

1147 SMITH, STEPHEN C. "Online Current-Events Retrieval Services: Developments and Trends."
Library Hi Tech 1 (Spring 1984): 59-64.
Changes in the online market are noted,
including the demise of the NEW YORK TIMES INFOR-
MATION SERVICE, the introduction of such new news
services as VUTEXT and NEWSNET, and BRS and
DIALOG's developing interest in the home computer
user. The impact of the microcomputer is noted
in this context. Bibliography.

1148 "Software Library Can be Accessed." T.H.E.
Journal: Technological Horizons in Education
12 (March 1985): 22.
Searchmart Corporation announces that its
SOFTWARE LIBRARY is online, providing descriptions and purchase information for thousands of
software products. The database is reviewed and
log-on information is supplied.

1149 "'The Source' Aims at Libraries." Small Computers in Libraries 1 (December 1981): 6-7.
THE SOURCE, an online information utility
which originally catered to the home computer
user, has expanded its scope to include libraries
among its clientele. THE SOURCE is described and
reviewed with the librarian in mind.

1150 "Stolen Books, On-Line." Small Computers in
Libraries 2 (March 1982): 7.
BOOKLINE ALERT, a database listing bib-
liographic information concerning major library
thefts in the United States, England, France,
Australia, and New Zealand, went online in
September, 1981. Input and access information
are provided.

1151 TALAB, ROSEMARY STURDEVANT. "Databases of Microcomputer Software: An Overview." Library
Journal 110 (May 1, 1985): 101-02, 104; and
School Library Journal 31 (May 1985): 131-32,
134.

Evaluations of software are often difficult to find, but several databases accessible
through DIALOG, BRS, and other online vendors
offer reviews or references to reviews. COMPUTER
DATABASE, MICROCOMPUTER INDEX, MENU, and ONLINE
MICRO-SOFTWARE GUIDE AND DIRECTORY (File SOFT)
are reviewed in this article. Bibliography.

1152 TENOPIR, CAROL. "The Database Industry Today:
    Some Vendors' Perspectives." Library Journal
    109 (February 1, 1984): 156-57.
        Although concerning the database industry
in general, nearly half of this article is devoted to a recent survey concerning the problem
of downloading of information from online databases using microcomputers. Advantages to the
user are discussed; anticipated impact on the
vendor is considered.

1153 TENOPIR, CAROL. "Database Subsets." Library
    Journal 110 (May 15, 1985): 42-43.
        Some database producers are beginning to
offer subsets or portions of their databases for
sale on floppy disk, magnetic tape, or laser-
disk. A librarian may find this to be a partial
solution to the problems of excessive line
charges and demands from end users for online
search privileges. Several producers of subsets
are identified.

1154 TENOPIR, CAROL. "Dialog's Knowledge Index and
    BRS/After Dark: Database Searching on Personal
    Computers." Library Journal 108 (March 1,
    1983): 471-74.
        BRS/AFTER DARK and DIALOG's KNOWLEDGE
INDEX, online search services directed toward the
home micro enthusiast, are announced and described. Individual searching strategies are
briefly outlined for each, services are compared,
and their potential considered.

1155 TENOPIR, CAROL. "End User Search Services: A
    Comparison." Online '83 Conference Proceed-
    ings, Chicago, 10-12 October 1983. Weston,
    CT: Online, Inc., 1983. Pp. 280-85.

Five end user search services are reviewed and compared in terms of costs, databases, special services, searching techniques, help features, documentation, and ease of use. Included are KNOWLEDGE INDEX, BRS/AFTER DARK, THE SOURCE, COMPUSERVE, and DELPHI. A comparison chart brings basic information together for ease of use.

1156 WALKER, RUSSELL E. "Library Users of Microcomputers: An Emerging Database." Public Libraries 23 (Summer 1984): 46-47.

THE MICROCOMPUTER DATABASE OF LIBRARY USERS, a nationwide, regionally organized listing of resource people knowledgeable in the field of microcomputers, is introduced. The organization of the database is discussed, the goals and objectives are presented, and an application form is included.

1157 WARD, JOSEPH H., Jr. "Online Searching: The Future is Now With Knowledge Index." Educational Computer Magazine 3 (May/June 1983); 28-29.

KNOWLEDGE INDEX, DIALOG's low cost, after hours search service aimed at the home computer owner, is spotlighted, considering search strategies, database selection, log-on, data elements, and future developments.

1158 "Wilson Online." Library Systems Newsletter 5 (November 1985): 85.

The H. W. Wilson Company is pleased with the success of its online edition of the Readers' Guide to Periodical Literature, and announces the expansion of its WILSONLINE to include Library Literature, Art Index, and Vertical File Index.

1159 ZAHED, HYDER A. "B-I-T-S: An Innovative Approach to Information Delivery." Online '84 Conference Proceedings, San Francisco, 29-31 October 1984. Weston, CT: Online, Inc., 1984. Pp. 279-83.

BIOSIS Information Transfer System (BITS), a service of BioSciences Information Services, which provides subscribers with monthly updates of bibliographic data on magnetic tape or floppy disk, is reviewed and evaluated. Zahed considers hardware and software requirements, BITS characteristics, system advantages, and new features. Bibliography.

DATA AND FILE MANAGEMENT

1160 ARMSTRONG, C. J. "The Use of a Commercial Microcomputer Database Management System as the
Basis for Bibliographic Information Retrieval." Journal of Information Science 8
(June 1984): 197-201.
    Bibliographic storage and retrieval using
dBASE II software is the topic of this article
which considers file structure, capabilities of
the software, searching and output. The file, as
designed, is structured for journal indexing;
however, it appears adaptable as an automated
catalog for a small library. Bibliography.

1161 BAILEY, ALBERTA S. "Creating and Maintaining a
Database/Databank Comparison System With Lotus
1-2-3 On a (Most-of-the-Time) IBM Compatible
Micro." Online 9 (March 1985): 86-92.
    A project to transfer a Database Update
File, maintained at the University of Arkansas
Library, from card file to microcomputer is
described by the project director. A Lee Data
Series 700 Personal Workstation with LOTUS 1-2-3
software was used for the project. A sample of
the end product is provided. Bibliography.

1162 BAILEY, JOHN A.; HOOD, DAVID G.; and MARTINEZ,
SAMUEL J. "The Development of a Low-Cost Computerized Editorial Processing System." The
Information Age in Perspective. Proceedings
of the 41st ASIS Annual Meeting. White
Plains, NY: Knowledge Industry Publications,
1978, v. 15. Pp. 21-24.
    Development of the EDITORIAL PROCESSING
SYSTEM (EPS), a microcomputer-based system used
in creating Petroleum Abstracts, is described,
along with hardware and software configurations.

1163 BAXTER, PAUL. "Microcomputers and the Bibliographic Record." The Application of Mini-
and Micro-Computers in Information, Documenta-

284

tion and Libraries. Proceedings of the International Conference on the Application of
Mini- and Micro-Computers in Information,
Documentation and Libraries, Tel-Aviv, Israel,
13-18 March 1983. New York: North-Holland,
1983. Pp. 513-18.
The potential of a microcomputer for
handling bibliographic records increases in direct relation to the increase in its storage
capacity. This article considers the role of the
microcomputer in bibliographic data control in
small libraries and its adaptability for accessing large bibliographic utilities. The role
of the British Library's Research and Development
Department in developing microcomputer applications is discussed, and the future for microcomputers in the handling of bibliographic records
is predicted. Bibliography.

1164 BECK, JEAN C. "Information Technology for School
Children." IFLA Journal 10, no. 2 (1984):
145-50.
The SIR (Schools Information Retrieval)
Project, a British information retrieval system
for secondary schools intended to simulate the
research-oriented online search systems, is discussed in detail. Operation of the programs,
written for Research Machines Ltd 380Z microcomputers and consisting of search and database
manipulation functions, is illustrated through
discussion and examples.

1165 BECK, JEAN C. "Information Technology in Action."
The School Librarian 30 (December 1982): 307-
11.
A British school librarian briefly discusses implementation of a microcomputer program
in her school, describes and evaluates the British Library's SIR project, and considers the
selection process for information retrieval software.

1166 BENSON, DENNIS A.; STANDING, ROY A.; and GOLD-
STEIN, CHARLES M. "A Microprocessor-Based
System for the Delivery of Full-Text, Encyclo-

pedic Information." The Information Community: An Alliance for Progress. Proceedings of the 44th ASIS Annual Meeting. White Plains, NY: Knowledge Industry Publications, 1981, v. 18. Pp. 256-59.

This paper discusses a pilot full-text, microprocessor-based delivery system that has been developed at the Lister Hill National Center for Biomedical Communications. Employing a special 16-bit microprocessor, the PASCAL Micro-Engine, the project successfully combines high level language with low cost microprocessor equipment to produce a cost-effective delivery system. Bibliography.

1167 BERTRAND, D., and BADER, C. R. "Storage and Retrieval of Bibliographic References Using a Microprocessor System." International Journal of Bio-Medical Computing 11 (July 1980): 285-93.

FILOS, a microcomputer-based storage and retrieval program for bibliographic references is described in detail. Designed for the Department of Psychology of the University of Geneva (Switzerland) Medical School, the program runs on a dual disk drive microcomputer system, and provides access by key-word, author, and string matching. Bibliography.

1168 BESEMER, SUE, and GADIKIAN, RANDY. "Indexing Phone Directories With dBASE II." Small Computers in Libraries 4 (June 1984): 1.

Setting up an automated index for a collection of telephone directories using dBASE II software and a microcomputer is described, as is producing a printed list using dBASE II REPORT. Examples are included.

1169 BLAIR, JOHN C., Jr. "Creating Your Own Database." Database 5 (August 1982): 11-17.

Creating in-house databases using a database management system is the topic of this article which combines theory and practice. Data manipulation, data storage, and design of the data entry are discussed, along with suggested

available software packages suitable to perform
specific retrieval functions.

1170 BLAIR, JOHN C., Jr. "DISK-O-MANIA: Storing Your
Data." Online 6 (January 1982): 72-76.
Blair covers the topic of microcomputer
data storage, addressing terms, types of data
storage, the role and capabilities of the operating system, procedures, and equipment.

1171 BORDWELL, STEPHEN P. "dBASE II--Library Use of
a Microcomputer Database Management System."
Program 18 (April 1984): 157-65.
Database management software is discussed, and its adaptation to library applications is considered. dBASE II, a general database management system popular among libraries,
is used as an example, and its application to the
organization and indexing of a collection of
library trade literature at the Library of the
College of Librarianship Wales is explained.

1172 BORDWELL, STEPHEN P. "Interfacing Microcomputer
Software Using a Common File." Program 17
(January 1983): 14-20.
By designing systems in which unrelated
software programs share common files, greater
efficiency and greater use of data are achieved.
Methodology is explained and utility programs
which perform the function are considered. Bibliography.

1173 BURTON, PAUL F. "Microcomputer Applications and
the Use of Database Management Software."
Program 16 (July 1982): 180-90.
Library applications for PETAID, a database management system designed for the Commodore
Pet, are outlined by the librarian at Leith
Nautical College, where the program is used for
indexing, acquisitions, producing union catalogs,
and serial control.

1174 BURTON, PAUL F. "Microcomputer Applications in
Information Retrieval." ISG News 20 (April
1982): 5-7.

Burton considers the microcomputer's role in the development of databases, online searching, local networks, and other aspects of information storage, retrieval, and manipulation.

1175 BURTON, PAUL F. "Software Off the Shelf: In-House Information With a Micro." Aslib Proceedings 35 (September 1983): 335-45.
Burton analyzes the concept of the database management system, discusses limitations, options, and use, and recommends good DBMS programs available in Great Britain. Bibliography.

1176 CARNEY, RICHARD. "InfoTrac: An Inhouse Computer-Access System." Library Hi Tech 3, no. 2, issue 10 (1985): 91-94.
InfoTrac, a laserdisc system built by the Information Access Company for its automated journal index, is discussed and evaluated. Combining an IBM PC with a Pioneer laserdisc player and Hewlett-Packard ThinkJet printer, the system provides an in-house database in online format.

1177 CHENEY, HAL. "A 'd' Limiter to Beware of." OCLC Micro 1 (May 1985): 16-18.
Librarians using dBASE II software may eventually want to upgrade to dBASE III. This article addresses problems which may be encountered, and suggests advance procedures which may help circumvent the problems.

1178 COHILL, ANDREW. "Bibliophile Brings Microcomputer Order Out of Chaos." Online 8 (January 1984): 34-41.
A bibliophile who wanted an easily manipulated file system for his book list gives the details of a self-created file program which meets his needs far better and more economically than any commercial database package available.

1179 CRANE, ROGER, and POOLE, WALLACE. "Project Retrieve: The Banking of Instructional Development Resources at Brock University." Educational Computer Magazine 2 (March/April 1982): 46-47.

The development of an online information
retrieval system for the Instructional Development Committee of Brock University is outlined.
The system employs Commodore PET hardware and a
JINSAM 1.0 software package. The information
sources are housed in the University Library.

1180 DAEHN, RALPH M. "Methods and Software for Building Bibliographic Data Bases." Canadian Library Journal 42 (June 1985): 147-52.
The in-house database is considered in
relation to the online vendor alternative, and
systems for maintenance of in-house databases
are discussed. The author addresses data entry,
information retrieval, file security, software,
and downloading in his presentation.

1181 "Data Bases Management Systems." Small Computers
in Libraries 2 (March 1982): 2-5.
Theory behind data base management systems (DBMS), a programming concept which origi-
nated with turnkey systems but is gradually being
adapted to micros, accompanies an explanation of
DBMS use.

1182 EARL, BRIAN. "An Apple in the Library." School
Librarian 33 (March 1985): 12-17.
Uses for an Apple microcomputer with PFS:
FILE and PFS: REPORT software in a school library
are discussed by a practicing librarian. PFS:
FILE Options are presented, several library
applications are recommended, and a variety of
in-house databases are suggested.

1183 EDDISON, BETTY. "A Checklist for Defining Your
Needs." Database 8 (June 1985): 78-81.
Criteria for the selection of file management software for database operation and maintenance are discussed, and a checklist is provided for quick reference.

1184 FOX, KATHLEEN. "Database-Management Software for
Apple II Systems." Library Software Review 3
(September 1984): 346-61.
Functions and some suggested applications

for database management systems are reviewed briefly before the author launches into a model for evaluating DBMS software. Especially useful is an evaluation checklist which covers such characteristics as hardware/software compatibility, file size limitations, data manipulation capabilities, and output capabilities. Seven programs are reviewed. Bibliography.

1185 FREUND, ALFRED L. "Three Data Managers for the CBM 8032." Software Review 1 (October 1982): 171-74.
     The Ramapo Catskill Library System, Middletown, New York, has developed an acquisitions system, an information storage and retrieval file, inventories, and mailing lists using a Commodore 8032 micro and OZZ, JINSAM, and THE MANAGER software. The three programs are compared in chart format, but no recommendations are made.

1186 GARTEN, EDWARD D. "Fifty 'Best' Database and File Management Packages for Academic Libraries." Library Software Review 4 (March/April 1985): 59-62.
     Fifty database management programs have been selected and recommended for academic library use on the basis of adaptability to the academic library environment, compatibility with brands of microcomputer hardware, and price. Brief annotations provide information on compatibility, special features, and sources.

1187 GILLESPIE, JIM. "dBASE II: Better Than Sliced Bread." Small Computers in Libraries 4 (November 1984): 7-8.
     Gillespie describes nine applications for which dBASE software is used in the Nepean (Ontario) Public Library. These range from problem patron files to bindery lists to paperback acquisitions to a corporate authority file.

1188 GILLESPIE, JIM. "dBASE II at Nepean, Ont., Public Library." Canadian Library Journal 41 (December 1984): 339-43.

Gillespie considers the micro-automation
of the Nepean (Ontario) Public Library, using a
Xerox 820 II microcomputer and dBASE II software.
Patron files, billing files, bindery lists, and
acquisitions files are described. Advantages and
limitations of the program are addressed.

1189 HENKENS, ROBERT W. "Microcomputer-Assisted
     Information Retrieval." North Carolina Li-
     braries 40 (Fall/Winter 1982): 214-19.
          A chemistry professor at Duke University
describes a microcomputer-assisted information
retrieval system which runs on an Apple II micro
and uses commercially produced software. He then
describes a program which is currently under
development which will combine the features of
the commercial software into one dedicated program for bibliographic data retrieval and manipulation. Bibliography.

1190 HERTHER, NANCY K. "Data Base Management Software
     in Libraries & Information Centers." Small
     Computers in Libraries 3 (October 1983): 1-2.
          The versatility of database management
systems is discussed, and the advantages of using
dBASE in a library are told. Bibliography.

1191 HUBBARD, ABIGAIL. "Reprint File Management Soft-
     ware." Online 9 (November 1985): 67-73.
          Reprint files often become cumbersome and
unwieldy, but can easily be controlled with a
file management program. Hubbard provides guidelines for establishing such a file, and provides
information concerning ten file management software programs in useful chart format. Included
are: BIBLIOFILE, BIBLIOTEK, BOOKENDS, LIBRARY
MATE, NOTEBOOK II, PROFESSIONAL BIBLIOGRAPHIC
SYSTEM, QUICK SEARCH LIBRARIAN, SAPANA: CARDFILE,
SCI-MATE PERSONAL DATA MANAGER, and SEARCHLIT.

1192 "Interactive Information Retrieval Through an
     Intelligent Terminal." British Library
     Research and Development Newsletter 20 (May
     1980): 1.
          A research project to test information

retrieval techniques using a specifically developed microcomputer system at the University of London is briefly described.

1193 JOSLIN, ANN. "Beyond Circ and Serials; Database Management Programs in Libraries." Online 83' Conference Proceedings, Chicago, 10-12 October 1983. Weston, CT: Online, Inc., 1983. Pp. 140-45.
The basics of choosing a database management system for a library are presented simply, while raising several difficult questions which must be addressed in the selection process.

1194 KANTERS, BEN. "Microcomputers for Information Storage and Retrieval." Electronic Library 1 (July 1983): 187-95.
Aspects of library information storage and retrieval using microcomputer equipment and software are considered, including hardware, software, database creation, data entry, indexing, and searching. Advice on choosing and learning to use information storage and retrieval packages is added. Bibliography.

1195 KARARIA, KAMAL. "Microcomputer-Based Bibliographic Information Storage and Retrieval System." Journal of Library and Information Science 6 (June 1981): 29-44.
An early attempt at bibliographic control using a microcomputer and a locally produced database management system is described. Implemented at the Eicher Goodearth Ltd. Research Centre Library, the program was developed on an HCL-8C micro, built by Hindustan Computers Ltd. File structure, choice of an indexing language, and system limitations are addressed. Bibliography.

1196 KAZLAUSKAS, EDWARD JOHN. "Information Management Software: Categories and Criteria for Review." Library Software Review 3 (March 1984): 46-51.
The author identifies three categories of information management software as: general purpose, specific, and library application DBMS

packages. Criteria for reviewing off-the-shelf versions of these, and notes on comparing their applications and functions are provided.

1197 KENT, ANTHONY K. "Microcomputers for Database Management and Retrieval." Proceedings of the 6th International Online Information Meeting, London, 7-9 December 1982. Medford, NJ: Learned Information, 1982. Pp. 351-57.

Microcomputers are destined to have a tremendous impact on libraries, particularly in the area of information storage and retrieval, but progress has been slowed by the lack of a theoretical base to information science and the lack of appropriate microcomputer software. The author considers these factors and provides direction for development in each.

1198 KITTLE, PAUL W. "Source Code." Database 8 (December 1985): 85-87.

Kittle examines data management and retrieval for libraries using dBASE II software.

1199 LEVINSON, JUDITH, and WEIL, SUZIE. "Peachtree Software: Database Creation." M300 and PC Report 2 (April 1985): 7.

Staff of the Library and Technical Information Department of Soreq Nuclear Research Centre, Yavne, Israel, have introduced IBM PC XT hardware and Peachtree Software's LIST MANAGER into the Centre's operation, using the two to create databases for the Centre's technical reports and the publications of Soreq's scientists. The project is described and evaluated.

1200 MACEK, ROSANNE. "File Management at the Apple Library PFS: FILE." Software Review 2 (March 1983): 24-28.

The basics of manipulating PFS: FILE software are explained, and examples are provided for its application as a file management system for acquisitions and indexing.

1201 MANSON, CONNIE. "dBASE II, WordStar, BIS: Washington's Natural Resources Bibliographies."

Small Computers in Libraries 5 (June 1985): 22-23.

Washington State's Department of Natural Resources employs an IBM PC microcomputer, with dBASE II and WORDSTAR software, to prepare, edit, index, and maintain a current bibliography of Washington geology and mineral resources, and to produce periodic supplements for publication. Procedures are defined and plans for the future are discussed.

1202 MASON, ROBERT M. "Database Management Software." Library Journal 110 (November 15, 1985): 64-65.

Mason discusses the various types of database management architecture, including sequential files, hierarchical and network structures, and relational database managers. He then identifies and reviews database management software suitable for the IBM PC.

1203 McDONALD, DAVID R. "Database Management Systems: A Review." Library Software Review 4 (July/ August 1985): 188-92.

Database management systems are reviewed in layman's terms, considering purpose and architecture, library applications, selection, and administration. Bibliography.

1204 MILLER, ROBERT H. "'Information Master' and the Salem Public Library." ACCESS: Microcomputers in Libraries 1 (October 1981): 14-15.

The experience of creating a library mailing list using an Apple II Plus microcomputer and INFORMATION MASTER software is described, along with suggested additional applications and limitations of the INFORMATION MASTER program.

1205 "Production of Bibliographies by Micros." Online Review 8 (February 1984): 15-16.

Three Austrian librarians are compiling a multivolume bibliography of bibliographies, collective biographies, and general reference books, using hand-held microcomputers such as the Epson HX-20 for data gathering and manipulation, and a minicomputer for storage. The hardware configuration is described and the project explained.

1206 ROSS, JOHN D. "LITER: a LITERature Reference Information Retrieval Program." *Agricultural Engineering* 60 (November 1979): 16-17.
  LITER, a microcomputer-based storage and retrieval program for bibliographic information, is described. Built to operate on a Wang 2200C microcomputer, the program was developed to control documents in a U. S. Department of Agriculture office, but is adaptable to any subject. Bibliography.

1207 ROWBOTTOM, MARY. "Information Retrieval Project in the UK." *Small Computers in Libraries* 1 (September 1981): 7.
  Rowbottom describes a microcomputer-based information storage and retrieval system (the SIR project) for secondary schools in Great Britain.

1208 ROWLANDS, JIM. "Comsoft DMS DELTA: Library Applications at Scunthorpe Central Library." *Vine* no. 59 (December 1984): 27-31.
  A microcomputer system purchased by Humberside Leisure Services to support the Business Information Centre at Scunthorpe, has been adapted to several library applications, including circulation control, local information files, serials, and cataloging, using DELTA data management software.

1209 SAFFADY, WILLIAM. "Data Management Software for Microcomputers." *Library Technology Reports* 19 (September/October 1983): 451-592.
  Eighteen database management systems are reviewed in detail, with a lengthy introduction which provides general background concerning DBMS programs and discusses similarities among the programs evaluated.

1210 SEIDEN, PEGGY, and KIBBEY, MARK. "Information Retrieval Systems for Microcomputers." *Library Hi Tech* 3, no. 1, issue 9 (1985): 41-54.

The characteristics and capabilities of information retrieval software are discussed, and two powerful examples, SIRE and ZYINDEX, are reviewed.

1211 SHAYEVITZ, EVYATAR. "LIS-Library Information System for Mini/Micro Computers." The Application of Mini- and Micro-Computers in Infomation, Documentation and Libraries. Proceedings of the International Conference on the Application of Mini- and Micro-Computers in Information, Documentation and Libraries, Tel-Aviv, Israel, 13-18 March 1983. New York: North-Holland, 1983. Pp. 161-67.
LIS, a library-oriented information storage and retrieval system from Israel, is described. Functions and features of the system are addressed; data input, retrieval, updating, distribution, and security are discussed; user/ computer communication is illustrated.

1212 SHEROUSE, VICKI M. "Using a General Data Base Program." Educational Computer Magazine 3 (March/April 1983): 46-47, 59.
The basic structure and uses of a database management system in one school media center are explained by the media specialist, and advantages and savings in time are told.

1213 SMITH, SCOTT F.; JORGENSEN, WILLIAM L.; and FUCHS, PHILIP L. "PULSAR: A Personalized Microcomputer-Based System for Keyword Search and Retrieval of Literature Information." Journal of Chemical Information and Computer Sciences 21 (November 1981): 209-13.
PULSAR, a keyword search and retrieval system developed at Purdue University for bibliographic control of scientific literature, is described in considerable detail. Written for the TRS-80 II microcomputer, the program is intended for personal or departmental use, but certainly seems applicable to science libraries.

1214 TAGG, ROGER M. "Bibliographic and Commercial Databases--Contrasting Approaches to Data

Management with Special Reference to DBMS."
Program 16 (October 1982): 191-99.
    Bibliographic and commercial databases
are contrasted, the development of information
retrieval programs and database management systems for accessing the two are described, and
possibilities for combining the best of the
access modes are suggested. Bibliography.

1215 TENOPIR, CAROL. "Identification and Evaluation
of Software for Microcomputer-Based In-House
Databases." Information Technology and Libraries 3 (March 1984): 21-34.
    The author reviews the growing volume of
literature concerning evaluation and selection of
software for microcomputer-based in-house databases, provides a list of review sources, and
includes brief information on eight database management packages. Bibliography.

1216 TENOPIR, CAROL. "In-House Databases I: Software
Sources." Library Journal 108 (April 1,
1983): 639-41.
    Deciding what files to automate and
determining appropriate software packages are
major considerations of this article, which provides good evaluations of several directories and
reviewing tools for software.

1217 TENOPIR, CAROL. "In-House Databases II: Evaluating & Choosing Software." Library Journal
108 (May 1, 1983): 885-88.
    The process of selecting data management
software is reviewed, from the basic needs
assessment to implementation and training, with
special emphases on software evaluation. Seven
packages are examined briefly. Bibliography.

1218 TOCATLIAN, JOCQUES, and ROSE, JOHN B. "Unesco's
General Information Programme and the Application of Information Mangement Software for
Microcomputers." Microcomputers for Information Management 1 (December 1984): 257-67.
    The need for data storage, management,
and exchange in developing countries is address-

ed, and the role of Unesco's General Information
Programme in encouraging the development of
microcomputer-based systems is explained. A program to aid member states in developing information systems is described. Bibliography.

1219 URBANEK, VAL. "INFORM: Library Information at
Your Fingertips." Information Technology and
Libraries 1 (December 1982): 336-41.
INFORM, a microcomputer-based turnkey
system for information storage and retrieval, is
outlined, illustrated, and evaluated. Although
the system is adaptable to other-than-library
uses, it is especially suited to libraries and
is being marketed as a stand alone system and as
a complement to the CLSI public access catalog.

1220 VAN STYVENDAELE, B. J. H. "The Making of an RNA
Phage Bibliography with Personal Information
Retrieval by Microcomputer." Methods of Information in Medicine 18 (July 1979): 158-64.
The development of a bibliography concerning RNA phages using a micro and database
software is described. Data conversion, record
structure, revision, updating, sorting, searching, and retrieval are considered. Bibliography.

1221 VAUGHAN, SHEILA, and EDMUNDS, LLOYD. "Making a
Micro Mighty in a Library." Australian Library News 12 (November 1982): 6.
Excerpts from the Vaughan and Edmunds
article, which appeared in Library Association
Record, October 1982, constitute the major portion of this news item.

1222 VAUGHAN, SHEILA, and EDMUNDS, LLOYD. "Relaxed,
Experimental Approach Proves Our Retrieval
System Viable." Library Association Record
84 (October 1982): 349-50.
The development of an information retrieval system for the University of Manchester's
Department of Administrative Studies Library is
related. The system employs dBASE software with
an Apple microcomputer modified to accommodate
the dBASE package.

1223 WAGNER, JUDY. "Data Base Management System
Design for Library Automation: A Look Inside
File Structure." ACCESS: Microcomputers in
Libraries 1 (July 1981): 13-14, 21.
This article considers file structure
along with major characteristics and uses of data
base management systems, then stresses the need
for development of systems geared to library
functions and the raising of librarians' awareness of the importance of such systems. Bibliography.

1224 WALDRON, C. B., and COOKE, DEBORAH M. "A Personal On-Line Reference Retrieval Program for
Microcomputers." Journal of Information
Science 4 (July 1982): 155-60.
An online bibliographic retrieval system
for researchers at St. Thomas' Hospital, London,
is described. Objectives, system requirements,
programming, and system access are detailed.
Bibliography.

1225 WALKER, STEPHEN. "An Information Retrieval Package for Microcomputers." Program 16 (July
1982): 171-79.
The development of FIRS, a free-text
information retrieval system, is outlined. System imposed constraints, file structure, and system configuration are briefly described. Bibliography.

1226 WARDEN, WILLIAM H., III, and WARDEN, BETTE M.
"An Introduction to Database Management
Systems." Library Hi Tech 2, no. 3, issue 7
(1984): 33-40.
Basics of a database management system
are considered, along with factors which should
influence system selection. The authors describe
a method for comparing systems and illustrate its
application. Bibliography.

TECHNOLOGY, HARDWARE, AND OPERATING SYSTEMS

1227 "The ASCII Code." Small Computers in Libraries
     1 (May 1981): 2-4.
          The American Standard Code for Informa-
     tion Interchange (ASCII), the code used in micro-
     computers to represent information stored in mem-
     ory, is charted, described, and its use explained
     in simple terms.

1228 "Advice on Micros." Library Systems Newsletter
     1 (November 1981): 38-39.
          In response to a request to identify
     inexpensive micros suitable for library use, the
     editors of LSN recommend the DEC VT18X, Hewlett-
     Packard 85, IBM Personal Computer, Intertec
     Superbrain, NEC America PC-8012A, Xerox 820, and
     Zenith X89.

1229 "Apple Upgrades." Small Computers in Libraries
     2 (July 1982): 5.
          The Apple II and Apple II Plus microcom-
     puters may seem to be losing ground as new and
     more powerful models come onto the market; how-
     ever, a variety of add-on hardware offers instant
     upgrade. A few of the most popular peripherals
     are mentioned here.

1230 ARMSTRONG, C. J.; GUY, R. F.; and PAINTER, J. D.
     "Microcomputers or Word Processors in the
     Library?" Reprographics Quarterly 14 (Summer
     1981): 98-103.
          The authors compare microcomputer and
     word processing systems in relation to their
     adaptability to library functions. The charac-
     teristics of both are described, advantages and
     limitations are reviewed, and present and future
     applications are suggested. Bibliography.

1231 BEISER, KARL. "Alternatives to the IBM Key-
     board." Small Computers in Libraries 5
     (July/August 1985): 10-12.

The IBM PC keyboard is the least functional part of an otherwise high quality machine. Beiser points out the problems, recommends the Key Tronic as a viable alternative, and justifies his recommendations.

1232 BEISER, KARL. "Can't Get Enough--Some Words About Memory." Small Computers in Libraries 5 (September 1985): 6-7.

Beiser considers the increasing need for greater quantities of random access memory (RAM); why and how the need occurs; how it may be satisfied; and how much memory is really enough.

1233 BEISER, KARL. "Microcomputing." Wilson Library Bulletin 60 (December 1985): 42-43.

Beiser discusses the growth of the IBM compatible market since 1981, and analyzes the products for quality, service, advice, software availability, and other criteria.

1234 BENDIG, MARK. "Not for Novices: Take Control of Your Printer." OCLC Micro 1 (July 1985): 6-7, 19.

Unless you purchase a printer that is configured to operate with your microcomputer, the printer or certain of its features may not function. Bendig suggests two techniques which will give the operator greater control over the printer, each method outlined in step-by-step detail.

1235 BIRKENHEAD, TOM, and ALLEN, DAVID. "Common Pitfalls in Data Processing; Mainframe Lessons for Micro Users." ACCESS: Microcomputers in Libraries 2 (January 1982): 3-4, 28.

Fourteen mistakes common to mainframe and minicomputer installations are discussed in terms of microcomputer systems, along with methods of averting the problems.

1236 BLAIR, JOHN C., Jr. "The Application of Small Computers in Libraries." Special Libraries Association Florida Chapter Bulletin 15 (July 1983): 121-27.

Blair addresses considerations and pitfalls in automating with small computers, emphasizes the importance of the operating system, and recommends UNIX and PICK.

1237 BLAIR, JOHN C., Jr. "A Bevy of Micros. . .A Shopping List of Specific Systems." Online 7 (May 1983): 46-53.
Blair discusses advantages of single-user versus multi-user microcomputer systems, then reviews eight systems adaptable to library functions.

1238 BLAIR, JOHN C., Jr. "One Possible Information Center Microcomputer Configuration: The 'Plain Vanilla' Apple II Plus." Online 6 (May 1982): 69-77.
The Apple II Plus microcomputer is basically a hobbyist's machine. Through the addition of peripherals it may be upgraded to serve minimally in an information center environment. These add-ons are described, along with certain recommended software packages.

1239 BOSS, RICHARD W. "Integrating and Interfacing Library Systems." Electronic Library 3 (April 1985): 124-31.
Microcomputers are essentially single function machines. Boss recommends functional integration in order to allow single function systems to share a common database. Considering turnkey, mini, and micro systems, he discusses interfaces, linking both homogenous and heterogenous systems, the role of vendors, and other related apsects of the topic. Bibliography.

1240 BOSS, RICHARD W. "Microcomputers in Libraries." Sourdough 19 (July 1982): 5, 23.
The 8-bit microcomputer is discussed in relation to its usefulness in libraries. It is recommended for word processing, scheduling, bookkeeping, and online searching, but not for such library functions as circulation and serials control, which demand large data storage capacities.

1241 BRANSCOMB, LEWIS M. "The Computer's Debt to
       Science." Library Hi Tech 2, no. 3, issue 7
       (1984): 7-18.
       The computer industry is still in its
infancy, but is growing at about 15% per year.
This growth is largely the result of scientific
discoveries and developments in computer technology, which allows the industry to continuously
offer improved products. The author considers
developments in disk storage, programming, end
user interfaces, and other areas of development
which sustain growth. He also considers limits.

1242 BRENNAN, PATRICIA B. M., and SILVERBERG, JOEL S.
       "Will My Disks Go Floo If I Take Them
       Through?" College and Research Libraries News
       46 (September 1985): 423-24.
       In order to determine the effects of
library magnetic security systems on data stored
on floppy disks, disks were exposed to extreme
conditions. Only one of the four experiments
performed--exposure to the sensitizer unit--
resulted in any loss or damage to data. The
experiment is detailed.

1243 BRODERSEN, MARGARET. "Electronic Typewriters/
       Printers." Small Computers in Libraries 2
       (December 1982): 7.
       The author describes the interface of a
Royal SE 5010 model electronic typewriter with an
Apple microcomputer to achieve letter quality
printing at an affordable price.

1244 BROERING, NAOMI C. "Minicomputer and Micro-
       computer Versions of Georgetown University's
       Library Information System (LIS)." Second
       National Conference on Integrated Online Li-
       brary Systems Proceedings, Atlanta, 13-14
       September 1984. Canfield, OH: Genaway & Asso-
       ciates, 1984. Pp. 169-74.
       Georgetown University's Library Infor-
mation System (LIS), an integrated system developed for the minicomputer and installed in 1981,
has been adapted for use on microcomputer hardware. This article provides information on both

the minicomputer version which runs on a PDP 11/23, and the microcomputer version which runs on a Motorola 6800 supermicro. Features and limitations are discussed.

1245 BROUSSARD, HARRY C. "Child's Play." Information Technology and Libraries 1 (September 1982): 203-05.
    Since 1970 the microcomputer has emerged as a major influence in libraries because of its simplicity, low cost, and versatility. Lack of standards has been a major problem; however, the author considers merits of the technology and predicts a solution which will make inexpensive library computing a reality.

1246 "Buying a Second-Hand Computer: Checklist." Small Computers in Libraries 4 (December 1984): 10.
    Guidelines are provided for checking out a used microcomputer prior to purchase.

1247 CARLSON, DAVID H. "The Perils of Personals: Microcomputers in Libraries." Library Journal 110 (February 1, 1985): 50-55.
    Written for the purpose of assessing the role of the microcomputer in the library, this article compares it to the larger and more powerful minis and mainframes, presents its limitations, discusses new advances and developments, and lists library functions which lend themselves to microcomputer applications. Bibliography.

1248 COLE, DAVID H. "More Ways to Print Than Meet the Eye." Small Computers in Libraries 4 (September 1984): 6-8.
    ASCII, the standard language for storing, printing, or transmitting computer data, is discussed, with several hypothetical situations in which ASCII is used in library situations.

1249 COLE, DAVID H. "Your New Library IBM Microcomputer: Unpleasant Surprises." M300 and PC Report 2 (November 1985): 1-4.
    Cole addresses microcomputer problems,

including common software, telecommunications, printer, and hard disk malfunctions.

1250 CORTEZ, EDWIN M. "New and Emerging Technologies for Information Delivery." Catholic Library World 54 (December 1982): 214-18.
A variety of new technological developments are discussed, including Viewdata and Teletext, video disc technology, and online catalogs. Microcomputers are considered for their potential in distributed computing, communications, single function activities such as acquisitions, and networking. Bibliography.

1251 "Cost Estimates for Integrated Micro-Systems." Library Systems Newsletter 4 (June 1984): 41-43.
Interest in microcomputer-based integrated systems for libraries is increasing; however, vendors are often reluctant to help in planning, setting up, and maintaining these relatively low-cost installations. Library Systems Newsletter editors discuss two types of available systems and identify vendors who offer each for sale.

1252 CRAWFORD, WALT. "Common Sense and Low-Cost Printers; or, Does Your System Have Impact?" Library Hi Tech 3, no. 2, issue 10 (1985): 29-38.
Printers often represent the most troublesome and frustrating component of a microcomputer system. Crawford identifies and discusses several common printer problems and reviews two inexpensive but serviceable dot matrix printers: the Star Micronics Gemini-10 and the Hewlett-Packard ThinkJet.

1253 "DOS 2.0 for the IBM PC." Small Computers in Libraries 4 (February 1984): 1-2.
The development of the IBM PC Disk Operating System (PC-DOS) is traced through the 1.0, 1.1, and 2.0 versions. Changes and refinements are pointed out, and reasons for upgrading to the 2.0 version are provided.

1254 DAVIS, R. H.; RINALDI, C.; and NEVES, J. "Evaluation of Alternative Microcomputer Systems for Retrieval of Scientific References." Online Review 6 (December 1982): 539-44. The Cromemco System 3, Apple II, and Telima 1000 operating systems are tested, evaluated, and compared in a simulated information retrieval situation. Bibliography.

1255 "Developments on the Hardware Front." Small Computers in Libraries 4 (September 1984): 11-12. Refinements on the Macintosh and the PCjr are described; the Apple IIc, Sears' color TV/computer monitor, and Hewlett-Packard's lazer printer are announced.

1256 DEWEY, PATRICK R. "Apple Sider: Affordable Hard Disk Storage for Small Libraries." Library Hi Tech 3, no. 1, issue 9 (1985): 79-81. The Apple Sider, a 10-megabyte hard disk drive for the Apple microcomputer is evaluated and recommended for libraries with large storage needs.

1257 "Disk Units." Small Computers in Libraries 1 (June 1981): 2-4. Tapes and disks are compared as storage media; differences in types of disks are explained.

1258 DOLL, CAROL A. "The Care & Handling of Micro Disks." School Library Journal 32 (November 1985): 45. Microcomputer disks, the mainstay of a library's software program collection, are fragile and easily damaged or destroyed. The author explains the effects of fingerprints, food, paperclips, dust, magnets, pencils, heat, and humidity on disks. Ways of avoiding damage are suggested. Making backup copies is recommended.

1259 ENSIGN, DAVID. "Hewlett-Packard's ThinkJet Printer and the OCLC M300 Workstation." M300 and PC Report 2 (September 1985): 1-4.

Hewlett-Packard's ThinkJet printer is reviewed in terms of its use with the OCLC M300 Workstation. The author considers compatibility with the M300 and other hardware, capabilities, configuration, costs, and control codes. Problems are addressed, but the evaluation is positive.

1260 "The Evolution of Library Microcomputers." Small Computers in Libraries 2 (July 1982): 3-4.
       A review of developments in microcomputer technology calls attention to the proliferation of greatly refined hardware and simplified software on the market.

1261 "Expanding the Memory of Your PC." Small Computers in Libraries 4 (December 1984): 10.
       Suggestions and cautions are offered for those considering expansion of the memory on an IBM PC or PC compatible.

1262 FALANGA, ROSEMARIE. "What Mother Never Told You. . .About Printers." Library Software Review 4 (May/June 1985): 143-44.
       The microcomputer literature contains a wealth of information on printer evaluation and selection which Falanga recognizes as worthwhile. However, she suggests six additional grassroots questions that the shopper may want to ask before doing an invoice voucher.

1263 FALK, HOWARD. "Hardware Corner." Electronic Library 2 (July 1984): 158-60.
       The Fujitsu microcomputer is reviewed; ink-jet and letter quality dot matrix printers are considered; and volume storage methods are discussed, including Eastman Kodak's 10 million character floppy and the Micro-Magnum, with a removable hard disk.

1264 FALK, HOWARD. "Multi-User Microcomputers." Electronic Library 3 (April 1985): 107-10.
       Falk compares costs for a multiple terminal network and a multi-user microcomputer. He describes how multi-user systems operate, pro-

vides cost estimates for purchase and installation, and recommends specific systems to consider.

1265 FREEDMAN, MARY, and CARLIN, LARRY. "More Definitions." Library Journal 110 (November 1,
1985): 40-41.
Freedman and Carlin's earlier article,
"A Warm Boot Cannot Be Ordered from L. L. Bean,"
is continued, with definitions of such microcom-
puter-related terms as Addresses and Ports, Communications, CPU, Software, Integrated Software,
and Machine Language.

1266 FREEDMAN, MARY, and CARLIN, LARRY. "There's No
Copy Like Hard Copy!" Library Journal 110
(June 1, 1985): 100-01.
Printer basics are addressed, including
the differences between dot matrix, letter quality, and laser printers; the differences between
parallel and serial printers; computer-printer
compatibility; the function of a buffer, and
other questions.

1267 FREEDMAN, MARY, and CARLIN, LARRY. "A Warm Boot
Cannot Be Ordered from L. L. Bean." Library
Journal 110 (October 1, 1985): 76-77.
Freedman and Carlin define and explain
several common, but sometimes confusing, microcomputer terms, including Boot Up, Operating System, Bit, Byte, and File.

1268 GAFFNER, HAINES B. "Videotex in Your Organization." Videotex--Key to the Information
Revolution. Proceedings of Videotex '82: The
International Conference and Exhibition on
Videotex, Viewdata, and Teletext, New York,
28-30 June 1982. London: Online Conferences,
Ltd., 1982. Pp. 525-29.
There are four functional microcomputer
applications to videotex technology: 1) videotex
terminal, 2) information provider workstation,
3) host, and 4) gateway. Gaffner explains these
four functions and discusses the convergence of
videotex with other computer systems.

1269 GATES, HILARY. "Multi-User Microcomputers for Small Libraries: Progress Report on the Project at the Cairns Library." Vine no. 53 (April 1984): 43-44.

A project to investigate the potential of a multi-terminal microcomputer system is reported on as it nears completion. The final choice is an ALTOS microcomputer with PICK operating system and BOOKSHELF software. The system is reviewed briefly.

1270 GILMAN, PETER. "The Ambiguity of Computer Language." Small Computers in Libraries 5 (September 1985): 8-10.

This inaugural number of a column which will appear regularly in Small Computers in Libraries deals with technological differences in microcomputer development and technical terminology in the United States and Great Britain, and the difficulties in sharing information because of these differences.

1271 GILNER, DAVID J. "Printing OCLC Diacritical Marks." Small Computers in Libraries 3 (March 1983): 5-6.

When this article was written, no commercially produced printer existed which would produce diacritical markings. However, the Hebrew Union College Library has had an Epson MX-80FT modified to indicate the necessary symbols through a combination of printed squares. The problem is discussed; the solution is illustrated and evaluated.

1272 GOLDSMITH, GERRY, and WILLIAMS, PHILIP W. "User Interface-Handwriting Recognition." Program 17 (April 1983): 86-89.

Several types of data input devices are discussed and evaluated, including handwriting recognition devices, the touch screen, light pens, bit pads, and voice recognition devices.

1273 GOOD, PHILLIP I. "Maintaining Your Micro--All Year." Computer Decisions 14 (December 1982): 82, 84.

Hints on maintaining a microcomputer, a word on maintenance contracts, and several products which make maintenance easier are discussed in this practical article.

1274 GORDON, HELEN A. "CD-ROM at ALA: Where It's At." Online 9 (September 1985): 9.
CD-ROM, a compact disc information storage system that is accessed via personal computer, was demonstrated in prototype at the 1985 American Library Association conference held in Chicago. The technology is briefly reported, and its future anticipated.

1275 GROSCH, AUDREY N. "Configuring a Professional Microsystem for Information Processing." Microcomputers for Information Management 1 (March 1984): 15-29.
Hardware is the major concern of this article which addresses each component of a microsystem individually, with suggestions on compatibility and adaptability.

1276 GROSCH, AUDREY N. Distributed Computing and the Electronic Library: Micros to Superminis. White Plains, NY: Knowledge Industry Publications, 1985. 203p.
The state of the art in library distributed computing using small systems is examined from the perspective of the librarian seeking basic information. Trends and issues are addressed; the future is predicted. Hardware and software are discussed, and several domestic and foreign integrated library systems are described. Bibliography.

1277 GROSCH, AUDREY N. "Distributive Data Processing in Information Systems--Myth or Reality?" Information Choices and Policies. Proceedings of the 42nd ASIS Annual Meeting. White Plains, NY: Knowledge Industry Publications, 1979, v. 16. P. 354.
Technological advances, particularly in the area of inexpensive microcomputers, have accelerated the move to decentralized computer

access, made possible computer-to-computer links
between libraries and bibliographic utilities and
search services, and moved the library world
closer to the day when distributive data processing becomes a reality.

1278 HAMMER, CARL. "Bringing Electronics to Our Libraries." Information: Reports and Bibliographies 10, no. 3 (1981): 3-7.
In the keynote address to the 23rd Mili-
tary Librarians' Workshop, Carl Hammer considers
data management through computer technology,
places appropriate emphasis on the development of
the silicon chip, and places the impact of the
microcomputer on library management into perspective. Bibliography.

1279 HANE, PAULA. "How to Cope When Your Computer
is Orphaned. . .Update from an Osborne User."
Database 7 (February 1984): 74-76.
When the Osborne Computer Company filed
for bankruptcy in 1983, individuals, businesses,
and libraries using Osborne microcomputers faced
the problem of immediate obsolescence of their
equipment. The author discusses availability of
service, user support, and software in light of
the bankruptcy proceedings.

1280 "Hard-Disk Drives for Micros." Small Computers
in Libraries 1 (November 1981): 2-4.
The hard-disk drive, which permits the
implementation of relatively large and sophisticated library micro-based systems, is discussed.
The technology is described, suggested applications and examples are provided, and a list of
manufacturers is included for follow-up purposes.

1281 "Hard Discs for Micros." Library Systems Newsletter 1 (December 1981): 46-47.
The major disadvantage to automating with
a microcomputer has been the limited storage
capacity of the floppy disk. The article introduces the Winchester hard disk drive, estimates
costs, and discusses the problem of getting guidance in implementation.

1282 "The Hardware Dilemma: Which System and Why?"
Electronic Learning 2 (January 1983): 51-64.
Major microcomputer brands and models are
reviewed and compared for the shopper. They are
grouped by price range: (1) Under $500, (2) $500-
1,000, (3) $1,000 and above, and (4) other major
micros.

1283 HARMAN, DEBBIE, and NEVINS, KATE. "The OCLC M300
Workstation." Information Technology and Libraries 3 (March 1984): 47-53.
The development of the OCLC M300 Workstation is considered in some detail, various
MICRO ENHANCER software packages are described,
and use of the workstation as a microcomputer is
discussed.

1284 HESSLER, DAVID W. "Interactive Optical Disc
Systems: Part 1: Analog Storage." Library Hi
Tech 2, no. 4, issue 8 (1984): 25-32.
Optical disc systems are considered for
data storage. Definitions, advantages, system
levels, and configurations are discussed. Microcomputer access and control are described.

1285 "The Ideal Printer." Small Computers in Libraries 1 (July 1981): 6-7.
Qualities to keep in mind when shopping
for a printer to provide microcomputer output
are listed and discussed.

1286 JENSEN, KEN, and BALL, ALAN J. S. "A Novelty
Whose Time Has Come." Canadian Library Journal 38 (August 1981): 199-205.
Primarily concerned with the development
of Videotex information networks based on mini
or mainframe computers, this article contains
some interesting alternative plans utilizing
Apple II microcomputers in order to reduce system
costs. Bibliography.

1287 JONES, EDWARD. "Computer Peripherals: What to
Buy." School Library Journal 31 (November
1984): 50-54.
The author considers several types of

add-ons to the basic computer, including four
varieties of printer, two types of video monitor, modems, touch pads, the mouse, power fil-
ters, and computer furniture.

1288 KITTLE, PAUL W. "You Don't Necessarily Need a
Big One." Small Computers in Libraries 4
(September 1984): 9-10.
The 8-bit microcomputer is recommended
for home or office use where large files and
sophisticated programs are not required.

1289 KLOEPPER, DAN C. "Maxi-, Mini-, Micro; Microcomputers in Libraries." Nebraska Library Association Quarterly 9 (Winter 1977): 30-32.
The differences between maxi-, mini-, and
microcomputers are explained, and the types of
library functions best suited to each are discussed.

1290 KUBITZ, WILLIAM J. "Computer Technology: A Fore-
cast for the Future." The Role of the Library
in an Electronic Society. Proceedings of the
1979 Clinic on Library Applications of Data
Processing. Urbana: University of Illinois
Graduate School of Library Science, 1980,
v. 16. Pp. 135-61.
Integrated circuit technology, the basics
for microcomputer electronics, is explained simply but in some detail; then present and future
technologies are described, including optical
disc, video disc, and optical digital disc computer systems. The microcomputer's relationship
to new technologies is revealed. Bibliography.

1291 LaRUE, JAMES. "The Computer Backlash: Why I Hate
IBM." Wilson Library Bulletin 59 (March
1985): 447-49.
The microcomputer industry is developing
so rapidly that a system is often obsolete before
it is paid for, and sometimes before it is purchased. LaRue considers this phenomenon, discusses functions for which 8-bit processors are
adequate, and recommends upgrading only if necessary.

1292 "Learning About Hard Disks the Hard Way." OCLC
Micro 1 (September 1985): 4, 6.
When the FEDLINK Center added a new hard
disk to an existing microcomputer system, a
problem arose with a cartridge drive. The problem is explained, and a way of avoiding it is
suggested.

1293 LISANTI, SUZANA. "OP SYS: Computer Operating
Systems." Library Software Review 4 (July/
August 1985): 214-16.
DOS, one of several popular operating
systems for microcomputers, is discussed in this
article written for the layperson. It is defined; its operation is described; versions are
differentiated; and the reader is encouraged to
learn its operation prior to considering microcomputer applications.

1294 LYONS, RAY. "Word's Worth." OCLC Micro 1 (September 1985): 35-36.
Lyons presents the basic concepts of
microcomputer input and output, along with the
functions of the disk operating system and applications software.

1295 MASON, ROBERT M. "All About Diskettes." Library
Journal 109 (March 15, 1984): 558-59.
Mason deals with the topic of floppy
disks very matter of factly, describing how they
are made, how to protect them from damage, the
value of the disk in relation to the information
stored on it, and new developments and trends in
the technology.

1296 MASON, ROBERT M. "Artificial Intelligence: Promise, Myth, and Reality." Library Journal 110
(April 15, 1985): 56-57.
Machine intelligence has been a favorite
science fiction topic for decades, but it is
becoming reality, according to Mason, who discusses developments in the area of artificial
intelligence and the role of the microcomputer
in the phenomenon, putting it all in a library
perspective.

1297 MASON, ROBERT M. "Current and Future Microcomputer Capabilities: Selecting the Hardware." Microcomputers for Information Management 1 (March 1984): 1-13.
Guidelines for hardware selection, trends in the microcomputer industry, and projected developments through 1998 are discussed, and some practical suggestions are made to the practicing librarian.

1298 MASON, ROBERT M. "The Micro Marketplace: Have the Principles of Selecting a Micro Changed?" Library Journal 109 (January 1984): 60-61.
Since IBM began producing and marketing the PC, the XT, and the PCjr, many shoppers consider them the standards against which other microcomputers should be compared and judged. However, Mason reiterates his earlier published criteria for choosing a microcomputer, and recommends that they be followed, with IBM simply considered an additional option in the marketplace.

1299 MASON, ROBERT M. "The New IBM PC AT, IBM and Apple LANs." Library Journal 109 (October 15, 1984): 1903-04.
The new IBM PC AT microcomputer is reviewed and compared with the PC and XT, and the IBM local area network (LAN) is described. Apple's local area network, called the Apple Bus, is briefly noted but not reviewed since it was not available for purchase or review when the article was written.

1300 MASON, ROBERT M. "Printer Options/New Products at ALA." Library Journal 109 (August 1984): 1428-29.
Recent developments in printer technology are discussed, including new jet and lazer models. These are briefly compared with the more common letter quality and dot matrix impact printers currently in wide use in offices and libraries. The author's impressions of new microcomputer products announced at ALA are appended.

1301 MATTHEWS, JOSEPH R. "The Automated Library
System Marketplace, 1982: Change and More
Change!" Library Journal 108 (March 15,
1983): 547-53.
    The library automated system marketplace
is examined in terms of the turnkey system, the
library developed system, and the microcomputer
system. Volume, software costs, and source information are included. Trends in library automation are discussed.

1302 MATTHEWS, JOSEPH R. "Competition & Change: The
1983 Automated Library System Marketplace."
Library Journal 109 (May 1, 1984): 853-60.
    The automated library system marketplace
is considered, including turnkey, library-devel-
oped, and microcomputer systems, with notes on
vendors, the COM catalog market, and integrated
systems. Tables and charts present statistics
graphically and list vendors.

1303 McCORMAC, MIKE. "Converging Technologies: The
Teleputer Terminal." Aslib Proceedings 35
(January 1983): 24-30.
    In this paper presented at the 55th Aslib
Annual Conference, the British Teleputer Three
terminal is introduced, and its functions as a
television receiver, a microcomputer, a videotex
terminal, and an access terminal for interchange
of data with other computers are described.

1304 MELBY, ALAN K. "Extending Word Processing for
Foreign Characters." Drexel Library Quarterly
20 (Fall 1984): 74-86.
    Problems in word processing non-English
text using the ASCII character set are identified. Two solutions to the production of non-
English characters are provided. Bibliography.

1305 MERRILL, PAUL F., and BENNION, JUNIUS L. "Videodisc Technology in Education: The Current
Scene." NSPI Journal 18 (November 1979): 18-
19, 22-26.
    The state of the art in videodisc tech-
nology is defined, the advantages of a videodisc/

microcomputer interface are detailed, and eleven related research projects having education and/ or library implications are described. Bibliography.

1306 "Microcomputer Buzzwords--Part I: Hardware." Small Computers in Libraries 1 (September 1981): 3-5.
The terminology of microcomputer hardware is identified and defined in layman's English.

1307 "A Microcomputer Facility for Small Libraries." Vine no. 46 (December 1982): 40-41.
A project to develop an integrated microcomputer system for small libraries, utilizing commercially available applications software, is discussed briefly. Plans for the project are reviewed, but no findings or conclusions are announced.

1308 "Microcomputers 101." ACCESS: Microcomputers in Libraries 1 (July 1981): 15-16, 21.
The basics of microcomputer technology are explained in language that a novice should understand. A glossary of terms also proves useful.

1309 MISCHO, LARE, and HEGARTY, KEVIN. "Videotex-- The Library of the Future." Information Technology and Libraries 1 (September 1982): 276-77.
A preview of future library technology offering home access to library service was presented by Boeing Computer Services for the Tacoma (WA) Public Library. Microcomputers were used as access terminals.

1310 MONTJAR, BONNIE D. "Major League Information Retrieval on a Little League System: BRS on a Microcomputer System." Second National Conference on Integrated Online Library Systems Proceedings, Atlanta, 13-14 September 1984. Canfield, OH: Genaway & Associates, 1984. Pp. 270-76.
Kennametal, Inc.'s Technology Information

Center, established to support the company's research and development activities, sought to develop an integrated system as powerful as the online search systems available through dial access. This was accomplished using an IBM PC with a hardware adaptation which allowed BRS/SEARCH to be implemented on the in-house microcomputer. System configuration, details of the hardware upgrade, and the future of the system are discussed.

1311 MOORE, CATHY. "WILS' Cathy Moore Reports on the Reluctant Serial Printer." M300 and PC Report 2 (February 1985): 6-7.
    Librarians who use a serial printer with an M300 Workstation may experience difficulty when trying to print using certain software programs. The problem stems from incompatibility between the machine and the software, which permits the software to route the print command to the wrong serial port. Moore explains the problem and recommends a solution.

1312 NEITZKE, CURT. "The Library Tinker's Tool Kit." Technicalities 4 (October 1984): 14-15.
    The author provides a checklist of tools and supplies which are necessary for maintenance of audiovisual equipment and computer hardware. The cost should run $150-$200.

1313 "New Technology for the Library Microcomputer." Small Computers in Libraries 5 (April 1985): 7-10.
    Writers for The Library Corporation consider prospects for Compact Disc Read Only Memory (CD-ROM), a recently introduced laser data storage medium which is accessed via microcomputer. The technology is described, and applications are discussed. Bibliography.

1314 NOERR, KATHLEEN T. BIVINS, and NOERR, PETER L. "Distributed Processors and Processing with Microcomputers." Electronic Library 1 (July 1983): 197-201.
    The authors consider the next generation

in microcomputing, with such developments as improved machine-human interfaces, speech recognition, synthesis and voice responses, and machine-
machine interfaces which make possible microcomputer networks and distributed processing.

1315 Online Terminal/Microcomputer Guide & Directory
1982-83. 3rd Edition. Weston, CT: Online,
Inc., 1982. 286p.
  A handbook concerning terminals and microcomputers, this volume combines feature articles on such topics as selection criteria, with
specifications for individual models of print and
video terminals, micros, modems, and printers.
Directories of brokers, manufacturers, consultants, sales and service sources are extremely
valuable.

1316 "Optical Disks for Micros Available." Small
Computers in Libraries 4 (December 1984): 4.
  Reference Technology of Boulder, Colorado, announces the development of a microcomputer
driven optical disc storage system which may soon
be appearing in libraries, since H. W. Wilson,
OCLC, RLG, CLSI, and other companies are investi-
gating the technology.

1317 "PL/1 for Library Microcomputers." Small Computers in Libraries 2 (September 1982): 6.
  Programming Language/One (PL/1), a general purpose computer language that is adaptable
to microcomputer programming, is discussed and
recommended.

1318 "Personal Computers." Online 5 (April 1981):
70-71.
  New hardware by Apple Computer, Sinclair
Research Ltd., Hewlett-Packard, Radio Shack, and
Intelligent Systems Corp. is announced and re-
viewed briefly.

1319 POWELL, ANTOINETTE. "Installing a Modem in the
M300." M300 and PC Report 2 (April 1985):
3-4.
  The Agriculture Library of the University

of Kentucky received one of the first M300 Workstations. In order to use it for other than OCLC
access, necessary peripherals were purchased and
installed. This article describes the selection
and installation of the communication modem, a
relatively straightforward task which proved
frustrating.

1320 "Power Back-Ups for Micros." Small Computers in
Libraries 2 (January 1982): 6.
Two short-term power supply devices are
currently available to help the microcomputer
user save his data in the event of a power failure. Apple-Juice, a battery operated unit, will
supply from 5 to 20 minutes of additional power;
Datasaver provides approximately 5 minutes.

1321 "Printer Prices Falling." Small Computers in
Libraries 2 (February 1982): 3.
Several high quality, low priced, formed
character printers are discussed as alternatives
to the expensive Diablo, Qume, or NEC models.

1322 "Printers for Micros." Small Computers in
Libraries 1 (July 1981): 2-6.
Differences between dot matrix and formed
character printers are explained, along with
types of printer connections, baud rate, and
other topics. A comparison chart by brand name
may prove useful.

1323 RAUDENBUSH, JEANNE. "Chip Though the Eye of the
Needle." Online 6 (March 1982): 72-73.
Hardware and basic software requirements
are considered for a customized, in-house microcomputer-based information system.

1324 REINFELDS, JURIS. "Software for Microcomputers."
Proceedings of the National Conference on
Library and Bibliographic Applications of
Minicomputers, Sydney, August 22-24, 1979.
Sydney, Australia: University of New South
Wales School of Librarianship, 1979. Pp. 191-
202.
Operating systems and algorithms, partic-

ularly for the microprocessor based TERAK system,
are the concerns of this paper, which considers
library needs and applications only briefly.

1325 RICHERSON, MICHAEL E. "The Strength of PASCAL
Structures." ACCESS: Microcomputers in
Libraries 3 (Spring 1983): 5-6.
        PASCAL is briefly compared to other com-
puter languages. Its structure, which constitutes its major advantage, is described and
illustrated.

1326 SAFFADY, WILLIAM. "Portable Computers: An Introduction to Available Systems." Computer
Equipment Review 5 (July/December 1983):
134-46.
        Saffady presents an overview of available
portable computers, discussing designs, key-
boards, video display units, operating systems,
programming languages, available software, and
price.

1327 SCHAEFER, MARY TONNE. "Leading-Edge, High Technology Information Devices Examined by National Agricultural Library." Information Retrieval and Library Automation 20 (December
1984): 1-4.
        Four new technological developments at
the National Agricultural Library are described.
Among the four is a stand-alone laser video-
disc/microcomputer system which is being used
for full text storage of the Pork Industry Handbook and related bibliographic citations from the
AGRICOLA database.

1328 "Service for Micros." Library Systems Newsletter
3 (May 1983): 39.
        This brief article provides advice on
microcomputer maintenance and service contracts,
with 1983 cost information on non-warranty service and repair.

1329 "Shopping Around for a Printer?" OCLC Micro
1 (September 1985): 21-23.
        Choosing an appropriate printer for use

with an M300 Workstation may pose problems and require possible choices and tradeoffs. This article considers the attributes of the parallel versus the serial printer, the need for printing characters in the OCLC character set, and the possibility of sharing or adapting an old printer to M300 specifications. Tips on selecting and ordering a printer are included.

1330 SONNEMANN, SABINE S. "The Videodisc as a Library Tool." Special Libraries 74 (January 1983): 7-13.

An experimental videodisc project sponsored by the National Library of Canada to demonstrate the ability of the videodisc to store and present library materials in a variety of formats, to demonstrate the use of the videodisc as a practical research tool, and to demonstrate the information retrieval capability of a videodisc/-microcomputer system is outlined. Apple II microcomputer hardware is used.

1331 STICHA, PHIL. "Low-Cost Laser Printers." Library Hi Tech 3, no. 2, issue 10 (1985): 41-52.

Laser printers are beginning to make an impact on the office machine industry because of their quality of print and gradually decreasing price tag. This article considers laser printer technology and reviews two affordable models: the Hewlett-Packard LaserJet and the ALMOST TYPESET. Bibliography.

1332 STURM, REBECCA. "High Tech Breakthrough: Interactive Videodisc." Wilson Library Bulletin 59 (March 1985): 450-52.

An overview of videodisc technology is presented, library applications are discussed, and recommendations are made for furthering development of interactive video technology.

1333 "Testing Floppy Disks: Which One to Buy." Small Computers in Libraries 4 (December 1984): 9.

A recent consumer report on floppy disks for microcomputers identifies the best and worst

in a three-point test for discoloration, strength
of the electrical signal transferred to the disk,
and tightness of the hub around the center hole.

1334 THOMAS, KEN. "Testing. . .One. . .Two. . ."
OCLC Micro 1 (March 1985): 8-9.
OCLC staff have tested several add-ons to
the M300 Workstation. Among those tested and
recommended are the AST SixPakPlus and the Quad-
board 2 multifunction boards. The IBM PC Color/
Graphics Monitor Adaptor was also tested, and
appears to be functional, although staff are
less certain of its adaptability.

1335 TRAUTMAN, RODES. "Storage Media for Microcomputers." Online 7 (November 1983): 19-28.
A brief but thorough introduction to
microcomputer storage methods describes various
options. Microchips, floppy disks, hard disks,
optical discs, secondary storage, magnetic tape
and other topics are considered. Bibliography.

1336 UNREIN, DAN. "So You Are Thinking About Hard
Copy: A Few Considerations Concerning Printers." ACCESS: Microcomputers in Libraries 2
(January 1982): 10-11, 24.
Four major considerations--methods of
data transmission, input/output capabilities,
the print mechanism, and the manner in which the
characters are to be printed--should determine
the type of printer chosen to accompany a microcomputer. Unrein examines these considerations.

1337 "Video Disks and Micros." Small Computers in
Libraries 2 (February 1982): 1.
The differences between capacitance and
laser optical type videodiscs are explained, and
applications of laser optical technology with
microcomputer access are explored.

1338 WARDEN, WILLIAM H., III, and WARDEN, BETTE M.
"Dot Matrix Impact Printers: An Overview and
Guide." Library Hi Tech 1 (Fall 1983): 14-27.
Dot matrix impact printers are differen-
tiated from other types of printers, and their

installation, use, and maintenance are discussed.
Thirty-one models produced by twelve different
companies are considered in text and chart form.

1339 WARDEN, WILLIAM H., III, and WARDEN, BETTE M.
"Microcomputers for Libraries: An Overview."
RSR: Reference Services Review 10 (Winter
1982): 81-87.
Characteristics to consider in choosing
a library microcomputer are reviewed, including
word length, memory size and capacity, CPU speed,
peripherals, and software. Fourteen models are
reviewed and compared, with recommendations.
Bibliography.

1340 WARDEN, WILLIAM H., III, and WARDEN, BETTE M.
"Microcomputers for Libraries: Features,
Descriptions, Evaluations." Library Hi Tech
1 (Summer 1983): 25-39.
Major features to consider in evaluating
microcomputers (word size, memory, disk size and
capacity, CPU speed, peripherals, and software)
are discussed in detail. Nineteen systems are
described individually then compared with one
another. Extensive bibliography.

1341 WASHINGTON, CURTIS. "Printer Pointers." Small
Computers in Libraries 5 (July/August 1985):
13-16.
Criteria for selecting a microcomputer
printer are provided and discussed, with insight
into specific needs of the library or office.

1342 "What's a Hex?" Small Computers in Libraries 2
(June 1982): 2-3.
The hexadecimal numbering system is defined and compared to the decimal and binary systems. Its value to programmers is explained.

1343 WILLIAMS, JAMES G. "8-, 16- and 32-Bit Processors: Characteristics and Appropriate Applications." Library Hi Tech 2, no. 2, issue 6
(1984): 51-59.
Components of a microcomputer are defined; characteristics of 8-bit, 16-bit, 32-bit,

and multiple-bit systems are considered; and
library applications for each type architecture
are discussed.

1344 WOOD, R. KENT, and WOOLLEY, ROBERT D. "An Overview of Videodisc Technology and Some Potential Applications in the Library, Information,
and Instructional Sciences." Arlington, VA:
ERIC Document Reproduction Service, ED 206
328, 1980.
    The state of the art in videodisc micro-
computer technology is explored. Types of systems, applications, and major faults are considered. A review of the literature and extensive
bibliography are useful to the reader seeking
further information.

1345 WOOD, R. KENT; WOOLLEY, ROBERT D; and ZSIRA,
STEPHEN W. "Videodisc/Microcomputer Research
Opens New Horizons for Libraries." American
Libraries 12 (April 1981): 208-09.
    The Videodisc Innovation Projects spon-
sored by Utah State University have produced
several firsts in library instruction, indexing,
and preservation of library materials. The projects are described briefly.

1346 WOOLLEY, ROBERT D. "A Videodisc/Portable Computer System for Information Storage." Educational and Industrial Television 11 (May
1979): 38-40.
    The possibilities for application of
videodisc technology to library processes seem
endless, and Woolley advocates research and
investigation to determine this potential. As
an example he cites and describes a microcom-
puter/videodisc system for library instruction.

1347 YOUNG, JACKY. "Supermicros and Unix--A New
Option for Automated Library System Users."
Library Software Review 4 (September/October
1985): 271-73.
    The supermicro combines the computing
power and multi-user capabilities of the minicomputer with the compactness and economy of the

micro to offer many options for library use.
Combined with UNIX, an equally powerful and versatile operating system which is fast becoming an
an international standard, supermicro technology
may affect revolutionary changes in the library.
The supermicro and UNIX are described, and their
impact on the library is considered.

1348 ANDRESON, DAVID. "The WLN PC: Local Processing in a Network Context." Information Technology and Libraries 3 (March 1984): 54-58.
     WLN's adoption of a modified IBM PC as a standard terminal for local access to the WLN database is discussed, along with terminal and nonterminal uses and suggestions for further utilization of the hardware.

1349 "Any Micro You Want as Long as It's IBM." Technicalities 4 (February 1984): 1.
     OCLC's decision to adopt a modified IBM PC as its new M300 Workstation is criticized in light of the diverse marketplace and the broad choice of hardware available.

1350 BIRMINGHAM, MARY TREACY. "Regional Micro-Based Information Networks Demand New Human Relationships." Microcomputers for Information Management 1 (June 1984): 109-23.
     Microcomputer networks offer options for developing local systems to address local needs. Birmingham considers the technological possibilities, but emphasizes the importance of human communications and networking to make such a project fully effective. Bibliography.

1351 BLAIR, JOHN C., Jr. "Systems Suitable for Information Professionals." Online 7 (July 1983): 36-43, 46-48.
     A recent trend in microcomputing is the development of multi-unit systems. Blair evaluates appropriate operating systems, microchips, and CPUs, then discusses local area networks (LANs), distributed processing, and requirements for a fully configured system.

1352 BOSS, RICHARD W. "Operating Systems for Multi-User/Tasking Micros." Software Review 2 (June 1983): 78-83.

Boss reviews briefly the function of an operating system, discusses the problems with, and additional demands made on multi-user systems, and compares UNIX, ZENIX, OASIS, and MP/M.

1353 CARON, BARBARA. "Microcomputers at the Morgantown, West Virginia Library." Small Computers in Libraries 4 (April 1984): 2-3.
The director of the Morgantown (WV) Public Library describes the selection of microcomputer software and equipment to implement a local area network connecting the branch libraries with the central library. An equipment list is included, and software packages--MULTIMATE, LOTUS 1-2-3, PEACHTREE ACCOUNTING MODULES, and dBASE II--are evaluated in relation to how well they meet the needs of the library.

1354 CHEN, CHING-CHIH. "MicroWatch." Microcomputers for Information Management 1 (March 1984): 75-76.
News of the microcomputer industry, with announcements of new and forthcoming developments in hardware and software constitutes the major portion of this regular column.

1355 COLLIER, MEL. Local Area Networks: The Implications for Library and Information Science. Library and Information Research Report, no. 19. London: British Library, 1984. 45p.
A microcomputer-based local area network is considered a viable option, instead of a minicomputer, for certain large data-processing activities. Collier presents information gathered from a research project funded by the British Library, in which he introduces the concept of the local area network, describes technology and configurations, and discusses its roles in a library/information science setting. Bibliography.

1356 COLLIER, MEL. "Microcomputer Networking in Libraries I: Background and Aims of the Project." Vine no. 48 (May 1983): 21.
The British Library Research and Develop-

ment Department and the Department of Industry
have jointly awarded a contract to the Polytechnic of Central London to investigate the potential of microcomputer-based local area networks
in libraries. Aims of the project and networking
basics are discussed. This article accompanies
one by Gillian Venner and Stephen Walker, "Microcomputer Networking in Libraries II: a Public
Access Catalogue System."

1357 COLLIER, MEL. "Microcomputer Networks for Library Applications: Research at the Polytechnic of Central London." Microcomputers for
Information Management 2 (March 1985): 33-42.
     A research grant to the Polytechnic of
Central London Library for development of an online public access catalog employing local area
network technology is described by one of the
major researchers. LAN background information is
summarized, objectives of the project are explained, and the basics of the research are revealed. Bibliography.

1358 COLLIER, MEL. "Microprocessor Networking in
Libraries." Library and Information News 5
(September 1982): 11-13.
     A project sponsored by the British Li-
brary Research and Development Department, to
investigate the application of local area networks (LANs) in libraries, is outlined and justified. Bibliography.

1359 COPELAND, JOYCE M. "Local Area Networks I:
Introductory Definition." Vine no. 55
(October 1984): 36-38.
     This first of two articles concerning
local area networks and their applications to
libraries, provides definitions necessary for an
understanding of the subject.

1360 COPELAND, JOYCE M. "Local Area Networks II."
Vine no. 55 (October 1984): 39-40.
     A continuation of "Local Area Networks
I," this article addresses LAN applications in
special libraries and information centers.

1361 COPELAND, JOYCE M., and FLOOD, STEPHEN. "Users
and Local Area Networks: Opportunities for
Information Transfer." Electronic Library
2 (October 1984): 273-77.
A research project on the use of local
area networks (LANs) in British special libraries
is reported. Issues and problems are discussed,
including organizational implications, which are
often overlooked in view of greater technological
concerns. Bibliography.

1362 CUADRA, CARLOS A. "Integrating the Personal Computer into a Multi-User Database Environment."
Proceedings of the 6th National Online Meeting, New York, 30 April-2 May 1985. Medford,
NJ: Learned Information, 1985. Pp. 111-16.
Microcomputer users in large organizations are beginning to see the advantages of
sharing information and are seeking methods of
interfacing computers to create in-house networks. Cuadra discusses the trend toward in-
house online databases, the advantages and disadvantages of multi-user computers, and a method
of linking existing microcomputers to a multi-
user system when one is installed.

1363 "EASy Cuts EDUMAIL Costs." Edunet News 23
(Spring 1981): 6.
The advantages of using the EDUNET Network Access System in conjunction with the University of Wisconsin's electronic mail network
are outlined for member libraries.

1364 "Empowerment at the Local Level." OCLC Newsletter no. 156 (February 1985): 12.
OCLC's commitment to the development of
local systems which can interface with their
central computers is discussed, and two new
microcomputer-based services, MICROCON and SC
350, are announced.

1365 FARR, RICK C. "LANs: A New Technology to Improve
Library Automation." Drexel Library Quarterly
20 (Fall 1984): 56-63.
The basics of a microcomputer-based local

area network are explained, with definitions, theory, configuration, and communication protocols addressed. Bibliography.

1366 FARR, RICK C. "The Local Area Network (LAN) and Library Automation." Library Journal 108 (November 15, 1983): 2130-32.
The concept of the microcomputer-based Local Area Network (LAN) is explained, along with applications to library management and automation. Advantages are described; problems and costs are considered. Bibliography.

1367 "First OCLC M300 Workstation Installed." Wilson Library Bulletin 58 (May 1984): 621-22.
The installation of the first M300 Workstation is announced by OCLC and Hillsdale College. Hillsdale's plans for its use and OCLC's plans for expansion of the program are outlined.

1368 "First OCLC M300 Workstation Installed at Hillsdale College." OCLC Newsletter no. 152 (May 1984): 3.
The Learning Resources Center of Hillsdale College, Hillsdale, MI, was the first library in the United States to receive an OCLC M300 Workstation. This announcement describes Hillsdale College, summarizes plans for use of the terminal, and estimates OCLC's installation schedule for the future.

1369 "Foundation Grant Buys a Micro Network." Library Journal 110 (April 15, 1985): 12.
Seventy-three libraries in North Central Iowa have received grants to help purchase the microcomputer hardware and software necessary to access the database of book holdings in the region, which is resident on an IBM AT as the Central Regional Library in Mason City.

1370 "IBM PC Chosen for WLN Terminal Decentralization Aid Foreseen." Library Journal 108 (September 15, 1983): 1750.
In preparation for possible decentraliza-

tion of certain of its processing functions, the
Washington Library Network has chosen the IBM
Personal Computer for local installations.

1371 IVIE, EVAN L. "Designing Microcomputer Networks." Drexel Library Quarterly 20 (Fall
1984): 48-55.
Placing the sum of human knowledge at
mankind's fingertips is a goal which may be
achieved through microcomputer, storage, and
networking technology, according to the author.
Ivie contemplates the possibilities, which he
considers achievable through microcomputer
networking, and suggests network criteria and
designs which may advance progress toward the
goal. Bibliography.

1372 LEVERT, VIRGINIA M. "Applications of Local Area
Networks of Microcomputers in Libraries."
Information Technology and Libraries 4 (March
1985): 9-18.
The concept of the microcomputer-based
local area network (LAN) is reviewed, and its
application to library uses is considered.
Existing LANs in special, academic, and public
libraries are described, and suggestions for
choosing a library LAN are provided. Bibliography.

1373 "Local Area Networks for Data Communications."
Library Systems Newsletter 4 (September 1984):
65-69.
The concept of the local area network is
explained; circuitry, access methods, topology,
bandwidth, and other topics are addressed.

1374 LOVECY, IAN. "A Library Implementation of a
LAN." Vine no. 59 (July 1985): 35-39.
The University of Reading (UK) Library
has implemented a local area network (LAN) using
microcomputers in conjunction with the library's
minicomputer. The LAN concept is explained,
background concerning the University of Reading
Library is provided, and hardware and applications are discussed.

1375 MASON, ROBERT M. "Automation and LANS at ALA."
Library Journal 109 (September 15, 1984):
1736-37.
    Mason discusses local area networks,
describes the file server and cable system approaches to networking, explains why LANs have
become popular, and expresses hope for networking
with the next generation of microcomputers. Networking products displayed at ALA 1984 are reviewed.

1376 MASON, ROBERT M. "OCLC Chooses IBM." Library
Journal 108 (September 1, 1983): 1666.
    The choice of IBM to produce the OCLC
Model 300 terminal is announced; modifications
required by OCLC are listed; optional uses for
the terminal are discussed.

1377 MASON, ROBERT M. "Should You Consider a PC Local
Area Network?" Library Journal 110 (June 15,
1985): 42-43.
    The concept of the local area network is
explained, advantages and disadvantages are
addressed, other options are considered, and
some factors for decision making are suggested.

1378 MATTHEWS, JOSEPH R. "Local Area Networks."
Online '84 Conference Proceedings, San Francisco, 29-31 October 1984. Weston, CT: Online, Inc., 1984. Pp. 172-74.
    The concept of the local area network is
explained, addressing technology, system architecture, and access.

1379 "Micros in Tech Services." Small Computers in
Libraries 3 (September 1983): 1-2.
    Choice of the IBM PC as system standards
by OCLC, WLN, and possibly RLIN is supported for
the sake of compatibility. Possible trouble
spots for intercommunication among networks
caused by hardware adaptations is considered.

1380 "Multi-User Small Computer Systems in the U.S.;
Report of a Study Visit." Vine no. 49 (May
1983): 30-36.

The state of the art in microcomputer-based multi-user library automation systems is summarized from the British perspective, based on data gathered during a study visit to the United States by a British researcher.

1381 "New Network Terminal: The WLN PC." Information Retrieval and Library Automation 21 (June 1985): 5-6.
The Washington Library Network announces the availability of the new WLN PC, and the first installation at Ganzaga University Law Library. A modified IBM PC designed to expedite access to the WLN database, the hardware provides multi-functional capabilities in addition to network access.

1382 "New OCLC Terminal to be IBM PC." Small Computers in Libraries 3 (July 1983): 5.
OCLC's announcement that the new Model 300 terminal, to be available in early 1984, will be a modified IBM Personal Computer, has caused considerable speculation in the library world. Pertinent questions are asked concerning the new terminals.

1383 "OCLC Selects IBM Personal Computer." Wilson Library Bulletin 58 (October 1983): 92.
OCLC announces the selection of IBM to manufacture the new M300 Workstation. The M300 is a customized IBM PC which permits users to interact with OCLC's mainframes as well as perform off-line data manipulation.

1384 "OCLC Will Offer Customized IBM PC for Network Access." Information Intelligence Online Libraries and Microcomputers 1 (September 1983): 9.
OCLC's M300 Workstation is announced and described, and availability is set for Spring, 1984.

1385 "RLG Announces IBM PC Version of RLIN Terminal." Information Technology and Libraries 4 (September 1985): 273-74.

The Research Libraries Group (RLG) announces the availability of software which will enable the IBM PC microcomputer to emulate an RLIN terminal and access the RLIN database. The necessary hardware configuration is outlined, and plans for further development are told.

1386 "RLIN to Go With IBM PC After All." Small Computers in Libraries 4 (October 1984): 11-12.
After long deliberation the Research Libraries Information Network (RLIN) has chosen the IBM PC for its system standard. The decision is explained and justified, and implications for the future are discussed.

1387 "Special Section: The IBM PC as a Terminal." Information Technology and Libraries 3 (March 1984): 47-68.
Four articles printed under one title in symposium style discuss the adoption of the IBM PC microcomputer by OCLC, WLN, and LCS as the terminal standard for each network. A fourth article concerns the Faxon Company's efforts to incorporate the IBM PC into their DataLinx network. Bibliography.

1388 TOWNLEY, CHARLES T. "ODIN: A Multifunction, Multitype Library Microcomputer Network." Information Technology and Libraries 3 (June 1984): 174-76.
ODIN, a microcomputer-based library network in the Harrisburg, Pennsylvania area was established in 1982 to provide greater access to local databases, to expedite interlibrary loans, and to provide access to commercial databases. Progress toward each goal is considered and evaluated individually, and future directions are set. Bibliography.

1389 TRUDELL, LIBBY. "New Technologies for Electronic Communication." Proceedings of the 4th National Online Meeting, New York, 12-14 April 1983. Medford, NJ: Learned Information, 1983. Pp. 553-59.
The concept of the local area network is

considered. Two configurations--the host-computer system and the microcomputer-based node-to-node network--are compared. Applications to libraries are briefly addressed. Bibliography.

1390 "Tying It All Together." Technicalities 4 (November 1984): 1.
     As microcomputers become prevalent in the library workplace, the desirability of linking them together into a network becomes greater. The editors allude briefly to some potential problems in networking, and recommend asking for and sharing help and information as new skills and techniques are developed.

1391 "WLN Selects IBM PC as New Network Terminal." Information Retrieval and Library Automation 19 (December 1983): 7-8.
     The Washington Library Network's selection of a modified IBM Personal Computer to replace the Hazeltine terminal as network standard is announced.

1392 "WLN Selects IBM Personal Computer." Wilson Library Bulletin 58 (September 1983): 8.
     The Washington Library Network (WLN) announces the selection of a modified IBM PC for its standard network terminal. Modifications are explained, and justification for the choice is briefly noted.

MICROCOMPUTER OPERATION

1393 ALBERICO, RALPH. "Macros for Micros." Small
Computers in Libraries 5 (December 1985): 4-6.
Macros are defined, and their value in
online searching is explained. PROKEY and SUPER-
KEY, two high quality macro processor software
packages are recommended.

1394 ANDERSON, ERIC S. "Eric (not ERIC): Tending the
Orchard." OCLC Micro 1 (November 1985): 9-10.
A word on adjusting the disk speed of a
microcomputer accompanies recommendations for
several useful utility programs. These include
DIVERSICOPY, for making archival and backup
disks; LIFESAVER, for recovering data and re-
building bad sectors on disks; and GPLE (Globe
Program Line Editor), for replacement of the
APPLESOFT (BASIC) editor.

1395 AUSTIN, CHARLES. "It's Time to Organize Those
Sloppy Disks!" Popular Computing 3 (March
1984): 156.
As a microcomputer user's data files
grow, the problem of finding a specific file
becomes more and more time consuming. Austin
tells how he has organized and indexed his data
for easy retrieval, using his micro to perform
the task.

1396 "Backup Procedures." Small Computers in Libraries 2 (May 1982): 2-3; and ACCESS: Microcomputers in Libraries 2 (October 1982): 15-16.
The advisability of maintaining backup
files for data is stressed, and three methods of
accomplishing the task are outlined.

1397 BEISER, KARL. "Getting the Most from IBM PC-
DOS." M300 and PC Report 2 (January 1985):
6-8.
Twenty-seven PC-DOS commands are listed,
and their functions briefly summarized. To fur-

337

ther aid the user, they are grouped into three categories: "The Essentials," "Worth Knowing," and "Occasionally Userful."

1398   BEISER, KARL.   "Getting the Most from IBM PC-DOS, Part II."   M300 and PC Report 2 (February 1985): 9-11.
        Beiser identifies useful features of PC-DOS and explains what each one does. Among those topics considered are the editing keys, uses of the copy command, and batch file commands.

1399   BEISER, KARL.   "Getting the Most from IBM-PC DOS: Part III."   M300 and PC Report 2 (March 1985): 6-8.
        The third in a series of aids for the PC-DOS user, this article identifies terms and functions used in redefining the operating environment and moving data.

1400   BEISER, KARL.   "Getting There from Here."   Small Computers in Libraries 5 (October 1985): 9-13.
        The problems encountered in transferring data from program to program or system to system often seem insurmountable. Beiser suggests several possible methods of system to system transfer including disk format conversion, modem transfer, and serial cable transfer. Program to program transfer, while less complex, can also be frustrating. Many programs provide a transfer function. If none is available, operating environments such as Microsoft's WINDOWS and IBM's TOPVIEW offer an alternative. Other options are mentioned and conversion utility programs are suggested.

1401   BENDIG, MARK.   "DOS-Tips."   OCLC Micro 1 (November 1985): 3-4, 6.
        Keeping track of the contents of a hard disk can be time consuming and frustrating, but PC-DOS (versions 2.0 and above) offers the option of setting up subdirectories to aid in managing hard disk files. Bendig explains the rationale, the procedure, and the use of the PROMPT and PATH commands.

1402 BENDIG, MARK. "DOS-Tips: Batch Files a la Mode."
OCLC Micro 1 (May 1985): 3-4, 6.
Bendig defines batch files, provides an
example, and explains how they are created and
executed.

1403 BENDIG, MARK. "DOS-Tips: Does Anybody Really
Know What Time It Is?" OCLC Micro 1 (July
1985): 3.
Bendig explains the reason for entering
date and time of day each time a user boots up a
microcomputer program, and he demonstrates how to
change the familiar A> prompt, should a user need
to do so.

1404 BENDIG, MARK. "Not for Novices: Printer Control
Revisited." OCLC Micro 1 (September 1985):
33-34.
In an earlier article Bendig presented
several methods of transmitting printer commands
from an IBM PC or M300. This article explains another method, which Bendig calls verified printer
setup. Technique and results are considered.

1405 BENDIG, MARK. "Not for Novices: The 'Let's Pre-
tend' Disk." OCLC Micro 1 (November 1985):
26-27.
PC-DOS Version 3.1 features a virtual
disk or RAM disk which the user may not understand, but which may prove useful. Once the RAM
disk is installed, the microcomputer will function as though it has an extra disk drive, which
may be used in the same ways that any disk drive
is used. Bendig explains the installation and
functions of the RAM disk, along with warnings
and limitations concerning its use.

1406 BUCKLAND, LAWRENCE F. "Data Input for Libraries:
State-of-the-Art Report." Arlington, VA: ERIC
Document Reproduction Service, ED 200 216,
1980.
Data input by four different methods--
optical character recognition, microcomputer,
minicomputer, and word processor--are described
and compared.

1407 CAPPUZZELLO, PAUL. "Printing the OCLC Basics
Logfile with Serial Printers." OCLC Micro
1 (March 1985): 15.
The OCLC M300 Workstation ordinarily de-
faults to the parallel printer port when running
OCLC Basics. Step-by-step instructions are provided for accomplishing the printing task with a
serial printer.

1408 CHAN, GRAHAM. "Problems in Printing With an
Apple Microcomputer." Vine no. 49 (August
1983): 26-27.
Using an Anadex DP 9501 printer with an
Apple III microcomputer, the Liverpool (UK) Polytechnic Library encountered problems with special
features such as underlining and super-scripting,
and with the printer sometimes producing garbage.
Chan identifies the problems, explains the reasons for the malfunctions, and suggests remedies
for the problems.

1409 CHENEY, HAL. "Using DOS and dBASE III to Organize Your File Directories." OCLC Micro 1
(December 1985): 16-17.
Cheney provides step-by-step instructions
on setting up and maintaining a data file, based
on a diskette directory, using dBASE III software.

1410 COX, BRUCE. "M300 and PC Report: Software Tutorial: Modifying OCLC Terminal Software for Hard
Disk Use." M300 and PC Report 2 (July/August
1985): 1-3.
OCLC terminal software version 2.00 may
be loaded onto hard disk for easier access and
operation by making a few modifications to the
software batch files. Cox outlines the modifications and the procedure.

1411 "DOS-Tips: Efficient Use of the DIRECTORY Command." OCLC Micro 1 (September 1985): 12.
DIR, the directory command for the Disk
Operating System (DOS), may be one of the most
useful commands to the micro operator. However,
it may also become very frustrating when the di-

rectory becomes large. This article explains how
to modify the DIR command to pause when a screen
is full, to display only file names and extensions, and to display specific types of files.

1412 DeYOUNG, BARBARA. "Resource Sharing of Micro
Software; or, What Ever Happened to All That
CP/M Compatibility?" Microcomputers for Information Management 1 (December 1984): 313-
24.
Microcomputer compatibility is considered and the major reason for incompatibility is
explored. Bibliography.

1413 "Disk Space Requirements for Libraries." Small
Computers in Libraries 2 (May 1982): 4-5.
Valuable information on figuring disk
storage needs for automated circulation, cataloging, and indexing projects is combined with useful advice on hardware and software needs for
large programs.

1414 "A Dose of DOS: AUTOEXEC.BAT." M300 and PC
Report 5 (December 1985): 3-6.
PC-DOS functions can save the operator
time and energy if properly set up and executed.
An AUTOEXEC.BAT program can cut corners in execu-
ting repetitious commands. This article gives
instructions on creating and installing AUTOEXEC.
BAT files and their uses.

1415 "Downloading the '12-Pitch Printing' Command to
Epson Printers." OCLC Micro 1 (September
1985): 8.
In this short article written with the
M300 user in mind, procedures are outlined for
changing to 12-pitch from 10-pitch printing,
which is standard on Epson FX-80 Epson FX-100,
and LQ 1500 printers.

1416 FOSDICK, HOWARD. "Microcomputer Programming in
the Information Center." Special Libraries 74
(July 1983): 211-21.
PL/I and COBOL have traditionally been
the most popular languages for programming main-

frame computers to perform library functions; however, librarians are programming their micros using BASIC and Pascal. Attempting to discover reasons for the change, Fosdick characterizes BASIC, Pascal, and PL/I, and compares the three languages in terms of adaptability to librarians' programming needs. Bibliography.

1417 FREEDMAN, MARY, and CARLIN, LARRY. "What To Do When It All Goes Wrong." Library Journal 110 (December 1985): 72-73.
    When computers are introduced into the workplace, it becomes inevitable that there will eventually be hardware breakdowns. Freedman and Carlin consider what to do when a computer malfunctions, with emphasis on identifying and defining the problem.

1418 "Funny File Names." Small Computers in Libraries 4 (February 1984): 4-5.
    The difference between a program and a data file is explained, the construction of file names using different operating systems is discussed, and the use of extensions is reviewed.

1419 "Getting Started--Part I." Small Computers in Libraries 3 (June 1983): 2-4.
    The basics of getting started in microcomputing are considered, from unpacking the hardware to determining the principal disk drive if the system has more than one. A section on operating systems is readable and informative.

1420 "Getting Started--Part II." Small Computers in Libraries 3 (July 1983): 2-4.
    The function and use of utilities programs, which enable the microcomputer user to do formatting, diskette copying, system generation, and configuration, are explained in simple terms.

1421 GILLMAN, PETER L. "User-Friendly: The Phrase That Launched a Thousand Slips." Small Computers in Libraries 4 (September 1984): 5-6.
    The discrepancy between impressions given in commercials and advertisements for microcom-

puters and their operation in actual practice is discussed, along with improvements needed in programming, hardware operation, and documentation.

1422 "Goof-Proof Disk Insertion." Small Computers in Libraries 2 (June 1982): 6.
This article provides a helpful hint on how to avoid damage to public-use disks because of improper insertion into the disk drive.

1423 HART, LAVON G., and GILLEY, GEORGE. "Simple Remedies for a Malfunctioning Computer." Indiana Media Journal 7 (Spring 1985): 25-27.
Problems common to microcomputer equipment are considered, and possible in-house solutions are suggested.

1424 HOCTER, KEITH. "Protect Yourself from the 'Glitches'." OCLC Micro 1 (September 1985): 23.
Power surges and loss of power for an extended period of time may result in loss of data. Hocter suggests saving data frequently and the installation of surge protectors as two methods of minimizing losses.

1425 "How to Trash Your Disk Files." Small Computers in Libraries 4 (May 1984): 1.
An easily made mistake while copying data disk-to-disk may result in garbled files. This article explains how the error occurs and suggests a simple tactic which will help prevent it.

1426 HUNTER, ERIC J. The ABC of BASIC: An Introduction to Programming for Librarians. London: Clive Bingley, 1982. 120p.
The basics of terminal operation and an introduction to the BASIC programming language are presented in a clear and precise manner, with library-related examples and simulations.

1427 HUSTING, STEVE. "Put the Buffer to Use." OCLC Micro 1 (July 1985): 18-19.
The IBM PC and the M300 Workstation have 20-character buffers which can be used to stack

commands or type ahead of the data processing function of the system. The function of the buffer is explained and its use is described.

1428 "Installation Problems With Micros." Small Computers in Libraries 1 (December 1981): 6.
Static electricity, humidity, power surges, and sudden jars are identified as sources of problems with microcomputers, and ways of alleviating the problems are suggested.

1429 "Insuring Your Micros." Small Computers in Libraries 4 (November 1984): 3-4.
The possibility of microcomputer theft is addressed, and precautions are suggested such as being certain that all equipment is on the school's inventory. The loss of data might be an even greater loss than the hardware. Daily backups stored away from the terminal are recommended as a safeguard.

1430 KANE, MATTHEW J. "A Benefit of Learning BASIC." Small Computers in Libraries 3 (September 1983): 2-3.
The district consultant for the Blair County (PA) Library System discusses the advantages of knowing BASIC in order to write programs for specific needs, then backs up his arguments with a specific example involving data manipulation for decision making.

1431 KUPERSMITH, JOHN. "Using the Radio Shack Model 100." Small Computers in Libraries 5 (June 1985): 10-11.
It is possible to transfer data between the Radio Shack Model 100 and the Apple Macintosh, which enables an operator to prepare files on the notebook size Model 100 for uploading, editing, and printing on the Macintosh. This procedure is described, and appropriate word processing, DBMS, spreadsheet, and function software are suggested.

1432 LISANTI, SUZANA. "Batch Files." Library Software Review 4 (September/October 1985): 285-90.

Lisanti deals with the concept of batch files, defining the term, differentiating between AUTOEXEC and designated .BAT files, describing the creation of .BAT files, and providing details of maintenance, manipulation, and execution.

1433 MAY, SCOTT. "Getting Organized." OCLC Micro 1 (September 1985): 26-27.
As the use of the microcomputer increases, it becomes increasingly more difficult to retrieve files. This article stresses the importance of always supplying system date and time when signing on, suggests standard naming practices, recommends the use of file name extensions, and encourages the maintenance of backup files to ease the problems of file retrieval.

1434 MAY, SCOTT. "Getting Organized, Part 2." OCLC Micro 1 (November 1985): 22-23.
The second part of a continued article on microcomputer file management concerns the setting up of subdirectories and paths in order to keep the system's root directory manageable. May discusses the theory, then illustrates with examples from his own experience.

1435 MESSERSMITH, PAUL. "Memory Needs and Storage Systems." ACCESS: Microcomputers in Libraries 1 (October 1981): 16-17.
A formula for estimating data storage needs for efficient microcomputer utilization is followed by a comparison of floppy and hard disk systems and brief suggestions on choosing hardware to accommodate needs and estimated usage.

1436 "Micro News: Radio Shack's 100 and the Macintosh." Small Computers in Libraries 5 (January 1985): 3.
Radio Shack's Model 100 lap computer is reported 100% compatible with Apple's Macintosh, and a data transfer routine is described in order to illustrate.

1437 MILLER, BILL. "Printing from an Applications Program." OCLC Micro 1 (November 1985): 12.

Printers wired to M300 Workstations may work when in OCLC mode but fail to respond to commands from applications software. Miller analyzes the reason for the failure, and suggests remedies for the problem.

1438 MOORE, CATHY. "Epson Utility Programs." OCLC Micro 1 (September 1985): 3-4.
A utility diskette soon to be available through OCLC's OMPX program is described for Epson printer users. The diskette, designed to expedite print commands, contains BASIC programs for printer control which ease the task of programming for special print jobs.

1439 MOORE, CATHY. "PC-File Timesavers." OCLC Micro 1 (September 1985): 3.
Moore explains the advantages to using the repeat key and the smart keys on the IBM-PC and M300 when using PC-FILE software.

1440 POWER, LEE. "Software Integration Without Integrated Software." OCLC Micro 1 (November 1985): 13-15.
Integrated results can often be achieved without integrated software if the data is in a standard ASCII text file delimited with carriage-return and line-feed characters. Power explains the procedure, cautions against problems, and provides many helpful hints.

1441 QUINT, BARBARA. "Protect Your Micro and its Data: Locking the Barn Door First." Small Computers in Libraries 5 (October 1985): 5-8.
Quint considers mechanical and human-generated problems which can befall a library microcomputer, and provides several suggestions for preventing them. Bibliography.

1442 "RAMdisks." Small Computers in Libraries 4 (February 1984): 6-7.
A technique has been developed to allow use of excess internal memory in a microcomputer for data manipulation. This is accomplished through the use of a program which fools the

micro into treating the excess memory as though
it were a third disk drive. Advantages and
disadvantages are discussed.

1443 SMITH, WESLEY. "Eleven Pipers Piping. . ." OCLC
Micro 1 (December 1985): 14-15.
Smith discusses the DOS DIRectory command, and identifies nineteen variations which
are handy, but not well known.

1444 STAPLES, BRIAN. "The Importance of Making Back-
ups; or, How to Get Out of a Strawberry Jam."
OCLC Micro 1 (July 1985): 16-17.
The importance of backup copies of programs and data is stressed, and procedures for
copying files are provided.

1445 SWEDA, VICKI. "One Little, Two Little. . .Ten
System Users." OCLC Micro 1 (November 1985):
20-21, 23.
A secretary in OCLC's corporate offices
outlines her own file system for organizing data
on an IBM XT.

1446 "Tips for PCs in the Library." Small Computers
in Libraries 4 (December 1984): 9-10.
John Ganz, author of the Naked Computer
and editor of Tech Street Journal offers ten tips
for making the best use of your micro.

1447 "WILS: More About M300 Printing." M300 and PC
Report 2 (January 1985): 4-5.
Printing while logged on to OCLC with an
M300 micro/terminal is quite different than
printing with the older OCLC 100 or 105 terminals. Various print options are explained and the
appropriate commands for each option are reviewed.

MICROCOMPUTER OPERATORS

1448 BLAIR, JOHN C., Jr. "The Psychology of the Human Interface With a Microcomputer: Machine-
Friendly Humanware." Online 6 (November
1982): 83-87.
      The concept of becoming machine-friendly
is explored, and suggestions for improving understanding and developing greater rapport with the
microcomputer are presented.

1449 BUSCH, JOE. "Got the VDT's?" Small Computers in
Libraries 4 (May 1984): 7.
      A survey of work environments of video
display terminal operators indicates that a
proper work environment is frequently lacking.
Busch reports his findings and suggests that
administrators and supervisors evaluate the work
place for possible causes of health and vision
problems.

1450 CHENEY, HAL. "Continuity, Context, and Your VDU:
The Big Picture Through a Small Window." Library Software Review 4 (May/June 1985): 145-
49.
      When doing large jobs on a microcomputer,
the operator may have to deal with the problem of
textual disorientation because of the limited
amount of text that is visible on the screen at
any time. The author considers the problem and
suggests techniques for coping, if not remedies
for the situation.

1451 CIPOLLA, KATHARINE G. "A Touch of Heresy." Ohio
Media Spectrum 34 (Spring 1982): 26-27.
      Cipolla responds to the naive question,
"What'll the librarians do when the computer
checks out books."

1452 FARKAS, DAVID L. "Computer Furniture. . .An
Expert's Guide on How to be Comfortable at
Your Micro." Online 8 (May 1984): 43-49.

Mismatched and makeshift office furniture may contribute to fatigue and other physical problems among video display terminal operators. This article, in conjunction with one by T. J. Springer which accompanies it, provides specifications for properly proportioned VDT furniture and offers suggestions for greater comfort in the workplace.

1453 FREEDMAN, MARY, and CARLIN, LARRY. ". . .And Now Press ENTER ." Library Journal 110 (August 1985): 68-69.
The authors consider the psychology of the microcomputer shopper, circa 1985, and discuss methods of teaching new owners and operators the basics of machine operations.

1454 "Girls' Computer Anxiety is Library Workshop Focus." School Library Journal 31 (September 1984): 14-15.
A series of microcomputer workshops for girls held at the Rye (NY) Free Reading Room is evaluated and found to be worthwhile. The workshops were started after the children's librarian noted a 4:1 ratio of boys to girls using the library's microcomputer equipment and consulted with a specialist who attributed the reluctance of girls to use the equipment to early childhood inhibitions.

1455 HARTER, STEPHEN P. "The Meaning of Microcomputers." Technicalities 4 (March 1984): 7-9, 15.
The microcomputer is put into perspective by a writer who considers himself no computer hack, but derives considerable pleasure from micro ownership and use. He discusses the fascination that the micro holds for him, some of the problems he has encountered, and the constant sense of discovery and excitement it brings.

1456 LUCE, RICHARD E., and HARTMAN, SUSAN. "Telecommuting to Work: Using Technology to Work at Home." Library Hi Tech 2, no. 4, issue 8 (1984): 79-83.

In 1982 the Boulder (CO) Public Library experimented with a "Work-at-Home Project" for selected management and support personnel, one day per week, using a variety of equipment including microcomputers and dumb terminals. The experiment is reviewed and positive benefits are reported. Bibliography.

1457 MASON, ROBERT M. "Ergonomics: The Human and the Machine." Library Journal 109 (February 15, 1984): 331-32.

After stating and justifying his thesis that the workplace can influence productivity by 10 to 25 percent, Mason discusses the microcomputer workstation, including desk, chair, keyboard, screen, and lighting.

1458 MASON, ROBERT M. "Micros, White Collar Workers & the Library." Library Journal 109 (November 15, 1984): 2132-33.

Employment forecasts for the future indicate a decline in the number of clerical jobs because of office automation, and a broadening of skills required of clerical workers to perform a wider range of functions. The implications for libraries are discussed, along with a challenge to libraries to change their structures to accommodate the new technologies.

1459 MILLER, ROSALIND E. "Just When You Thought It Was Safe to Go Back In the School Library, In Comes a Microcomputer." Catholic Library World 54 (November 1982): 146-47.

Miller deals briefly with the psychology of adjusting to technological change, then disspells three widely held myths concerning microcomputers.

1460 MUSHRUSH, JAN. "Micro Training-Over Easy?" OCLC Micro 1 (September 1985): 24-25.

The author airs some personal peaves concerning the training of people in the use of microcomputers, and makes some valid and positive suggestions for the improvement of computer training/education in general.

1461 SCHLIEVE, PAUL LYNN. "Perceived Microcomputer
Professional Development Needs of Wisconsin
Public School Library/Media Specialists."
Ph. D. dissertation, Southern Illinois University at Carbondale, 1981.
An instrument designed to assess the perceived needs of library/media specialists concerning microcomputers was designed and adminis-
tered to 1333 Wisconsin library/media personnel
in 1981. Major needs were identified to be programming skills, knowledge of hardware and software compatibility, computer languages, teaching
methods, and software selection criteria. Bibliography.

1462 "Telecommuting and Libraries: The Next Challenge." Technicalities 4 (May 1984): 1, 16.
The microcomputer, equipped with a modem
and communications software, opens up the possibility for librarians and library staff to work
at home. The editors address the topic and predict that it will be one of many micro-related
concepts that libraries will have to recognize
and resolve in the future.

1463 TOROK, ANDREW G. "Ergonomics Considerations in
Microcomputing." Microcomputers for Information Management 1 (September 1984): 229-50.
The impact of the microcomputer on the
workplace and its effect on the welfare of the
worker are addressed in detail, with several
practical recommendations for dealing with micros
in a library environment. Bibliography.

1464 VANDERHOEF, JOHN, and GALLINA, PAUL. "Ergonomics
of VDTs." Canadian Library Journal 40 (October 1983): 285-87.
The microcomputer has drastically increased the use of computer technology in library
functions and has drawn attention to the need for
greater effort in integrating the video display
terminal into the workplace. The authors suggest
a human systems approach with recommendations
which should lead to a healthier, safer, and more
comfortable work environment. Bibliography.

1465 VAVREK, BERNARD. "Beware of Microcomputeritis."
Library Journal 110 (November 1, 1985): 164-
65; and School Library Journal 32 (November
1985): 152-53.
Vavrek characterizes the compulsive computer hack, describes ten symptoms to use for
self-diagnosis, and provides a three-part pre-
scription for the malady.

1466 WALTON, ROBERT A. "The Microcomputer Age: Understanding Its Effect in Library & Information
Center Environments." Online '83 Conference
Proceedings, Chicago, 10-12 October 1983.
Weston, CT: Online, Inc., 1983. Pp. 305-08.
Integration of a microcomputer program
into a library, and its effect on the organization, particularly the staff, are considered in
terms of addressing and planning for staff
anxieties.

SOFTWARE

1467 "Accessory Programs for PC-DOS and MS-DOS."
Electronic Library 3 (April 1985): 86.
Head Computers Ltd., announces seven new
software utilities of possible interest to librarians.

1468 "Almost Free Software." Small Computers in
Libraries 5 (March 1985): 4.
The Folklife Terminal Club, an international support group for Commodore users,
announces the publication of its new catalog of
public domain software, with instructions on how
to join the club and begin receiving programs.

1469 AMERICAN ASSOCIATION OF SCHOOL LIBRARIANS. COM-
MITTEE FOR STANDARDIZATION OF ACCESS TO LI-
BRARY MEDIA RESOURCES. "Microcomputer Software and Hardware--An Annotated Source List;
How to Obtain, How to Evaluate, How to Catalog, How to Standardize." School Library
Media Quarterly 12 (Winter 1984): 107-19.
A report of the AASL Committee for Standardization of Access to Library Media Resources
addresses the problems of obtaining, evaluating,
and cataloging software, and standardizing such
aspects of the software industry as packaging and
numbering. A list of software producers is included, and a sample evaluation form is provided.

1470 ANDERSON, ERIC S. "Eric (Not ERIC): The One-on-
One Defense." OCLC Micro 1 (July 1985): 4-5.
Anderson issues a strong reminder to budget for software; he recommends shareware as an
inexpensive software alternative; and he provides
a logical and reasonable interpretation of what
is and is not legal under copyright.

1471 ANDERSON, ERIC S. "Software Selection Considerations." ACCESS: Microcomputers in Libraries 2
(July 1982): 10-11, 17, 23.

Anderson enumerates and expands upon the five major considerations for microcomputer software selection: 1) hardware configuration, 2) program soundness, 3) machine capability, 4) ease of use, and 5) documentation. Bibliography.

1472 "Apple Library Software." Small Computers in Libraries 4 (February 1984): 2.
Micro Library Software announces the addition of COMPUTER CAT to its line of library/information management software, and the release of two new programs: MLS APPL-CAT and MLS APPL-CIRC in early 1984. The employment of Betty Costa as a consultant is also announced.

1473 BARRETTE, PIERRE P. "Selecting Digital Electronic Knowledge: A Process Model." School Library Media Quarterly 10 (Summer 1982): 320-36.
A model is suggested for the evaluation and selection of information sources and various instructional media accessible via microcomputer. The article has a school curriculum and media orientation but is adaptable to other uses. Bibliography.

1474 BAUGHMAN, SUSAN. "Microcomputer Software—What It Is—How to Select It—Where to Buy It." Education Libraries 5 (Winter 1980): 33-34.
Baughman provides general guidelines for software selection and purchase, with a brief annotated bibliography of microcomputer software reviewing sources and journals.

1475 BAUGHMAN, SUSAN. "Software Collection Management." Education Libraries 9 (Spring 1984): 17, 30.
Baughman identifies three components in collection management and applies them to a software collection. She deals with software description, organization, and control, with emphasis on storage methods.

1476 BEAUMONT, JANE. "UTLAS Microcomputer Products." Library Software Review 4 (May/June 1985): 150-53.

UTLAS, Inc., a supplier of library automation products and services, is adding a line of
microcomputer products. The article reviews the
InfoQUEST family of systems which operates on IBM
PC hardware, and considers the UTLAS IBM PC Intelligent Workstation.

1477 BELLIN, DAVID. "After the Purchase: Software
Maintenance and Outside Support." Software
Review 2 (June 1983): 69-72.
Maintenance contracts are standard for
microcomputer hardware, but less popular for
software, although there is a growing need for
ongoing maintenance, enhancement, and support.
Bellin addresses these services, notes functions
in which outside help might be required, and
reviews factors in choosing a consultant.

1478 BLAIR, JOHN C., Jr. "Software Applications Packages and the Role of the Computer Applications
Specialist." Online 6 (March 1982): 64-69.
Choosing microcomputer software for specific functions is a time consuming and demanding
task which requires expertise. The author summarizes the tasks of a computer applications
specialist, reviews the steps in choosing a software package, considers vendor and user responsibilities, and discusses software characteristics
and compatibility.

1479 BLAIR, JOHN C., Jr. "A Tutorial in Representative Apple Software." Database 5 (June
1982): 72-79.
Four of the best commercial software
packages available for the Apple microcomputer
are reviewed. These are DB MASTER for database
management, SUPER-TEXT II for word processing,
VISITERM for communciations, and VISIPLOT for
graphics. An overview of each type of software
is followed by a review of a specific program.

1480 BLAND, BARBARA B. "Evaluation: The Key to
Selecting Quality Microcomputer Courseware for
School Media Collections." North Carolina
Libraries 40 (Fall/Winter 1982): 191-97.

Bland addresses the problem of making good software choices when unexpected funds for microcomputer equipment and software become available. Media specialist/librarian involvement, quality, sources, and selection criteria are discussed, and selection procedures and criteria are summarized in an appendix.

1481 "Bowker Assigning ISBNs to Software." Wilson Library Bulletin 58 (September 1983): 10.
R. R. Bowker Company, U. S. Administrator of the ISBN agency, announces the use of International Standard Book Numbers for identification of software programs.

1482 BROERING, NAOMI C. "An Affordable Microcomputer Library Information System Developed by Georgetown University." Microcomputers for Information Management 1 (December 1984): 269-83.
The Library Information System (LIS), an integrated minicomputer software package developed for Georgetown University, has been adapted for microcomputer, and libraries are being sought as demonstration sites. The system is reviewed. Bibliography.

1483 "Building a Software Library: How Do You Create a Library of Software That Meets Your Needs-- and Doesn't Break Your Budget?" Electronic Learning 3 (October 1983): 77-87.
Four school principals and two media specialists consider the problem of starting and maintaining a software collection on a limited budget. A basic collection of thirty-one programs is recommended, and Glenn Fisher reviews ten publications which review software.

1484 BURTON, PAUL F., and GATES, HILARY. "Library Software for Microcomputers." Program 19 (January 1985): 1-19.
A number of software packages are now available for every library application, making review, comparison, and evaluation necessary prior to purchase. To aid in the process, Burton

and Gates review requirements and features of
various types of software, including information
retrieval, online searching, online catalogs,
acquisitions, serials, and circulation. Bibliography.

1485 BUSICK, CHRIS. "Microcomputers in Libraries."
Colorado Libraries 9 (Autumn 1983): 41-42.
A program for compiling bibliographies
and another listing serial holdings, both created
by members of the library reference staff at the
University of Colorado for use with the Radio
Shack TRS-80, are described and discussed.

1486 CAMPBELL, PATRICIA B. "Preliminary Guidelines
for Selecting Computer Software." Interracial
Books for Children Bulletin 15, no. 5 (1984):
15, 14.
Guidelines for selecting software for
children and youth are presented and discussed,
with equity being a major criterion. Violence/
non-Violence, Passivity/Empowerment, Competition/
Cooperation, and Failure/Success are considered
along with content, language, and graphics.

1487 CHEN, CHING-CHIH. MicroUse Directory: Software.
West Newton, MA: MicroUse Information, 1984.
440p.
Information concerning 1,500 library-
specific and library-related microcomputer software programs is provided in brief database
management format, including vendor name and
address, cost, hardware requirements, operating
system, language, memory requirements, peripherals, and a brief description of the program.
Based on the MICROUSE database compiled at
Simmons College, this is the first of several
planned volumes to be produced from MICROUSE
data.

1488 CHRISTIAN, DEBORAH. "Library Programmers: Creators or Copycats?" ACCESS: Microcomputers in
Libraries 3 (Spring 1983): 4, 11.
The need for library software is addressed, as is the tendencies of programmers to main-

tain a mainframe or minicomputer mindset and seek
to improve standard software rather than create
new and innovative programs for the micro.

1489 CIBBARELLI, PAMELA; TENOPIR, CAROL; and
KAZLAUSKAS, EDWARD JOHN. Directory of Information Management Software For Libraries,
Information Centers, Record Centers. Studio
City, CA: Cibbarelli and Associates, 1983.
133p.
Fifty-five software packages designed for
library applications are described in detail.
Fifty-four others are listed. The volume includes mainframe, mini, and micro packages. Bibliography.

1490 CLYDE, LAUREL A., and JOYCE, D. JOAN. "Selecting
Computer Software for School Libraries."
School Library Media Quarterly 13 (Spring
1985): 129-37.
Criteria for selection of library software are examined from the perspective of both
the library manager and the collection development librarian. General and specific criteria
are considered; review sources are discussed.
Bibliography.

1491 COHAN, KIM. "Documentation: Feared by All."
ACCESS: Microcomputers in Libraries 2 (April
1982): 5.
Cohan makes a plea for improved and
simplified instruction manuals.

1492 "Copyright for Software in Australia." Electronic Library 2 (October 1984): 213-14.
The Australian Government has extended
copyright to include software in a stop-gap measure to encourage research and development in
automation until the question of software protection is resolved.

1493 "Copyright Law Sets Limits on Computer Program
Copying." Library Journal 110 (November 15,
1981): 1670.
Public Law 96-517, which sets the rights

and limitations on the copying of computer software, is quoted and interpreted for the computer
user, programmer, or librarian seeking to get the
greatest possible use from software purchases,
within the limits of the law.

1494 "Copyright Protection for Software." Electronic
Library 3 (January 1985): 18-19.
Some problems concerning national and
international copyright of computer software are
addressed, and a method of preventing unauthorized copying, called shrink wrap licensing, is
introduced.

1495 DAVIES, JOHN. "Copyright and Computer Software:
The Publishers' View." Aslib Proceedings 35
(November/December 1983): 444-48.
The British copyright law is considered
in light of the growing computer software industry. The government's reluctance to enact firm
legislation is noted, and publishers' methods of
protecting their products from piracy are discussed. Bibliography.

1496 DEMAS, SAMUEL. "Microcomputer Software Collections." Special Libraries 76 (Winter 1985):
17-23.
Demas presents an overview of the major
considerations in developing a software collection, addressing selection and acquisition, processing, and circulation. Included is a section
on copyright and other laws affecting software
lending. Bibliography.

1497 DEWEY, PATRICK R. "High Resolution Adventure
Games for Use With Library Patrons." Library
Software Review 4 (September/October 1985):
294-97.
Interactive fiction, or adventure games
based on stories, have become popular with microcomputer users, and Dewey considers them reasonable additions to a public library's software
collection. He discusses games with high resolution graphics, and briefly reviews thirty-two
titles.

1498 DEWEY, PATRICK R. "Searching for Software: Looking for Bargains." Library Software Review 3 (September 1984): 390-93.

A librarian on a budget can still offer a variety of microcomputer programs by taking advantage of free and inexpensive software sources. In this article Dewey differentiates between free and public domain software and identifies several sources for each, including software clubs, state agencies which maintain clearinghouses, and bulletin boards. Glossbrenner's How to Get Free Software, and other print titles are suggested.

1499 DEWEY, PATRICK R. "Simulations for the Apple: Rat Control in Ancient Sumer." Library Software Review 4 (January/February 1985): 18-20.

The benefits of microcomputer simulation games are pointed out, several commercial games suitable for libraries are reviewed, and readers are encouraged to write new games or alter existing games to fit their needs.

1500 EAGER, VIRGINIA W. "Something for (Almost) Nothing." Small Computers in Libraries 4 (October 1984): 6-7.

Andrew Fluegeleman, author of PC-TALK, has devised a unique "try-it-pay-if-you-like-it" method of merchandising for his program. Recently authors of several other programs have tried and liked Fluegeleman's idea. The method is described, and four software programs are described which are available on those terms.

1501 EDGERTON, MARY. "Computer Literacy for Library Staff: OCLC's Keymap Program." M300 and PC Report 2 (July/August 1985): 3-4.

One annoyance in using an M300 Workstation with applications programs is that the keys on the OCLC keyboard don't always perform the function they indicate. KEYMAP, a macro program written to correct the problem, is described.

1502 EMARD, JEAN-PAUL. "Software Hang-ups and Glitches: Problems to be Faced & Overcome." Online 7 (January 1983): 18-23.

The Vice-President of Online, Inc.,
offers some practical advice on purchasing,
using, and protecting microcomputer software.

1503 "Evaluation of Computer Software." Scan 1, no. 4
(1982): 3-4.
This article, published by the Library
Services Division of the New South Wales Department of Education, enumerates and discusses ten
criteria for the teacher-librarian to apply in
software evaluation and selection.

1504 EVANS, RICHARD W. "Primary and Secondary Stages
in the Courseware Evaluation Process: An
Application to Computer-Aided Basic Skills
Training." Software Review 1 (February 1982):
58-67.
The associate director of SUNY Farming-
dale's microcomputer lab considers the problem of
software evaluation and selection, and proposes
guidelines which are applicable to his own lab,
and adaptable to others.

1505 FABIAN, WILLIAM M., and COURTNEY, MARJORIE S.
"An Apple for the Librarian: Microcomputers
in Instruction." Show-Me-Libraries 33 (March
1982): 5-8.
The founding of the CALICO microcomputer
software firm and the use and evaluation of two
of CALICO's library instruction programs are the
focus of this article. An evaluative questionnaire for use with students is included.

1506 FALANGA, ROSEMARIE. "Generic or Canned Software?" Library Software Review 4 (March/
April 1985): 97-98.
The question of adapting off-the-shelf
software to library purposes is addressed, advantages and disadvantages are identified, and methods for achieving the greatest use from commercial packages are suggested.

1507 FALANGA, ROSEMARIE. "A Little Demonstration. . ."
Library Software Review 4 (July/August 1985):
220-21.

The problem of selecting software is addressed, and the value of demonstration disks
made available by some software producers is
considered.

1508 GARBER, MARVIN. "How Safe is Safe? Backup Protection With an Apple II." Library Software
Review 4 (July/August 1985): 217-19.
Microcomputer users are encouraged to
make backup copies of datafiles, but the greater
problem of backup copies for commercial software
is the major topic of this article. Copy protection practices of software vendors are discussed
and suggestions are made which may save the
microcomputer user considerable inconvenience
should a software diskette be damaged.

1509 GAROOGIAN, RHODA. "Pre-Written Software: Identification, Evaluation, and Selection." Software Review 1 (February 1982): 11-34.
Commercially available software systems
and their applications to library functions are
emphasized in this article, which also provides
information sources, a list of vendors, and a
discussion of evaluative techniques. Both turnkey and micro packages are considered. Bibliography.

1510 GARTEN, EDWARD D., and McMEEN, GEORGE R. "A
Roundtable of Concerns: Microcomputer Software in the Library." Library Hi Tech 1
(Winter 1983): 99-102.
An acquisitions librarian, a collection
development librarian, a cataloger, a public services librarian, and others discuss the problems
posed by software circulation and services in the
library. Several software packages and sources
are reviewed.

1511 GASAWAY, LAURA N. "Nonprint Works and Copyright
in Special Libraries." Special Libraries 74
(April 1983): 156-70.
Focusing on computer programs, online
databases, and electronically published materials, this article by a librarian and law profes-

sor analyzes usage and library copying practices in relation to the Copyright Revision Act of 1976 as amended. Bibliography.

1512 GATES, HILARY. A Directory of Library and Information Retrieval Software for Microcomputers. Brookfield, VT: Gower, 1985. 59p.
Approximately 250 microcomputer software packages specifically designed for library applications are listed and described, with purchase information. Function and hardware indexes enhance the usefulness of the volume.

1513 GATES, HILARY. Library Software for Microcomputers. British Library Research & Development Report, no. 5798. London: British Library, 1984. 78p.
175 library-specific microcomputer programs are listed, with purchase information, hardware requirements, applications, and brief notes. This is a British publication which contains a mix of British and American products.

1514 GEFFNER, BONNIE. "Software: What's Available." Software Review 1 (October 1982): 178-96.
Forty software packages are discussed in this article concerning programs for library, business, and educational applications. Turnkey and microcomputer software are considered.

1515 GERHARDT, LILLIAN N. "Introducing CAI Software Reviews: Made in North Carolina." School Library Journal 31 (September 1984): 40-41.
A new monthly column intended to provide reviews of current software suitable for computer aided instruction is announced. The reviews will be provided by the staff of the Media Evaluation Center of North Carolina, whose previous work and background are the topic of this article.

1516 GILMAN, JAMES A. "The 'Soft' Option." Library Association Record 86 (January 1984): 23-26.
Software services offered by libraries are considered from the British perspective. Copying rather than lending is an option, as is

dial-up software service. Management, compatibility, and copyright problems are addressed.

1517 GLOSSBRENNER, ALFRED. How to Get Free Software; The Master Guide to Free Programs for Every Brand of Personal or Home Computer. New York: St. Martin's Press, 1984. 436p.

There is a wealth of microcomputer software in the public domain, which the creator is willing to share at little or no cost. Glossbrenner addresses this material, discussing types of software, quality, support, and techniques for obtaining free programs. However, the real value in this book is in the hundreds of sources of free and inexpensive software which the author identifies and evaluates. These sources include user groups, bulletin board services, online search services, journals, and libraries.

1518 GLOTFELTY, RUTH. "Stalking Microcomputer Software." School Library Journal 28 (March 1982): 91-94.

The problem of locating appropriate microcomputer software for school libraries and media centers is addressed, along with evaluations and purchasing information for several worthwhile programs, and a plea to vendors to revise their marketing practices to allow prepurchase previews.

1519 GORDON, ANITRA, and ZINN, KARL. "Microcomputer Software Considerations." School Library Journal 28 (August 1982): 25-27.

The authors discuss criteria and other considerations involved in the selection of microcomputer software for the media center.

1520 GRIFFIS, JOAN E. "The Challenge of Computer Software Evaluation." Catholic Library World 55 (April 1984): 403-04.

The problems of locating and evaluating computer software are presented, standard review sources such as Booklist, Learning, and MICROSIFT are mentioned, and negotiating with producers for evaluation privileges is discussed.

1521 "Group Debates Software Numbering." Publishers
     Weekly 227 (February 22, 1985): 79-80, 82.
          In 1983 the American National Standards
     Committee (ANSC) appointed a subcommittee to
     write standards for numbering computer software.
     Meanwhile, R. R. Bowker Company and others began
     using the International Standard Book Number
     (ISBN) scheme. Now that the ANSC committee has
     completed its work, attributes of the two sys-
     tems are being considered by publishing groups.
     This article represents arguments for both
     schemes presented at a meeting of the Associa-
     tion of American Publishers.

1522 HAKES, BARBARA. "Selecting Microcomputer Soft-
     ware." Wyoming Library Roundup 39 (Spring/
     Summer 1984): 46-48.
          Criteria for the selection of microcom-
     puter software are considered, with the school or
     library media center in mind. Such general cri-
     teria as educational value, content, and user
     interaction are listed, but seven less obvious
     considerations are discussed in greater detail.
     These are (1) allowance for instruction of heter-
     ogeneous groups, (2) provision of immediate feed-
     back, (3) diagnosis and prescription, (4) adapt-
     ive and interactive qualities, (5) locus of con-
     trol (6) revisability, and (7) previous success
     of the program.

1523 HALL, HAL W. "A Roundtable of Concerns: Micro-
     computer Software in the Library, Continued."
     Library Hi Tech 2, no. 1, issue 5 (1984):
     99-101.
          An earlier discussion edited by Garten
     and McMeen is continued. Problems posed by the
     introduction of software into an academic library
     are identified and discussed; unfortunately,
     there are more problems than solutions.

1524 HANE, PAULA. "Public Domain Software: A Boon for
     Libraries." Online 8 (September 1984): 31-34.
          Disadvantages of public domain software
     are presented, yet it is recommended as a viable
     source of inexpensive programs. Two user's

groups for CP/M based software are mentioned,
and their clearinghouse services are described.
Finally, a half-dozen public domain utility programs are reviewed.

1525 HANE, PAULA. "Public Domain Software: Part II."
Online 9 (January 1985): 13-16.
In a continuation of an earlier article
concerning public domain software, Hane compares
INDEX.COM, a public domain indexing program, with
a similar commercial program called DOCUMATE/
PLUS; and the public domain dictionary, SPELLM20.
COM, with the commercial program, SPELLGUARD.

1526 HANNIGAN, JANE ANNE. "The Evaluation of Microcomputer Software." Library Trends 33 (Winter
1985): 327-48.
The evaluation and selection of software
for libraries is treated thoroughly in this
article which considers types of software individually, then applies general guidelines for
software purchase. Bibliography.

1527 HART, EARL. "Selection of Computer Software."
Louisiana Library Association Bulletin 46
(Summer 1983): 17-21.
Guidelines to assist the school librarian
in microcomputer software selection are enumerated, and a handy sample evaluation form is
included. Bibliography.

1528 HENDERSON, MADELINE M. "Protecting Computer
Programs." American Society for Information
Science Bulletin 9 (February 1983): 5, 26.
The status of microcomputer software pro-
tection under the copyright law is summarized,
along with software/copyright court cases and the
Register's Report to Congress.

1529 "IBM PC Program Exchange." Small Computers in
Libraries 3 (September 1983): 5.
The Graduate Library School of the University of Arizona announces the initiation of a
clearinghouse/distribution service for public
domain microcomputer programs written for the IBM

PC. The service is described, standards for
programs are outlined, and order guidelines are
provided.

1530 "IBM PCjr Software." Library Software Review 3
(March 1984): 72-77.
Seventeen software packages designed for
the IBM PCjr are briefly described. More than
half are games, but an operating system, communications package, word processing software, and
other useful tools are included.

1531 "ISBN Agency Making More Software Assignments."
Wilson Library Bulletin 58 (June 1984):
698-99.
Emery Koltay, Director of the U. S. ISBN
Agency, reports on the growing use of International Standard Book Numbers by software producers for standard numbering and identification
of software.

1532 "ISBN Expands to Micro Software." American
Society for Information Science Bulletin 9
(June 1983): 5.
The R. R. Bowker Company announces its
decision to assign International Standard Book
Numbers to microcomputer software to expedite
identification and control. The ISBN system
is explained for better user understanding.

1533 "ISBN Numbers for Micro Software Affirmed by
International Body." Library Journal 109
(September 1, 1984): 1591.
The International ISBN Agency announces
the extension of the ISBN numbering system to
include microcomputer software, and offers a free
instruction manual concerning use of the numbers.

1534 "ISBN System Assigned to Microcomputer Software."
Information Retrieval and Library Automation
19 (October 1983): 7.
The R. R. Bowker Company's decision to
use International Standard Book Numbers for
software identification is announced. The ISBN
system is explained briefly.

1535 "ISBN System Expands to Microcomputer Software."
     Publishers Weekly 223 (May 20, 1983): 132.
            The R. R. Bowker Company's decision to
     assign International Standard Book Numbers to
     microcomputer software is announced.

1536 "ISBN Use Defended for Computer Software." Li-
     brary Journal 110 (February 15, 1985): 95.
            In November, 1984 the National Informa-
     tion Standards Organization announced a standard
     numbering scheme to be applied to computer soft-
     ware; however, many software producers had al-
     ready begun using International Standard Book
     Numbers for identification. In this article use
     of the ISBN is defended.

1537 "International Software Copyright." Small Com-
     puters in Libraries 5 (June 1985): 4.
            New Jersey Senator Frank Lautenberg has
     proposed copyright legislation to maintain inter-
     national protection of software, despite move-
     ments in some countries to weaken or abandon pro-
     tection. The bill is briefly summarized.

1538 "International Standard Program Numbers." Online
     Review 7 (August 1983): 282.
            The International Standard Program Number
     (ISPN), a scheme for identification and control
     of software, similar to the ISBN and ISSN, is
     announced by International Software, the British
     Company responsible for the International Soft-
     ware Database.

1539 "Interview: Ted Hines." ACCESS: Microcomputers
     in Libraries 1 (October 1981): 6, 19.
            Dr. Theodore C. Hines, former Professor
     of Library Science and Educational Technology at
     the University of North Carolina at Greensboro,
     discusses his interests in developing microcom-
     puter software for libraries.

1540 JACOB, MARY ELLEN. "Why Microcomputer Numbering?
     A White Paper Prepared by Mary Ellen Jacob for
     the NISO Program Committee." Library Hi Tech
     News no. 13 (February 1985): 11-19.

This white paper prepared for the National Information Standards Organization Z39BB subcommittee charged with devising a standard identification numbering scheme for software, justifies the committee's assignment, presents a draft of the committee's work, and compares their proposed Standard Computer Software Number (SCSN) to the International Standard Book Number (ISBN).

1541 JENKINS, KAY. "Microcomputer Software for Library Management." Ohio Media Spectrum 36 (Winter 1984/1985): 36-39.
 A school media specialist provides lists of commercial software suitable for use in cataloging, circulation, and list management. She identifies those she has used, and states her preferences.

1542 KENDALL, DAVID. "Program Generators; or, Flying Without the Stick." Small Computers in Libraries 2 (August 1982): 4-5.
 Program generators, software packages designed to permit programming in layman's terms, are now available for microcomputers. Kendall tells how to test and evaluate them for appropriateness to your needs.

1543 KLEINSMITH, LEWIS J. "Writing Software for Multiple Computers." Small Computers in Libraries 5 (January 1985): 7-9.
 Since it is unlikely that the microcomputer industry will produce and adhere to standards for programming languages, operating systems, and memory maps in order to make software interchangeable from system to system, software producers must create a version of their program for each brand of micro. Kleinsmith discusses the problems and disadvantages of such an arrangement.

1544 KLUCKAS, WILLIAM F., and D'ALLEGRO, JOSEPH M. "Evaluating Software Packages." Electronic Library 1 (July 1983): 162-65.
 A questionnaire devised to aid in software evaluation may be useful in software selec-

tion when applied to individual programs and used
as a basis for comparison.

1545 KNAPP, LINDA ROEHRIG. "How to Get Free Software." Popular Computing 3 (December 1983):
226, 228, 230.
Public domain microcomputer software is
defined, arguments are presented for and against
it, and sources are identified and discussed.

1546 KOMOSKI, KENNETH. "Push Ed Software Out of the
Comfort Zone." School Library Journal 31
(November 1984): 56, 58-59.
Computers are the educational fad of the
1980s, and little attention is being paid to why
they are added to a curriculum or how they are
being used. Komoski speaks out against using
technology to teach what can be taught as well
with a workbook, and provides several tips for
librarians to use in evaluating teaching programs
for possible purchase.

1547 "LC Weighs Software Copyright." Library Journal
108 (August 1983): 1402, 1404.
The Copyright Office of the Library of
Congress is reviewing mandatory deposit requirements for copyright of software at the instiga-
tion of copyright owners, who fear the loss of
trade secrets through the depository system.
Arguments are presented.

1548 LARSON, ANDREW. "Follett Replies." Small Computers in Libraries 3 (April 1983): 1-2.
The director of Follett Book Company's
Microcomputer Division explains Follett's preview
and return policies for software available from
that company.

1549 LaRUE, JAMES. "Documentation: Writing is Reason-
ing." Library Software Review 3 (June 1984):
202-06.
The value of good microcomputer documentation is emphasized, improvement in documentation of commercial software is noted, and the
ultimate, "self-documenting software," is dis-

cussed. Documentation tailored to a library's
specific applications must be written locally,
and the author offers suggestions for accomplishing the task.

1550 LaRUE, JAMES. "Steal This Program!" Library
Software Review 4 (September/October 1985):
298-301.
LaRue considers the software copyright
dilemma from a personal perspective, presenting
the point of view of both the user and the producer, differentiating between copy protection
and software warranty, and constructing a reason-
ably workable code of ethics for the user.
Trends are noted.

1551 LATHROP, ANN. "Building the Software Collection." Educational Computer Magazine 1
(November/December 1981): 23, 30.
Selection criteria for microcomputer
software are considered.

1552 LATHROP, ANN. "Building the Software Collection:
Part III." Educational Computer Magazine 2
(January/February 1982): 16-17, 52-53.
This article, a tutorial for learning
software evaluation criteria and techniques, uses
CALICO's PERIODICAL INDEXES program as an exam-
ple.

1553 LATHROP, ANN. "Microcomputer Courseware: Selection and Evaluation." Top of the News 39
(Spring 1983): 265-74.
The problem of selecting microcomputer
courseware is addressed, and evaluation criteria
are suggested. Sources of evaluation instruments
and courseware reviews and a sample evaluation
form are appended.

1554 LATHROP, ANN. "San Mateo County Office of Educa-
tion of Computer-Using Educators SOFTSWAP."
Computing Teacher 9 (April 1982): 16-31.
SOFTSWAP, a project of the San Mateo
County (CA) Office of Education and the Computer-
Using Educators' Microcomputer Center, gathers

and distributes public domain software to educators. The program is outlined, how to receive
copies of software is explained, and dozens of
programs are listed. An order form is included.

1555 LATHROP, ANN. "Software. . .PREviewing and RE-
viewing." Educational Computer Magazine 1
(September/October 1981): 14.
The need for a media coordinator to preview microcomputer software prior to purchase is
emphasized; the reluctance of most producers to
send preview programs is reported; and ten methods for gathering evaluative data on software are
suggested.

1556 LATHROP, ANN. "The Terrible Ten in Educational
Programming (My Top Ten Reasons for Automatically Rejecting a Program)." Educational Computer Magazine 2 (September/October 1982): 34.
Lathrop lists and discusses ten negative
factors to look for in evaluating microcomputer
courseware for possible school library or classroom use. Among these are rewarding failure,
technical problems, inadequate instructions, sar-
castic or derogatory responses, and poor documentation.

1557 LATHROP, ANN, and MARSHALL, JANICE. "Mail-Order
Software Distributors with Liberal On-Approval
Policies." Computing Teacher 12 (June 1985):
31-33.
Discriminating teachers, administrators,
and media specialists are beginning to seek software distributors who sell on approval, offer a
variety of popular software, screen programs
before listing them in their catalogs, and provide catalogs free of charge. The authors provide profiles of thirteen companies that meet
these criteria.

1558 LEIMBACH, JUDY. "Spotlight on Computers: Students in Control." School Library Journal 28
(August 1982): 37.
The microcomputer is an ideal teaching
tool for the gifted, according to this teacher of

gifted intermediate students who has included
computer literacy in her curriculum. In addition
to use of the computer, she teaches programming,
and places the student-produced programs in the
school library for the entire faculty, staff, and
student body to use.

1559 LETTNER, LORETTA. "A Library Software Sampler."
Library Journal 110 (May 1, 1985): 124, 126-
30; and School Library Journal 31 (May 1985):
154, 156-60.
A good selective bibliography of microcomputer software for a variety of library applications is provided by one of Library Journal's
assistant editors. Categorized by application,
the entries include bibliographic information and
brief annotations.

1560 LEVERT, VIRGINIA M. "Library Software Update."
Library Hi Tech News 1 (September 1984): 1,
13-14.
Microcomputer use in libraries is increasing dramatically, and with it the number of
library-specific microcomputer programs. Levert
analyzes the availability of general use and
library-specific applications programs, the hardware on which they run, and development trends
for the future. Bibliography.

1561 LEVERT, VIRGINIA M. "Library-Specific Microcomputer Software." Library Software Review 4
(March/April 1985): 79-81.
Levert analyzes the library software marketplace, addressing both generic applications
programs and library-specific software. Commercial producers are considered, and trends in
the hardware market are touched upon. Bibliography.

1562 "Libraries Not Hazardous to Your Disks." Small
Computers in Libraries 1 (December 1981): 5.
Following an inquiry concerning the
negative effects on software of theft-detection
systems in libraries, detection machines in air-
ports, and microwave ovens in kitchens, the

editors of <u>SCIL</u> offer a selection of reader responses which are far from conclusive.

1563 "Library Administration Program." <u>Small Comput-</u>
<u>ers in Libraries</u> 1 (June 1981): <u>1</u>.
    Several library-oriented microcomputer
programs available for Apple II, TRS-80, and most
other standard hardware brands are listed, with
their sources.

1564 LISANTI, SUZANA, and DUNKLE, REBECCA. "Software
Review Index." <u>Library Hi Tech</u> 2, no. 1,
issue 5 (1984): <u>95-98</u>.
    Fifty-two reviews of new software prod-
ucts which have appeared in five popular computer
magazines are listed in this on-going column.
Several word processing, spreadsheet, and database management systems are included.

1565 LISANTI, SUZANA, and DUNKLE, REBECCA. "Software
Review Index." <u>Library Hi Tech</u> 2, no. 3,
issue 7 (1984): <u>101-04</u>.
    Fifty reviews of education and library
related software are listed in this on-going
column.

1566 LOERTSCHER, DAVID V. "Analyzing Microcomputer
Software." <u>School Library Journal</u> 29
(November 1982): 28-32.
    Loertscher encourages librarians and
media specialists to write microcomputer courseware, provides practical advice on developing
ideas, and suggests some good examples of courseware which the beginning programmer might use as
patterns.

1567 LOERTSCHER, DAVID V. "In-House Production of
Computer Software." <u>Drexel Library Quarterly</u>
20 (Winter 1984): 16-26.
    Teacher-made materials have long been a
part of every school library media center; thus,
locally produced software should be no exception.
Loertscher identifies the media specialist's role
in adapting commercial software to local needs,
selecting public domain software when appropri-

ate, and assisting in the writing of new programs
when required. Bibliography.

1568 LOHNER, WOLFGANG, and KOCH, WALTER. "Portable
Software Packages for Microcomputers to be
Installed in Developing Countries Under Unesco's Sponsorship." IFLA Journal 11, no. 2
(1985): 124-28.
   A Unesco program to identify and distribute appropriate microcomputer software to libraries and information centers in developing countries, is described. Specifications for selection of software are noted, and the functioning
and administration of the program are addressed.

1569 LOOK, HUGH EVISON. "Evaluating Software for Microcomputers." Electronic Library 2 (January
1984): 53-60.
   Eight major and nine secondary criteria
for choosing microcomputer software are outlined
and discussed.

1570 "Low-Cost Commodore Programs." Small Computers
in Libraries 3 (March 1983): 7.
   The Folklife Terminal Club announces the
availability of more than 5,000 public domain
software programs which may be obtained through
the club offices.

1571 LUNDEEN, GERALD, and TENOPIR, CAROL. "Microcomputer Software for In-House Databases. . .
Four Top Packages Under $2000." Online 9
(September 1985): 30-38.
   Database management software for the library is addressed, selection criteria are considered, and four database management programs--
CAIRS, IN-MAGIC, SCI-MATE, and SIRE--are reviewed
and compared.

1572 LYTLE, SUSAN S., and HALL, HAL W. "Software,
Libraries, & the Copyright Law." Library
Journal 110 (July 1985): 33-39.
   The decision to offer microcomputer capa-
bilities as an integral part of library services
at Texas A & M University Library have forced li-

brary staff to address copyright issues. Two
A & M staff members provide insight into the
copyright law, licensure and contracts, making
of archival copies, vendor disclaimers, piracy,
and other copyright issues. Bibliography.

1573 MANLEY, WILL. "Facing the Public." Wilson
Library Bulletin 57 (March 1983): 588-89.
A columnist for Wilson Library Bulletin
takes a strong stance against circulation of
video game cartridges from the public library.

1574 MARSHALL, PETER. "The Strange Case of 'Software
Lending Right'." Library Association Record
85 (July/August 1983): 269.
In Great Britain the pirating of microcomputer software through lending and subscription libraries is an increasing problem for the
software industry. The problem is defined, copyright is addressed, and some likely actions by
software manufacturers are noted.

1575 MASON, ROBERT M. "Choosing Spreadsheet & Database Management Software." Library Journal
110 (October 15, 1985): 54-55.
Mason reviews software selection criteria, uses, and functional requirements, then
reviews three spreadsheets and one database management package. Reviewed are: LOTUS 1-2-3,
SUPERCALC3, VP-PLANNER, and REFLEX.

1576 MASON, ROBERT M. "Searching for Software: Finding & Buying the 'Right Stuff'." Library
Journal 108 (April 15, 1983): 801-02.
The advantages and limitations of commercial, public domain, custom made, and mail order
software are considered; software guides are
listed; methods of obtaining previewing privileges for software are suggested; and a method of
software storage is recommended.

1577 MASON, ROBERT M. "Software Copyright and Copy
Protection; Laser Disk Systems at ALA."
Library Journal 110 (September 15, 1985):
58-59.

Mason considers software copyright and
copy protection from an economic, an ethical,
and a practical point of view, then considers
the future, including the impact that local area
networks will have on the issue. A short column
is appended concerning laser disk systems which
were exhibited at the 1985 American Library
Association Conference.

1578 MASON, ROBERT M. "A Software Primer: Information
for the First Time User." Online '83 Conference Proceedings, Chicago, 10-12 October 1983.
Weston, CT: Online, Inc., 1983. Pp. 189-92.
Mason reviews some software basics, including function, types, sources, and selection.

1579 MASON, ROBERT M. "Software Wars." Library
Journal 110 (May 15, 1985): 40-41.
Competition is becoming intense in the
software marketplace as Adam Osborne launches his
new company, Paperback Software International
(PSI), intending to offer quality software at
reasonable prices. The first PSI production,
PAPERBACK WRITER, is reviewed, and other PSI
products are discussed briefly. The competition
between integrated and specialized software such
as SYMPHONY and FRAMEWORK is also noted.

1580 McCALLUM, SALLY. "Standards: Software Numbering." RTSD Newsletter 9, no. 8 (1984): 95-96.
Drafts of three new standards are announced by the National Information Standards
Organization (NISO). The standard for numbering
software, which has a rather stormy history, is
described, and background information concerning
the numbering controversy is included.

1581 McELROY, A. RENNIE, and BARCLAY, KENNETH A. "Request." Program 15 (October 1981): 233-37.
SIR (Simple Information Retrieval), an
information processing package being developed
jointly by the Library and the Department of Computer Studies at Napier College for use with a
North Star Horizon 64K microcomputer, is described. Comments are invited.

1582 MEAD, CHERYL L. "States to Watch: North Carolina: A Software Evaluation Plan With National Implications." Electronic Learning 3 (October 1983): 32, 39-40.
The Media Evaluation Services of North Carolina's State Department of Public Instruction are described, and North Carolina's plan for cataloging software is presented.

1583 MICHELS, FREDRICK; HARRISON, NEIL; and SMITH, DOUGLAS. "User-Supported Software for the IBM PC." Library Hi Tech 3, no. 2, issue 10 (1985): 97-106.
The authors present the concept of user-supported software (often called freeware), and review four high quality user-supported software programs for the IBM personal computer: PC-FILE III, PC-CALC, PC-WRITE, and PC-TALK II. Bibliography.

1584 MILLER, INABETH. "Microcomputers in Media Centers--Selecting Software." Collection Building 5 (Summer 1983): 3-17.
The selection of microcomputer software for schools and libraries is treated thoroughly in this article which identifies sources of software and software reviews, offers advice on choosing a vendor, details preview techniques, and provides evaluation criteria. Several educational software series are reviewed, research is cited, and the educational value of computer games is discussed. Bibliography.

1585 "More on Loaning Programs." Small Computers in Libraries 4 (April 1984): 4-5.
United Computer Corporation, a California based company which rents out commercially produced software, has been sued by MicroPro, the publishers of WORDSTAR word processing software, for permitting unauthorized copying of MicroPro products. The suit has been settled out of court. United Computer now has a license to rent MicroPro software, and all United Computer rentals are protected against unauthorized copying with PROLOK disks.

1586 MOSKOWITZ, MICKEY. "Developing a Microcomputer Program to Evaluate Library Instruction." School Library Media Quarterly 10 (Summer 1982): 351-56.
The author describes the procedure for developing a microcomputer program using a self-produced library instruction evaluation program as a model to demonstrate the process. Bibliography.

1587 "National Software Library." Software Review 2 (September 1983): 184.
PC Telemart, Inc., announces the establishment of the National Software Library, in Fairfax, Virginia. It is a research and reference facility, with memberships sold on a subscription basis.

1588 NAUMER, JANET NOLL. "Microcomputer Software Packages--Choose With Caution." School Library Journal 29 (March 1983): 116-19.
This annotated bibliography of microcomputer software suitable for library applications is arranged by function for easy comparison. Bibliography.

1589 NOLAN, JEANNE M. "Database Management Software off the Shelf vs. Customized Packages. Which is the Best Route?" Online '84 Conference Proceedings, San Francisco, 29-31 October 1984. Weston, CT: Online, Inc., 1984. Pp. 187-90.
Off the shelf database management packages are compared with semi-customized and fully customized software, taking into consideration the time required to learn the program, design, debug, document, and implement the system. Bibliography.

1590 NOLAN, JEANNE M. "Integrated Software." Electronic Library 3 (January 1985): 36-37.
Nolan explains the concept of integrated software, identifies several integrated packages, and provides addresses, phone numbers, and other information for each producer or distributor.

1591 NOLAN, JEANNE M. Micro Software Evaluations.
Torrance, CA: Nolan Information Management
Services, 1984. 176p.
Thirty-four library specific software
packages, most of them compatible with microcom-
puter hardware, are evaluated.

1592 NOLAN, JEANNE M. Micro Software Report. Library
Edition. Torrance, CA: Nolan Information Management Services, 1982. Annual.
An alphabetical listing of library oriented software programs for microcomputers, this
useful reference series provides brief descriptions, hardware requirements, review sources, and
order information for commercially available
software packages.

1593 NOLAN, JEANNE M. "Microcomputer Software for
Libraries: A Survey." Electronic Library 1
(October 1983): 275-78.
A survey of commercial software suitable
for library use indicates numbers of programs
available for major library functions, and identifies high interest, high demand areas for development in the near future.

1594 "Other Approaches to Universal Software Identification." Software Review 2 (September 1983):
180-81.
Registering and recording microcomputer
software is becoming a growing problem as the
software market expands. R. R. Bowker Company is
using International Standard Book Numbers (ISBN);
compilers of the International Standard Database
have devised International Standard Program Numbers (ISPN); while the National Information
Standards Organization (NISO) Z39 committee, has
appointed a subcommittee to design a standard
numbering system.

1595 PAUL, SANDRA K. "Update on the Z39 Software Numbering Standard." American Society for Information Science Bulletin 10 (June 1984): 10,
12.
The chairperson of the National Informa-

tion Standards Organization Z39.BB subcommittee,
which has been given the charge to devise a
standard numbering scheme for computer software,
provides a brief overview of the proposed system
and outlines the future work of the committee in
seeking its adoption.

1596 "Periodicals Wholesalers Assn. Backs ISBN for
Software." Library Journal 110 (April 1,
1985): 28.
Harold Paulsen, representing some 350
wholesale periodical distributors, presented
arguments supporting use of the International
Standard Book Number (ISBN) for software identification and control to the National Information
Standards Organization, according to this brief
news note.

1597 PHILLIPS, BRIAN. "'Shareware'. . .Make It Your
First Software Purchase." Online 9 (May
1985): 33-36.
The concept of "shareware" or "freeware"
is explained. PC-WRITE, PC-FILE III, and PC-
TALK, three popular shareware programs, are
reviewed.

1598 PLANTON, STANLEY. "Hacking at the Apple Tree:
How to Duplicate Software." Library Journal
110 (November 1, 1985): 156-59; and School
Library Journal 32 (November 1985): 144-47.
A brief introduction to copyright and
copy protection of software precedes an analysis
of typical protection schemes used by software
manufacturers and reviews of three software programs designed to copy software in spite of copy
protection. Suggestions for copying are included.

1599 POLLY, JEAN ARMOUR. "Selecting Really Excellent
Software for Young Adults." Voice of Youth
Advocates 8 (June 1985): 114-15.
Polly writes briefly about planning and
budgeting for microcomputer software in a public
library, and provides good criteria for collection building.

1600 POST, RICHARD. "Selected Shareware for Library-
        Media Administrative Applications." Ohio
        Media Spectrum 36 (Winter 1984/1985): 12-15.
            The shareware concept of software market-
        ing is explained, and five shareware programs are
        reviewed briefly. Included are PC-WRITE, PC-FILE
        III, PC-TALK III, FREECALC, and PC PICTURE GRAPH-
        ICS SYSTEM.

1601 "Product Announcements." Small Computers in Li-
        braries 2 (October 1982): 4-5.
            A variety of microcomputer software is
        announced, including the CATALOG CARD AND LABEL
        WRITER and the LIBRARY CIRCULATION SYSTEM, from
        K-12 MicroMedia; A-V MANAGEMENT PROGRAMS from
        Edward Tennen; and several Apple programs from
        Richmond Micro Software.

1602 "Program Protection Scheme Available." Small
        Computers in Libraries 4 (March 1984): 6.
            The Vault Corp. announces a new product,
        called Prolok, which prevents copying of micro-
        computer software. Libraries can purchase disks
        programmed with the Prolok system, produce copies
        of software for circulation using those disks,
        and be certain that copyright protected software
        will not be reproduced.

1603 "Programs and Versions and Revisions." Small
        Computers in Libraries 1 (December 1981): 2.
            The author tells how to identify variant
        versions and revisions of commercial software.

1604 "Public Domain Software: Another Source Report-
        ed." Library Journal 109 (May 1, 1984): 847.
            A national clearinghouse for public do-
        main software is announced by Microcomputer Li-
        braries and the Highsmith Company, Inc.

1605 RAITHEL, FREDERICK J. "Small Computer Software
        Sharing Program." Show-Me Libraries 30 (July
        1979): 43-44.
            Instantext, a software sharing program
        instituted by Mid-Missouri librarians in 1977,
        is described by one of its founders.

1606 RAITHEL, FREDERICK J., and KLOEPPER, DAN C.
"'Instantext' Opened to Nebraska Librarians."
Nebraska Library Association Quarterly 11
(Spring 1980): 6-7.
Instantext, a microcomputer software exchange service initiated by a group of Mid-Missouri librarians in 1977, is described. Access
to the exchange is explained; a sample program
is provided.

1607 RAPPAPORT, SUSAN. "Logo in the Libraries." Library Journal 110 (November 15, 1985): 66-67.
Logo, a unique programming language particularly useful in teaching situations, is discussed, and its value in a library situation is
explored.

1608 RAPPAPORT, SUSAN. "Software Collecting: Method
for Madness." Library Journal 110 (April 1,
1985): 56-57.
Rappaport considers the dearth of good
software, and draws attention to the problems of
identifying, reviewing, and getting good programs
into the hands of the teacher. She provides the
librarian with eleven guidelines for software
selection.

1609 "Reading Manuals and Documentation." Small Computers in Libraries 4 (January 1984): 6-7.
The problem of interpreting microcomputer
manuals and software documentation is addressed
briefly, and several terms common in microcomputer literature are defined and discussed.

1610 "Reference Technology Software Solves Optical
Disk Incompatibility Problems." Electronic
Library 3 (July 1985): 151.
One of the major problems with data storage on optical disk has been incompatibility
among computer storage disks, operating systems,
and host processors. Reference Technology, Inc.,
announces a major breakthrough with the development of STA/F File System software. The software
is described, uses are discussed, and purchase
information given.

1611 ROSENBERG, VICTOR. "Selling Software: An Inside
Viewpoint." Wilson Library Bulletin 58 (May
1984): 636-38.
The creator of the PERSONAL BIBLIOGRAPHIC
SYSTEM discusses the creative process, including
the value of customer feedback in planning and
decision making and the reputation of the creator
in software evaluation and selection.

1612 SAFFADY, WILLIAM. "Electronic Spreadsheet and
Data Management Software for Microcomputers."
Library Technology Reports 20 (July/August
1984): 431-608.
Saffady provides a general introduction
to the genre, then reviews twelve electronic
spreadsheets, one graphics generator, and eight
data management systems.

1613 SCHEPPKE, JIM. "Software Hints for Public Library
Micros." Unabashed Librarian 49 (1983): 14.
Purchasing educational software for public library use demands special skill because
most educational software is designed for the
school or home computer market. Scheppke identifies six desirable qualities for educational
software in public libraries, and recommends that
software selection be made with those qualities
in mind.

1614 SELL, JOANNE. "Microcomputer Software Fair."
Media Spectrum 9 (Third quarter 1982): 15-17.
Organizing and presenting a microcomputer
software fair is described by a media specialist
with first-hand experience in the activity.

1615 "Software Copying Protection: Defendisk's Signa-
ture Method." Small Computers in Libraries
4 (December 1984): 10-11.
A new method of copy protection for software, developed by Defendisk, Inc., of Denver,
Colorado, is described briefly.

1616 "Software Digest: Integrated Software Testing."
Library Hi Tech News no. 13 (February 1985):
4.

The results of a comparative evaluation
of popular integrated software programs are summarized. Performed by the staff of Software
Digest and reported in that publication's Ratings
Newsletter, the survey evaluates each program on
ease of learning, ease of use, performance, versatility, and other criteria.

1617 "Software for Micros and Minis." Library Systems
Newsletter 1 (August 1981): 14
The importance of off-the-shelf software
is increasing steadily because of the high cost
of producing or purchasing customized software.
Some surprising cost estimates are quoted.

1618 "The Software Line-Up: What Reviewers Look for
When Evaluating Software." Electronic Learning 2 (October 1982): 44-48.
A two page form for use in evaluating
microcomputer courseware is presented, and its
application to software selection is explained.

1619 "Software Numbering Progress Announced." Library
Software Review 3 (June 1984): 149-50.
The American National Standards Committee
Z39, Subcommittee on Software Numbering, has
announced agreement on a registration and numbering system for software. The system will be similar to the International Standard Book Number
(ISBN), with the number representing the regis-
trant, the product, the delivery medium, and a
check digit.

1620 "Software Numbering System Under Development."
Information Retrieval and Library Automation
19 (February 1984): 3-4.
The American National Standards Committee
Z39 Subcommittee BB, charged with developing a
standard numbering system for computer software,
presents a brief report of its work through 1983.

1621 "Software Publishers Assn. Report Criticizes
Software Evaluation Service." School Library
Journal 31 (April 1985): 10.
The newly formed Software Publishers

Association has produced and distributed a report sharply critical of the Educational Computer Service and the National Education Association, its founder, for its structure, fees, and licensing requirements. The criticisms are discussed at length in this news article.

1622 "Some Library Management Programs." Electronic Learning 2 (March 1983): 70-71.
Twenty microcomputer programs designed to perform specific library functions are presented in brief chart format for easy comparison.

1623 "Sorting for BASIC Users." Small Computers in Libraries 2 (February 1982): 2.
The article explores problems encountered with most sort programs written in BASIC. SORT/ B, a workable and efficient program that can be incorporated into standard BASIC software, is reviewed.

1624 STAPLES, BRIAN. "OMPX: On the Trail of 'Just Right' Software." OCLC Micro 1 (March 1985): 12-14.
OMPX, the OCLC Microcomputer Program Exchange, is discussed, and its services are described in some detail.

1625 SURPRENANT, THOMAS. "On the High Tech Frontier: An Interview With W. Krag Brotby." Library Software Review 4 (March/April 1985): 92-96.
An interview with W. Krag Brotby, founder of the Vault Corporation, provides an introduction to software and data security, addressing security systems, liability, librarians' rights, and other issues.

1626 SWIGGER, KEITH. "Ways to Look Before You Leap." Educational Computer 4 (January 1984): 16-17.
Previewing software before purchase is often difficult, but Swigger suggests several methods, including ordering programs on approval, attending conventions where distributors exhibit, and visiting other computer users who already own the software.

1627 TAGG, W., and TEMPLETON, RAY. Computer Software:
Supplying It and Finding It. Library and
Information Research Report, no. 10. London:
British Library, 1983. 53p.
Tagg and Templeton consider software acquisition and collection management from a British perspective. Included are listings of associations that supply software as well as printed
sources of software information and reviews. A
portion of the book is devoted to cataloging,
copyright, and other issues. Bibliography.

1628 TALAB, ROSEMARY STURDEVANT. "Copyright, Micro
Software, and the Library Media Center."
School Library Media Quarterly 12 (Summer
1984): 285-88.
The Copyright Revision Act of 1976, and
its impact on microcomputer software use in library media centers is the subject of this article which explains the law in relation to software, discusses copyright infringement, provides
suggestions for safeguarding the school's liability in case of infringement, and discusses the
media specialist's responsibilities in encouraging and insuring legal uses of library software.
Bibliography.

1629 "Technical Services and Circulation Software for
Micros." Library Systems Newsletter 4 (December 1984): 94-96.
Development of software to support library functions is increasing steadily, as evi-
denced by the number of programs available for
technical services and circulation. The editors
briefly summarize the 1985 offerings of eight
producers of library software.

1630 TEDD, LUCY A. "Software for Microcomputers in
Libraries and Information Units." Electronic
Library 1 (January 1983): 31-48.
A general introduction to the topic of
microcomputer software discusses operating systems and points for consideration in purchasing
software. A variety of library applications are
discussed, with features of specific programs

described. Applications include word processing,
data management, in-house information retrieval,
online searching, library-specific functions, and
financial management. Bibliography.

1631 TEDD, LUCY A. "Software for Microcomputers in
Libraries and Information Units." Proceedings
of the 6th International Online Information
Meeting, London, 7-9 December 1982. Medford,
NJ: Learned Information, 1982. Pp. 482-83.
The previous article is summarized.

1632 TEMPLETON, RAY. "'Public Domain' Software."
Aslib Proceedings 35 (November/December 1983):
440-43.
The term, public domain, is defined, and
its application to microcomputer software is discussed. The software library maintained by the
Advisory Unit for Computer Based Education is
described, along with its collection of public
domain software which is available for copy.
Bibliography.

1633 TENOPIR, CAROL. "Evaluation of Library Retrieval
Software." Communicating Information. Proceedings of the 43rd ASIS Annual Meeting.
White Plains, NY: Knowledge Industry Publications, 1980, v. 17. Pp. 64-67.
Criteria and guidelines for the evaluation and selection of online retrieval software
for microcomputers are presented for the librarian with limited background in automation.

1634 TOOMBS, WILLIAM W. "Software Copyright, Piracy
and Libraries." Small Computers in Libraries
4 (November 1984): 10-11.
Toombs considers the copyright law and
the ethics of software piracy, discusses producers' attempts at protecting their products, and
recommends a stance for libraries on the issue.
Bibliography.

1635 TREBAS, DAVE. "Documentation for the Compleat
Programmer." ACCESS: Microcomputers in Libraries 2 (April 1982): 15-16.

Trebas presents a simple formula for writing effective microcomputer program documentation.

1636 TREVELYAN, A., and ROWAT, MARTIN J. _An Investigation of the Use of Systems Programs in Library Applications of Microcomputers._ Library and Information Research Report, no. 12. Boston Spa: British Library Lending Division, Publications Section, 1983. 158p.
  The feasibility of using commercial or readily available software to implement microcomputer-based automated systems for libraries is investigated by a team of researchers who concentrated on six areas: circulation, acquisitions, cataloging, notification of patrons, database management, and periodical circulation. Bibliography.

1637 TREVELYAN, A., and ROWAT, MARTIN J. "Systems Programs in Library Applications of Microcomputers." _Vine_ no. 40 (October 1981): 31-32.
  In 1981 Martin Rowat received a grant from the British Library Research and Development Department to study the use of system programs in developing library application software. This is an interim report which summarizes the literature search, specifications for the project, and plans, but contains no data or conclusions.

1638 TRUETT, CAROL. "Evaluating Software Reviews: A Review of the Reviews." _Library Software Review_ 3 (September 1984): 371-78.
  One of the most important functions a librarian can perform is locating reviews of materials being considered for purchase. This is particularly important for microcomputer software. Truett outlines ten criteria by which to evaluate a review, and briefly reviews fourteen journals that review software.

1639 TRUETT, CAROL. "The Search for Quality Micro Programs: Software & Review Sources." _School Library Journal_ 30 (January 1984): 35-37.
  The school librarian's role in providing

guidance to teachers selecting microcomputer
software is discussed, the value of directories
and review journals is pointed out, and an annotated bibliography of thirty-five directories,
review journals, and sources is included.

1640 "Unisist's Inventory of Software." Electronic
Library 1 (January 1983): 11.
        UNESCO's General Program for Information
(UNISIST), has announced its intention to compile
an inventory of basically noncommercial software
for mainframe, mini, and microcomputers, according to this news item.

1641 "Universal Software Market Identifiers." Software Review 2 (June 1983): 102.
        Technique Learning Corp. announces the
development of the Universal Software Market
Identifier (USMI) for the purpose of registering
and identifying microcomputer software.

1642 "Use of Microcomputers in Libraries: BHRA Awarded
Research Grant." Online Review 5 (April
1981): 193.
        In 1981 the British Library awarded a one
year research grant to BHRA Fluid Engineering to
underwrite research on the adaptation of systems
programs to microcomputer uses in libraries. The
project is explained; procedures are outlined.

1643 "Using Program Packages in Libraries." Small
Computers in Libraries 3 (November 1983): 6.
        A research project compares the use of
generic software for library functions with the
purchase or creation of dedicated programs.

1644 WALKER, DAVID D. "Towards a National Software
Library." Educational Media International
no. 3 (1981): 20-24.
        The Director of the Scottish Microelec-
tronics Development Programme advocates establishment of a National Software Library, and
identifies some of the problems to be solved,
including hardware compatibility, documentation,
and bibliographic control.

1645 WALL, C. EDWARD. "Microcomputer Software Identification: The Search for Another Numbering Standard." Library Hi Tech News no. 13 (February 1985): 1, 11.

Wall briefly traces the development of a standard identification and control scheme for microcomputer software, and includes Mary Ellen Jacob's white paper, "Why Computer Numbering," which was prepared for the National Information Standards Organization subcommittee charged with devising a numbering mechanism.

1646 WALTON, ROBERT A. "How to Protect Yourself--and the Library--When Shopping for Software." Technicalities 4 (January 1984): 15-16.

The three basic approaches of libraries in acquiring software have been to purchase turnkey systems, to buy and adapt generic software programs to local needs, and to contract for customized programs to perform specific functions. Walton addresses the problem of contracting for customized programs and suggests several vital points, including ownership, copyright, performance standards, documentation, and specific responsibilities of the library and the programmer, which should be addressed during contract negotiation.

1647 WALTON, ROBERT A. "Micro Communications Software: Things to Look For." Technicalities 4 (July 1984): 14-15.

Eight features to look for in evaluating and choosing communications software are identified and discussed.

1648 WALTON, ROBERT A. "Microcomputer Applications for the Library." Online '82 Conference Proceedings, Atlanta, 1-3 November 1982. Weston, CT: Online, Inc., 1982. Pp. 215-20.

A realistic approach to microcomputer software evaluation is recommended, integrated function and single function software are differentiated, and several good examples of library applications software are provided in both categories.

1649 WALTON, ROBERT A. "Poor Micro Documentation--
A Survivors' Guide." Technicalities 4 (September 1984): 12-13.
Documentation for microcomputer software
has been traditionally weak. Walton identifies
reasons and provides seven points to consider in
evaluating and identifying good documentation.

1650 WALTON, ROBERT A. "Technical Services Software
for Microcomputers." Technicalities 4 (November 1984): 8, 12.
Brief entries, including name, distributor, supported equipment, and approximate price,
are supplied for twenty-three cataloging and
thirteen acquisitions micro software packages.

1651 WARRICK, THOMAS S. "Legal Aspects of Purchasing
Microcomputer Software." American Society for
Information Science Bulletin 10 (August 1984):
9-12.
Copyright is defined, the purpose of the
copyright law is explained, and application of
the law to the regulation of software copying is
presented. The rights of the software purchaser
are discussed, and the purchaser is urged to
insist on a written contract spelling out those
rights at the time of purchase.

1652 WICHERT, M. LOU. "The Computer Software Evaluation Challenge for Media Specialists." Media
Spectrum 9 (Second quarter 1982): 8-9.
The author lists and elaborates on
twenty-one points for consideration in evaluating
microcomputer software.

1653 WOOLLS, BLANCHE E. "Another Approach to Selecting Microcomputer Software." Indiana Media
Journal 6 (Spring 1984): 23-26.
Increased availability of educational
software permits the media specialist greater
variety in program selection; thus, selection
criteria have changed. Woolls provides a new
set of selection guidelines, mentions negative
characteristics to avoid, and discusses weeding
the collection of old and outdated programs.

1654 WOOLLS, BLANCHE E. "Selecting Microcomputer
Software for the Library." Top of the News
39 (Summer 1983): 321-27.
Although the software industry is boom-
ing, library management programs are in short
supply. The author discusses local development
of software and selection of adaptable commercial
programs as two solutions to the problem, giving
pros and cons and helpful hints for both alternatives. Bibliography.

1655 WOOLLS, BLANCHE E., and LOERTSCHER, DAVID V.
"Some Sure-Fire Microcomputer Programs."
School Library Journal 28 (August 1982): 22-
24.
An annotated bibliography of twenty
microcomputer programs suitable for use in public
schools provides the media specialist with a
basic selection of high quality software covering
a variety of curriculum areas.

1656 YERKEY, A. NEIL. "Small Business Microcomputer
Programs: Tools for Library Media Center Management." School Library Media Quarterly 12
(Spring 1984): 212-16.
Off-the-shelf software is recommended for
many school library management functions. Database management, word processing, software design, and spreadsheet software are discussed, and
several specific programs are recommended for
each function.

1657 "Z39 Establishes Software Subcommittee 'BB'."
Information Retrieval and Library Automation
19 (November 1983): 5.
The establishment of a subcommittee by
the American National Standards Committee (ANSC)
to design a standard numbering system for computer software is announced.

1658 AMERICAN LIBRARY ASSOCIATION. RESOURCES AND
TECHNICAL SERVICES DIVISION. COMMITTEE ON
CATALOGING: DESCRIPTION AND ACCESS, CATALOGING
AND CLASSIFICATION SECTION. Guidelines for
Using AACR2 Chapter 9 for Cataloging Microcomputer Software. Chicago: American Library
Association, 1984. 32p.
    Guidelines for standardized cataloging of
computer software are provided in this supple-
mental volume to AACR2. Intended to be used in
conjunction with AACR2, these guidelines make
frequent reference to Chapter 9, "Machine-Readable Data Files," of the original volume.

1659 ANDERSON, ERIC S. "The Software Nightmare."
Classroom Computer News 3 (April 1983): 74.
    The problems of library software storage
and protection are considered, and some safe-
guards are suggested.

1660 BAKER, PATTI R. "Adoption of a Computer Software
Cataloging System at an Elementary School."
School Library Media Quarterly 13 (Summer
1985): 208-14.
    An elementary teacher explains her online
cataloging system for software, based on PFS:
FILE. She describes its implementation and acceptance by other teachers. Bibliography.

1661 BEST, BEVERLY. "Cataloging Computer Software."
CMC News (Winter 1982): 6-7.
    Two methods of cataloging microcomputer
software are described and illustrated.

1662 BULLERS, DAVID L., and WADDLE, LINDA L. Processing Computer Software for the School Media
Collection. 2nd edn. Waterloo, IA: David L.
Bullers, 1984. 20p.
    Technical processing procedures for
adding a software program to a school library

is outlined here, including ordering, checking in, copying, cataloging, and processing for circulation. Good illustrations enhance the text.

1663 COHEN, DOREEN. "The Software Library." Small Computers in Libraries 5 (October 1985): 26-27.
The Reference Librarian/Computer Coordinator for the Menlo Park (CA) Library discusses processing, storage, and use of microcomputer software in the library's public computer room.

1664 DAVIES, DENISE M. "The Organization of a Computer Software Collection Using an Information Storage and Retrieval Package." Microcomputers for Information Management 2 (September 1985): 201-10.
Davies discusses the development of an automated database for the University of Hawaii Graduate School of Library Studies' software collection using INMAGIC database management software. Record design, input, searching, output, documentation, and physical organization of the collection are considered. Bibliography.

1665 DEWEY, PATRICK R., and GARBER, MARVIN. "Organizing and Storing Diskettes." School Library Journal 30 (April 1984): 32.
Advice on storing software, protecting it from damage, and a simple but effective method of accessing a library's software collection are offered.

1666 DODD, SUE A. Cataloging Machine-Readable Data Files: An Interpretive Manual. Chicago: American Library Association, 1982. 247p.
AACR2 rules for cataloging machine-readable data files are interpreted, with examples. Microcomputer programs are considered, with other forms of machine-readable text.

1667 DODD, SUE A. "Changing AACR2 to Accommodate the Cataloging of Microcomputer Software." Library Resources and Technical Services 29 (January/March 1985): 52-65.

The entry of book publishers into the software market and the interest of librarians in expanding collections to include software have brought about a demand for cataloging rules to accommodate this new medium. This article addresses changes which have been made to Chapter 9 of the Anglo-American Cataloguing Rules, Second Edition (AACR2), which deals with cataloging machine-readable data files, as well as changes which are pending, and further changes which need to be made. Bibliography.

1668 DODD, SUE A. "What Do Drivers of Cars and Users of Microcomputers Have in Common? A Cataloger's Commentary." Technicalities 5 (February 1985): 10-11.

Dodd responds to the statement, "You don't need to understand the mechanics of a car in order to drive it," and draws an analogy between automobiles and microcomputers which she uses to reinforce her stance on AACR2 full record cataloging for software.

1669 DODD, SUE A., and SANDBERG-FOX, ANN M. Cataloging Microcomputer Files: A Manual of Interpretation for AACR2. Chicago: American Library Association, 1985. 272p.

A thorough interpretive guide for cataloging microcomputer data files, this volume is based on chapter 9 of the Anglo-American Cataloguing Rules, second edition (AACR2) and Guidelines for Using AACR2 Chapter 9 for Cataloging Microcomputer Software. The volume summarizes the development of cataloging rules for machine-readable data files, analyzes the bibliographic elements necessary to describe and catalog a microcomputer data file, and provides examples of data file cataloging.

1670 FLETCHER, BONNIE L. "Cataloging Microcomputer Software." Idaho Librarian 36 (April 1984): 30-32.

Fletcher discusses the problems of applying AACR2, Chapter 9 to cataloging microcomputer software, and the work of the RTSD Committee on

Cataloging: Description and Access Task Force in preparing software cataloging guidelines. She then considers the essential data elements in cataloging a software program and illustrates the application of cataloging rules. Bibliography.

1671 FLETCHER, BONNIE L. "Cataloging Microcomputer Software: Rules, Guidelines, and Trends." Library Software Review 3 (December 1984): 486-96.
Cataloging machine-readable data files, particularly software programs, has become a growing problem in libraries as microcomputers have proliferated. This article reviews the background of the problem, provides an example of software cataloging following AACR2, and notes trends which may affect the future. Bibliography.

1672 GILBERT, BETSY. "Organizing Your Software Library." Popular Computing 2 (April 1983): 153-54.
Organizing a software collection for efficient use, whether in a home, business, or library setting, is considered by the author, who recommends utility and simplicity and the use of a database management program. There are no cataloging rules here, but several good suggestions for arrangement, storage, and security for software, data disks, and documentation.

1673 Guidelines for Cataloging Microcomputer Software. Manitowoc, WI: Wisconsin Educational Media Association, 1982. 7p.
An introduction, nine cataloging rules, and nine examples constitute this useful but basic guide for cataloging microcomputer software in compliance with the Anglo-American Cataloguing Rules, 2nd ed.

1674 Guidelines for Processing and Cataloging Computer Software for Schools and Area Education Agencies. Chicago: American Association of School Librarians, 1983. 13p.
A brief but useful guide for cataloging

and processing computer software for public
schools, the text refers to AACR2 and the AECT
Standards for Cataloging Nonprint Materials for
authority. Especially useful are several pages
of examples, including catalog cards, pockets,
and labels.

1675 HAWLEY, STEVEN C. "Developing a Directory for a
Software Collection." Ohio Media Spectrum 36
(Winter 1984/1985): 7-11.
Hawley describes the application of dBASE
II database management system to the development
of a software catalog. Record construction,
identification of components, compilation of the
directory, and indexing are considered.

1676 HORSNELL, VERINA. "Cataloguing Computer Software." Library Association Record 84 (July/
August 1982): 251.
The lack of cataloging standards for
computer software is noted, and recommendations
from a meeting sponsored by the British Library
Research and Development Department on the problem are shared.

1677 INTNER, SHEILA S. "Problems and Solutions in
Descriptive Cataloging of Microcomputer Software." Cataloging and Classification Quarterly 5 (Spring 1985): 49-56.
The problem of software cataloging has
been addressed by a Task Force of ALA's Committee
on Cataloging: Description and Access, but all
problems have not been solved. Intner reviews
the problems of terminology, physical description, and hardware notes as they were dealt with
by the Task Force in Guidelines for Using AACR2
Chapter 9 for Cataloging Microcomputer Software,
then addresses the problem of determining when
the Guidelines should be applied. Bibliography.

1678 INTNER, SHEILA S. "Suggestions for the Catalog-
ing of Machine-Readable Materials." Library
Resources and Technical Services 27 (October/
December 1983): 366-70.
The cataloging of floppy disks is con-

sidered, and each bibliographic component is reviewed in light of AACR2 cataloging rules and peculiarities of the item to be cataloged. Suggestions are made which permit catalogers greater flexibility and provide greater accommodation for cataloging of new products. Bibliography.

1679 MERRITT, MEREDITH. "Racter the Author?" Library Journal 110 (November 1, 1985): 160; and School Library Journal 32 (November 1985): 148.

Warner Software/Warner Books has announced the publication of a volume of poetry and prose created by a computer, which opens up debate on how it should be cataloged. The Library of Congress' treatment of the book is discussed, and various other options are considered.

1680 "Micro Software Guidelines Okayed." American Libraries 15 (February 1984): 102.

Finalization of AACR2 guidelines for cataloging microcomputer software is announced.

1681 MILLER, BRUCE CUMMINGS. "Disk Library Programs." M300 and PC Report 2 (November 1985): 5.

Miller addresses the problem of bibliographic control of a growing microcomputer software collection, and recommends a quick and easy solution using a public domain program called DIRLIB, found on an electronic bulletin board.

1682 MITCHELL, JOAN S. "Subject Access to Microcomputer Software." Library Resources and Technical Services 29 (January/March 1985): 66-72.

Although cataloging of microcomputer software has become an issue in libraries since 1980, emphasis has been on descriptive cataloging rather than subject analysis. In 1984 the cataloging and classification section of ALA appointed a Subject Analysis Subcommittee to study the problem of subject classification of software. This article reports on the subcommittee's preliminary work, which consists of setting goals and identifying problems. Bibliography.

1683 NASATIR, MARILYN. "Machine-Readable Data Files
and Networks." Information Technology and
Libraries 2 (June 1983): 159-64.
Bibliographic control of machine-readable
data files and microcomputer software is addressed in relation to the MARC format and OCLC
cataloging. Standards and data elements for
descriptive cataloging are discussed, as is the
progress being made in developing standard cataloging formats and practices. Bibliography.

1684 OLSON, NANCY B. "Cataloging Micro Software."
OCLC Newsletter no. 144 (December 1982): 6-7.
A group of cataloging experts met in
November, 1982 to discuss cataloging of microcomputer software. Reports on the state of the
art led to a request for a task force to draw up
guidelines for software processing.

1685 OLSON, NANCY B. Manual of AACR2 Examples for
Microcomputer Software and Video Games. Lake
Crystal, MN: Soldier Creek Press, 1983. 30,
51, 18p.
This manual for cataloging microcomputer
software provides rules based on AACR2, with
examples of covers and printed packaging for commercial software programs, and original cataloging performed for those programs.

1686 OLSON, NANCY B. "Microcomputer Software Cataloging Task Force Meets at OCLC." OCLC Newsletter no. 146 (April 1983): 3.
A Task Force of the Resources and Technical Services Division of ALA has been charged
with the task of writing microcomputer software
cataloging rules, with guidelines to be used
until the rules can be published. The delibera-
tions of the first meeting of the Task Force are
reported.

1687 RICHARDS, MARY. "Issues in Microcomputer Software Cataloging and Processing." Wisconsin
Library Bulletin 78 (Summer 1983): 68-69.
The author briefly describes state-of-
the-art software cataloging in 1983. The prob-

lems of physical description and program altera-
tions are the major concerns of the article,
although dealing with backup copies of software
is also considered. Bibliography.

1688 ROLAND, LEON. "Software Organization." Computing Teacher 12 (March 1985): 39-40.
The author discusses three methods of
organizing a school's software collection, one
of which is cataloging it for the library/media
collection. He describes bibliographic data collection, data storage, and data retrieval for
each method.

1689 RORVIG, MARK E. "The 'Bibliographic' Control of
Microcomputer Software." Electronic Library
2 (July 1984): 183-95.
Rorvig provides a rationale for cataloging and bibliographic control of software within
a library, and reviews seven commercially produced software directories useful in the cataloging process. Bibliography.

1690 SKOMAN, LUCIA. "Organizing a Microcomputer Software Collection." Computing Teacher 9 (October 1981): 55-56.
A librarian at Regional Educational Media
Center #16 in Ann Arbor, Michigan, describes the
center's classification scheme and descriptive
cataloging format for microcomputer software.

1691 SKOMAN, LUCIA. "Organizing a Software Collection." Classroom Computer News 2 (September/
October 1981): 36-37.
The same article appeared, with editorial
changes, in Computing Teacher, October 1981.

1692 "Software Union List Developed by Massachusetts
Library Group." Library Journal 109 (July
1984): 1280.
Massachusetts is taking the lead in
developing a union catalog of microcomputer software, and is working on a cooperative purchasing
program for software, according to this news
brief.

1693 TEMPLETON, RAY, and WITTEN, ANITA. Study of Cataloguing Computer Software: Applying AACR2 to Microcomputer Programs. Library and Information Research Report, no. 28. London: British Library, 1984. 77p.

A British research project aimed at determining problems in applying AACR2 to the cataloging of microcomputer software is described, with findings and solutions. Appendices cover such topics as "Microcomputer Software Packages—Standard Description and Bibliographic Control," "Recommendations for Ammendments to AACR2, Chapter 9," "Cataloging Microcomputer Software: A Simple Guide," and "Machine-Readable Cataloging (MARC)." Bibliography.

1694 THOMPSON, GLENN J. " Guidelines for Cataloging Microcomputer Software." Alexandria, VA: ERIC Document Reproduction Service, ED 247 930, 1983.

Software cataloging guidelines recommended by the Wisconsin Educational Media Association are presented and illustrated with examples.

1695 TOOTH, JOHN. "Cataloging Microcomputer Software: The State of the Art." School Libraries in Canada 5 (Winter 1985): 5-7.

Tooth deals briefly with the state of the art in software cataloging, and reviews the literature of the topic from the Canadian and United States perspectives.

CIRCULATION OF HARDWARE AND SOFTWARE

1696 "Apple Software Circulated by Public Library in N. Y." Library Journal 109 (September 1, 1984): 1589.
        The Liverpool (NY) Public Library reports a successful software lending project. The lending policy is summarized, and protective packaging for check-out is described.

1697 ARMOUR, JEAN. "Software Circulation Success." Small Computers in Libraries 4 (September 1984): 6.
        Liverpool (NY) Public Library's successful software circulation service is described and evaluated, problems are discussed, and popular titles are mentioned.

1698 BROWN, R. WILLIAM. "A Cooperative Software Library." Classroom Computer News 3 (May/June 1983): 29.
        In 1982 several schools in southwestern Colorado formed a cooperative software library. This article discusses its establishment, and use trends which have been noted.

1699 BRYANT, DAVID S. "Circulating Personal Computers." Library Journal 110 (November 1, 1985): 161-63; and School Library Journal 32 (November 1985): 149-51.
        The Belleville (NJ) Public Library began circulating microcomputers in the summer of 1983. This article outlines the library's plan for microcomputer service, their publicity coverage, and results of the program. Results of a survey provides information concerning users and the success of the program.

1700 CHANDLER, DENIS, and O'TOOLE, PAT. "Computer Software Loan Experiment." Audiovisual Librarian 10 (Summer 1984): 146-47.
        In 1983 the Cambridgeshire (UK) Libraries

began lending microcomputer software from one
of its branches on an experimental basis. The
project was monitored by questionnaire. This
article briefly describes the loan project and
summarizes demographic and user needs data from
the survey.

1701 "Circulating Software: A Report from Minneapolis
Public Library." Technicalities 5 (February
1985): 15.
   A software circulation project at the
Minneapolis (MN) Public Library is described, and
such problems as licensing agreements and protection of diskettes are addressed.

1702 "Circulating Software; or, Let the End User Beware." Technicalities 4 (December 1984): 1.
   The editors of Technicalities address the
question of libraries circulating commercial microcomputer software, particularly those programs
which are sold with license agreements. Only the
problem is raised; no solutions or recommendations are presented.

1703 "Cloquet, Minn. to Loan Micros & Teach 'Computer
Literacy'." Library Journal 107 (September
15, 1982): 1694.
   Through a matching grant from the Blandin
Foundation, the Cloquet (MN) Public Library has
established a circulating microcomputer hardware
and software collection aimed at increasing
computer literacy in the community.

1704 "Faculty Checkout." Popular Computing 1 (October
1982): 22.
   The Faculty Computer-Familiarity Program,
a microcomputer lending project at the University
of Wisconsin/Madison is described and evaluated.

1705 GEDDES, GEORGE. "How an Education College Library Uses Computer Software." Library Association Record 86 (October 1984): 425, 427.
   The library of the Jordanhill College of
Education, the largest teacher training facility
in Scotland, has made a commitment to supply

microcomputer software for in-service teaching, demonstration, campus coursework, and general use. The software collection, facilities, and circulation of software are addressed, as are some of the difficulties encountered in the venture. Bibliography.

1706 "Library Circulates Software." Small Computers in Libraries 3 (March 1983): 4.
The North Central (WA) Regional Library's mail order circulation program for microcomputer software is described briefly.

1707 "Loaning of Micro Software in Libraries?" Small Computers in Libraries 3 (October 1983): 2-3.
Some of the apparent problems in circulating software from libraries are identified, including costs, hardware specific programs, damage, and piracy. Some solutions and alternatives are suggested.

1708 MALAKUNAS, MILDA. "Software-Lending and the Law." Library Association Record 86 (May 1984): 225.
A trend in Great Britain toward the lending of microcomputer software by libraries prompted this article which deals with piracy, copyright, and copy protection systems.

1709 "Montgomery Co.'s Apple Popular With All Ages." School Library Journal 30 (May 1984): 12.
An Apple II Plus microcomputer purchased by the Montgomery County (PA) Public Library is available on a rental basis to children and adults. User policy is briefly stated, and popular programs are mentioned.

1710 "Portsmouth, N. H., Library Program: Circulating Computers, Workshops." Library Journal 108 (March 1, 1983): 438.
The Portsmouth (NH) Public Library reports and evaluates its micro lending program.

1711 "Renting Micros at Kansas City." Library Journal 110 (October 15, 1985): 24.

A micro rental program at the Kansas City Public Library is described, with a statement of policy and partial listing of available programs.

1712 ROCKMAN, ILENE. "Microcomputer Circulation in Libraries." Library Software Review 3 (December 1984): 497-500.
Circulation of microcomputer hardware has become an issue in libraries since 1980. Rockman reviews the literature on the topic and provides insight into loan policies, user eligibility, user fees and overdue charges, equipment, orientation, and other related issues. Bibliography.

1713 SAVAGE, EARL R. "A 'Computer Library'." T.H.E. Journal: Technological Horizons in Education 11 (October 1983): 121-22; and Educational Microcomputing Annual 1 (1985): 114-15.
A Title IV-C grant provided the funds for the Colonial Beach (VA) School District to purchase forty-eight microcomputers to form the nucleus of a computer literacy program and a circulating computer library for the school. Establishment of the center is considered, along with policies, procedures, and plans for the future.

1714 "School's Micro Library Circulates to Students." School Library Journal 31 (December 1984): 15.
The Colonial Beach (VA) School System's circulating computer library, consisting of forty-eight Texas Instrument, Commodore, and Radio Shack micros, is described, with a brief policy statement and evaluation of the program.

1715 SMISEK, THOMAS. "Circulating Software: A Practical Approach." Library Journal 110 (May 1, 1985): 108-09; and School Library Journal 31 (May 1985): 138-39.
The Minneapolis (MN) Public Library's venture into building and circulating a software collection is shared. The project is evaluated.

1716 "Software Acquired & Loaned by Minneapolis Public Library." Library Journal 109 (September 15, 1984): 1712.

A software lending program at the Minneapolis (MN) Public Library is described, subject areas are listed for which software is available, and policies are briefly summarized.

1717 "Software Comes by Mail in Wenatchee, Wash." Library Journal 110 (April 1, 1985): 29.
Washington State's North Central Regional Library owns a collection of more than 3,000 public domain software programs which it lends through the mail on order from patrons who select from the library's printed catalog. Details are provided in this brief news article.

1718 WALCH, DAVID B. "The Circulation of Microcomputer Software in Academic Libraries and Copyright Implications." Journal of Academic Librarianship 10 (November 1984): 262-66.
The results of a survey of 296 academic libraries indicates trends in circulation of microcomputer software to students and faculty. The possibility of software pirating is considered and copyright is discussed. Bibliography.

1719 "Arizona GLS Gets Micro." Small Computers in Libraries 1 (July 1981): 7.
This news note announces the acquisition of an Intertec Superbrain 64K RAM microcomputer by the Graduate Library School of the University of Arizona. Justification for the purchase of the particular system and proposed uses are outlined.

1720 ARMSTRONG, C. J., and LARGE, J. A. "The Design and Implementation of a Microcomputer Teaching Package for Online Bibliographic Searching." The Application of Mini- and Micro-Computers in Information, Documentation and Libraries. Proceedings of the International Conference on the Application of Mini- and Micro-Computers in Information, Documentation and Libraries, Tel-Aviv, Israel, 13-18 March 1983. New York: North-Holland, 1983. Pp. 189-94, and Education for Information 2 (March 1984): 35-42.
The authors consider instructional aids developed and employed at the College of Librarianship Wales, and emphasize the importance of microcomputers in teaching and development. A specific microcomputer program, which emulates the DIALOG database for purposes of teaching online search procedures, is described in considerable detail. Bibliography.

1721 ARMSTRONG, C. J., and LARGE, J. A. "Designing and Implementing a Microcomputer Training Package for Online Bibliographic Searching." Information Technology: Research and Development 2 no. 2 (1983): 65-72.
A microcomputer-based online bibliographic searching emulation developed at the College of Librarianship Wales, is described, along with a justification for its development and a discussion of the problems encountered in its design and construction.

1722 ARMSTRONG, C. J., and LARGE, J. A. A Microcomputer Teaching Package for Online Biblio-
raphic Searching: Manual. British Library
Research & Development Reports, no. 5740.
London: British Library, 1984. 150p.
    A manual for teaching online searching
via microcomputer, this publication accompanies
a tutorial program on three diskettes, which consists of questions and answers concerning online
searching and emulates DIALOG search procedures.
A British publication, the programs are written
to run on a Research Machines 380Z microcomputer
with at least 56K of memory.

1723 ARMSTRONG, C. J., and LARGE, J. A. A Microcom-
puter Teaching Package for Online Biblio-
raphic Searching: Workbook. British Library
Research & Development Reports, no. 5741.
London: British Library, 1984. 26p.
    This workbook accompanies Armstrong and
Large's A Microcomputer Teaching Package for
Online Bibliographic Searching: Manual.

1724 ARMSTRONG, C. J., and LARGE, J. A. "A Microdata-
base for Online Search Training." Proceedings
of the 5th International Online Meeting, London, 8-10 December 1981. Medford, NJ: Learned
Information, 1981. Pp. 397-407.
    A program which emulates DIALOG online
search procedures is compared with similar
simulation programs. The emulation program is
described, reviewed, and illustrated; advantages
and limitations are discussed; and the program
is judged to be successful in a teaching situation. Bibliography.

1725 "Atari at Alabama." Small Computers in Libraries
2 (March 1982): 6.
    An Atari 400, 16K microcomputer, has been
purchased by the University of Alabama Library
School, although no uses for it have been announced.

1726 BUXTON, ANDREW B. "Online Training Courses in
the UK." Proceedings of the 8th International

Online Information Meeting, London, 4-6 December 1984. Medford, NJ: Learned Information,
1984. Pp. 503-09.
    The report of a survey by the United
Kingdom Online User Group, Subcommittee on Education and Training, evaluates various types of
online searching courses and workshops, considering location, duration, cost, coverage, format,
practice facilities, and documentation. Bibliography.

1727 "Computers for Rural Libraries." LJ/SLJ Hotline
    10 (March 2, 1981): 4.
    The establishment of a microcomputer lab-
oratory by Clarion State College's Center for the
Study of Rural Librarianship is announced in this
brief news note.

1728 DAY, J. M., and TEDD, LUCY A. "Computer Software
    for Education and Training: Developments in
    UK Schools of Librarianship and Information
    Science." Proceedings of the 7th Internation-
    al Online Information Meeting, London, 6-8
    December 1983. Medford, NJ: Learned Informa-
    tion, 1983. Pp. 471-81.
    British schools of library and informa-
tion science have produced several computer-based
teaching programs for use on minis, micros, and
mainframes. This paper describes the development
of programs and the creation of CALLISTO, a
microcomputer-based directory for disseminating
information on the packages developed. Bibliography.

1729 "GLS-Chicago Gets Altos Micro." Small Computers
    in Libraries 1 (June 1981): 7.
    This news item announces the purchase of
and Altos ACS-8000 and an Apple by the University
of Chicago Graduate Library School to support
research on information storage and retrieval and
to use in the teaching of computer programming.

1730 GUY, R. F. "Short Courses in Online Searching:
    Continuing Education and the Library School."
    Proceedings of the 6th International Online

Information Meeting, London, 7-9 December 1982. Medford, NJ: Learned Information, 1982. Pp. 143-54.

Library schools' responsibilities for providing instruction in online searching are established and justified; factors in course design are discussed; and short courses offered at the College of Librarianship Wales, some using microcomputer equipment as terminals, are described. Bibliography.

1731 GUY, R. F.; LARGE, J. A.; and ARMSTRONG, C. J. "Microcomputer Simulations of Online Bibliographic Systems for Teaching Purposes." Proceedings of the 2nd National Online Meeting, New York, 24-26 March 1981. Medford, NJ: Learned Information, 1981. Pp. 261-70.

A tutorial package developed at the College of Librarianship Wales to aid in the teaching of online database searching is described in detail. The program, which includes an introductory question and answer section, a prompted controlled search, and an unstructured search option is amply illustrated with examples. Bibliography.

1732 HERRING, JAMES E. "Placement by Micro." Scottish Library Association News 182 (July/August 1984): 25, 27, 29.

A microcomputer-based DBMS file maintained by the School of Librarianship and Information Studies at Robert Gordon's Institute of Technology, Aberdeen, Scotland, contains profiles of all British libraries that accept student librarians for fieldwork. The file, which runs on an Apple II or Apple IIe micro with KWIRS software, is explained and illustrated.

1733 JOHNSON, D. K. Report on the Conversion of an On-Line Information Retrieval System Simulator for Use on an ITT 2020 (Apple) Microcomputer. British Library Research and Development Report, no. 5580. London: British Library, 1980. 44p.

Information storage and retrieval pro-

grams originally resident in a Digico MTS16 minicomputer were converted to an ITT 2020 (Apple)
microcomputer by members of the Loughborough
University Department of Library and Information
Studies faculty for use in teaching online
searching techniques. With a database of bibliographic records loaded into the micro, simulation of an online search program is achieved.

1734 KEENAN, STELLA. "Education for Online Information Retrieval in British Library Schools."
Information Interaction. Proceedings of the
45th ASIS Annual Meeting. White Plains, NY:
Knowledge Industry Publications, 1982, v. 19.
Pp. 147-48.
Methods of teaching online information
retrieval in British library schools are surveyed, and the trend toward greater use of microcomputers is noted. Bibliography.

1735 LARGE, J. A., and ARMSTRONG, C. J. "The Microcomputer as a Training Aid for Online Searching." Online Review 7 (January 1983): 51-59.
A microcomputer-based training and simulation package for teaching online searching is
described. The package, developed at the College
of Librarianship Wales, runs on a Research Machines 380Z micro. Bibliography.

1736 LARGE, J. A., and GUY, R. F. "Microcomputers in
Library Education." Media in Education and
Development 15 (September 1982): 111-13.
The importance of the computer in library
functions is stressed, common computer applica-
tions are identified, and the use of micro-
computers in teaching library processes in the
College of Librarianship Wales is described.
Bibliography.

1737 "Microcomputer Lab Set Up in Pennsylvania."
Library Journal 106 (May 15, 1981): 1022.
A news item announces the establishment
of a micro lab at Clarion State College in the
Center for the Study of Rural Librarianship.

1738 SCHLESSINGER, BERNARD S., and SCHLESSINGER, JUNE
H. "The Use of Microcomputers in Education
for Librarianship and Information Science."
The Application of Mini- and Micro-Computers
in Information, Documentation and Libraries.
Proceedings of the International Conference
on the Application of Mini- and Micro-Computers in Information, Documentation and Libraries, Tel-Aviv, Israel, 13-18 March 1983.
New York: North-Holland, 1983. Pp. 177-82;
and Education for Information 2 (March 1984):
29-34.
A survey of accredited library schools in
the United States indicates increasing use of microcomputers in library and information science
curricula, and supports a prediction of continued
development and growth, particularly in simulation, library programming, statistical analysis,
library management education, and tutorials.
Bibliography.

1739 SCOTT, ALDYTH D. "Mini- and Microcomputers in
Education and Training for Library and Information Work." The Application of Mini- and
Micro-Computers in Information, Documentation
and Libraries. Proceedings of the International Conference on the Application of Mini-
and Micro-Computers in Information, Documentation and Libraries, Tel-Aviv, Israel, 13-18
March 1983. New York, North-Holland, 1983.
Pp. 183-88.
The status of mini and microcomputers in
British schools of library and information science is discussed; their use as training tools is
considered; research and development are described. Bibliography.

1740 SPELLER, BENJAMIN F., Jr., and BOWIE, GEORGE F.,
III. "Microcomputing in Library Education."
North Carolina Libraries 40 (Fall/Winter
1982): 220-23.
The growing use of microcomputers leads
naturally to the question of computer use in library education programs. This article reports
on a survey of library education in North Caro-

lina conducted in 1982. Hardware, software, and
applications are addressed. Bibliography.

1741 STIEHL, RUTH E., and ANDERSON, EDWIN. "Media
Center Builds Media Packages to Teach Basic
Microcomputer Skills." Computing Teacher 11
(August 1983): 45-47.
    Oregon State University's Media Faculty
has developed a series of programs for teaching
microcomputer skills to students in the university's School of Education. The programs are
described; advantages and limitations are noted.

1742 STIRLING, KEITH H. "A Micro-Based Emulator for
Online Search Services." Drexel Library Quarterly 20 (Fall 1984): 87-97.
    DIALTWIG, a program which runs on the IBM
PC and emulates the DIALOG Online Retrieval System, is used by the School of Library and Information Science at Brigham Young University to
teach the basics of online searching. Applications and features of the program are presented,
and its performance is evaluated. Bibliography.

1743 SUGRANES, MARIA R., and SNIDER, LARRY C. "Microcomputer Applications for Library Instruction:
Automation of Test and Assignment Scoring, and
Student Record Keeping." Microcomputers for
Information Management 2 (September 1985):
171-88.
    As library training programs have been
developed for information retrieval systems, the
management of data generated by the programs has
become labor-intensive and costly. This article
describes a program designed to manage library
training program data for University 100, a one-
unit required course at the California State
University, Long Beach. Hardware and software
are considered; the system is described; implementation is discussed. Bibliography.

1744 SWANSON, DON R. "Miracles, Microcomputers, and
Librarians." Library Journal 107 (June 1,
1982): 1055-59.
    In 1981 the Graduate Library School at

the University of Chicago purchased an Altos ACS-8000 microcomputer to support teaching and research. Through a software package called ASYNC, interactive capabilities with the university's mainframe computer were achieved. This led to the development of an in-house online retrieval system which the author recommends as a model for use with small files in a decentralized library setting. Bibliography.

1745 "Syracuse to Train 'Computer Coordinators'." School Library Journal 30 (October 1983): 76.
     A new program to train school computer coordinators is announced. Offered by the School of Information Studies at Syracuse University, the program starts in the fall of 1984.

1746 "TRS-80 for Rural Libraries Center." Small Computers in Libraries 1 (May 1981): 1.
     The establishment of a microcomputer lab at the Center for the Study of Rural Librarianship at Clarion State College is announced.

1747 TEDD, LUCY A. "Teaching Aids Developed and Used for Education and Training for Online Searching." Online Review 5 (June 1981): 205-16.
     Various methods of teaching online database searching in British schools of librarianship are described, including use of audio and digital recording devices, audiovisual materials, and printed matter. Of special interest to this bibliography is information concerning local information retrieval systems, and communications programs for providing online experience, using both dumb terminals and microcomputer software. Bibliography.

1748 TEDD, LUCY A. The Teaching of Online Cataloguing and Searching and the Use of New Technology in U. K. Schools of Librarianship and Information Science. British Library Research & Development Report, no. 5616. London: British Library, 1981. 120p.
     Tedd reports a survey of sixteen British schools of library and information science con-

ducted to determine methods and utilization of
new technologies in teaching cataloging and online searching. Although a variety of methods
are indicated, the role of the microcomputer
appears significant and on the increase. Bibliography.

1749 TEDD, LUCY A. "Use of Minis, Micros and Terminals in the Education of Librarians and Information Scientists." Minis, Micros and Terminals for Libraries and Information Services.
Proceedings of the Conference Organized Jointly by the Institute of Information Scientists
and the Information Retrieval Specialist Group
of the British Computer Society, Held at the
National Computing Centre, Manchester, 6-7
November 1980. London: Heyden and Son, 1980.
Pp. 111-18.
Computers and terminals provide options
for hands-on experience in online searching, cataloging, and other functions in Great Britain's
sixteen library schools. Tedd describes several
educational applications. Bibliography.

CONFERENCES, WORKSHOPS, USER GROUPS, ETC.

1750 ALDER, KATE. "Introducing Teacher-Librarians to
        Computers." Australian School Librarian 19
        (Winter 1982): 53-55.
            A three day microcomputer workshop,
    sponsored by the Professional Guidance Section,
    Library Branch, of the Education Department of
    Victoria, and held at Melbourne State College in
    1981, is described. One day of formal learning
    and two days of hands-on experience provided
    teacher-librarians with perspective and first
    hand experience in setting up a data file, with a
    basic introduction to programming included.

1751 ALLEY, BRIAN. "On the Conference Circuit: LITA,
        Micros and Milwaukee." Technicalities 3
        (February 1983): 9, 11.
            A LITA workshop, "Small Bytes & Little
    Bits--The Microcomputer in Libraries," is sum-
    marized. Workshop speakers included Ted Hines
    and Rosemary Collins, J. Darlene Myers, Lawrence
    Woods, and Richard Thompson.

1752 ANDERSON, ERIC S. "Eric (Not ERIC): A Tale of
        Two Sites." OCLC Micro 1 (September 1985):
        9-10.
            Anderson summarizes the programs of the
    IBM PC Library Users Group and Apple Library
    Users Group, both of which met during the 1985
    ALA Conference in Chicago. Impressions of each
    is recorded and the two are briefly compared.

1753 "Apple/Library User Group." Small Computers in
        Libraries 3 (October 1983): 3.
            The establishment of the Apple Library
    User Group by Apple Computer, Inc., is announced;
    purpose of the group is told; membership and
    benefits are discussed.

1754 "Apple Library Users Group Formed." Online 7
        (November 1983): 89.

A user group for librarians using Apple microcomputers in the workplace is announced by Apple Computers, Inc. Membership details are provided.

1755 "BRS' Marovitz Predicts that Search Services Must Change in the Future. . .Microcomputers the Hot Topic of ONLINE '82." Online 7 (January 1983): 9.
A brief review of the Online '82 Conference, held in Atlanta November 1-3, emphasizes the impact of micros on online search services.

1756 BEISER, KARL. "Microcomputing." Wilson Library Bulletin 60 (October 1985): 46-47.
The automation exhibits at the American Library Association's 1985 Conference are reviewed, including the BIBLIOFILE CD-ROM cataloging system, EASYLAN and LANLINK local area network software, and several other new software and hardware products.

1757 BERGLUND, PATRICIA. "School Library Technology." Wilson Library Bulletin 59 (September 1984): 48-49, 79.
Ann Lathrop's influence on the introduction of microcomputer technology into schools is related, and the establishment of the California Library Media Consortium for Classroom Evaluation of Media Courseware, under her leadership, is told. Consortium activities are summarized.

1758 BRITISH LIBRARY. RESEARCH AND DEVELOPMENT DEPARTMENT. Libraries and Computer Materials. Report of a Seminar Held at the White Horse Hotel, Dorking, 13-14 March 1981. British Library Research & Development Report, no. 5690. London: British Library Board, 1982. 42p.
The impact on libraries of the rapid changes in computer materials was the subject of this British seminar. Edited versions of three presentations--"Libraries and Computer Materials," "The CEDAR Project," and "The Hertfordshire County Council Advisory Unit for Computer Based

Education"--along with synopses of discussions, conclusions, and recommendations are included.

1759 "Computer Club Kits Available from Apple." School Library Journal 30 (March 1984): 85.
Apple Computer, Inc., announces computer club kits to be distributed free to the first 10,000 schools to request them.

1760 CONGER, LUCINDA D. "1982 Online: A Review." Online 7 (May 1983): 39-43.
At the 1983 District of Columbia Online Weekend, Conger proclaimed 1982 the year of the microcomputer, then reviewed changes in online services which improved searching in 1982.

1761 CORDON, MYRT M. "Plum of a Program." Unabashed Librarian no. 49 (1983): 27-28.
A computer fair held at the Stanislaus County (CA) Free Library is described. A sample news release concerning the event and a letter of invitation to exhibitors are included.

1762 "Covering the Floor: ALA Midwinter Exhibits." Wilson Library Bulletin 59 (March 1985): 465-66.
New technology displayed at ALA Midwinter 1985 is reviewed, including the DataPhase EAST-WIND MICRO CIRCULATION SOFTWARE, OCLC's SC-350 and MICROCON, and Faxon's MICROLINX.

1763 DEWEY, PATRICK R. "Illinois Librarians Gather for Public Access Microcomputer Conferences." Educational Computer Magazine 3 (March/April 1983): 60-61.
More than ninety people gathered at the Chicago (IL) Public Library's Cultural Center on November 12, 1982, for a one day workshop, "Public Computing: A Look at Public Access Microcomputers." Activities of the day are summarized, and the major presentations are highlighted.

1764 DEWEY, PATRICK R. "Seeing Software and Finding Help: On Joining a Microcomputer User Group." Library Software Review 3 (June 1984): 175-78.

Various activities of microcomputer user groups are described, and the benefits of membership are discussed, including meetings, information exchange, directories, database access, and newsletters.

1765 "Downloading/Uploading Conference at St. John's." Library Hi Tech News no. 16 (May 1985): 1, 12.

Downloading and uploading of online databases and catalogs was the theme of the 1985 Congress of Librarians, sponsored by the Division of Library and Information Science of St. John's University. Papers presented by Barbara Ferrante, Helen Wilbur and Kathy Niemeier, James Brewer, Mary Ellen Jacob, and others are briefly summarized.

1766 ELLINGEN, DANA. "Computer Shows and Software: First National Software Show, Tenth International Information Management Exposition and Conference." Library Software Review 3 (March 1984): 63-71.

Impressions of two software shows are reported. Ellingen discusses their merits, reviews the activities of the First National Software Show, and briefly reviews the best of the software displayed.

1767 FERRIS, DAVE. "Computer Software and Copyright, 23 March 1984." Audiovisual Librarian 10 (Autumn 1984): 216-17.

Ferris summarizes the proceedings of a one day seminar sponsored by the Library Association and the Library Association's Audiovisual Group concerning the issues of computer software and copyright in Great Britain. Among the speakers were Geoff Crabb, Peter Marshall, and Nick Alexander.

1768 GAULD, MARGARET. "MEETINGS: Using Microcomputers in Libraries--AVSCOT 1-Day Course, 28 November 1984." Audiovisual Librarian 11 (Spring 1985): 112.

A one day workshop for novice microcomputer users, held at Queen Margaret College

Library, Edinburgh, is reported. Presentations
are summarized, including "Bits and Pieces: An
Introduction to the Micro," by Kenneth Clark;
"The Micro in Library Housekeeping," by Paul
Burton; and "Software for Information Retrieval:
An Introduction," by Douglas Anderson.

1769 HARRISON, HELEN P. "'Software on the Shelf:
Computer Materials in the Library'. A One-
Day Course Organized by the Library Association and the LA Audiovisual Group, 28 October
1982." Audiovisual Librarian 9 (Winter 1983):
45-48.
A workshop sponsored by the British Library Association and the LA Audiovisual Group is
reported. Paul Burton, John Eyre, and Robert
Salkeld addressed issues, including storage and
handling of software, copyright, cataloging, and
hardware. Case studies of three libraries com-
mitted to microcomputer use present insight into
applications, problems, and advantages.

1770 "Home Computers for the Library." Technicalities
2 (March 1982): 1.
The lure of the microcomputer at the ALA
1982 Midwinter Conference is noted, despite
recession and hard times in many local libraries.

1771 HUND, FLOWER. "Micro Conference in Kansas City."
Small Computers in Libraries 3 (June 1983):
1-2.
A joint meeting of the Heart of America
Chapter of ALA and the Kansas City Online Users
Group is reported by one of the participants.
The program, titled "How to Get a Bit of Information out of a Byte of Data Processing," was
conducted by Frederick Raithal, who dealt with
the history of information management and implementing a successful automation project, and
Silas Kelly, who discussed networking and the
future of microcomputing.

1772 "IBM PC Library User Group Formed." Small Computers in Libraries 4 (November 1984): 11.
The formation of an IBM PC user group

for librarians is announced. Objectives of the
group are presented, with the name and address of
a contact person.

1773 "IBM PC Library Users' Group Forms." Electronic
Education 4 (January 1985): 35.
The formation of an IBM PC user group
is announced; the goals of the group are listed;
and plans for regular meetings and regional chapters are told.

1774 "IBM PC Library Users Group News." Small Computers in Libraries 5 (March 1985): 5.
The IBM PC Library Users Group, founded
at the 1984 Library Software Conference, announces the appointment of interim staff, publishes proposed goals, and designates the M300
and PC Report as its communication medium.

1775 "IBM PC Library Users Group Plans Chicago Meeting
in July." M300 and PC Report 2 (March 1985):
3-4.
Preliminary organization of the IBM PC
Library Users Group is announced, along with a
proposed meeting to be held in conjunction with
the American Library Association's Annual Conference in July, 1985. Approval of a charter and
goals are slated for the meeting.

1776 KESSELMAN, MARTIN. "National Online Meeting."
Wilson Library Bulletin 57 (June 1983):
838-41.
The Fourth National Online Meeting held
in New York, April 12-14, 1983, is reported in
detail, with emphases on legal and ethical questions of downloading data from online databases,
fee structures for downloading, and new developments in microcomputer technology.

1777 KESSELMAN, MARTIN. "National Online Meeting Held
in New York." Wilson Library Bulletin 56
(June 1982): 754-56.
The proceedings of the Third National
Online Meeting held in New York, March 30-April
1, 1982, are summarized. The first day was

devoted to microcomputer technology, with presentations by Theodore C. Hines, Anthony Kent, Leonard Fisher, and others.

1778 KESSELMAN, MARTIN. "Online Update." _Wilson Library Bulletin_ 58 (February 1984): 430-31.
       Kesselman presents highlights of the Online '83 meeting, held in Chicago in October, 1983. The microcomputer hardware and software theme is carried through by such authorities as Christopher Morgan and Donald Wismer. Emerging technologies such as electronic mail and videodisc data storage are also addressed.

1779 KESSELMAN, MARTIN. "Online Update." _Wilson Library Bulletin_ 59 (April 1985): 540-41.
       Kesselman presents highlights of the Eighth International Online Information Meeting, held in London, December 4-6, 1984.

1780 LEE, MISSY. "Microcomputers and the Library." _Mississippi Libraries_ 47 (Summer 1983): 42-43.
       Missy Lee reports on a workshop conducted by Robert Walton at the Mississippi Research and Development Center on March 11, 1983. Walton presented a practical program, demonstrating how microchips are made, and discussing such topics as purchasing a micro, types of programs, printers, and software storage and care.

1781 "MUGLNC: Micro User Group Designed for Libraries." _Library Journal_ 108 (August 1983): 1414.
       The Microcomputer Users' Group for Librarians in North Carolina (MUGLNC) is announced, and its purpose and activities are outlined briefly.

1782 MAGUIRE, CARMEL. "Managing the Micro: Seminar Report." _LASIE_ 11 (May/June 1981): 11-13.
       A LASIE seminar on microcomputer management is reported. Presentations by microcomputer specialists Allan Thompson, Alan R. Marshall, Andrew Newell, Ian Webster, and three micro users are summarized.

1783 MAGUIRE, CARMEL. "Micro Systems Information Ex-
change." LASIE 15 (July/August 1984): 25-28.
The 1984 Midyear Meeting of the American
Society for Information Science is reported.
Papers by J. J. Hayden, William Saffady, Adam
Cohen, Hal Borko, and others are summarized
briefly. The theme was "The Micro Revolution."

1784 "Managing Micros for the Masses Critical New
Media-Center Skill." American Libraries 13
(September 1982): 530, 532.
A 3½ hour session entitled "Supervising
the Computer Revolution," sponsored by the Ameri-
can Association of School Librarians for the 1982
ALA Conference in Philadelphia, is summarized
with highlights from presentations by Marge
Kosel, Judith K. Meyers, Richard Casabonne, Grace
Shope, Theodore C. Hines, Charles G. Forsythe,
and F. Curtis May.

1785 MELIN, NANCY. "A Day on the Floor: ALA Exhibits." Wilson Library Bulletin 60 (September
1985): 28-32.
The exhibits at the 1985 American Library Association Conference are reviewed, with
emphasis on new technology and developments.
Among those products which drew attention were
Brodart's LE PAC online catalog, Library Corporation's BIBLIOFILE, and H. W. Wilson's WILSEARCH.

1786 "Micro 'Summer Camp' in N. C. Teaches Computing
Basics." Library Journal 109 (February 1,
1984): 133.
A summer workshop, sponsored by MUGLNC
(Microcomputer Users' Group for Libraries in
North Carolina) and attended by sixty-eight
librarians, is reported favorably.

1787 "'Micros and Medicine' Fair Draws 300 in Houston." Library Journal 109 (April 15, 1984):
762.
A microcomputer fair sponsored by the
Houston Academy of Medicine-Texas Medical Center
featured microcomputer applications for medical
education, research, and office management during

a six day conference which drew an audience of
three-hundred people.

1788 MOREO, STANLEY D. The Microcomputer: What Is It?
How Does It Function? What Is Its Possible
Role in the Library? Champaign, IL: CATALIST,
1983. 89p.
A study guide written for a microcomputer
workshop for librarians in 1983, this publication
addresses library staff and patron use of micros,
software, hardware, information sources, and
other topics. Bibliography.

1789 MORRISON, PEGGY. "Fourth Online Conference
Held." Library of Congress Information Bulletin 42 (January 31, 1983): 34-36.
The Fourth Annual Online Conference, held
in Atlanta in November, 1983, is summarized. The
conference focused on microcomputers and highlighted hardware, user friendliness, and downloading of online searches.

1790 "New Illinois Micro User Group Plans Extensive
Member Services." Library Journal 109
(November 15, 1984): 2108.
The founding of the Central Illinois
Libraries Users Group is told, and its objectives
are reviewed.

1791 "New Microcomputer Group Formed in New England."
Library Journal 109 (March 1, 1984): 422.
NEMICRO, a new microcomputer user group
in the New England states, is introduced. An address is provided if more information is desired.

1792 NYREN, KARL. "ASIS at Midyear 1980." Library
Journal 105 (July 1980): 1479-85.
The ninth American Society for Information Science (ASIS) Midyear Conference, held May
15-17, 1980, is reported, including a one day
workshop on microcomputers, with presentations
concerning the EASY DATA CIRCULATION SYSTEM,
TERAC at Dartmouth College, Chicago Public
Library's public access program, and other micro
related topics.

1793 "Online '83 Stresses Microcomputer Uses." <u>Small</u>
<u>Computers in Libraries</u> 3 (June 1983): 6-7.
ONLINE '83, the fifth annual conference
for online database users, scheduled for Chicago,
October 10-12, is previewed briefly.

1794 PLOTNIK, ARTHUR. "Many Just Starting Out on Road
to Micro-topia." <u>American Libraries</u> 14 (April
1983): 176.
A microcomputer seminar, "Microcomputers
in Action," held at St. John's University, February 21, 1983, is reported and briefly summarized.

1795 RAITT, DAVID. "International Conference on the
Application of Mini- and Microcomputers in Information, Documentation and Libraries, 1983,
March 13-18, Tel-Aviv, Israel." <u>Electronic</u>
<u>Library</u> 1 (July 1983): 177.
A one week conference on mini and microcomputer applications to information science and
libraries is reported and reviewed.

1796 "Rallying Library Support With a Microcomputer."
<u>Library Journal</u> 110 (April 1, 1985): 20.
Donald Wismer reports on a project of the
Maine Library Association to target library supporters and solicit their aid in such activities
as lobbying Congress to oppose the reduction of
LSCA funds. He describes the use of a microcomputer in maintaining address files, producing
form letters, and other functions of the project.

1797 RENWICK, KEITH. "The Audiovisual Library
Environment: A Report of the 1981 <u>Audiovisual</u>
<u>Librarian</u> Study School and Conference." <u>Audio-</u>
<u>visual Librarian</u> 7 (Autumn 1981): 15-22.
The 1981 meeting of the Audiovisual Group
of the Library Association is summarized. A half
day was devoted to microcomputers, with Paul
Hickling, Tim O'Shea, and Robert Salkeld making
presentations.

1798 "Rosary Workshop Attracts Many Librarians."
<u>Educational Computer Magazine</u> 3 (March/April
1983): 61.

A one day workshop, "Public Access Microcomputers: Selection and Management," is reported. Patrick Dewey, Arlene Santoro, Leslie
Edmonds, and Marvin Garber made presentations on
assessment needs, user agreements, staff training, and special projects at the North-Pulaski
Branch of the Chicago Public Library.

1799 ROSS, MARGARET A., and MEADOWS, SHARON L.
"Microcomputers and School Libraries: The
Nova Scotia Workshop." School Libraries in
Canada 5 (Fall 1984): 8-10.
The Canadian School Library Association's
workshop, "Microcomputers and School Libraries,"
held May 3-5, 1984, is reviewed in detail, including information on background and planning,
as well as program, participants, and leaders.

1800 ROWAT, MARTIN J. "Use of Systems Programs in Library Applications of Microcomputers: A Brief
Note." Vine no. 45 (October 1982): 51-52.
A seminar sponsored by the British Library Research and Development Division to promote interest in adapting existing microcomputer
systems to library use is summarized by the
organizer of the seminar.

1801 ROYAN, BRUCE, and McELROY, A. RENNIE. Minis and
Micros: Smaller Computers for Smaller Libraries. Cambridge: Library Association, College
of Further and Higher Education Group, 1981.
44p.
The partial proceedings of a conference
sponsored by the Scottish Section of the Colleges
of Further and Higher Education Group of the Library Association, this publication consists of
one long article, "Readymade Systems for the
Smaller Library," by Bruce Royan, concerning
mainframe and minicomputers, and a bibliography,
"Mini- and Micro-computers in Libraries," by
A. Rennie McElroy.

1802 "Rural Library Conference to Focus on OCLC and
Microcomputers." OCLC Newsletter no. 155
(November 1984): 12.

A one day conference on the theme, "OCLC and Microcomputers: Linking Their Use in Rural Libraries," sponsored by the Center for the Study of Rural Librarianship, is reported, with Jeanne Isacco and Mark Bendig as speakers.

1803 SALOMON, KRISTINE. "Microcomputer Workshop." Nebraska Library Association Quarterly 12 (Summer 1981): 29-30.

A microcomputer workshop held at Nebraska Wesleyan University in February, 1981 is reported in this news item.

1804 "School Media Librarians Recount the Ways of Computers." American Libraries 14 (September 1983): 530, 532.

The proceedings of the joint meeting of the AASL Microcomputer Utilization for School Library Media Centers Discussion Group and the AASL Online School Libraries Users Group are reported. Speakers were Zhita Elvord Rea, Hugh Durbin, Joanne Troutner, and Nancy Minnich.

1805 "Seminars for Georgia Librarians on Micros and Library Automation." Library Journal 108 (March 15, 1983): 539.

Four two day microcomputer workshops for Georgia public librarians are reported.

1806 SMITH, DUNCAN, and BURGIN, ROBERT. "Micros in the Carolinas." Public Libraries 23 (Summer 1984): 61-62.

A computer camp for librarians, held in August, 1983, is reviewed and evaluated. Sponsored by the Microcomputer Users Group for Libraries in North Carolina (MUGLNC) the camp was intended to provide hands-on experience for librarians with little or no prior computer background. Other MUGLNC activities are also described.

1807 SNELSON, PAMELA. "Library Instruction and the Computer." Small Computers in Libraries 5 (September 1985): 11-12.

Two sessions of the ACRL Microcomputer Services

in Academic Libraries Discussion Group, held at
the 1985 ALA Conference in Chicago, are summarized. Adhering to the public access/public
service interests of the group, speakers presented papers on "Copyright, Licensing and Software,"
"Micros and Software in Libraries," "Two Kinds of
Computer Use for Libraries," and "Computer Literacy and Software Use."

1808 "Teleconference With Rural Libraries." Electron-
     ic Library 3 (January 1985): 12.
          A one day conference, "OCLC & Microcom-
     puters: Linking Their Use in Rural Libraries,"
     sponsored by the Center for the Study of Rural
     Librarianship at Clarion University, demonstrated
     the use of microcomputers in accessing OCLC. The
     conference was broadcast simultaneously to the
     Northwest Regional Library System in the Sioux
     City, Iowa area.

1809 TENOPIR, CAROL. "Full-text, Downloading, & Other
     Issues." Library Journal 108 (June 1, 1983):
     1111-13.
          The proceedings of the 4th National On-
     line Meeting are highlighted, with two of the
     issues being availability and access to full-text
     databases and the implications of downloading on
     the future of the online information market.

1810 "Users' Group for M300 and IBM PC Formed." Elec-
     tronic Library 3 (January 1985): 24.
          The formation of the IBM PC Library Users
     Group is announced, with its goals, meeting
     schedule, and an address for more information.

1811 "Vendor Turnout at UC-San Diego Focuses on End-
     User Searching." Library Journal 109 (July
     1984): 1280.
          This news item reports a one day confer-
     ence at the University of California-San Diego
     focusing on online searching by the end user,
     employing microcomputer technology as the medium.

1812 WATSTEIN, SARAH B. "No Crystal Ball Gazing Here:
     A Report on the Metro Workshop on Microcomput-

ers in Library Reference Services." Library
Hi Tech News no. 17 (June 1985): 24-25.
        The enhancement of library reference ser-
vices through the use of microcomputers was the
theme of a one day workshop sponsored by the New
York Metropolitan Reference and Research Library
Agency on 16 May 1985. Addresses by Thomas
Surprenant and J. Robert Verbessey are summa-
rized; accounts of four workshops are reported.

1813 WOOD, NEVILLE. "AVSCOT Mighty Micro Meeting."
Audiovisual Librarian 9 (Summer 1983): 147.
        A meeting of AVSCOT, held in Glasgow, is
briefly reported. The meeting, entitled "Handling and Managing Computer Software," dealt with
compatibility, copyright, cataloging, and other
topics of concern.

BIBLIOGRAPHY

1814 ABI/SELECTS: The Annotated Bibliography of
     Computer Periodicals. Louisville, KY: Data
     Courier, 1983. 576p.
          533 computer-related journals are listed
     and annotated, with complete bibliographic and
     subscription information.

1815 ADAMS, JOHN, and ADAMS, ROBIN. "Layman's Guide
     to Personal Computing." RSR: Reference Serv-
     ices Review 10 (Spring 1982): 7-17.
          Interest in microcomputers is running
     high, and the literature is proliferating. John
     and Robin Adams discuss the wide variety of
     microcomputer literature on the market and choose
     a sampling of the best for their bibliography.

1816 ADLER, ANNE G.; BABER, ELIZABETH A.; LEE, LI AI
     L.; MARSALES, RITA M.; and SWANSON, JEAN R.
     Automation in Libraries: A LITA Bibliography,
     1978-82. Ann Arbor, MI: Pierian Press, 1983.
     177p.
          This bibliography on the broad topic of
     library automation contains in excess of 2,500
     citations, with substantial sections on micro-
     computers and microcomputer software.

1817 ALBERGHENE, JANICE M. "A Baker's Dozen of New
     Magazines, Part 2: Computer Magazines."
     School Library Journal 30 (May 1984): 38-39.
          Six quality microcomputer magazines suit-
     able for a school library are reviewed. Preceding
     the reviews is a discussion of computer magazines
     in general, and the criteria used in choosing the
     six to be included. Part 1, which appeared in
     School Library Journal, April, 1984, reviewed
     low-tech magazines.

1818 ALBRECHT, BOB, and FIREDRAKE, GEORGE. "Computer-
     Town, USA." Computing Teacher 8, no. 1 (1980-
     81): 18-19.

A handout originally produced to accompany a presentation at a National Council of Teachers of Mathematics conference, this article concerning ComputerTown, USA provides a good basic subscription list for Commodore PET and TRS-80 users.

1819 ANDERSON, ERIC S; DEWEY, PATRICK R.; and SPILLMAN, NANCY Z. "Computer Books." Booklist 80 (May 1, 1984): 1223-25.
A list of recommended microcomputer books suitable for teens and adults is presented, with complete bibliographic information and annotations.

1820 BECK, SUSAN J., and BENSON, JAMES A. "Bibliography of Downloading and Uploading for Microcomputer Users, Librarians, and Information Specialists." Downloading/Uploading Online Databases and Catalogs. Proceedings of the Congress for Librarians, St. John's University, Jamaica, New York, 18 February 1985. Library Hi Tech Special Studies Series, no. 1. Ann Arbor, MI: Pierian Press, 1985. Pp. 102-23.
This 380 item bibliography is a comprehensive listing of the literature of downloading and uploading for the years 1974 through 1984. References are categorized by topic, but not annotated. An author index is appended.

1821 BEISER, KARL. "Microcomputer Periodicals for Libraries." American Libraries 14 (January 1983): 43-48.
This annotated list of sixty-two periodicals is representative of the current literature of microcomputing. A good distribution of general, library-oriented, and special interest titles is included.

1822 BLACKHURST, ERIC W. "Books for Teachers." Classroom Computer Learning 5 (November/December 1984): 36-37.
Nine classic microcomputer books for the computing teacher are listed and annotated.

1823 BREAM, ELIZABETH. "Microcomputers." Emergency
Librarian 11 (September/October 1983): 37-38.
Nine recommended microcomputer journals
are listed for the librarian with a limited budget. Each title is annotated; order information
is included. The list is priced under $175.

1824 BURKE, BARBARA, and McNAMARA, LINDA. "Electronic
Bulletin Boards: An Annotated Bibliography."
Small Computers in Libraries 5 (June 1985):
17-21.
The first installment in a series concerning electronic bulletin boards, this article
introduces the topic and the series and presents
a twenty-six item annotated bibliography of bulletin board software.

1825 BURKE, BARBARA, and McNAMARA, LINDA. "Electronic
Bulletin Boards: An Annotated Bibliography,
Part II." Small Computers in Libraries 5
(July/August 1985): 20-21.
Part II of an annotated bibliography,
which began in the June 1985 issue of SCIL, looks
at electronic bulletin board directories.

1826 BURKE, BARBARA, and McNAMARA, LINDA. "Electronic
Bulletin Boards: An Annotated Bibliography,
Part III." Small Computers in Libraries 5
(September 1985): 16-20.
Part III of a bibliography concerning
electronic bulletin boards, this selection of
forty-seven articles covers general information.

1827 BURKE, BARBARA, and McNAMARA, LINDA. "Electronic
Bulletin Boards: An Annotated Bibliography,
Part IV." Small Computers in Libraries 5
(October 1985): 22-25.
Thirty-six annotated references to spe-
cific electronic bulletin board systems cover the
literature of the topic through Fall, 1984.

1828 BURKE, BARBARA, and McNAMARA, LINDA. "Electronic
Bulletin Boards: An Annotated Bibliography,
Part V." Small Computers in Libraries 5
(November 1985): 17-19.

1829 BURKE, BARBARA, and McNAMARA, LINDA. "Electronic
     Bulletin Boards: An Annotated Bibliography,
     Part VI." Small Computers in Libraries 5
     (December 1985): 11-14.
         The final installment of a six-part
     annotated bibliography on electronic bulletin
     board systems lists thirty-three articles con-
     cerning the setting up of local bulletin board
     facilities.

1830 "Catching Up." Small Computers in Libraries 1
     (April 1981): 2-3.
         This short annotated bibliography of
     microcomputer books from the early 1980s is a
     representative sampling of early micro literature
     aimed at the novice.

1831 CHAMBERS, VAL; HAYCOCK, KENNETH R.; et al.
     "Microcomputers: A Guide to Periodicals for
     Teachers and Librarians." Emergency Librarian
     10 (January/February 1983): 18-22.
         This classified and annotated bibliog-
     raphy of 125 microcomputer related journals is a
     valuable tool for the librarian seeking to build
     a microcomputer collection, or the novice com-
     puter enthusiast seeking information on available
     publications.

1832 CLYDE, LAUREL A, and JOYCE, D. JOAN. Computers
     and School Libraries: An Annotated Bibliogra-
     phy. Wagga Wagga, New South Wales: Riverina
     College of Advanced Education, Center for
     Library Studies, 1983. 176p.
         Three hundred annotated references to
     works concerning microcomputers in school li-
     braries constitute this useful bibliography from
     Australia.

1833 COLSHER, WILLIAM L. "Special-Interest Microcom-
     puting Publications." onComputing 2 (Fall
     1980): 60-64, 66-67.
         Reviews of approximately thirty period-
     icals devoted to microcomputers provide evalua-
     tive statements and order information valuable to
     librarians interested in microcomputer litera-

ture, although no titles concerning microcomputer
use in libraries are included.

1834 "Computer Book Roundup." School Library Journal
31 (August 1985): 25-27.
Twenty-three 1984 and 1985 computer books
for children from pre-school through high school
age are reviewed with the school librarian in
mind.

1835 CRAWFORD, WALT. "Common Sense and Computer
Magazines; or, What's the Good Word, Part I:
Periodicals." Library Hi Tech 2, no. 4
(1984): 61-69.
Sixty microcomputer magazines available
for purchase at newsstands in September, 1984,
are considered in this compartative bibliographic
essay which reviews twenty-two titles individually, and recommends eight for library purchase.

1836 DELLIT, JILLIAN. "Computer Networking in School
Library/Resource Centres: A Bibliography."
Society for Mass Media and Resource Technology
Journal 12 (December 1982): 21-24.
Networking in the school library is the
topic of this fifty item bibliography which in-
cludes articles on mainframe, mini, and micro-
based systems. Annotations are not provided.

1837 DEMPSEY, DENISE P. "Microcomputing in Libraries:
An Annotated Bibliography." North Carolina
Libraries 40 (Fall/Winter 1982): 225-32.
This sixty-two item bibliography of
selected articles concerning microcomputers in
libraries provides a good survey of early
writings on the topic.

1838 DEWEY, PATRICK R. "Microcomputer Dictionaries--
Buzzwords, Lexicons, and Glossaries: Definitions You Can Byte Into." Library Journal 110
(February 1, 1985): 59-61.
Twenty-seven printed and six software
dictionaries of microcomputer terms are listed,
with complete bibliographic and order data and
brief annotations.

1839 DEWEY, PATRICK, R. "Microcomputer Magazines for
       Libraries: An Update." American Libraries 16
       (April 1985): 267.
          Fifteen new microcomputer journals are
     annotated in this bibliographic update of an
     earlier compilation which appeared in American
     Libraries, January, 1983.

1840 DEWEY, PATRICK R. "Microcomputers and Tele-
       communications: A Checklist of Books and
       Journals." American Libraries 15 (October
       1984): 631-32, 649.
          An annotated bibliography of thirty-
     three books and eleven journals point out the
     best available sources of printed information on
     microcomputer communication technology.

1841 DEWEY, PATRICK R. "Searching for Software: A
       Checklist of Microcomputer Software Direc-
       tories." Library Journal 109 (March 15,
       1984): 544-46.
          Dewey addresses the problem of locating
     reliable software reviews and purchase infor-
     mation through an annotated checklist of soft-
     ware directories, including both hard copy and
     online formats.

1842 ENGLISH, RANDALL. "What's New in 001.64." Book
       Report 1 (September/October 1982): 42-43.
          A school librarian recommends a selective
     list of microcomputer books and journals for the
     school media center.

1843 GEFFNER, BONNIE. "Bibliography." Software
       Review 1 (February 1982): 84-93.
          This substantial bibliography of general
     sources concerning computers and software in
     education and in libraries is the first of a
     planned series to appear in Software Review.

1844 GORDON, HELEN A. "A Guide for Reading--A Selec-
       ted Annotated Bibliography for Understanding
       Microcomputer Hardware, Software and Peripher-
       als." Online 7 (May 1983): 30-34.
          This excellent, fifty item annotated bib-

liography concentrates on microcomputer hardware,
software, printers, modems, and disk drives.

1845 GRAHAM, BARBARA S. "Software Reviews: A Guided
Tour." Education Libraries 9 (Spring 1984):
13-16.
Graham has compiled an annotated guide to
books, journals, and online sources which review
or index reviews of microcomputer software.

1846 HANLEY, KAREN STANG. "Books for Kids." Classroom Computer Learning 5 (November/December
1984): 32-34, 36.
The best computer books for children and
young people are grouped into elementary, junior
high, and high school categories, and briefly
annotated for the busy librarian. This article
updates "The Best Computer Books for Children,"
which appeared in the November, 1983 issue of
Classroom Computer Learning.

1847 HAWKINS, DONALD T. "Online Information Retrieval
Bibliography: Seventh Update, Part I." Online
Review 8 (June 1984): 247-77.
931 references to articles published
between 1982 and 1984 make up this thorough bibliography covering all aspects of information
retrieval, including microcomputer and minicomputer applications.

1848 HAWKINS, DONALD T. "Online Information Retrieval
Bibliography: Seventh Update, Part II." Online Review 8 (August 1984): 325-81.
Author and permuted title indexes
complete the information retrieval bibliography
which appeared in Online Review, June, 1984.

1849 HAYCOCK, KENNETH R. "Microcomputers: A Guide to
Periodicals for Librarians, Media Specialists
and Teachers." Pacific Northwest Library Association Quarterly 48 (Spring 1984): 36-48.
An impressive list of microcomputer magazines and journals is categorized by emphasis and
annotated with brief descriptive statements and
subscription information.

1850 HAYNES, EVELYN. "Computer Assisted Library
        Instruction: An Annotated Bibliography."
        Colorado Libraries 11 (Spring 1985): 31-35.
            This bibliography covering the literature
    of library instruction via computer from 1967 to
    1985 includes mainframe and mini as well as mi-
    crocomputer projects, and is particularly valu-
    able for its broad perspective and well written
    annotations.

1851 HERB, BETTY. "Books About Computer Technology."
        School Library Journal 31 (November 1984):
        38-39, 42, 44-49.
            This annotated bibliography of thirty-
    nine computer books for upper elementary through
    high school levels covers general information,
    games, programming instruction, and aids for the
    teacher/librarian.

1852 HORSNELL, VERINA, and PRITCHARD, ALAN. "Micro-
        computers in Libraries and Information Serv-
        ices: A Reading List." Audiovisual Librarian
        9 (Winter 1983): 55-57.
            Twenty-six works concerning microcomput-
    ers in libraries provides a good selective read-
    ing list from the British perspective.

1853 HUTCHINSON, BECK, and HUTCHINSON, LINT. "What
        to Read: An Annotated Bibliography." Instruc-
        tional Innovator 28 (February 1983): 17-20.
            This annotated bibliography of thirty-
    eight serial titles provides a good selective
    list of microcomputer periodicals for the micro
    enthusiast or general library collection.

1854 "Introductory Articles." Small Computers in
        Libraries 1 (June 1981): 4.
            This short bibliography of microcomputer
    articles provides annotations and evaluations of
    early general microcomputer literature.

1855 JOYCE, D. JOAN, and CLYDE, LAUREL A. "Computers
        and School Libraries: A Preliminary Bibliog-
        raphy." Society for Mass Media and Resource
        Technology Journal 12 (December 1982): 25-32.

A bibliography of materials concerning computer use in school libraries is presented from an Australian perspective. No annotations are included.

1856 "Keeping Up." Small Computers in Libraries 1 (April 1981): 3.
A brief annotated listing of microcomputer journals provides a sound subscription list for the small library or individual wishing to remain current in microcomputer technology. All of the titles are still published.

1857 KESSELMAN, MARTIN. "Online Update." Wilson Library Bulletin 59 (March 1985): 477-78.
A brief annotated bibliography concerning microcomputer communications and online searching is intended as a purchasing guide and resource for librarians.

1858 KILPATRICK, THOMAS L. "Annotated Bibliography: Microcomputers in Libraries." ACCESS: Microcomputers in Libraries 3 (Spring 1983): 12, 33-52.
This annotated bibliography of more than 300 items covers the literature of microcomputer applications to library processes through the fall of 1982.

1859 LANKFORD, MARY D. "Microcomputers." Booklist 78 (October 1, 1981): 242-44.
In 1980 the Irving (TX) Independent School District launched a search for information concerning microcomputers prior to purchasing micro equipment for classrooms and media centers. This article is the result of that search, and contains an annotated bibliography of books and articles, evaluation criteria for software selection, program evaluations, and a short list of software suppliers.

1860 LANKFORD, MARY D. "Microcomputers: Software Evaluations and Print Resources." Booklist 78 (April 1, 1982): 1028-29.
Ten microcomputer programs suitable for

library instruction are reviewed along with an
equal number of print resources concerning microcomputers.

1861 LATHROP, ANN. "Microcomputer Software for
Instructional Use: Where Are the Critical
Reviews?" Computing Teacher 9 (February
1982): 22-26.
    Lathrop lists and annotates thirty micro-
computer related journals which review educational software for teachers, librarians, and media
specialists.

1862 LATHROP, ANN. "Recommended Books for Elementary
and Junior High School Library Media Centers."
Educational Computer Magazine 2 (November/
December 1982): 30-31, 62.
    An annotated bibliography of microcom-
puter books suitable for elementary and junior
high school students provides guidance for the
media specialist/librarian seeking to build a
microcomputer collection.

1863 LYON, SALLY. "End-User Searching of Online Databases: A Selective Annotated Bibliography."
Library Hi Tech 2, no. 2, issue 6 (1984): 47-
50.
    The literature of end user online search-
ing is reviewed, and twenty-six selected articles
on search services, end-user/intermediary searching, and end user training are listed and annotated.

1864 MANDELL, PHYLLIS LEVY. "AV Programs for Computer
Know-How." School Library Journal 31 (February 1985): 23-28.
    Forty-four audiovisuals suitable for use
in microcomputer education are reviewed, with
purchase information. Films, videocassettes,
filmstrips, and audiocassettes are included.

1865 MANSFIELD, RICHARD. "PET Newsletters and Magazines." Compute 4 (June 1982): 90.
    Subscription information is provided for
five journals concerning the Commodore PET.

1866 McLAUGHLIN, PAMELA. "Microcomputer Software
Evaluation: A Selected ERIC Bibliography."
Education Libraries 9 (Spring 1984): 18, 30.
A bibliography of citations selected from
ERIC's Resources in Education and Current Index
to Journals in Education provides bibliographic
information and annotations for journal articles
and ERIC documents concerning microcomputer software evaluation.

1867 "Microcomputer Periodicals." Small Computers in
Libraries 1 (November 1981): 5-6.
A bibliography of forty microcomputer
journals, with subscription information and
annotations, might prove valuable to the librarian or the personal computer buff, although more
current data may be available.

1868 "Microcomputer Software Catalog List." Media
and Methods 18 (April 1982): 8.
A brief bibliography of microcomputer
software catalogs may prove of some use to
librarians looking for sources of software.

1869 MILLER, INABETH, and STURROCK, ALLAN. Microcomputers and the Media Specialist: An Annotated
Bibliography. Syracuse, NY: ERIC Clearinghouse on Information Resources, 1981. 70p.
This annotated bibliography of print
resources concerning microcomputers in the media
center covers hardware, software, educational
applications, games, and other related topics, as
well as library applications.

1870 MITCHELL, LORNA; BURKHOLDER, SUE; and KOWALCZYK,
BRIDGET. Library Applications of Microcomputers: A Bibliography. Columbia, MO: Missouri
Library Association, 1984. 59p.
Compiled by the Computer and Information
Technology Committee of the Missouri Library
Association, this bibliography covers materials
published between 1982 and 1984. Approximately
800 entries are arranged in broad subject categories, including various applications, hardware,
software, and peripherals. There is no index.

1871 "New Books of Interest." Small Computers in
     Libraries 4 (February 1984): 7.
          This short annotated bibliography of
     microcomputer books contains titles which are
     worthy additions to general library collections.

1872 NEWMARK-KRUGER, BARBARA. "All the Things You
     Need to Know About Microcomputers and Were
     Afraid to Ask: A Bibliography." Top of the
     News 39 (Summer 1983): 341-46.
          Some seventy journal and book titles,
     mostly of a general nature, constitute this anno-
     tated bibliography of materials concerning the
     microcomputer, which should be useful as a basic
     buying guide for small libraries.

1873 NEWMARK-KRUGER, BARBARA. "Microcomputer Bibliog-
     raphy." Hot Off the Computer 1 no. 10, pp.
     27-30.
          Thirty-one titles, with annotations, con-
     stitute this selective bibliography concerning
     microcomputers prepared for public library use.

1874 NICITA, MICHAEL, and PETRUSHA, RONALD. The
     Reader's Guide to Microcomputer Books. 2nd
     ed. Brooklyn, NY: Golden-Lee, 1984. 473p.
          This bibliography of more than 1,000
     microcomputer books is categorized by broad sub-
     ject area for quick reference. Complete bibliog-
     raphic information is supplied; book annotations
     are included; and each book is rated for quality
     on a scale of 1 to 100. Most of the entries are
     1983 or 1984 editions.

1875 PATERSON, MARJORIE T. Microcomputers and Micro-
     processors. Readers' Guide, no. 18. Chippen-
     ham, Wiltshire: Library Association, Public
     Libraries Group, 1979. 47p.
          An early microcomputer bibliography com-
     piled by a British librarian emphasizes tech-
     nology, with little notice of library applica-
     tions.

1876 "Peripheral Press." Electronic Library 3 (April
     1985): 142-44.

Twenty-seven articles from journals not directly concerned with library applications of electronics are listed and annotated.

1877 POOL, GAIL. "Magazines." Wilson Library Bulletin 56 (January 1982): 376-78.
The first installment of a regular column to be featured in Wilson Library Bulletin, this article concerns computer magazines. Included is a brief description of the market and reviews of six high quality titles from a large selection.

1878 POPENOE, CRIS. Book Bytes: The User's Guide to 1200 Microcomputer Books. New York: Pantheon, 1984. 233p.
This annotated bibliography of microcomputer books includes works on the fundamentals of microcomputing, specific brands of hardware, applications, and programming. A broad selection is included, but not always the most current titles.

1879 PRATT, ALLAN D. A Selective Guide to the Microcomputer Literature. Tucson, AZ: Graham Conley Press, 1983. 60p.
A representative selection of microcomputer journals and monographs is listed and annotated in this early bibliography. An appendix provides addresses for small and hard-to-locate publishers.

1880 PUGH, W. JEAN, and FREDENBURG, ANNE M. "Decisions, Decisions, Decisions: Help in Choosing Microcomputer Software and Hardware." Online 9 (January 1985): 18-30.
A useful bibliography of 167 hardware and software reviews is indexed to help match up reviews of compatible equipment and programs and similar products for comparative purposes.

1881 RAHLFS, KIM POWELL; RAHLFS, THOMAS; and UNDERHILL, ROBERT G. "Microcomputers in Educational Settings: A Categorization of ERIC ED Documents Through December 1982." Arlington, VA: ERIC Document Reproduction Service, ED 237 080, 1982.

Approximately 200 ERIC documents concerning microcomputer use in education (including libraries) constitute this annotated bibliography covering the years 1976 to 1982. Variables and identifiers are included and have been compiled into a subject listing for easy use of the bibliography.

1882 "Recently Published Articles." Small Computers in Libraries 5 (March 1985): 10.
A brief, selective bibliography of microcomputer articles of interest to librarians is provided for quick reference.

1883 "Recently Published Articles." Small Computers in Libraries 5 (April 1985): 6.
Five articles from Library Software Review and Wilson Library Bulletin are recommended for librarians' professional reading.

1884 ROBERTS, JUSTINE. "An Elite Microdozen." Library Journal 110 (May 1, 1985): 99-100; and School Library Journal 31 (May 1985): 129-30.
Twelve of the best microcomputer books published in 1984/85 are reviewed for the discriminating librarian.

1885 SHADDUCK, GREGG. "IBM Books." M300 and PC Report 2 (May 1985): 9-10.
Four books--three on IBM software; one on data and file management--are listed and annotated.

1886 SHIRINIAN, GEORGE N. "Microcomputer Publications: An Overview." Serials Librarian 9 (Spring 1985): 19-24.
The rate of increase in microcomputer literature is noted, types of journals are discussed, and problems (some common to serials; others unique to microcomputer titles) are identified. A selective list of recommended microcomputer journals is included.

1887 "Softalk, Other Magazines Fold." Small Computers in Libraries 4 (October 1984): 8.

This article identifies ten microcomputer
journals that have ceased publication or merged
with other titles to form new publications.

1888 THOMPSON, JAMES E., and WILHELM, DENNIS.
"Selected Annotated Bibliography on Micro-
Computer Software." Indiana Media Journal
7 (Winter 1984): 24-26.
Software evaluation and selection are
continuing problems for librarians faced with
the task of building software collections. This
bibliography lists journals, directories, databases, and other sources of software reviews,
with purchase information and brief annotations.

1889 TROUTNER, JOANNE JOHNSON. "How to Develop a
Computer Book Collection." School Library
Journal 31 (November 1984): 31-32.
A brief review of criteria for selection
of computer books for children and young people
accompanies a selective bibliography of twenty-
two books suitable for elementary through high
school grade levels.

1890 TROUTNER, JOANNE JOHNSON. "Microcomputer Books
for Core Collections." School Library Journal
30 (September 1983): 41-44.
A selective bibliography of thirty-two
books about microcomputing suitable for use with
children and young people represent the best of
more than 200 books examined. General guidelines
used in selecting the books are discussed, and
each title is annotated.

1891 TWADDLE, DAN R. "Microcomputers in Public Libraries and School Media Centers: A Selected
Survey of Periodical Literature." Kentucky
Libraries 47 (Spring 1983): 18-25.
This selective, annotated bibliography of
the literature of microcomputers in public and
school libraries provides an overview of the
classic writings in a new and active discipline.

1892 "Update on Micro Books." Small Computers in
Libraries 1 (October 1981): 6-7.

This early bibliography of recommended microcomputer books might be of interest to the micro enthusiast or the reference librarian, although the subject and the literature have changed greatly since it was compiled.

1893 WALLACE, W. H. What's In Print: The Subject Guide to Microcomputer Magazines. Blue Ridge Summit, PA: TAB Books, 1984. 461p.

An index to articles in seventy-five general and hardware-specific microcomputer journals, this book may be useful to the librarian or patron seeking printed information on specific brands and models of microcomputer. However, arrangement of data is confusing on first opening the volume, and entries lack authors' first names, volume numbers, and paging for the articles.

1894 WALLER, EDWARD M. "A Microcomputer Bibliography for Librarians." Library Hi Tech 2, no. 1 (1984): 73-76.

Twenty-two books concerning microcomputer applications in libraries make up this selective basic bibliography for librarians.

1895 WRIGHT, WILLIAM F., and HAWKINS, DONALD T. "Information Technology: A Bibliography." Special Libraries 72 (April 1981): 163-74.

This eighty-six item selective bibliography concerning information technology in libraries contains a section on mini and microcomputers.

1896 ZSIRAY, STEPHEN W., Jr. "Microcomputers in the School Library Media Center: Building the Media Collection." School Learning Resources 1 (June 1982): 15-17.

Zsiray has developed a bibliography of microcomputer books, audiovisuals, and journals to support a school computer literacy program. Each reference is annotated; and although the references are somewhat dated, the work may provide guidance in developing computer collections in school libraries and media centers.

DIRECTORIES AND INFORMATION SOURCES

1897 "Addresses of Interest." ACCESS: Microcomputers
in Libraries 3 (Spring 1983): 13, 52-53.
Addresses of distributors or producers
of library oriented microcomputer software,
journals, databases, and other resources are
listed by type of resource or service provided.

1898 "AMIGOS's Micro Program." M300 and PC Report 2
(April 1985): 5.
The AMIGOS Bibliograhic Council announces
a program of training and technical support for
selected business and library application software. The program, scheduled to start in July,
1985, features software for IBM PCs and PC compatibles, with training and troubleshooting service, sold on a subscription basis.

1899 "AMIGOS' Micro Program." Small Computers in
Libraries 5 (April 1985): 3.
The AMIGOS Bibliographic Network an-
nounces a microcomputer support program for
AMIGOS members.

1900 BURTON, PAUL F. Microcomputer Applications in
Libraries and Information Retrieval: A Directory of Users. Edinburgh, Scotland: Leith
Nautical College, 1981. 46p.
This directory of microcomputer installations in sixty British libraries was compiled to
expedite the sharing and exchange of microcomputer information. Entries provide hardware, software, and application information, and the name
of a contact person.

1901 "Buyers Guide." Electronic Education 2 (March/
April 1983): 29-67.
A valuable aid for year-end or year-
round purchases, this microcomputer buyers' guide
lists software, books, catalogs, films and filmstrips, furniture, storage systems, peripherals,

and hardware. Brief annotations and purchase information are provided.

1902 "The Cataloguing and Exchange of Computer Software." Electronic Library 1 (January 1983): 11-12.
       A selected list of people and organizations in Great Britain who are involved in the cataloging or exchange of microcomputer software is provided by Varina Horsnell, Bibliographic and Information Systems Officer for Britain's Library Association.

1903 DEACON, JAMES. "Computer Software for Library/ Media Center Applications [and] An Update." Arlington, VA: ERIC Document Reproduction Service, ED 233 716, 1983.
       Deacon has compiled a directory of library skills and library function software, arranged by producer.

1904 "The Electronic Learning Software Directory: A Guide to 200 Producers of Educational Programs." Electronic Learning 1 (May/June 1982): 63-72.
       Sources of educational software are listed, with addresses, types of programs produced, hardware for which the programs are written, and price range.

1905 FU, TINA C. "Microcomputer Information Exchange in Wisconsin." Online '83 Conference Proceedings, Chicago, 10-12 October 1983. Weston, CT: Online, Inc., 1983. Pp. 65-69.
       In 1982 the Automation Committee of the Wisconsin Association of Academic Librarians established a microcomputer information exchange, which has been automated using an Apple II Plus microcomputer and LIST HANDLER software. A survey of Wisconsin libraries provided basic information on microcomputer applications, which is analyzed and shared.

1906 HART, THOMAS L. "Microcomputer Software and Hardware--An Annotated Source List: How to

Obtain, How to Evaluate, How to Catalog, How
to Standardize." School Library Media Quarterly 12 (Winter 1984): 107-19.
The title tells it all. This report from
the AASL Committee for Standardization of Access
to Library Media Resources provides sources of
information on such problems as cataloging of
software, along with a list of some 250 producers
and distributors from which software may be obtained.

1907 HENSINGER, JAMES SPEED. "There are Demos and
Demos." OCLC Micro 1 (September 1985): 4.
The Bibliographical Center for Research
(BCR) in Denver, Colorado, maintains a collection
of demonstration software for loan to BCR members. Hensinger discusses characteristics of
demonstration software and provides advice on
evaluating programs based on demos.

1908 HORSNELL, VERINA. "Microcomputers in Libraries
and Information Services: A List of Contacts."
Audiovisual Librarian 9 (Spring 1983): 104-07.
Twenty-four British research and development projects are listed and briefly described.

1909 HORSNELL, VERINA. "The Who and Where of Micro: A
Brief Guide to Sources." Library Association
Record 84 (March 1982): 100.
Sources of microcomputer information in
Great Britain are listed and described, including
resource people, publications, research projects,
organizations, and libraries.

1910 HOWDEN, NORMAN. "A Community Grows." Louisiana
Library Association Bulletin 46 (Summer 1983):
23-24.
Communication exchange is essential to
making maximum use of microcomputer equipment in
libraries. Howden lists sources of microcomputer
information available to Louisiana librarians,
stresses the leadership roles of the Louisiana
State University School of Library and Information Science and the Louisiana State Library in
providing information, and suggests new ways of

heightening microcomputer awareness in the state.
Bibliography.

1911 "Information Technology Centre." Vine no. 45
(October 1982): 47-48.
In 1982 the Polytechnic of Central London
established its Information Technology Centre to
house and demonstrate developments from the
entire field of information technology. The
hours, location, and programs are announced.

1912 JONES, MAXINE. "Computer Resources for the
School Librarian." American Libraries 13
(April 1982): 276-77.
Publications about microcomputers; producers of microcomputer programs for students,
faculty, and librarians; software producers; and
microcomputer manufacturers are listed in this
useful resource for school librarians.

1913 KENT, EBEN L. "A Microcosmic Examination of
Microcomputers Resources in Illinois."
Illinois Libraries 65 (October 1983): 507-10.
A survey of microcomputer literature
available in Illinois libraries indicates strong
holdings in the subject and general accessibility
of the materials. Monographs, journals, online
databases, and nontraditional sources such as
user groups and computerized bulletin boards are
considered.

1914 "Library Micro Clearinghouse." Library Software
Review 3 (March 1984): 6-7.
A national clearinghouse for library management applications of general purpose software
is announced by its founders, Microcomputer Libraries and The Highsmith Company. The purpose
of the clearinghouse is to promote good microcomputer library management through the exchange
of library application templates for readily
available software.

1915 "Library Micro Clearinghouse Begun." Small
Computers in Libraries 4 (January 1984): 1.
The Highsmith Company and Microcomputer

Libraries have announced their collaboration in a
clearinghouse project to make available library
management applications of standard microcomputer
software. The concept is explained and sources
of more information are provided.

1916 "MCR Announces Availability of Videotapes on
      Microcomputers." Technicalities 4 (August
      1984): 10.
          Six new videotapes concerning microcom-
      puter use are announced by Metrics Research Cor-
      poration, with purchase information.

1917 MAY, F. CURTIS, and LATHROP, ANN. "Microcomput-
      ers. . .Tools for New Action and Interaction
      in Our Library Media Centers." CMLEA Journal
      6 (Fall 1982): 9-11.
          The San Mateo (CA) Educational Resources
      Center established a microcomputer center in 1980
      to serve the needs of educators in the county.
      Services are discussed, including hands-on exper-
      ience with hardware and software, public domain
      software exchange, and software evaluation.

1918 "Micro Consulting Service Launched by WLN."
      Library Journal 109 (September 1, 1984): 1590.
          The new WLN Microcomputer Consulting
      Service is announced, services are listed, and
      availability of services and products are told.

1919 "Micro Software Exchange Begins." OCLC News-
      letter no. 155 (November 1984): 8.
          The OCLC Microcomputer Program Exchange,
      formerly the LIS/PX program begun by Allan Pratt
      at the University of Arizona, is announced and
      briefly described.

1920 "Micro Software Sources and Directories." LITA
      Newsletter no. 21 (Summer 1985): 7-8.
          ALA's Library and Information Technology
      Association provides a listing of thirty-one
      sources of information concerning microcomputer
      software. Included are directories, databases,
      lending libraries, reference centers, and
      catalogs.

1921 "Micro Support from AMIGOS: Training, Consulting,
     Technical." Library Journal 110 (June 1,
     1985): 72.
          The AMIGOS program of support for IBM PC
     and PC compatible micros is announced and briefly
     described.

1922 "Microcomputers in Libraries--An Information
     Blackhole?" Vine no. 50 (October 1983): 40-
     41.
          Dissemination of information concerning
     microcomputers is a growing problem as micro-
     computers proliferate. The author lists several
     British organizations and institutions which pro-
     vide microcomputer information, then concentrates
     on FIRM, a small group of information specialists
     committed to information sharing. Names and ad-
     dresses of FIRM members are provided.

1923 "Micros in Public Libraries Survey." Small Com-
     puters in Libraries 4 (March 1984): 7.
          The Public Library Association Task
     Force, "Microcomputers in Public Libraries,"
     announces the compilation of a database of North
     American micro users to expedite information ex-
     change and communication.

1924 "MicroSIFT Software Evaluations." ACCESS: Micro-
     computers in Libraries 2 (January 1982): 13-
     16.
          The Northwest Regional Educational Lab-
     oratory, of Portland, Oregon, began publishing
     software reviews in the October, 1981, issue of
     its newsletter, MicroSIFT News. This article
     described the format and content of the reviews
     and includes evaluative summaries of twelve soft-
     ware packages that have been reviewed in greater
     detail in MicroSIFT News.

1925 "Minister Opens Software Showcase for Librar-
     ians." Library Association Record 84
     (December 1982): 421.
          The opening and dedication of an Infor-
     mation Technology Centre on the campus of the
     Polytechnic of Central London is reported. The

Centre, funded jointly by the British Library
Research and Development Department and the
British Department of Industry, is primarily a
a research demonstration and referral center for
microcomputers and other technology.

1926 "New Source for Public Domain Software for IBM PC
    Micro." Library Journal 109 (April 1, 1984):
    620.
        The University of Arizona's Graduate
Library School announces its LIS/PX program, an
exchange program for public domain software and
other free and inexpensive materials for use with
the IBM PC.

1927 "OCLC Begins Microcomputer Exchange." Wilson
    Library Bulletin 59 (December 1984): 250, 252.
        OCLC's Microcomputer Program Exchange,
(OMPX) is announced, and materials and services
are described.

1928 "OCLC Launches Program: Micro Software Exchange."
    Library Journal 110 (February 1, 1985): 31.
        OCLC announces the initiation of a pro-
gram to collect and distribute public domain
software, written for the IBM PC, which might be
of value to M300 Workstation users.

1929 "OCLC Microcomputer Exchange Begins." Informa-
    tion Technology and Libraries 4 (March 1985):
    65-66.
        OCLC announces the OCLC Microcomputer
Program Exchange (OMPX), which provides public
domain and shareware programs for the IBM PC.

1930 "OCLC Starts Program Exchange for PC/M300."
    Small Computers in Libraries 4 (October
    1984): 10-11.
        The Library and Information Services
Program Exchange (LIS/PX), which was started by
Allan Pratt at the University of Arizona Graduate
Library School, is now the OCLC Microcomputer
Program Exchange (OMPX), according to this arti-
cle which describes OMPX, lists services, and
provides access information.

1931 "Ohio Libraries Eye Proposal for Microcomputer
   Center." Library Journal 108 (May 1, 1983):
   864.
       An Ohio Library Association proposal for
   a microcomputer center to provide micro-related
   services to its membership is explained.

1932 "PALINET Starts Micro Center." Small Computers
   in Libraries 4 (May 1984): 4-5.
       The Pennsylvania Library Network (PALI-
   NET) announces a Microcomputer Support Services
   Program (MSSP) to provide software and hardware
   information, a training laboratory, and current
   reviews to PALINET members. PALINET supported
   software is listed.

1933 "Program Exchange Update." Small Computers in
   Libraries 4 (May 1984): 6-7.
       The LIS/PX exchange program for public
   domain software written for IBM PC and PC look-
   alikes is reported, and several available programs are listed.

1934 "San Mateo Microcomputer Center." Small Computers in Libraries 2 (January 1982): 2.
       A joint project of the San Mateo County
   (CA) Office of Education and a group of teachers
   called Computer-Using Educators, the San Mateo
   Microcomputer Center is a cooperative demonstration facility containing a variety of microcomputer systems and software donated for review and
   evaluation. Their operation is described and
   evaluated.

1935 SHEARIN, JOHN W. "Microcomputer Evaluation and
   Resource Center." Indiana Media Journal 4
   (Summer 1982): 9-13.
       The Microcomputer Evaluation and Resource
   Center (MERC), maintained by the Indiana Department of Public Instruction's Division of Federal
   Resources and School Improvement, is introduced
   and discussed. The Center's philosophy is presented, regulations and procedures are outlined,
   equipment is described, and access information is
   provided.

1936 SHEARIN, JOHN W. "One Stop Computer Sampling."
Book Report 1 (September/October 1982): 38-39.
The services of a microcomputer evaluation center located in the Indiana State Department of Education are evaluated.

1937 SIMMONS, PETER. "Microcomputer Applications Form
Data Base in British Columbia." Canadian
Library Journal 42 (April 1985): 81-86.
COMPULINE, a telephone reference service
designed to provide information about microcomputer hardware and software, is examined and
evaluated. Sponsored by the British Columbia
Library Association and the University of British Columbia's School of Library, Archival, and
Information Studies, COMPULINE provides free services to requestors within British Columbia.

1938 SIMMONS, PETER. "Micros in British Columbia
Libraries." Small Computers in Libraries 4
(October 1984): 1-2.
COMPULINE, a microcomputer applications
reference service for libraries in British Columbia, is described in some detail, with telephone
access information provided.

1939 SNELSON, PAMELA. "The Academic Computer."
Library Software Review 4 (March/April 1985):
90-91.
Computers have become a major force in
higher education, and several professional
associations have enlarged the scope of their
interests and activities to include this new
area. Snelson considers some of these associations and their publications which regularly
provide computer information.

1940 "SOLINET Area Micro User Group Will Handle Micro
Information." Library Journal 109 (February
15, 1984): 312.
The SOLINET Microcomputer Users Group
(SMUG) has taken over the responsibility of
responding to queries concerning microcomputer
software and use which were formerly addressed
to SOLINET. A contact person is identified.

1941 TODD, WIN. "Microcomputers in Schools: A List
of Information Sources." School Librarian
31 (March 1983): 223-25.
British microcomputer organizations,
educational programs, projects, and user groups
are listed, with addresses and brief descriptions
of activities.

1942 "User Groups." Small Computers in Libraries 3
(October 1983): 7.
The proliferation of microcomputer user
groups is noted, themes and benefits are considered.

1943 "Virginia Software Library." Library Journal
109 (September 15, 1984): 1716.
The PC National Software Reference
Library in Fairfax, Virginia, is briefly
described.

1944 "WLN Microcomputer Consulting Service." Library
Software Review 3 (September 1984): 305.
The Washington Library Network (WLN)
announces its new consulting service which will
offer assistance to member libraries needing help
in hardware or software selection, local area
network development, online communication training, and other functions as needed.

SOFTWARE AND SYSTEMS REVIEWS

Acquisitions

ACQ 350

1945 "OCLC to Offer Micro-Based Acquisitions Sys-
      tem." OCLC Newsletter no. 157 (April 1985):
      9.

1946 "OCLC Developing Micro-Based Acquisitions Sys-
      tem." Library Systems Newsletter 5 (June
      1985): 43-44.

1947 "OCLC to Offer Micro-Based Acquisitions Sys-
      tem." Wilson Library Bulletin 59 (June
      1985): 649-50.

1948 "OCLC to Offer Micro-Based Acquisitions Sys-
      tem." Electronic Library 3 (July 1985): 161.

1949 "M300 News//From Dublin: MicroBased Acquisition
      System." M300 and PC Report 2 (July/August
      1985): 4.

1950 "OCLC to Offer Micro-Based Acquisitions Sys-
      tem." Information Technology and Libraries
      4 (September 1985): 276.

1951 GABEL, LINDA. "ACQ350 and the Future of Online
      Acquisitions." OCLC Newsletter no. 159
      (October 1985): 11.

BIB-BASE/ACQ

1952 "Micro-Based Acquisitions System Announced."
      Small Computers in Libraries 4 (April 1984):
      7.

1953 "Small Library Computing: Bib-Base/Acq--A
      Microcomputer On-Line Acquisitions System."
      Library Hi Tech News 1 (May 1984): 3.

1954 "Small Library Computing. . ." College and
Research Libraries News 45 (June 1984): 316-
17.

1955 "Library Administration." Library Software
Review 3 (September 1984): 441-42.

DTI ACQUISITIONS

1956 "DTI Data Trek." Small Computers in Libraries
2 (October 1982): 6-7.

ETTACQ

1957 "More Automation Options for Micros." Library
Systems Newsletter 5 (September 1985): 67-
69.

GS 500 ACQUISITIONS SYSTEM

1958 "Gaylord's Stand-Alone Micro-Based Acquisition
System." Library Journal 108 (October 1,
1983): 1836.

1959 BULLARD, SCOTT R. "Gaylord's Acquisitions System GS-500." Library Acquisitions: Practice
and Theory 8, no. 3 (1984): 207-15.

LIBRARY ACQUISITIONS APPLICATION MODULE

1960 SHEROUSE, VICKI M. "Library Acquisitions
Application Module." Booklist 81 (January
1, 1985): 658.

SCOLAS

1961 "Small Computer On-Line Acquisitions System
(SCOLAS). Small Computers in Libraries 3
(February 1983): 2.

Audiovisual

AV CATALOG WRITER

1962 ANDERSON, ERIC S. "AV Catalog Writer." Book-
      list 79 (June 1, 1983): 1287-88.

1963 ANDERSON, ERIC S. "AV Catalog Writer." Com-
      puting Teacher 11 (October 1983): 45-46.

1964 ANDERSON, ERIC S. "AV Catalog Writer." Book-
      list 80 (January 1, 1984): 693.

1965 DEWEY, PATRICK R. "Managing the Small Li-
      brary." Wilson Library Bulletin 59 (Janu-
      ary 1985): 353.

A/V HANDLER

1966 "Media Booking on a Micro." Library Systems
      Newsletter 5 (March 1985): 20.

A/VION

1967 "Software for Film/Video Distribution and
      Audiovisual Library Administration." Soft-
      ware Review 2 (September 1983): 196-97.

AUDIO-VISUAL EQUIPMENT

1968 GARTEN, EDWARD D. "Using a Micro to Learn AV
      Equipment Operation." Library Hi Tech 1
      (Spring 1984): 110-11.

AUDIO-VISUAL INVENTORY

1969 "Audio-Visual Inventory for Apple II +." Small
      Computers in Libraries 3 (March 1983): 4.

AUDIOVISUAL EQUIPMENT INVENTORY

1970 "Audiovisual Equipment Inventory." School
      Library Journal 31 (March 1985): 127.

AUDIOVISUAL EQUIPMENT SCHEDULING

1971 HOWELL, SHARON. "Audiovisual Equipment Sched-
       uling Program." Book Report 3 (September/
       October 1984): 62.

1972 "Audiovisual Equipment Scheduling." School
       Library Journal 31 (March 1985): 127-28.

MEDIA AND EQUIPMENT MANAGEMENT

1973 "Media and Equipment Management." Electronic
       Education 3 (September 1983): 43.

RECORD LIBRARY

1974 GEFFNER, BONNIE. "'Book Library' and 'Record
       Library' Disk-Based Catalogs for the Apple II."
       Software Review 1 (October 1982): 181.

VIDEO TAPE TRACKER

1975 "Library." Library Software Review 3 (March
       1984): 103.

1976 PICHETTE, W. H. "Video Tape Tracker." Educa-
       tional Technology 24 (September 1984): 55-
       56.

Bibliography

BIBLIOGRAPHY

1977 JUDY, JOSEPH R. "Four for Text Handling: Note-
      book, IBR, Bibliography, Footnote." Online
      Review 8 (October 1984): 427-30.

1978 "Worth Noting: TECH Takes a Look at Notebook
      II." Technicalities 5 (July 1985): 13.

BIBLIOGRAPHY WRITER

1979 ANDERSON, ERIC S. "Bibliography Writer."
      ACCESS: Microcomputers in Libraries 3
      (Spring 1983): 14.

1980 ANDERSON, ERIC S. "Bibliography Writer." Book
      Report 2 (May/June 1983): 58.

1981 ANDERSON, ERIC S. "Bibliography Writer." Book-
      list 80 (September 1983): 104.

1982 DEWEY, PATRICK R. "Managing the Small Li-
      brary." Wilson Library Bulletin 59 (Janu-
      ary 1985): 353.

1983 "Bibliography Writer." School Library Journal
      31 (March 1985): 128.

BIBLIOTEK

1984 "BIBLIOTEK Literature Management System."
      Small Computers in Libraries 1 (November
      1981): 4.

1985 BJORNER, SUSAN N. "BIBLIOTEK: The Bibliograph-
      ic Management System." Small Computers in
      Libraries 2 (July 1982): 2-3.

1986 MITLIN, LAURANCE R. "Bibliotek: Designed for
      Handling Bibliographies." Electronic Li-
      brary 2 (October 1984): 239-41.

1987 FELTEN, SUZANNE Y., and VAN CAMP, ANN J.
      "BIBLIOTEK, the Bibliographic Management
      Software." Online 8 (November 1984): 47-50.

BOOKENDS

1988 CUSHING, MATTHEW, Jr. "Software Evaluation:
      Bookends." M. D. Computing 1 (May 1984): 35.

1989 SHEROUSE, VICKI M. "Bookends." Booklist 81
      (September 1, 1984): 82.

1990 DEWEY, PATRICK R. "Database Management Simpli-
      fied." Wilson Library Bulletin 59 (June
      1985): 701.

FICTION FINDER

1991 FABIAN, WILLIAM M. "CALICO: Skills Programs to
      Promote Library Use." American Libraries 15
      (April 1984): 264.

1992 ANDERSON, ERIC S. "Fiction Finder." Booklist
      81 (September 1, 1984): 82.

1993 DEWEY, PATRICK R. "Customized Requests."
      Wilson Library Bulletin 59 (November 1984):
      222.

1994 LETTNER, LORETTA. "Fiction Finder." Library
      Journal 110 (May 1, 1985): 128; and School
      Library Journal 31 (May 1985): 158.

LIBRARIAN

1995 "Library." Library Software Review 3 (March
      1984): 103-04.

PERSONAL BIBLIOGRAPHIC SYSTEM

1996 "New Programs Released." Small Computers in
      Libraries 3 (June 1983): 6-7.

1997 ROSENBERG, VICTOR. "Personal Bibliographic
      System: A System for Creating and Maintain-

ing Bibliographies." Information Technology and Libraries 2 (June 1983): 184-87.

1998 "Micro Program for Bibliographies Created by Michigan Library School." Library Journal 108 (July 1983): 1306.

1999 "Personal Bibliographic System Available." Electronic Library 1 (July 1983): 171.

2000 "Personal Bibliographic System Available." Technicalities 3 (July 1983): 6.

2001 "Software to Aid Bibliographers." Library Systems Newsletter 3 (July 1983): 54.

2002 "Software to Aid in the Compilation of Bibliographies." Software Review 2 (September 1983): 195-96.

2003 "New Bibliography Program for Micros." Electronic Library 1 (October 1983): 230-31.

2004 DICKINSON, DONALD, and PRATT, ALLAN D. "Personal Bibliographic System (PBS)--Review." Small Computers in Libraries 3 (November 1983): 3-4.

2005 ALLEY, BRIAN, and CARGILL, JENNIFER. "Worth Noting: Personal Bibliographic System." Technicalities 4 (January 1984): 3, 6.

2006 ANDERSON, ERIC S. "Personal Bibliographic System." Booklist 80 (January 1, 1984): 690.

2007 ANDERSON, ERIC S. "Personal Bibliographic System." Booklist 80 (January 1, 1984): 693.

2008 ROSENBERG, VICTOR. "Personal Bibliographic System: A 'Front End' to the Online Library." American Libraries 15 (January 1984): 46, 48.

2009 "New Micro Software Versions of Bibliographic Data System." Library Journal 109 (February 15, 1984): 314.

2010 "Language Processing." <u>Library Software Review</u>
3 (June 1984): 273-74.

2011 YOUNG, CAROL G. "Personal Bibliographic System." <u>Library Software Review</u> 3 (June
1984): 248-49.

2012 RUSHINEK, SARA. "Personal Bibliographic System." <u>Educational Technology</u> 24 (July
1984): 56.

2013 "Software System Generates Bibliographies."
<u>Information Retrieval and Library Automation</u>
20 (July 1984): 8-9.

2014 SAFFADY, WILLIAM. "Personal Bibliographic System." <u>Library Technology Reports</u> 20 (July/
August 1984): 579-84.

2015 DEWEY, PATRICK R. "Inhouse Bibliographer."
<u>Wilson Library Bulletin</u> 59 (October 1984):
143.

2016 GROSCH, AUDREY N. "Personal Bibliographic System and Data Transfer System Software Review." <u>Collegiate Microcomputer</u> 2 (November
1984): 309-15.

PROFESSIONAL BIBLIOGRAPHIC SYSTEM

2017 DEWEY, PATRICK R. "Inhouse Bibliographer."
<u>Wilson Library Bulletin</u> 59 (October 1984):
143.

2018 "Personal Bibliographic Software, Inc.: The
Professional Bibliographic System and Bib-
lio-Link." <u>Library Hi Tech News</u> 1 (October/
November 1984): 30-31.

2019 "New Products Announced." <u>Technicalities</u> 4
(November 1984): 15.

2020 "New Bibliography Programs Out." <u>Small
Computers in Libraries</u> 4 (November 1984):
4.

2021 "Personal Bibliographic Software, Inc. Announces Two New Software Packages." Library
Software Review 4 (January/February 1985):
47-48.

2022 McNAMARA, FRANCES. "MicroSystems Software Program to Offer FINDER and PBS." OCLC Newsletter no. 158 (July 1985): 8.

2023 "Personal Bibliographic Software Announces
Three New Products." Electronic Library 3
(July 1985): 158.

2024 SAFFADY, WILLIAM. "BIBLIO-LINK/ Professional
Bibliographic System." Library Technology
Reports 21 (July/August 1985): 381-84.

2025 "Bibliographic System for Macs." Small Computers in Libraries 5 (September 1985): 21.

2026 "OCLC to Offer Professional Bibliographic System." OCLC Newsletter no. 159 (October
1985): 10.

2027 TENOPIR, CAROL. "Software for Online Searching." Library Journal 110 (October 15,
1985): 52-53.

2028 "M300 News//From Dublin: Professional Bibliographic System." M300 and PC Report 2
(November 1985): 4.

2029 FETTERS, LINDA K. "A Guide to Seven Indexing
Programs. . .Plus a Review of the 'Profes-
sional Bibliographic System'." Database 8
(December 1985): 31-38.

2030 "OCLC Offers New Bibliographic Software."
Wilson Library Bulletin 60 (December 1985):
9-10.

Cataloging

BIB-BASE/MARC

2031 "Small Library Computing." <u>Small Computers in Libraries</u> 5 (February 1985): 5.

BIB-BASE/TEXT

2032 "Small Library Computing." <u>Small Computers in Libraries</u> 5 (February 1985): 5.

BOOK TRAK CATALOG CARD AND LABEL SYSTEM

2033 ANDERSON, ERIC S. "Book Trak Catalog Card and Label System." <u>Book Report</u> 3 (January/February 1985): 63-64.

C. C. WRITER

2034 FOX, KATHLEEN. "C. C. Writer." <u>Library Software Review</u> 4 (May/June 1985): 173-74.

CARD

2035 "New Microcomputer Software for Libraries." <u>Electronic Library</u> 1 (January 1983): 9.

CARD AND LABEL MANAGER (CALM)

2036 "Be C.A.L.M. With Your Apple." <u>Small Computers in Libraries</u> 4 (March 1984): 7.

2037 "Card and Label Software Program Created by Presbyterian College." <u>Library Journal</u> 109 (April 1, 1984): 620.

2038 "CALM Eases Catalog Card and Label Production." <u>American Libraries</u> 15 (September 1984): 603.

2039 ANDERSON, ERIC S. "Card and Label Manager." <u>Book Report</u> 3 (January/February 1985): 62.

2040 ANDERSON, ERIC S. "Card and Label Manager."
Book Report 3 (January/February 1985): 64.

2041 "Card and Label Manager/Booklist." School
Library Journal 31 (March 1985): 128-29.

2042 "Card and Label Manager (CALM)." Small Computers in Libraries 5 (March 1985): 9.

2043 ANDERSON, ERIC S. "Card and Label Manager."
Booklist 81 (May 1, 1985): 1268.

2044 LETTNER, LORETTA. "Card and Label Manager."
Library Journal 110 (May 1, 1985): 127;
and School Library Journal 31 (May 1985):
157.

CARDPREP

2045 ANDERSON, ERIC S. "Cardprep." Book Report
3 (January/February 1985): 64.

2046 LETTNER, LORETTA. "Cardprep." Library Journal
110 (May 1, 1985): 127; and School Library
Journal 31 (May 1985): 157.

2047 "Cardprep Produces Cards, Labels, and Lists."
American Libraries 16 (June 1985): 450.

CARDPRO

2048 "Card Catalog Printing Program." Small
Computers in Libraries 2 (November 1982):
7.

2049 MASON, ROBERT M. "More Bargains & Osborne's
Executive." Library Journal 108 (May 15,
1983): 981-82.

2050 "Cardpro." School Library Journal 31 (March
1985): 129.

2051 LETTNER, LORETTA. "Cardpro." Library Journal
110 (May 1, 1985): 127; and School Library
Journal 31 (May 1985): 157.

CARDS

2052 MASON, ROBERT M. "Software: Increasing Capa-
      bilities." Library Journal 109 (May 15,
      1984): 956-57.

2053 ANDERSON, ERIC S. "Cards." Book Report 3
      (January/February 1985): 64.

2054 LETTNER, LORETTA. "Cards." Library Journal
      110 (May 1, 1985): 127; and School Library
      Journal 31 (May 1985): 157.

2055 "CARDS." Small Computers in Libraries 5
      (September 1985): 23.

CATALOG CARD AND LABEL WRITER

2056 SILVERSTEIN, JOAN. "Catalog Card and Label
      Writer." Hot Off the Computer 1 no. 10,
      pp. 22-23.

2057 BJORNER, SUSAN N. "Catalog Card Production: A
      Comparison of Two Software Packages." Small
      Computers in LIbraries 2 (July 1982): 1.

2058 SHEROUSE, VICKI M. "The Catalog Card and Label
      Writer." Booklist 79 (November 1, 1982):
      390.

2059 "Library Administration." Library Software
      Review 3 (September 1984): 441-42.

2060 "Update to Cat Card & Label Writer." Small
      Computers in Libraries 4 (October 1984): 1.

2061 ANDERSON, ERIC S. "K-12 Catalog Card and
      Label Writer." Book Report 3 (January/
      February 1985): 63.

2062 "Catalog Card and Label Writer." School Li-
      brary Journal 31 (March 1985): 129.

2063 LETTNER, LORETTA. "Catalog Card & Label
      Writer." Library Journal 110 (May 1, 1985):

127; and School Library Journal 31 (May 1985): 157.

CATALOG CARD ASSEMBLER

2064 SHEROUSE, VICKI M. "Catalogue Card Assembler." Booklist 80 (January 1, 1984): 689.

2065 "Catalog Card Assembler." School Library Journal 31 (March 1985): 129-30.

2066 NICHOLSON, MARILYN. "Card Catalogue Assembler II." Book Report 4 (May/June 1985): 59-60.

CATALOGING BY COMPUTER

2067 ANDERSON, ERIC S. "Cataloging By Computer." Book Report 3 (January/February 1985): 63.

CATALOGIT!!!

2068 DEWEY, PATRICK R. "Simple Library Applications." Wilson Library Bulletin 59 (February 1985): 418.

2069 LETTNER, LORETTA. "Catalogit!!" Library Journal 110 (May 1, 1985): 127; and School Library Journal 31 (May 1985): 157.

COMPUTER CATALOGING: QUICK 'N EASY

2070 "Computer Cataloging: Quick 'n Easy." Small Computers in Libraries 3 (May 1983): 5.

2071 ANDERSON, ERIC S. "Computer Cataloging Quick 'N Easy." Book Report 3 (January/February 1985): 63.

CORTEX

2072 CHAPMAN, PATRICIA, and NOERR, PETER L. "BLAISE CORTEX: A Microprocessor System for Libraries." Information Processing and Management 19, no. 2 (1983): 77-81.

GENCAT/3

2073 "Knowledge Industry: GENCAT/3." Library Hi
      Tech News no. 18 (July/August 1985): 14-15.

2074 "GENCAT/3 Available from KIPI." Small Computers
      in Libraries 5 (October 1985): 3.

HOME CATALOGER

2075 ANDERSON, ERIC S. "Home Cataloger." Booklist
      81 (April 1, 1985): 1131.

LIBRARIAN'S HELPER

2076 "Low Cost Catalog Card Program." Small Com-
      puters in Libraries 4 (October 1984): 5-6.

2077 "Low Cost Catalog Card Program Out." Small
      Computers in Libraries 4 (November 1984): 6.

2078 LETTNER, LORETTA. "The Librarian's Helper."
      Library Journal 110 (May 1, 1985): 128; and
      School Library Journal 31 (May 1985): 158.

2079 "More Automation Options for Micros." Library
      Systems Newsletter 5 (September 1985):
      67-69.

2080 SWAN, JOHN C. "Computers & Catalog Cards."
      Library Journal 110 (September 15, 1985):
      60.

2081 DEWEY, PATRICK R. "Software for Libraries."
      Wilson Library Bulletin 60 (October 1985):
      61.

2082 "Scarecrow Enters Software Field With Librar-
      ian's Helper." American Libraries 16 (Octo-
      ber 1985): 669.

LIBRARY PROCESSES SYSTEM

2083 "Catalog Cards on the TRS-80." Small Computers
      in Libraries 1 (November 1981): 4.

2084 "Catalog Card System from EDUCOMP." Small Computers in Libraries 2 (August 1982): 5.

2085 "Educomp Pockets/Labels Program Out." Small Computers in Libraries 4 (October 1984): 7.

2086 LETTNER, LORETTA. "Library Processes System." Library Journal 110 (May 1, 1985): 129; and School Library Journal 31 (May 1985): 159.

MLS100

2087 "TRS-80 as OCLC Terminal." Information Technology and Libraries 1 (September 1982): 302-03.

2088 "Maxwell Software Makes TRS80 Into an OCLC Terminal." Library Journal 107 (September 1, 1982): 1589-90.

2089 "TRS-80 Library Programs Available." Small Computers in Libraries 2 (November 1982): 7.

2090 "Software for TRS-80 Allows OCLC Access." Electronic Library 1 (January 1983): 9.

2091 WILBURN, GENE. "Terminal Emulator Software for the TRS-80 Model III. A Look at Eight Telecommunication Programs." Software Review 2 (March 1983): 14-23.

2092 "TRS-80/OCLC Emulator Out." Small Computers in Libraries 3 (April 1983): 7.

MICRO-CONVERT

2093 McQUEEN, JUDY, and BOSS, RICHARD W. "Micro Library Software." Library Technology Reports 20 (March/April 1984): 233-34.

MICRO-RECON

2094 WLN Retrospective Conversion Software." Library Hi Tech News no. 14 (March 1985): 14.

2095 "Washington Library Network's Micro-Recon." M300 and PC Report 2 (March 1985): 5.

2096 "WLN Introduces Micro-Recon." Wilson Library Bulletin 59 (March 1985): 445.

2097 "WLN Introduces Micro-Recon." Electronic Library 3 (April 1985): 86-87.

2098 "WLN's Micro-Recon for IBM or Apple." Small Computers in Libraries 5 (April 1985): 4.

2099 "WLN Introduces Micro-Recon." Information Technology and Libraries 4 (June 1985): 179-80.

2100 "WLN's Micro-Recon Software for IBM and Apple Micros." Library Journal 110 (June 1, 1985): 72.

2101 GORDON, HELEN A. "WLN Offers Micro-Recon." Online 9 (July 1985): 82.

MICROCHECK

2102 "MicroCheck Retrospective Conversion System." American Libraries 16 (February 1985): 133.

2103 ALLAN, ANN, and KREYCHE, MICHAEL. "MicroCheck: For Catalog Conversion and Updating." Electronic Library 3 (April 1985): 90-91.

MICROCON

2104 "MICROCON: A New Conversion Option from OCLC." Library Systems Newsletter 5 (January 1985): 8.

2105 "MICROCON for Conversion Work." M300 and PC Report 2 (February 1985): 5.

2106 "Microcomputer-Based Retrospective Conversion Service Now Available." OCLC Newsletter no. 156 (February 1985): 12.

2107 "OCLC's MICROCON and SC350." Small Computers in Libraries 5 (February 1985): 1.

2108 "OCLC Introduces Micro-Based Services." Information Technology and Libraries 4 (March 1985): 69-70.

2109 "SC-350 and MICROCON." Wilson Library Bulletin 59 (March 1985): 466.

2110 "MICROCON: Microcomputer-Based Retrospective Conversion from OCLC." Information Retrieval and Library Automation 20 (April 1985): 6.

2111 "OCLC and Retro Conversion." Library Journal 110 (June 1, 1985): 75.

MITINET/RETRO

2112 EPSTEIN, HANK. "MITINET/retro: Retrospective Conversion on an Apple." Information Technology and Libraries 2 (June 1983): 166-73.

2113 EPSTEIN, HANK. "MITINET: A System for Retrospective Conversion." American Libraries 15 (February 1984): 113-14.

2114 BOCHER, ROBERT F. "MITINET/Retro in Wisconsin Libraries." Information Technology and Libraries 3 (September 1984): 267-74.

2115 EPSTEIN, HANK. "MITINET: Retrospective Conversion to a MARC Data Base." Online '84 Conference Proceedings, San Francisco, 29-31 October 1984. Weston, CT: Online, Inc., 1984. Pp. 109-12.

2116 LETTNER, LORETTA. "MITINET." Library Journal 110 (May 1, 1985): 128; and School Library Journal 31 (May 1985): 158.

MOLLI

2117 "MOLLI: Automated Searching, Cataloging, and Indexing." American Libraries 16 (September 1985): 597.

OCLC MICRO ENHANCER (CATALOGING)

2118 McNAMARA, FRANCES. "Cataloging Micro Enhancer
      for M300 Undergoing Field Testing." OCLC
      Newsletter no. 155 (November 1984): 8.

2119 LETTNER, LORETTA. "OCLC Cataloging and Inter-
      library Loan Micro Enhancers." Library
      Journal 110 (May 1, 1985): 128; and School
      Library Journal 31 (May 1985): 158.

2120 McNAMARA, FRANCES. "OCLC's Cataloging Micro-
      Enhancer Software." Library Software Review
      4 (July/August 1985): 193-95.

ORICAT

2121 ADLER, ELHANAN. "Original Cataloging Via
      Microcomputer." Small Computers in Li-
      braries 3 (May 1983): 2-3.

PAPERBACK PROGRAM

2122 SHEROUSE, VICKI M. "Paperback Program." Book-
      list 79 (November 1, 1982): 391.

PET COMPUTER LIBRARY CARD MAKER

2123 SHIRINIAN, GEORGE N. "Review--Catalog Card
      Maker." Small Computers in Libraries 3
      (February 1983): 5-6.

QUICK CARD

2124 ANDERSON, ERIC S. "Quick Card." Book Report
      3 (January/February 1985): 64.

2125 RATHJE, LINDA. "Quick Card." Computing
      Teacher 13 (November 1985): 49.

RILEY'S CATALOG CARDS

2126 ANDERSON, ERIC S. "Riley's Catalog Cards."
      Book Report 3 (January/February 1985):
      64.

2127 LETTNER, LORETTA. "Riley's Catalog Cards."
Library Journal 110 (May 1, 1985): 129; and
School Library Journal 31 (May 1985): 159.

TELEMARC III

2128 BJORNER, SUSAN N. "Catalog Card Production: A
Comparison of Two Software Packages." Small
Computers in Libraries 2 (July 1982): 1.

2129 KEPROS, STEVE. "Telemarc Catalog Card Program." Small Computers in Libraries 3
(March 1983): 6.

2130 LETTNER, LORETTA. "Telemarc III." Library
Journal 110 (May 1, 1985): 129; and School
Library Journal 31 (May 1985): 159.

TERMMARC

2131 "Small Library Computing." Small Computers in
Libraries 5 (February 1985): 5.

ULTRACARD

2132 "Ultracard." American Libraries 14 (October
1983): 625.

2133 "Card Preparation Program for the PC." Small
Computers in Libraries 3 (October 1983): 3.

2134 MAXWELL, MARGARET. "ULTRACARD Card Preparation
Program--Review." Small Computers in Libraries 3 (November 1983): 3.

2135 "ULTRACARD Program Available." Technicalities
3 (December 1983): 2.

2136 "ULTRACARD--The Ultimate Catalog Card Production Program." Library Hi Tech News 1
(January 1984): 21; and Library Hi Tech News
1 (March 1984): 21.

2137 KEPPLE, ROBERT J. "The Vendors' Corner: Ultracard." Library Software Review 3 (September
1984): 394-98.

2138 "Ultracard Version 3." <u>Library Software Review</u>
4 (January/February 1985): 46.

2139 "Small Library Computing." <u>Small Computers in
Libraries</u> 5 (February 1985): 5.

UNIFACE

2140 MASON, ROBERT M. "More Bargains & Osborne's
Executive." <u>Library Journal</u> 108 (May 15,
1983): 981-82.

WRITEBAR

2141 "Do It Yourself Bar Codes." <u>Small Computers in
Libraries</u> 5 (February 1985): 10.

Circulation

AUTOMATED LIBRARY II

2142 "An Atari-Based School Library Circ System."
American Libraries 16 (April 1985): 270.

2143 LETTNER, LORETTA. "Automated Library II."
Library Journal 110 (May 1, 1985): 127; and
School Library Journal 31 (May 1985): 157.

BOOK TRAK ONLINE CIRCULATION SYSTEM

2144 ANDERSON, ERIC S. "Book Trak Online Circulation System." *Booklist* 80 (November 1,
1983): 436.

2145 "Book Trak Online Circulation System." *Library
Software Review* 4 (July/August 1985): 222-
24.

BOOKWORM

2146 "Small Scale Circ Program Announced." *Small
Computers in Libraries* 1 (September 1981):
5.

2147 "J. L. Hammett's Bookworm." *Library Journal*
108 (October 1, 1983): 1835.

2148 ANDERSON, ERIC S. "Bookworm." *Booklist* 80
(November 1, 1983): 436-37.

2149 "Bookworm." *School Library Journal* 31 (March
1985): 128.

CTI AUTOMATED LIBRARY SYSTEM

2150 "New Circulation Systems." *Library Systems
Newsletter* 1 (August 1981): 11-12.

2151 "Automated Library System for Minis and
Micros." *Software Review* 1 (February
1982): 97-98.

2152 SIMONDS, MICHAEL J. "MicroComputer Based Cir-
      culation Systems." Connecticut Libraries
      24 (November 1982): 6.

CIRCA I and CIRCA II

2153 "Circ Systems from Highsmith." Small Computers
      in Libraries 3 (June 1983): 5.

2154 "New Microcomputer-Based Circulation Systems
      for Libraries." Software Review 2 (Septem-
      ber 1983): 197-98.

2155 "Highsmith's Apple Circulation System." Li-
      brary Journal 108 (October 1, 1983): 1835.

2156 "Highsmith's Apple Circulation Systems: Circa I
      and Circa II." Library Journal 108 (Novem-
      ber 1, 1983): 2012.

CIRCULATION MANAGEMENT SYSTEM

2157 "Apple Circulation System." Small Computers in
      Libraries 3 (February 1983): 5.

2158 LETTNER, LORETTA. "Circulation Management Sys-
      tem." Library Journal 110 (May 1, 1985):
      127; and School Library Journal 31 (May
      1985): 157.

CIRCULATION MANAGER

2159 "Media Circulation System." Small Computers in
      Libraries 4 (January 1984): 3.

2160 LETTNER, LORETTA. "Circulation Manager."
      Library Journal 110 (May 1, 1985): 127; and
      School Library Journal 31 (May 1985): 157.

2161 "Free Software Program Offered." Electronic
      Education 5 (October 1985): 22.

CIRCULATION PLUS

2162 "Library Software Company." College and Resear-
      ch Libraries News 45 (October 1984): 503.

2163 LETTNER, LORETTA. "Circulation Plus." Library Journal 110 (May 1, 1985): 127; and School Library Journal 31 (May 1985): 157.

2164 EVANS, NELL. "Circulation Plus." Library Software Review 4 (July/August 1985): 247-48.

DATE DUE

2165 SHIRINIAN, GEORGE N. "Review: Date Due Library Circulation Program." Small Computers in Libraries 3 (October 1983): 4-5.

EASTWIND

2166 "EastWind Blows in from Kansas." American Libraries 15 (October 1984): 655-56.

2167 "Data Phase Announces Microcomputer Software." Information Technology and Libraries 3 (December 1984): 419.

2168 "Data Phase's Eastwind Circ System." Small Computers in Libraries 5 (February 1985): 3.

2169 "Eastwind Micro Circulation." Wilson Library Bulletin 59 (March 1985): 465-66.

2170 LETTNER, LORETTA. "Eastwind Full Circulation." Library Journal 110 (May 1, 1985): 127-28; and School Library Journal 31 (May 1985): 157-58.

GS 100

2171 "Gaylord to Market New Circ System." Small Computers in Libraries 2 (February 1982): 4.

2172 SIMONDS, MICHAEL J. "MicroComputer Based Circulation Systems." Connecticut Libraries 24 (November 1982): 6.

INFOQUEST-PAC

2173 CAMPBELL, BONNIE. "InfoQUEST: An Online Catalog for Small Libraries." Library Hi Tech
2, no. 3, issue 7 (1984): 41-46.

2174 "UTLAS Announces Availability of InfoQUEST."
Wilson Library Bulletin 59 (September
1984): 9.

2175 LETTNER, LORETTA. "InfoQUEST-PAC." Library
Journal 110 (May 1, 1985): 128; and School
Library Journal 31 (May 1985): 158.

LIBRARIAN

2176 MEADLEY, PAT. "The Librarian: A Computer Program for Elementary Schools." Emergency
Librarian 11 (January/February 1984): 15-
16.

LIBRARY CIRCULATION MANAGEMENT PROGRAM

2177 "Circulation Control Program." Small Computers
in Libraries 2 (October 1982): 4.

2178 SHEROUSE, VICKI M. "Library Circulation Management Program." Booklist 80 (January 1,
1984): 690.

2179 FOX, KATHLEEN. "Library Circulation Manager."
Library Software Review 3 (June 1984): 245-
46.

LIBRARY HELPER 'OVERDUES'

2180 "Software." Wilson Library Bulletin 59 (October 1984): 157.

2181 LETTNER, LORETTA. "Library Helper 'Overdues'."
Library Journal 110 (May 1, 1985): 128; and
School Library Journal 31 (May 1985): 158.

2182 "Software." Wilson Library Bulletin 60 (October 1985): 77-78.

2183 "Office Management." Electronic Learning 5 (November/December 1985): 76.

LIBRARY MICROTOOLS: OVERDUES

2184 "Library Program Handles Overdues." T.H.E. Journal: Technological Horizons in Education 13 (October 1985): 58.

LIBRARY MONITOR

2185 "New Programs Released." Small Computers in Libraries 3 (June 1983): 6-7.

2186 LETTNER, LORETTA. "The Library Monitor." Library Journal 110 (May 1, 1985): 128; and School Library Journal 31 (May 1985): 158.

LIBRARY OVERDUE MATERIALS RECORD

2187 "New Programs Released." Small Computers in Libraries 3 (June 1983): 6-7.

2188 LETTNER, LORETTA. "Library Overdue Materials Record." Library Journal 110 (May 1, 1985): 128; and School Library Journal 31 (May 1985): 158.

THE LIBRARY SYSTEM

2189 "More Library Automation Options for Micros." Library Systems Newsletter 5 (September 1985): 67-69.

LISTEN

2190 "LISTEN, an Under $20K System at St. Charles City-County, Mo." Library Journal 108 (December 15, 1983): 2286.

MACBETH CIRCULATION SYSTEM

2191 "Microcomputer Based Systems for Smaller Libraries." Vine no. 48 (May 1983): 27-29.

MICRO-CIRC

2192 McQUEEN, JUDY, and BOSS, RICHARD W. "Micro Library Software." Library Technology Reports 20 (March/April 1984): 233-34.

NONESUCH

2193 SAFFADY, WILLIAM. "Ringgold Nonesuch Circulation System." Library Computer Equipment Review 2, no. 2 (1981): 120-25.

2194 MARCUM, DEANNA H., and BOSS, RICHARD W. "Information Technology." Wilson Library Bulletin 55 (June 1981): 764-65.

2195 "$29,000 Micro-Based Circ System Announced." Small Computers in Libraries 1 (December 1981): 1.

OVERDUE BOOKS

2196 DEWEY, PATRICK R. "Simple Library Applications." Wilson Library Bulletin 59 (February 1985): 418.

2197 LETTNER, LORETTA. "Overdue Books." Library Journal 110 (May 1, 1985): 129; and School Library Journal 31 (May 1985): 159.

OVERDUE COLLECTOR

2198 DEWEY, PATRICK R. "Managing the Small Library." Wilson Library Bulletin 59 (January 1985): 353.

THE OVERDUE WRITER

2199 "New Low Cost Circ System." Small Computers in Libraries 1 (December 1981): 7.

2200 ANDERSON, ERIC S. "The Overdue Writer." Electronic Learning 2 (April 1983): 80-81.

2201 ANDERSON, ERIC S. "Overdue Writer." Booklist 80 (January 1, 1984): 693.

2202 SKAPURA, ROBERT. "Overdue Writer: Overdue Notice Program for Small Libraries." American Libraries 15 (May 1984): 340.

2203 DEWEY, PATRICK R. "Managing the Small Library." Wilson Library Bulletin 59 (January 1985): 353.

OVERDUEMASTER

2204 LETTNER, LORETTA. "OVERDUEmaster." Library Journal 110 (May 1, 1985): 129; and School Library Journal 31 (May 1985): 159.

UNICORN

2205 YOUNG, JACKY, and ZIMMERMAN, JULIA. "Unicorn: A Unique On-Line Circulation System." Southeastern Librarian 32 (Winter 1982): 85-86.

2206 WARDEN, WILLIAM H., III. "Microcomputer Based Circulation: Sirsi Corporation's Unicorn System." Library Hi Tech 1 (Winter 1983): 44-46.

Communications

ASCII PRO

2207 SAFFADY, WILLIAM. "ASCII PRO." Library Tech-
      nology Reports 21 (July/August 1985): 375-
      80.

APPLE-IBM CONNECTION

2208 "Alpha Software Introduces the Apple-IBM Con-
      nection." Software Review 2 (June 1983):117.

ASCOM

2209 MASON, ROBERT M. "Telecommunications Pro-
      grams--The Osborne Executive--DEC's Rainbow
      100 Plus." Library Journal 108 (November 1,
      1983): 2034-35.

BBS-PC

2210 "New BBS Program for IBM PC." Bulletin Board
      Systems 3 (June 1985): 3-4.

BRS/SEARCH

2211 "BRS to Market New Database Management Software
      for Micros. . .Aimed at Libraries and Legal
      Applications." Online 6 (September 1982):
      11.

2212 "BRS to Sell Its Search Software." American
      Society for Information Science Bulletin 9
      (February 1983): 7.

2213 "BRS/SEARCH Software Now Available for Main-
      frame, Mini and Micro Applications." Online
      7 (May 1983): 14, 67.

2214 "BRS/SEARCH Information Retrieval Software
      Available." Information Technology and
      Libraries 2 (June 1983): 216-17.

2215 "BRS/Search Information Retrieval Software Now Available for Mainframe, Mini, and Microcomputer Applications." Online Review 7 (June 1983): 204.

2216 BRUNELLE, BETTE. "The Vendor's Corner: The BRS/SEARCH System." Software Review 2 (December 1983): 245-54.

2217 LUNDEEN, GERALD, and TENOPIR, CAROL. "Microcomputer-Based Library Catalog Software." Microcomputers for Information Management 1 (September 1984): 215-28.

2218 SNOW, CARL E., and CANGANELLI, PATRICK W. "Front End Software: BRS/SEARCH." Library Software Review 4 (September/October 1985): 311-14.

BIBLIO-LINK

2219 "Personal Bibliographic Software, Inc.: The Professional Bibliographic System and Biblio-Link." Library Hi Tech News 1 (October/November 1984): 30-31.

2220 "New Bibliography Programs Out." Small Computers in Libraries 4 (November 1984): 4.

2221 "New Products Announced." Technicalities 4 (November 1984): 15.

2222 "Professional Bibliographic Software, Inc. Announces Two New Software Packages." Library Software Review 4 (January/February 1985): 47-48.

2223 "Personal Bibliographic Software, Inc." College and Research Libraries News 46 (February 1985): 79.

2224 "Personal Bibliographic Software Announces Three New Products." Electronic Library 3 (July 1985): 158.

2225 SAFFADY, WILLIAM. "BIBLIO-LINK/Professional
Bibliographic System." Library Technology
Reports 21 (July/August 1985): 381-84.

2226 TENOPIR, CAROL. "Software for Online Searching." Library Journal 110 (October 15,
1985): 52-53.

BIOSUPERFILE

2227 "Biosis Introduces New Microcomputer Software
Package for BITS Users." Online Review 8
(February 1984): 22.

2228 "BIOSIS Downloading Software Offers User-
Friendly Access." Library Journal 109
(February 15, 1984): 312.

2229 "Database Creation Software from Biosis."
Online Review 8 (April 1984): 123.

BLAST

2230 "BLAST Lets Micros, Minis Transfer Files."
Software Review 2 (September 1983):
187.

BRIDGE-IT

2231 "WLN Software Downloads Bibliographic Records
to Microcomputers." Electronic Library 3
(July 1985): 157.

CAPITAL PC REMOTE BULLETIN BOARD SYSTEM

2232 "Electronic Bulletin Board Accessed by Home
Micros." Library Journal 109 (May 15,
1984): 938.

COMMSCAN

2233 FENICHEL, CAROL HANSEN. "COMMSCAN." Library
Software Review 4 (March/April 1985): 103-
04.

COMMUNICATIONS PLUS

2234 "DTI Data Trek Announces Communications Plus."
Library Hi Tech News 1 (January 1984): 20.

CONNECT

2235 "Integrated Communication Software Packages:
Connect." Online Review 8 (June 1984): 196.

COPYLINK

2236 "Copylink." Library Software Review 3 (March
1984): 93.

CROSSTALK

2237 GEFFNER, BONNIE. "CROSSTALK and LINK--Data
Communications Software for Micros." Software Review 1 (October 1982): 188.

2238 MASON, ROBERT M. "Telecommunications Pro-
grams--The Osborne Executive--DEC's Rainbow
100 Plus." Library Journal 108 (November 1,
1983): 2034-35.

2239 HOLLAND, MAURITA PETERSON. "Communications
Software: Experiences with Perfect Link and
Crosstalk XVI." Online 8 (July 1984): 75-80.

2240 FENICHEL, CAROL HANSEN. "Software Reviews:
Communications." Library Software Review
4 (May/June 1985): 160-63.

DATA TRANSFER SYSTEM

2241 "OCLC/RLIN Down-Load Program." Small Computers
in Libraries 3 (December 1983): 7.

2242 "Data Transfer System." Library Hi Tech News
1 (February 1984): 5.

2243 "New Micro Software Versions of Bibliographic
Data System." Library Journal 109 (February
15, 1984): 314.

2244 "Data Transfer Software for Online Library
      Catalogues." Electronic Library 2 (April
      1984): 74.

2245 "Downloading Made Simple." American Libraries
      15 (October 1984): 656.

2246 GROSCH, AUDREY N. "Personal Bibliographic
      System and Data Transfer System Software
      Review." Collegiate Microcomputer 2 (Novem-
      ber 1984): 309-15.

DATALINK

2247 "Datalink-PC." Library Software Review 3
      (March 1984): 93-94.

DATAPATH

2248 "Datapath Enhanced for IBM PC." Electronic
      Library 2 (October 1984): 225.

FINDERLINK

2249 AARON, ROBERT, and SMITH, JUDITH ANN. "FINDER,
      FINDERlink and Search Companion: Software
      for Uploading and Downloading (Abstract)."
      Downloading/Uploading Online Databases and
      Catalogs. Proceedings of the Congress for
      Librarians, St. John's University, Jamaica,
      New York, 18 February 1985. Library Hi Tech
      Special Studies Series, no. 1. Ann Arbor,
      MI: Pierian Press, 1985. Pp. 28-29.

GEORGE

2250 SAFFADY, WILLIAM. "GEORGE Communications Soft-
      ware." Library Technology Reports 21 (July/
      August 1985): 385-89.

GRAM-A-SYST

2251 "Gram-a-Syst Links Micros to Telex Net." Soft-
      ware Review 2 (September 1983): 199.

HAYES TERMINAL PROGRAM

2252 HANIFAN, THOMAS. "Hayes Terminal Program."
Small Computers in Libraries 3 (February
1983): 3-4.

HELLO CENTRAL!

2253 GEFFNER, BONNIE. "'HELLO CENTRAL!'--Data Communications for the Apple II." Software
Review 1 (October 1982): 189.

2254 ANDERSON, ERIC S. "Hello Central." Booklist
80 (March 1, 1984): 1003.

I/O EXPRESS

2255 ELLINGEN, DANA. "I/O Express." Library Software Review 3 (March 1984): 66.

2256 SAFFADY, WILLIAM. "I/O EXPRESS." Library Technology Reports 21 (July/August 1985): 395-
400.

IMPERSONATOR

2257 SAFFADY, WILLIAM. "THE IMPERSONATOR." Library
Technology Reports 21 (July/August 1985):
390-94.

IN-SEARCH

2258 "In-Search. . .Latest Front-End Search Package
for DIALOG." Online 8 (May 1984): 10, 75.

2259 SCHRADER, DAVID B., and PORTOGHESE, CHRISTINE
P. "In-Search: Bringing Dialog to the End
User." Information Today 1 (July/August
1984): 17, 29.

2260 "Software Packages: More on Menlo." Online
Review 8 (October 1984): 407.

2261 TENOPIR, CAROL. "Database Access Software."
Library Journal 109 (October 1, 1984):
1828-29.

2262 LEVY, LOUISE R. "Gateway Software: Is It For You?" Online 8 (November 1984): 67-79.

2263 "Professional Version of In-Search Released by Menlo Corp." Online 9 (March 1985): 12.

2264 FENICHEL, CAROL HANSEN. "IN-SEARCH." Library Software Review 4 (March/April 1985): 101-03.

2265 RUDIN, JOAN; HAUSELE, NANCY; STOLLAK, JAY; and SONK, JOSEPH. "Comparison of In-Search, Scimate and an Intelligent Terminal Emulator in Biomedical Literature Searching." Proceedings of the Sixth National Online Meeting, New York, 30 April-2 May 1985. Medford, NJ: Learned Information, 1985. Pp. 403-08.

INSTANTCOM

2266 LASBO, PAUL. "Upload on a Micro Application." Online 8 (January 1984): 12-17.

2267 "Announcing the Release of INSTANTCOM Version 3.1." Online Review 8 (April 1984): 119.

2268 "Integrated Communication Software Packages: Instantcom." Electronic Library 2 (July 1984): 142-43.

2269 STIGLEMAN, SUE. "Instantcom: For Online Communications." Online Review 8 (December 1984): 539-42.

2270 MILLER, RALPH. "Designing Your Own Low Cost Front-End Software." Online 9 (March 1985): 94-98.

2271 ROBINSON, ANN. "A Comparison of PC-TALK and Instantcom for Uploading and Downloading." Proceedings of the Sixth National Online Meeting, New York, 30 April-2 May 1985. Medford, NJ: Learned Information, 1985. Pp. 391-402.

INTERLYNC

2272　MASON, ROBERT M.　"Telecommunications Programs--The Osborne Executive--DEC's Rainbow 100 Plus." Library Journal 108 (November 1, 1983): 2034-35.

IT

2273　"New System for Unskilled Users to Search Information Databases." Electronic Library 3 (January 1985): 17.

LANLINK

2274　"LAN on a Disk Networks PCs." T.H.E. Journal: Technological Horizons in Education 12 (June 1985): 36.

2275　"The Software Link Puts LAN on a Disk." Electronic Library 3 (July 1985): 158-59.

LAPCOM

2276　"Communications." Library Software Review 3 (June 1984): 252-53.

LEXIS/NEXIS

2277　"LEXIS/NEXIS Communication Software." OCLC Micro 1 (September 1985): 30.

LINK

2278　GEFFNER, BONNIE.　"CROSSTALK and LINK--Data Communications Software for Micros." Software Review 1 (October 1982): 188.

MICRO LINK II

2279　SAFFADY, WILLIAM.　"MICRO LINK II." Library Technology Reports 21 (July/August 1985): 401-04.

MICRO SEARCH/SAVE

2280 SPELLER, BENJAMIN F., Jr., and BOWIE, GEORGE
F., III. "Microcomputer Based Search/Save
System for the Lockheed Information System
(DIALOG)." Information Processing and Man-
agement 18, no. 3 (1982): 161-62.

MICROCAMBRIDGE

2281 "CSA Announces microCambridge." Online Review
8 (June 1984): 200.

2282 "Cambridge Scientific Introduces Micro Search
Package." Online 9 (March 1985): 101-02.

2283 "MicroCambridge Facilitates CSA Database
Searching." Online Review 9 (June 1985):
189-90.

MICRODISCLOSURE

2284 EAGER, VIRGINIA W. "MicroDISCLOSURE--Software
for the IBM PC/XT Enduser." Database 7
(June 1984): 79-84.

2285 LEVY, LOUISE R. "Gateway Software: Is It For
You?" Online 8 (November 1984): 67-79.

MICROSEARCH

2286 ANDERSON, ERIC S. "MICROsearch." Booklist 81
(June 1, 1985): 1414.

MICROTERM

2287 WILBURN, GENE. "Terminal Emulator Software for
the TRS-80 Model III: A Look at Eight Telecommunication Programs." Software Review 2
(March 1983): 14-23.

MIGHTY MAIL

2288 "Mighty Mail." Online Review 8 (June 1984):
196.

2289 "Mighty Mail." Electronic Library 2 (July
1984): 143.

2290 "Mighty Mail Communications Packages to Aid
Online Searchers." Online 8 (September
1984): 95-96.

MIKROTEL

2291 "ESA-IRS's Mikrotel Software Available."
Online Review 9 (October 1985): 367; and
Electronic Library 3 (October 1985): 239-40.

MITE

2292 MASON, ROBERT M. "Telecommunications Pro-
grams--The Osborne Executive--DEC's Rainbow
100 Plus." Library Journal 108 (November 1,
1983): 2034-35.

2293 "Communications Packages." Software Review 2
(December 1983): 271-72.

2294 GORDON, HELEN A. "Mycroft Labs Introduces
Menu-Driven Datacom Package." Online 8
(July 1984): 94.

2295 FENICHEL, CAROL HANSEN. "Software Reviews:
Communications." Library Software Review
4 (May/June 1985): 160-63.

2296 SAFFADY, WILLIAM. "MITE." Library Technology
Reports 21 (July/August 1985): 405-10.

MODEM 7

2297 MASON, ROBERT M. "Telecommunications Pro-
grams--The Osborne Executive--DEC's Rainbow
100 Plus." Library Journal 108 (November 1,
1983): 2034-35.

2298 HANE, PAULA. "MODEM 7 and Downloading." Online 9 (November 1985): 57-64.

MODEM80

2299 WILBURN, GENE. "Terminal Emulator Software for
the TRS-80 Model III: A Look at Eight Tele-

communications Programs." Software Review
2 (March 1983): 14-23.

NET-SEARCH

2300 "Informatics Introduces Net-Search." Library
Software Review 3 (December 1984): 460.

OL'SAM

2301 "Micro Supports On-Line Searches." Small
Computers in Libraries 1 (June 1981): 7.

2302 "More on OL'SAM." Small Computers in Libraries
1 (August 1981): 6.

2303 TOLIVER, DAVID E. "OL'SAM: An Intelligent
Front-End for Bibliographic Information
Retrieval." Information Technology and
Libraries 1 (December 1982): 317-26.

OMNILINK

2304 "Micro-Mainframe." Library Software Review 3
(June 1984): 274.

OMNIMICRO

2305 "Micro-Mainframe." Library Software Review 3
(June 1984): 274.

ONLINE PRICING SIMULATOR

2306 "Package Projects Online Costs." Information
Today 1 (July/August 1984): 21.

2307 "Online Pricing Software for Micros Introduced." Online 8 (September 1984): 95; and
Electronic Library 2 (October 1984): 224-25.

OZMOSIS

2308 GEFFNER, BONNIE. "'OZMOSIS'--Data Communications for the Osborne 1 and CP/M-Based
Micros." Software Review 1 (October 1982):
188-89.

PC-DIAL

2309 SAFFADY, WILLIAM. "PC-DIAL." Library Technology Reports 21 (July/August 1985): 411-15.

PC/NET-LINK

2310 "New Telecomm Program." Small Computers in Libraries 4 (May 1984): 4.

2311 "Information General Corporation." College and Research Libraries News 45 (June 1984): 316.

2312 "PC Software Reduces Online Time." Online Review 8 (June 1984): 199-200.

2313 "PC Software Reduced Online Time." Electronic Library 2 (July 1984): 145.

2314 "PC/NET-LINK Promises Fast Database Selection & Access." Library Journal 109 (August 1984): 1388.

2315 "Auto-Logon/Database Directory Software Introduced by Informatics." Online 8 (September 1984): 97.

2316 "Informatics: PC/NET-LINK Software." Library Hi Tech News no. 13 (February 1985): 22.

2317 LETTNER, LORETTA. "PC/NET-LINK." Library Journal 110 (May 1, 1985): 126; and School Library Journal 31 (May 1985): 156.

2318 "PC/Net-LINK's Online Demo." Small Computers in Libraries 5 (May 1985): 4.

PC-TALK

2319 "Free/Cheap IBM PC Programs." Small Computers in Libraries 3 (September 1983): 7.

2320 POST, RICHARD. "Selected Shareware for Library-Media Administrative Applications."

Ohio Media Spectrum 36 (Winter 1984/1985): 12-15.

2321 ROBINSON, ANN. "A Comparison of PC-TALK and Instantcom for Uploading and Downloading." Proceedings of the 6th National Online Meeting, New York, 30 April-2 May 1985. Medford, NJ: Learned Information, 1985. Pp. 391-402.

2322 MICHELS, FREDRICK; HARRISON, NEIL; and SMITH, DOUGLAS. "User-Supported Software for the IBM PC." Library Hi Tech 3, no. 2, issue 10 (1985): 97-106.

2323 "PC-TALK III." Information Processing and Management 21, no. 2 (1985): II.

2324 PHILLIPS, BRIAN. "'Shareware'. . .Make It Your First Software Purchase." Online 9 (May 1985): 33-36.

2325 SAFFADY, WILLIAM. "PC-TALK III." Library Technology Reports 21 (July/August 1985): 416-20.

PDS/1.

2326 "New Microbased System Developed." Journal of Library Automation 12 (June 1979): 187-88.

PEOPLE'S MESSAGE SYSTEM

2327 DEWEY, PATRICK R. "Software for Libraries." Wilson Library Bulletin 59 (April 1985): 554-55.

PERFECT LINK

2328 HOLLAND, MAURITA PETERSON. "Communications Software: Experiences with Perfect Link and Crosstalk XVI." Online 8 (July 1984): 75-80.

PLEASE

2329 "Micro-Mainframe." Library Software Review 3 (June 1984): 274.

PRIMATE

2330 LEFKOVITZ, DAVID. "PRIMATE: A Microcomputer System for Host Mediation and Private File Text Search." Information Interaction. Proceedings of the 45th ASIS Annual Meeting. White Plains, NY: Knowledge Industry Publications, 1982, v. 19. Pp. 162-64.

2331 "ISI to Market Micro/Database Linkage Program." Small Computers in Libraries 3 (January 1983): 1-2.

PRO-SEARCH

2332 "MENLO: Pro-Search." Library Hi Tech News no. 16 (May 1985): 8.

2333 LETTNER, LORETTA. "Pro-Search." Library Journal 110 (May 1, 1985): 126; and School Library Journal 31 (May 1985): 156.

2334 "Menlo Corporation Produces Pro-Search for the Information Professional." Online Review 9 (June 1985): 187-88.

2335 "Search Software." Small Computers in Libraries 5 (June 1985): 16.

2336 BLANCHARD, MARK. "RE:Views." OCLC Micro 1 (July 1985): 20.

2337 "Micromedia Limited: Pro-Search." Library Hi Tech News no. 18 (July/August 1985): 15.

2338 SAFFADY, WILLIAM. "PRO SEARCH." Library Technology Reports 21 (July/August 1985): 421-27.

2339 "Menlo: Pro-Search." Library Hi Tech News no. 20 (October 1985): 17.

2340 TENOPIR, CAROL. "Software for Online Searching." Library Journal 110 (October 15,
1985): 52-53.

READITERM

2341 "Communications Packages." Software Review 2
(December 1983): 271-72.

RELAY

2342 "Communications Packages." Software Review 2
(December 1983): 271-72.

2343 "Communications." Library Software Review 3
(June 1984): 252-53.

RESPOND

2344 GORDON, HELEN A. "RESPOND for Async and
Synchronous Communications." Database 8
(June 1985): 70.

2345 SAFFADY, WILLIAM. "RESPOND/TTY and RESPOND/
ASYNC." Library Technology Reports 21
(July/August 1985): 428-33.

REVITEL

2346 "Communications Software for Micros." Online
Review 9 (October 1985): 367-68; and Electronic Library 3 (October 1985): 238-39.

ST80 III

2347 WILBURN, GENE. "Terminal Emulator Software for
the TRS-80 Model III: A Look at Eight Telecommunication Programs." Software Review 2
(March 1983): 14-23.

SCI-MATE

2348 GARFIELD, EUGENE. "Sci-Mate: A User-Friendly
Information Storage and Retrieval System for
Microcomputers." The Application of Mini-

and Micro-Computers in Information, Documentation and Libraries. Proceedings of the International Conference on the Application of Mini- and Micro-Computers in Information, Documentation and Libraries, Tel-Aviv, Israel, 13-18 March 1983. New York: North-Holland, 1983. Pp. 79-84.

2349 "Software for Searching and Storing." American Libraries 14 (May 1983): 327.

2350 "New Technology." College and Research Libraries News 44 (May 1983): 164-65.

2351 "ISI Introduces Two Software Packages for Information Retrieval and File Management." Online 7 (May 1983): 13-14.

2352 STOUT, CATHERYNE, and MARCINKO, THOMAS. "Sci-Mate: A Menu-Driven Universal Online Searcher and Personal Data Manager." Online 7 (September 1983): 112-16.

2353 "Bits and Sci-Mate Now Compatible." Online Review 8 (August 1984): 301.

2354 LUNDEEN, GERALD, and TENOPIR, CAROL. "Microcomputer-Based Library Catalog Software." Microcomputers for Information Management 1 (September 1984): 215-28.

2355 LEVY, LOUISE R. "Gateway Software: Is It For You?" Online 8 (November 1984): 67-79.

2356 RUDIN, JOAN; HAUSELE, NANCY; STOLLAK, JAY; and SONK, JOSEPH. "Comparison of In-Search, Scimate and an Intelligent Terminal Emulator in Biomedical Literature Searching." Proceedings of the 6th National Online Meeting, New York, 30 April-2 May 1985. Medford, NJ: Learned Information, 1985. Pp. 403-08.

2357 LETTNER, LORETTA. "Sci-Mate." Library Journal 110 (May 1, 1985): 130; and School Library Journal 31 (May 1985): 160.

2358 PILACHOWSKI, DAVID. "Universal Online Searcher; Personal Data Manager." Library Software Review 4 (May/June 1985): 163-64.

2359 LUNDEEN, GERALD, and TENOPIR, CAROL. "Microcom-
puter Software for In-House Databases. . .
Four Top Packages Under $2000." Online 9
(September 1985): 30-38.

SEARCH

2360 "Search Before Going Online." Online Review 8
(August 1984): 300.

SEARCH COMPANION

2361 "Software Update." M300 and PC Report 2 (January 1985): 9.

2362 AARON, ROBERT, and SMITH, JUDITH ANN. "FINDER,
FINDERlink and Search Companion: Software
for Uploading and Downloading (Abstract)."
Downloading/Uploading Online Databases and
Catalogs. Proceedings of the Congress for
Librarians, St. John's University, Jamaica,
New York, 18 February 1985. Library Hi Tech
Special Studies Series, no. 1. Ann Arbor,
MI: Pierian Press, 1985. Pp. 28-29.

SEARCH HELPER

2363 "Information Access Co. Announces New Microcomputer and Optical Disk Products." Information Intelligence Online Libraries and
Microcomputers 1 (September 1983): 4-5.

2364 JOHNSON, GRETCHEN L. "Search Helper." RQ 23
(Fall 1983): 96-97.

2365 "Online Search Assistance." Small Computers in
Libraries 4 (February 1984): 3.

2366 ENSOR, PAT, and CURTIS, RICHARD A. "Search
Helper: Low-Cost Online Searching in an Academic Library." RQ 23 (Spring 1984): 327-31.

2367 NIEMEIER, KATHY. "Online Searching--A Case
      History." Proceedings of the 5th National
      Online Meeting, New York, 10-12 April 1984.
      Medford, NJ: Learned Information, 1984.
      Pp. 247-50.

2368 "Claim for SEARCH HELPER: Online Search Costs
      Cut." Library Journal 109 (April 15, 1984):
      761-62.

2369 "Search Helper a New, Easy and Inexpensive Way
      to Search Six Databases." Online Review 8
      (June 1984): 199.

2370 SMITH, RITA H., and PHILLIPS, LINDA L. "Search
      Helper: An Online Service for Undergrad-
      uates." RSR: Reference Services Review 12
      (Fall 1984): 31-34.

2371 LEVY, LOUISE R. "Gateway Software: Is It For
      You?" Online 8 (November 1984): 67-79.

2372 "SEARCH HELPER Pricing Options." Small Com-
      puters in Libraries 4 (December 1984): 11.

2373 "IAC: Search Helper Pricing Options." Library
      Hi Tech News no. 11/12 (December 1984/Jan-
      uary 1985): 41.

2374 NIEMEIER, KATHY. "SEARCH HELPER: IAC's Online
      Searching Aid." Downloading/Uploading On-
      line Databases and Catalogs. Proceedings
      of the Congress for Librarians, St. John's
      University, Jamaica, New York, 18 February
      1985. Library Hi Tech Special Studies
      Series, no. 1. Ann Arbor, MI: Pierian
      Press, 1985. Pp. 25-27.

2375 "Menu-Driven, Self-Coaching Online Search Aid
      Now Directed at Moderate-User Market."
      Information Retrieval and Library Automation
      20 (January 1985): 5-6.

2376 LETTNER, LORETTA. "Search Helper." Library
      Journal 110 (May 1, 1985): 127; and School
      Library Journal 31 (May 1985): 157.

SEARCHMASTER

2377 "SDC Search Service Becomes SDC Information
Services. . .Announces a New Microcomputer
Package." Online 7 (July 1983): 66.

2378 WILBUR, HELEN L. "The ORBIT SearchMaster Sys-
tem: A Search Management Tool." Download-
ing/Uploading Online Databases and Catalogs.
Proceedings of the Congress for Librarians,
St. John's University, Jamaica, New York,
18 February 1985. Library Hi Tech Special
Studies Series, no. 1. Ann Arbor, MI:
Pierian Press, 1985. Pp. 22-24.

SEARCHWARE

2379 TENOPIR, CAROL. "Software for Online Searching." Library Journal 110 (October 15,
1985): 52-53.

SMART TERMINAL

2380 LIVESEY, BRIAN. "Information Retrieval on a
Tandy." Proceedings of the 6th International Online Information Meeting, London,
7-9 December 1982. Medford, NJ: Learned
Information, 1982. Pp. 255-62.

SMARTCOM II

2381 "Telecommunications for Micros, Minis." T.H.E.
Journal: Technological Horizons in Education
12 (January 1985): 35.

2382 FENICHEL, CAROL HANSEN. "Software Reviews:
Communications." Library Software Review 4
(May/June 1985): 160-63.

2383 SAFFADY, WILLIAM. "SMARTCOM II." Library
Technology Reports 21 (July/August 1985):
434-39.

SMARTERM 100

2384 SAFFADY, WILLIAM. "SMARTERM 100." Library
     Technology Reports 21 (July/August 1985):
     440-46.

STRAIGHT TALK

2385 MEADOR, JIM, and BUTLER, BECKY. "Straight Talk
     for the Macintosh--In Mouse Language."
     Database 8 (August 1985): 104-10.

SUPERTERM

2386 "Communications." Library Software Review 3
     (March 1984): 92-94.

TELCOM

2387 WILBURN, GENE. "Terminal Emulator Software for
     the TRS-80 Model III: A Look at Eight Tele-
     communication Programs." Software Review 2
     (March 1983): 14-23.

TELETERM

2388 MASON, ROBERT M. "Telecommunications
     Programs--The Osborne Executive--DEC's Rain-
     bow 100 Plus." Library Journal 108 (Novem-
     ber 1, 1983): 2034-35.

TELIOS

2389 SAFFADY, WILLIAM. "TELIOS." Library Technol-
     ogy Reports 21 (July/August 1985): 447-51.

TERMEXEC

2390 CONNELL, WILLIAM SCOTT. "Communications for
     the Apple II: TermExec." Online Review 8
     (October 1984): 438-39.

TRANSEND

2391 "Communications Packages." Software Review 2
     (December 1983): 271-72.

504 / SOFTWARE AND SYSTEMS REVIEWS

2392 ANDERSON, ERIC S. "Transend 1." Booklist 80
(May 1, 1984): 1266.

UNITERM

2393 WILBURN, GENE. "Terminal Emulator Software for
the TRS-80 Model III: A Look at Eight Telecommunication Programs." Software Review 2
(March 1983): 14-23.

VIDTEX EXECUTIVE

2394 WILBURN, GENE. "Terminal Emulator Software for
the TRS-80 Model III: A Look at Eight Telecommunication Programs." Software Review 2
(March 1983): 14-23.

VISITERM

2395 BLAIR, JOHN C., Jr. "A Tutorial in Representative Apple Software." Database 5 (June
1982): 72-79.

2396 GEFFNER, BONNIE. "'VisiTerm'--Data Communications for the Apple II." Software Review 1
(October 1982): 187-88.

VTERM

2397 SAFFADY, WILLIAM. "VTERM II." Library Technology Reports 21 (July/August 1985): 452-
56.

WILSEARCH

2398 "H. W. WILSON: Software for Direct Patron
Access to Wilson Databases." Library Hi
Tech News no. 19 (September 1985): 15-16.

2399 "WILSEARCH Software Announced." Database 8
(December 1985): 74.

Database Management Systems

ADAPT

2400 BUCKLEY, JO ANN. "Adapt." Library Software
Review 4 (July/August 1985): 237-38.

ADMINISTRATOR

2401 "WordPlus for PC, Rainbow Among Five Micro
Packages." Software Review 2 (June 1983):
121.

AUTOMATIC FILER

2402 "Database Management System for the TI 99/4A."
Software Review 2 (March 1983): 51.

BANK STREET FILER

2403 SHEROUSE, VICKI M. "Bank Street Filer." Booklist 82 (November 1, 1985): 432.

2404 OLDS, HENRY F., Jr. "Bank Street Filer." Classroom Computer Learning 6 (November/December
1985): 14-16.

CCA DATA MANAGEMENT SYSTEM

2405 SEAVEY, CHARLES A. "CCA Data Management System." RQ (Summer 1983): 413-14.

CARDFILE

2406 GEFFNER, BONNIE. "'CARDFILE'--Electronic Index
Cards." Software Review 1 (October 1982):
186.

2407 SHALETTE, ALAN. "Cardfile." Peelings II 4,
no. 2 (1983): 28-29.

2408 SAFFADY, WILLIAM. "Cardfile." Library Technology Reports 19 (September/October 1983):
461-66.

CONDOR 20

2409 SAFFADY, WILLIAM. "Condor 20." Library Tech-
      nology Reports 19 (September/October 1983):
      467-76.

D-SIRE

2410 "D-SIRE for Info Retrieval." Small Computers
      in Libraries 5 (February 1985): 4.

2411 LETTNER, LORETTA. "D-Sire (Data Research Sys-
      tem for Information Retrieval)." Library
      Journal 110 (May 1, 1985): 126; and School
      Library Journal 31 (May 1985): 156.

DB MASTER

2412 BLAIR, JOHN C., Jr. "A Tutorial in Representa-
      tive Apple Software." Database 5 (June
      1982): 72-79.

2413 BOCKMANN, FRED. "D. B. Master." Booklist 79
      (January 1, 1983): 626-27.

2414 WILLIAMS, BRIAN. "Microcomputer Based Cata-
      logs--DB Master and dBASE II." Online '83
      Conference Proceedings, Chicago, 10-12
      October 1983. Weston, CT: Online, Inc.,
      1983. Pp. 309-13.

2415 ANDERSON, ERIC S. "DB Master." Booklist 80
      (January 1, 1984): 692.

2416 ANDERSON, ERIC S. "DB Master (Version 4)."
      Booklist 80 (January 1, 1984): 690.

2417 ELLINGEN, DANA. "Advanced DB Master." Library
      Software Review 3 (March 1984): 65.

2418 TALLY, ROY. "DB Master for the Apple." Small
      Computers in Libraries 4 (March 1984): 1-3.

2419 FOX, KATHLEEN. "DB Master." Library Software
      Review 3 (September 1984): 351-54.

2420 ANDERSON, ERIC S. "DB Master 4 Plus." Booklist 81 (January 1, 1985): 655.

2421 ANDERSON, ERIC S. "DB Master 4 Plus." Booklist 81 (January 1, 1985): 661.

DATA BASE MANAGER II--THE INTEGRATOR

2422 "Software for PC Integrates Spreadsheet, WP
Programs." Software Review 2 (September
1983): 198-99.

2423 SAFFADY, WILLIAM. "Data Base Manager II--The
Integrator." Library Technology Reports 20
(July/August 1984): 552-59.

DATA DESIGN

2424 GEFFNER, BONNIE. "'DATA DESIGN'--Database Manager for the IBM Personal Computer." Software Review 1 (October 1982): 182.

2425 "Insoft Has Released DATA DESIGN." Educational
Computer 3 (July/August 1983): 44.

2426 ELLINGEN, DANA. "Data Design." Library Software Review 3 (March 1984): 65.

2427 SAFFADY, WILLIAM. "Data Design." Library
Technology Reports 20 (July/August 1984):
560-66.

DATA FACTORY

2428 FOX, KATHLEEN. "Data Factory." Library Software Review 3 (September 1984): 354-55.

DATA REPORTER

2429 FOX, KATHLEEN. "Data Reporter." Library
Software Review 3 (September 1984): 355.

DATABANK

2430 GEFFNER, BONNIE. "'DATABANK'--CP/M Based In-

formation Filing and Processing." <u>Software
Review</u> 1 (October 1982): 185.

DATADEX

2431 "Data Base Management Systems from IUS." <u>Soft-
ware Review</u> 2 (September 1983): 203.

DATAEASE

2432 SHEPHERD, CLAYTON A. "Dataease." <u>Library Software Review</u> 4 (March/April 1985): 99-101.

DATAFAX

2433 "Datafax." <u>Software Review</u> 2 (June 1983): 122.

2434 SAFFADY, WILLIAM. "Datafax." <u>Library Technology Reports</u> 20 (July/August 1984): 567-72.

DATAFILER

2435 MOORE, CATHY. "DataFiler." <u>Library Software
Review</u> 4 (May/June 1985): 164-67.

DATAFLEX

2436 SAFFADY, WILLIAM. "Dataflex." <u>Library Technology Reports</u> 19 (September/October 1983):
477-84.

DATAMANAGER

2437 "Micro-Based Data Entry Software Introduced."
<u>Information Retrieval and Library Automation</u>
20 (August 1984): 7.

dBASE

2438 "dBASE II in Libraries." <u>Small Computers in
Libraries</u> 2 (June 1982): 1.

2439 JOLLY, JOHN. "dBASE II at Glendora (Ca.)
Public Library." <u>Small Computers in
Libraries</u> 3 (February 1983): 1.

2440 CHAN, ANNA. "dBASE II in a Small Library."
Small Computers in Libraries 3 (August
1983): 4-5.

2441 SAFFADY, WILLIAM. "dBASE II." Library Technology Reports 19 (September/October 1983):
485-95.

2442 WILLIAMS, BRIAN. "Microcomputer Based Cat-
alogs--DB Master and dBASE II." Online '83
Conference Proceedings, Chicago, 10-12 October 1983. Weston, CT: Online, Inc., 1983.
Pp. 309-13.

2443 GORDON, HELEN A. "dBase II Now Multi-User."
Online 8 (July 1984): 94.

2444 GORDON, HELEN A. "dBase III Announced."
Online 8 (September 1984): 104.

2445 RADIKIAN, RANDOLPH. "dBASE II in Libraries."
Library Software Review 3 (December 1984):
521-26.

2446 SULLIVAN, JEANETTE. "Using dBASE II for Bibliographic Files." Online 9 (January 1985):
46-51.

2447 BEISER, KARL. "Feature Software Review: dBASE
II." Library Software Review 4 (March/April
1985): 82-89.

EASYDATA

2448 GEFFNER, BONNIE. "'EASYTEXT' and 'EASYDATA'--
Word Processing and Database Management
Software for the IBM Personal Computer."
Software Review 1 (October 1982): 183-84.

EASYFILER

2449 "Data Base Management Systems from IUS."
Software Review 2 (September 1983): 203.

FYI 3000

2450 McCLEARY, HUNTER. "FYI 3000: The Unconventional Database Management Program." Database 7 (December 1984): 49-53.

2451 STEWART, LINDA GUYOTTE; CURTIS, HOWARD; and MARKIEWICZ, JIM. "Feature Software Review: FYI 3000." Library Software Review 4 (May/June 1985): 154-59.

FAMULUS

2452 BATTY, DAVID. "FAMULUS: A Successful File Management System Reviewed." The Information Community: An Alliance for Progress. Proceedings of the 44th ASIS Annual Meeting. White Plains, NY: Knowledge Industry Publications, 1981, v. 18. Pp. 235-36.

FAST FACTS

2453 SAFFADY, WILLIAM. "Fast Facts." Library Technology Reports 20 (July/August 1984): 573-78.

FILEMANAGER +

2454 SAFFADY, WILLIAM. "Filemanager +." Library Technology Reports 19 (September/October 1983): 496-500.

FINDER

2455 "FINDER: A New Retrieval System." Small Computers in Libraries 4 (May 1984): 4.

2456 "Database." Library Software Review 3 (June 1984): 253-54.

2457 "Full Text Database System for Micros." Online Review 8 (June 1984): 198-99; and Electronic Library 2 (July 1984): 144-45.

2458 LUNDEEN, GERALD, and TENOPIR, CAROL. "Microcomputer-Based Library Catalog Software." Microcomputers for Information Management 1 (September 1984): 215-28.

2459 "Data Base Software for Micros." Library Systems Newsletter 5 (January 1985): 6-7.

2460 AARON, ROBERT, and SMITH, JUDITH ANN. "FINDER, FINDERlink and Search Companion: Software for Uploading and Downloading (Abstract)." Downloading/Uploading Online Databases and Catalogs. Proceedings of the Congress for Librarians, St. John's University, Jamaica, New York, 18 February 1985. Library Hi Tech Special Studies Series, no. 1. Ann Arbor, MI: Pierian Press, 1985. Pp. 28-29.

2461 McNAMARA, FRANCES. "MicroSystems Software Program to Offer FINDER and PBS." OCLC Newsletter no. 158 (July 1985): 8.

2462 "Finder." Electronic Library 3 (October 1985): 238.

FIRS

2463 "FIRS: A Free Text Information Retrieval System for Microcomputers." Program 16 (January 1982): 39-40.

1stBASE

2464 "Administration." Electronic Learning 4 (November/December 1984): 78.

FLEXFILE

2465 SILVERMAN, STAN. "Software Review: Flex File." Electronic Learning 1 (May/June 1982): 60.

2466 SHIRINIAN, GEORGE N. "Review: Flexfile 2.0." Small Computers in Libraries 3 (August 1983): 2-3.

FOXBASE

2467 RAUH, EDWARD M. "FoxBASE, Database Management Software 5 to 22 Times Faster than dBASE II --A Review." Online 9 (September 1985): 73-74.

FRAMEWORK

2468 GORDON, HELEN A. "Framework Announced by
     Ashton-Tate." Online 8 (July 1984): 92-94.

FREE FILER

2469 SCOTT, JAMES F. "Free Filer." Library Soft-
     ware Review 4 (May/June 1985): 167-68.

GENERAL MANAGER

2470 SAFFADY, WILLIAM. "General Manager." Library
     Technology Reports 19 (September/October
     1983): 501-06.

2471 FOX, KATHLEEN. "The General Manager." Library
     Software Review 3 (September 1984): 355-56.

GOLDEN RETRIEVER

2472 "Golden Retriever Is Not a Dog." Small Com-
     puters in Libraries 1 (April 1981): 6.

2473 "Capital Systems Group to Market CLASS Pro-
     grams." Small Computers in Libraries 2
     (March 1982): 7.

2474 GEFFNER, BONNIE. "'CLASS' Library Micro-
     computer System for the TRS-80." Software
     Review 1 (October 1982): 180-81.

2475 "Golden Retriever In a Class of Its Own."
     Electronic Library 1 (July 1983): 174-75.

2476 SAFFADY, WILLIAM. "Golden Retriever." Library
     Technology Reports 19 (September/October
     1983): 507-12.

2477 LUNDEEN, GERALD, and TENOPIR, CAROL. "Micro-
     computer-Based Library Catalog Software."
     Microcomputers for Information Management
     1 (September 1984): 215-28.

2478 CLINE, SHARON D. "The Vendor's Corner: Golden

Retriever." Library Software Review 4 (Jan-
uary/February 1985): 24-27.

INCREDIBLE JACK

2479 FOX, KATHLEEN. "The Incredible Jack." Library
      Software Review 3 (September 1984): 356.

INFOBASE

2480 "Control Data UK to Market IR Software."
      Online Review 8 (August 1984): 302.

INFOPRO

2481 "WordPlus for PC, Rainbow Among Five Micro
      Packages." Software Review 2 (June 1983):
      121.

INFOSTAR

2482 SAFFADY, WILLIAM. "Infostar." Library Tech-
      nology Reports 19 (September/October 1983):
      513-20.

2483 "Database Manager Coordinates Records." T.H.E.
      Journal: Technological Horizons in Education
      12 (April 1985): 50.

INFOTRAC

2484 "IAC Automated Literature Search System."
      Library Hi Tech News no. 13 (February 1985):
      21-22.

INMAGIC

2485 "INMAGIC." Library Systems Newsletter 1
      (August 1981): 15.

2486 GEFFNER, BONNIE. "'INMAGIC' Now Available for
      Micros." Software Review 1 (October 1982):
      178.

2487 "INMAGIC for Micros." Library Systems News-
      letter 3 (October 1983): 76.

2488 "INMAGIC for Data Base Creation and Access."
Software Review 2 (December 1983): 257.

2489 LUNDEEN, GERALD, and TENOPIR, CAROL. "Microcomputer-Based Library Catalog Software."
Microcomputers for Information Management
1 (September 1984): 215-28.

2490 "New Derivative of Inmagic Text Retrieval System." Electronic Library 3 (April 1985):
85-86.

2491 LETTNER, LORETTA. "Inmagic." Library Journal
110 (May 1, 1985): 126; and School Library
Journal 31 (May 1985): 156.

2492 BEISER, KARL. "Feature Software Review: 2,
INMAGIC." Library Software Review 4 (July/
August 1985): 229-35.

2493 LUNDEEN, GERALD, and TENOPIR, CAROL. "Microcom-
puter Software for In-House Databases. . .
Four Top Packages Under $2000." Online 9
(September 1985): 30-38.

IRMA

2494 SAFFADY, WILLIAM. "IRMA." Library Technology
Reports 19 (September/October 1983): 521-24.

JINSAM

2495 GEFFNER, BONNIE. "'JINSAM' DBMS for School Libraries." Software Review 1 (October 1982):
180.

KWIC-REF/1

2496 CATHCART, GERALD. "KWIC-REF/1 for Document
Storage and Retrieval." Electronic Library
3 (April 1985): 92-93.

LETUS A-B-C

2497 LETTNER, LORETTA. "Letus A-B-C." Library

Journal 110 (May 1, 1985): 126; and School
Library Journal 31 (May 1985): 156.

LIBRARIAN

2498 GEFFNER, BONNIE. "'The Librarian'--Information
Retrieval Package for the Apple II." Software Review 1 (October 1982): 181.

2499 "A New Librarian." Electronic Library 1 (January 1984): 10.

2500 "Librarian Version 2.0." Electronic Library 2
(July 1984): 139.

THE LIBRARY MATE

2501 "Document Indexing on the Apple." Small Computers in Libraries 2 (October 1982): 6.

2502 GARTEN, EDWARD D. "Library Mate Database Manager." Library Hi Tech 2, no. 4, issue 8
(1984): 109.

2503 GARTEN, EDWARD D. "Library Mate: Database with
Keyword Indexing." Electronic Library 2
(October 1984): 242-43.

2504 LETTNER, LORETTA. "Library Mate." Library
Journal 110 (May 1, 1985): 126; and School
Library Journal 31 (May 1985): 156.

LIST HANDLER

2505 SHEROUSE, VICKI M. "List Handler." Booklist
80 (March 1, 1984): 1004.

2506 FOX, KATHLEEN. "List Handler." Library Software Review 3 (September 1984): 356-58.

LISTMAKER

2507 GEFFNER, BONNIE. "'LISTMAKER'--List Management
for the TRS-80, Apple and Atari." Software
Review 1 (October 1982): 187.

2508 "List Management Program for Apple Computers [TRS-80 Too]." Software Review 2 (June 1983): 113-14.

2509 SHEROUSE, VICKI M. "ListMaker." Booklist 81 (September 1, 1984): 84.

MANAGER

2510 ELLINGEN, DANA. "Manager." Library Software Review 3 (March 1984): 67.

MARCON

2511 "Data Base Software for Micros." Library Systems Newsletter 5 (January 1985): 6-7.

2512 "Marcon." Electronic Library 3 (October 1985): 237-38.

MAXIMANAGER

2513 "TRS-80 Library Programs Available." Small Computers in Libraries 2 (November 1982): 7.

2514 LIVESEY, BRIAN. "Information Retrieval on a Tandy." Proceedings of the 6th International Online Information Meeting, London, 7-9 December 1982. Medford, NJ: Learned Information, 1982. Pp. 255-62.

MICRO-CAIRS

2515 "Micro-Cairs Information Management Software." Electronic Library 2 (July 1984): 139.

2516 SABOE, MICHAEL S. "CAIRS--An Information Retrieval System for Any Organization." Online '84 Conference Proceedings, San Francisco, 29-31 October 1984. Weston, CT: Online, Inc., 1984. Pp. 212-18.

2517 LUNDEEN, GERALD, and TENOPIR, CAROL. "Microcomputer Software for In-House Databases. . . Four Top Packages Under $2000." Online 9 (September 1985): 30-38.

MICRORIM

2518 "Transportable DBMS for IBM PC." Software
     Review 2 (June 1983): 115.

MIDOC

2519 KOWARSKI, IRENE, and MICHAUX, CHRISTIAN.
     "MIDOC: A Microcomputer System for the
     Management of Structured Documents." Infor-
     mation Processing '83. Proceedings of the
     International Federation for Information
     Processing 9th World Computer Conference,
     Paris, 19-23 September 1983. New York:
     North-Holland, 1983. Pp. 567-72.

2520 "'User-Friendly' Document Management System for
     Microcomputers." Information Retrieval and
     Library Automation 19 (March 1984): 8.

MIKRO POLYDOC

2521 "Mikro Polydoc." Electronic Library 1 (April
     1983): 91-92; and On-Line Review 7 (April
     1983): 83.

2522 "Samsom Provides Software for Own Databank Con-
     struction." Online Review 7 (October 1983):
     375-76.

MIRABILIS

2523 "Samson Provides Software for Own Databank Con-
     struction." Online Review 7 (October 1983):
     375-76.

MOLLI

2524 "More Automation Options for Micros." Library
     Systems Newsletter 5 (September 1985): 67-
     69.

NOTEBOOK

2525 JUDY, JOSEPH R. "Four for Text Handling: Note-
     book, IBR, Bibliography, Footnote." Online
     Review 8 (October 1984): 427-30.

2526 "Database Manager is Text Oriented." T.H.E.
      Journal: Technological Horizons in Education
      12 (March 1985): 47.

2527 "Worth Noting: TECH Takes a Look at Notebook
      II." Technicalities 5 (July 1985): 13.

NUTSHELL

2528 "Information Mangement Systems: Nutshell."
      Electronic Library 3 (October 1985): 237.

OFFICE FILER

2529 SAFFADY, WILLIAM. "Office Filer." Library
      Technology Reports 19 (September/October
      1983): 534-39.

OMNIS

2530 "Database Designed for Macintosh Use." T.H.E.
      Journal: Technological Horizons in Education
      12 (June 1985): 36.

PC-FILE

2531 "Free/Cheap IBM PC Programs." Small Computers
      in Libraries 3 (September 1983): 7.

2532 "New LIS/PX Disk Available--PC-FILE 9.1."
      Small Computers in Libraries 3 (December
      1983): 2.

2533 "PC-FILE Data Base System--Review." Small Com-
      puters in Libraries 3 (December 1983): 2-3.

2534 POST, RICHARD. "Selected Shareware for
      Library-Media Administrative Applications."
      Ohio Media Spectrum 36 (Winter 1984/1985):
      12-15.

2535 MICHELS, FREDRICK; HARRISON, NEIL; and SMITH,
      DOUGLAS. "User-Supported Software for the
      IBM PC." Library Hi Tech 3, no. 2, issue
      10 (1985): 97-106.

2536 PHILLIPS, BRIAN. "'Shareware'. . .Make It Your
First Software Purchase." Online 9 (May
1985): 33-36.

2537 SHIRINIAN, GEORGE N. "PC-File III." Library
Software Review 4 (July/August 1985): 238-
40.

PDQ

2538 "PDQ Released." Software Review 2 (March
1983): 53.

PFS: FILE and REPORT

2539 SAFFADY, WILLIAM. "PFS: FILE and REPORT."
Library Technology Reports 19 (September/
October 1983): 540-47.

2540 SKAPURA, ROBERT. "PFS: File/PFS: Report."
Booklist 80 (January 1, 1984): 692.

2541 CROSSFIELD, NANCY L. "PFS and PFS Report:
Adaptable Library Tools." Small Computers
in Libraries 4 (April 1984): 1-2.

2542 FOX, KATHLEEN. "PFS: File and PFS: Report."
Library Software Review 3 (September 1984):
358-61.

2543 BARALOTO, R. ANTHONY. "Scholastic PFS: FILE
and Life Science Data Bases." Electronic
Learning 5 (November/December 1985): 56-57.

PERSONAL DATA BASE

2544 SAFFADY, WILLIAM. "Personal Data Base."
Library Technology Reports 19 (September/
October 1983): 548-53.

PHI BETA FILER

2545 KLAWITTER, PAMELA AMICK. "Phi Beta Filer."
Classroom Computer Learning 5 (September
1984): 16-17.

PLEASE

2546　STURR, NATALIE. "Please." Library Software
　　　　Review 4 (May/June 1985): 168-71.

POWER-BASE

2547　MASON, ROBERT M. "Database Management Soft-
　　　　ware." Library Journal 110 (November 15,
　　　　1985): 64-65.

PRACTIBASE

2548　GORDON, HELEN A. "PractiBase for IBM PCs and
　　　　Compatibles." Online 9 (September 1985):
　　　　106.

QBASE

2549　SAFFADY, WILLIAM. "QBase." Library Technology
　　　　Reports 20 (July/August 1984): 585-94.

QUESTEXT III

2550　SAFFADY, WILLIAM. "Questext III." Library
　　　　Technology Reports 19 (September/October
　　　　1983): 554-59.

2551　"Questext III." Online Review 8 (June 1984):
　　　　199.

QUICK-SEARCH LIBRARIAN

2552　"Quick-Search Librarian." Software Review 2
　　　　(June 1983): 125.

2553　BETTS, FRANCIS M., III. "Quick Search Librar-
　　　　ian Fast but Frustrating." Electronic
　　　　Library 2 (July 1984): 153-55.

2554　LETTNER, LORETTA. "Quick-Search Librarian."
　　　　Library Journal 110 (May 1, 1985): 126-127;
　　　　and School Library Journal 31 (May 1985):
　　　　156-57.

QUICKFILE

2555 "Quickfiling Apple." Software Review 2
(December 1983): 270-71.

R: BASE

2556 SAFFADY, WILLIAM. "R: BASE SERIES 4000."
Library Technology Reports 20 (July/August
1984): 595-601.

2557 MASON, ROBERT M. "Database Management Software." Library Journal 110 (November 15,
1985): 64-65.

REFLEX

2558 MASON, ROBERT M. "Choosing Spreadsheet & Database Management Software." Library Journal
110 (October 15, 1985): 54-55.

reQUEST

2559 "Database Management." Library Software Review
3 (March 1984): 99.

2560 "Database Management." Library Software Review
3 (September 1984): 434-36.

REVELATION

2561 MASON, ROBERT M. "Database Management Software." Library Journal 110 (November 15,
1985): 64-65.

SAPANA: CARDFILE

2562 "SAPANA: CARDFILE Program Available for IBM."
Small Computers in Libraries 4 (May 1984):
5.

2563 FORCE, RON. "Sapana: Cardfile." Library Software Review 4 (July/August 1985): 240-42.

SAVVY PC

2564 SAFFADY, WILLIAM. "Savvy." Library Technology
Reports 20 (July/August 1984): 602-08.

2565 SHEPHERD, CLAYTON A. "SAVVY PC." Library
Software Review 4 (July/August 1985): 242-
45.

SEARCHLIT

2566 "SearchLit Retrieval Program Offered." Small
Computers in Libraries 4 (January 1984): 3.

2567 "Searchlit (Version 2.0): A Literature Filing
System for the IMB-PC." Electronic Library
2 (July 1984): 141.

SEEK

2568 KESNER, RICHARD M. "Seek: A Database Manager,
Information Retrieval Software." American
Archivist 46 (Fall 1983): 475-76.

SEEKEASY

2569 VOGT, SJOERD. "Seekeasy." Electronic Library
2 (October 1984): 237-38.

SELECTOR

2570 SAFFADY, WILLIAM. "Selector." Library Technology Reports 19 (September/October 1983):
560-69.

SIRE

2571 KOLL, MATTHEW B.; NOREAULT, TERRY; and McGILL,
MICHAEL J. "Enhanced Retrieval Techniques
on a Microcomputer." Proceedings of the 5th
National Online Meeting, New York, 10-12
April 1984. Medford, NJ: Learned Informa-
tion, 1984. Pp. 165-70.

2572 "SIRE--Advanced Information Retrieval for
Micros." Information Technology and Libraries 3 (December 1984): 421.

2573 SEIDEN, PEGGY, and KIBBEY MARK. "Information
Retrieval Systems for Microcomputers."
Library Hi Tech 3, no. 1, issue 9 (1985):
41-54.

2574 "Data Base Software for Micros." Library
Systems Newsletter 5 (January 1985): 6-7.

2575 LETTNER, LORETTA. "Sire." Library Journal 110
(May 1, 1985): 127; and School Library
Journal 31 (May 1985): 157.

2576 GORDON, HELEN A. "SIRE for Bibliographic
Retrieval Available." Database 8 (June
1985): 70.

2577 LUNDEEN, GERALD, and TENOPIR, CAROL. "Microcom-
puter Software for In-House Databases. . .
Four Top Packages Under $2000." Online 9
(September 1985): 30-38.

2578 PORTOGHESE, CHRISTINE P., and SCHRADER, DAVID
B. "SIRE: Information Storage and Searching." Electronic Library 3 (December 1985):
314-16.

STATUS

2579 "Status of Status." Electronic Library 3
(January 1985): 17; and Online Review 9
(February 1985): 34.

2580 KISSEL, RICH. "STATUS: Free Text Retrieval."
Electronic Library 3 (July 1985): 172-73;
and Online Review 9 (August 1985): 287-
88.

2581 PRINCE, E. TED. "Comments from the Producers
of STATUS: Free Text Retrieval." Electronic
Library 3 (July 1985): 173-74.

2582 PRINCE, E. TED. "Comments from the North American Distributors of STATUS: Free Text
Retrieval." Online 9 (August 1985): 288-
89.

SUPERBASE 64

2583 SMITH, DAVID FAY. "Superbase 64." Publishers
Weekly 226 (August 24, 1984): 43.

SUPERFILE

2584 "Superfile for Indexing--A Review." Small
Computers in Libraries 2 (December 1982):
4-6.

2585 SAFFADY, WILLIAM. "Superfile." Library Technology Reports 19 (September/October 1983):
570-76.

T.I.M. III

2586 SAFFADY, WILLIAM. "T.I.M. III." Library Technology Reports 19 (September/October 1983):
577-84.

TOTL. INFOMASTER

2587 "Database." Library Software Review 3 (June
1984): 253-54.

TRAKKER

2588 ELLINGEN, DANA. "Trakker." Library Software
Review 3 (March 1984): 67.

ULTRAFILE

2589 YERKEY, NEIL A. "Ultrafile for Predefined
Data." Electronic Library 2 (October 1984):
233-36.

VISIDEX

2590 KENDALL, DAVID. "Keys to In-House Information." Small Computers in Libraries 2
(August 1982): 1-2.

2591 GEFFNER, BONNIE. "Electronic Filing--Elec-
tronic Index Cards VisiFile and VisiDex for

the Apple II." Software Review 1 (October
1982): 185-86.

VISIFILE

2592 GEFFNER, BONNIE. "Electronic Filing--Elec-
tronic Index Cards VisiFile and VisiDex for
the Apple II." Software Review 1 (October
1982): 185-86.

2593 SAFFADY, WILLIAM. "Visifile." Library Technology Reports 19 (September/October 1984):
585-92.

ZYINDEX

2594 ELLINGEN, DANA. "ZyIndex." Library Software
Review 3 (March 1984): 68.

2595 SEIDEN, PEGGY, and KIBBEY, MARK. "Information
Retrieval Systems for Microcomputers."
Library Hi Tech 3, no. 1, issue 9 (1985):
41-54.

2596 PORTOGHESE, CHRISTINE P., and SCHRADER, DAVID
B. "ZyINDEX: A Powerful Indexing & Searching Package." Electronic Library 3 (January
1985): 30-33.

2597 WILLIAMS, WENDY S. "Comments from the Producers of ZyINDEX." Electronic Library 3
(January 1985): 33-34.

2598 "ZyLAB: Expanded File Capacities for ZyINDEX."
Library Hi Tech News no. 14 (March 1985):
16.

2599 HOLLAND, MAURITA PETERSON. "ZyINDEX: Full Text
Retrieval Power." Online 9 (July 1985): 38-
42.

2600 GORDON, HELEN A. "ZyIndex Plus Announced."
Database 8 (August 1985): 87.

Dictionaries

BANK STREET SPELLER

2601   CAREY, DORIS. "Bank Street Speller." Computing Teacher 12 (December 1984/January 1985): 31-32.

CORRECTSTAR

2602   "Spelling Corrector for WordStar Users." T.H.E. Journal: Technological Horizons in Education 12 (November 1984): 81.

2603   BEISER, KARL. "MicroPro Axes Program." Small Computers in Libraries 5 (December 1985): 7-10.

DICTIONARY

2604   SKAPURA, ROBERT, and ANDERSON, ERIC S. "Dictionary." Booklist 80 (January 1, 1984): 692.

THE DICTIONARY

2605   ANDERSON, ERIC S. "The Dictionary." Booklist 80 (November 1, 1983): 437.

HAYDEN: SPELLER

2606   BRANNIGAN, PATRICK. "Spelling Checker: Hayden: Speller." Library Software Review 4 (September/October 1985): 314-15.

MAGIC WORDS

2607   "Magic Words." Software Review 2 (June 1983): 123.

PFS: PROOF

2608   "PFS:PROOF." School Library Journal 31 (December 1984): 52.

SENSIBLE SPELLER

2609 GEFFNER, BONNIE. "'SENSIBLE SPELLER'--Spelling
      Verification." Software Review 1 (October
      1982): 184.

2610 SKAPURA, ROBERT. "Sensible Speller." Booklist
      80 (January 1, 1984): 692.

2611 SMITH, DAVID FAY. "Sensible Speller for Pro-
      DOS." Publishers Weekly 226 (August 24,
      1984): 41, 43.

2612 DEWEY, PATRICK R. "Fewer Misteaks." Wilson
      Library Bulletin 59 (December 1984): 286.

2613 SHEROUSE, VICKI M. "Sensible Speller IV."
      Booklist 81 (April 1, 1985): 1132.

SPELLER

2614 "Language Arts." Library Software Review 3
      (June 1984): 271-73.

SPELLING PROOFREADER

2615 "SPELLING PROOFREADER." Software Review 2
      (June 1983): 124.

TOTL.SPELLER

2616 "Word Processing." Library Software Review 3
      (March 1984): 114-16.

VISISPELL

2617 "Word Processing for IBM PC." Software Review
      2 (June 1983): 117-18.

WEBSTER'S NEW WORLD SPELLING CHECKER

2618 "Spelling Checked for 40,000 Words." T.H.E.
      Journal: Technological Horizons in Education
      12 (January 1985): 47.

Graphics

APPLE II BUSINESS GRAPHICS

2619 "Apple II Business Graphics." Software Review
2 (June 1983): 122.

dGRAPH

2620 "dBase II Graphics." Software Review 2 (September 1983): 200.

DR. CAT GRAPHIX DISK

2621 "Public Domain Apple Graphics Routines." Software Review 2 (June 1983): 121-22.

EP-PLOT

2622 "Graphics." Library Software Review 3 (June 1984): 260-62.

ENHANCED BUSINESS GRAPHICS

2623 "Graphics Package Converts Spreadsheet Data." Software Review 2 (September 1983): 201.

FAST GRAPHS

2624 SAFFADY, WILLIAM. "FAST GRAPHS." Library Technology Reports 20 (July/August 1984): 547-50.

GRAPH 'N' CALC

2625 "Graph 'N' Calc." Software Review 2 (September 1983): 202.

GRAPHICS GENERATOR

2626 "Graphics Generator." Software Review 2 (June 1983): 125.

GRAPHICS MAGICIAN

2627 CALLAMARAS, PETER V. "The Graphics Magician."
      Software Review 2 (March 1983): 10-13.

GRAPHMASTER

2628 "Graphmaster." School Library Journal 31
      (March 1985): 130.

GRAPHTRIX

2629 "Graphics." Library Software Review 3 (March
      1984): 100-01.

INFOGRAPH 100

2630 "Graphics." Library Software Review 3 (June
      1984): 260-62.

MACDRAW

2631 JOHNSON, HARRIETT, and JOHNSON, RICHARD D.
      "Enter MacDraw." Small Computers in Li-
      braries 5 (December 1985): 18-22.

MIRRORGRAPH

2632 "Graphics Package for IBM PC." Software Review
      2 (September 1983): 202.

PC-GRAPH

2633 "'Shareware' Software Gaining." Small Com-
      puters in Libraries 5 (March 1985): 4.

PC PICTURE GRAPHICS SYSTEM

2634 POST, RICHARD. "Selected Shareware for Library-
      Media Administrative Applications." Ohio
      Media Spectrum 36 (Winter 1984/1985): 12-15.

PICTURE PERFECT

2635 GEREN, PHYLLIS. "Picture Perfect." Booklist
      81 (July 1985): 1583.

THE PRINT SHOP

2636 DEWEY, PATRICK R. "Software for Libraries."
Wilson Library Bulletin 59 (January 1985):
352.

2637 EVERHART, NANCY, and HARTZ, CLAIRE. "Creating
Graphics with 'The Print Shop'." Library
Journal 110 (May 1, 1985): 118-20; and
School Library Journal 31 (May 1985): 148-
50.

2638 GEREN, PHYLLIS. "The Print Shop." Booklist
81 (June 1985): 1583.

2639 "Printing Program Adds New Features." T.H.E.
Journal: Technological Horizons in Education
13 (October 1985): 52.

VCN EXECUVISION

2640 ELLINGEN, DANA. "VCN ExecuVision." Library
Software Review 3 (March 1984): 68.

VISIPLOT

2641 BLAIR, JOHN C., Jr. "A Tutorial in Representative Apple Software." Database 5 (June
1982): 72-79.

Indexing

ANSWER

2642 ANDERSON, CHARLES. "ANSWER: An 'Off-the-Shelf'
Program for Computer-Aided Indexing."
Indexer 13 (October 1983): 236-38.

AUTHEX

2643 "An Indexing System with Authority File."
American Libraries 16 (May 1985): 350.

2644 HARTER, STEPHEN P. "Printed Index Production."
Online Review 9 (December 1985): 451-53.

2645 DEWEY, PATRICK R. "Periodical Indexing System." Wilson Library Bulletin 60 (December
1985): 58-59.

BNS COMPUTER-ASSISTED INDEXING PROGRAM

2646 FETTERS, LINDA K. "A Guide to Seven Indexing
Programs. . .Plus a Review of the 'Profes-
sional Bibliographic System'." Database 8
(December 1985): 31-38.

BOOKDEX

2647 "Book and Newspaper Index Programs Available."
Small Computers in Libraries 2 (January
1982): 3.

2648 "New Microcomputer Software for Libraries."
Electronic Library 1 (January 1983): 9.

2649 "Indexing Software for Micros." Online Review
8 (August 1984): 301; and Electronic Library
2 (October 1984): 222.

2650 "Microcomputer Software for Libraries." Information Technology and Libraries 3 (September
1984): 311.

2651 FETTERS, LINDA K. "A Guide to Seven Indexing
      Programs. . .Plus a Review of the 'Profes-
      sional Bibliographic System'." Database 8
      (December 1985): 31-38.

FOXON-MADDOCKS INDEX PREPARATION SYSTEM

2652 FETTERS, LINDA K. "A Guide to Seven Indexing
      Programs. . .Plus a Review of the 'Profes-
      sional Bibliographic System'." Database 8
      (December 1985): 31-38.

THE INDEX EDITOR

2653 FETTERS, LINDA K. "A Guide to Seven Indexing
      Programs. . .Plus a Review of the 'Profes-
      sional Bibliographic System'." Database 8
      (December 1985): 31-38.

INDEX PLUS

2654 "Personal Bibliographic Software Announces
      Three New Products." Electronic Library 3
      (July 1985): 158.

INDEX PREPARATION SYSTEM

2655 FETTERS, LINDA K. "A Guide to Seven Indexing
      Programs. . .Plus a Review of the 'Profes-
      sional Bibliographic System'." Database 8
      (December 1985): 31-38.

INDIX

2656 VEANER, ALLEN B., and KLEMENT, SUSAN P. "Indix:
      Index-Making for Computer-Wise Users."
      Electronic Library 3 (April 1985): 94-98.

ININDEX

2657 FETTERS, LINDA K. "A Guide to Seven Indexing
      Programs. . .Plus a Review of the 'Profes-
      sional Bibliographic System'." Database 8
      (December 1985): 31-38.

MACINDEX

2658 "Boston Software Publishers: Software for Mac-
      intosh." Library Hi Tech News no. 20 (Octo-
      ber 1985): 16-17.

MACREX

2659 FETTERS, LINDA K. "A Guide to Seven Indexing
      Programs. . .Plus a Review of the 'Profes-
      sional Bibliographic System'." Database 8
      (December 1985): 31-38.

MICREX

2660 FETTERS, LINDA K. "A Guide to Seven Indexing
      Programs. . .Plus a Review of the 'Profes-
      sional Bibliographic System'." Database 8
      (December 1985): 31-38.

MICRO INDEXING SYSTEM

2661 FETTERS, LINDA K. "A Guide to Seven Indexing
      Programs. . .Plus a Review of the 'Profes-
      sional Bibliographic System'." Database 8
      (December 1985): 31-38.

NEWSDEX

2662 "Book and Newspaper Index Programs Available."
      Small Computers in Libraries 2 (January
      1982): 3.

2663 "New Microcomputer Software for Libraries."
      Electronic Library 1 (January 1983): 9.

2664 "Indexing Software for Micros." Online Review
      8 (August 1984): 301; and Electronic Library
      2 (October 1984): 222.

2665 "Microcomputer Software for Libraries." Infor-
      mation Technology and Libraries 3 (September
      1984): 311.

2666 FETTERS, LINDA K. "A Guide to Seven Indexing

Programs. . .Plus a Review of the 'Professional Bibliographic System'." <u>Database</u> 8 (December 1985): 31-38.

POPPYTIME INDEX BUILD

2667 "Poppytime Index Build System." <u>Electronic Library</u> 2 (July 1984): 140-41.

TAPIT: APPLE PERIODICALS

2668 SHEROUSE, VICKI M. "TAPIT: Apple Periodicals." <u>Booklist</u> 81 (June 1, 1985): 1415.

ADLIB2

2669 "Launch of ADLIB2 on Unix." Electronic Library
      3 (January 1985): 19.

ADVANCE

2670 "Advanced Library Concepts." Small Computers
      in Libraries 5 (February 1985): 3.

AMERICANA SOFTWARE LIBRARY

2671 ANDERSON, ERIC S. "Americana Software
      Library." Booklist 82 (October 1, 1985):
      282.

APPLEWORKS

2672 ANDERSON, ERIC S. "The Library Works." Book
      Report 3 (September/October 1984): 28, 67.

2673 TURNER, JACK. "AppleWorks." Computing Teacher
      12 (October 1984): 34-35.

2674 ANDERSON, ERIC S. "Appleworks." Booklist 81
      (January 1, 1985): 652.

2675 ANDERSON, ERIC S. "Appleworks." Booklist 81
      (January 1, 1985): 661.

2676 OLDS, HENRY F., Jr. "AppleWorks." Classroom
      Computer Learning 6 (September 1985): 33-34.

AURA

2677 "AURA DBMS Takes New Approach." Software
      Review 2 (December 1983): 278-79.

AUTOLIB

2678 LETTNER, LORETTA. "Autolib." Library Journal

110 (May 1, 1985): 126; and School Library Journal 31 (May 1985): 156.

AUTOMATED LIBRARY SYSTEM

2679 "Micro-Based Automated Library System for Schools." Software Review 2 (September 1983): 192-93.

2680 LETTNER, LORETTA. "Automated Library System (ALS)." Library Journal 110 (May 1, 1985): 129; and School Library Journal 31 (May 1985): 159.

BOOK TRAK

2681 McQUEEN, JUDY, and BOSS, RICHARD W. "Book Trak." Library Technology Reports 20 (March/April 1984): 134.

2682 "Book Trak." School Library Journal 31 (November 1984): 85.

BOOKSHELF

2683 "BOOKSHELF: An Integrated, Modular Package for the Smaller Library." Vine no. 54 (June 1984): 37-38.

2684 "BookshelF for Library Automation." Electronic Library 3 (April 1985): 87.

CARD DATALOG

2685 "Card Datalog Adds Acquisitions Capabilities." Library Systems Newsletter 2 (October 1982): 80.

2686 "Data Trek Inc's New Dimension in Microcomputer Software." Electronic Library 1 (July 1983): 176-77.

2687 McQUEEN, JUDY, and BOSS, RICHARD W. "Card Datalog." Library Technology Reports 20 (March/April 1984): 134-36.

2688 LUNDEEN, GERALD, and TENOPIR, CAROL. "Microcomputer-Based Library Catalog Software."
Microcomputers for Information Management
1 (September 1984): 215-28.

2689 LETTNER, LORETTA. "Card Datalog Library
System." Library Journal 110 (May 1, 1985):
129; and School Library Journal 31 (May
1985): 159.

CONCORD

2690 "Concord: A Free-Text Retrieval System for the
Apricot/IBM Range." Online Review 9 (June
1985): 190.

HEAD COMPUTERS INTEGRATED SYSTEM

2691 "A Complete Practical Library System for
£4000." Electronic Library 3 (January
1985): 18.

KNOWLEDGEMAN

2692 "Knowledge Manager." Software Review 2
(September 1983): 202.

2693 SAFFADY, WILLIAM. "KNOWLEDGEMAN." Library
Technology Reports 20 (July/August 1984):
460-70.

2694 "Lan Version of KnowledgeMan Available."
Electronic Library 3 (July 1985): 160-
61.

LIBRARIAN: LIACQUIRE, LICAT, LICIRCULATE & LISERIAL

2695 "LIBRARIAN Option for Library Automation."
Library Systems Newsletter 5 (January
1985): 5-6.

2696 LETTNER, LORETTA. "Librarian: LiAcquire,
LiCat, LiCirculate, & LiSerial." Library
Journal 110 (May 1, 1985): 129; and School
Library Journal 31 (May 1985): 159.

LIBRARY INFORMATION SYSTEM

2697　"Georgetown University Medical Center's Library
　　　Information System." Software Review 2
　　　(December 1983): 260-64.

MICROLIBRARY

2698　"Mini Functionality on a Micro." Electronic
　　　Library 3 (April 1985): 87.

2699　PEGG, NIGEL. "Micro Library: An Integrated
　　　System for Small to Medium Sized Libraries."
　　　Vine no. 59 (July 1985): 26-34.

MICROMARC

2700　DUE, STEPHEN C. "MICROMARC: The Microcomputer
　　　in a School Library." Australian School
　　　Librarian 19 (September 1982): 100-01.

2701　"Australian Writes School Library Software
　　　Package." Australian Library News (December
　　　1982): 2.

2702　"School Library Micro System Developed by Aus-
　　　tralian." Library Journal 108 (July 1983):
　　　1306.

MIDWEST AUTOMATED TECHNICAL SERVICES SOFTWARE

2703　LETTNER, LORETTA. "Midwest Automated Technical
　　　Services Software." Library Journal 110
　　　(May 1, 1985): 130; and School Library
　　　Journal 31 (May 1985): 160.

MIST

2704　"Microcomputer Information Support Tools."
　　　Online Review 8 (June 1984): 197; and
　　　Electronic Library 2 (July 1984): 143-44.

OCELOT LIBRARY SYSTEM

2705　BALL, ALAN J. S. "The Vendor's Corner: The

Ocelot Library System." Library Software
Review 3 (December 1984): 538-46.

PC-DESK

2706 "Freeware//PC-DESK." M300 and PC Report 2 (May
      1985): 6.

PC/FOCUS

2707 "Database Management." Library Software Review
      3 (September 1984): 434-36.

PROJECT VIKING

2708 "UNIX for IBM PC." Software Review 2 (June
      1983): 120-21.

RICHMOND LIBRARY MANAGEMENT SYSTEM

2709 "'Dream' Library Management May Be Reality."
      Electronic Education 2 (February 1983): 27.

2710 "Richmond Library Management System." Elec-
      tronic Learning 2 (March 1983): 88.

SCHOOL LIBRARY MANAGEMENT SYSTEM

2711 LETTNER, LORETTA. "School Library Management
      System." Library Journal 110 (May 1, 1985):
      130; and School Library Journal 31 (May
      1985): 160.

SCRIBE LIBRARY SYSTEM

2712 LETTNER, LORETTA. "Scribe Library System."
      Library Journal 110 (May 1, 1985): 130; and
      School Library Journal 31 (May 1985): 160.

STAR

2713 CUADRA, RUTH LANDAU. "A Case Study--Use of the
      Star Microcomputer Data Entry and Retrieval
      System." Proceedings of the 2nd National
      Online Meeting, New York, 24-26 March 1981.

Medford, NJ: Learned Information, 1981.
Pp. 159-60.

2714 "Cuadra Assocs Announce Full IR System." Small Computers in Libraries 1 (May 1981): 6.

2715 CUADRA, NEIL G. "STAR: A Microcomputer System for Data Entry, Retrieval, and Publication Support." Electronic Publishing Review 1, no. 2 (1981): 131-38.

2716 "Database Management." Library Software Review 3 (March 1984): 99.

2717 LUNDEEN, GERALD, and TENOPIR, CAROL. "Microcomputer-Based Library Catalog Software." Microcomputers for Information Management 1 (September 1984): 215-28.

2718 "Data Base Software for Micros." Library Systems Newsletter 5 (January 1985): 6-7.

2719 "Cats or Dogs or Pigs or Cows or Chickens or Elephants." Information Retrieval and Library Automation 20 (March 1985): 4-5.

2720 LETTNER, LORETTA. "Star." Library Journal 110 (May 1, 1985): 130; and School Library Journal 31 (May 1985): 160.

SYSTEM 23

2721 "CLSI Micro-Based System 23 Now Installed in 13 Libraries." Library Journal 108 (December 15, 1983): 2286, 2288.

ULTIMATE

2722 "Seven Functions are Integrated." T.H.E. Journal: Technological Horizons in Education 12 (April 1985): 30.

UNICORN

2723 "A PC Unicorn." Library Systems Newsletter 5 (October 1985): 76.

VISION

Interlibrary Loan

A-C-C-E-S-S

2725 "Apple-Based ILL System Out." Small Computers
in Libraries 1 (May 1981): 6.

2726 LETTNER, LORETTA. "A-C-C-E-S-S." Library
Journal 110 (May 1, 1985): 126; and School
Library Journal 31 (May 1985): 156.

BOOKPATH

2727 "Micro-Based Interlibrary Loan Request System
from Colorado." Library Systems Newsletter
4 (June 1984): 46.

F.I.L.L.S.

2728 BEN-SHIR, RYA. "ILL Program for IBM PC."
Small Computers in Libraries 3 (December
1983): 4.

2729 "ILL Software for IBM-PC." Library Journal 109
(May 1, 1984): 842.

2730 BEN-SHIR, RYA. "F.I.L.L.S.: Fast Inter-Library
Loans and Statistics." American Libraries
15 (June 1984): 454.

2731 GORDON, HELEN A. "F.I.L.L.S. Software for
Interlibrary Loans." Online 8 (July 1984):
94.

2732 "More PC-Based ILL Support." Library Systems
Newsletter 4 (July 1984): 56; and Library
Systems Newsletter 4 (August 1984): 64.

2733 "Small Net Borrowers Offered New ILL Software
for IBM PCs." Library Journal 109 (August
1984): 1387.

2734 "ILL Software Package." Information Technology
and Libraries 3 (September 1984): 311.

2735 "New ILL Program Available for PC, M300."
Small Computers in Libraries 4 (October
1984): 7-8.

2736 WITTERS, MARYANNE. "Interlibrary Loans With a
Micro. . .Clean and Quick." Online 8
(November 1984): 53-57, 60-61.

2737 "F.I.L.L.S. Second Enhanced Release." Small
Computers in Libraries 4 (December 1984):
12.

2738 BROOKS, JO ANN. "F.I.L.L.S., Fast Library Loans
& Statistics." Electronic Library 3 (January 1985): 28-29.

2739 "Software Package Saves Libraries Time, Money."
Technicalities 5 (January 1985): 2.

2740 LETTNER, LORETTA. "F.I.L.L.S. 2.0 (Fast Inter
Library Loans and Statistics, 2nd Release."
Library Journal 110 (May 1, 1985): 128; and
School Library Journal 31 (May 1985): 158.

2741 BEN-SHIR, RYA. "Fast Inter Library Loans and
Statistics: The Second, Enhanced Release."
Library Software Review 4 (May/June 1985):
132-38.

2742 GORDON, HELEN A. "F.I.L.L.S. Version 2
Released." Database 8 (June 1985): 70.

2743 "MacNeal Hospital: Enhanced Inter-Library Loan
Software Includes Telecommunications Op-
tions." Library Hi Tech News no. 18 (July/
August 1985): 15.

2744 "F.I.L.L.S. Enhanced Version." M300 and PC
Report 2 (September 1985): 6.

2745 "Enhanced FILLS Software Includes Telecommunications Option." Electronic Library 3
(October 1985): 239.

2746 "Software." Wilson Library Bulletin 60 (October 1985): 77-78.

ILL FORM PRINTER

2747 "ILL Form Printer Program." Small Computers in
      Libraries 3 (October 1983): 5.

2748 "ILL Forms Printer for Apples." Small Comput-
      ers in Libraries 3 (November 1983): 7.

2749 LETTNER, LORETTA. "ILL Forms Printer." Library
      Journal 110 (May 1, 1985): 128; and School
      Library Journal 31 (May 1985): 158.

ILL3 DATAFILE

2750 "ILL3 Datafile." Small Computers in Libraries
      5 (September 1985): 23.

2751 "Expanding Your Computer: ILL3 Datafile." M300
      and PC Report 2 (November 1985): 4.

OCLC MICRO ENHANCER (INTERLIBRARY LOAN)

2752 NEVINS, KATE F. "Microcomputers and OCLC
      Access." OCLC Newsletter no. 145 (February
      1983): 5.

2753 NEVINS, KATE F. "Microcomputers and OCLC
      Access." Small Computers in Libraries 3
      (April 1983): 3.

2754 "OCLC Micro Access." American Libraries 14
      (May 1983): 326.

2755 "OCLC Micro Enhancer." Library Systems News-
      letter 3 (September 1983): 72.

2756 "OCLC Micro Enhancer Software Wins ILL Perform-
      ance Raves." Library Journal 109 (February
      15, 1984): 309.

2757 SNIDER, LARRY C. "OCLC and ME: A User's
      Evaluation of the Interlibrary Loan Micro
      Enhancer." OCLC Newsletter no. 152 (May
      1984): 6-7.

2758 "ILL Micro Enhancer Borrows Time for You, Makes You a Net Supplier of Better Service." OCLC Newsletter no. 152 (May 1984): 8.

2759 "Interlibrary Loan Micro Enhancer Now Available for IBM Personal Computers." OCLC Newsletter no. 153 (June 1984): 15.

2760 "OCLC Markets Micro Enhancer." Information Today 1 (July/August 1984): 21.

2761 "OCLC: Interlibrary Loan Micro Enhancer for IBM PC." Library Hi Tech News 1 (September 1984): 6.

2762 CAPPUZZELLO, PAUL. "Interlibrary Loan Micro Enhancer Now Available for M300 Workstations." OCLC Newsletter no. 154 (September 1984): 10.

2763 "Micro Enhancer for Inter-Library Loans." Electronic Library 2 (October 1984): 225.

2764 LETTNER, LORETTA. "OCLC Cataloging & Interlibrary Loan Micro Enhancers." Library Journal 110 (May 1, 1985): 128; and School Library Journal 31 (May 1985): 158.

2765 CAPPUZZELLO, PAUL. "Version 2 of ILL Micro Enhancer Now Available for M300 Workstations." OCLC Newsletter no. 159 (October 1985): 14.

Library Skills

ADVANCED DEWEY DECIMAL SYSTEM

2766 ROSS, JANE E. "Advanced Dewey Decimal System."
      School Library Journal 31 (November 1984):
      68.

ALMANACS

2767 FABIAN, WILLIAM M. "CALICO: Skills Programs to
      Promote Library Use." American Libraries
      15 (April 1984): 264.

2768 ROSS, JANE E. "Almanacs." School Library
      Journal 31 (November 1984): 68.

ANSWERING QUESTIONS LIBRARY STYLE

2769 SHEROUSE, VICKI M. "Answering Questions Library
      Style." Booklist 81 (September 1, 1984):
      81-82.

2770 ROSS, JANE E. "Answering Questions Library
      Style." School Library Journal 31 (November
      1984): 68-69.

2771 LETTNER, LORETTA. "Answering Questions Library
      Style." Library Journal 110 (May 1, 1985):
      124; and School Library Journal 31 (May
      1985): 154.

BARTLETT'S FAMILIAR QUOTATIONS

2772 LANKFORD, MARY D. "Bartlett's Familiar Quota-
      tions." Booklist 79 (November 1, 1982):
      389-90.

2773 FABIAN, WILLIAM M. "CALICO: Skills Programs to
      Promote Library Use." American Libraries 15
      (April 1984): 264.

2774 ROSS, JANE E. "Bartlett's Familiar Quotations."
School Library Journal 31 (November 1984):
69.

BASIC FICTION SKILLS

2775 ROSS, JANE E. "Basic Fiction Skills." School
Library Journal 31 (November 1984): 69.

BIBLIOGRAPHY

2776 ROSS, JANE E. "Bibliography." School Library
Journal 31 (November 1984): 69.

BIOGRAPHIES

2777 ROSS, JANE E. "Biographies." School Library
Journal 31 (November 1984): 69.

BOOK SHELF

2778 LANKFORD, MARY D. "Bookshelf." Booklist 79
(September 1, 1982): 58.

2779 ROSS, JANE E. "Book Shelf." School Library
Journal 31 (November 1984): 69-70.

CALL NUMBER

2780 FABIAN, WILLIAM M. "CALICO: Skills Programs to
Promote Library Use." American Libraries 15
(April 1984): 264.

2781 ROSS, JANE E. "Call Number." School Library
Journal 31 (November 1984): 70.

CARD CATALOG

2782 ROSS, JANE E. "Card Catalog." School Library
Journal 31 (November 1984): 70.

CURRENT BIOGRAPHY

2783 LANKFORD, MARY D. "Current Biography." Booklist 79 (November 1, 1982): 389-90.

548 / SOFTWARE AND SYSTEMS REVIEWS

2784 FABIAN, WILLIAM M. "CALICO: Skills Programs
to Promote Library Use." American Libraries
15 (April 1984): 264.

2785 ROSS, JANE E. "Current Biography." School
Library Journal 31 (November 1984): 70.

DICTIONARY GUIDE WORDS

2786 LANKFORD, MARY D. "Dictionary Guide Words."
Booklist 78 (October 1, 1981): 243.

2787 ROSS, JANE E. "Dictionary Guide Words."
School Library Journal 31 (November 1984):
70.

DICTIONARY SKILLS

2788 ROSS, JANE E. "Dictionary Skills." School
Library Journal 31 (November 1984): 70.

ELEMENTARY LIBRARIES

2789 DeLAURENTIIS, EMILIANO C. "Elementary Libraries." Educational Technology 22 (June
1982): 38.

ELEMENTARY LIBRARY MEDIA SKILLS

2790 ANDERSON, ERIC S. "Elementary Library Media
Skills: Level 1." Electronic Learning 3
(May 1984): 94-96.

2791 ANDERSON, ERIC S. "Elementary Library Media
Skills (ELMS)." Booklist 80 (May 1, 1984):
1263.

2792 ANDERSON, ERIC S. "Elementary Library Media
Skills." Book Report 3 (May/June 1984): 64.

2793 ROSS, JANE E. "Elementary Library Media
Skills." School Library Journal 31 (November 1984): 70.

2794 TROUTNER, JOANNE JOHNSON. "Elementary Library

Media Skills." School Library Media
Quarterly 13 (Winter 1985): 80-81.

2795 LETTNER, LORETTA. "ELMS (Elementary Library
Media Skills)." Library Journal 110 (May
1, 1985): 124; and School Library Journal
31 (May 1985): 154.

ENCYCLOPEDIA KEY WORDS

2796 ROSS, JANE E. "Encyclopedia Key Words."
School Library Journal 31 (November 1984):
70.

HOW CAN I FIND IT?

2797 TROUTNER, JOANNE JOHNSON. "How Can I Find It
If I Don't Know What I'm Looking For."
School Library Media Quarterly 14 (Fall
1985): 44.

2798 "Library Skills." Electronic Learning 5
(November/December 1985): 61-62.

HOW TO SEARCH OCLC

2799 "Program Uses Video Games to Train OCLC Users."
American Libraries 16 (November 1985): 749.

INFORMASTER

2800 "Micro 'Knowledge Explorer'." American Libraries 15 (October 1984): 656.

2801 "Informaster." School Library Journal 31
(March 1985): 130-31.

LEARNING ABOUT CATALOG CARDS

2802 ROSS, JANE E. "Learning About Catalog Cards."
School Library Journal 31 (November 1984):
70.

LEARNNG TO LOCATE BOOKS ON THE SHELF

2803 ROSS, JANE E. "Learning to Locate Books on the

Shelf." School Library Journal 31 (November 1984): 70-71.

LEARNING TO UNDERSTAND THE CARD CATALOG

2804 ROSS, JANE E. "Learning to Understand the Card Catalog." School Library Journal 31 (November 1984): 71.

LEARNING TO UNDERSTAND THE COPYRIGHT NOTICE

2805 ROSS, JANE E. "Learning to Understand the Copyright Notice." School Library Journal 31 (November 1984): 71.

LEARNING TO USE AN INDEX

2806 ROSS, JANE E. "Learning to Use an Index." School Library Journal 31 (November 1984): 71.

LEARNING TO USE THE TABLE OF CONTENTS

2807 ROSS, JANE E. "Learning to Use the Table of Contents." School Library Journal 31 (November 1984): 71.

LIBRARY CATALOG

2808 FABIAN, WILLIAM M. "CALICO: Skills Programs to Promote Library Use." American Libraries 15 (April 1984): 264.

2809 ROSS, JANE E. "Library Catalog." School Library Journal 31 (November 1984): 72.

LIBRARY IQ

2810 "Library IQ." Electronic Learning 2 (March 1983): 88.

LIBRARY/MEDIA SKILLS

2811 ANDERSON, ERIC S. "Library/Media Skills." Booklist 81 (September 1, 1984): 84.

LIBRARY SEARCH AND SOLVE

2812 LETTNER, LORETTA. "Library Search and Solve."
Library Journal 110 (May 1, 1985): 124; and
School Library Journal 31 (May 1985): 154.

2813 "Students Learn to Search Resources." T.H.E.
Journal: Technological Horizons in Education
13 (September 1985): 56.

LIBRARY SKILLS

2814 "Teaching Library Skills." Software Review 2
(June 1983): 108.

LIBRARY SKILLS

2815 BYNON, GEORGE. "Library Skills." Computing
Teacher 11 (February 1984): 33-34.

LIBRARY SKILLS

2816 SHEROUSE, VICKI M. "Library Skills." Booklist
81 (August 1985): 1683.

LIBRARY SKILLS: OVERVIEW, REFERENCE AND CLASSIFICATION

2817 ROSS, JANE E. "Library Skills." School
Library Journal 31 (November 1984): 72.

2818 LETTNER, LORETTA. "Library Skills: Overview,
Reference and Classification." Library
Journal 110 (May 1, 1985): 124; and School
Library Journal 31 (May 1985): 154.

LIBRARY SKILLS: WHAT'S THERE AND HOW TO FIND IT

2819 LATHROP, ANN. "Library Skills: What's There
and How to Find It!" Computing Teacher 8,
no. 7 (1980-81): 39-40.

2820 TURRENTINE, BONNIE. "Library Skills." School
Microware Reviews 1 (Winter 1982): 8-9.

2821 "Library Skills: What's There and How to Find

It." ACCESS: Microcomputers in Libraries 2
(January 1982): 14.

2822 "Library Skills: What's There and How to Find
It (Continuation)." ACCESS: Microcomputers
in Libraries 2 (April 1982): 2.

2823 BROWN, MARIJKE. "Library Skills." RQ 22 (Summer 1983): 414-15.

2824 ROSS, JANE E. "Library Skills: What's There
and How to Find It." School Library Journal
31 (November 1984): 72.

2825 LETTNER, LORETTA. "Library Skills." Library
Journal 110 (May 1, 1985): 124; and School
Library Journal 31 (May 1985): 154.

2826 HANDY, ALICE. "Library Skills." Book Report 4
(May/June 1985): 61.

LIBRARY TERMS

2827 LANKFORD, MARY D. "Library Terms." Booklist
78 (October 1, 1981): 243.

2828 "Software to Avoid." School Library Journal
30 (November 1983): 6.

2829 ROSS, JANE E. "Library Terms." School Library
Journal 31 (November 1984): 72.

LIBRARY USAGE SKILLS

2830 ANDERSON, ERIC S. "Library Usage Skills."
Booklist 80 (November 1, 1983): 438.

2831 ROSS, JANE E. "Library Usage Skills." School
Library Journal 31 (November 1984): 72.

2832 LETTNER, LORETTA. "Library Usage Skills."
Library Journal 110 (May 1, 1985): 124, 126;
and School Library Journal 31 (May 1985):
154, 156.

PERIODICAL INDEXES

2833 LATHROP, ANN. "Building the Software Collection: Part III." Educational Computer Magazine 2 (January/February 1982): 16-17, 52-
53.

2834 FABIAN, WILLIAM M. "CALICO: Skills Programs to
Promote Library Use." American Libraries 15
(April 1984): 264.

2835 ROSS, JANE E. "Periodical Indexes." School
Library Journal 31 (November 1984): 72.

POETRY INDEXES

2836 LANKFORD, MARY D. "Poetry Indexes." Booklist
79 (November 1, 1982): 389-90.

2837 FABIAN, WILLIAM M. "CALICO: Skills Programs to
Promote Library Use." American Libraries 15
(April 1984): 264.

2838 ROSS, JANE E. "Poetry Indexes." School Library Journal 31 (November 1984): 72.

PUTTING FICTION BOOKS IN ALPHABETICAL ORDER

2839 LANKFORD, MARY D. "Putting Fiction Books in
Alphabetical Order." Booklist 78 (October
1, 1981): 244.

2840 ROSS, JANE E. "Putting Fiction Books in
Alphabetical Order." School Library Journal
31 (November 1984): 72.

READING POWER

2841 ROSS, JANE E. "Reading Power." School Library
Journal 31 (November 1984): 72.

REFERENCE SKILLS--DICTIONARY

2842 ROSS, JANE E. "Reference Skills--Dictionary."
School Library Journal 31 (November 1984):
72.

REFERENCE SKILLS--LIBRARY

2843 ROSS, JANE E. "Reference Skills--Library."
      School Library Journal 31 (November 1984):
      72.

RIPLEY'S BELIEVE IT OR NOT: LIBRARY RESEARCH SKILLS

2844 ANDERSON, ERIC S. "Ripley's Believe It or Not:
      Library Research Skills." Booklist 81 (June
      1985): 1414.

2845 TOLBERT, PATRICIA H., and RIDEOUT, MARY P.
      "Ripley's Believe It or Not Library Research
      Skills." Library Software Review 4 (July/
      August 1985): 249-50.

SHELVING BOOKS THE LC WAY: A SELF TEST

2846 "Southwestern Oregon CC Offers Shelving Test
      Software." Library Journal 110 (February
      15, 1985): 102.

2847 ANDERSON, ERIC S. "Shelving Books the LC Way:
      Self-Test." Booklist 81 (May 1, 1985): 1270.

SKILLS MAKER

2848 ANDERSON, ERIC S. "Skills Maker." Book Report
      3 (January/February 1985): 61-62.

2849 ANDERSON, ERIC S. "Skills Maker." Booklist 81
      (May 1, 1985): 1270.

USING AN INDEX TO PERIODICALS

2850 TROUTNER, JOANNE JOHNSON. "Using an Index to
      Periodicals." School Library Media Quarter-
      ly 13 (Spring 1985): 155.

2851 "Software." Wilson Library Bulletin 59 (March
      1985): 510-11.

2852 ANDERSON, ERIC S. "Using an Index to Periodi-
      cals, Level I and II." Booklist 81 (May 1,
      1985): 1271.

USING REFERENCE TABLES IN AN ALMANAC

2853 ROSS, JANE E. "Using Reference Tables in an Almanac." School Library Journal 31 (November 1984): 74.

WHERE IS IT?

2854 DEWEY, PATRICK R. "Library Instruction." Wilson Library Bulletin 60 (November 1985): 57.

WHERE THE RAINBOW ENDS

2855 "Apple Reading Program Out." Small Computers in Libraries 3 (July 1983): 4.

WONDERQUEST

2856 "Micro 'Knowledge Explorer'." American Libraries 15 (October 1984): 656.

Mailing List

ABLE ONE MAILING LIST

2857 "Mailing Lists." Library Software Review 3
     (September 1984): 442-43.

BULK MAILER

2858 "Bulk Mailer." Software Review 2 (June 1983):
     124.

BUSINESS ADDRESS MANAGER

2859 ROSENBERG, VICTOR. "Business Address Manager."
     Library Software Review 4 (March/April
     1985): 104-05.

FCM: FILING, CATALOGING, AND MAILING SYSTEM

2860 ANDERSON, ERIC S. "FCM: Filing, Cataloging,
     and Mailing System." Booklist 80 (July
     1984): 60.

IBR

2861 JUDY, JOSEPH R. "Four for Text Handling:
     Notebook, IBR, Bibliography, Footnote."
     Online Review 8 (October 1984): 427-30.

KEYMAILER

2862 SPILLMAN, NANCY Z. "KeyMailer." Booklist 81
     (May 1, 1985): 1269.

MAGIC MAILER

2863 "Magic Mailer." Software Review 2 (June 1983):
     123.

MAIL-DEX

2864 "Mail-Dex." Software Review 2 (September
     1983): 203-04.

MAILIST

2865 "Mailing Lists." Library Software Review 3
(September 1984): 442-43.

MAILMERGE

2866 PRATT, ALLAN D. "Mailmerge for WordStar--
Review." Small Computers in Libraries 2
(August 1982): 3-4.

MEMBERS PROGRAM

2867 "Members Program." Software Review 2 (June
1983): 126.

NAME & ADDRESS LIST MANAGEMENT SYSTEM

2868 "Name & Address List Management System." Software Review 2 (June 1983): 124.

NAMOR MAIL LIST PROGRAM

2869 "Mail List Program." Software Review 2 (June
1983): 114.

2870 "Mail Lists." Software Review 2 (September
1983): 203.

POST MASTER

2871 GEFFNER, BONNIE. "'POST MASTER'--Mailing List
Software for the NEC PC-8000." Software
Review 1 (October 1982): 186-87.

WORDPRO-MAIL LIST

2872 "WordPlus for PC, Rainbow Among Five Micro
Packages." Software Review 2 (June 1983):
121.

Miscellaneous

DECISION-ANALYST

2873   MASON, ROBERT M.   "Computer-Aided Decisions,
       Users' Groups."   Library Journal 108
       (December 1, 1983): 2224-25.

GRAMMATIK

2874   GEFFNER, BONNIE.   "'GRAMMATIK' Enhances Your
       Text Editor by Checking for Common Errors."
       Software Review 1 (October 1982): 184-85.

2875   MEER, JEFFREY.   "Grammatik: Beyond Spelling."
       Online Review 8 (October 1984): 433-35.

PC LENS

2876   "Two Aids for the Visually Handicapped."   Small
       Computers in Libraries 4 (October 1984):
       4-5.

2877   "Software Update."   M300 and PC Report 2 (Jan-
       uary 1985): 9.

PC VOICE

2878   "Software Update."   M300 and PC Report 2 (Jan-
       uary 1985): 9.

RANGEFINDER

2879   DESROCHES, RICHARD A., and RUDD, MARIE.   "Shelf
       Space Management: A Microcomputer Applica-
       tion."   Information Technology and Libraries
       2 (June 1983): 187-89.

2880   "'Rangefinder' Stack Management Program."
       Small Computers in Libraries 3 (November
       1983): 4.

READABILITY ANALYSIS PROGRAM

2881 GOCHENOUR, GERALD A. "Readability Analysis
     Program." Educational Technology 22 (April
     1982): 55-56.

READABILITY CALCULATIONS

2882 ANDERSON, ERIC S. "Readability." Booklist 80
     (September 1, 1983): 107.

2883 "Readability Program Measures Grade Levels."
     American Libraries 15 (October 1984): 667.

2884 DEWEY, PATRICK R. "Removing the Tedium."
     Wilson Library Bulletin 59 (November 1984):
     222-23.

2885 LETTNER, LORETTA. "Readability Calculations."
     Library Journal 110 (May 1, 1985): 129; and
     School Library Journal 31 (May 1985): 159.

READABILITY FORMULAS

2886 "Readability Formulas." School Library Journal
     31 (November 1984): 87.

READABILITY INDEX

2887 ISAACSON, DAN. "Readability Index." Computing
     Teacher 8, no. 5 (1980-81): 42-43.

2888 WOOD, IRENE. "Readability." Booklist 79
     (April 1, 1983): 1048.

READING LEVEL ANALYSIS

2889 "Reading Level Analysis." School Library
     Journal 31 (November 1984): 87-88.

RIGHTWRITER

2890 MASON, ROBERT M. "Human Resources and the
     Micro System." Library Journal 110 (March
     15, 1985): 44-45.

2891 "Proofreader Works on PC Documents." T.H.E.
Journal: Technological Horizons in Education
12 (April 1985): 45.

TALKING PROGRAM

2892 "Two Aids for the Visually Handicapped." Small
Computers in Libraries 4 (October 1984):
4-5.

WAGES

2893 BOYDEN, PATRICK C. "Wages." Small Computers
in Libraries 4 (June 1984): 2.

Online Catalogs

BOOK LIBRARY

2894 GEFFNER, BONNIE. "'Book Library' and 'Record
Library' Disk-Based Catalogs for the Apple
II." Software Review 1 (October 1982):
181.

COMPULOG

2895 EMBAR, INDRANI. "COMPULOG: An Online Catalog."
Small Computers in Libraries 4 (June 1984):
5-6.

2896 LETTNER, LORETTA. "Compulog." Library Journal
110 (May 1, 1985): 126; and School Library
Journal 31 (May 1985): 156.

COMPUTER CAT

2897 "COMPUTER CAT is Now Available in Multi-User
Version." Apple Educator's Newsletter 4
(February 1983): 9-10.

2898 "Multi-User Computerized Card Catalog." ACCESS:
Microcomputers in Libraries 3 (Spring 1983):
32.

2899 BERGLUND, PATRICIA. "School Library Technology
Wilson Library Bulletin 59 (January 1985):
336-37.

MICRO-PAC

2900 "Micro Catalog for Libraries." T.H.E. Journal:
Technological Horizons in Education 11
(March 1984): 120.

2901 McQUEEN, JUDY, and BOSS, RICHARD W. "Micro
Library Software." Library Technology
Reports 20 (March/April 1984): 233-34.

561

OPAC

2902   GENIER, G. "On-Line Micro Catalog in Ottawa."
       Small Computers in Libraries 4 (March 1984):
       5.

TEQLIB

2903   LUNDEEN, GERALD, and TENOPIR, CAROL. "Micro-
       computer-Based Library Catalog Software."
       Microcomputers for Information Management
       1 (September 1984): 215-28.

Serials

CHECKMATE

2904 "CLASS Offers Microcomputer Serials System."
Wilson Library Buletin 56 (September 1981):
13.

2905 "Capital Systems Group to Market CLASS Programs." Small Computers in Libraries 2
(March 1982): 7.

2906 "Gaylord to Distribute CLASS Programs." Small
Computers in Libraries 2 (October 1982): 2.

2907 GEFFNER, BONNIE. "'CLASS' Library Microcomputer
System for the TRS-80." Software Review 1
(October 1982): 180-81.

2908 MARCUM, DEANNA H., and BOSS, RICHARD W. "Information Technology." Wilson Library Bulletin 57 (October 1982): 154-55.

2909 McQUEEN, JUDY, and BOSS, RICHARD W. "Checkmate." Library Technology Reports 20
(March/April 1984): 136-44.

2910 "Class Announces Multi-User Library Software."
Small Computers in Libraries 4 (April 1984):
7.

2911 "CLASS Offers Multi-User Serials Software."
Wilson Library Bulletin 58 (May 1984): 617.

2912 "Multi-User Version of Serials System." Small
Computers in Libraries 4 (May 1984): 5.

2913 "CHECKMATE Available in Multi-User Configuration." Library Systems Newsletter 4 (June
1984): 46.

2914 "CLASS: Multi-User Version of Serials System."
Library Hi Tech News 1 (June 1984): 4-5.

563

2915   "CLASS." College and Research Libraries News
       45 (June 1984): 315.

2916   GORDON, HELEN A. "CLASS Introduces Multi-
       User Version of CHECKMATE." Online 8
       (July 1984): 94.

2917   "Faxon, the PC XT, and CLASS." M300 and PC
       Report 2 (January 1985): 5.

GS 600 SERIALS CONTROL SYSTEM

2918   "Gaylord Introduces Apple IIe-Serials Control
       System." Small Computers in Libraries 3
       (August 1983): 3.

2919   "Gaylord's Newest: Serials Control on an
       Apple." Library Journal 108 (October 1,
       1983): 1836.

2920   "Gaylord Tests New Serials Control System."
       Wilson Library Bulletin 58 (February 1984):
       395.

2921   "Gaylord's Apple-Based Serials System Now in
       Field Testing." Library Journal 109 (April
       1, 1984): 619.

MLS204

2922   McQUEEN, JUDY, and BOSS, RICHARD W. "Maxwell
       Library Systems." Library Technology
       Reports 20 (March/April 1984): 216.

MAG/BASE

2923   SAFFADY, WILLIAM. "MAG/BASE." Library Tech-
       nology Reports 19 (September/October 1983):
       525-33.

MAGAZINE CONTROL SYSTEM

2924   ANDERSON, ERIC S. "Magazine Control." Book-
       list 79 (April 1, 1983): 1047-48.

2925 ANDERSON, ERIC S. "Magazine Control System."
     Book Report 2 (May/June 1983): 58-59.

2926 ANDERSON, ERIC S. "Magazine Control System."
     Computing Teacher 11 (September 1983): 58-
     59.

2927 ANDERSON, ERIC S. "Magazine Control System."
     Booklist 80 (January 1, 1984): 693.

MICRO-PER

2928 McQUEEN, JUDY, and BOSS, RICHARD W. "Micro
     Library Software." Library Technology
     Reports 20 (March/April 1984): 233-34.

MICROLINX

2929 "Faxon's MicroLinx." Small Computers in Li-
     braries 5 (February 1985): 3.

2930 "MICROLINX." Wilson Library Bulletin 59 (March
     1985): 466.

2931 "FAXON: Financing Plans for MicroLinx." Li-
     brary Hi Tech News no. 22 (December 1985):
     4.

PS SERIAL CONTROL SYSTEM

2932 McQUEEN, JUDY, and BOSS, RICHARD W. "Profes-
     sional Software's Serial Control System."
     Library Technology Reports 20 (March/April
     1984): 266-68.

2933 LETTNER, LORETTA. "Serials Control System."
     Library Journal 110 (May 1, 1985): 130; and
     School Library Journal 31 (May 1985): 160.

PERIODICALS MANAGEMENT APPLICATION MODULE

2934 SHEROUSE, VICKI M. "Periodicals Management
     Application Module." Booklist 81 (January
     1, 1985): 658.

REMO

2935　"Read-More IBM Serials System." M300 and PC
　　　　Report 2 (April 1985): 6.

ROUTING

2936　"EBSCO's New Software Packages." Library Soft-
　　　　ware Review 3 (June 1984): 158.

2937　"EBSCO Announces New Software Package." Infor-
　　　　mation Technology and Libraries 3 (September
　　　　1984): 316.

SC 350 SERIALS CONTROL SYSTEM

2938　"OCLC Introduces SC 350." Wilson Library
　　　　Bulletin 59 (February 1985): 379.

2939　"OCLC Introduces SC 350--A Microcomputer-Based
　　　　Serials Control System." OCLC Newsletter
　　　　no. 156 (February 1985): 13.

2940　"OCLC SC 350." Library Hi Tech News no. 13
　　　　(February 1985): 20.

2941　"OCLC's MICROCON and SC 350." Small Computers
　　　　in Libraries 5 (February 1985): 3.

2942　"SC 350 Micro Serials Control." M300 and PC
　　　　Report 2 (February 1985): 5.

2943　"OCLC's SC 350 Serials System." Library Sys-
　　　　tems Newsletter 5 (February 1985): 12.

2944　"OCLC's New Micro-Based Serials Subsystem."
　　　　Library Journal 110 (February 15, 1985):
　　　　100.

2945　"SC 350 from OCLC." Small Computers in Li-
　　　　braries 5 (February 1985): 5.

2946　"OCLC Introduces Micro-Based Services." Infor-
　　　　mation Technology and Libraries 4 (March
　　　　1985): 69-70.

2947 "SC-350 and MICROCON." Wilson Library Bulletin
59 (March 1985): 466.

SERIALS CONTROL SYSTEM

2948 "Serials Control Software." Library Systems
Newsletter 3 (July 1983): 55.

2949 McQUEEN, JUDY, and BOSS, RICHARD W. "Meta-
Micro Serials Control System." Library
Technology Reports 20 (March/April 1984):
217-33.

SERIALS MANAGEMENT SYSTEM

2950 "Serials Management System (SMS) on a PC."
Electronic Library 3 (July 1985): 160.

Spreadsheets

CALCSTAR

2951 SAFFADY, WILLIAM. "CALCSTAR." Library Technology Reports 20 (July/August 1984): 437-44.

DESKTOP/PLAN

2952 "Desktop/Plan II." Software Review 2 (June 1983): 124.

EASYCALC

2953 SAFFADY, WILLIAM. "EASYCALC." Library Technology Reports 20 (July/August 1984): 445-52.

EASYPLANNER

2954 SAFFADY, WILLIAM. "EASYPLANNER." Library Technology Reports 20 (July/August 1984): 453-59.

EXCEL

2955 TANGORRA, JOANNE. "New Microsoft Spreadsheet Heats Up Mac Wars." Publishers Weekly 227 (May 17, 1985): 69.

EXECUCALC

2956 "Spreadsheet." Library Software Review 3 (September 1984): 445-46.

FREECALC

2957 POST, RICHARD. "Selected Shareware for Library-Media Administrative Applications." Ohio Media Spectrum 36 (Winter 1984/1985): 12-15.

GENERAL LEDGER

2958 "General Ledger." Software Review 2 (June
      1983): 122.

HOT ACCOUNTS

2959 "Accounting." Library Software Review 3 (March
      1984): 89-90.

LOTUS 1-2-3

2960 "Lotus' 1-2-3." Software Review 2 (June 1983):
      119.

2961 McINTYRE, DONALD M. "Spreadsheets, Database
      Management, and Graphics: As Easy as 1-2-3."
      Online 7 (November 1983): 31-40.

2962 MASON, ROBERT M. "Software: Increasing Capa-
      bilities." Library Journal 109 (May 15,
      1984): 956-57.

2963 SAFFADY, WILLIAM. "LOTUS 1-2-3." Library
      Technology Reports 20 (July/August 1984):
      471-80.

2964 MASON, ROBERT M. "Choosing Spreadsheet &
      Database Management Software." Library
      Journal 110 (October 15, 1985): 54-55.

MASTER PLANNER

2965 "Financial Modelling for Micros." Electronic
      Library 1 (January 1983): 10-11.

MULTIPLAN

2966 GARTEN, EDWARD D., and McMEEN, GEORGE R.
      "MULTIPLAN." Library Hi Tech 1 (Winter
      1983): 101.

2967 SAFFADY, WILLIAM. "MULTIPLAN." Library Tech-
      nology Reports 20 (July/August 1984): 481-
      89.

NUMBER CRUNCHER

2968   "Number Cruncher Runs in 64K Memory." Software
       Review 2 (September 1983): 201.

PC-CALC

2969   MICHELS, FREDRICK; HARRISON, NEIL; and SMITH,
       DOUGLAS. "User-Supported Software for the
       IBM PC." Library Hi Tech 3, no. 2, issue 10
       (1985): 97-106.

PFS: PLAN

2970   MILLER, MICHAEL J. "PFS: PLAN: A Spreadsheet
       for the People, This Program Emphasizes Ease
       of Use Rather Than Sophisticated Features."
       Popular Computing 4 (December 1984): 140-42,
       144.

PEACHCALC

2971   SAFFADY, WILLIAM. "PEACHCALC." Library Tech-
       nology Reports 20 (July/August 1984): 490-
       96.

PERFECT CALC

2972   SAFFADY, WILLIAM. "PERFECT CALC." Library
       Technology Reports 20 (July/August 1984):
       497-505.

PLANNERCALC

2973   "Financial Modelling for Micros." Electronic
       Libraries 1 (January 1983): 10-11.

PRACTICALC

2974   SMITH, DAVID FAY. "PractiCalc II." Publishers
       Weekly 226 (June 29, 1984): 78.

REPORT MANAGER

2975   "Spreadsheet." Library Software Review 3 (Sep-
       tember 1984): 445-46.

SITE MANAGER

2976 "New Programs Released." Small Computers in
Libraries 3 (June 1983): 6-7.

2977 LETTNER, LORETTA. "The Site Manager." Library
Journal 110 (May 1, 1985): 129; and School
Library Journal 31 (May 1985): 159.

SUPERCALC

2978 "Spreadsheet Programs." Small Computers in
Libraries 2 (September 1982): 3-4.

2979 SAFFADY, WILLIAM. "SUPERCALC." Library Technology Reports 20 (July/August 1984): 506-
15.

2980 SAFFADY, WILLIAM. "SUPERCALC2." Library Technology Reports 20 (July/August 1984): 516-
26.

2981 SAFFADY, WILLIAM. "SUPERCALC3." Library Technology Reports 20 (July/August 1984): 527-
38.

2982 MASON, ROBERT M. "Choosing Spreadsheet & Database Management Software." Library Journal
110 (October 15, 1985): 54-55.

TIMBERLINE SPREADSHEET

2983 "Timberline Spreadsheet." Software Review 2
(June 1983): 119.

20/20

2984 GORDON, HELEN A. "20/20 Integrated Spreadsheet
Announced." Online 9 (May 1985): 76.

VP-PLANNER

2985 MASON, ROBERT M. "Choosing Spreadsheet & Database Management Software." Library Journal
110 (October 15, 1985): 54-55.

VISICALC

2986 SCHUYLER, MICHAEL. "VisiCalc: Library Uses
     for a Business Standard." ACCESS: Micro-
     computers in Libraries 2 (January 1982): 9,
     17-19, 27.

2987 SCHUYLER, MICHAEL. "A Review of VISICALC."
     Software Review 1 (February 1982): 68-77.

2988 "Spreadsheet Programs." Small Computers in
     Libraries 2 (September 1982): 3-4.

2989 "VisiCalc Advanced Version." Software Review
     2 (June 1983): 125.

2990 ANDERSON, ERIC S. "VisiCalc." Booklist 80
     (January 1, 1984): 692.

2991 SAFFADY, WILLIAM. "VISICALC." Library
     Technology Reports 20 (July/August 1984):
     539-46.

CREATE

2992 SMITH, DANA E. "Create: Customized Reference
Statistics Programs." American Libraries 15
(March 1984): 179.

OUTPUTM

2993 LETTNER, LORETTA. " OUTPUTM (Output Measures
for Public Libraries." Library Journal 110
(May 1, 1985): 128-29; and School Library
Journal 31 (May 1985): 158-59.

SPEEDSTAT

2994 "New Products: SpeedSTAT." ACCESS: Microcomputers in Libraries 3 (Spring 1983): 32.

STATS PLUS

2995 "Statistics Package." Software Review 2
(September 1983): 195.

STATSTAR

2996 KELLER, LISA. "Library Statistics in Massachusetts." Small Computers in Libraries 3
(January 1983): 7.

Word Processing

APPLE WRITER

2997   BOCKMANN, FRED. "Applewriter 2.0." Booklist
79 (September 1, 1982): 56.

2998   BJORNER, SUSAN N. "Worth Noting." Technicalities 3 (August 1983): 2, 10.

2999   BLOCK, DAVID, and KALYONCU, AYDAN. "Selection
of Word Processing Software for Library
Use." Information Technology and Libraries
2 (September 1983): 252-60.

3000   SHEROUSE, VICKI M. "Apple Writer IIe." Booklist 80 (March 1, 1984): 1002.

BANK STREET WRITER

3001   BOUDROT, THOMAS E., and LOOFBORO, DEBBY. "The
Bank Street Writer." Electronic Learning 2
(February 1983): 92-94.

3002   "The Bank Street Writer." Classroom Computer
News 3 (April 1983): 76.

3003   WETZEL, KEITH. "The Bank Street Writer."
Computing Teacher 11 (August 1983): 36-37.

3004   FORD, BARBARA G. "The Bank Street Writer."
Classroom Computer Learning 4 (October
1983): 61.

3005   SHEROUSE, VICKI M. "The Bank Street Writer."
Booklist 80 (November 1, 1983): 436.

3006   GARTEN, EDWARD D. "Word Processing for the
Computer-Shy." Library Hi Tech 2, no. 4,
issue 8 (1984): 109-10.

3007   COSTA, BETTY; SKAPURA, ROBERT; and ANDERSON,
ERIC S. "Bank Street Writer." Booklist
80 (January 1, 1984): 692.

3008 WETZEL, KEITH. "Bank Street Writer." Computing Teacher 12 (December 1984/January 1985):
30-31.

3009 "Word Processing." Electronic Learning 5
(October 1985): 74.

3010 SHEROUSE, VICKI M. "The Bank Street Writer
II." Booklist 82 (October 1, 1985): 282-83.

CUT AND PASTE

3011 ANDERSON, ERIC S. "Cut and Paste." Booklist
80 (July 1984): 1560.

3012 KAPLAN, HOWARD. "Cut and Paste." Classroom
Computer Learning 5 (September 1984): 17-18.

3013 "Cut and Paste." School Library Journal 31
(December 1984): 49.

DATATEXT

3014 "Datatek Intros WP Package for IBM PC." Software Review 2 (September 1983): 201-02.

DISPLAYWRITER 2

3015 POLLARD, RICHARD. "Word Processing for Microcomputers: An Assessment of Current Trends
and Future Potential." Microcomputers for
Information Management 2 (September 1985):
189-200.

DOCUWRITER

3016 "Docuwriter." Classroom Computer Learning 5
(October 1984): 66.

EASYTEXT

3017 GEFFNER, BONNIE. "'EASYTEXT' and 'EASYDATA'--
Word Processing and Database Management
Software for the IBM Personal Computer."
Software Review 1 (October 1982): 183-84.

EASYWRITER

3018 HUNTER, C. BRUCE, and WOLD, ALLEN L. "Easy-
      Writer." Media and Methods 21 (September
      1984): 31-32.

EDIT

3019 "EDIT, Public Domain Software." Small Com-
      puters in Libraries 5 (September 1985):
      23.

EXPRESS

3020 "Letter Processing Package is Available."
      T.H.E. Journal: Technological Horizons in
      Education 12 (June 1985): 47.

FINAL DRAFT

3021 "Word Processor Caters to Users." T.H.E.
      Journal: Technological Horizons in Education
      12 (June 1985): 49.

FINALWORD

3022 VEANER, ALLEN B. "The FinalWord." Library
      Software Review 3 (September 1984): 400-
      10.

FOOTNOTE

3023 GEFFNER, BONNIE. "'FOOTNOTE' and 'PAIR' En-
      hance 'WORDSTAR'." Software Review 1
      (October 1982): 185.

3024 JUDY, JOSEPH R. "Four for Text Handling: Note-
      book, IBR, Bibliography, Footnote." Online
      Review 8 (October 1984): 427-30.

FORMAT

3025 SMITH, STEVE. "Word Processors: Format II."
      Library Software Review 4 (September/October
      1985): 316-18.

HOMEWORD

3026 SMITH, DAVID FAY. "The Homeword: The Personal
Word Processor." Publishers Weekly 225
(February 10, 1984): 169.

3027 ANDERSON, ERIC S. "Homeword." Booklist 80
(March 1, 1984): 1003.

3028 KAPLAN, HOWARD. "Homeword." Classroom Computer Learning 4 (April/May 1984): 66-67.

3029 HUNTER, C. BRUCE, and WOLD, ALLEN L. "Home-
Word." Media and Methods 21 (September
1984): 30-31.

3030 "Homeword." School Library Journal 31 (December 1984): 50.

3031 ANDERSON, ERIC S. "Homeword." Booklist 81
(January 1985): 661.

HORIZON WORDPROCESSING

3032 "Word Processing for UNIX." Software Review 2
(June 1983): 120.

KAMAS

3033 LaRUE, JAMES. "KAMAS." Library Software
Review 4 (September/October 1985): 318-21.

LEADING EDGE WORD PROCESSOR

3034 "Word Processor for IBM PC." T.H.E. Journal:
Technological Horizons in Education 12
(November 1984): 60.

MAGIC SLATE

3035 "Magic Slate: A Word Processing Program for a
Wide Range of Levels." Electronic Learning
4 (January 1985): ESR4.

3036 ANDERSON, ERIC S. "Magic Slate." Booklist 82
(November 1, 1985): 434.

MAGIC WAND

3037 BLOCK, DAVID, and KALYONCU, AYDAN. "Selection
of Word Processing Software for Library
Use." Information Technology and Libraries
2 (September 1983): 252-60.

MAGIC WINDOW

3038 "Magic Window II." Software Review 2 (June
1983): 123.

3039 SKAPURA, ROBERT. "Magic Window II." Booklist
80 (January 1, 1984): 692.

MICROSOFT WORD

3040 POLLARD, RICHARD. "Word Processing for Microcomputers: An Assessment of Current Trends
and Future Potential." Microcomputers for
Information Management 2 (September 1985):
189-200.

3041 HYER, DIANNE. "Software Side By Side: Word
Processing Software." Electronic Learning
5 (November/December 1985): 44-45.

MULTIMATE

3042 POLLARD, RICHARD. "Word Processing for Microcomputers: An Assessment of Current Trends
and Future Potential." Microcomputers for
Information Management 2 (September 1985):
189-200.

3043 DEEMER, SELDEN S. "Multimate Professional Word
Processor (version 3.30)." Library Software
Review 4 (September/October 1985): 321-24.

MY WORD

3044 BABITS, ANN. "My Word." Library Software
Review 4 (September/October 1985): 324-
26.

NEWSCRIPT

3045 "Word Processing on TRS-80." Software Review 2
(June 1983): 105-06.

NEWWORD

3046 McCARTHY, MICHAEL. "NewWord: A Powerful Chal-
lenger to WordStar." Computers & Electronics 22 (June 1984): 46, 48, 96-97.

3047 LaRUE, JAMES. "NewWord." Library Software
Review 4 (September/October 1985): 326-
30.

PC WRITE

3048 POST, RICHARD. "Selected Shareware for Library-Media Administrative Applications."
Ohio Media Spectrum 36 (Winter 1984/1985):
12-15.

3049 MICHELS, FREDRICK; HARRISON, NEIL; and SMITH,
DOUGLAS. "User-Supported Software for the
IBM PC." Library Hi Tech 3, no. 2, issue 10
(1985): 97-106.

3050 MILLER, RALPH. "Designing Your Own Low Cost
Front-End Software." Online 9 (March 1985):
94-98.

3051 PHILLIPS, BRIAN. "'Shareware'. . .Make It Your
First Software Purchase." Online 9 (May
1985): 33-36.

PFS: WRITE

3052 "PFS: WRITE." School Library Journal 31
(December 1984): 52.

3053 SHEROUSE, VICKI M. "Scholastic PFS: Write."
Booklist 82 (October 1, 1985): 285.

3054 HYER, DIANNE. "Software Side By Side: Word
Processing Software." Electronic Learning
5 (November/December 1985): 44-45.

PAPERBACK WRITER

3055 MASON, ROBERT M. Paperback Writer." Library
      Journal 110 (May 15, 1985): 40.

PEACHTEXT

3056 "Peachtext Word Processor." Software Review 2
      (June 1983): 123.

PEACHY WRITER

3057 SHEROUSE, VICKI M. "Peachy Writer." Booklist
      80 (November 1, 1983): 440.

PIE WRITER

3058 "PIE Writer Word Processing and New Applesoft
      Compiler from Hayden." Software Review 1
      (February 1982): 98.

3059 DEWEY, PATRICK R. "Easy as PIE." Wilson
      Library Bulletin 59 (December 1984): 286.

PROFESSIONAL WRITER'S PACKAGE

3060 "Dedicated Power in Word Processor." T.H.E.
      Journal: Technological Horizons in Education
      12 (June 1985): 36.

QUILL

3061 EVANS, NELL. "QUILL." Library Software Review
      4 (September/October 1985): 330.

RGS WRIGHT +

3062 "Word Processor." Electronic Learning 5
      (November/December 1985): 74, 76.

RIGHTWRITER

3063 GORDON, HELEN A. "RIGHTWRITER--An Expert at
      Your Fingertips." Database 8 (December
      1985): 53-56.

3064 BAUER, DALE L. "RightWriter: Document Analysis." Electronic Library 3 (December 1985): 318-19.

SAMNA WORD

3065 MASON, ROBERT M. "Software: Increasing Capabilities." Library Journal 109 (May 15, 1984): 956-57.

3066 "Word Processor Does Calculations." T.H.E. Journal: Technological Horizons in Education 12 (May 1985): 52.

3067 POLLARD, RICHARD. "Word Processing for Microcomputers: An Assessment of Current Trends and Future Potential." Microcomputers for Information Management 2 (September 1985): 189-200.

SCREEN WRITER

3068 BLOCK, DAVID, and KALYONCU, AYDAN. "Selection of Word Processing Software for Library Use." Information Technology and Libraries 2 (September 1983): 252-60.

3069 ANDERSON, ERIC S., and SKAPURA, ROBERT. "Screen Writer II." Booklist 80 (January 1, 1984): 692.

SELECT

3070 GARTEN, EDWARD D., and McMEEN, GEORGE R. "SELECT." Library Hi Tech 1 (Winter 1983): 101.

3071 "Word Processing." Library Software Review 3 (March 1984): 114-16.

3072 VEANER, ALLEN B. "SELECT Word Processor and SELECT Write." Library Software Review 4 (September/October 1985): 302-07.

SKIWRITER

582 / SOFTWARE AND SYSTEMS REVIEWS

3073 "Word Processing: SKIWRITER II." Electronic
Learning 4 (November/December 1984): 80.

SUPER-TEXT

3074 BLAIR, JOHN C., Jr. "A Tutorial in Representative Apple Software." Database 5 (June
1982): 72-79.

3075 GEFFNER, BONNIE. "SUPER-TEXT 40/56/70--Word
Processing for the Apple II." Software
Review 1 (October 1982): 183.

SUPERSCRIPTSIT

3076 HYER, DIANNE. "Software Side By Side: Word
Processing Software." Electronic Learning
5 (November/December 1985): 44-45.

SUPERWRITER

3077 GEFFNER, BONNIE. "'SuperWriter'--Integrated
Text Processing for Micros." Software
Review 1 (October 1982): 184.

SYTEXT

3078 "Word Processor Serves Multi-Users." T.H.E.
Journal: Technological Horizons in Education
12 (March 1985): 45.

THOR

3079 HERTHER, NANCY K. "Thor." Library Software
Review 4 (July/August 1985): 259-61.

VISIWORD

3080 "Word Processing for IBM PC." Software Review
2 (June 1983): 117-18.

VOLKSWRITER

3081 SPILLMAN, NANCY Z. "Volkswriter 1.2." Booklist 80 (January 1, 1984): 691-92.

3082   EVANS, WAYNE A. "Volkswriter Scientific." Li-
       brary Software Review 4 (September/October
       1985): 330-34.

WORD JUGGLER

3083   SHEROUSE, VICKI M. "Word Juggler IIe/Lexicheck
       IIe." Booklist 81 (September 1, 1984): 85.

3084   "Word Juggler." Electronic Learning 5 (Septem-
       ber 1985): 87.

WORD WORKER

3085   COATES, RENATE G. "The Word Worker: Word Pro-
       cessing Programs." ACCESS: Microcomputers
       in Libraries 2 (October 1982): 24-25.

WORDMARC

3086   ROBERTS, JUSTINE. "WordMARC." Library Soft-
       ware Review 4 (September/October 1985): 334-
       36.

WORDPERFECT

3087   POLLARD, RICHARD. "Word Processing for Micro-
       computers: An Assessment of Current Trends
       and Future Potential." Microcomputers for
       Information Management 2 (September 1985):
       189-200.

3088   SCHELKOPF, NANCY C. "WordPerfect." Library
       Software Review 4 (September/October 1985):
       336-38.

3089   HENSINGER, JAMES SPEED. "RE:Views: WordPerfect
       4.0." OCLC Micro 1 (December 1985): 24-25.

WORDPLUS

3090   "WordPlus for PC, Rainbow Among Five Micro
       Packages." Software Review 2 (June 1983):
       121.

WORDSTAR

3091 LIKINS, JOHN. "Worth Noting." Technicalities
      3 (August 1983): 10.

3092 BLOCK, DAVID, and KALYONCU, AYDAN. "Selection
      of Word Processing Software for Library
      Use." Information Technology and Libraries
      2 (September 1983): 252-60.

3093 HUNTER, C. BRUCE, and WOLD, ALLEN L. "Word-
      Star." Media and Methods 21 (September
      1984): 32.

3094 "Micropro Debuts WordStar 2000 Software."
      Library Software Review 4 (January/February
      1985): 41-42.

3095 "New Software: WordStar 2000." Library Journal
      110 (February 15, 1985): 125.

3096 GORDON, HELEN A. "WordStar 2000 & 2000 Plus
      Released by MicroPro International." Online
      9 (March 1985): 109-10.

3097 SANDLER, COREY. "Wordstar 2000." Publishers
      Weekly 227 (May 17, 1985): 71.

3098 POLLARD, RICHARD. "Word Processing for Micro-
      computers: An Assessment of Current Trends
      and Future Potential." Microcomputers for
      Information Management 2 (September 1985):
      189-200.

3099 POWELL, ANTOINETTE. "WordStar 2000." Library
      Software Review 4 (September/October 1985):
      238-42.

3100 BEISER, KARL. "MicroPro Axes Program." Small
      Computers in Libraries 5 (December 1985):
      7-10.

WORDVISION

3101 "WordVision Word Processor--Review." Small
      Computers in Libraries 4 (January 1984): 2.

WRITE CHOICE

3102 ANDERSON, ERIC S. "The Write Choice." Book-
         list 81 (March 1, 1985): 1005-06.

WRITE STUFF

3103 "The Write Stuff." School Library Journal 31
         (December 1984): 53.

WRITING WORKSHOP: THE MILLIKEN WORD PROCESSOR

3104 DEWEY, PATRICK R. "A Magic Typewriter." Wil-
         son Library Bulletin 59 (November 1984):
         223.

3105 "The Milliken Word Processor." School Library
         Journal 31 (December 1984): 51.

3106 SHEROUSE, VICKI M. "The Writing Workshop: The
         Milliken Word Processor." Booklist 81 (May
         1, 1985): 1271.

3107 HYER, DIANNE. "Software Side By Side: Word
         Processing Software." Electronic Learning 5
         (November/December 1985): 44-45.

WRITING WORKSHOP: PREWRITING

3108 TROUTNER, JOANNE JOHNSON. "The Writing Work-
         shop: Prewriting." Booklist 82 (October 1,
         1985): 286.

HARDWARE REVIEWS

AT&T

3109 "IRD Report: AT&T Safari." <u>Library Hi Tech</u>
<u>News</u> no. 14 (March 1985): 2.

ADDS

3110 FALK, HOWARD. "Tongues, Tilts, and Tones."
<u>Electronic Library</u> 3 (January 1985): 38.

ALTOS

3111 "16-Bit Micros Challenge Minis." <u>Library Sys-</u>
<u>tems Newsletter</u> 2 (March 1982): 23-24.

APPLE

3112 SAFFADY, WILLIAM. "Apple II and Apple II Plus
Computers." <u>Library Computer Equipment</u>
<u>Review</u> 1 (January/June 1980): 33-38.

3113 SAFFADY, WILLIAM. "The Apple III Personal Computer System." <u>Computer Equipment Review</u> 3
(July 1981): 90-98.

3114 "Apple II Plus." <u>Electronic Learning</u> 2 (January 1983): 60.

3115 "Apple Announces Two New Micros." <u>Small Com-</u>
<u>puters in Libraries</u> 3 (April 1983): 2.

3116 MASON, ROBERT M. "Traveling, Apple's LISA,
Public Micros." <u>Library Journal</u> 108 (June
15, 1983): 1235-36.

3117 WALTON, ROBERT A. "Walton Interviews Walton--
The Apple Macintosh." <u>Technicalities</u> 4
(April 1984): 13-14.

3118 GORDON, HELEN A. "Apple Unveils LISA 2
Series." <u>Online</u> 8 (May 1984): 82.

3119 GORDON, HELEN A. "Macintosh Added to Apple
Line." Online 8 (May 1984): 81-82.

3120 GORDON, HELEN A. "Apple Brings Out Its Transportable IIc for 'Serious' Home Applications." Online 8 (July 1984): 91-93.

3121 MASON, ROBERT M. "Apple's 'Fat Mac'." Library
Journal 109 (November 15, 1984): 2133.

3122 GORDON, HELEN A. "Apple's 512K Macintosh Released." Online 9 (January 1985): 92.

3123 MASON, ROBERT M. "Summer Potpourri." Library
Journal 110 (August 1985): 66-67.

APRICOT

3124 GORDON, HELEN A. "Apricot XI Unveiled." Online 8 (November 1984): 90-92.

ATARI

3125 SAFFADY, WILLIAM. "Atari 800 Microcomputer."
Computer Equipment Review 4 (January/June
1982): 36-41.

3126 "Atari 400." Electronic Learning 2 (January
1983): 52.

3127 "Atari 800." Electronic Learning 2 (January
1983): 56.

CLSI

3128 "Products and Services." Wilson Library
Bulletin 59 (January 1985): 365.

CANON

3129 "Canon Desktop Is All-In-One Computer." Electronic Learning 4 (January 1985): 61.

3130 GORDON, HELEN A. "Canon PC is IBM Compatible."
Online 9 (January 1985): 91-92.

CASIO

3131 "Casio." Electronic Learning 2 (January 1983):
63.

CHEMCORP

3132 "Chemcorp Icon Micro Operates in a Network."
Electronic Learning 4 (October 1984):
78.

COMMODORE

3133 SAFFADY, WILLIAM. "Commodore PET, CBM, Super-
PET and VIC-20 Microcomputers." Computer
Equipment Review 4 (January 1982): 14-29.

3134 "VIC-20." Electronic Learning 2 (January
1983): 55.

3135 "Commodore PET." Electronic Learning 2 (January 1983): 57.

3136 "Commodore 64." Electronic Learning 2 (January 1983): 58.

3137 "Commodore Has Two New Models." Electronic
Learning 4 (October 1984): 78.

COMPAQ

3138 SAFFADY, WILLIAM. "Compaq Portable Computer."
Computer Equipment Review 5 (July/December
1983): 161-65.

3139 GORDON, HELEN A. "TELECOMPAQ Available in Six
Models." Online 9 (September 1985): 105.

CONTROL DATA

3140 "CDC Micro has Timeshare, Standalone Uses."
Library Systems Newsletter 2 (March 1982):
24.

CONVERGENT TECHNOLOGIES

3141 DAVIS, CHARLES H. "Portable Micros: Potentials
for Information Management." Microcomputers
for Information Management 1 (March 1984):
57-65.

CORONA

3142 FALK, HOWARD. "Multi-User Microcomputer."
Electronic Library 3 (January 1985): 40.

CORVUS

3143 "Corvus Systems." Electronic Learning 2 (January 1983): 63.

CROMEMCO

3144 "Cromemco." Electronic Learning 2 (January
1983): 63.

DEC RAINBOW

3145 GARTEN, EDWARD D. "DEC Rainbow 100 Microcomputer User Critique and Application in
a University Library." Collegiate Microcomputer 1 (May 1983): 173-76.

3146 MASON, ROBERT M. "Telecommunications Pro-
grams--The Osborne Executive--DEC's Rainbow
100 Plus." Library Journal 108 (November 1,
1983): 2034-35.

DATA GENERAL

3147 GORDON, HELEN A. "Data General 10-LB. Portable
Announced." Online 9 (January 1985): 91.

DIGITAL MICROSYSTEMS

3148 SAFFADY, WILLIAM. "Digital Microsystems' HiNet
Microcomputer Network." Computer Equipment
Review 4 (July/December 1982): 154-59.

EPSON

3149 DAVIS, CHARLES H. "Portable Micros: Potentials

for Information Management." <u>Microcomputers</u> <u>for Information Management</u> 1 (March 1984): 57-65.

3150 EDGE, LEWIS A., Jr. "QX-10 is Complete, Ready-to-Run Micro." T.H.E. <u>Journal: Technological</u> <u>Horizons in Education</u> 12 (March 1985): 16-17.

FRANKLIN

3151 "Franklin ACE 1000." <u>Electronic Learning</u> 2 (January 1983): 61.

HEATHKIT/ZENITH

3152 "Heathkit/Zenith Educational Systems." <u>Elec-</u><u>tronic Learning</u> 2 (January 1983): 63-64.

3153 FALK, HOWARD. "IBM/PC Compatibles." <u>Elec-</u><u>tronic Library</u> 3 (January 1985): 38.

HEWLETT-PACKARD

3154 "Microcomputer Runs Mini Software." <u>Library</u> <u>Systems Newsletter</u> 1 (August 1981): 14.

3155 "Hewlett Packard Upgrades Touchscreen PCs." <u>Electronic Library</u> 3 (July 1985): 164-65.

3156 GORDON, HELEN A. "Hewlett-Packard Portable Weighs 9 Lbs." <u>Database</u> 8 (August 1985): 87.

IBM

3157 "IBM Personal Computer." <u>Computer Equipment</u> <u>Review</u> 3 (July 1981): 99-108.

3158 "IBM Goes Small." <u>Library Systems Newsletter</u> 1 (September 1981): 17-18.

3159 "IBM Announces Small Business System. . .Personal Computer Next?" <u>Online</u> 5 (October 1981): 10, 83.

3160 SAFFADY, WILLIAM. "IBM Displaywriter Word Processor." Computer Equipment Review 4 (January/June 1982): 42-50.

3161 "IBM Personal Computer Looks Good." Small Computers in Libraries 2 (March 1982): 6.

3162 "The IBM Personal Computer." Electronic Learning 2 (January 1983): 61-62.

3163 SAFFADY, WILLIAM. "An Update Report: The IBM Personal Computer XT." Computer Equipment Review 5 (July/December 1983): 175-79.

3164 "IBM's Peanut Announced." Small Computers in Libraries 3 (November 1983): 5.

3165 GROSCH, AUDREY N. "IBM Personal Computer and the IBM Extended Personal Computer." Library Technology Reports 20 (January/February 1984): 61-84.

3166 "IBM Announces Its New IBM PCjr." Library Hi Tech 1 (Spring 1984): 86-88.

3167 "IBM Introduces New Personal Computer." Wilson Library Bulletin 59 (October 1984): 92.

3168 "IBM Personal Computer AT." Library Hi Tech News 1 (October/November 1984): 27-28.

3169 "IBM PCjr." Library Hi Tech News 1 (October/November 1984): 28-29.

3170 "IBM Introduces Personal Computer AT." Library Software Review 3 (December 1984): 457-58.

3171 FALK, HOWARD. "The IBM Portable Computer." Electronic Library 3 (January 1985): 40.

3172 FALK, HOWARD. "The Powerful IBM/AT." Electronic Library 3 (January 1985): 40-41.

3173 MASON, ROBERT M. "Update on the PC Jr." Library Journal 110 (February 15, 1985): 125.

3174   "The IBM PC Family." Library Systems News-
       letter 5 (March 1985): 23-24.

INTELLIGENT SYSTEMS

3175   "Intelligent Systems." Electronic Learning 2
       (January 1983): 64.

KAYPRO

3176   MASON, ROBERT M. "More Bargains & Osborne's
       Executive." Library Journal 108 (May 15,
       1983): 981-82.

3177   MASON, ROBERT M. "Traveling, Apple's LISA,
       Public Micros." Library Journal 108 (June
       15, 1983): 1235-36.

3178   SAFFADY, WILLIAM. "Kaypro II Portable Com-
       puter." Computer Equipment Review 5 (July/
       December 1983): 151-54.

3179   "Kaypro 2X Enhances Drives." Electronic Learn-
       ing 4 (October 1984): 78.

3180   "Kaypro Word Processor Has Full System." Elec-
       tronic Learning 4 (January 1985): 61.

LNW

3181   KITTLE, PAUL W. "An Alternative to the Higher-
       Priced Spread." Small Computers in Librar-
       ies 4 (April 1984): 5-6.

MONROE

3182   "Monroe." Electronic Learning 2 (January
       1983): 64.

3183   GORDON, HELEN A. "Monroe's System 2000--CP/M
       and MSDOS Included." Online 8 (July 1984):
       92.

NEC

3184 "Nippon Electric Company, Ltd." _Electronic Learning_ 2 (January 1983): 64.

3185 DAVIS, CHARLES H. "Portable Micros: Potentials for Information Management." _Microcomputers for Information Management_ 1 (March 1984): 57-65.

3186 "IBM Compatible." _Electronic Library_ 2 (October 1984): 246.

OCLC M300 WORKSTATION

3187 THOMAS, KEN. "Evolution of Library Use: More Than a Terminal: The M300 Workstation Will Give Users Formidable Computing Power." _OCLC Newsletter_ no. 149 (November 1983): 4-5.

3188 "New OCLC Terminal Specifications Announced." _Small Computers in Libraries_ 3 (November 1983): 1.

3189 THOMAS, KEN. "Libraries Field Test M300 Workstation." _OCLC Newsletter_ no. 152 (May 1984): 2-3.

3190 "OCLC's New M300 Workstation." _Electronic Library_ 2 (July 1984): 146.

OSBORNE

3191 "The Osborne I--A Brief Review." _Small Computers in Libraries_ 2 (June 1982): 6-7.

3192 "Osborne." _Electronic Learning_ 2 (January 1983): 64.

3193 MASON, ROBERT M. "More Bargains & Osborne's Executive." _Library Journal_ 108 (May 15, 1983): 981-82.

3194 SAFFADY, WILLIAM. "Osborne 1 Portable Computer." _Computer Equipment Review_ 5 (July/December 1983): 147-50.

3195 MASON, ROBERT M. "Telecommunications Pro-
      grams--The Osborne Executive--DEC's Rainbow
      100 Plus." Library Journal 108 (November 1,
      1983): 2034-35.

PANASONIC

3196 "Panasonic's 'Super' Sr. Partner Computer."
      Library Hi Tech News 1 (October/November
      1984): 29.

RADIO SHACK/TANDY

3197 "New Radio Shack Computer Announced." Small
      Computers in Libraries 2 (February 1982): 1.

3198 "16-Bit Micros Challenge Minis." Library Sys-
      tems Newsletter 2 (March 1982): 23-24.

3199 "TRS-80 Color Computer." Electronic Learning 2
      (January 1983): 54.

3200 "TRS-80 MODEL III." Electronic Learning 2
      (January 1983): 58-59.

3201 "Radio Shack." Electronic Learning 2 (January
      1983): 64.

3202 SAFFADY, WILLIAM. "TRS-80 Model 16 Small Busi-
      ness Computers." Computer Equipment Review
      5 (January/June 1983): 83-91.

3203 DAVIS, CHARLES H. "Portable Micros: Potentials
      for Information Management." Microcomputers
      for Information Management 1 (March 1984):
      57-65.

3204 "Tandy 1000 Is IBM-Compatible." Electronic
      Learning 4 (January 1985): 61.

3205 "New 256-Kbyte Micro Introduced." T.H.E.
      Journal: Technological Horizons in Education
      12 (January 1985): 123.

3206 FALK, HOWARD. "New Personal Computers." Elec-
      tronic Library 3 (April 1985): 100.

ROLM

3207 GORDON, HELEN A. "Cedar, Juniper Desktops
Announced by ROLM." Online 9 (March 1985):
108.

SHARP

3208 "Sharp." Electronic Learning 2 (January 1983):
64.

3209 FALK, HOWARD. "A Sharp Portable." Electronic
Library 3 (January 1985): 39.

SONY

3210 "Sony." Electronic Learning 2 (January 1983):
64.

TSC

3211 "TSC/Houghton-Mifflin." Electronic Learning 2
(January 1983): 64.

TELCON

3212 SAFFADY, WILLIAM. "Zorba and Nomis Portable
Computers." Computer Equipment Review 5
(July/December 1983): 155-60.

TEXAS INSTRUMENTS

3213 "TI 99/4A." Electronic Learning 2 (January
1983): 53.

3214 SAFFADY, WILLIAM. "Texas Instruments Professional Computer." Computer Equipment
Review 5 (July/December 1983): 166-74.

3215 "TI's Portable." Library Hi Tech 1 (Spring
1984): 85-86.

3216 DAVIS, CHARLES H. "Portable Micros: Potentials
for Information Management." Microcomputers
for Information Management 1 (March 1984):
57-65.

3217 GORDON, HELEN A. "Texas Instruments Offers
         Briefcase-Size PC." Database 8 (February
         1985): 84.

3218 FALK, HOWARD. "Computer in a Briefcase."
         Electronic Library 3 (April 1985): 100.

3219 GORDON, HELEN A. "Texas Instrument's Business
         Pro Announced." Online 9 (July 1985): 83.

TIMEX/SINCLAIR

3220 "Super-Cheap Micros." Small Computers in Li-
         braries 2 (September 1982): 7.

3221 "Timex-Sinclair 1000." Electronic Learning 2
         (January 1983): 53-54.

3222 MASON, ROBERT M. "More Bargains & Osborne's
         Executive." Library Journal 108 (May 15,
         1983): 981-82.

VICTOR

3223 GROSCH, AUDREY N. "The Victor 9000 Micro-
         computer: A Professional Personal Computer
         System." Library Technology Reports 19
         (March/April 1983): 189-214.

XEROX

3224 SAFFADY, WILLIAM. "Xerox 820 Microcomputer."
         Computer Equipment Review 4 (January/June
         1982): 30-35.

ZAISAN

3225 FALK, HOWARD. "Computer Plus Telephone."
         Electronic Library 3 (January 1985): 38.

BOOK REVIEWS

ABI/SELECTS: The Annotated Bibliography of Computer
    Periodicals. David Bond, ed. Louisville, KY:
    Data Courier, 1983. 576p.

3226 "SELECT-ing Computer Periodicals." Software
    Review 2 (September 1983): 208.

3227 EMARD, JEAN-PAUL, and GORDON, HELEN A. Online
    8 (March 1984): 90-91.

AMERICAN LIBRARY ASSOCIATION. COMMITTEE ON CATALOG-
    ING: DESCRIPTION AND ACCESS. Guidelines for
    Using AACR2, Chapter 9 for Cataloging Microcom-
    puter Software. Chicago: American Library
    Association, 1984. 32p.

3228 Journal of Academic Librarianship 10 (November
    1984): 304.

3229 "For Cataloging Software. School Library
    Journal 31 (February 1985): 37.

3230 OLSON, NANCY B. Library Software Review 4
    (May/June 1985): 180.

ANDRESEN, DAVID. Printers. . .Printers. . .Printers;
    A Guide to Selection for the PC. Olympia, WA:
    Washington Library Network, 1984. 35p.

3231 "Printers. . .Printers. . .Printers." Tech-
    nicalities 5 (April 1985): 1.

3232 OCLC Micro 1 (September 1985): 29.

Automation in Libraries: A LITA Bibliography, 1978-
    1982. Compiled by Anne G. Adler, Elizabeth A.
    Baber, Li Ai L. Lee, Rita M. Marsales and Jean R.
    Swanson. Ann Arbor, MI: Pierian Press, 1983.
    177p.

3233 Journal of Academic Librarianship 9 (January 1984): 370.

3234 VOCINO, MICHAEL. Library Hi Tech 1 (Spring 1984): 102-03.

3235 "Software Resources in Print." Library Software Review 3 (March 1984): 126-27.

3236 VASATURO, RONALD. "Worth Noting." Technicalities 4 (March 1984): 2.

3237 CONAWAY, CHARLES WILLIAM. Technical Services Quarterly 2 (Spring/Summer 1985): 146-47.

BEAUMONT, JANE, and KRUEGER, DONALD R. Microcomputers for Libraries: How Useful are They? Ottawa: Canadian Library Association, 1983. 124p.

3238 SHIRINIAN, GEORGE N. "Microcomputers for Libraries: How Useful Are They?--A Review." Small Computers in Libraries 3 (May 1983): 4.

3239 RICHMOND, RICK. "Microcomputer Applications." Library Journal 108 (June 1, 1983): 1114.

3240 RICHMOND, RICK. Journal of Academic Librarianship 9 (September 1983): 243.

3241 GARTEN, EDWARD D. Library Hi Tech 2, no. 1, issue 5 (1984): 84-85.

3242 DAWSON, ANDY. Library Review 33 (Spring 1984): 53.

3243 DAWSON, ANDY. Journal of Academic Librarianship 10 (September 1984): 237.

BEECHHOLD, HENRY F. The Plain English Repair and Maintenance Guide for Home Computers. New York: Simon and Schuster, 1984. 265p.

3244 "Mending Micros." American Libraries 15 (June 1984): 466.

Bowker/Bantam 1984 Complete Sourcebook of Personal
    Computing. New York: R. R. Bowker, 1983. 646p.

3245 "Growing Personal Computer Boom Captured in
        Bowker 'Sourcebook'." Library Journal 108
        (October 15, 1983): 1917.

Bowker's 1985 Complete Sourcebook of Personal Com-
    puting. New York: R. R. Bowker, 1984. 1050p.

3246 RETTIG, JAMES. Wilson Library Bulletin 59
        (March 1985): 499.

BRAND, STEWART. Whole Earth Software Catalog. Garden
    City, NY: Quantum/Doubleday, 1984. 208p.

3247 CURTIS, HOWARD. Special Libraries 76 (Spring
        1985): 161-62.

3248 CURTIS, HOWARD. Journal of Academic Librarian-
        ship 11 (July 1985): 175.

BROWN, EBEN. Timex-Sinclair 1983 Directory; Where to
    Find Practically Everything for the Timex-
    Sinclair Computer. Alexandria, MN: E. Arthur
    Brown Company, 1983. 90p.

3249 "Timex-Sinclairs in Libraries." Small Comput-
        ers in Libraries 3 (July 1983): 6.

BROWN, FRED. Brown Book. Santa Barbara, CA: Fred
    Brown Associates, 1984. 285p.

3250 "Computer 'Blue Books' for Used Micros." Small
        Computers in Libraries 5 (January 1985): 4.

BRUMAN, JANET L. Communications Software for Micro-
    computers. San Jose, CA: CLASS, 1983. 25p.

3251 "Communications Software for Microcomputers."
        Small Computers in Libraries 3 (March 1983):
        6.

3252 "Communications Software--Review." Small
        Computers in Libraries 3 (July 1983): 5.

3253 LOOK, HUGH EVISON. Electronic Library 1 (October 1983): 243-44.

3254 "Book Reviews." Library Hi Tech 2, no. 1, issue 5 (1984): 84-85.

BULLERS, DAVID L., and WADDLE, LINDA L. Processing Computer Software for the School Media Collection. Waterloo, IA: David L. Bullers, 1981. 16p.

3255 PERRY-HOLMES, CLAUDIA. Library Hi Tech News 1 (February 1984): 22.

3256 "Cataloging Software." School Library Journal 31 (September 1984): 51.

3257 Wilson Library Bulletin 59 (October 1984): 156.

BURTON, PAUL F. Microcomputer Applications in Academic Libraries. Library and Information Research Report, no. 16. London: British Library, 1983. 125p.

3258 CORBETT, LINDSAY. Library Review 33 (Autumn 1984): 187.

3259 CORBETT, LINDSAY. Journal of Academic Librarianship 11 (March 1985): 52.

3260 Journal of Academic Librarianship 11 (November 1985): 312.

BURTON, PAUL F. Microcomputer Applications in Libraries and Information Retrieval: A Directory of Users. Edinburgh, Scotland: Leith Nautical College, 1981. 46p.

3261 Vine no. 40 (October 1981): 30.

3262 Electronic Library 1 (January 1983): 29.

BURTON, PHILIP E. A Dictionary of Minicomputing and Microcomputing. New York: Garland STPM Press, 1982. 346p.

3263 BAGLEY, CAROLE A. Educational Technology 22
(July 1982): 42.

CHARTRAND, MARILYN J., and WILLIAMS, CONSTANCE D.
Educational Software Directory: A Subject Guide
to Microcomputer Software. Littleton, CO:
Libraries Unlimited, 1982. 292p.

3264 "Ed Software Directory." Small Computers in
Libraries 2 (November 1982): 7.

3265 "New Educational Software Directory Out."
Small Computers in Libraries 2 (December
1982): 4.

3266 Journal of Academic Librarianship 9 (March
1983): 56-57.

3267 Booklist 79 (April 1, 1983): 1049.

3268 FAY, JIM. "Worth Noting." Technicalities 3
(July 1983); 3-4.

CHEN, CHING-CHIH. MicroUse Directory: Software. West
Newton, MA: MicroUse Information, 1984. 440p.

3269 "Ching-chih Chen Issues Library Applications
Software Directory." Library Journal 109
(November 15, 1984): 2109.

3270 "MicroUse Database Publishes First Directory
on Software." OCLC Newsletter no. 156
(February 1985): 7.

3271 RAITT, DAVID. Electronic Library 3 (April
1985): 117-18.

3272 GARTEN, EDWARD D. Library Hi Tech News no. 17
(June 1985): 10.

3273 GORDON, HELEN A. Online 9 (September 1985):
79-80.

CHEN, CHING-CHIH, and BRESSLER, STACEY E. Microcomputers in Libraries. New York: Neal-Schuman
Publishers, 1982. 259p.

3274 "New Title from Neal-Schuman." Small Computers in Libraries 2 (May 1982): 5.

3275 VAUGHAN, SHEILA. "Applying the Mighty Micro." Library Association Record 84 (December 1982): 437.

3276 CASWELL, JERRY V. RQ 22 (Winter 1982): 213-14.

3277 RAITT, DAVID. Electronic Library 1 (January 1983): 26-27.

3278 GORDON, HELEN A. Online 7 (March 1983): 44-45.

3279 SHIRINIAN, GEORGE N. "Microcomputers in Libraries--A Review." Small Computers in Libraries 3 (April 1983): 5.

3280 CASWELL, JERRY V. Journal of Academic Librarianship 9 (May 1983): 121.

3281 SESSIONS, JUDITH A. College and Research Libraries 44 (May 1983): 271-72.

3282 MAYS, A. H. Journal of Academic Librarianship 9 (September 1983): 243.

3283 LISANTI, SUZANA. Journal of Academic Librarianship 9 (November 1983): 305.

3284 BEAUMONT, JANE. Canadian Library Journal 40 (December 1983): 390.

3285 TROUTNER, JOANNE JOHNSON. "Information About Micros." School Library Journal 30 (February 1984): 39.

3286 BEAUMONT, JANE. Journal of Academic Librarianship 10 (May 1984): 111.

CHRISTIE, LINDA GAIL, and CHRISTIE, JOHN. The Encyclopedia of Microcomputer Terminology: A Source Book for Business and Professional People. Englewood Cliffs, NJ: Prentice-Hall, 1984. 336p.

3287 T.H.E. Journal: Technological Horizons in Education 12 (November 1984): 84.

CIBBARELLI, PAMELA; TENOPIR, CAROL; and KAZLAUSKAS, EDWARD JOHN. Directory of Information Management Software: For Libraries, Information Centers, Record Centers. Studio City, CA: Cibbarelli and Associates, 1983. 133p.

3288 "New Selection Guide." Small Computers in Libraries 3 (June 1983): 7.

3289 Library Software Review 3 (March 1984): 125.

3290 CHWEH, STEVEN S. Library Hi Tech News 15 (April 1985): 11-12.

3291 "Information Management Software Directory." Information Retrieval and Library Automation 21 (November 1985): 10.

CLARK, PHILIP M. Microcomputer Spreadsheet Models for Libraries: Preparing Documents, Budgets, and Statistical Reports. Chicago: American Library Association, 1985. 118p.

3292 College and Research Libraries News 46 (July/ August 1985): 368.

3293 GROSCH, AUDREY N. OCLC Micro 1 (September 1985): 31.

3294 Journal of Academic Librarianship 11 (September 1985): 249.

3295 MILLER, R. BRUCE. Journal of Academic Librarianship 11 (November 1985): 302.

3296 CIARKOWSKI, ELAINE F. Library Hi Tech News no. 21 (November 1985): 13.

CLYDE, LAUREL A., and JOYCE, D. JOAN. Computers and School Libraries: An Annotated Bibliography. Wagga Wagga, New South Wales, Australia: Centre for Library Studies; Riverina College of Advanced Education, 1983. 176p.

3297 "Bibliography from Down Under." Small Computers in Libraries 4 (April 1984): 5.

COLLIER, MEL. Local Area Networks: The Implications for Library and Information Sciences. London: British Library, 1984. 53p.

3298 Journal of Academic Librarianship 11 (November 1985): 315.

Computer-Readable Databases: A Directory and Data Sourcebook. Chicago: American Library Association, 1985. 2v.

3299 "Database Directory Extends Coverage in New Edition." Small Computers in Libraries 4 (March 1984): 5.

COSTA, BETTY, and COSTA, MARIE. A Micro Handbook for Small Libraries and Media Centers. Littleton, CO: Libraries Unlimited, 1983. 216p.

3300 "Two New Micro Books." Small Computers in Libraries 3 (May 1983): 7.

3301 "Microcomputers in Small Libraries." American Libraries 14 (September 1983): 565.

3302 "New Books." Educational Computer Magazine 3 (October 1983): 65.

3303 Journal of Academic Librarianship 9 (November 1983): 305.

3304 GORDON, HELEN A. Online 8 (March 1984): 92.

3305 LOERTSCHER, DAVID V. "About Micros." School Library Journal 30 (March 1984): 120.

3306 VERBESEY, J. ROBERT. Library Hi Tech 1 (Spring 1984): 100-01.

3307 ANDERSON, M. ELAINE. RQ 23 (Spring 1984): 378.

3308 NASH, JOHN C., and NASH, MARY M. Canadian Library Journal 41 (April 1984): 100.

3309 ATTIG, BARBARA. *School Library Media Quarterly* 12 (Summer 1984): 311.

3310 NASH, JOHN C., and NASH, MARY M. *Journal of Academic Librarianship* 10 (July 1984): 175.

3311 BLANCHARD, MARK. *OCLC Micro* 1 (September 1985): 31-32.

CULOTTA, WENDY; ERCEGOVAC, Z.; and ROTH, D. *Local Area Networks and Libraries: The Los Angeles Chapter of ASIS Seminar Proceedings.* Studio City, CA: Pacific Information, 1985. 174p.

3312 *Journal of Academic Librarianship* 11 (November 1985): 315.

DAHMKE, MARK. *Microcomputer Operating Systems.* New York: Byte Books/McGraw-Hill, 1982. 227p.

3313 WACLENA, KEITH. *Information Processing and Management* 19, no. 3 (1983): 188.

DANIEL, EVELYN H., and NOTOWITZ, CAROL I. *Media and Microcomputers in the Library: A Selected, Annotated Resource Guide.* Phoenix, AZ: Oryx Press, 1984. 157p.

3314 "Guide to Nonprint Media Published." *Electronic Library* 2 (October 1984): 212.

3315 RAITT, DAVID. *Electronic Library* 2 (October 1984): 253.

3316 *American Libraries* 15 (November 1984): 748.

3317 JOHNSON, RICHARD D. *Journal of Academic Librarianship* 10 (January 1985): 359.

3318 McKINNIE, WILLIAM G. *Emergency Librarian* 12 (January/February 1985): 32.

3319 TERTELL, SUSAN M. *Library Software Review* 4 (January/February 1985): 38.

3320 FLORANCE, VALERIE. Information Technology and Libraries 4 (March 1985): 73-75.

3321 JOHNSON, RICHARD D. Journal of Academic Librarianship 11 (March 1985): 52.

3322 ROEDER, JOAN. "Micro Resource Guide." School Library Journal 31 (May 1985): 46.

3323 FLORANCE, VALERIE. Journal of Academic Librarianship 11 (July 1985): 175.

3324 ROEDER, JOAN. Journal of Academic Librarianship 11 (September 1985): 249.

Datapro Complete Guide to Dial-Up Databases. Delran, NJ: Datapro Research Corp., 1984. 1v. (Loose leaf).

3325 "Datapro Dial-Up Databases Guide." Small Computers in Libraries 5 (February 1985): 10.

DELLOW, DONALD, A., and POOLE, LAWRENCE H. Microcomputer Applications in Administration and Instruction. San Francisco: Jossey-Bass, 1984. 122p.

3326 Journal of Academic Librarianship 10 (January 1985): 368.

DEWEY, PATRICK R. Public Access Microcomputers: A Handbook for Librarians. White Plains, NY: Knowledge Industry Publications, 1984. 151p.

3327 American Libraries 15 (July/August 1984): 538.

3328 RAITT, DAVID. Electronic Library 2 (October 1984): 253-54.

3329 CORCOS, CHRIS. Library Hi Tech 2, no. 4, issue 8 (1984): 91.

3330 GORDON, HELEN A. Online 8 (November 1984): 98.

3331 BREWER, JAMES. RQ (Winter 1984): 241-42.

3332 STABLER, KAREN CHITTICK. Information Technology and Libraries 3 (December 1984): 425-26.

3333 SONFLIETH, SUSIE. RQ 24 (Spring 1985): 373-74.

3334 STABLER, KAREN CHITTICK. Journal of Academic Librarianship 11 (May 1985): 114.

3335 SULLIVAN, PEGGY. Library Software Review 4 (May/June 1985): 180-81.

3336 SONFLIETH, SUSIE. Journal of Academic Librarianship 11 (July 1985): 175.

Directory of Discount Computer Suppliers. New York: Discount America Publications, 1983. 30p.

3337 "Discover Discounts." American Libraries 14 (September 1983): 565.

Directory of Microcomputer Applications in Libraries. San Jose, CA: CLASS, 1984. 128p.

3338 "Micro Applications Directory." American Libraries 16 (February 1985): 132.

3339 "CLASS' Directory of Micro Applications." Small Computers in Libraries 5 (February 1985): 9.

3340 GORDON, HELEN A. Online 9 (September 1985): 80.

Directory of Microcomputers in Public Libraries in New York State. New York: New York Library Association Publications, 1984. 120p.

3341 "Micros in N. Y. Public Libraries." Library Journal 110 (February 1, 1985): 79.

3342 "Empire State Micros." American Libraries 16 (February 1985): 133.

The Directory of Public Domain (and User Supported) Software for the IBM Personal Computer. Santa

Clara, CA: PC Software Interest Group, 1984. 109p.

3343 "Public-Domain Entries." American Libraries 15 (June 1984): 465.

3344 College and Research Libraries News 45 (June 1984): 317.

DODD, SUE A. Cataloging Machine-Readable Data Files: An Interpretive Manual. Chicago: American Library Association, 1982. 247p.

3345 Journal of Academic Librarianship 9 (May 1983): 114.

3346 INTNER, SHEILA S. Information Technology and Libraries 2 (June 1983): 226-29.

3347 VASATURO, RONALD. Journal of Academic Librarianship 9 (July 1983): 168-69.

3348 VASATURO, RONALD. Journal of Academic Librarianship 9 (September 1983): 245-46.

3349 STAMELOS, ELLEN. Public Library Quarterly 4 (Fall 1983): 112-13.

3350 "Microcomputing." American Libraries 16 (November 1985): 748-49.

DOWLIN, KENNETH E. The Electronic Library: The Promise and the Process. New York: Neal-Schuman, 1984. 199p.

3351 "Search Aids & Publications." Online (March 1984): 82-83.

3352 Journal of Academic Librarianship 10 (May 1984): 111-12.

3353 GORDON, HELEN A. Online 8 (May 1984): 88.

3354 SAGER, DONALD J. "The Electronic Imperative." Library Journal 109 (May 15, 1984): 960.

3355 Library Software Review 3 (June 1984): 286.

3356 RAITT, DAVID. Electronic Library 2 (July 1984): 162.

3357 GARTEN, EDWARD D. Journal of Academic Librarianship 10 (July 1984): 164.

3358 McKEE, BOB. "Electronic Access." Library Association Record 86 (August 1984): 311.

3359 GARTEN, EDWARD D. Journal of Academic Librarianship 10 (September 1984): 237-38.

3360 JONES, ELLEN. Canadian Library Journal 41 (October 1984): 303.

3361 ROSENBERG, VICTOR. Library Quarterly 54 (October 1984): 428-29.

3362 PETERS, PAUL EVAN. Information Technology and Libraries 3 (December 1984): 426-27.

3363 JONES, ELLEN. Journal of Academic Librarianship 10 (January 1985): 368-69.

3364 ROSENBERG, VICTOR. Journal of Academic Librarianship 11 (March 1985): 52.

3365 PETERS, PAUL EVAN. Journal of Academic Librarianship 11 (May 1985): 114.

DYKSTRA, DAVID C. Easy Data Computer Comparisons; The Only Comprehensive Computer Buyer's Guide. Newport Beach, CA: Easy Data, 1983. 139p.

3366 "Computer Comparisons." ACCESS: Microcomputers in Libraries 3 (Spring 1983): 32.

EDISON-SWIFT, SUSAN, and EDISON-SWIFT, PAUL. Microcomputer Equipment Security. Manitowoc, WI: Wisconsin Educational Media Association, 1983. 30p.

3367 "Computer Security." School Library Journal 31 (September 1984): 51.

610 / BOOK REVIEWS

EISENBERG, MICHAEL. The Direct Use of Online Bibliographic Information Systems by Untrained End
Users: A Review of Research. Syracuse, NY: ERIC
Clearinghouse on Information Resources; Information Resources Publications, 1983. 40p.

3368 EMARD, JEAN-PAUL. Online 8 (September 1984):
107-08.

ELLSWORTH, SUSAN. User's Handbook of Personal Computer System Care. Oxnard, CA: Simplist's
Principle, 1984. 36p.

3369 "Media Resource Service." Small Computers in
Libraries 4 (June 1984): 4.

FOSDICK, HOWARD. Computer Basics for Librarians and
Information Specialists. Arlington, VA: Information Resources Press, 1981. 203p.

3370 THOMPSON, RICHARD E. "Worth Noting." Technicalities 3 (July 1983): 12.

FROEHLICH, ROBERT A. The Free Software Catalog and
Directory: The What, Where, Why and How of
Selecting, Locating, Acquiring, and Using Free
Software. New York: Crown Publishers, 1984.
475p.

3371 T.H.E. Journal: Technological Horizons in
Education 12 (January 1985): 72.

3372 DEWEY, PATRICK R. Booklist 81 (March 1, 1985):
924.

3373 CURRY, MARY CLARE. Book Report 4 (May/June
1985): 37.

GADER, BERTRAM, and NODAR, MANUEL V. Apple Software
for Pennies. New York: Warner, 1985. 303p.

3374 DEWEY, PATRICK R. Booklist 82 (September 1,
1985): 26.

GATES, HILARY. A Directory of Library and Information

Retrieval Software for Microcomputers. Brookfield, VT: Gower, 1985. 59p.

3375 COLLINGE, BRIAN. Electronic Library 3 (April
1985): 116-17.

3376 RAITT, DAVID. Electronic Library 3 (April
1985): 118; and Online Review 9 (June 1985):
202.

3377 "Microcomputer Software Directory Update."
Information Retrieval and Library Automation
21 (October 1985): 10.

3378 Journal of Academic Librarianship 11 (November
1985): 312, 314.

3379 GARMAN, NANCY J. Database 8 (December 1985):
84.

3380 WILLIAMS, THOMAS. Library Hi Tech News no. 22
(December 1985): 16.

GILMAN, JAMES A. Information Technology and the
School Library Resource Centre: The Microcomputer
as Resourcerer's Apprentice. London: Council for
Educational Technology, 1983. 289p.

3381 BOEHMER, M. CLARE. School Library Media Quarterly 12 (Fall 1984): 437-38.

3382 BOEHMER, M. CLARE. Journal of Academic Librarianship 10 (January 1985): 364.

GLOSSBRENNER, ALFRED. How to Buy Software: The Master
Guide to Picking the Right Program. New York:
St. Martin's, 1984. 648p.

3383 ANDERSON, ERIC S. Booklist 80 (May 1, 1984):
1224.

GLOSSBRENNER, ALFRED. How to Get Free Software: The
Master Guide to Free Programs for Every Brand of
Personal or Home Computer. New York: St.
Martin's, 1984. 436p.

3384 SMITH, DAVID FAY. Publishers Weekly 226
      (August 24, 1984): 41.

3385 "Microcomputing." American Libraries 15
      (November 1984): 746-47.

GOLDMAN, CARL A. Help, There's a Computer in the
      Office. San Francisco, CA: Rising Star Press,
      1979. 248p.

3386 KIPPERMAN, JACOB. Software Review 1 (February
      1982): 100-01.

GRIFFITHS, JOSE-MARIE. Application of Minicomputers
      and Microcomputers to Information Handling.
      Paris: General Information Programme and UNISIST,
      UNESCO, 1981. 94p.

3387 "Mini-Microcomputer Applications to Information
      Handling." Information Retrieval and Li-
      brary Automation 18 (June 1982): 7.

3388 Electronic Library 1 (April 1983): 104.

3389 KIRK, ARTEMIS G. Library Hi Tech 2, no. 2,
      issue 6 (1984): 88-89.

3390 KIRK, ARTEMIS G. Journal of Academic Librar-
      ianship 11 (March 1985): 52-53.

HAYCOCK, KENNETH R. Microcomputers: A Guide to Peri-
      odicals for Teachers, Librarians and Media Spe-
      cialists. Vancouver, BC: Association for Media
      and Technology in Education in Canada, 1984.
      25p.

3391 "New Guide from Canada." Small Computers in
      Libraries 4 (April 1984): 7.

HUNTER, ERIC J. "ABC" of BASIC: An Introduction to
      Programming for Librarians. London: Bingley,
      1982. 120p.

3392 Journal of Academic Librarianship 9 (March
      1983): 59.

IBM PC Expansion & Software Guide. Indianapolis, IN: Que Corporation, 1982. 250p.

3393 ALLEY, BRIAN. "Worth Noting." Technicalities 3 (November 1983): 15.

KAZLAUSKAS, EDWARD J. System Analysis for Library Microcomputer Applications. Studio City, CA: Pacific Information, 1985. 104p.

3394 Journal of Academic Librarianship 11 (November 1985): 314.

KEREN, CARL, and PERLMUTTER, LINDA. The Application of Mini- and Micro-Computers in Information, Documentation and Libraries. Proceedings of the International Conference on the Application of Mini- and Micro-Computers in Information, Documentation and Libraries, Tel Aviv, Israel, 13-18 March 1983. New York: North-Holland, 1983. 801p.

3395 KIRK, ARTEMIS G. Library Hi Tech 2, no. 2, issue 6 (1984): 88-89.

3396 "Small Computer Applications in Information, Documentation and Libraries." Information Retrieval and Library Automation 19 (February 1984): 10.

3397 BORKO, HAROLD. "Mini/Micro Menu." Library Journal 109 (April 15, 1984): 796.

3398 POTTER, WILLIAM GRAY. Information Technology and Libraries 3 (June 1984): 217-18, 220.

3399 BORKO, HAROLD. Journal of Academic Librarianship 10 (July 1984): 176.

3400 RAITT, DAVID. Electronic Library 2 (July 1984): 162.

3401 POTTER, WILLIAM GRAY. Journal of Academic Librarianship 10 (September 1984): 238.

3402 WRIGHT, GORDON, H. Canadian Library Journal
       41 (October 1984): 302.

3403 WRIGHT, GORDON H. Journal of Academic Librar-
       ianship 10 (January 1985): 369-70.

3404 KIRK, ARTEMIS G. Journal of Academic Librar-
       ianship 11 (March 1985): 52.

KEREN, CARL, and SERED, IRINA. International Inven-
    tory of Software Packages in the Information
    Field. Paris: UNESCO, 1983. 605p.

3405 "Recent Publication." Online Review 9 (Febru-
       ary 1985): 48.

3406 Journal of Academic Librarianship 11 (September
       1985): 249.

KESNER, RICHARD M. Automation for Archivists and
    Records Managers: Planning and Implementation
    Strategies. Chicago: American Library Associa-
    tion, 1984. 222p.

3407 CHEPESIUK, RON. "Archivists and Automation."
       Library Journal 109 (September 15, 1984):
       1738.

3408 MASLYN, DAVID C. Library Hi Tech 3, no. 1,
       issue 9 (1985): 114-15.

3409 BRICHFORD, MAYNARD. Online Review 9 (February
       1985): 45-46.

3410 WILSON, LOFTON. Information Technology and
       Libraries 4 (March 1985): 78, 80.

3411 DiCARLO, MICHAEL. Journal of Academic Librar-
       ianship 11 (May 1985): 99-100.

3412 STRATHERN, GLORIA M. Canadian Library Journal
       42 (June 1985): 165, 167.

3413 WILSON, LOFTON. Journal of Academic Librar-
       ianship 11 (July 1985): 189.

3414 MASLYN, DAVID C. Journal of Academic Librarianship 11 (September 1985): 259.

KESNER, RICHARD M., and JONES, CLIFTON H. Microcomputer Applications in Libraries: A Management Tool for the 1980's and Beyond. Westport, CT: Greenwood Press, 1984. 250p.

3415 "New Books & Guides Published." Small Computers in Libraries 4 (October 1984): 5.

3416 HERTHER, NANCY K. Library Software Review 4 (January/February 1985): 38-39.

3417 CRAWFORD, WALT. Information Technology and Libraries 4 (March 1985): 80-82.

3418 HAYDEN, LEE. RQ 24 (Spring 1985): 373.

3419 RAITT, DAVID. Electronic Library 3 (April 1985): 116.

3420 GUILFOYLE, MARVIN. Journal of Academic Librarianship 11 (May 1985): 98-99.

3421 BINKLEY, DAVID. Canadian Library Journal 42 (June 1985): 169.

3422 HAYDEN, LEE. Journal of Academic Librarianship 11 (July 1985): 187.

3423 BINKLEY, DAVID. Journal of Academic Librarianship 11 (September 1985): 259.

LEIBSON, STEVE. The Handbook of Microcomputer Interfacing. Blue Ridge Summit, PA: TAB Books, 1983. 261p.

3424 JEMELKA, JORG R. Library Hi Tech 1 (Winter 1983): 91.

LOOP, LIZA; ANTON, JULIE; and ZAMORA, RAMON. ComputerTown: Bringing Computer Literacy to Your Community. Reston, VA: Reston Publishing Co., 1983. 160p.

3425 Publishers Weekly 224 (August 5, 1983): 49.

LOVE, ROLLAND, and LIKENS, CHRIS. IBM Software Directory. New York: R. R. Bowker, 1984. 934p.

3426 DEWEY, PATRICK R. Booklist 81 (March 1, 1985): 924.

MASON, ROBERT M., and ENNISS, STEPHEN C. The Micro Consumer: Library Software, A Guide to Selection. Atlanta, GA: Metrics Research Corp., 1984. 110p.

3427 "'Micro Consumer' Software Buying Guides." Library Hi Tech News no. 16 (May 1985): 13-14.

3428 SMISEK, THOMAS. "Selecting Software." Library Journal 110 (August 1985): 71.

MASON, ROBERT M., and ENNISS, STEPHEN C. The Micro Consumer: Word Processing, A Guide to Selection. Atlanta, GA: Metrics Research Corp., 1984. 104p.

3429 "'Micro Consumer' Software Buying Guides." Library Hi Tech News no. 16 (May 1985): 13-14.

MATTHEWS, JOSEPH R. A Reader on Choosing an Automated Library System. Chicago: American Library Association, 1983. 390p.

3430 DOWLIN, KENNETH E. "Choosing Computers." Library Journal 109 (March 1, 1984): 463.

McCUNN, DONALD H. Write, Edit, and Print; Word Processing With Personal Computers. San Francisco: Design Enterprises of San Francisco, 1982. 527p.

3431 SCHUYLER, MICHAEL. ACCESS: Microcomputers in Libraries 2 (October 1982): 23.

3432 "Two Unusual Micro Books." Small Computers in Libraries 3 (May 1983): 4-5.

3433 COLLVER, RANDALL L. Information Technology and Libraries 2 (September 1983): 334-35.

MELLIN, MICHAEL, and HAYS, NANCY. The Book of IBM
    Software 1985. Los Angeles: Arrays, Inc., 1984.
    547p.

3434 ANDERSON, ERIC S. Booklist 82 (September 1,
        1985): 26.

Microcomputer Publications Survey. Norwalk, CT:
    International Resource Development, 1983. 120p.

3435 Library Review 33 (Summer 1984): 122-23.

3436 Journal of Academic Librarianship 10 (January
        1985): 370.

Microcomputers for Libraries: Product Review and Pro-
    curement Guide. Powell, OH: James E. Rush
    Associates, 1984. 1v. (Loose leaf).

3437 "Microcomputer Product Review." Small Com-
        puters in Libraries 4 (February 1984): 5.

3438 "Microcomputers for Libraries." Library Soft-
        ware Review 3 (September 1984): 426.

3439 CRAWFORD, WALT. "Two Books on Microcomputers
        for Libraries." Library Hi Tech 2, no. 2,
        issue 6 (1984): 83-85, 87-88.

3440 CRAWFORD, WALT. Journal of Academic Librar-
        ianship 11 (March 1985): 53.

3441 MIMNAUSH, ELLEN NULTY. Library Software Review
        4 (July/August 1985): 263-64.

Microcomputers in Education. Norwalk, CT: Inter-
    national Resource Development, 1983. 196p.

3442 "Legal Challenges Among the Issues Pegged in
        Forecast on Microcomputers." Library
        Journal 108 (April 15, 1983): 780.

MILLER, INABETH. Microcomputers and the Media
    Specialist: An Annotated Bibliography. Syracuse,
    NY: ERIC Clearinghouse on Information Resources,
    1981. 70p.

3443 ABBOTT, CAROL. School Library Media Quarterly
      11 (Spring 1983): 224.

3444 ABBOTT, CAROL. Journal of Academic Librarian-
      ship 9 (July 1983): 173.

MILLER, INABETH. Microcomputers in School Library
      Media Centers. New York: Neal-Schuman, 1984.
      165p.

3445 EMARD, JEAN-PAUL. Online 8 (May 1984): 89-90.

3446 "Micros in Media Centers." American Libraries
      15 (June 1984): 464.

3447 BLIGHT, MARILYN. School Library Media Quarter-
      ly 13 (Winter 1985): 77-78.

3448 WILLIAMS, LAURIE. Library Hi Tech News no. 15
      (April 1985): 14.

3449 BLIGHT, MARILYN. Journal of Academic Librarian-
      ship 11 (September 1985): 240.

MILLIOT, JIM. Micros at Work: Case Studies of Micro-
      computers in Libraries. White Plains, NY:
      Knowledge Industry Publications, 1985. 148p.

3450 RICHMOND, RICK. "Micro Case Studies." Library
      Journal 110 (October 1, 1985): 78.

NAUMER, JANET NOLL. Media Center Management With an
      Apple II. Littleton, CO: Libraries Unlimited:
      1984. 236p.

3451 "New Books & Guides Published." Small Com-
      puters in Libraries 4 (October 1984): 5.

3452 COSTA, BETTY. Computing Teacher 12 (November
      1984): 45.

3453 "Libraries Unlimited Media Center: Management
      With an Apple II." Library Hi Tech News
      no. 11/12 (December 1984/January 1985): 17.

3454 Classroom Computer Learning 5 (January 1985):
62.

3455 NASH, MARY M. Canadian Library Journal 42
(February 1985): 40.

3456 BUTTREY, TOM. Library Software Review 4
(March/April 1985): 111.

3457 NASH, MARY M. Journal of Academic Librarianship 11 (May 1985): 119.

NICITA, MICHAEL, and PETRUSHA, RONALD. Reader's Guide
to Microcomputer Books. 2nd ed. White Plains,
NY: Knowledge Industry Publications, 1984. 473p.

3458 BEAN, CHRISTOPHER A. Library Software Review
4 (May/June 1985): 181.

NOLAN, JEANNE M. Micro Software Evaluations. Torrance, CA: Nolan Information Management Services,
1984. 176p.

3459 BYNON, GEORGE. Information Technology and
Libraries 3 (September 1984): 320-21.

3460 BYNON, GEORGE. Journal of Academic Librarianship 11 (March 1985): 53.

3461 GATES, HILARY. Journal of Academic Librarianship 11 (July 1985): 176.

NOLAN, JEANNE M. Micro Software Report, Library
Edition, 2nd ed. Torrance, CA: Nolan Information
Management Services, 1984. 157p.

3462 "Micro Software Report/Review Resource Issued."
Information Retrieval and Library Automation
19 (February 1984): 8.

3463 BYNON, GEORGE. Information Technology and
Libraries 3 (September 1984): 320-21.

3464 BYNON, GEORGE. Journal of Academic Librarianship 11 (March 1985): 53.

OLSON, NANCY B. A Manual of AACR2 Examples for Microcomputer Software and Video Games. Lake Crystal,
MN: Soldier Creek Press, 1983. 69p.

3465 "Cataloging Software and Games." American
Libraries 14 (November 1983): 683.

3466 PERRY-HOLMES, CLAUDIA. Library Hi Tech News
1 (May 1984): 21.

OUVERSON, MARLIN D. A Glossary of Microcomputer
Terms; Plus How to Buy the Right Computer for
You. Menlo Park, CA: People's Computer Co.,
1983. 27p.

3467 "ComputerTown Announces New Books." Small
Computers in Libraries 3 (May 1983): 3.

PANTELIDIS, VERONICA SEXAUER. Microcomputer Essentials. Greenville, NC: East Carolina University
Department of Library Science, 1984. 83p.

3468 "Microcomputer Manual Released." Small Computers in Libraries 4 (March 1984): 4-5.

3469 "East Carolina University Library Science
Department Publishes Books on Microcomputers." School Library Media Quarterly
13 (Winter 1985): 5.

PETERSON, DALE. Microcomputer Q & A. Menlo Park,
CA: People's Computer Co., 1983. 29p.

3470 "ComputerTown Announces New Books." Small
Computers in Libraries 3 (May 1983): 3.

POPENOE, CRIS. Book Bytes: The User's Guide to 1200
Microcomputer Books. New York: Pantheon, 1984.
233p.

3471 DEWEY, PATRICK R. Booklist 80 (July 1984):
1518.

POYNTER, DAN. Computer Selection Guide. Santa
Barbara, CA: Para Publishing, 1983. 164p.

3472 American Libraries 14 (September 1983): 565.

PRATT, ALLAN D. A Selective Guide to the Micro-
     computer Literature. Tucson, AZ: Graham Conley
     Press, 1983. 60p.

3473 "Guide to Micro Literature Out." Small Com-
     puters in Libraries 3 (March 1983): 2.

3474 "Library Micro-Use Materials Offered by Graham
     Conley Press." Library Journal 108 (August
     1983): 1414.

3475 Journal of Academic Librarianship 9 (September
     1983): 244.

3476 PERRY-HOLMES, CLAUDIA. Library Hi Tech News
     1 (February 1984): 22.

The Public Domain Software Catalog. Woodland Hills,
     CA: Elliam Associates, 1984. 1v.

3477 "Public-Domain Entries." American Libraries 15
     (June 1984): 465-66.

3478 "Public Domain Software." Library Journal 110
     (February 1, 1985): 79.

RORVIG, MARK E. Microcomputers and Libraries: A Guide
     to Technology, Products and Applications. White
     Plains, NY: Knowledge Industry Publications,
     1981. 134p.

3479 PRATT, ALLAN D. "Microcomputers in Libraries--
     Review." Small Computers in Libraries 2
     (February 1982): 6-7.

3480 Journal of Academic Librarianship 8 (March
     1982): 58.

3481 GORDON, HELEN A. "Microcomputers and Li-
     braries." Online 6 (May 1982): 44-45.

3482 SCHUYLER, MICHAEL. Information Technology
     and Libraries 1 (September 1982): 307-09.

3483 DOWLIN, KENNETH E. Journal of Academic Librarianship 8 (November 1982): 320.

3484 SCHUYLER, MICHAEL. Journal of Academic Librarianship 8 (January 1983): 382.

3485 GROSCH, AUDREY N. Special Libraries 74 (January 1983): 102-03.

3486 SANDERS, GLENN. Journal of Academic Librarianship 9 (March 1983): 60.

3487 GROSCH, AUDREY N. Journal of Academic Librarianship 9 (May 1983): 122.

3488 McMURDO, GEORGE. Library Review 33 (Spring 1984): 53.

3489 McMURDO, GEORGE. Journal of Academic Librarianship 10 (September 1984): 242.

ROSENBERG, JERRY M. Dictionary of Computers, Data Processing and Telecommunications. New York: Wiley, 1984. 614p.

3490 "Dictionaries." Library Software Review 3 (March 1984): 128.

3491 "Crossfields Glossary Links Computers, Data Processing and Telecommunications." Information Retrieval and Library Automation 20 (August 1984): 10.

ROSENBERG, KENYON C. Dictionary of Library and Educational Technology. 2nd ed., revised. Littleton, CO: Libraries Unlimited, 1983. 185p.

3492 "Books in Brief." Library Software Review 3 (June 1984): 285.

SCHLOBIN, ROGER. Word Choice: An Advanced Guide to Selecting a CP/M Word Processor and a Microcomputer for Home, University, and Business. Lombard, IL: Quest Publishing, 1983. 86p.

3493 BARKER, THOMAS T. "Word Processing Selection
Material: A Book Review." Collegiate
Microcomputer 2 (August 1984): 267-68.

SCHWARTZ, NARDA LACEY. The Whole Computer Catalog.
Fullerton, CA: Designs III Publishers, 1983.
460p.

3494 "The Whole Computer Catalog." American Libraries 15 (April 1984): 268.

SHIRINIAN, GEORGE N. Microcomputing Periodicals: An
Annotated Bibliography. 8th ed. Toronto: The
Author, 1983. 98p.

3495 MORGAN, LYNN. Serials Librarian 9 (Fall 1984):
99-100.

SHIRINIAN, GEORGE N. Microcomputing Periodicals: An
Annotated Bibliography. 9th ed. revised and
expanded. Toronto: The Author, 1983. 141p.

3496 "New Edition of Micro-Periodicals Out." Small
Computers in Libraries 3 (October 1983): 7.

SIMPSON, GEORGE A. Microcomputers in Library Automation. McLean, VA: Metrek, A Division of the
MITRE Corp., 1978. 50p.

3497 DOWLIN, MAY. Public Library Quarterly 2
(Spring 1980): 65.

SINCLAIR, I. R. Inside Your Computer. Peterborough,
NH: Wayne Green Publications, 1983. 108p.

3498 MASON, ROBERT M. "More Books & Guidebooks."
Library Journal 108 (October 1, 1983):
1856-57.

The Software Encyclopedia. New York: R. R. Bowker,
1985. 2v.

3499 RETTIG, JAMES. Wilson Library Bulletin 60
(December 1985): 67.

624 / BOOK REVIEWS

Software Reports. Carlsbad, CA: Allenbach Industries, 1983. 1v. (Loose leaf).

3500 "Educational Software Reviews." American Libraries 14 (September 1983): 565.

3501 Booklist 80 (November 1, 1983): 441.

3502 SINESKY, MICHELE. Library Software Review 3 (June 1984): 288.

The Software Source. Plano TX: The Software Source, 1983. 1v. (Loose leaf).

3503 ALLEY, BRIAN. "Worth Noting." Technicalities 3 (November 1983): 15.

SPENCER, DONALD D. Spencer's Computer Dictionary for Everyone. New York: Scribner's, 1985. 290p.

3504 "Computer Dictionary for Everyone." T.H.E. Journal: Technological Horizons in Education 12 (November 1984): 89.

THOMASON, NEVADA WALLIS. Microcomputer Information for School Media Centers. Metuchen, NJ: Scarecrow Press, 1985. 334p.

3505 Journal of Academic Librarianship 11 (July 1985): 169-70.

3506 "Microcomputer Information for School Media Centers." T.H.E. Journal: Technological Horizons in Education 13 (September 1985): 66.

TIJERINA, LOUIS. Video Display Terminal Workstation Ergonomics. Dublin, OH: OCLC, 1984. 28p.

3507 "Workstation Ergonomics." Small Computers in Libraries 5 (February 1985): 9.

TREVELYAN, A., and ROWAT, MARTIN J. An Investigation of the Use of Systems Programs in Library Applications of Microcomputers. London: British Library, 1983. 156p.

3508 BURTON, PAUL F. Library Review 33 (Autumn
      1984): 185-87.

3509 BURTON, PAUL F. Journal of Academic Librarian-
      ship 11 (March 1985): 53.

TROUTNER, JOANNE JOHNSON. The Media Specialist, the
    Microcomputer, and the Curriculum. Littleton,
    CO: Libraries Unlimited, 1983. 181p.

3510 "Two New Micro Books." Small Computers in
      Libraries 3 (May 1983): 7.

3511 "New Book for Media Specialists." Small Com-
      puters in Libraries 4 (March 1984): 5.

3512 EMARD, JEAN-PAUL. Online 8 (May 1984): 89-90.

3513 "Micros in Media Centers." American Libraries
      15 (June 1984): 464.

3514 ROEDER, JOAN. "Micros in the Curriculum."
      School Library Journal 31 (September 1984):
      50.

3515 WALL, ELIZABETH. Electronic Education 4
      (March/April 1985): 62.

3516 POLGAR, JOAN J. School Library Media Quarterly
      13 (Winter 1985): 79.

TRUDELL, LIBBY; BRUMAN, JANET; and OLIVER, DENNIS.
    Options for Electronic Mail. White Plains, NY:
    Knowledge Industry Publications, 1984. 172p.

3517 McGEE, JENNY. Library Hi Tech News no. 17
      (June 1985): 10-11.

3518 GORDON, HELEN A. Online 9 (September 1985): 79.

TRUETT, CAROL, and GILLESPIE, LORI. Choosing Educa-
    tional Software: A Buyer's Guide. Littleton, CO:
    Libraries Unlimited, 1984. 202p.

3519 "Microcomputing." American Libraries 15
      (May 1984): 348.

WALTON, ROBERT A. Microcomputers: A Planning and
Implementation Guide for Librarians and Information Professionals. Phoenix, AZ: Oryx Press,
1983. 96p.

3520 Information Intelligence Online Libraries and
Microcomputers 1 (September 1983): 9.

3521 College and Research Libraries News 45 (February 1984): 104.

3522 GORDON, HELEN A. Online 8 (March 1984): 89-90.

3523 Library Software Review 3 (March 1984): 132-33.

3524 "Manual for Managing Micros." American Libraries 15 (March 1984): 185.

3525 RICHMOND, RICK. "Computer Procurement."
Library Journal 109 (March 15, 1984): 566.

3526 TYCKOSON, DAVID. "Worth Noting." Technicalities 4 (May 1984): 15.

3527 POTTER, WILLIAM GRAY. Information Technology
and Libraries 3 (June 1984): 217-18, 220.

3528 RICHMOND, RICK. Journal of Academic Librarianship 10 (July 1984): 176.

3529 BEAUMONT, JANE. Canadian Library Journal 41
(August 1984): 219.

3530 POTTER, WILLIAM GRAY. Journal of Academic
Librarianship 10 (September 1984): 238.

3531 HENDERSON, HELEN. Electronic Library 2
(October 1984): 252-53.

3532 BEAUMONT, JANE. Journal of Academic Librarianship 10 (November 1984): 303.

3533 GARTEN, EDWARD D. Library Hi Tech 2, no. 1,
issue 5 (1984): 84-85.

3534 TROUTNER, JOANNE JOHNSON. School Library Media
     Quarterly 13 (Spring 1985): 152-53.

3535 TROUTNER, JOANNE JOHNSON. Journal of Academic
     Librarianship 11 (November 1985): 314.

WEBSTER, TONY. Microcomputer Buyer's Guide. Los
   Angeles, CA: Computer Reference Guide, 1981.
   326p.

3536 "Micro Buyer's Guide Published." Library Sys-
     tems Newsletter 1 (November 1981): 39.

3537 RAGAN, TILLMAN J. Educational Technology 22
     (December 1982): 32.

3538 RETTIG, JAMES. Wilson Library Bulletin 57
     (June 1983): 883-84.

3539 COHEN, ALLEN. RQ 23 (Spring 1984): 367-69.

3540 DEWEY, PATRICK R. Booklist 81 (March 1, 1985):
     925.

WEBSTER, TONY, and CHAMPION, RICHARD. Microcomputer
   Software Buyer's Guide. New York: McGraw-Hill,
   1984. 422p.

3541 RETTIG, JAMES. Wilson Library Bulletin 59
     (December 1984): 292.

3542 ANDERSON, ERIC S. Booklist 81 (March 1, 1985):
     925.

WILLIS, JERRY. How to Use the Timex-Sinclair Computer. Beaverton, OR: Dilithium Press, 1983.
   124p.

3543 "Timex-Sinclairs in Libraries." Small Com-
     puters in Libraries 3 (July 1983): 6.

WILLIS, JERRY, and MILLER, MERYL. Computers for
   Everybody. 2nd ed. Beaverton, OR: Dilithium
   Press, 1983. 262p.

3544 PATRICK, PATTY. "Computers for Everybody--
     A Review." Small Computers in Libraries
     3 (March 1983): 2.

WOODS, LAWRENCE A., and POPE, NOLAN F. The Librar-
     ian's Guide to Microcomputer Technology and
     Applications. White Plains, NY: Published for
     ASIS by Knowledge Industry Publications, 1983.
     209p.

3545 "Microcomputer Usage." Library Journal 108
     (November 1, 1983): 2036.

3546 GARTEN, EDWARD D. Library Hi Tech 2, no. 1,
     issue 5 (1984): 84-85.

3547 CRAWFORD, WALT. "Two Books on Microcomputers
     for Libraries." Library Hi Tech 2, no. 2,
     issue 6 (1984): 83-85, 87-88.

3548 CROOK, ALISON. Journal of Academic Librarian-
     ship 10 (November 1984): 303.

3549 BUXTON, DAVID. Information Technology and
     Libraries 3 (December 1984): 434-36.

3550 GROSS, MARGARET B. Canadian Library Journal 41
     (December 1984): 352.

3551 GARDNER, TRUDY A. Medical Library Association
     Bulletin 73 (January 1985): 73.

3552 GORDON, HELEN A. Online 9 (January 1985): 100-
     01.

3553 SANDERS, JILL. College and Research Libraries
     46 (March 1985): 190-92.

3554 CRAWFORD, WALT. Journal of Academic Librarian-
     ship 11 (March 1985): 53.

3555 BUXTON, DAVID. Journal of Academic Librarian-
     ship 11 (May 1985): 115.

SERIALS REVIEWS

ACCESS: Microcomputers in Libraries, 1-3. 1981-1983.
    Quarterly. Oakridge, OR: DAC Publications.
    ISSN: 0277-0784.

3556 DOWLIN, KENNETH E. "Micro Mag." Library
        Journal 107 (February 1, 1982): 237.

3557 HINES, THEODORE C., and COLLINS, ROSANN W.
        Information Technology and Libraries 1
        (March 1982): 75-76.

3558 LATHROP, ANN. "Upcoming Library Conference,
        New Publications Announced." Educational
        Computer Magazine 2 (May/June 1982): 22.

Byte, 1- . 1975- . Monthly. Peterborough, NH:
    McGraw-Hill. ISSN: 0360-5280.

3559 POOL, GAIL. "Magazines." Wilson Library
        Bulletin 56 (January 1982): 376-78.

COINT Reports, 1- . 1980- . Bimonthly. Morton
    Grove, IL: Advertisement Digest. ISSN: 0198-
    8840.

3560 KATZ, BILL. "Software." Library Journal 109
        (June 15, 1984): 1226.

Collegiate Microcomputer, 1- . 1983- . Quarter-
    ly. Terre Haute, IN: Rose-Hulman Institute of
    Technology. ISSN: 0731-4213.

3561 "Micros-in-Colleges Journal." Small Computers
        in Libraries 2 (December 1982): 2.

3562 GARTEN, EDWARD D., and McMEEN, GEORGE R.
        Library Hi Tech 1 (Winter 1983): 101-02.

3563 "Collegiate Microcomputer." Library Software
        Review 3 (September 1984): 426.

629

Computer Blue Book, 1984–   . Semiannual. Durango, CO: Orion Research Corp.

3564 "Computer 'Blue Books' for Used Micros." <u>Small Computers in Libraries</u> 5 (January 1985): 4.

Computer Book Review, 1– . 1983–   . Bimonthly. Honolulu, HI: Comber Press. ISSN: 0737-0334.

3565 SHIRINIAN, GEORGE N. "Two Computer Book Selection Aids." <u>Small Computers in Libraries</u> 4 (April 1984): 4.

3566 KATZ, BILL. <u>Library Journal</u> 109 (September 1, 1984): 1620.

Computer Bookbase, 1– . 1982–   . Annual, with monthly and quarterly supplements. Cerritos, CA: Computer Bookbase Co. ISSN: 0740-2015.

3567 SHIRINIAN, GEORGE N. "Two Computer Book Selection Aids." <u>Small Computers in Libraries</u> 4 (April 1984): 4.

Computer Books and Serials in Print, 1984–   . Annual. New York: R. R. Bowker. ISSN: 0000-0779.

3568 <u>American Libraries</u> 15 (July/August 1984): 538.

3569 "New Books & Guides Published." <u>Small Computers in Libraries</u> 4 (October 1984): 5.

Computer Equipment Review, 1– . 1981–   . Semiannual. Westport, CT: Meckler Pub. Co. ISSN: 0278-260X.

3570 SCHULTHEISS, LOUIS A. <u>College and Research Libraries</u> 44 (March 1983): 154-55.

3571 SCHULTHEISS, LOUIS A. <u>College and Research Libraries</u> 45 (March 1984): 117.

Computer Shopper, 1– . 1981–   . Monthly. Titusville, FL: Patch Pub. Co.

3572 MASON, ROBERT M. "From the Mail Bag." Library Journal 108 (June 15, 1983): 1235-36.

Computer Software/Hardware Index, 1- . 1984- . Monthly. Haledon, NJ: Computer Software/Hardware Index. ISSN: 0882-5629.

3573 "Computer Review Index." American Libraries 15 (April 1984): 268-69.

3574 MIHRAM, DANIELLE. Library Hi Tech 2, no. 4, issue 8 (1984): 94.

3575 TERTELL, SUSAN M. Library Software Review 4 (March/April 1985): 109.

Creative Computing, 1- . 1974- . Monthly. Morristown, NJ: Creative Computing. ISSN: 0097-8140.

3576 POOL, GAIL. Magazines." Wilson Library Bulletin 56 (January 1982): 376-78.

Data Sources, 1- . 1981- . Quarterly. New York: Ziff-Davis Pub. Co. ISSN: 0744-1673.

3577 "Comprehensive Software Directory." Library Systems Newsletter 1 (September 1981): 19.

3578 MASON, ROBERT M. "More Books & Guidebooks." Library Journal 108 (October 1, 1983): 1856-57.

3579 GARTEN, EDWARD D. Library Hi Tech 2, no. 4, issue 8 (1984): 95.

Database, 1- . 1978- . Weston, CT: Online, Inc. ISSN: 0162-4105.

3580 TEGLER, PATRICIA. College and Research Libraries 45 (March 1984): 117.

Dial-Out, 1- . 1983- . Monthly. New York: Dial-Out.

3581 "More Microcomputer Newsletters." Software
      Review 2 (September 1983): 207.

Digest of Software Reviews: Education, 1- .
      1983- . Quarterly. Fresno, CA: School &
      Home CourseWare. ISSN: 0749-9302.

3582 ACCESS: Microcomputers in Libraries 3 (Spring
      1983): 32.

3583 Booklist 79 (April 1, 1983): 1049.

3584 Library Software Review 3 (March 1984): 119.

3585 Library Software Review 3 (June 1984): 288.

3586 KATZ, BILL. "Software." Library Journal 109
      (June 15, 1984): 1226.

3587 SKINNER, BARBARA J. School Library Media
      Quarterly 12 (Fall 1984): 436-37.

3588 "New Digest of Software Reviews: Education."
      Electronic Library 3 (January 1985): 16.

3589 Library Hi Tech News no. 22 (December 1985):
      11.

ETC, 1-3. 1982-1984. Monthly. San Francisco, CA:
      Far West Laboratory. ISSN: 0735-3723.

3590 ACCESS: Microcomputers in Libraries 3 (Spring
      1983): 32.

Hot Off the Computer, 1- . 1983- . 10 issues/
      year. Elmsford, NY: Westchester Library System.
      ISSN: 0747-8076.

3591 "More Microcomputer Newsletters." Software
      Review 2 (September 1983): 207.

3592 Library Hi Tech News 1 (March 1984): 21.

3593 OCLC Micro 1 (September 1985): 32.

ICP Directory, 1- . 1981- . Monthly, October
    through May. Indianapolis, IN: International
    Computer Programs. ISSN: 0736-282X.

3594 "Comprehensive Software Directory." Library
     Systems Newsletter 1 (September 1981): 19.

InCider, 1- . 1983- . Monthly. Peterborough,
    NH: 1001001, Inc. ISSN: 0740-0101.

3595 "InCider Begins Publication." Software Review
     2 (March 1982): 56.

Information Intelligence Online Libraries and Micro-
    computers, 1- . 1983- . 10 issue/year.
    Phoenix, AZ: Information Intelligence. ISSN:
    0737-7770.

3596 MACHOVEC, GEORGE, and HULEATT, RICHARD S.
     "Premiere Issue of Online Libraries and
     Microcomputers." Information Intelligence
     Online Libraries and Microcomputers 1
     (September 1983): 7.

3597 EMARD, JEAN-PAUL. Online 8 (January 1984):
     80-81.

3598 Library Hi Tech News 1 (March 1984): 21.

3599 "Micros and Libraries." Electronic Learning 4
     (October 1984): 77.

INFOSCAN, 1- . 1983- . Monthly. Mitchell, SD:
    SYNCOM.

3600 Library Hi Tech News 1 (January 1984): 16.

InfoWorld, 1- . 1979- . Weekly. Framingham, MA:
    Popular Computing. ISSN: 0199-6649.

3601 POOL, GAIL. "Magazines." Wilson Library
     Bulletin 56 (January 1982): 376-78.

jr, 1-1. 1984-1984. Monthly. Peterborough, NH:
    Wayne Green, Inc. ISSN: 0742-6607.

3602 "Two Mags for the IBMjr: Another Ceases."
Small Computers in Libraries 3 (December
1983): 1.

LAMP: Literature Analysis of Microcomputer Publications, 1- . 1983- . Bimonthly. Mahwah, NJ:
Soft Images. ISSN: 0735-9721.

3603 Library Hi Tech News 1 (January 1984): 22.

3604 TERTELL, SUSAN M. Library Software Review 4
(March/April 1985): 109.

LAN Newsletter, 1- . 1983- . Monthly. Brook-
line, MA: Information Gatekeepers. ISSN: 0735-
1844.

3605 "Local Area Networks Newsletter." Library Hi
Tech 1 (Spring 1984): 111.

Library Hi Tech, 1- . 1983- . Quarterly. Ann
Arbor, MI: Pierian Press. ISSN: 0737-8831.

3606 "Library Hi Tech is New Quarterly Journal."
Information Retrieval and Library Automation
19 (July 1983): 11.

3607 "Technology in Libraries." Software Review 2
(September 1983): 205-06.

3608 "Hi-Tech Mag." Library Journal 108 (December
15, 1983): 2314.

Library Software Review, 1- . 1982- . Bimonthly.
Westport, CT: Meckler Pub. Co. ISSN: 0742-5759.

3609 "Software for Libraries, Schools is Journal
Subject." Information Retrieval and Library
Automation 20 (June 1984): 8.

3610 GARMAN, NANCY J. Online 9 (July 1985): 57.

LOTUS, 1- . 1985- . Monthly. Cambridge, MA:
Lotus Development Corp. ISSN: 8756-7334.

3611 "Lotus Magazine to Debut in 1985." Small Computers in Libraries 5 (January 1985): 6-7.

M300 and PC Report, 1- . 1984- . Monthly, except July-August. Westport, CT: Meckler Pub. Co. ISSN: 0743-7633.

3612 "'Small Computers in Libraries' and 'M300 and PC Report'." Library Software Review 3 (September 1984): 303-05.

3613 Library Software Review 3 (September 1984): 422-24.

3614 Keeping Up With the M300 and Other Uses of the IBM PC." Library Systems Newsletter 5 (June 1985): 43.

Macworld, 1- . 1984- . Monthly. San Francisco, CA: PC World Communications. ISSN: 0741-8647.

3615 "Macintosh Mag." American Libraries 15 (March 1984): 185.

3616 "Macworld." Library Software Review 3 (September 1984): 424-25.

Micro-ROOTS, 1- . 1984- . Bimonthly. Wheaton, MD: Micro-ROOTS.

3617 "New Micro/Genealogy Journal Begun." Small Computers in Libraries 4 (November 1984): 7.

Micro Software Report, 1983- . Annual. Westport, CT: Meckler Pub. Co. ISSN: 8755-5786.

3618 SHIRINIAN, GEORGE N. "Micro Software Report: A Review." Small Computers in Libraries 2 (October 1982): 1-2.

3619 "New Ed. of Micro Software Report." Small Computers in Libraries 4 (January 1984): 7.

3620 PERRY-HOLMES, CLAUDIA. Library Hi Tech News 1 (February 1984): 22.

3621 NOERR, PETER L. <u>Electronic Library</u> 3 (April
      1985): 114-15.

3622 "Meckler: Micro Software Report." <u>Library Hi
      Tech News</u> no. 18 (July/August 1985): 12.

<u>Microcomputer Index</u>, 1- . 1980- . Bimonthly.
    Palo Alto, CA: Database Service. ISSN: 8756-
    7040.

3623 <u>Booklist</u> 80 (November 1, 1983): 441.

3624 TERTELL, SUSAN M. <u>Library Software Review</u> 4
      (March/April 1985): 109.

<u>Microcomputer Market Place</u>, 1982- . Annual. New
    York: Dekotek, Inc. ISSN: 0735-1925.

3625 <u>Hot Off the Computer</u> 1, no. 10, p. 20.

3626 <u>Wilson Library Bulletin</u> 57 (June 1983): 883-84.

3627 COHEN, ALLEN. <u>RQ</u> 23 (Spring 1984): 367-69.

<u>Microcomputers for Information Management</u>, 1- .
    1984- . Quarterly. Norwood, NJ: Ablex Pub-
    lishing Co. ISSN: 0742-2342.

3628 <u>Library Hi Tech News</u> 1 (January 1984): 16.

3629 <u>Library Software Review</u> 3 (March 1984): 119-20.

3630 "Microcomputers for Information Management."
      <u>Information Retrieval and Library Automation</u>
      19 (May 1984): 8.

3631 GARTEN, EDWARD D. <u>Library Hi Tech News</u> no. 15
      (April 1985): 11.

<u>MICROINDEX</u>, 1- . 1983- . Monthly. South Nashua,
    NH: Serious Personal Computing.

3632 GARTEN EDWARD D. "A Microindex Arrives on the
      Scene." <u>Library Hi Tech</u> 1 (Spring 1984):
      110.

National LOGO Exchange, 1- . 1982- . Monthly,
    September through May. Charlottesville, VA:
    Posy Pubs. ISSN: 0734-1717.

3633 "National Logo Exchange." Small Computers in
     Libraries 4 (January 1984): 3.

OCLC Micro, 1- . 1985- . Bimonthly. Dublin, OH:
    OCLC, Inc. ISSN: 8756-5196.

3634 "Micro. Again." M300 and PC Report 2 (January
     1985): 4.

3635 "Play It Again, Sam." M300 and PC Report 2
     (February 1985): 5.

3636 "OCLC to Publish Microcomputer Magazine." OCLC
     Newsletter no. 156 (February 1985): 14.

3637 "OCLC Micro: One More Time." M300 and PC
     Report 2 (March 1985): 4-5.

3638 "OCLC Introduces Microcomputer Magazine." Wil-
     son Library Bulletin 59 (March 1985): 442.

3639 "OCLC to Publish Microcomputer Magazine."
     Technicalities 5 (April 1985): 2, 12.

3640 "Micro Debuts." M300 and PC Report 2 (May
     1985): 4.

3641 "Keeping Up With the M300 and Other Uses of the
     IBM PC." Library Systems Newsletter 5 (June
     1985): 43.

3642 CARLSON, DAVID H. Library Hi Tech News no. 18
     (July/August 1985): 18-19.

Online, 1- . 1977- . Bimonthly. Weston, CT:
    Online, Inc. ISSN: 0146-5422.

3643 TEGLER, PATRICIA. College and Research Li-
     braries 45 (March 1984): 118-19.

Online Micro-Software Guide and Directory, 1983/

84- . Updated with Supplements. Weston, CT: Online, Inc. ISSN: 0734-5097.

3644 RAITT, DAVID. Electronic Library 1 (April 1983): 107.

3645 ALLEY, BRIAN. "Worth Noting." Technicalities 3 (November 1983): 15.

3646 DESROCHES, RICHARD A. Library Hi Tech 1 (Winter 1983): 92.

3647 BROGAN, LINDA. Medical Library Association Bulletin 72 (January 1984): 43-44.

3648 BROGAN, LINDA. Journal of Academic Librarianship 10 (July 1984): 175.

Online Review, 1- . 1977- . Bimonthly. New York: Learned Information. ISSN: 0309-314X.

3649 TEGLER, PATRICIA. College and Research Libraries 45 (March 1984): 119.

Online Terminal/Microcomputer Guide & Directory, 1982/ 83- . Triennial. Weston, CT: Online, Inc. ISSN: 1734-5100.

3650 "Online Guide Expands in New Edition." Information Retrieval and Library Automation 18 (June 1982): 8-9.

3651 BOSS, RICHARD W. "Book Review/Online Terminal Guide and Directory." Online 6 (September 1982): 57.

3652 SHIRINIAN, GEORGE N. "Online Terminal/Microcomputer Guide and Directory--Review." Small Computers in Libraries 2 (October 1982): 7.

3653 DESROCHES, RICHARD A. Library Hi Tech 1 (Winter 1983): 92-93.

PC Abstracts: Abstracts and Index of Periodical Literature for the IBM PC and PC Compatible User,

1- . 1983- . Annual. Jenks, OK: Artrice
Press. ISSN: 0743-2534.

3654 DEVIN, ROBIN B. Library Hi Tech News no. 18
(July/August 1985): 20-21.

PC Clearinghouse Software Directory, 1- . 1983- .
Biannual. Fairfax, VA: PC Clearinghouse. ISSN:
0736-4180.

3655 MASON, ROBERT M. "More Books & Guidebooks."
Library Journal 108 (October 1, 1983):
1856-57.

PC Free, 1- . 1986- . Harrod's Creek, KY: River-
side Data, Inc.

3656 "Micro News: PC Free." M300 and PC Report 2
(November 1985): 4.

PC Week, 1- . 1983- . Weekly. New York: Ziff-
Davis. ISSN: 0740-1604.

3657 TRAUTMAN, RODES. "Third Wave Complimentary
Newspaper." Small Computers in Libraries 4
(June 1984): 7.

PCjr, 1-1. 1984-1984. Monthly. New York: Ziff-
Davis. ISSN: 0740-7807.

3658 "Two Mags for the IBMjr: Another Ceases."
Small Computers in Libraries 3 (December
1983): 1.

Personal Computer News, 1-1. 1983-1983. Bimonthly.
Pt. Reyes Station, CA: Personal Computer News.
ISSN: 0736-5020.

3659 American Libraries 14 (September 1983): 565.

Personal Computing, 1- . 1977- . Hasbrouck
Heights, NJ: Hayden Publishing Co. ISSN: 0192-
5490.

3660 POOL GAIL. "Magazines." Wilson Library
Bulletin 56 (January 1982): 376-78.

Popular Computing, 1- . 1981- . Monthly. Peterborough, NH: McGraw-Hill. ISSN: 0279-4721.

3661 POOL, GAIL. "Magazines." Wilson Library Bulletin 56 (January 1982): 376-78.

Professional Computing, 1- . 1984- . Bimonthly. New York: John Wiley. ISSN: 0742-1036.

3662 "Hewlett-Packard Mag from Wiley." American Libraries 15 (March 1984): 185.

Program, 1- . 1966- . Bimonthly. London: Aslib. ISSN: 0033-0337.

3663 GORMAN, MICHAEL. "Recent Publications: Special Review." Information Technology and Libraries 4 (September 1985): 277-79.

Run, 1- . 1983- . Monthly. Peterborough, NH: Wayne Green, Inc. ISSN: 0741-4285.

3664 "New Magazine for VIC-20 and Commodore-64 Users." Small Computers in Libraries 3 (October 1983): 3.

Small Computer Program Index, 1- . 1982- . Bimonthly. Watford, UK: ALLM Books. ISSN: 0261-7102.

3665 "Small Computer Program Index Out." Small Computers in Libraries 3 (June 1983): 4.

Small Computers in Libraries, 1- . 1981- . Monthly. Westport, CT: Meckler Pub. Co. ISSN: 0275-6722.

3666 "Newsletter on Small Computers." Information Retrieval and Library Automation 17 (October 1981): 9.

3667 HINES, THEODORE C., and COLLINS, ROSANN W. Information Technology and Libraries 1 (March 1982): 75-76.

3668 "Newsletter Devoted to Library Micro Use."
Information Retrieval and Library Automation
18 (April 1983): 9.

3669 "'Small Computers in Libraries' and 'M300 and
PC Report'." Library Software Review 3
(September 1984): 303-04.

3670 WAY, HAROLD E. Database 8 (December 1985): 80-
81.

Social Science Micro Review, 1- . 1982- .
Quarterly. Raleigh, NC: North Carolina State
University. ISSN: 8755-3031.

3671 "Political Science Micro Review." Small Computers in Libraries 2 (October 1982): 3.

3672 "Social Science Micro Review." Classroom
Computer Learning 4 (March 1984): 84.

The Software Catalog: Microcomputers, 1983- .
Biannual. New York: Elsevier Science Pub. Co.
ISSN: 0736-2722.

3673 MASON, ROBERT M. "More Books & Guidebooks."
Library Journal 108 (October 1, 1983):
1856-57.

3674 ALLEY, BRIAN. "Worth Noting." Technicalities
3 (November 1983): 15.

3675 Library Hi Tech 1 (Winter 1983): 102.

3676 COHEN, ALLEN. RQ 23 (Spring 1984): 367-69.

3677 CHIANG, KATHERINE S. Special Libraries 76
(Spring 1985): 160-61.

3678 CHIANG, KATHERINE S. Journal of Academic Librarianship 11 (July 1985): 176-77.

3679 "Elsevier Science: New Edition of Microcomputer
Software Catalog." Library Hi Tech News
no. 18 (July/August 1985): 12.

The Software Finder, 1- . 1981- . Semiannual.
Dresden, ME: Dresden Associates.

3680 SINESKY, MICHELE. "Software Selection Aids."
Library Software Review 3 (June 1984):
290.

Software Reviews on File, 1- . 1985- . Monthly.
New York: Facts on File. ISSN: 8755-7169.

3681 "Facts on File: Software Reviews." Library Hi
Tech News no. 16 (May 1985): 13.

3682 RETTIG, JAMES. Wilson Library Bulletin 59
(June 1985): 706.

SpecialWare Directory: A Guide to Software Sources for
Special Education, 1983- . Annual. Columbus,
OH: LINC Associates. ISBN: 0-89774-200-1.

3683 PEET, WILLIAM. Computing Teacher 12 (March
1985): 66-67.

Teaching, Learning, Computing. 1- . 1983- .
Monthly during the school year. Placenta, CA:
Seldin Pub. ISSN: 0742-4930.

3684 "Teaching, Learning, Computing." American
Libraries 15 (April 1984): 269.

Telematics and Informatics, 1- . 1984- . Quarterly. New York: Pergamon Press. ISSN:
0736-5853.

3685 Library Hi Tech News 1 (January 1984): 16.

The Whole Earth Software Review, 1-1. 1984-1984.
Quarterly. Sausalito, CA: Point. ISSN: 0742-
0560.

3686 "Brand-Name Software Review." American Libraries 15 (March 1984): 185.

3687 GORDON, HELEN A. Online 8 (May 1984): 90.

<u>Wired Librarian's Newsletter</u>, 1- . 1984- .
   Monthly. Freeport, IL: Micro Libraries. ISSN:
   0884-593X.

3688 "On-line Librarians." <u>Instructional Innovator</u>
      30 (January 1985): 7.

Becker, Joseph. 676.
Bedfordshire County (UK) Library System. 296, 798.
Bednar, Colleen F. 408.
BEECHHOLD, HENRY F. The Plain English Repair and
    Maintenance Guide for Home Computers. 3244.
Beiser, Karl. 86, 334, 1231-1233, 1397-1400, 1756,
    1821, 2447, 2492, 2603, 3100.
Bell, A. J. 924.
Bell, Anne. 924.
Bell, Margaret. 1036.
Bell Communications Research, Inc. Information
    Research Center. 143.
Bell 212A (dialup connector). 409.
Belleville (NJ) Public Library. 1699.
Bellevue (NE) Public Library. 784.
Bellin, David. 1477.
Ben-Shir, Rya. 2730, 2741.
Bendig, Mark. 925, 1234, 1401-1405.
Benenfeld, Alan R. 707.
Bennett, Charles. 749.
Bennion, Junius L. 1305.
Benson, Dennis A. 1166.
Benson, James A. 926-928, 1820.
Benson, Laura M. 199.
Benson, Peggy. 1038.
Berglund, Patricia. 6, 200-202, 1757, 2899.
Bernhard, Keith E. 571.
Berry, John. 7, 87.
Bertrand, D. 1167.
Besemer, Sue. 1168.
Best, Beverly. 1661.
Best, Tim. 203.
Betts, Francis M., III. 2553.
Beversdorf, Anne. 530.
BIB-BASE/ACQ. 1952-1955.
BIB-BASE/MARC. 2031.
BIB-BASE/TEXT. 2032.
BIBLIO-LINK. 1038, 2219-2226.
BIBLIOFILE. 454, 615, 618, 1756, 1785.
Bibliographic Access. 360, 1224.
Bibliographic Control. 1160, 1163, 1167, 1178, 1180,
    1189, 1195, 1206, 1213.
Bibliographic Formatting Software. 863.
Bibliographic Instruction. 392, 900, 903-904, 915,
    918-919, 998, 1013, 1505, 1586, 1903.

Software. 910, 2766-2856.
Bibliographic Retrieval Service, see BRS.
Bibliographic Utilities. 941, 967, 1214.
Bibliographical Center for Research (BCR). 1907.
Bibliography.
 Microcomputer Audiovisuals. 1864.
 Microcomputer Books. 1819, 1822, 1830, 1834, 1838,
  1871, 1874, 1878, 1884-1885, 1892, 1894.
 Microcomputer Journals. 1814, 1817, 1821, 1823,
  1831, 1833, 1835, 1839, 1849, 1953, 1856, 1867,
  1877, 1886-1887.
 Microcomputer Literature. 1815, 1837, 1843, 1852,
  1858, 1859-1860, 1870, 1872-1873, 1875-1876,
  1879, 1882-1883, 1891, 1893.
 Production. 194, 649, 655, 954, 973, 1023, 1035-
  1036, 1201, 1205, 1220, 1485.
 Software. 1977-2030.
BIBLIOGRAPHY. 1977-1978, 2776.
BIBLIOGRAPHY WRITER. 1979-1983.
BIBLIOTEK. 1984-1987.
Bickerstaff, Mollie. 311.
Bielenberg, W. Larry. 409.
Bills, Linda G. 88.
Bindery Records. 333, 337, 660.
Binkley, David. 3421, 3423.
BIOGRAPHIES. 2777.
BioSciences Information Service. 1087, 1159.
BIOSIS. 1087-1090, 1159.
BIOSUPERFILE. 2227-2229.
Birkenhead, Tom. 1235.
Birmingham, Mary Treacy. 1350.
BITS. 1087-1090, 1159.
Bivins, Kathleen T. 709-714.
Bivins, Kathleen T., see also Noerr, Kathleen T.
 Bivins.
Bjorner, Susan N. 452, 1985, 2057, 2128, 2998.
Black, John B. 5, 8.
Blackhurst, Eric W. 1822.
Blair, John C., Jr. 9-10, 89, 335, 677, 929, 978,
 1169-1170, 1236-1238, 1351, 1448, 1478-1479,
 2395, 2412, 2641, 3074.
Blair, Marjorie. 750.
Blair County (PA) Library System. 1430.
Blanchard, Mark. 2336, 3311.
Bland, Barbara B. 1480.

CHECKMATE. 2904-2917.
CHEMCORP (micro). 3132.
Chemical Abstracts Service. 697, 1025.
Chen, Ching-chih. 17-19, 158, 343, 665, 1094-1095, 1354, 1487.
CHEN, CHING-CHIH. MicroUse Directory: Software. 3269-3273..
CHEN, CHING-CHIH, and BRESSLER, STACEY E. Microcomputers in Libraries. 3274-3286.
Cheney, Hal. 94, 1177, 1409, 1450.
Cheng, Chin-Chuan. 494.
Chepesiuk, Ron. 3407.
Cherokee County (SC) Public Library. 377.
Chiang, Katherine S. 3677-3678.
Chicago Public Library. 719.
    North Pulaski Branch. 439, 708, 715, 717-718, 723, 728, 758, 785, 788-790, 793, 871, 1798.
Children's Media Data Bank. 443.
Choi, Kun-Woo Park. 617.
Christian, Deborah. 290, 941, 1488.
CHRISTIE, LINDA GAIL, and CHRISTIE, JOHN. The Encyclopedia of Microcomputer Terminology. 3287.
Church Libraries. 620.
Chweh, Steven S. 3290.
Ciarkowski, Elaine F. 3296.
Cibbarelli, Pamela. 1489.
CIBBARELLI, PAMELA; TENOPIR, CAROL; and KAZLAUSKAS, EDWARD JOHN. Directory of Information Management Software. 3288-3291.
CIFER 2684 (micro), 1026, 1031.
Cimbala, Diane J. 761.
Cimpl, Kay. 634.
Cipolla, Katharine G. 344, 1451.
CIRCA I and CIRCA II. 2153-2156.
Circulation. 211, 279, 351, 354, 361, 363, 366, 392, 496, 500, 505, 509, 514, 611.
    Software. 504, 517, 1541, 2142-2206.
    Systems. 155, 350, 487-490, 492-493, 495, 497, 501-503, 508, 511-512, 515, 519-521.
CIRCULATION MANAGEMENT SYSTEM. 497, 2157-2158.
CIRCULATION MANAGER. 2159-2161.
CIRCULATION PLUS. 211, 2162-2164.
Citroen, Charles L. 942.
Clarion University. Center for the Study of Rural Librarianship. 162, 939, 1040, 1727, 1737, 1746, 1802, 1808.

Fox, Kathleen. 1184, 2034, 2179, 2419, 2428-2429, 2471, 2479, 2506, 2542.
Fox Valley Interlibrary Loan Network. 563.
FOXBASE. 2467.
FOXON-MADDOCKS INDEX PREPARATION SYSTEM. 2652.
FRAMEWORK. 1579, 2468.
FRANKLIN (micro). 3151.
  ACE 100. 209.
  ACE 1000. 3151.
Frazier, Kenneth L. 431.
Frechette, James. 413.
Fredenburg, Anne M. 1880.
FREE FILER. 2469.
Free Software. 1498, 1517, 1545.
Free-Text Information Retrieval. 1225.
FREECALC. 2957.
Freedman, Mary. 109-110, 1265-1267, 1417, 1453.
Freeman, Gretchen L. 407.
Freeman, Steve. 653.
Fresno County (CA) Free Library. 686.
Freund, Alfred L. 414, 574, 606, 1185.
Friend, Linda. 965.
FROEHLICH, ROBERT A. The Free Software Catalog and Directory. 3371-3373.
Front Ends. 961, 979, 994, 1020, 1058.
Frost, Ken. 5.
Frost, Stanley P. 1112.
Fu, Tina C. 1905.
Fuchs, Curtis Ray. 219-220.
Fuchs, Philip L. 1213.
FUJITSU (micro). 1263.
Full Text Document Delivery. 1166.

GS 100. 2171-2172.
GS 500 ACQUISITIONS SYSTEM. 1958-1959.
GS 600 SERIALS CONTROL SYSTEM. 2918-2921.
Gabel, David. 275.
Gabel, Linda. 1951.
GADER, BERTRAM, and NODAR, MANUEL V. Apple Software for Pennies. 3374.
Gadikian, Randy. 636, 1168.
Gadsden S. R. 553.
Gaffner, Haines B. 1268.
Gallina, Paul. 1464.
Galloway, Sarah Beth. 681.

Graphics. 178, 384, 440, 522-525, 1612.
   Software. 2619-2641.
GRAPHICS GENERATOR. 2626.
GRAPHICS MAGICIAN. 2627.
GRAPHMASTER. 2628.
GRAPHTRIX. 2629.
Gray, Robert A. 226.
Great Neck (NY) Public Library. 495.
Great River Regional Library, St. Cloud, MN. 301.
Green, Kevin E. 319.
Green, Lisa Ann. 683.
Greengrass, Linda. 1115.
Grieve, Ann. 246.
Grieves, Robert T. 1116.
Griffis, Joan E. 1520.
Griffith, Jeffrey C. 970-971.
Griffiths, Jose-Marie. 30, 116, 972.
GRIFFITHS, JOSE-MARIE. <u>Applications of Minicomputers and Microcomputers to Information Handling.</u> 3387-3390.
Grookett, Paula R. 227.
Grosch, Audrey N. 1276-1277, 2016, 2246, 3165, 3223, 3293, 3485, 3487.
Gross, Margaret B. 3550.
Grotophorst, Clyde W. 973-974.
Guilfoyle, Marvin. 3420.
Guskin, Alan E. 183.
Guy, R. F. 1230, 1730-1731, 1736.

Hackleman, Debbie. 459.
Hakes, Barbara. 1522.
Hales, David. 540.
Hall, Hal W. 1523, 1572.
Halperin, Michael. 975.
Hammer, Carl. 1278.
Handy, Alice. 2826.
Handzel, Ruth. 976.
Hane, Paula. 1279, 1524-1525, 2298.
Hanifan, Thomas. 355, 2252.
Hanley, Karen Stang. 1846.
Hannigan, Jane Anne. 1526.
Hanson, Mary. 228.
Hard Disks. 82, 413, 1256, 1263, 1280-1281, 1292, 1401, 1410, 1435, 1445.
Hardware. 6, 38, 95, 1275, 1306, 1315, 1318.

Rushinek, Sara. 2012.

SC 350. 1364, 1762, 2938-2947.
SDC. 1083.
ST80 III. 2347.
STA/F FILE SYSTEM. 1610.
Saboe, Michael S. 2516.
Sacramento (CA) Public Library. 472.
Saffady, William. 1041-1042, 1209, 1326, 1612, 2014,
    2024, 2193, 2207, 2225, 2250, 2256-2257, 2279,
    2296, 2309, 2325, 2338, 2345, 2383-2384, 2389,
    2397, 2408-2409, 2423, 2427, 2434, 2436, 2441,
    2453-2454, 2470, 2476, 2482, 2494, 2529, 2539,
    2544, 2549-2550, 2556, 2564, 2570, 2585-2586,
    2593, 2624, 2693, 2923, 2951, 2953-2954, 2963,
    2967, 2971-2972, 2979-2981, 2991, 3112-3113,
    3125, 3133, 3138, 3148, 3160, 3163, 3178, 3194,
    3202, 3212, 3214, 3224.
Sager, Donald J. 300, 3354.
St. Clair, Gloriana. 425.
St. Cloud Daily Times. 301.
St. John's University. Division of Library and Infor-
    mation Science. 1765, 1794.
St. Louis (MO) Public Library. 653.
St. Louis County (MO) Public Library. 347.
Salas, Ricardo. 478.
Salem (MA) High School Instructional Materials Center.
    508.
Salomon, Kristine. 1803.
SAMNA WORD. 3065-3067.
San Bernardino (CA) Public Library. 735, 864.
San Diego County (CA) Public Library. 772.
San Francisco (CA) Public Library. 510.
San Mateo County (CA) Office of Education. 1554,
    1917, 1934.
Sanders, Glenn. 3486.
Sanders, Jill. 3553.
Sandler, Corey. 3097.
SAPANA: CARDFILE. 2562-2563.
Sargeant, Arthur. 388.
Sather, Ruth. 865-866.
Satyanarayana, R. 64.
Saunders, Jeremy. 263.
Sauve, Deborah. 546.
Savage, Earl R. 1713.

SHIRINIAN, GEORGE N. Microcomputing Periodicals.
    3495-3496.
Shreeve, Robin. 152.
Shroder, Emelie J. 737-738.
Siegfried, Pat. 872.
Silverberg, Joel S. 1242.
Silverman, Karen Sandlin. 479.
Silverman, Stan. 2465.
Silverstein, Joan. 2056.
Simmons, Beatrice. 238.
Simmons, Debra. 268.
Simmons, Peter. 1937-1938.
Simmons, Rosetta. 873.
Simmons College. Graduate School of Library and
    Information Science. 1095, 1123, 1135-1136,
    1487.
Simonds, Michael J. 2152, 2172.
Simpson, George A. 68.
SIMPSON, GEORGE A. Microcomputers in Library Automa-
    tion. 3497.
Simulation. 572.
SINCLAIR, I. R. Inside Your Computer. 3498.
Sinesky, Michele. 3502, 3680.
Sinnett, Dennis. 912.
SIR (Schools Information Retrieval) Project. 1164,
    1207.
SIR (Simple Information Retrieval). 1581.
SIRE. 479, 1210, 2571-2578.
Site Design. 886.
SITE MANAGER. 2976-2977.
Skapura, Robert. 269-270, 513, 2202, 2540, 2604,
    2610, 3007, 3039, 3069.
SKILLS MAKER. 2848-2849.
Skinner, Barbara J. 3587.
SKIWRITER. 3073.
Sklarz, David P. 874-875.
Skoman, Lucia. 1690-1691.
Skopp, Sam. 480.
Skvaria, Donna. 876.
Sleeth, Jim. 1045.
Slides, 447.
Slingluff, Deborah. 1046.
Sloan, Bernard G. 153.
Small Computer Program Index. 3365.
Small Computers in Libraries. 3666-3670.

Copy Protection. 1585, 1602, 1615, 1625, 1708.
Copying. 1511, 1516, 1598.
Copyright. 2, 815, 1470, 1492-1495, 1511, 1528,
    1537, 1547, 1550, 1572, 1574, 1577, 1585, 1598,
    1627-1628, 1634, 1651, 1708, 1718, 1767.
Development. 374, 1488, 1539, 1543, 1566-1567,
    1586, 1593, 1611, 1617, 1642, 1646, 1654, 1728.
Directories. 1487, 1489, 1512-1513, 1592, 1689,
    1841, 1897, 1901, 1903-1904.
Documentation. 1491, 1549, 1609, 1635, 1649.
Evaluation and Selection. 856-857, 1471, 1474,
    1478, 1480, 1484, 1486, 1490, 1503, 1507, 1519-
    1520, 1522, 1526-1527, 1544, 1548, 1551-1553,
    1555-1556, 1569, 1582, 1584, 1599, 1608, 1613,
    1618, 1626-1627, 1630-1631, 1633, 1652-1654,
    1866, 1907.
Fairs. 1614, 1766.
Industry. 1579.
Licensing Agreements. 1701-1702.
National Clearinghouse. 1604, 1914-1915.
Piracy. 940, 1047, 1574, 1634, 1708.
Previewing. 1626, 1907.
Processing. 1662, 1674, 1684, 1692.
Review Sources. 1093, 1474, 1490, 1520, 1584,
    1638-1639, 1845, 1861, 1888.
Reviews. 1479, 1514-1515, 1530, 1559, 1565, 1583,
    1588, 1591, 1597, 1601, 1629, 1639, 1655, 1860,
    1880, 1924.
Sources. 1498, 1517, 1524, 1529, 1545, 1557, 1590,
    1604-1606, 1624, 1648, 1868, 1902-1904, 1906,
    1919-1920, 1926-1930.
Storage. 1659, 1665, 1672.
Standard Numbering Systems. 1521, 1531-1536, 1580,
    1594-1596, 1619-1620, 1641, 1645, 1657.
Software Catalog: Microcomputers. 3673-3679.
Software Digest. 1616.
Software Encyclopedia. 3499.
Software Finder. 3680.
SOFTWARE LIBRARY (database). 1111, 1148.
Software Publishers Association. 1621.
Software Reports. 3500-3502.
Software Reviews on File. 3681-3682.
Software Source. 3503.
SOLINET. 607, 1940.
Soltzberg, Leonard J. 19.

University of South Carolina College of Librarianship.
   377.
University of Strathclyde Library. 1026.
University of Toronto Department of Civil Engineering,
   Transportation Safety Collection. 313.
University of Winnipeg Library. 370.
University of Wisconsin.
   Eau Clair Library. 915.
   Madison Library. 431, 634, 649, 1704.
   Oshkosh Library. 968.
   Parkside Library. 850.
UNIX (operating system). 1236, 1347, 1352.
Unrein, Dan. 1336.
Urbanek, Val. 19, 1219.
User Groups and Clubs. 866, 1759, 1764, 1781, 1806,
   1942.
USERKIT. 1061-1062, 1069, 1073-1075.
USERLINK. 1063.
USING AN INDEX TO PERIODICALS. 2850-2852.
USING REFERENCE TABLES IN AN ALMANAC. 2853.
Utah State University Videodisc Innovation Projects.
   1345.
Utility Programs. 1394, 1420, 1438, 1467, 1524, 1623.
UTLAS IBM PC (workstation). 1476.
Utterback, Nancy. 1039.

VCN EXECUVISION. 2640.
VP-PLANNER. 2985.
Valente, Richard D. 914.
Van Arsdale, Dennis. 483.
Van Camp, Ann J. 1987.
Van Styvendaele, B. J. H. 1220.
Vanderhoef, John. 1464.
Vasaturo, Ronald. 3236, 3347-3348.
Vaughan, Sheila. 1221-1222, 3275.
Vavrek, Bernard. 161-162, 1465.
Veaner, Allen B. 163, 2656, 3022, 3072.
Vecht, Emma S. 963.
Venner, Gillian. 632.
Verbesey, J. Robert. 892, 3306.
Vertical File Index. 1158.
Veterans Administration Medical Center Library, New
   York, NY. 328.
Vickery, A. 76.
VICTOR (micro). 3223.